marketing

THIRD EDITION

Peter Chisnall

Prentice Hall

New York • London • Toronto • Sydney • Tokyo • Singapore

First edition published 1985
Second edition published 1989

This third edition first published 1995 by
Prentice Hall International (UK) Limited
Campus 400, Maylands Avenue
Hemel Hempstead
Hertfordshire, HP2 7EZ
A division of
Simon & Schuster International Group

Typeset in 10/12.5 pt Sabon by Photoprint, Torquay

Printed and bound in Great Britain
at the University Press, Cambridge

Library of Congress Cataloging-in-Publication Data

Available from the publisher

British Library Cataloguing in Publication Data

A catalogue record for this book is available from
the British Library

ISBN 0–13–203365–8

1 2 3 4 5 99 98 97 96 95

Strategic business marketing

Contents

Preface

The marketing of industrial, technical and professional goods and services to businesses of many kinds has developed significantly over the past decade, and comparatively few organisations are without specialist skills in this vital function of management. Yet there are still some whose ingrained attitudes and behaviour lead them either to ignore or to undervalue the contribution which professional marketing could make to the progress and success of their corporate activities.

This new edition – which has been thoroughly revised and extensively augmented – has been retitled in order to indicate clearly the value of this text to management students and practitioners who seek expert knowledge of marketing theory and applications over a wide spectrum of industry, business and commerce, as well as in the public services. Of the many topics covered, special attention has been given to international business strategies, the growth of 'regionalism', including the evolution of the European Union, innovation strategies and corporate identity programmes. Other salient issues explored are environmental policies, business ethics, total quality management (TQM) and product liability.

Business is undoubtedly increasing in its complexity, and competition has sharpened in virtually every market. While change is inevitable, bringing new opportunities as well as problems, productive relationships need to be established between suppliers and buyers in both home and overseas markets. Skilful negotiation is based on sound knowledge of products, markets and people; strategies should never be designed in abstract terms.

As before, references are fully listed at the end of each chapter for easy consultation. Throughout the text, many practical examples are given of specific applications of marketing theory. I have benefited from consulting leading authors, whose publishers have kindly permitted me to include specific tables and diagrams. I am also grateful to Charles Sammonds of the University of Wolverhampton for the exchange of ideas on the growing importance of business ethics in practice. In particular, I gratefully acknowledge the assistance of Dr Darach Turley in drafting the well-focused questions at the end of each chapter.

With pleasure, I acknowledge the professional and friendly help of my publishers, and I dedicate this volume to Charles and Georgina, although their present reading tastes are certainly unlikely to extend to it.

Peter M. Chisnall

CHAPTER ONE

Marketing principles and practice

INTRODUCTION

Modern communities are knowledgeable and sophisticated: many goods and services are demanded to satisfy their dynamic needs. These increasingly involve the products and services of the newer industries, such as computers, electronics, telecommunications, aerospace, petrochemicals and pharmaceuticals, as well as the traditional industries like steel-making, textiles and engineering.

Needs are more than physical; in economies of affluence the tendency is for increasing emphasis to be given to satisfying psychological needs. These psychogenic (also known as emotional or psychological) needs reflect the complexity of human behaviour in modern society. As Maslow[1] has pointed out: 'Man . . . is a perpetually wanting animal. Ordinarily the satisfaction of these wants is not altogether mutually exclusive, but only tends to be.' Human needs are dynamic: as soon as one is satisfied, yet another replaces it to continue the never-ending spiral of satisfactions.

Needs may originate from personal and domestic consumption, from the factory floor or from the hospital operating theatre. Organisations are of many types – industrial, commercial, public sector services, charities, etc. – and their needs range widely, from immense capital investments to relatively low-cost items. (See Chapter 2 for further discussion.)

Experienced buyers – whether acting in their personal roles as consumers or as professionals in an organisation – put increasing pressure on manufacturers, distributors and suppliers of goods and services to provide them with acceptable solutions to their problems and needs. Inevitably, expectations rise and new demands are made related, perhaps, to product safety features or after-sales service. Sir Christopher Hogg of Courtaulds[2] has stated that companies survive because they do things for their customers which are distinctive and which their customers want. BMW[3] has declared that it does not 'sell cars', but aims to satisfy people's motoring aspirations. JCB, the UK's largest manufacturer and exporter of earth-moving and materials-handling equipment, believes that the company's success has been largely because it understands customers' needs and endeavours to meet them.

PRINCIPAL TASKS OF MANAGEMENT

Three tasks face those in charge of organisations, whether they are primarily motivated by profits or by social objectives:

1. Decide on the nature and extent of the products and/or services that are to be offered to identified customers/clients.
2. Arrange the production of those specific products or services.
3. Organise the availability of those products and services (this includes selling and distribution strategies). (See Figure 1.1.)

With the growth of mass markets and more sophisticated patterns of consumption, organisations have become larger and more complex. To control these types of resources, specialised formations of management have developed, covering key responsibilities such as research and development, production, finance and accounting, personnel and marketing.

These tasks are so fundamental to the existence and continuity of any organisation that they demand professional expertise. Sophisticated techniques of management in production, costing, financial control or personnel are vital, but they cannot by themselves produce success in an environment which is growing increasingly competitive. It is the role of marketing to interpret and assess the needs, both present and emergent, of specific markets, and to stimulate activities within an organisation to develop relevant products/services.

The prime responsibility of management is to organise corporate resources so that they achieve the objectives which have been agreed by the policy-makers. The successful management of a business calls for entrepreneurial qualities: the function of marketing is to assume the role and responsibilities of the entrepreneur, whose traditional role has been to interpret market requirements and relate these to the resources which are currently available or which it may be feasible to acquire within the medium and long term. Without entrepreneurial energy and leadership, business are unlikely to prosper, particularly in the highly competitive environment which typifies most industries today.

The activities of a business or, indeed, of any type of organisation can be viewed as an input–output model (see Figure 1.2). In the case of commercial companies,

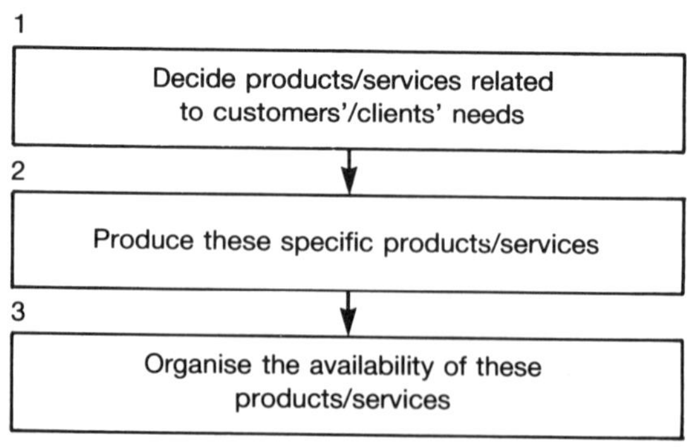

FIGURE 1.1 Sequential approach to principal tasks of management

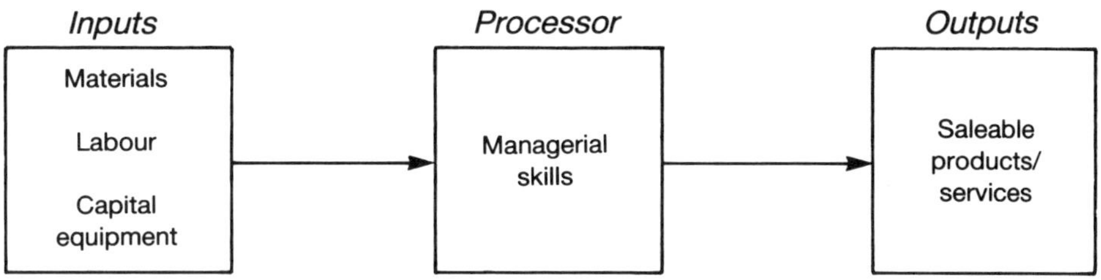

FIGURE 1.2 Simple input–output model of market-directed organisational efforts

inputs into the 'pipeline' will be capital equipment and manufacturing resources such as labour, raw and processed materials, components, etc.; the nature of these inputs and their 'mix' will, of course, vary according to industries and individual companies. These productive inputs need to be organised and controlled: such duties are the responsibility of management (as shown in the centre box of Figure 1.2). The results of all these co-ordinated activities are products which, if a business is market orientated, are attractive to certain kinds of buyer – consumers, industrial, public sector, etc.

Figure 1.2 obviously simplifies the often intricate and complex flow of activities within a firm or other type of organisation. But the basic pattern clearly remains the same, and all production, as Adam Smith stipulated many years ago, should always be undertaken with the needs of the customer constantly in mind. With classical elegance, he observed: 'The maxim is so perfectly self-evident that it would be absurd to attempt to prove it.'[4] Precept and practice often fail to coincide, not least in large-scale organisations. The logic and 'self-evidence' which were so appealing to Adam Smith appear to have had little influence on the behaviour of many firms, until they are forced by competition to change entrenched and outmoded ways of dealing with customers. (The vital interrelationship of the various specialised functions of management is discussed in some detail later.)

NATURE OF MARKETING

Marketing has two aspects:

1. A business philosophy.
2. A management function.

BASIC BUSINESS PHILOSOPHY

As a basic philosophy of business, the marketing concept is simple and as old as the hills: it is inspired by the wish to serve customers well so that they will buy (and continue to buy) the goods and services offered to them by individual and competing suppliers. Customer orientation, as the famous founder of economic theory[4] noted, should be the motivating force behind businesses of all kinds.

When businesses were small and their customers few, there was no need for specialised functions of management. The owners of these enterprises were in almost daily contact with their customers and knew their needs intimately. But as firms became larger and their markets expanded, information about customers was less immediate, and there was the growing danger of distance distorting the view held of customers' needs. In his wisdom, Adam Smith reminded these entrepreneurs of the way to business success: think first of what your customer really wants and then organise your resources to satisfy these particular needs.

There is nothing new or revolutionary in what is termed 'marketing orientation'; it might well be called plain business common sense. However, common sense tends not to be so commonly distributed, and even today some organisations seem sadly unaware that their eventual success lies in their customers' hands.

The consumer goods industries were the first to take note of the marketing concept: that 'market orientation' meant more than mouthing anodyne phrases – it required action. This entailed research, planning and the many other activities now regarded as essential parts of an integrated marketing strategy.

To be able to produce goods was not enough; the new philosophy entailed ensuring that those goods were likely to appeal to certain kinds of customer – identified, perhaps, by social class, age, family life style, geographical area, etc. As Levitt has remarked: 'A product is something people will buy. If they don't buy it it's not a product (or a service). It's a museum piece.'[5]

Hence, marketing as a business philosophy is profitable only if it is practised by ensuring that the whole organisation is motivated by recognising its dependence upon clients, customers, patrons (or however else those who buy its 'outputs' are described) for its survival and growth. Peter Drucker commented some years ago: 'If we want to know what a business is we have to start with its purpose . . . There is only one valid definition of business purpose: to create a customer . . . The customer is the foundation of a business and keeps it in existence.'[6]

Du Pont, the giant US chemical and energy business, is getting to grips with the challenges of the 1990s: 'We have to get nearer to our customers and look at things from their point of view; their health is incredibly important to us'.[7] (See Chapter 6 outlining Du Pont's market segmentation strategy.)

MANAGEMENT FUNCTION

As a specialised function of management, marketing has a key role to play in generating profitable business. It has far-spanning interests and responsibilities across the whole spectrum of industry, commerce and, indeed, the public services. Marketing is the entrepreneurial force in a company: this may be directed towards the launching of a new product range, a novel type of insurance policy or a new leisure facility. In relatively small organisations, the owner or general manager will assume these types of responsibility, but as companies grow larger, the function of marketing becomes more sophisticated and specially trained management is necessary.

Despite the lead given by consumer goods industries, many industrial and service firms have shown a marked reluctance to acknowledge that marketing is a legitimate function of management, relevant to their activities. The view often taken seems to be that marketing is probably very useful for fast-moving consumer goods seen on the shelves of supermarkets, but that its value to technical and industrial firms is distinctly limited. Further, it has no place at all in non-profit-motivated organisations such as the public health and welfare services, charities or cultural organisations.

This blinkered view of the role of marketing was not shared by the Machine Tools Economic Development Committee, which, more than 20 years ago, initiated a two-year intensive study of the British machine tool industry at manufacturing and distribution levels. It was noted that successful firms were characterised by their total commitment to servicing customers' needs. 'Every executive in these companies – from top management down through the entire management structure – was personally oriented towards the customer. Marketing attitudes generated the specific motivation of these successful companies.'[8]

A report on industrial innovation by the Institute of Mechanical Engineers also stated that among the major factors detracting from a higher rate of innovation in the United Kingdom was 'a lack of appreciation of marketing techniques in middle and lower engineering management'.[9]

These reports become almost monotonous in their messages: ignore marketing skills and place your business at risk. Whole industries, like the British motorcycle industry, have virtually disappeared because they have lost touch with their customers and what they really want. Technical cleverness and sophistication are not by themselves able to provide effective answers to world competition. Inventiveness needs to be harnessed to commercial skills such as marketing to bring about successful innovation. (See Chapter 7 for extended discussion of this important theme.)

MARKETING AND COLLECTIVE ATTITUDES

Apart from the techniques, marketing involves adopting certain standards which affect behaviour throughout an organisation. 'Marketing covers the collective attitudes of management to markets as well as the operation itself.'[10] This attitudinal orientation should be shared by everyone in the organisation, irrespective of their functional responsibilities. A team spirit should be fostered: a willingness to work at all levels and across all functions of a business in order to win customers and their continued patronage.

In Levitt's words: 'Marketing is not just a business function. It is a consolidating view of the entire business process.'[5] It is more than mechanistic; it goes to the heart of an organisation and should affect everyone who works for it.

Successful marketing managers act as catalysts in their businesses, causing attitudinal and behavioural changes in all departments. Selling is not confined by them to products or services: they sell actively *within* their companies and encourage new standards of customer care to be adopted.

Industrial product manufacturers sometimes seem to suffer mental blocks when introducing their products to customers. Most of their managerial time and energy appears to be expended at the development and production stages; the planning of market entry is often haphazard and distinctly at variance with the professional attention given earlier. Clearly, products should be effectively designed and well made, but the task of management is by no means ended.

> Products must be planned, not just designed. It means that the people charged with selling the product must participate in its creation at the outset, not just after they get it from the manufacturing department . . . this spells an end to the rigid separation between R&D and marketing, between engineering and marketing, and even between advertising and sales promotion . . .[5]

Organisations are managed by people. Acting in their various vocational roles, people decide the fate of the organisation to which they belong. 'The enterprise is a community of human beings. Its performance is the performance of human beings.'[6] To be successful, organisations need balanced inputs from the different sectors of management so that wealth-producing resources, in the case of commercial firms, are allocated to achieve organisational goals. In commercial terms, this means securing profitable business by offering customers goods and services which they are willing and able to buy. Individual efforts should be co-ordinated into team performance, with the goals of the organisation clearly in focus. The health of an organisation, like the human body, depends on the right functioning of its many parts. If sickness or inefficiency occurs in one area, the entire organism may malfunction; the disease may be so contagious and lethal that unless drastic surgery is possible there is little hope of survival.

The need for much greater teamwork within organisations, especially between people in different functions, has been 'one of the most popular managerial leitmotifs of the last five years in Europe and the United States',[11] but very few companies have actually operated like this. Multidisciplinary teams, task forces and project groups have all been acclaimed as excellent ideas, which some companies like Ford, Xerox and JCB have eventually adopted. But the easing of departmental sensitivities, and the relaxing of professional attitudes and long-held habits, are essential for the success of such efforts.

It is a sad fact that in many organisations corporate resources are never really co-ordinated effectively. In some cases, the spirit of competition exists more *inside* an organisation than in behaviour towards its market. Managerial energies are sapped and frustrated by corrosive campaigns of internecine warfare waged between different departments. Frequently, hostility is not just covert, and employees have been known to speculate whether they all work for the same organisation. Customers and clients may also become aware of the conflict within the organisation which professes to serve them. It does not inspire them with confidence and may well cause them to look elsewhere for their supplies. Goodwill is largely the willingness which an organisation is perceived to display towards satisfying the needs of its market. Apart from physical products or actual services, the 'constellation of benefits' offered to customers should include the pleasantness of doing business. This behavioural factor may well be the paramount influence, particularly when there is little real or observable difference between products or services of a generic type.

The complex pattern of inputs and outputs in an organisation cannot be left to develop haphazardly. Productive working in all branches of corporate activity rests largely on the articulation of a coherent policy. This calls for vision and leadership from top management, a thorough appreciation of the resources of the organisation, and an awareness of market opportunities. These are exacting criteria; but they are the recipe for effective management of organisations of all types. As Robert Heller has observed with his customary vigour:

> In effect, management is a far more homely business than its would-be scientists suggest, more closely allied to cookery than any other human activity. Like cooking, it rests on a degree of organisation and on adequate resources. But just as no two chefs run their kitchens the same way, so no two managements are the same – even if they all went to the same business (or cookery) school. You can teach the rudiments of cooking, as of management: you cannot make a great cook or a great manager.[12]

As observed earlier, in most small and in many medium-sized organisations the function of marketing tends to be closely related to that of general management. Often, the chief executive assumes these dual roles and as the organisation grows his or her responsibilities extend into many areas, although, of course, the chief executive's managerial time is not elastic. Further, the chief executive's early working years may have been largely spent in specific functions such as production or engineering to which he or she may continue to pay special attention. As the organisation gets bigger, the problems of production, financing and marketing become more complex and mistakes can have more disastrous effects. As long as the managing director can keep his or her finger firmly on the pulse of the organisation, its progress can be monitored. Because of the managing director's status, he or she can intervene effectively in day-to-day operations, and a degree of flexibility exists which would be unusual in larger undertakings. Since the foundation of the business, this type of managing director (who displays all the attributes of the textbook entrepreneur) is likely to have built up a cadre of executives who show strong personal loyalty as well as professional commitment in their managerial roles.

This tightly knit organisation tends to suffer under the strains imposed by expansion beyond the boundaries of the close personal management of its founder or his or her corporate successor. In particular, the efficiency of the whole organisation may be endangered because the chief executive relinquishes direct mangerial responsibility in certain activities such as production or marketing. The chief executive is likely to have appointed, perhaps through internal promotion, executives to take some of the load off his back. This new phase of organisational life is critical and requires expert handling if growth is to continue: the seeds of decay may easily be scattered by careless (this may not, of course, be deliberate or malicious) planning and direction. The role of marketing, for instance, may never have been formalised; it rested largely on the personal negotiating style of one person who over the years had acquired considerable insight into the behaviour of 'his' or 'her' customers. These close personal relationships had resulted in satisfactory business, largely because of the bargaining position of the chief executive in the environment and also within the organisation.

If the marketing function is now formalised by the appointment of an executive with specific responsibilities in this area, he or she may well face peculiar difficulties within the company. The executive will not have the authority of the managing director, but will be expected to achieve even greater marketing success. This dilemma may be compounded, if the executive is a newcomer, by his or her ignorance of the informal as well as the formal relationships existing between other functional areas of management. That the executive has been appointed at all may be perceived by other members of the staff as a threat to their status and career prospects. Unless the role of marketing is understood by everyone in an organisation, misunderstanding is bound to arise. This is particularly likely where the functions of marketing have never been identified separately from those of the general manager.

The transition from 'personalised' marketing to 'professionalised' marketing will not be easy: it will present problems that will challenge managerial stamina. But these problems can be controlled, if not eradicated, by effective communications. It should be explained – and this responsibility rests with the chief executive of the developing organisation – that marketing management is just as vital to the success of a firm (or other corporate organisation) as production is. It is not intended to usurp other managerial roles and certainly not to cause them to disintegrate.

DEFINITION OF MARKETING

The Chartered Institute of Marketing has defined marketing as follows: 'Marketing is the management process responsible for identifying, anticipating and satisfying customer requirements profitably.'

This definition emphasises that marketing is concerned with supplying the specific needs of identified target markets at a profit. This is one of the hallmarks of marketing that differentiates it from just selling: the latter can be accomplished and actually result in a loss, whereas marketing focuses on profitable opportunities suitable for the resources of a company.

The essence of the marketing concept is to be responsive to customers and their many needs; this cannot happen unless quite a lot is known about customers (present and prospective) and the types of business they run.

Because the value of creative marketing is not restricted to commercial undertakings, the Institute of Marketing's definition might usefully be extended to state that marketing is necessarily concerned with achieving the objectives of an organisation – and these may well not be dedicated to producing profits, as in the case of charities, public sector health, welfare and recreational services, etc. (This aspect of marketing's responsibilities is discussed later.)

In industrial markets, there are particular characteristics of products which reflect the essential investment nature of such purchases, as noted in Chapter 2.

Marketing is involved not just with today or this week, but with planning for tomorrow and next year as well. It seeks to find out, and to understand more about, the factors affecting demand for products and services. Anticipation of needs is another responsibility of marketing management; some needs will be long-standing and overt, others may be latent and as yet undeveloped. The problems (and opportunities) of innovation are discussed at some length in Chapter 7; at this time, it can be said that anticipating what people will buy at some future time is one of the most difficult tasks facing marketing management. If it were otherwise, many manufacturers and distributors would reap rich harvests without undue effort.

Working closely with other functions of management, marketing management has to provide a product or service that will satisfy specific customer needs and whose market value exceeds its cost. Value is, to a considerable extent, subjective, and related to utility and desirability. Successful firms are able to market products of superior value, competitively priced, that will attract business and result in profits. This is the key to corporate survival and growth. Exchange of values is at the heart of all industrial and commercial life: planning profitable exchanges is the particular responsibility of marketing management. To quote Adam Smith again: 'Every man . . . lives by exchanging, or becomes in some measure a merchant.'[4]

Whether those who buy products and services are known as clients, customers, patrons or consumers is not important: what is vital is that their expectations are understood and met. Merchants of all kinds have prospered over the ages because they have ensured that what they offer is what their customers find attractive. Beauty may well be in the eye of the beholder; value is certainly in the mind of the customer.

> Customers buy products and services because they offer benefits greater than the price of buying, installing and using the product or service – not because they offer technology . . . Many vendors, in fact, confuse technology or product features with benefits . . . marketing decisions need to be transparent, comprehensible and clearly rooted in a common desire to discover, deliver and communicate customer benefits.[13]

Based on sound marketing research, customer benefits should be specifically designed into products; technological excellence itself is no guarantee of business success, as a vehicle manufacturer found out rather painfully. It had redesigned the engine of a military vehicle so that it took up only half the space of the earlier model, but sales did not rise spectacularly. Users preferred a competitor's engine that was much larger but decidedly easier to maintain. Keeping vehicles in commission was far more important than the physical dimensions of the engine. Sadly, the wrong benefits had been offered because of lack of understanding of the real needs of actual users.

CRITICAL FACETS OF MARKETING MANAGEMENT

Earlier it was noted that marketing is both a philosophy and an activity: the former should inspire and motivate every person – at whatever level they work – in a business or other type of organisation; the latter demands professional expertise and dedication to ensure that corporate aspirations are put into practice.

In common with their colleagues in other functional areas of management, marketing managers have four specific responsibilities. These tend to overlap in real life but are distinguished here for purposes of discussion:

1. Analysis.
2. Planning.
3. Control.
4. Implementation.

ANALYSIS

The first function of marketing management relates to finding out about markets in which a company operates at present or which it is planning to enter. Without valid and reliable data, marketing cannot be successful. Through systematic marketing research, present and emergent needs will be identified, analysed and evaluated. This evaluation will cover both quantitative and qualitative assessments related to specific markets and special segments judged to be of value to the business. The interpretation of market needs carries heavy responsibility; it demands, among other managerial qualities, the ability to assess risk and to cope with uncertainty.

Marketing decisions are peculiarly difficult to make; there are so many factors in the environment, such as the level of competitive activity or the effect of fiscal policies, which are almost entirely outside the control of the marketer. The marketing manager is expected to possess entrepreneurial flair and judgement without which he or she is unlikely to be successful. To rely solely on inspiration would, of course, be totally inadequate; professional marketing calls for a blend of analytical and creative skills, especially in the highly competitive conditions which characterise most markets today. (Detailed consideration of market research techniques is given in Chapter 4.)

PLANNING

The second facet of marketing management – planning – follows logically from the analytical approach which, in particular, characterises professional marketing.

Strategic planning involves choosing markets, developing products and services, devising attractive and effective marketing strategies, organising marketing resources and forecasting levels of demand. These are certainly far-reaching responsibilities which demand expertise of a high order.

The success of many industrial firms rests in the ingenuity of their design and marketing staff in offering feasible solutions to the problems of their customers. By collaborating closely with customers in solving, for example, production bottlenecks, suppliers can build up a store of goodwill which will stand them in good stead in competitive markets. Colt International, the air-conditioning equipment specialist, has explained: 'We don't look at ourselves as sellers of heating and ventilating equipment. Our marketing approach is to design whole systems to solve a customer's problems. Our task then is to seek solutions. Obviously there is great scope for new approaches.' Colt places particular stress on the contribution which value analysis has made in approaching customers' problems. 'The VA (value analysis) approach has also led to a distinct improvement in interdepartmental relations. Problems are no longer looked at in isolation but in the context of the whole enterprise, beginning with supplies and ending with after-sales service.'[14] (The techniques of value analysis are also referred to in Chapter 11.)

Technological change and planned obsolescence have intruded into industrial markets. It is no longer safe for industrial product manufacturers to assume that the environment in which they seek business is immune from the instability and dynamic activity which often characterise consumer markets. Sometimes managements fall so much in love with the technological beauty of their product that they fail to observe what is happening in the world outside – the market. Steam locomotive manufacturers, convinced that steam would never lose its prime position, were dismayed to find their 'unchallengeable' market suddenly taken over by diesel electric engines. They had failed to recognise that technological developments had resulted in a more efficient method of rail traction, and that the traditional solution of steam power was no longer acceptable to their customers. The natural law dictates that organisms which fail to adjust to a changing environment eventually perish. If organisations do not modify their products or their methods of marketing, they run the risk of market extinction. In general, there is no shortage of production capacity in modern economies; there is still plenty of scope for industrial and service organisations to adopt a realistic approach to their markets, based on the principles of marketing which have been proved successful in other product fields.

As the sales directors of a large petroleum company observed: 'Whatever product an organisation is marketing – whether it be detergents, ladies' lingerie or motor fuels – all have common problems and often similar marketing objectives. For each there is a constant struggle for optimum profits and market share in a competitive environment, related to supply/demand factors, price, quality and costs. Each is irrevocably linked to the consumer and his changing needs.'[15]

Strategic planning (see Chapters 5–9) is vital: it sets the direction and pace for the whole business – not just for the marketing staff. Decisions about products and services will be formalised in a marketing plan and this can be really successful only if all the other departments of a company are consulted and made aware of the projected market objectives.

CONTROL

The third facet of marketing management – control – is essential to marketing productivity. Standards of performance such as territory sales quotas, market share ratios, cost/sales ratios, advertising/sales ratios, new product budgets, etc. provide critical measures of performance. An efficient feedback system should be devised in collaboration with financial colleagues. The entire span of marketing activities must be monitored and made cost-effective. As with production, standards should be drawn up in marketing operations so that corporate objectives are achieved within given constraints of time and cost.

Other useful marketing control tools will be customer profitability analysis orders stratified by industry and customer size; the ratio of standard to specially manufactured products, etc.

The discipline of cost-effectiveness can be applied to marketing management with notable success. Large volume orders may be very seductive to sales staff, but to the professional marketing executive their effects on profits could be disastrous. No company can continue to operate for long without a reasonable level of profits; orders of dramatic size may help to fill production lines in the short term and it will be a matter of policy whether or not to accept them, but in the long term, only profitable business will ensure that the business continues to exist.

IMPLEMENTATION

This final facet of marketing management entails implementation of the overall marketing strategy and direction of the supporting tactics, ensuring, for example, that selling activities are efficiently targeted and fully co-ordinated; that pricing policies are reflected realistically across ranges and types of products and services; and that promotional plans are fully developed in terms of specific media, advertising appeals, target audiences, frequency of appearance, etc. (See Chapter 5 for further discussion.)

Detailed attention must be given to every aspect of implementing marketing efforts. Nothing should be left to chance, although, of course, environmental changes, such as competitors' behaviour, will occur and demand rapid evaluation. At all costs, bureaucratic rigidity should be avoided; instead, flexibility and leadership are required, so that people in different departments and at all levels are made aware of what the organisation is trying to achieve and how they can help to ensure sucess. One of America's leading management writers and consultants, Russell L. Ackoff, has shrewdly observed that 'the effectiveness of employees can be maximised only if their values and those of the organization are not in conflict'.[16]

Management is essentially concerned with people: it is their performance which builds successful enterprises and distinguishes them from the 'also-rans'.

This brief review of the competences required for professional marketing will indicate that a well-balanced synthesis of skills makes marketing a far more sophisticated area of management responsibility than selling. Marketing is essentially strategic, whereas selling is tactical. This is not in any way to debase the value of selling – which is an important and vital operation – but rather to emphasise that merely to relabel the sales manager a 'marketing manager' is not necessarily going to guarantee that the far wider responsibilities of marketing will be accepted and the corresponding duties performed.

DUAL ROLES OF MARKETING MANAGEMENT

Marketing managers are obviously busy people who are expected to know what is going on in the many markets in which their companies transact business. Their knowledge must be up to date, relevant and reliable, and they must possess analytical talent, creative flair, good social skills and organising ability.

Hence, *two particular roles* have to be fulfilled by marketing managers, in whatever kind of market they operate. They should act as:

1. Interpreters.
2. Integrators.

Again, these roles are not distinct in actual management; at times, one particular activity will tend to become the focus of attention.

INTERPRETER

The role of interpreter means that marketing management have to analyse and evaluate market behaviour and interpret these findings not just to the marketing and sales staff, but to *all* the functions of management which contribute to the firm's existence and development. Everyone in the business should know what markets are at present being supplied and what markets it is planned to enter.

The requirements of these markets in terms of quality, price, delivery and after-sales service should also be known.

INTEGRATOR

The responsibilities of the marketing manager cover the vital function of integrating the marketing plans with all the other activities of the organisation. Adventurous marketing schemes will fall flat on their faces (and so will the marketing managers involved) if this critical stage of integration is neglected. Not the least important market skill is the ability to work in partnership with other managers and to encourage their whole-hearted co-operation through every stage of the marketing operation. This covers the early stages of innovation when an idea is translated into a feasible product or service, through to production on test plant and finally on to regular production lines. It includes budgeting, financial control and all the associated activities which are routine in modern organisations.

Specific aspects of the interface between marketing management and other areas of an organisation will now be discussed in some detail because the integrative function appears often to be overlooked, if not ignored, in many organisations. It may be thought by some marketing managers that this function is not really in their province; nothing is more erroneous. Who else in the organisation should (or could) assume this responsibility if they do not accept it? Certainly not the financial accountant or the production director or the purchasing director or even the personnel director. The managing director will have the overall responsibility of ensuring the efficiency of the organisation but, except in a relatively small firm, he or she is unlikely to have the close personal contact with the various markets in which the organisation operates. The other directors' experience and qualifications are related to areas of expertise different from those of the marketing person. The responsibility to act both as an interpreter *and* as an integrator must be the marketing manager's, who should develop fully his or her managerial skills in both directions.

CORPORATE INTERFACES OF MARKETING

PURCHASING–MARKETING INTERFACE

Marketing management and purchasing management should work closely together, for they share a common responsibility: the efficient application of specific expertise in order to contribute to overall corporate success. Buyers need to understand their suppliers; marketers need to understand their customers. In both cases this is achieved through establishing close links.

The products marketed by many companies – for example, motor vehicles or electrical engineering – depend heavily for their reputation and efficiency on the contributions made by component suppliers. Standards of quality and reliability of delivery are major factors in purchasing strategies and eventually affect the success of marketing plans. Apart from components, other bought-in supplies such as packaging can frustrate marketing efforts. It is not an uncommon experience, unfortunately, for ex-factory deliveries of finished products to fall dramatically because of shortage of vital kinds of packaging. Dual-sourcing – alternative supply sources – has tended to become widely adopted to overcome to some extent the danger of relying exclusively on one supplier whose own production and distribution arrangements may be upset by economic or industrial difficulties.

Christopher Lorenz of the *Financial Times*[17] has drawn attention to 'two powerful but contrasting concepts which just happen to be slightly connected', i.e. *supplier networks* (known in the USA as vendor networks) and *time-to-market*. After 20 years or so, the first is still not commonly adopted, and refers to the establishment of close relationships between a company and a few carefully selected, long-term suppliers who, in turn, have their own networks of sub-suppliers. This has evolved into *partnership sourcing*, as pioneered by IBM, Hewlett-Packard and other large companies in the USA, and which is now attracting increasing interest from British industry. The second concept – *time-to-market* – is concerned with speeding up the complicated process of new product development. (See Chapter 7 for extended discussion of the problems of innovation.)

Both concepts, as Lorenz noted, focus on the need to build close relationships with external suppliers, so as to cut the time taken to bring new products to market.

In the planning of new products, purchasing and marketing should co-operate closely; some novel products may have component parts which place rigorous demands on supplying firms because of new types of raw material or finishing process. The level of stocks to be held and the anticipated rate of deliveries are critical matters to be discussed between production, purchasing, finance and marketing. Supplies must be assured *before* new products are introduced into the regular manufacturing and selling lists. One large pharmaceutical chemical company, because of restricted storage at one of its factories, holds a working-stock of a vital material sufficient for only one week's production. But it has taken great care to ensure that supplies of this material are regularly shipped to the company on a tightly controlled delivery schedule.

Just-in-time (JIT) methods involve holding absolutely minimum levels of stocks of specific components, etc., which are dispatched by suppliers according to tight schedules imposed by their customers. JIT can result in reduced inventory costs, faster response to product modifications, lower wastage rates, and very close relationships between buyers and sellers.

Suppliers are contracted to deliver, on a daily or more frequent basis – under one hour in some instances – relatively small quantities of essential supplies. Delivery schedules must be strictly adhered to, and consistently high standards of quality maintained.

In America, JIT was adopted by General Motors largely because of threatening competition from Japanese car-makers. In the UK, Nissan has developed the system into *synchronised supply*, which entails delivery of components direct to the assembly line just as they are needed. When Ford, over a period of three years, planned production of the Mondeo, which is assembled at Genk in Belgium and at Kansas City in the USA, it drastically cut the number of suppliers to only 200 component-makers. JIT methods were also adopted: about 15 suppliers set up production within about 20 miles of the Genk plant, which is fed with synchronised deliveries of components.

Another valuable contribution which can be made by purchasing management relates to the expert evaluation of trends in, for instance, world commodity markets which are likely to affect sources of raw materials. Production and marketing plans may have to be modified drastically unless adequate buffer stocks have been built up. The soaring costs of some basic materials and the consequent increase in the replacement values of manufacturing stocks are matters which also demand the attention of financial experts in the organisation.

From time to time, suppliers will develop new materials or improve the design of the components which are bought in. If close links are established between marketing, production and purchasing departments, these improvements and innovations can be fully explored. Recognition of the interdependence of the various functional areas of management in modern organisations should help to break down the barriers of professional chauvinism that still tend, regrettably, to feature in managerial behaviour. Innovation is difficult enough without its risks being intensified by a lack of constructive communication between functional areas of management.

Hakansson[18] has noted that some industrial companies encourage an extensive exchange of technical information with suppliers. One strategy, termed 'follow-my-leader', involves buying from the leading supplier in order to obtain early knowledge of technical developments. The other strategy – 'open house' – encourages several suppliers to have ready access to the customer's factory to help in solving technical problems and to develop appropriate products. Suppliers are used, in effect, as extensions of the customer's own technical skills, and if this joint development occurs both parties are likely to benefit significantly.

Two further strategies adopted by some firms' buying departments are: (1) 'market orientation' – continuous monitoring of different sources of supply through close co-operation with several suppliers; and (2) 'environmental anchoring', which involves intensive commercial interaction with one important supplier.

Purchasing management in collaboration with production management may need to investigate the alternatives of make-or-buy; the economies require careful assessment by the financial and costing experts. The security of continued supplies of critical components should not be overlooked. Multiple-sourcing is a favoured buying strategy in order to protect a firm's own markets. In these discussions, the marketing side of the organisation should be consulted so that an overall view of the implications of the proposed new buying strategy can be objectively taken.

Marketing management have the responsibility of advising purchasing departments of the trends in sales of the various products marketed. Maximum/minimum stock levels and ordering quantities of dependent components may have to be adjusted to avoid stock losses and tying up capital in abnormally high stocks.

PRODUCTION–MARKETING INTERFACE

> While marketing is the essential background for business policy, not all of the decisions governed by policy are marketing decisions . . . Many decisions about the management of company resources can be defined as problems of plant layout, materials handling, inventory control, quality control, labour relations or administrative organisation.[19]

Marketing efforts need the firm back-up given by an efficient and co-operative production management. Likewise, production is not an end in itself: its function is to supply products and services which have been designed and made to meet the specified needs of customers, as interpreted by marketing management. As with purchasing, production and marketing efficiency cannot, realistically, be viewed separately. There must necessarily be a spin-off between these sections of an organisation which affects the roots of policy.

If, for instance, marketing management plan to enter a higher-quality market, where customers are likely to be more experienced and sophisticated in their buying behaviour, one of the first steps to take is to ensure that production people are fully aware of the need to upgrade the quality of some product ranges. Higher prices will no doubt be charged, so greater added value should be contributed to products or the whole marketing operaton will prove to be a disastrous flop. It may be necessary to use higher grades of raw materials, to redesign some products, to adopt different manufacturing techniques, and to arrange for stricter standards of quality at every stage of production. Marketing and production efforts should be synchronised; only by sharing the responsibilities of meeting customers' needs are inconsistencies in marketing and production policies to be avoided. Expensive promotional campaigns are wasteful and counterproductive if the goods fail to give satisfaction, or if they are not available to inspect and buy. Companies still fall into the trap of publicising their products on a national scale before ensuring that production resources are adequate to meet the anticipated demand and that the logistics of distribution have been carefully planned well in advance.

Marketing management should allocate part of their time to discussing problems with their production colleagues. As with purchasing, the likely levels of demand for specific products should be fully explored. Limitations in immediate production capacity may mean that the introduction of new products should be carefully phased, perhaps on a regional basis. Essentially, an equilibrium should be established between production and marketing efforts.

Blois[20] has stated that the marketing and manufacturing parts of a business have the same ultimate goal, which is the welfare of the enterprise; this depends on the enterprise's ability to create value. Conflict arises between these functional areas of management because of their 'compartmentalisation', the fact that measures of efficiency are related to departmental and not overall effort, and disagreement as to whether marketing or manufacturing is the most cost-effective way of producing value. The first two problems are said to be well known, but the third is little discussed, despite its critical nature.

The more specialised manufacturing becomes, the more restricted are the end-use markets for the resultant products; marketers must appreciate that such relatively narrow markets can be catered for only if profitable prices are obtainable. An equally important way in which marketing and manufacturing can work well together is for marketing to identify new applications for existing products so that full profit potential is achieved through exploiting experience in production.

It is valuable from time to time for production and marketing management to check manufacturing lists together; stock levels should be compared with sales achieved over certain time periods. One manufacturer once discovered that stocks of a component which was still on their active manufacturing list were sufficient, at present rate of sales, to last for at least 40 years.

Inevitably, management problems are perceived and evaluated according to specific professional responsibilities and experience. Ackoff[16] instances a paper mill whose output was seriously depleted because sales staff were booking orders which covered increasing numbers of different types of paper. This resulted in shorter production runs with resultant high set-up costs; also, many of the products produced no profit. The production manager called in a research team to help solve the problem, which he felt was not his responsibility. Despite opposition from him, the investigators proposed to the marketing manager that certain unprofitable products should be eliminated. This was resisted on the grounds that the business might lose valued customers, so a different solution was put forward: a new system of remuneration for sales staff was devised, which was profit based as distinct from the existing volume-based system. Profitable lines offered the potential for earning increased sales commissions, but non-profitable lines carried no commissions at all. This creative and pragmatic approach was adopted and resulted in increases in profitability, in the incomes of sales staff, and in production efficiency. (See also Chapter 5.)

By working closely with production colleagues, marketing managers not only with break down prejudices and suspicious (the 'them and us' syndrome), but they will also develop a deeper understanding of the whole operation of their organisations. This fuller knowledge will help them in negotiation with customers, and will enable them to suggest feasible solutions to customers' problems which lie within the resources of their firms. Marketing recommendations about product development, for instance, are more likely to attract production management's interest if they take into account the realities of manufacturing, including the constraints under which all firms inevitably have to operate.

Associated closely with production are the research and development activities of companies, particularly those in science-based and technically advanced industries. The critical role of successful new products as a source of corporate development underlines the need for marketing management to keep closely in touch with their R&D colleagues. (Chapter 7 discusses the management of innovation.) Marketing managers should appreciate the problems and processes involved in the development of new products from the idea stage to test-plant production and eventually, perhaps, to commercialisation. It is no use grousing about the nature or rate of new product development if no real interest has been displayed by marketing management in the inevitable frustrations and problems of this exacting task. Marketing knowledge of the needs of particular types of customer should be shared fully with the R&D people so that they have some useful guidelines in their work. They should also know of the contribution which marketing research could make in the evaluation of new products. Sharing of knowledge by the commercial and technical managers involved in new products would reduce the risks which are an inseparable part of an enterprising product strategy.

To quote again from the report of the Institution of Mechanical Engineers to the Advisory Council for Applied Research and Development:

> To define a saleable product requires contact between designer and purchaser. In too many cases these two extremes of the production process fail to meet. Engineers responsible for design should, ideally, have marketing experience. Failing that, they should be in day-to-day contact with the sales force to ensure that essential requirements are not overlooked or lost in transmission.[9]

PERSONNEL–MARKETING INTERFACE

This aspect of a marketing manager's general interest in the efficiency of his or her organisation should not be regarded as of little impact on providing customers with acceptable goods and services. As was observed earlier, people make up organisations and their actions decide the destinies of these firms or other types of corporate undertaking.

Marketing managers are clearly interested in the methods of selecting, training and motivating personnel who work directly in the marketing function. Personnel managers need to be briefed about the nature of the tasks involved in marketing at different levels so that the right kind of staff can be recruited. But apart from this direct influence on personnel policies, marketing management may be able to contribute to the staff training programmes to ensure that a consistent corporate image is reflected to the environment. The telephone operator and receptionist, for example, occupy immensely important links in the chain of corporate communications; often, regrettably, these tend to be the weakest links. Marketing and personnel managers might well tackle this kind of problem, because unless they do so it is unlikely that other functional areas of management will regard it as their responsibility.

FINANCE–MARKETING INTERFACE

Marketing has been defined as profit-generating activity as distinct from selling, which is primarily concerned with sales volume. Since marketing management are motivated by profit, it necessarily follows that they should have a professional interest in efficient methods of budgetary control and costing. The interrelationships between costs, sales volume and profits must be appreciated, while thorough knowledge of the mechanics of cash flow needs to be acquired.

Marketing managers should encourage financial executives to take part in drawing up marketing strategies. A regular flow of financial information related to market performance should prove of immense benefit in directing marketing activities. Financial and marketing people have a great deal in common: the profitable exploitation of corporate resources. Much greater efficiency could result in most organisations from the mutual exchange of knowledge in these vital functions in management.

Pricing policies, for example, while based on accurate systems of costing, are also subject to expert evaluation of market trends. Experts in both financial and marketing areas need to understand the nature and limitations of the inputs which they can contribute to the final policy decisions. (See Chapters 2 and 5 for further discussion of price.)

Marketing involves expenses – sometimes, in the case of advertising campaigns, involving large sums of money. Marketing management should accept the primary discipline of managerial accountability and co-operate in a system of budgetary control. The responsibility of management is to use corporate resources efficiently. Because marketing inputs are often extremely difficult to measure for their effectiveness, particular care is needed to control expenditure in this area of management.

The short- and long-term costs of entering new markets call for several skills in evaluating likely success. Market shares, for example, may be increased quite remarkably, but overall profitability may decline. In dynamic marketing conditions, management expertise should be subscribed from many specialities; that marketing management and financial management are able to offer complementary knowledge and skills should be acknowledged by practical managerial involvement.

CO-ORDINATING AND INTEGRATING MARKETING

Through discussion of the interface relationships of marketing, an attempt has been made to widen the traditional perspective of its responsibilities and to emphasise the need for the various managerial disciplines to co-operate actively in pursuit of the declared objectives, i.e. policy, of an organisation. (See Figure 1.3.)

The parochial activities which tend to drive wedges between areas of management cannot be tolerated. Marketing management should not be viewed as hatching some kind of sinister takeover scheme for their organisations. All organisations must serve their publics or eventually they will fail in economic terms as well as in the social benefits they plan to confer. To be successful, organisations should keep in touch with the environment; this is the specific task of marketing, particularly in large organisations which have lost the personal antennae with which the small business could so usefully check its sphere of operations.

At a given period in the life of an organisation, certain constraints are the principal limiting factors. In the case of industrial concerns, these could relate to production capacity or skilled labour, or availability of specific qualities of raw materials. The immediately available corporate resources must be used to greatest advantage, while in the long term, production and marketing plans are devised which will ensure the growth and prosperity of the organisation. Stability must be ensured before expansion is feasible. Objective analysis of market opportunities will give management guides as to where the organisation can 'plug into' the market.

Marketing strategies rarely succeed in isolation; marketing managers should not regard themselves as solo performers in the environmental arena. They need the

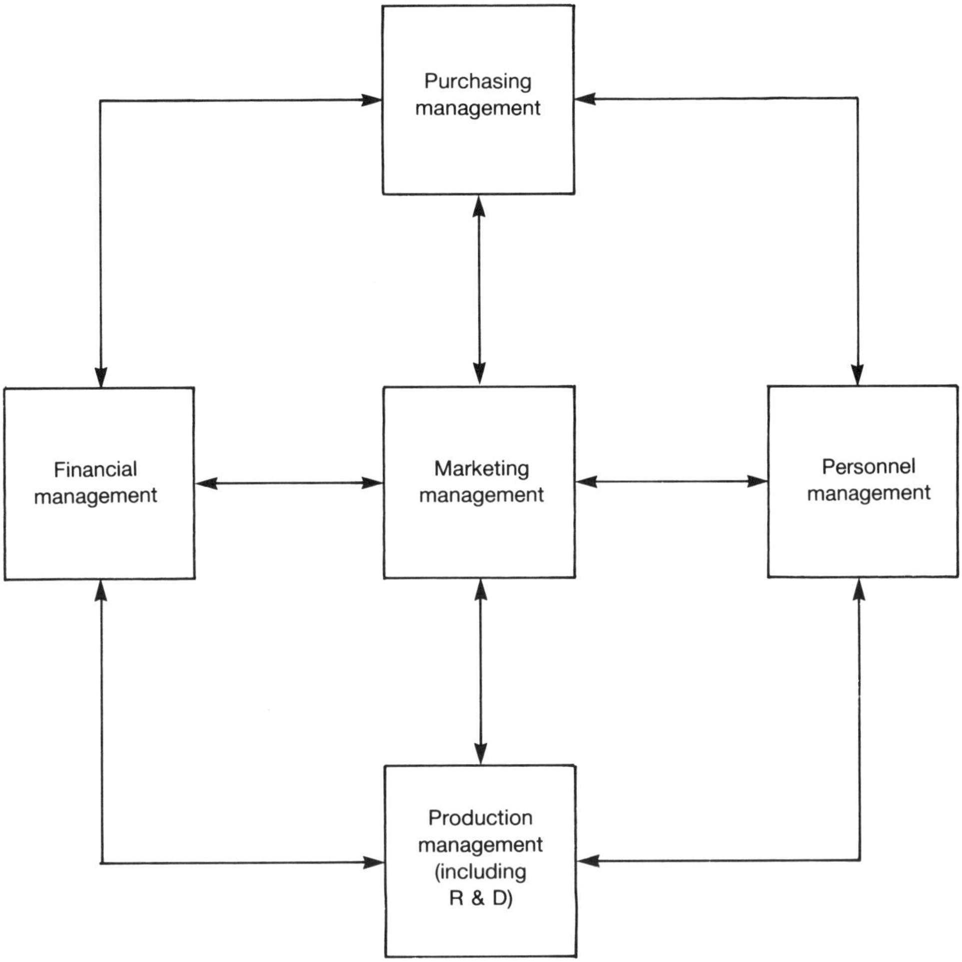

FIGURE 1.3 Corporate interface of marketing

professional expertise and personal support of other departmental executives. It is time that managers were educated in the art and science of intra-organisational negotiation.

To quote Ackoff again: 'The performance of any system, therefore of a company, is never equal to the sum of the performance of its parts taken separately. *It is the product of their interactions*.'[16] The core of successful operations in any organisation lies in the effectiveness with which *interactions* are managed within departments and throughout the entire span of activities. While functional specialisms in management demand specialised knowledge, skills and expertise, managerial attitudes and behaviour should always encourage the development of 'working partnerships', which enable information to be shared readily, problems discussed creatively, and opportunities assessed objectively.

As Michael Porter[21] has stated in his monumental text *The Competitive Advantage of Nations*, there is no shortage of explanations why some nations are competitive and others are not. So, also, with the companies which contribute to these various economies. But to survive – and, indeed, grow – under the unrelenting pressures of contemporary trading conditions, is a direct challenge to the ingenuity of management, particularly those who have to win business against world-wide competition.

CORPORATE PERFORMANCE: VITAL INPUTS AND RELATIONSHIPS

So far in this chapter the nature of marketing, its range of responsibilities and specific functions have been discussed. Further, the interdependence of the specialised areas of management expertise have been described in some detail.

These vital managerial inputs and relationships are shown in Figure 1.4: the six principal areas of management expertise make distinctive contributions to

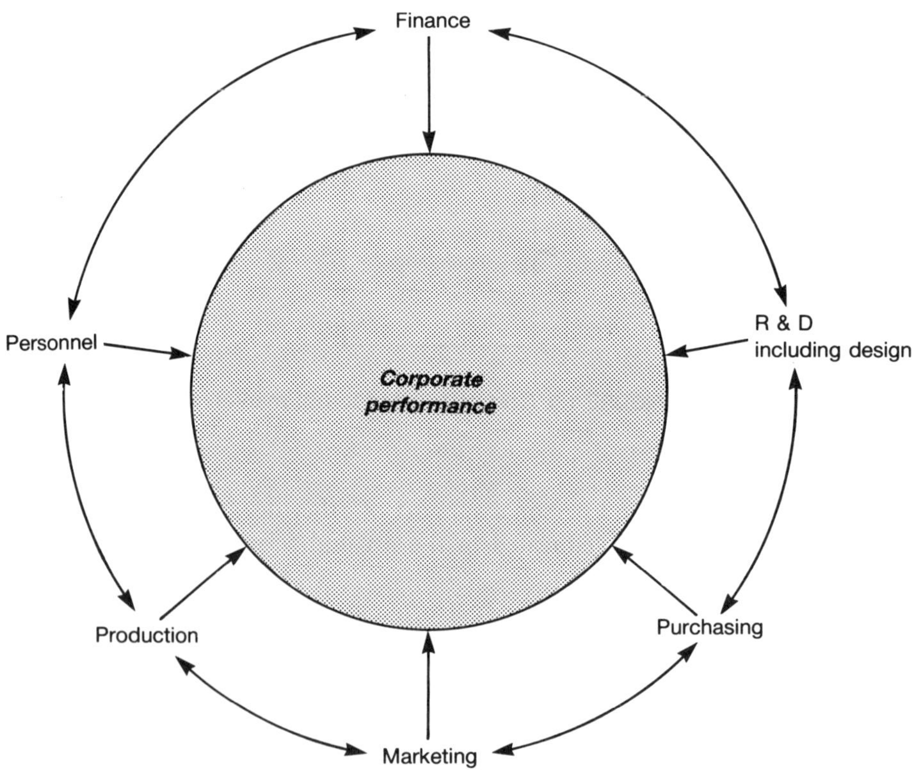

FIGURE 1.4 Vital inputs to corporate performance

corporate performance. Together they form a coherent and balanced set of specialised skills; one weak performer in this 'circle of competences' can frustrate overall performance and even result in corporate losses being incurred.

Management specialists are inevitable in complex organisations; each functional area of management can make its own unique contribution to the general prosperity of an organisation. Marketing expertise is a necessary but not sufficient condition for success in competitive environments. Whole-hearted enthusiastic backing from *all* managers and staff is critical for significant corporate performance. Linkages between management specialisms should be actively forged and encouraged to develop.

Marketing management should make sure that everyone in their company is aware of the nature of the markets at which their products are targeted, so that a real team effort takes place through every department, and at every level, of the firm. Every cog in a wheel makes a vital contribution to the efficient meshing of the mechanism.

Information about markets, drawn from first-hand marketing research, should be discussed with designers, production engineers, purchasing officers, etc. Marketing research should not be hoarded and used solely by the marketing departments: full value should be extracted from such important and often expensive data, so that, for example, product improvements and product innovations can be planned to satisfy the specific needs of identified market segments. There are, as the chairman of Courtaulds noted in his company's report two aspects of any company that determine its future: *what* it does and *how* it does it.

> There is a tendency for business commentators to overemphasise the first of these – to imply, for example, that participation in a growth industry, whether pharmaceuticals or electronics, is by itself sufficient to ensure profits growth. But the fact is that how well a company operates in its business is just as important as what it does, if not more so.[22]

The curious ambivalence of senior industrial management towards the role of marketing in their companies was noted in a survey commissioned by a leading firm of chartered accountants and management consultants. Although senior executives stated that marketing was their primary concern in planning the development of their companies, organisational commitment to marketing was often lacking. They comment that 'clearly there is a gap between good intentions and effective marketing action'.[23]

The report observes that the creation of a strong market orientation is far too important to be left to specialists; it should demand the attention and enthusiasm of the chief executive, who is 'personally committed to the marketing concept and is prepared to encourage changes in attitudes and working practices aimed at improving marketing performance *throughout the company*'. Industrial companies in particular are urged to adopt this 'top-down' and 'company-wide' approach to marketing. Engineering component manufacturers, for instance, frequently work to tight technical specifications. To do this profitably, market research, financial control, production efficiency, effective distribution and sound technical sales back-up are all essential; 'a total team approach and commitment to the customer' is the only way to ensure success.

Sir Douglas Hague, a former chairman of the Economic and Social Research Council, strongly endorses this integrated view of marketing which should be actively propagated at board level:

> In a sense, marketing is concerned with every aspect of the business . . . It does not mean that marketing is the most important function in the business. It does mean that the firm's top management must be sure that the firm is so organised that marketing problems are seen as problems of the whole firm . . . It is from the effectiveness of its marketing policy that the biggest influence on the firm's total profitability and growth will come.[24]

APPLICATIONS OF ORGANISATIONAL MARKETING

Marketing expertise can be applied in a diverse range of organisations. In Chapter 2, the UK economy is described as a service economy and this phenomenon is explored at some length.

In the language of economics, both goods and services provide 'utilities' which possess value-in-exchange. The production of tangible goods dominated the earlier years of industrialisation and provided the main source of employment in the United Kingdom and other developed countries. Although manufacturing industry is still a significant part of the UK economy, the tertiary or service section of the economy has achieved prominence both as a source of employment and as a major contributor to the national income. It is, therefore, very relevant to consider marketing in its relationship to the service industries.

At the same time it would be well to bear in mind, as Sir Monty Finniston noted in a lecture given at the Royal Society of Arts, that although services 'are necessary to the conduct of wealth creation and may conserve wealth – e.g. doctors, nurses, firemen, postmen, sewage operatives – they are not, with some exceptions – e.g. consultancy and project management – primary agents for wealth creation'.[25] However, such services need efficient management, perhaps more so if they are in the public sector.

MARKETING OF SERVICES RELATIVELY NEGLECTED

The role of marketing in the service industries has tended to be neglected; management literature has largely confined marketing theory and applications to products, the majority of which have been concerned with consumer markets. Discussion of how marketing techniques can be useful in the service sector has generally been limited to banking over the past decade or so. Now it is advisable to extend the discussion to a much wider range of services because of the importance they have assumed in modern economics. It will be useful to lead this enlarged discussion by a brief look at the nature of services and some of the ways in which they could be defined and helped by marketing action.

In 1964 Robert C. Judd,[26] writing in the *Journal of Marketing*, deplored that although 'the dollar volume of marketing services continues to increase, yet the definition of what constitutes a service remains imprecise.' His article was followed about two years later by that of another American marketing professor, who noted: 'The marketing discipline has a strong "goods" orientation. In academic courses in marketing, tangible goods are considered, but rarely services to any extent. Yet services represent an area of economic activity that accounts for 30–40 per cent of consumer dollar expenditures.'[27] Today, of course, the contribution of services to modern economies such as that of the United States has risen very significantly.

In 1972 Aubrey Wilson presented the case for adapting and applying marketing techniques to achieve greater efficiency in professional services such as banking, consultancy, architecture and accountancy, to which he confined his constructive text. Apart from the wide spectrum of professional services, there are, of course, many other non-tangible inputs into the national economy. Further, Wilson's definition of professional services – 'A professional service is one purchased by industry and institutions from individuals and organisations'[28] – appeared to overlook that professional services (such as legal services) are used by individuals as well as by corporate undertakings. Moreover, the nature and extent of the services which attract the label 'professional' are not at all clear. After protracted study, the Monopolies Commission report on professional services' activities could only go so far as to comment: 'We have not found it possible to define them precisely or to establish a definitive list of professions. We do not in any case think such a definition necessary.'[29]

TYPES OF SERVICE

Services may be classified in two broad areas: commercial services (corporate clients) and consumer services (private clients); these are not mutually exclusive.

Commercial services are provided to organisations to enable them to achieve their corporate objectives, which, in the case of industrial and commercial companies, generally relate to profit targets. However, services are consumed by non-profit organisations because the entire economic system requires services of many kinds to keep it viable. Financial, insurance, legal, transport, security and communications services typify those which are indispensable to organisations, whether profit-motivated or not. Organisational buyers in the public service and in industry may differ in their prime motivation, but they share the same responsibilities: to procure goods and services for use in their organisations as opposed to personal consumption.

Consumer services, on the other hand, are those provided direct to satisfy personal needs. These are of many kinds – legal, financial, medical, technical, insurance, hairdressing, etc. Expenditure on services, as noted earlier, has increased significantly over the past 30 years or so. (See Chapter 2 for further discussion.)

Some kinds of service, e.g. legal, are of course used for both personal and organisational benefit, although for different tasks.

Services may also be viewed along a continuum from complex to simple. At one extreme, there are services such as air-conditioning or airlines; at the other pole, the delivery of domestic milk or newspapers. It is suggested that services often tend to devolve from complex to relatively simple projects. Domestic central heating installations, for example, have been simplified by automatic boiler equipment and small-bore piping. Air transport has been simplified ('air-shuttle' operations) and there is, therefore, a move across the continuum. Computer installations, although instrinsically complex, can offer a wide variety of data services, from relatively simple analyses to highly complex statistical manipulations. Programs may, therefore, range across the whole continuum.

Services could also be typified according to the time they are administered. Several commercial and consumer services could be rendered: pre-sales → during sales → post-sales. Pre-sales services would include advertising, point of purchase displays, demonstrations, exhibitions and related activities. Also included would be the provision of technical data, submission of quotations and specimen products. The intermediate services cover negotiations – which may be a lengthy and involved series of discussions – leading to the booking of acceptable business. After-sales service is a vital element of the product–service mix. Many products require efficient after-sales service; manufactures can reassure customers through offering effective back-up services. 'In several industrial product markets, "package deals" involving the supply, installation and servicing of equipment help to overcome buyers' legitimate anxieties and confirm their judgement in selecting particular suppliers.'[30] Dissonance reduction should be one of the main objectives of a planned system of servicing.

Levitt[31] points out that prospective buyers of services are generally forced to depend on surrogates to assess what they are likely to get. For instance, they can gaze at glossy brochures depicting distant holiday locations; they can consult current users of a certain software program about its performance; or they can ask existing clients of solicitors or management consultants about their levels of satisfaction with the services provided. Whereas tangible products can often be directly handled and even tested in advance of commitment to purchase, it is usually difficult, if not impossible, to do the same with intangible products. It may of course be possible, as with hotels, to book a weekend stay as a preliminary to a longer holiday, and this may test the facilities.

The complexity of some services may inhibit their diffusion; sometimes there are too many variables to consider before a decision can be taken. The popularity of package-deal holidays supports the argument for simplifying the adoption processes in services. The method of acquiring several other services could be simplified with advantage – for example, life assurance. The growth of credit usage in Britain in recent years has been greatly influenced by the introduction of bank credit cards. This credit service offers customers a relatively easy method of acquiring a financial loan to purchase goods at stores and other outlets which are parties to the credit card franchise. This is a decidedly more flexible approach by the banks to customers seeking credit than the rather cumbersome enquiries which, at one time, characterised the granting of an overdraft.

MARKETING TECHNIQUES FOR SERVICES

As with products, the markets for services are dynamic, and so services should be designed to keep abreast of changing needs. Hence, *marketing research* should be undertaken to analyse and evaluate market behaviour. This systematic and analytical approach uses the same methodologies as applied for many years in researching product markets. Whether products are tangible or intangible, buying motivations (for example) should be identified before attempting to influence people or organisations to acquire them (see Chapter 4).

Some American researchers[32] were interested in determining the degree of market orientation by service firms in the United States. It was believed that, generally, service firms lagged behind manufacturing firms in market orientation. From a mail survey of 1,000 service firms randomly chosen from the 1982 edition of Dun and Bradstreet's *Million Dollar Directory*, an effective sample of 323 firms from a variety of service industries was obtained. Firms were asked to rate on a five-point scale nine statements which were chosen as indicators of marketing orientation: for example, 'When a customer is dissatisfied with our service, we perform the service again at no charge.' The findings of this study showed that service firms 'are quite heterogeneous with respect to their degree of marketing orientation'. Local firms were significantly less marketing orientated than non-local firms; so also were consumer service firms compared with firms which 'had above average competitive positions'.

The researchers concluded that service firms which neglect marketing are 'exceedingly vulnerable', especially when new entrants challenge established businesses. Although this particular research was done over 20 years ago, its findings appear to be still highly relevant today.

Service industries cannot neglect marketing expertise and expect to survive in the free-for-all that now characterises their markets, as well as tangible goods markets.

International banking, for example, has undergone a vast change over recent years, and competition is now of a new order and virulence. In a striking review in *Long Range Planning*, Graham Turner analysed the future ambitions of Japan's financial giants, indicating that no fewer than 27 of the world's 50 largest banks, among which there is intense competition, are Japanese. Now they have their corporate eyes firmly focused on investment or merchant banking, which they are particularly eager to exploit because 'some of their best clients have been picked off by American houses like Salomon Brothers' during the last few years. 'Powerful and effective overseas bases are also important to the great Japanese financial institutions because they are crucial in helping to bridge the vast cultural and language gap which currently exists between Japan and the West and which must be closed if they are to become truly global players.'[33] Truly, the rules of the game are radically different and the banking arena is certainly full of vigorous players.

After using marketing research, the next marketing technique that can be applied to the service industries is *strategic planning* (see Chapters 5–9).

Planning, whether of tangible or intangible products, is the foundation of an effective marketing strategy. Again, the principles are the same across diverse markets; the 'marketing mix' or combination of marketing inputs may well vary, according to the nature of specific services and market environments. Market planning entails the design and development of services aimed to satisfy the needs of particular kinds of client, as identified through market research.

Strategic planning should be done thoroughly: it includes the setting of objectives, market target figures, promotional policies, distributive arrangements (e.g. branch network related to market potential), tactical selling operations (this may involve sales training programmes), etc. The planning stage should include the development of new services: innovation in the service industries is as vital as in product markets. Over recent years, many new services have become available to industrial and private users: containerised shipments, roll-on/roll-off loaders, cash dispensing machines, launderettes, private health insurance, abolition or rationalisation of bank charges, option mortgages, barge-aboard catamarans and special banking arrangements for students. Marketers of services should monitor their markets and be prepared to innovate by offering new or improved services.

At the planning stage, the communications policy has to be worked out; from this will develop the corporate image upon which the future success of a bank, building society or technical service will largely depend (see Chapter 10).

An effective communications strategy makes full use of the varied forms of publicity available in modern communities. These include media advertising, editorial comment and public relations activities of various kinds. With financial services in particular, the location and appearance of offices is important in building an acceptable corporate image. The joint-stock banks have adopted corporate symbols which clearly distinguish their branch offices and give psychological reassurance to clients.

In the past, the joint-stock banks have tended to ignore the marketing concept; they have not responded quickly enough to the more critical expectations of their clients, both corporate and personal. Efforts to attract customers have been sporadic and not very well organised. The phenomenal growth of US banks in the United Kingdom and the development of other financial houses indicate the dynamic, competitive nature of modern financial services markets. The rapid growth of unit trusts in the United Kingdom was largely due to highly trained and motivated sales people who were able to communicate effectively with target audiences.

Telephone banking is an innovation in British banking services which is spreading rapidly. *First direct* was launched by Midland Bank in 1989 and is claimed to be attracting 4,000–5,000 new customers a month; this was followed, in 1991, by *Prime Line* backed by National Westminster. These new banking ventures offer a full range of financial services, from savings accounts to unsecured loans and share dealing, independent of local branch accounts. Other types of tele-banking are associated with existing branch-based accounts, and are run by several banks, including TSB (Speedline) and NatWest (Actionline).

Since 1987, the joint-stock banks have faced growing competition from building societies, whose operations have been permitted to be extended into unsecured lending, insurance, second mortgages, etc. In particular, dynamic marketing programmes have been devised by Halifax, Nationwide Anglia, Abbey National and Leeds Permanent, with the avowed ambition of their becoming major banks. In retaliation, the clearing banks entered the house mortgage market, and started to pay interest on current account balances. At last, it seems they recognise that, as a senior banker once said, they are in a highly price-sensitive, commodity market with a lot of new entrants of determined professionalism.

Two essential marketing techniques – *research and planning* – have been discussed relative to service industries. A third technique, *marketing control*, is applicable; an organised feedback system is necessary to evaluate the performance of marketing strategies. In dynamic market conditions, strategic targets and tactical operations should be under continuous appraisal, so that an organisation retains the initiative in its markets. Strategy links the needs of the client with the objectives of the organisation to achieve the optimum allocation of corporate resources. While it is obviously necessary to formulate plans covering activities some time ahead, rigidity should be guarded against; the development of alternative strategies ensures that management has a flexible approach to changes in the environment.

The marketing information system referred to earlier should incorporate control data to ensure that marketing efforts are effectively deployed.

SERVICE INDUSTRIES AND THE 'MIXED' ECONOMY

In the United Kingdom, the private sector and the public sector are closely meshed and form what is termed the 'mixed economy'. (See Chapter 2 for further discussion.) The public services of health, welfare, education, communications and the road network system form an indispensable part of the infrastructure of a sophisticated community.

Management is not a term to which the 'caring professions' take readily: to be asked to accept marketing as a specialised activity of management is likely to result in a state of acute hypertension. But the health care systems in the United Kingdom are under stress and their efficiency is being openly challenged. Old attitudes die hard in old professions, while new commercial stances are viewed with suspicion if not downright hostility. The Office of Fair Trading (OFT) is exerting pressure on doctors' and dentists' professional organisations, which impose severe advertising restrictions on their members. The Law Society has already relaxed, to some degree, its rules on professional publicity. Competition is gradually appearing in the professions. 'So far the furthest the BMA has gone down the marketing road has been to issue guidelines advising doctors of ways to impart information to patients.'[34] Dentists, however, have been allowed more leeway: since 1986 they have been able to conduct limited forms of advertising, no doubt influenced by the OFT's view that it was desirable for patients to have better information about their services.

Private sector businesses and public sector undertakings differ in their philosophies and market behaviour, but they are all concerned with meeting specific needs at both corporate and personal levels. The efficient allocation of scarce resources should be a matter of concern for all management, wherever they may exercise their responsibilities.

It has been argued elsewhere[35] that government and social planners should make far greater use of marketing research in the design of the public services. Many of these, such as health care, intimately affect the minds, bodies and lives of people of all ages and social groups. Such vital services should not be designed without objective enquiry about patients' health and social needs, life styles, expectations, etc. Good intentions are no substitute for decisions which have been based on systematic research.

In the United States, where the organisation of the health services is different from the UK system, marketing research is quite widely used to assess market needs. Since the roots of marketing research in the United Kingdom lie deep in social investigations by such pioneers as Booth, Bowley and Rowntree, application of market research to the areas of health and the other public services should certainly not be regarded as unacceptable.

Objective survey enquiries have helped in the development of services for the disabled[36] by identifying the nature and extent of certain kinds of disablement and the ways in which people of various ages are able to cope with the ordinary tasks of living in their own households. There are many other areas of human activity where marketing research can be most usefully applied to give insight and guidance to policy-makers and professional workers. Vast programmes of public health and social welfare should not be undertaken without systematic research at both national and regional levels.

The publicly administered services are not subject to the management discipline of generating profit. Standards of efficiency should be drawn up, therefore, related to the expectations and needs of the specific communities catered for by these services.

Clearly, the provision of services in response to the needs of modern society should not be undertaken without heed to the costs involved; this particularly applies to service monopolies which are not primarily affected by commercial constraints.

In planning services, whether these are associated with commercial activities or with the public sector, more attention should be given to input/output measurement. Otherwise, there is a very real danger that services may become over-elaborated and wastefully administered, devouring resources out of proportion to their contribution to the efficiency of an organisation or to the welfare of a community.

The public and private sectors in the United Kingdom are in tandem, and are substantially interdependent. Managers in both sectors should establish mutual respect and understanding of their individual roles in the economy: partnership is preferable to partisanship.

Later discussion in this text highlights the critical dependency of several private sector industries on the public sector. In addition, political factors may intervene and largely determine the fates of certain industries or even companies.

Government intervention in industrial activities is no longer unique. Regional policies have been developed to influence, both directly and through various incentives, the location of new factories, in an attempt to balance the decline of some of the United Kingdom's traditional industries such as coal mining, textiles and shipbuilding.

The complexity of the public sector, which frequently endures internal conflict between public accountability, commercial viability, and political pressures, places particular stresses on the provision and management of services affecting the welfare of individuals as well as those influencing the development of business and industry. For instance, alternative ways of financing the development of new motorways in the UK have been discussed for several years, and schemes have been proposed by leading commercial contractors that would enable expansion of these major networks to continue within the constraints of public sector budgetary expenditure.

MARKETING IN A POST-INDUSTRIAL SOCIETY

The wealth of a nation is built up from the contributions made by its productive resources. In a developed country like the UK, these resources are many and complex. Radical changes have affected the structure of the industrial and commercial base; the older industries of steel, coal, shipbuilding and textiles have shrunk, while newer industries – based, for example, on electronics, computer technology or sophisticated technical and advisory services – have become significant contributors to the national wealth.

In this competitive, dynamic environment, British industry and commerce should use all the talents and energies of the workforce. Production resources relate to both tangible and intangible products; to the public sector and to the private sector industries; to goods and services marketed for profit, and to those provided by national and regional administrations. Various management disciplines have evolved to handle efficiently the production and exchange of goods and services.

Marketing is one of these vital managerial functions necessary to ensure that organisations across the whole spectrum of economic and social activity provide people in industry and elsewhere with acceptable products and services.

Professor Derek Abell of IMEDE has stressed that the failure to be market driven can be felt right through the whole of a company's operations. Some 15 years ago, a large mechanical engineering company, renowned over 75 years for the quality of its industrial products and technological expertise, experienced loss of market share, competitive superiority and price competitiveness. 'For nearly five years, the company anguished over slipping sales and market share while profits turned to losses.'[37] Eventually, its problems were recognised to stem from product features and ranges that were no longer acceptable to their customers. They were also woefully out of touch with the changed segmentation of their markets, which now demanded new combinations of high-value-added products, technology and service in some sectors, while in more mature sectors, mostly concerned with standardised products, success depended on offering low prices and prompt deliveries.

Following this analysis, a cost-cutting exercise and improved manufacturing techniques were introduced. However, the company clearly needs to sustain a long-term drive to assure its future prosperity.

SUMMARY

Marketing is a specialised function of management which is not restricted to consumer products: it has a vital role in many types of organisation – industrial, commercial, public sector services, charities, etc. The techniques of marketing cover four areas of activity: analysis, planning, control and implementation; these tend to overlap in real life. The analytical approach involves marketing research and interpretation of data; the planning factor follows logically, and involves choices of markets, development of products and services, organising effective marketing strategies and tactics, etc.; the control element is essential for marketing productivity: setting of performance standards – market share ratios, territory sales quotas, etc.

Marketing management have two roles: (1) interpreter; and (2) integrator. The first role concerns analysis and evaluation of markets and communicating findings in terms of quality, price, service, etc., so that the whole business is responsive to customers' needs. The second role covers the important task of integrating marketing plans with all the other activities of the business. The corporate interfaces of marketing necessitate close relationships with other specialised functions of management, such as purchasing, finance, personnel, production, R&D and design. All these specialised skills contribute to corporate performance; a balanced team is imperative for success.

Apart from physical products, marketing has valuable applications in service industries, and its techniques, such as marketing research, can be applied to improve market knowledge and in the preparation of strategic plans. There is immense scope for effective marketing in modern service economies. As well as profit-motivated services, the public sector services of health, education and social welfare can improve their efficiency and offer more relevant benefits through using, for example, market and social research to guide the design of patient-care programmes.

REFERENCES

1. Maslow, A. H., 'A theory of human motivation', *Psychological Review*, vol. 50, 1943.
2. Montagnon, Peter, 'What makes the top dogs tick', *Financial Times*, 29 September 1992.
3. Newland, M., 'The art and science of service', *Marketing Business*, 1992.
4. Smith, Adam, *Wealth of Nations*, Rawdon House Inc., New York, 1937.
5. Levitt, Theodore, *Marketing for Business Growth*, McGraw-Hill, New York, 1974.
6. Drucker, Peter F., *The Practice of Management*, Heinemann, London, 1961.
7. Marsh, Peter, 'Marketing higher value niches', *Financial Times*, 22 January 1990.
8. Machine Tools Economic Development Committee, *A Handbook for Marketing Machinery*, HMSO, London, October 1970.
9. 'Industrial innovation: a submission to the Advisory Council for Applied Research and Development', The Institute of Mechanical Engineers, 24 October 1979.
10. National Economic Development Office, *The Plastics Industry and its Prospects.* A Report of the Plastics Working Party of the Chemicals EDC, HMSO, London, July 1971.
11. Lorenz, Christopher, 'Teamwork is tricky', *Financial Times*, 1 October 1990.
12. Heller, Robert, *The Naked Manager*, Barrie and Jenkins, London, 1971.
13. Nevens, Michael, 'When the going gets tough, the tough excel at marketing', *Electronic Business*, Reed Publishing, 1 January 1987.
14. Tavernier, Gerard, 'Where value analysis is a way of life', *International Management*, February 1975.
15. Smolden, Wilfred, 'Increasing penetration in consumer markets', in *Long Range Planning for Marketing and Diversification*, ed. G. Wills and B. Taylor, Bradford University Press/Crosby/Lockwood, London, 1971.
16. Ackoff, Russell, *Management in Small Doses*, John Wiley, New York, 1986.
17. Lorenz, Christopher, 'A daunting menu for managers', *Financial Times*, 14 August 1992.
18. Hakansson, Hakan (ed.), *International Marketing and Purchasing of Industrial Goods: An interaction approach*, Wiley, Chichester, 1983.
19. Alderson, Wroe, *Marketing Behaviour and Executive Action*, Richard D. Irwin, Homewood, Ill. 1957.
20. Blois, K. J., 'The manufacturing/marketing orientation and its information needs', *European Journal of Marketing*, vol. 14, no. 5/6, 1980.
21. Porter, Michael, *The Competitive Advantage of Nations*, Macmillan, London, 1990.
22. Hogg, Sir Christopher, Courtaulds PLC Company Report and Accounts, 1986/7.
23. Tellick, Jan, and Mason, Andrew, 'Facing the market', *Arthur Young Business View*, ed. R. Buckley, no. 12, spring/summer 1986.

24. Hague, Sir Douglas, *Managerial Economics: Analysis for business decisions*, Longman, London, 1977.
25. Finniston, Sir Monty, 'Creative management,' *Journal of the Royal Society of Arts*, vol. 126, no. 5263, 1978.
26. Judd, Robert C., 'The case for redefining services', *Journal of Marketing*, vol. 28, 1964.
27. Rathmell, John M., 'What is meant by services?' *Journal of Marketing*, vol. 30, 1966.
28. Wilson, Aubrey, *The Marketing of Professional Services*, McGraw-Hill, Maidenhead, 1972.
29. Monopolies Commission, *A Report on the General Effect on the Public Interest of Certain Restrictive Practices so Far as they Prevail in Relation to the Supply of Professional Services*, Part 1, HMSO, London, 1970.
30. Chisnall, Peter M. *Marketing: A behavioural analysis*, McGraw-Hill, Maidenhead, 1975.
31. Levitt, Thedore, 'Marketing intangible products and product intangibles', *Harvard Business Review*, vol. 59, no. 3, 1981.
32. Parasuraman, A., Berry, Leonard L., and Zeithaml, Valerie A., 'Service firms need marketing skills', *Business Horizons*, vol. 26, no. 6, 1983.
33. Turner, Graham, 'The future ambitions of Japanese financial giants', *Long Range Planning*, vol. 20, no. 5, 1987.
34. McEwan, Geona, 'Nibbling at marketing', *Financial Times*, 3 December 1987.
35. Chisnall, Peter M., 'Market research', *Management for Health Service Administrators*, ed. D. Allen and J. G. Hughes, Pitman Medical, London, 1983.
36. Chisnall, Peter M., 'Market research applied to health and social welfare: a study of health and disability in a UK metropolitan borough', *Esomar*, Barcelona, August/September 1983.
37. Abell, Derek F., 'The middleman: an imperative for market driven organizations', *Perspectives for Managers*, no. 2, IMEDE, Lausanne, 1988.

REVIEW AND DISCUSSION QUESTIONS

Q1 What do you consider to be the more significant features of marketing as a business philosophy?

Q2 Why, in your view, has the marketing concept been slower to emerge in industrial firms than in those producing consumer goods and services?

Q3 Are there any specific difficulties which marketing managers of industrial firms encounter in their dealings with managers who have other functional responsibilities?

Q4 How might the four functions of management apply to the marketing manager of a firm marketing fax machines?

Q5 Take two organisations with which you are familiar and compare the degree to which corporate interface relations are encouraged in each.

Q6 How might the distinction between industrial products and industrial services affect the activities of a marketing manager in the corporate banking sector?

CHAPTER TWO

Characteristics of industrial markets

BRITISH INDUSTRIAL TRENDS

For many generations, Britain, the oldest industrialised nation, once dubbed the 'Workshop of the World', dominated world manufactures; the traditional pattern was for British imports of food and raw materials to be offset by large-scale exports of manufactured products of many kinds. For example, in the late nineteenth century, British textile machinery makers enjoyed 80 per cent of world trade and there was virtually no import penetration into the country. 'From 1868 to 1872 the country passed through a roaring boom which Disraeli described as a "convulsion of prosperity", but in 1873 there was a financial crash';[1] from 1873 to 1896, British industry suffered a 'great depression', and it was alleged that foreigners were stealing business. The rising industrial powers of the United States and Germany directly challenged Britain's long-held trading supremacy, which has never been regained.

After the Second World War, a radical restructuring of world trade took place. The United Kingdom in common with the other developed economies of the western world faced new competition in manufactured products from production centres set up in the newly industrialised countries, such as Taiwan, the Philippines, Singapore, Brazil and Turkey. Raw materials were processed into semi-manufactures, while new plants making, for example, electronic products and cars were built from scratch.

Meanwhile, the UK's trading position was increasingly threatened by high inflation, low productivity, soaring energy costs and poor labour relations: over the period 1950–80, GDP increased by less than 2 per cent per annum. Several economists and politicians have expressed concern about what is termed the 'de-industrialisation' of the UK over the post-war years. In 1960 manufacturing output accounted for over 40 per cent of GDP, but by 1988 this figure had fallen dramatically to under one-quarter. Currently, the UK share of world trade is around 7 per cent – just about half of what it was in 1964. Import penetration of manufactured goods like machine tools, as well as many types of consumer product, continues to threaten the UK economy. Textile machinery, as noted earlier, was once firmly in the hands of British firms; but by 1975 the world leader was Germany, followed by Switzerland and Japan. Between 1970 and 1975, almost nine out of ten textile manufacturers in the UK bought foreign machines, and a survey found that 45 per cent said that these imports worked better and were of more advanced design, while 38 per cent stated that there was no suitable British machine available; 9 per cent felt that foreign firms seemed to understand the user better and gave superior service. It is instructive to note that only 4 per cent gave price as a reason for purchase.

CLASSICAL ANALYSIS OF INDUSTRIAL ACTIVITIES

Economists have traditionally divided the activities of working populations into three main groups: primary, secondary and tertiary. The primary or extractive sector covers agriculture, mining, forestry and fishing, which are particularly significant occupations in relatively mature economies. The secondary or manufacturing sector refers to the manufacturing and construction industries which, as a country's industrial development evolves, compete with and finally supplant the primary sector as the major source of economic wealth. The tertiary sector relates to the service and distributive trades – to those employed in what has been termed 'incorporeal production'.

The shift from growing products to making products and then to offering services, often closely associated with specific types of product, characterises all advanced economies. In what has been termed the post-industrial society, the tertiary sector of the economy has become the major source of new employment. Increasingly, the service sector has focused on knowledge-related services for professional and business needs.

BIRTH OF A SERVICE ECONOMY

As already noted in Chapter 1, a service economy reflects a relatively wealthy society which has the major proportion of its employment in the tertiary sector. Sophisticated products, such as those based on chemicals and electronics, advance while the older industrial activities, like coal mining and textile manufacture, assume less importance to the overall national economy. The industrial revolution has been reactivated by far-reaching technological changes, automation and improvements in managerial systems of administration and control which have profoundly changed industrial and commercial life. With improved standards of health, education, welfare and conditions of employment, and, in general, rising levels of real income, a new industrial society has been created. 'In a poor society, there is insufficient wealth to provide capital for social services, scientific and industrial research, and the many opportunities of an advanced economy.'[2]

Obviously, the increasing dependence of modern economies on the efficiency of the service industries is a matter of particular interest to marketing executives. Service industries will increasingly absorb more spending power, while being responsible for a greater proportion of national economic progress.

Over 50 years ago, Colin Clark[3] drew attention to the trends in service employment: 'Careful generalisation of available fact shows . . . the most important concomitant of economic progress to be the movement of working population from agriculture to manufacture, and from manufacture to commerce and services.'

The United States, by virtue of its trends in employment and economic activities, claims to be the first nation to have a 'service economy'; in 1985, 68 per cent of the nation's gross national product (GNP) and 71 per cent of its employment were derived from the service sector. By 1991, 72 per cent of America's GDP, almost 80 per cent of employment, and 30 per cent of exports were accounted for by the service sector. Over the period 1980–91, employment in the private sector services increased markedly: in legal services by 106 per cent, business services by 67 per cent, health by 59 per cent, and recreation by 53 per cent.[4]

A NEDO publication noted:

> If transport is included in the service sector, by 1966 the UK just about qualified for admission to the exclusive club of service economies, since services claimed, for the first time, half the labour force. Reckoned on the basis of full-time equivalents, the proportion of the labour force in services was slightly less than half; this reflected the sector's disproportionate reliance on part-time workers.[5]

DISTINCTION BETWEEN GOODS AND SERVICES

It is perhaps unfortunate that economic activity has been traditionally, and rather arbitrarily, divided by professional economists into the goods and service sectors. This dichotomy is not altogether satisfactory, as NEDO pointed out: 'No criterion is likely to provide a clear cut distinction between the two sectors.'[5] This view is shared by the American National Bureau of Economic Research: 'The boundary between service and goods production is very difficult to draw, and probably no division based on industrial classifications would be completely satisfactory'.[6] Judd had defined services as 'market transactions where the object of the exchange is something other than the transfer of a tangible commodity'.[7] Such transactions involve the provision of transport systems, cash security and transfer (banks), public utility undertakings, etc.

Service industries tend to be labour intensive, employing, in particular, relatively large numbers of female and part-time workers. Services have been traditionally described as being perishable in nature ('unstockable'), intangible, and having close relationship to consumers. But these characteristics do not satisfactorily delineate services: it is often difficult – if not impossible – to separate the contribution of a service from the satisfaction given by the ownership of a particular product. Service is frequently an intrinsic part of the package of benefits offered to the customer. So interrelated are the benefits derived from some products and their surrounding or dependent services that it would be futile to attempt to differentiate between the value of the goods provided and the services rendered: for instance, 'retailing and the goods sold, or legal services and the house acquired'; or the service rendered may be reflected in the tangible product – 'teeth fabricated by a dentist'.[5] The growing trend towards the leasing of equipment illustrates how difficult it becomes to differentiate satisfactorily between goods and services. To benefit from the use of such equipment, the customer does not have to become the owner.

Increasingly, customers expect an efficient servicing back-up with the products they buy. These services, such as arrangement of finance, or after-sales maintenance, provide a constellation of benefits which attract business. Service becomes an essential elements in the marketing mix; attractive complementary services help to differentiate products and win customers.

A 1992 OECD report[8] indicated that services and manufacturing are increasingly interconnected: manufacturers buy more inputs from service firms, while, in turn, the latter buy increasingly from manufacturers. The biggest single supplier to General Motors was reported[4] to be a health service company, Blue Cross–Blue Shield, and one of GM's biggest 'products' is financial and insurance services, which, with computer services, account for 20 per cent of total revenue. Sony also derives 20 per cent of its turnover from film and music activities; if design, marketing, finance and after-sales service functions are also included, services probably represent at least half of Sony's business.

As *The Economist* acutely observes: 'Computers would be useless without software writers. Nobody would buy a car if there were no petrol stations. Indeed, the distinction between industry and services is now largely meaningless. In rich countries, over half the workers in a typical manufacturing firm do service-type jobs – design, distribution, financial planning; only a minority makes things on the factory floor.'[9]

DEPENDENCE OF ADVANCED ECONOMIES ON SERVICE INDUSTRIES

That an advanced economy depends increasingly on the contribution of the service industries is clearly evident from this discussion. Without an efficient system of transport or effective methods of communication, or the availability of adequate power supplies, the whole economy would grind to a catastrophic halt. In addition, the health, education and welfare services add immeasurably to the well-being and also the efficiency of the population. The public sector, with far-reaching responsibilities in town planning, slum clearance, recreational facilities and related welfare services, contributes the major part of the services in the United States and in the United Kingdom. The mixed economy of modern industrialised communities seems, in fact, to depend on an essential equilibrium being maintained between the production of tangible goods by industry and the provision of complementary services by public sector organisations.

At the same time, it should be recognised that the services provided by the central government and local authorities are financed from taxation, borrowing or, in some instances, European funding, and not from trading activities. Private sector businesses and personal taxpayers ultimately have to bear the burden of costs involved in public sector spending, although over recent years some attempts are being made to market, on a more or less commercial basis, specific public sector services.

The service sector, as Quinn and Gagnon note in the *Harvard Business Review*,[10] is a major market for high technology; about 80 per cent of the computing, communications and related information technologies equipment sold in the United States during 1982, and 70 per cent of all computer systems sold in the United Kingdom during 1984, were accounted for by the service sectors of these economies.

The Labour Government of the immediate post-war years in the UK introduced a wide-spanning programme of nationalisation involving, for example, coal mining, steel production, and the energy generation industries; state corporations covering, for instance, telecommunications, were also established. In 1979 the Conservative Government directly challenged the status quo through a radical restructuring of these large-scale undertakings by means of extensive privatisation. For instance, the British Gas Corporation, which had monopolised the gas supply industry for several years, was transformed into a public company as British Gas plc. Under strict regulatory control, this new company continues to exercise a virtual monopoly in the supply of gas from the British fields in the North Sea and also from Norway. However, under pressure from the Government, British Gas, in 1992, agreed to reduce its industrial and commercial market share to 40 per cent by 1995, and also to run its pipelines as an arm's-length business serving itself and other suppliers on equal terms. Up to the early 1980s, British Steel suffered from overcapacity in some sectors; following extensive rationalisation, involving plant closures and job losses, it was profit earning by the end of the decade and was then privatised.

In 1989 the 10 water authorities of England and Wales also became public limited companies, with extensive responsibilities for water supply, land drainage, sewage disposal and recreational facilities. The Central Electricity Generating Board was divided into two companies: National Power and Powergen, with the National Grid becoming jointly owned by a number of private sector distribution companies, which had evolved from the former area electricity boards; these, in turn, have become regional electricity companies. British Telecom plc (BT) emerged from the transformation of telecommunications in the 1980s, to face privatisation in 1984 and the challenge of competition from a new entrant, Mercury Communications, a Cable and Wireless subsidiary. In February 1993, Ionica, a privately owned company in Cambridge, was granted a licence to run a radio-based telecommunications system across the country. Other companies are in the process of seeking official agreement to operate systems directly competing with BT and Mercury.

Despite these fundamental changes, the public sector of the UK economy disburses vast sums in capital and current expenditure. Official statistics reveal, for example, that in 1988/89 the National Health Service accounted for £25,170m, Education for £22,140m, Social Security for £48,500m, and Housing for £56m.

Local authorities also significantly influence the social and economic development of their regions: in 1987/88, for instance, their total expenditure amounted to £59,827.3 million in the UK.

Public sector employment is another important factor affecting modern economies. In 1961 there were 24.5 million in the UK workforce, of which 3.7 million were employed in central government and 2.2 million in public corporations; in 1988 the UK workforce totalled 25.9 million, public corporation employees had fallen to one million, but central government workers had actually risen by nearly 46 per cent to 5.4 million (*Annual Abstracts*, 1992).

Over the UK economy as a whole, the service industries have grown steadily and currently account for around 63 per cent of GNP, compared with 1.4 per cent contributed by agriculture, and just under 36 per cent by industry. From 1971 to 1989 the numbers employed in banking, finance, insurance, business services and leasing increased, while those working in transport and communications declined. In 1911, 6 million UK employees worked in the service industries; 50 years later this figure had more than doubled; and by 1990 nearly 16 million were in the service sector (*Annual Abstracts*, 1992).

Part-time employment is a notable characteristic of the service industries, and female workers are particularly evident: 82 per cent of female employees are in service industries. These trends are becoming more marked, and were highlighted in January 1993, when the Burton retailing group announced that it was converting 1,000 full-time jobs into 3,000 part-time ones. It has been suggested[11] that more people will, in fact, develop *'portfolio' jobs* – two or three smaller jobs or projects which may be combined to provide the equivalent income from a full-time post. This radical development reflects the traditional working arrangements of many professionals, like writers and artists, over some years. Another development is the growing tendency for companies to contract out many of their 'non-core' activities. 'Portfolio' jobs are likely to provide new opportunities in a depressed labour market.

The tertiary sector, including both the public and private services, has important effects on manufacturing industry. Contracts for supplies and equipment for the steel, coal, gas, electricity and railway services are responsible for a substantial proportion of the total economic activity in the private sector of the economy. Some industries, although not actually in the public sector, are virtually dependent on business from public undertakings. Motorway construction, sewers, bridge building and telecommunications equipment are examples of 'dependent' industries.

Over 50 per cent of total demand and half of total expenditure on research and expenditure on the UK electronics industry are dependent on the Ministry of Defence and also British Telecom.

For many years, the near-monopoly of BT had resulted in the three leading telecom equipment suppliers (GEC, Plessey and STC) being almost totally dependent on one buyer in the UK. As we have seen, some degree of competitive activity has followed the entry of Mercury Communications, and additional competition comes from cellular mobile phones, such as Racal's Vodaphone.

IMPORTANCE OF SERVICES IN BALANCE OF PAYMENTS

Traditionally, services have rendered invaluable assistance to the United Kingdom's export performance. Without the contribution of invisible exports such as insurance, banking, merchanting and brokerage, the balance of payments would have been even more precarious.

Since 1948 invisible exports, i.e. earnings from insurance and financial services provided by the City of London, professional and management consultancy fees, films, books, videos, licensing and patents, have made significant contributions to the UK's overall balance of payments. In 1990 (net) invisibles amounted to +£4,295 million against (net) visible trade of −£18,675 million (*Annual Abstracts*, 1992).

Far from being 'non-productive', the financial and other services play a dynamic role in the economy, even though they have not prevented debit balances of trade since 1986. However, some concern is now being expressed[12] on how much longer invisibles will be able to remain positive, because of dwindling overseas investment income from shrinking foreign assets.

NATURE OF ORGANISATIONAL PRODUCTS

In Chapter 1 it was observed that organisations are of many kinds; some have commercial objectives, while others, for example, may be primarily concerned with health and social needs.

Market behaviour affecting the demand for organisational products and services is, in general, very different from that experienced with consumer supplies. There are basic differences which directly influence strategic and tactical operations. These fundamental characteristics relate to factors such as demand, supply, pricing, concentration ratios and special trading policies. In this section the significance of these special features will be outlined and discussed, so that a useful foundation will be laid for the subsequent study of buying behaviour.

Compared with many consumer supplies, organisational supplies tend to be complex and sophisticated, e.g. computer installations, power stations and automated processing plants. This particularly applies to capital equipment, which is also characterised as having relatively high durability. Such products tend to be bought fairly infrequently by any one organisation; furthermore, they are distinctly different from high-frequency purchases of consumer products such as food in that purchase can often be postponed for long periods of time. Admittedly, this may eventually lead to problems in industrial efficiency, but in the short term, at least, buyers of industrial equipment are able to exercise their prerogative as to *when* they buy specific equipment. Industrial markets are, therefore, subject to policy decisions on investment which may be affected by many factors, such as political events, outside the control of market suppliers.

Within particular industrial markets, the complexity and costs of products vary considerably; some suppliers may be limited to relatively low-cost products like components, while others specialise in complete package deals, such as the design and building of a major institution like a hospital or airport – these are usually referred to as turnkey contracts.

Technological advances and the rate of innovation vary across industrial markets. Lead time has been cut drastically and, in general, industrial products are now sharing some of the dynamic character traditionally associated with consumer products. Over 25 years ago, the president of Du Pont acknowledged: 'Lead time is gone. There is no company so outstanding technically today that it can expect a long lead in a new discovery.'[13] When Du Pont invented nylon in the 1930s, it experienced a virtual monopoly for years, but when it introduced Delrin in 1960, it was only a year before Celanese marketed a rival product. Today the pace of change is remorseless, as is particularly evident in the electronics field. (The problems of innovation are considered in some detail in Chapter 7.)

TYPES OF INDUSTRIAL PRODUCT

It is difficult to classify organisational goods definitively; there are almost bound to be borderline cases, so that mutually exclusive groupings are virtually impossible. One approach would be to start at the fundamental point of basic raw materials and then to proceed through semi-processed products, components and eventually to completely finished equipment. This was the foundation of the classifications adopted by the Industrial Marketing Research Association[14] based on analyses[15] of the functions of marketing research in industrial markets. Three categories of products (and services) were noted:

1. Capital goods: 'sold as an inherent whole to further production, in machines, accessories or components'.
2. Primary products: 'basic materials like steel, chemicals, or aluminium bars sold to manufacturers'.
3. Intermediate products: 'such as tubes, castings or building materials which have to undergo some major change of form'.

Other researchers have adopted various criteria for classifying industrial products. For example, Kotler,[16] who refers to the 'producer market (also called industrial market)' as 'the market consisting of individuals and organisations who acquire goods and services to be used in the production of further products and services for sale or rental to others', has three main methods of classifying goods:

1. *Goods entering the product completely – materials and parts.*
   (a) Raw materials:
      (i) farm products (wheat, etc.);
      (ii) natural products (fish, crude petroleum, iron ore).

   (b) Manufactured materials and parts:
      (i) component materials (steel, cement, wire, textiles);
      (ii) component parts (small motors, tyres, castings).
2. *Goods entering the product partly – capital items.*
   (a) Installations:
      (i) buildings and land rights (factories, offices);
      (ii) fixed equipment (generators, computers, elevators).
   (b) Accessory equipment:
      (i) portable or light factory equipment and tools (hand tools, lift trucks);
      (ii) office equipment (typewriters, desks).
3. *Goods not entering the products – supplies and services.*
   (a) Supplies:
      (i) operating supplies (lubricants, typing paper);
      (ii) maintenance and repair items (paint, nails, brooms).
   (b) Business services:
      (i) maintenance and repair services (window cleaning, typewriter repairs);
      (ii) business advisory services (legal, management consulting, advertising).

Stanton states that industrial goods are differentiated from consumer goods because of their ultimate use. 'Industrial goods are those intended for use in making other products, or for rendering a service in the operation of a business or institutional enterprise.'[17] He classifies industrial products as follows:

1. Raw materials.
2. Fabricating materials and parts.
3. Installations.
4. Accessory equipment.
5. Operating supplies.

These five categories are based on the broad uses of products in contrast to the classification of consumer products on the basis of buying habits:

1. *Raw materials*: 'industrial goods which will become part of another physical product and which have received no processing at all, other than that necessary for economy or protection in physical handling', e.g. (a) minerals, land; (b) wheat, cotton, tobacco, fruit and vegetables, livestock and animal products such as eggs and raw milk.
2. *Fabricating materials and parts*: become actual parts of the finished product; already processed to some extent. Fabricating *materials*, e.g. pig iron, yarn, will undergo further processing. Fabricating *parts* will be assembled with no further change in form, e.g. spark plugs, fan belts, buttons.
3. *Installations*: manufactured industrial products – the long-lived expensive major equipment of an industrial user, e.g. large generators, factory building,

jet aeroplanes for airlines. 'The differentiation characteristic of installations is that they set the scale of operation in a firm.'

4. *Accessory equipment*: used to aid production operations of an industrial user, but it does not have a significant influence on the scale of operations in a firm, and does not become an actual part of the finished product. Its life is shorter than installations (3) and longer than operating supplies (5). Examples are office equipment, small power tools and forklift trucks.
5. *Operating supplies*: 'convenience goods' of the industrial field; short-lived, low-priced items usually purchased with a minimum of effort. They help firm's operations but do not become part of finished product. Examples are lubricating oils, stationery and heating fuel.[17]

Marrian[18] classified industrial goods as those commodities (goods and services) purchased, hired or leased for use either directly in the production of other goods and services destined for either the industrial or ultimate consumer markets (domestic and export), or for rendering services to organisations engaged in serving the industrial or ultimate consumer markets. She made four 'broad' distinctions in industrial goods:

1. Industrial equipment (buildings, installation equipment, necessary equipment – operating equipment, tools and instruments, furnishings and fittings).
2. Industrial materials (new materials, processed materials, fabricated materials, fabricating materials).
3. Industrial supplies (packaging, operating supplies, spares and replacements).
4. Industrial services (equipment services, facilitating services, advisory and consultative services).

Marrian also characterised industrial buyers as those who buy on behalf of commercial, professional and institutional organisations; they act to further organisational rather than personal goals. Within organisational buying, three main divisions are made: industrial, institutional and intermediate buyers. These are briefly as follows:

1. *Industrial buyers* are those 'buying goods and services for some tangible productive and commercially significant purpose', e.g. manufacturers, primary (extractive) producers, agricultural, forestry, fishery and horticultural producers.
2. *Institutional buyers* are those buying goods and services for institutional (in the sense of providing a service which is often intangible) and not necessarily commercially significant purposes, e.g. schools, hospitals, local government, professions, hotels.
3. *Intermediate buyers* are those buying goods and services for resale or for facilitating the resale of other goods, in the industrial or ultimate consumer markets, for commercial purposes, e.g. distributors, dealers, wholesalers, retailers, service trades.

McCarthy's typology of industrial goods has six categories. The first two are closely comparable to Kotler's second category; the third and fourth can be readily related to Kotler's first category; while the fifth and sixth compare with Kotler's third category, as follows:

Categories of industrial goods	*cf. Kotler*[16]
1. Installations	2
2. Accessory equipment	2
3. Raw materials	1
4. Component parts and materials	1
5. Supplies	3
6. Services	3

McCarthy states that, while consumer goods classification 'is tentative and perhaps arbitrary, the industrial goods classification is keyed directly to the way industrial purchasing departments and accounting control systems operate day by day. Buyers, for example, often specialise by product categories.'[19]

Hill *et al.*[20] offer the following 'general classifications' of industrial products which can be usefully compared with McCarthy's and Kotler's typologies:

Classifications	*cf. McCarthy*[19]	*Kotler*[16]
1. Major equipment	1	2
2. Accessory equipment	2	2
3. Fabricating or component parts	4	1
4. Process material	5	3
5. Operating supplies	6	3
6. Raw materials	3	1

Hill *et al.* further differentiate these categories of industrial product. For example, major equipment is of two general types: multipurpose or standard machines, and special or single-purpose machines (e.g. McCarthy's custom-built or standard).

These various systems of industrial product classification have much in common, as can be noted from this brief review.

Products are viewed in different ways according to their function in diverse industries. The use to which a product is put biases it towards a particular classification. Car accessories supplied as original equipment would attract a different classification from 'replacement' sales to fleet-owners or distributors.

NATURE OF DEMAND FOR ORGANISATIONAL PRODUCTS

VERTICAL DEMAND VERSUS HORIZONTAL DEMAND

The demand for organisational products will be significantly affected by their end-use. *Analysis of the end-uses* of such products leads to the development of effective methods of market segmentation. Some products have many applications in industry and commerce; others have distinctly limited market opportunities. Vertical demand applies where a product has virtually only one market: suppliers of specific equipment for the nuclear fuel industry, for example, must obtain most of their business in the UK from the public sector. Less extreme instances relate to steel-making equipment and supplies, where in the United Kingdom the market is largely represented by the British Steel Corporation; or to potters' clay, which has relatively few buyers in the United Kingdom and of which two groups account for almost 60 per cent of the tableware section of the ceramic industry.

Vehicle component manufacturers have distinctly limited outlets for their production. In general, the greater the concentration of demand for a particular product, the more likely is the demand in that market to be vertical. Suppliers who experience only limited markets for their products should weigh up their business opportunities very carefully: the old adage of 'too many eggs in one basket' suggests that such firms should actively seek new uses for their products and also develop new types of product within their manufacturing competences.

Other products experience horizontal demand and have applications over many markets in different industies, e.g. weighing machines, first-aid kits, steel, forklift trucks and chemicals such as ethano-lamines. Zinc die castings have many applications: automotive components, builders and domestic hardware are major end-use markets; others are toys and sports equipment, commercial and office equipment, domestic appliances and instruments; minor end-use markets include audio-visual equipment, cutlery and ornamental goods.

Woven narrow fabrics (tapes, bindings and webbings) made of different materials and in several widths and finishes are of various types according to the needs of the many industries in which they are used. For instance, glass fibre and polyester tapes are used in the aeronautical industry, for plastics reinforcement, and electrical and thermal insulation; acrylic/polypropylene webbings are used in the manufacture of leisure and equestrian equipment, clothing, luggage, seat belts and boat rigging lines; cotton tapes have applications in the electrical industry and in a whole range of domestic products, such as ties for aprons and loose-covers, as well as providing trimmings for the fashion industry; 'touch and close' fastener tapes are used in the leisure, equestrian and garment industries, and also with Ministry of Defence equipment and medical products.

In addition, there are vertical segments within horizontal markets, as occurs with fire protection products. These are sold to practically every industry, but some specific items, such as fire engines, are limited to relatively few buyers which are almost entirely in the public sector. (See Chapter 6 on product portfolio and market segmentation strategies.)

Inputs from the huge petrochemicals industry are to be found in a wide variety of industries: plastics, synthetic fibres, solvents, synthetic rubber, fertilisers and agricultural chemicals. In turn, these supply industrial customers in other production plants, such as those making packaging, clothing, carpets, tyres, soaps and detergents, and also have applications in dry cleaning, printing, petroleum refining, etc. From these industries, diverse ranges of products are marketed, including paints, containers, fashion clothing, upholstery fabrics, cleaning fluids, petrol, lubricants, belting, footwear and animal feedstuffs.

VARIETY OF USES FOR PRODUCT

Marketers of products enjoying horizontal demand may advantageously plan to apportion their sales over market sectors to minimise trading risks and the effect of cyclical or other trend phenomena. China clay, for example, originally experienced a vertical demand from the pottery industry, but the pattern of demand is now horizontal because of the many uses of this mineral in modern industry. These include paper, pharmaceuticals, paint, rubber, plastics and agricultural chemicals. The paper industry is, in fact, the major user of china clay, accounting for about three-quarters of total market sales.

Another product with diverse applications is carbon dioxide, which is 'used as a carbonating agent in the brewing industry, as a refrigerant in food processing, as an inert atmosphere in oil refineries, and for welding in the engineering industries'.[21] Each of these market segments has its own distinctive pattern of demand and buying behaviour.

To market carbon dioxide successfully it is important to acquire knowledge about user industries, e.g. specific rates of growth and the diverse structures which will affect negotiations. 'You do not have the same type of marketing problem in selling to, say, the brewing industry, as you do with, say, electronics.' Not only are the structures of the industries different, but the whole pattern of buying behaviour also varies, as do the specialist media of advertising.

The plastics division of ICI manufactures a very wide range of plastics which are based on substantially different technologies and are used in a large number of industries in the manufacture of their products (see Table 2.1).

ICI considers that its business 'can be and is regarded as a number of separate businesses at the vital marketing stage, although further back there are a number of common functions which gather considerable strength from being part of a large organisation'.[21]

DERIVED DEMAND

With many industrial products, demand is directly dependent on the rate of usage, which may be several stages from the initial purchaser. Companies may contribute part of the finished product or, perhaps, only the packaging. The demand for capital equipment, for example, is largely dependent on the prospective demand for the goods (industrial or consumer) which this plant will be capable of producing. This will be likely to refer not only to short-term demand patterns but also to estimates of demand extending over 20 years or even longer. Associated with these problems are the lead times necessary to design, develop and produce new capital

TABLE 2.1 Consumption of plastics by industry sector

Sector	*Percentage of total consumption*
Packaging	21.7
Building	20.9
Electrical	7.8
Automotive	4.3
Housewares	4.1
Other transport	3.5
Furniture	3.5
Clothing (including footwear)	3.0
Toys, fancy goods, etc.	3.0
Mechanical engineering	2.8
Consumer durables	2.0
Agriculture	1.6
Miscellaneous and unidentified	21.8
	100.0

Source: Owen.[21]

equipment. In general, industrial products tend to have longer manufacturing cycles than consumer goods.

Similarly, the demand for the materials and components used in the manufacture of capital goods will depend heavily on the rate of sales in the equipment market.

The demand for extinguishant gases, such as Halon, is directly dependent on the number of fire protection appliances sold to users. Sheet metal demand is generated by the demand for products which are made from it. The demand for safety-belt webbing will derive from the sales of car safety belts which, in turn, are now almost entirely dependent on the level of demand for new cars.

The pattern of derived demand affecting industrial raw materials is illustrated in Figure 2.1. Forecasts of demand at the ultimate level, i.e. finished product, will significantly influence the volume of demand throughout the entire industrial pipeline. Markets do not exist in isolation; their interrelationships and dependencies need to be carefully studied and evaluated.

The impact of derived demand on the chemical industry is given in Figure 2.2.

It is apparent, therefore, that a complex mix of economic, social, political and other factors affect patterns of demand: for example, the total demand for earth-moving equipment is influenced significantly by public sector construction activities, private sector new home building, etc.; interest rates, regional economic plans, world trade movements, environmental regulations and energy costs are also influential.

Inevitably, the dependency of derived-demand products on factors outside the control of those marketing the products indicates that such companies should become acquainted with trends in markets beyond the one in which they are directly active. Clearly, there is a great amount of interdependence between industrial firms; sometimes, unfortunately, there is a danger that component

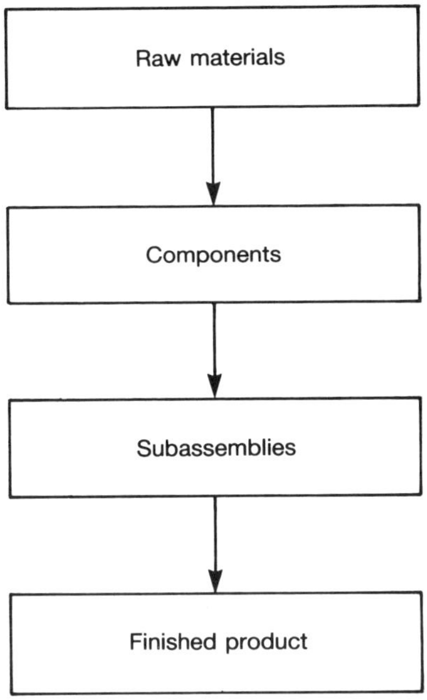

FIGURE 2.1 Pattern of derived demand for industrial raw materials

manufacturers degenerate into 'captive suppliers' to large assembly plants. On the other hand, industrial buyers tend to become heavily dependent on the performance of their suppliers: the ability to adhere to strict standards of quality and scheduled deliveries becomes of vital importance in allocating available business.

Marks and Spencer's trading success depends largely on the effective management of its suppliers, many of whom (like S. R. Gent, manufacturers of women's wear) derive 90 per cent of turnover from this retail giant. If, as has happened in the past, clothing sales are sluggish, the effects are felt not only in the primary suppliers but also in the sales of their own suppliers – those involved in yarns, packaging, printing, etc.

It is important that industrial marketers understand the uses to which their products are applied in various markets. As Hakansson and his co-researchers have observed: 'The firm has to be both an expert in its products as a component as well as the function of that component in the larger product.'[23] Product and process knowledge are critical to success in competitive markets. In the industrial detergents market, it was found that the technical advice of suppliers is a pronounced marketing input. Also, the production and technical staff of customers are much more heavily involved in the product selection stage than with many other products.

Companies marketing products which experience derived demand may actively intervene lower down the 'demand chain' in order to stimulate demand for their

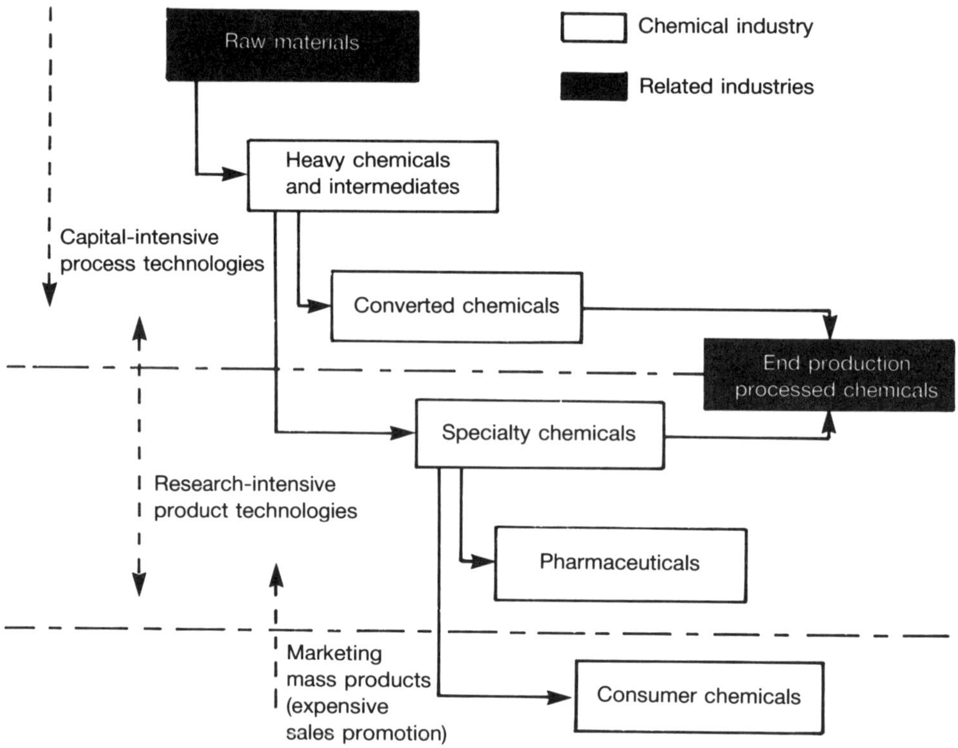

FIGURE 2.2 Chemical industry's pattern of derived demand (Source: Eugster[24])

products. Fibre manufacturers such as Courtaulds undertake systematic marketing research at several levels of the fashion industry; they also advertise directly to consumers with the objective of gaining insight into trends in demand and of influencing, to some degree, the derived demand for synthetic yarns. This type of market intervention is termed 'back-pressure' selling, or 'reverse' selling.

Packaging manufacturers, for instance, co-operate closely with food processors in the development of improved types of materials, closures, etc. Technical advisory services are an essential part of the marketing effort of industrial marketers; through this type of co-operation, goodwill is built up over the years of personal involvement in customers' problems. Research could usefully identify areas in which suppliers might offer technical assistance to promote business.

Some companies like Coats, the large-scale producers of yarns and threads now merged to form Coats Viyella, developed vertically integrated structures to increase their influence on the pattern of demand at several stages of production and distribution. Horizontal integration, adopted by other companies, is designed to reduce competition at the manufacturing stage in specific industrial markets by rationalising production methods and product ranges, and by lowering overall costs. Research should endeavour to trace the organisational pattern of particular companies and evaluate the extent of influence exercised on demand.

Associated with the phenomenon of derived demand is the *acceleration effect*, which occurs when changes in demand further down the demand chain result in a magnification of demand earlier in the production processes and distribution arrangements involved in a particular product. This could, for instance, happen when a 25 per cent increase in final consumption of an item leads to 40 per cent extra demand for the specific raw materials used in its manufacture. The magnified demand results from changes in the inventory levels of the firms engaged at various levels of the derived demand chain, such as: raw materials → components → finished product → merchant → final user. Hence, if final consumption increases by 25 per cent, merchants would need to adjust their stocks to cope with the expanded demand. Allowing for a nominal five weeks' stockholding and, for ease of calculation, a 50-week year, the following equation results:

$$25\% + (25\% \times \frac{5}{50}) = 27\tfrac{1}{2}\%$$

Manufacturers, in turn, would need to adjust their stocks as follows (on the projected basis of 10 weeks' normal stockholding):

$$27\tfrac{1}{2}\% + (27\tfrac{1}{2}\% \times \frac{10}{50}) = 33\%$$

At the next stage back of derived demand, component suppliers' stocks would be adjusted thus (allowing for projected five weeks' stocks):

$$33\% + (33\% \times \frac{5}{50}) = 36\tfrac{1}{3}\%$$

Finally, raw materials suppliers, with average stocks of five weeks, would need to adjust their holdings as follows:

$$36\tfrac{1}{3}\% + (36\tfrac{1}{3}\% \times \frac{5}{50}) = \text{approx. } 40\%.$$

Conversely, a reduction in the level of demand for a specific product may cause orders to fall off steeply further back through the various levels of derived demand, i.e. a *deceleration effect* is experienced, as stocks are quickly adjusted by the various suppliers involved.

ELASTICITY OF DEMAND

Classical economic theory postulates that as price falls demand tends to rise, and vice versa; the extent of this movement is termed the *elasticity of demand* and is graphically indicated by a downward-sloping curve (see Figure 2.3).

In effect, a demand curve is a considered estimate of the likely outcome of the demand for a product at different levels of price. Certain assumptions about buying behaviour are necessarily incorporated.

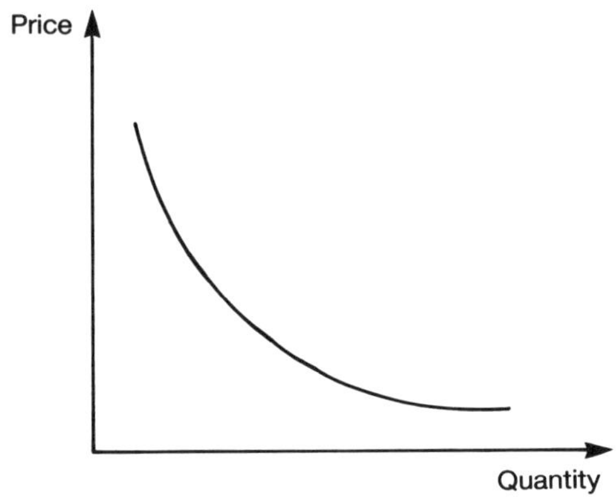

FIGURE 2.3 Simplified model of elastic demand

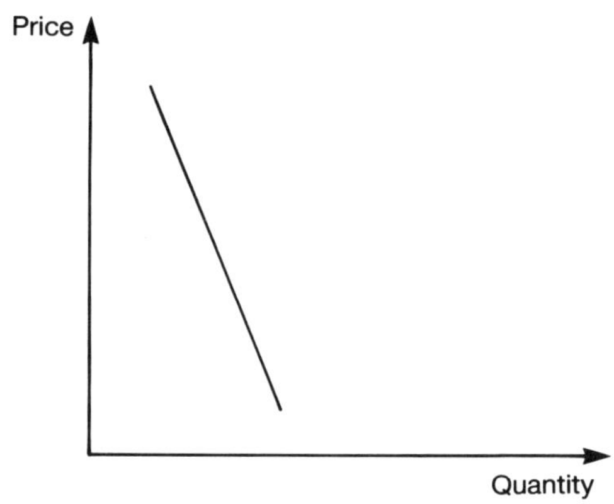

FIGURE 2.4 Simplified model of inelastic demand

The alternative model of demand refers to those buying situations where only relatively small changes in demand follow from price alterations (see Figure 2.4).

In consumer markets, price reductions are designed to attract an immediate response (e.g. washing machines, cookers, colour television sets), but market behaviour in industrial products is different; and although lower prices may suggest, for instance, that certain kinds of equipment are now feasible, spontaneous ordering would be unlikely because of the more complicated decision-making processes involved and the need to plan a series of dependent events.

In general, industrial products with derived-demand characeristics do not benefit from relatively small price reductions. The demand for several industrial products tends to show a reverse elasticity in the short term; hence, industrial marketers are seldom able to expand demand significantly merely by reducing price.

In expectation of further price reductions, industrial buyers may be able to delay purchasing if they hold adequate stocks of certain materials or components. A price increase, on the other hand, may lead to increased demand from buyers anxious, and able, to stock up, since they believe that prices may suddenly start to soar in the near future.

This behaviour contrasts sharply with the general behaviour of demand in consumer product markets, where price variations tend to affect levels of consumption inversely. The relative freedom of competitive consumer product manufacturers to increase market share through price reductions is largely not the experience of industrial marketers.

But, as Stacey and Wilson[25] emphasise, it is important to distinguish between the price elasticity of an industry and that of an individual manufacturer who may hope to increase its turnover, if only for the time being, by reducing its prices below current market levels.

Because of the dependent nature of derived demand, it is possible for reductions in the prices of a particular supplier to be accompanied by reduced sales if the general level of demand experienced by the industrial customer is falling.

Where the product being supplied represents only a relatively minor element in the total cost structure of the finished product, reductions in price are not likely to increase demand; when components represent a major cost factor, price will, of course, be far more critical. If, for example, the price of stainless steel fell appreciably, new or extended applications could result which would increase overall market demand.

Substitution may also affect the level of demand for certain products at existing prices. Synthetic yarns have been instrumental in capturing a large share of the traditional carpet market, and have also expanded overall demand considerably. Leather upholstery in cars has largely been replaced by synthetic coverings. In many areas of industrial activity, the by-products of the petrochemical industries have dramatically changed traditional buying preferences. Shortages of some natural raw materials, emphasised by price rises, have accelerated the rate of substitution.

Elasticity of demand refers, therefore, to sales volume in specific segments of the total market for a product, and it follows that different elasticities may operate in various sectors. Market segments, and individual customers within them, should be analysed and rated for their likely sensitivity to price changes. For example, aluminium has many applications, such as airframes, saucepans, kettles and cooking foil. In airframe constructions, aluminium offers unique advantages (light weight related to strength, ductility and anti-corrosion properties), so that even at higher prices it would still be in great demand (see Figure 2.4). However, aluminium foil is in competition with other types of wrapping (waxed paper, cellulose film, etc.) and unless it can establish unique advantages (as with cooking), price levels are likely to influence market growth.

The latitude with which an individual supplier may vary its price will relate, as far as the buyer is concerned, to its market position (major, average or marginal supplier), the degree of essentiality of its product/service, the general level of competition in a specific market, and the extent to which it may be able to differentiate its product. (See Chapters 5 and 6 for further discussion of price).

The interaction of demand and supply, and, hence, price, will be affected in many cases by the intensity of demand at various stages of the demand chain (see the discussion above).

As noted, the trading structure of an industry affects the bargaining power of individual suppliers. Conditions can vary from those approximating a perfect market, as theorised by economists, to a situation of virtual monopoly. In the first case, many firms of about the same size may be active in a market which has minimal barriers to entry; in the second case, one or two very large firms may dominate an industry and make entry to that market extremely difficult.

In practice, the majority of industries tend to be characterised by a mixture of large, medium and small firms, with price competition significantly affected by the balance existing between the various firms of a particular size. The more equitably market shares are distributed within an industry, the more marked will be the tendency for price competition to be active. (See Chapter 5 for Porter's analytical model.)

Industrial buyers may be sensitive to factors in the marketing mix other than price. The reputation of a supplier, the availability of efficient servicing, acceptable delivery dates, design leadership, etc. are non-price factors which research should identify as being significant in certain markets.

In the short term, supplies of many industrial goods and services are relatively fixed; price competition may, therefore, be inhibited. However, new methods of production, improved technology or better-designed products may enable industrial marketers to challenge the existing price structure in a market. Marketers should take note of the nature and level of competition, including the pace of technological innovation in specific industrial markets.

TRENDS IN DEMAND

The nature and extent of trends in demand functions of particular organisational product and service markets require careful evaluation. Trend analyses are concerned with isolating and identifying market movements so that a better understanding of market behaviour may be obtained.

It may be possible to establish the causes of significant market movements; these may be attributable to technological, fiscal, financial, economic, political, cultural or demographic changes. One particularly dramatic category of long-term trend has become known as the Kondratieff cycle.

In 1925 Nicolai Dimitriyevich Kondratieff, after some years of research into long-term trends in selected economic indicators, stated that 50-year cycles existed; his findings, published in Germany, were translated into English in 1935.

Sahal[26] notes that in 1913, Van Gelderen, followed by Kondratieff about a decade later, advanced the thesis that economic development occurred in the form of long waves of about half a century consisting of 'spring-tides' of prosperity and 'ebb-tides' of relative scarcity. Schumpeter, he says, contended that the origin of such long waves (Kondratieff cycles) lay in the clustering of fundamental innovations over certain periods of time.

Drucker has observed that, in the last decades of one of these cycles, old and mature industries appear to be exceptionally successful, whereas 'they are already in decline, for what looks like record profits is in fact underinvestment and the distribution of no-longer-needed capital'.[27]

The first Kondratieff cycle (1787–1842) sprang mainly from innovations resulting from the development of steam power; the second (1843–97) from innovations focused around railroads; and the third (1898–1953) through the development of electric power and the internal combustion engine.

Sahal adds that the importance of Schumpeter's pioneering work cannot be overemphasised, but it requires further verification. This view is supported by Ray,[28] who also observes that neither Kondratieff nor Schumpeter lived long enough to witness the peak of the upswing in the 1960s, which was 'probably attributable to a combination of major innovations in the chemical industries (catalytic cracking, synthetic materials and fibres, antibiotics); in aircraft (jet engine, helicopters); in the electrical/electronics industry (TV, computers); and perhaps even in the peaceful application of nuclear power'. He speculates that the next great innovatory cycle will centre on the microprocessor.

Industries based on new technologies, aimed at new markets, may largely offset the declining demand and resultant economic impact experienced by old industries. Drucker[27] notes that 'as Schumpeter and others have shown', the Kondratieff trough identified in Britain and France in the late nineteenth century 'simply did not happen in the United States or Germany'. Old and mature industries declined, of course, but overall economic growth continued because of the rapid spread of new technologies. Technical innovation was harnessed to entrepreneurial energy and pulled the United States out of the threatening trough.

However, as Drucker observes later, in the last 20 years of the Kondratieff cycle, the mature industries eventually 'all but collapse overnight', and the newer technologies are not yet able to generate sufficient jobs or absorb enough new capital to compensate for the dramatic decline. He notes that the smokestack industries in the USA and western Europe 'do seem to conform to the Kondratieff cycle'; in Japan the same trend is observable, although lagged by a few years.

But Drucker states that new employment prospects arising from entrepreneurial and innovative business activities in the USA are not compatible with traditional Kondratieff theory. Instead, there appears to be 'a remarkable resemblance to the "atypical Kondratieff wave" of Germany and the US after 1873 – 25 years of great turbulence in these countries and of economic and social change, but also 5 years of rapid economic growth'.[29] (Refer to the discussion at the opening of this chapter.)

A sharp critic of the Kondratieff cycle is Mathias, who states that its existence in more than price terms is 'far from proven'. Further, there is certainly no agreement about the variables used in the research.

> The inherent periodicity and replicability of the Kondratieff long-swing has been challenged no less than its characteristics and structural unity. This being so, in the present state of research, it is wise to refrain from interpreting trends in the British economy between 1873 and 1896 as the structural dynamics of the downswing phase of a Kondratieff cycle.[30]

Emphatic criticism also comes from Sam Brittan of the *Financial Times*, who pungently commented: 'There are mysterious Kondratieff cycles or other inexorable rhythms which preside over our affairs. But human fallibility remains. Although a lot has been learned since the 1930s, political economy is still more an art than a science.'[31]

Even though Kondratieff's theory may be held in some dispute, it is a fact that during certain periods of time innovations had profound effects on technologies, and the direction and pace of industrial activities were fundamentally affected. (The impact of innovation on marketing strategies is discussed at some length in Chapter 7.)

Four general categories of demand trend have been noted: secular (or 'normal'), seasonal, cyclical and erratic. Expert marketing research will help in providing data over time which will guide management on investment policy, marketing strategy, etc.

In all markets there is a typical demand trend: this is described as the secular or normal trend and refers to the smooth or regular movement of a series of data observed over a fairly long period of time. Some industrial products, e.g. machine tools, are subject to relatively violent changes in demand over a period of years ranging from 5 to 20. This trend is typified as cyclical; certain industries tend to 'lead' a general upswing in economic activity and are also likely to be the first to experience a downturn in demand. The wave-like movements observable in cyclical variations involve periods of prosperity, recession, depression and recovery, and are caused by factors other than the weather or cultural or social behaviour. Cyclical fluctuations may be manifested at several levels: national economy, industries or sectors of industries, and individual firms. Many explanations of business cycles – some ingenious – have been offered: these range over real, psychological and monetary theories. No simple explanation is really possible; there is not just *one* type of cycle. Individual business cycles require separate evaluations, although the anticipation of these strong movements remains exceedingly difficult.

The significance of seasonal trends also needs careful appreciation; peak demand may have to be met from buffer stocks, but since these tie up capital, a reliable assessment of the level and duration of demand is obviously desirable. 'Seasonal' variation is not necessarily related to seasons of the year, but refers to any kind of variation of a recurrent nature where the period of time involved is not longer than one year. Sales of fertilisers, wines, paint, heating fuels and holiday travel are typical.

The last category of demand trend – erratic – is not predictable from marketing research. Experience and sensitive observation of market behaviour may suggest, however, that some unusual trend is likely to occur. Irregular trends could be triggered off by some unusual natural disaster or economic event, such as blizzards, droughts, wars or strikes. OPEC, for instance, has had immense impact on the economics of the whole of the western world. The cataclysmic oil price rises of the 1970s shattered the developed world and triggered off the so-called energy crisis. Yet it was early in 1970 that the US Cabinet Task Force on Oil commented that they did not predict a substantial price rise in world oil markets over the next ten years.

NATURE OF SUPPLY

PRODUCTS

Categories of industrial products were discussed earlier, when it was seen that these range from complex, sophisticated and costly equipment to relatively simple, low-cost components or routine supplies. In some cases repeat purchases are regular features of the market, e.g. lubricating oils, while in other instances one-off deals, such as the installation of a major industrial plant, are the order of the day.

Custom-built or specially designed products tend to be more evident in industrial than in consumer markets. Often, these types of product involve considerable development time and costs, e.g. designing and building a new passenger liner or a major process plant, or opening up a new ore mine. Suppliers require expert skills related to particular user-industries, and so are able to build customer loyalty because their products often become so closely integrated with the businesses of their customers that a high degree of mutual dependency arises. Food manufacturers, for example, rely heavily on the efficiency of food-processing machines for the profitability of their operations. Some of these machines may, of course, be standard designs, although in certain cases considerable modifications may have rendered them virtually custom-built.

Standard products are, generally speaking, more open to competitive activities. They may be generic in nature, so differentiation across alternative sources of supply is not particularly marked. In cases like this, supplies are almost at the level of 'commodity products', with the resultant disadvantages for marketers. Often, industrial products are from standard ranges; research could usefully identify the optimum width of the product range of specific types of goods. Customers' specifications could be related to standard products and an acceptable degree of product rationalisation could be attempted.

Industrial inventory policies are critical factors in the successful operation of businesses. The problem of maintaining adequate stocks has already been alluded to; another aspect refers to the sensitive relationship between changes in the stocks held by customers and those of their suppliers. If customers change their consumption patterns radically because of increased sales, component suppliers may suddenly be faced with heavily increased demands both to satisfy the immediate production needs of their customers and to build up larger working stocks. This is also likely to escalate stockholdings at the supplying firm in the expectation of future increased business. (Refer to the discussion of derived demand on pp. 47–51).

If a market decline sets in, the impact on component suppliers will probably be immediate and severe as customers run down their heavy stocks before reordering.

A carefully articulated inventory policy is an important factor which contributes to the success of a business undertaking. Since most industrial production is in anticipation of demand, management has to accept the responsibility of balancing supply with demand, endeavouring to eliminate, as far as possible, tying up capital in abnormal stocks while at the same time avoiding loss of orders because of inability to deliver in an acceptable time.

Expectations of buyers' demands will be helped by closely studying the trends of user-industries, noting the impact of new technologies on their products and of new markets that their customers may be developing. As noted earlier, derived demand is a typical characteristic of industrial markets, so it will pay industrial suppliers to be aware of what is happening in consumer product markets; new tastes may cause significant changes in some industrial supplies.

Industrial products are frequently made to BSS or other accepted standards, so that, superficially at least, there is little to choose between competitive suppliers. In such instances, the astute marketer builds into his or her product other reasons why people should buy *this* version rather than those offered by competitors. This approach will be considered in the next section.

AUGMENTED OR EXTENDED PRODUCTS

The augmented or extended product concept is a particularly valuable one for industrial marketers. Simply stated, it is that a product or service is more than just a simple transaction: it provides not merely the physical benefits inherent in its use, but can be designed to give a cluster of benefits that are attractive to specific kinds of buyer. The application of this concept can help suppliers of basic commodity-type products to differentiate their market offerings and so win business through a positive strategy of adding new values to their deals with customers. In other words, they offer a package deal as against trying to compete with a product that is virtually identical to that sold by several other firms – moreover, often relying solely on sharp pricing to attract orders.

Of course, many shrewd suppliers of basic products already ensure that their customers receive good back-up service and regular supplies of essential raw materials. But this concept of the augmented product could be used far more widely in industrial markets, particularly because in several product fields competition is not just from home-based suppliers but from many ambitious overseas firms which are able to provide products of comparable technical quality. Kotler[16] has distinguished three levels of product (see Figure 2.5): (1) the core product; (2) the formal product; and (3) the augmented product.

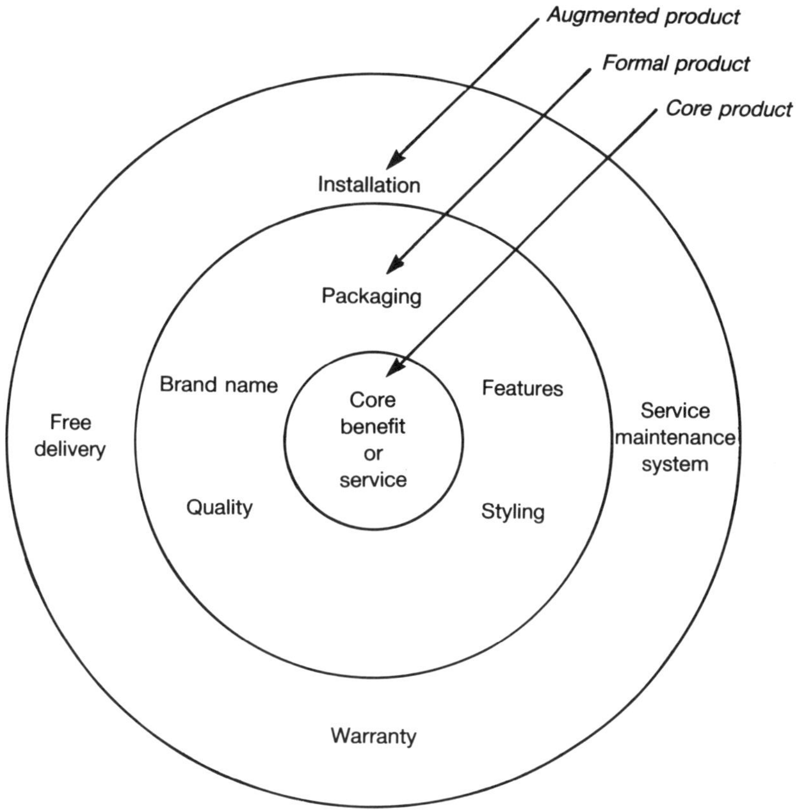

FIGURE 2.5 Three levels of product (Source: Kotler[16])

These categories correspond closely to those offered by Levitt,[32] who added a fourth dimension: (1) the generic product; (2) the expected product; (3) the augmented product; and (4) the potential product.

Basically, these two well-known writers are projecting the same message: competing products may be physically identical, but one can be more acceptable than the other because of some additional reason or reasons which motivate customers to buy. One large chemical company found, for example, that its excellent technical data provided with the product frequently contributed to its marketing success.

Taking the various 'levels' of a product further, the core product or service refers to the basic or minimum benefit provided, such as transportation by a car, the facility to deposit or withdraw money at a bank, or the ability of a screwdriver to fit certain sizes of screw. These are the fundamental qualities of products or services that are largely taken for granted and are available from many sources.

At the next level a product is designed to offer additional benefits, such as branding (which helps to control risk in buying), convenient packaging (which may protect a product from accidental damage or give it prolonged life) or distinctive styling (which may make a product aesthetically more pleasing, or ergonomically designed to give better value in use). Price competition is now being diluted by adding attractive new benefits to appeal to certain market segments.

The augmented level of a product adds extra values, such as delivery and installation services, well-designed maintenance systems and first-class warranties.

Cunningham and Roberts[33] have shown the importance of service in the valve and pump industry. They classified service as (1) convenience; and (2) reliability; these related to what are usually described as before- and after-sales service. The former refers to features such as technical advice in selecting the right product for a particular task, credit facilities and reliable delivery information. The latter helps to reduce the uncertainty attached to a buying decision through offering, for example, user training courses, good repair facilities and technical back-up after the product is bought.

These researchers found that 'buyers were not only prepared to pay for a more reliable service but also were reluctant to change suppliers for a reduction in price of less than 5 per cent'. This led them to believe either that the market may be 'service-elastic' in that the better the quality of the service, the greater the likelihood of business; or, alternatively, that the customer may be able to impose certain standards of service on its most important suppliers.

This UK study was followed up by Banting,[34] who conducted a similar study of Canadian pump and valve manufacturers. Delivery, reliability, prompt quotation and provision of technical advice were found to be the most important aspects of service which suppliers of forgings and castings could offer pump and valve makers.

Both the UK and Canadian surveys found that delivery reliability ranked first with this industrial sector; in second ranking for the United Kingdom was technical advice, compared with prompt quotation for the Canadian industry; test facilities achieved third ranking in the United Kingdom was given to replacement guarantee and, in Canada, to discounts. Overall, some divergent values were apparent: 'much more than minor shuffling is manifested', and further research would be advisable, particularly in view of the fairly low response (21 per cent) to the Canadian survey. However, there is evidence that Canadian pump and valve manufacturers can be segmented according to service expectations: valve makers are more concerned about the provision of technical advice, ease of contact with suppliers and replacement guarantees, and are more generally satisfied with their metals suppliers, whereas pump manufacturers are more interested in discounts and after-sales service.

The trend towards building non-price incentives into products, such as speedy and reliable delivery, and technical back-up services, is growing in both home and domestic markets. (See also Chapter 5 for pricing factors in industrial buying.) Many companies marketing industrial and technological products now recognise that competitive strengths can be greatly enhanced by paying attention to the expanded needs of their customers. TI, the large engineering group, attributed half of the income it derives from manufacturing seals to the after-sales service, installation and monitoring offered to customers; the Japanese company Fujitsu acquired the British computing group ICL, 'mainly because of its skills in software and systems integration rather than hardware'.[35] The computer industry, as a whole, is going through a fundamental reappraisal of its product and marketing strategies: from being technology driven to becoming customer driven.

Services are progressively being integrated into product deals, with the emphasis on offering comprehensive solutions to customers' problems. Successful companies will be those which can effectively combine the 'hard' manufacturing skills with the 'soft' service skills:[35] this can result in a realistic type of industrial synergy.

Product augmentation offers many opportunities to industrial marketers; the 'added benefit' should be based on adequate market research to identify and evaluate customers' behaviour in relation to specific supplies. Buyers' expectations are dynamic in competitive markets, so information should be up to date. Creative marketing strategies can lift a product out of the rut of being a commonplace, basic good and reposition it so that it is perceived by buyers to be a more useful product. This enhanced product will give the supplier greater negotiating advantages and may lead to systems selling.

SYSTEMS SELLING

This concept is closely related to that of the augmented product; a complete package of products and/or services is designed and offered to identified target customers. This differentiation strategy may involve, for example, the design, installation and servicing of a complex production facility; or a combination of hardware and software computer services including the training of personnel, as IBM has done for some years.

Levitt[36] has described how the term 'systems selling' actually originated with the buyer and not the seller. The US federal military contracts office 'developed the practice of buying major weapons and communications packages through a single prime contractor'; this simplified the placing of contracts. In practice, however, this method of buying had been used for some time in public works contracts, although not formally described as 'systems selling'.

Increasingly, the complexity of many industrial products has meant that their efficiency depends on expert servicing, so 'package deals' have grown substantially over the past few years. Customers are seeking comprehensive solutions to their problems and the reduction of risk and uncertainty.

The service aspect of selling products has, therefore, become far more important in the strategies of organisational market suppliers. From being considered as a rather secondary business activity, servicing has now attracted special attention because it can be a most effective marketing tool.

Systems selling can be developed as a very effective competitive marketing strategy to attract and keep customers who would often rather deal with one firm that is able to offer a comprehensive package than have to search for several sources of supply.

DISTRIBUTION

With consumer products, a sophisticated network of distributive trades channels the goods from manufacturers to consumers. These intermediaries are frequently highly specialised (e.g. food, fashion clothing, household furniture), and serve the needs of a vast population spread over the whole country.

The efficiency of 'traditional' methods of supplying certain industrial markets also deserves attention. Some companies have experimented successfully with alternative marketing operations, such as franchise deals and telephone selling.

In industrial markets, the channels of distribution are generally direct, apart from functions such as steel stockholding, builders' merchants or agricultural machinery distributors. Selling is mainly by direct contact between manufacturers and their customers, and often demands considerable technical knowledge. Orders are likely to be of large volume and entail commitments over a fairly long period of time.

Distribution decisions in industrial markets may take years to develop; management should, therefore, give adequate thought to this important factor in successful marketing. Steel stockholders, for example, fulfil a vital role in stocking a wide range of steel for quick delivery to diverse industries. The tasks involved in the physical flow of products from manufacturers through to end-users are sometimes referred to as the logistics of supply. In some very large organisations, this responsibility has developed into a specialist function of management. (See further discussion of industrial distributive strategies in Chapter 5.)

CONCENTRATION FACTORS

On the whole, transactions covering the supply of industrial goods and services are more complicated than in consumer markets. Also, the actual number of buyers for specific products is smaller and there tend to be greater differences between buyers.

The range of buying extends from virtually monopsonistic (single buyer) power to where there are many buyers, so that no individual buyer is able to dictate terms of business. The nature of price competition is related to the degree of concentration of buying power and the structure of the supplying industry (see Chapter 5 on market bargaining factors).

The pattern and strength of competition in an industry depend on the number of firms and also their relative sizes. If a small number of firms produce a large proportion of an industry's output, *high concentration* is present, and those companies possess *market power* in the sense that their decisions can affect the quality of goods and the prices at which they are offered for sale. Where there are large numbers of small firms in an industry, fragmentation occurs, and any change in the output of a single supplier will have virtually no effect on price.

Nevertheless, small firms can enhance their *market power* by identifying and supplying specific market segments with special types of product. In these market niches, small producers may well have distinct advantages because of the highly specialised nature of their supplies. This strategic strength often permits them to charge prices somewhat above those of the commodity-type products offered by large firms.

GEOGRAPHICAL CONCENTRATION

Industries may be clustered geographically, with a few large firms dominating the total output: for example, the British pottery industry is centred around Stoke-on-Trent where two large groups, Wedgwood and Royal Doulton, account for about 60 per cent of total sales of tableware. Industrial clustering of cutlery manufacturing is still evident, though on a reduced scale, in Sheffield, and of motor vehicle production in the Birmingham and Coventry areas, but dispersion has followed the entry of the Japanese manufacturers, Honda, Nissan and Toyota, who have set up car assembly plants in the 'non-traditional' areas of Swindon, Teesside and Derbyshire. These European-based competitors are, as noted in Chapter 1, operating JIT and synchronised supply systems, which encourage component suppliers to locate feeder plants within easy travelling distance of their prime customers. However, some other important industries, e.g. electronics, man-made fibres and pharmaceuticals, are not clustered geographically.

ANCILLARY INDUSTRY CLUSTERING

Industrial concentrations related to specific types of product tend to attract localised ancillary or service industries. These related industries add to the density of specialised industrial activities and are a significant factor in planning industrial marketing strategies.

US RESEARCH INTO INDUSTRIAL CONCENTRATION

For nearly 70 years, the professional sales journal *Sales and Marketing* has published regular surveys into the marketing and business environment of the USA. The resultant statistics indicate current population levels, effective buying power, retail sales trends and general economy activity. Regionally clustered industries are identified, so that marketing campaigns can be effectively targeted, including the planning of sales territories, and also the selection of appropriate advertising media. It has been found, for example, that regional concentration patterns influence at least half of the industries making up the US economic structure; highly concentrated industries include cigarettes, motor vehicles, certified air transportation, aircraft guided missiles and space vehicles, and blast furnaces and steel mills. While there are substantial differences in the scale of their respective turnovers, the degree of their concentration does not vary greatly.

CONCENTRATION RATIOS BY SIZE OF FIRM

Industries tend to be populated by many relatively small-scale producers and to be described as having low levels of concentration, e.g. furniture, leather goods and timber; or they are characterised by mass production, e.g. vehicles and heavy capital intensive production plants such as chemicals. In these cases, high levels of concentration are said to be present.

Channon's[37] research on UK industrial concentrations over the period 1970–8 revealed an overall trend towards higher concentration (see Table 2.2). By 1978, 55 (35.2 per cent) of 156 industry segments had a five-firm concentration ratio greater than 60 per cent. (This ratio refers to the percentage of net output for the industry segment represented by the five largest enterprises.)

From the early 1960s concentration gradually increased until the mid-1970s, when the pace accelerated somewhat.

Taking into account earlier research into the concentration ratios of British industry, there was a decided swing during the period 1958–63 (see Table 2.3). Of the 209 industries listed, which accounted for approximately half of all sales by manufacturing industries during 1958 and 1963, five firms made over 50 per cent and more of the total sales in 120 industries; by 1963 this figure had increased to 127 industries.

Concentration again increased over the period 1963–8: five firms covered 75 per cent and over of total sales in 99 industries in 1963, whereas in 1968 this figure jumped to 127 industries.

The above data, and others given by these researchers, are viewed as 'almost certainly an understimate of the true position, since they do not (and cannot) take account of the fact that one firm may operate in several industries, and so a large firm may dominate a number of industries'.[38] Since 1935 the shares of the largest firms of both net output and of employment have grown very significantly. The

TABLE 2.2 Five-firm industry concentration ratios

Concentration ratio (%)	*Industry segments*							
	1970		*1970 cumulative*		*1978**		*1978 cumulative*	
	No.	*%*	*No.*	*%*	*No.*	*%*	*No.*	*%*
0–9	1	0.7	1	0.7	2	1.3	2	1.3
10–19	13	8.7	14	9.4	15	9.6	17	10.9
20–9	21	14.1	35	23.5	13	8.3	30	19.2
30–9	22	14.8	57	38.3	23	14.8	53	34.0
40–9	31	20.8	88	59.1	28	18.0	81	52.0
50–9	17	11.4	105	70.5	20	12.8	101	64.8
60–9	11	7.4	116	77.9	13	8.3	114	73.1
70–9	9	6.0	125	83.9	15	9.6	129	82.7
80–9	15 } 44	10.1	140	94.0	17 } 55	10.9	146	93.6
90–100	9	6.0	149	100.0	10	6.4	156	100.0
	149	100.0			156	100.0		

*1978 – no data given for sugar industry.
Source: Channon.[37]

TABLE 2.3 Distribution of five-firm ratios (based on sales), 1958–63

Concentration ratio (%)	*1958*		*1963*	
	No. of industries	*Sales (%)*	*No. of industries*	*(%)*
Under 25	30	16.5	16	8.4
25–50	59	25.3	66	28.3
50–75	66	33.3	67	35.4
75+	54	24.9	60	27.9
	209	100.0	209	100.0

Changes 1958–63

Concentration	*Number of industries*	*Share of sales*	
		1958 (%)	*1963 (%)*
Increased	128	69.0	67.7
No change	25	10.1	11.4
Decreased	56	20.9	20.9
	209	100.0	100.0

Source: Aaronovitch and Sawyer.[38]

dramatic increase in British industry concentration is of particular interest to marketing management and, of course, to economic and social policies in general.

Earlier, it was noted that industrial markets are often dominated by a relatively limited number of enterprises with aggregate sales accounting for the bulk of industry sales in specific markets, a trend accentuated over recent years by industrial mergers in many industries, e.g. brewing, shipbuilding, carpet production and electronic engineering. Buyers in these large firms wield considerable power in purchasing a wide range of products and services. The 80/20 rule has increasingly become evident in industrial markets. For instance, over 80 per cent of the capital products turnover of the UK-owned electronics companies is accounted for by a few manufacturers, such as GEC, Thorn-EMI, Racal and Ferranti. In chemicals and pharmaceuticals, ICI and Glaxo dominate the UK sector; however, apart from these and Smith-Kline Beecham and Wellcome, most companies are relatively small and focus on niche markets or supply largely generic products.

Some industries, however, remain considerably fragmented, such as house building, or road haulage in which (as a survey revealed) 55 per cent of total turnover was accounted for by the 150 largest companies, the balance being covered by 18,000 enterprises:

> High concentration of buying power inevitably leads to demands for special terms, priority in deliveries, and other preferential treatment from suppliers to these large organisations. There is a substantial danger, of course, that, for example, component manufacturers, as noted earlier, may become 'captive-

suppliers' to their very big customers; marketing strategists should carefully evaluate the risks of accepting contracts for very high proportions of their total outputs.[13]

Fewer sources of supply will be open to buyers of several types of product or service. This might encourage some finished product manufacturers to acquire suppliers of strategic components in order to safeguard their own production lines, or it could accelerate the noticeable trend in some industries to scan world markets for suitable sources of supply. This global-scanning approach to buying may extend as 'traditional' customers become more concerned about their lines of supply, and has been referred to as 'multiple sourcing'.

Industrial clustering has wide repercussions. It may foster new styles of negotiation between supplier and customer which recognise their interdependence, and the fact that 'bargaining is not the same as fighting, because suppliers made weak by systematic, unfairly based contracts represent a real danger to the long-term profitability of the firms they do business with.'[13]

Hakansson,[24] whose interaction model of industrial buying is discussed in Chapter 3, has referred to the power-dependence relationship that exists between suppliers and their customers, the state of conflict or co-operation and the overall closeness or distance of the relationship. Both parties hold expectations; the business environment is dynamic, and buyer and seller interact and establish distinctive patterns of behaviour. Among the establishment and development of mutually satisfactory trading relationships, buyers whose firms represent significant proportions of an industry's total production may exert considerable bargaining powers against their suppliers, both prospective and present. Skilful negotiation is clearly imperative in industrial marketing; cultivation of the right 'atmosphere' ensures that bargaining does not deteriorate into bickering.

On the other hand, industrial suppliers should adopt a creative approach to their customers and offer to work alongside them in product development and testing. In this way goodwill will be engendered and unique insights obtained into market opportunities. From technical collaboration, commercial 'partnerships' are likely to grow to the advantage of both parties.

CHARTING CONCENTRATION RATIOS

A useful method of representing the degree of specific concentration ratios is by the use of what is termed the Lorenz Curve (see Figure 2.6). If all firms in an industry were of equal size, they would be represented by the diagonal which is described as the line of absolute equality. The extent to which the Lorenz Curve deviates from this line indicates the relative concentration; the area between the Lorenz Curve and the diagonal is generally termed the area of concentration or inequality. The flatter the Lorenz Curve, the less is the degree of concentration, i.e. the more equitably the total production of a specific industry is distributed over various sizes

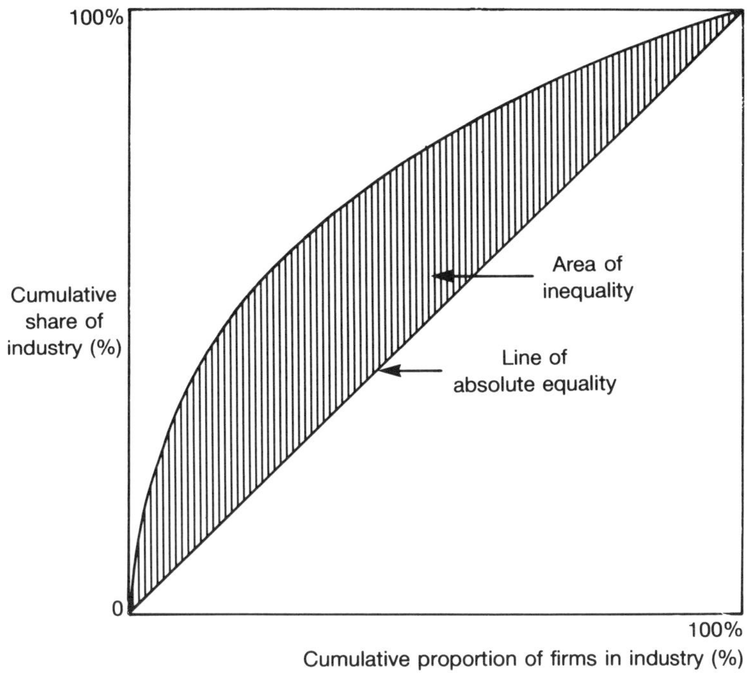

FIGURE 2.6 Typical Lorenz Curve

of firms. The construction of a Lorenz Curve conveys graphically the actual structure of a given industry.

PUBLIC SECTOR MARKETING

Earlier in this chapter the growing importance of the public sector in modern 'mixed economies' was discussed; marketing management need to know more about these important sources of business and the methods of negotiation involved.

Public corporations like British Coal, British Rail, the Post Office, the BBC and the new town corporations, and also local government services, exercise very considerable buying power in the purchase of goods and services of many kinds. Many also play an influential role in the development and application of quality standards by their suppliers. (See also Chapter 11.) Considerable speculation now exists about the future patterns of ownership and operations of most of the large industrial and commercial undertakings which are at present in the public sector.

Local government in England and Wales was reorganised as from 1 April 1974, the most drastic restructuring since 1888, replacing 1,385 local councils by just over 450 with greatly increased financial and administrative responsibilities. County boundaries were also altered; some new counties, like Avon and Cleveland, emerged, while old names such as Westmorland disappeared. Within the county structures, new 'district councils' took over the duties of city corporations, county and non-county boroughs, and urban and rural districts. It is likely that, in the near future, the restructuring arrangements will be modified, particularly related to the re-introduction of certain historic county names.

In May 1975, reorganisation of local authorities in Scotland reduced their number from 431 to 65, distributed as follws: 9 Regions; 53 Districts; 3 Island Areas.

The total industrial demand generated by local authorities, now controlled by a relatively small number of large councils, demands professional marketing efforts by suppliers. Standards of negotiation are likely to improve as local authorities increasingly acquire more expertise in bulk buying of goods related to their diverse responsibilities in education, social services, housing, street lighting, leisure activities, refuse collection, etc. (Bid pricing is considered in Chapter 5.) Privatisation of local authority services, such as refuse collection, has already been introduced in some areas. But this process has encountered hostility from certain councils, especially those controlled by left-wing politicians.

The sensitivity of public administration to political and economic factors deserves some reflection by industrial marketing management. Road construction programmes, for instance, may be suddenly curtailed, with serious repercussions on private industrial planning and profitability. The interdependence of the public sector and the private sector is discussed in the next chapter, and the need for much closer sharing of forward planning is stressed.

Because of the magnitude of spending by the public sector and the reverberations this has throughout the whole economy, policy decisions should be made much more carefully than, unfortunately, sometimes appears to be the case. Management in both sectors of the economy are working under constraints which, multiplying in their complexity and effects, emphasise the need for an objective approach to the management of resources. On mutual understanding and co-operation rest the fragile structure and future of the economic system in which the public sector and the private sector are in permanent partnership.

Over recent years there has been a rigorous evaluation by UK central government of the management and role of the public services, and the doctrine of 'accountability' and strict budgetary control has been imposed from Whitehall. Vigorous commercial policies are being adopted, although not without political and social repercussions.

SPECIAL TRADING PRACTICES

RECIPROCAL TRADING

Reciprocal trading (reciprocity) is a factor which influences some industrial markets. Similar to bilateral trading agreements between countries, reciprocal business agreements between firms occur when, as far as practicable, intertrading takes place in certain defined products. Pressure may be exerted by the more dominant 'trading partner', so that equitable reciprocal business is not in practice transacted, and there may be occasions when firms could buy more advantageously from an 'outside' supplier. Reciprocity may inhibit buying practices, rendering it difficult for new suppliers to enter some markets.

An oligopolistic market situation (where there are only a few producers or sources of supply of a particular commodity) favours reciprocal trading because the options open to buyers are limited.

A type of reciprocity may occur involving a third party. A firm may suggest or designate where one of its suppliers should obtain specific materials or components to be used in the manufacture of goods on order.

Intergroup trading is practised in some industrial organisations with diverse manufacturing activities. This tends to occur with companies which are organised in some form of vertical integration.

JOINT VENTURES

Joint ventures usually involve large industrial and commercial organisations which pool their substantial combined resources to attain specific objectives, such as infiltration into a highly competitive overseas market. (These activities are discussed in more detail in Chapter 8.)

Volvo BM, the farming, earth-moving and forestry equipment subsidiary of Volvo, set up a joint venture with Poclain, the French manufacturer of hydraulic excavators and mobile cranes, to market their products (with the exception of farm machinery). The managing director of Volvo BM was reported as saying that this strategy was

> intended to meet competition from the US companies which dominated in the field . . . Poclain will distribute Volvo BM products in France, while Volvo BM takeover Poclain's Swedish subsidiary and the marketing of the French company's products in Sweden . . . In addition, Poclain's West German subsidiary, Deutsche Poclain, will market Volvo BM products in West Germany and a new subsidiary is to be found in Austria, in which Volvo will have the majority.[39]

These companies will now be able to market complementary ranges of equipment.

Volkswagen was reported[40] to be building a 70 per cent stake in Skoda Automobila, the Czech car company, with the intention of breaking even in 1992 and producing profits from 1993. Domestic sales have been boosted by the introduction of an upgraded 'Sports-Line' model, and also because of tariff changes which have resulted in imported cars costing more. Skoda has also increased sales to Germany, mostly to the eastern provinces. In 1995, when Volkswagen will have acquired its full 70 per cent stake, as agreed under the joint venture arrangements with the Czech Government, further negotiations will probably result in the remaining shares being offered to both local and foreign investors; but certain constraints are likely to be imposed.

The terms of joint ventures should be specific and agreed by both parties; one company may be responsible for the bulk of finance while the other provides technological or marketing expertise. Joint buying arrangement may sometimes be effected.

CONSORTIA

In certain markets, particularly related to the construction industries, a number of companies may form a consortium or voluntary association for a limited time period to secure large contracts, the demands of which would be outside the limits of individual resources. Specialised skills can be fully deployed while capital commitment and risk are shared, presumably, in equitable proportions. Such consortia may exercise very considerable buying influence. Consortia may be restricted to nationally based companies, or membership could be extended to include foreign companies which may have special access to certain overseas markets, as in civil engineering contracts.

LEASING OF EQUIPMENT

Most industrial equipment is sold outright to the customer, but over recent years there has been a growing tendency to offer certain kinds of machinery on a rental basis. Some particular types of equipment, e.g. Rank Xerox copying machines and shoe machinery, were once only available through leasing agreements, although Xerox's market policy has been modified over recent years.

Where equipment entails considerable capital costs and may be used only intermittently, users may benefit substantially from leasing. Leasing also allows entrepreneurs to enter markets which would not otherwise be open to them. The construction industry, for example, uses leased equipment on a fairly wide scale, thus reducing fixed investment.

Some leasing agreements allow customers to exercise an option to lease or buy after a stipulated period of time.

Leased equipment is occasionally supplied on the understanding that supplies of materials or parts are ordered exclusively from the lessor. This is usually ensured by designing equipment which will operate only with specific branded supplies. In many cases, equipment is provided at nominal cost in order to stimulate sales of dependent materials.

Dynamic examples of leasing which have enabled one company to build a profitable new business and the other to get back on to its feet, resulting in the earning of substantial export revenues, relate to two airline carriers, Tempair International Airlines and British Midland Airways. These companies 'wet lease' aircraft, i.e. supply other carriers with jet aircraft plus the aircrews and the supporting ground staff.

Tempair originated in the mid-1960s as a brokerage service dealing in the sale and lease of second-hand airliners. As developing nations progressed, they aspired to operate long-range international air services but lacked the expertise to do so. Wet leasing of jet aircraft was an attractive proposition to countries such as Burma, Bangladesh and Indonesia; it enabled them to test the market without incurring heavy capital investment. As countries develop, leases can gradually be 'dried out', so that the deal no longer includes the supply of trained personnel.

British Midland Airways were forced to look for new opportunities when they were 'left with two unmarketable Boeing 707s on their hands'[41] following the severe setback in 1972 of the North Atlantic charter market. They decided to repaint the aircraft in neutral colours and enter the wet leasing business, securing a contract with Sudan Airways.

British Midland hires its own fleet by a dry lease method and pays on an hourly utilisation basis, thus eliminating capital repayment costs.

PROJECT MANAGEMENT (TURNKEY OPERATIONS)

With large capital investment projects, often overseas, marketing strategies tend to become highly specialised. A large power station or hospital will entail the application of many skills over a long period of time. Design could take two years and construction a further three or four years. Professional expertise and diverse manufacturing facilities contribute to these multimillion pound contracts; such resources have to be co-ordinated so that projects are completed satisfactorily.

The essence of project management is handling complexity over a period of limited duration. Often, a 'turnkey contractor' is appointed who has total responsibility for both design and construction. This strategy offers new opportunities for contractors to develop project management skills and to market this type of expertise related to specific kinds of capital project. STC[42] was successful in obtaining a very large project because it had anticipated the buyer's needs and over some years had undertaken preparatory studies which enabled the company to be well placed to win the contract. Its long-term planning typifies the strategic approach necessary to secure these highly valuable contracts.

On a rather different scale, Perkins Engines views the marketing of its diesel engines as having 'a large element of project management'.[43] In selling to original equipment manufacturers – such as vehicle builders, agricultural and mechanical handling equipment manufacturers, and producers of generating sets and compressors – a great deal of co-ordination is necessary.

LICENSING

This method of operation is discussed in Chapters 7 and 8, in connection with innovation strategies and international marketing strategies.

SUMMARY

Classical economic theory has traditionally divided industrial activities into three main groups: primary, secondary and tertiary. The tertiary or service sector grows in importance in developed economies.

It is difficult to distinguish satisfactorily between goods and services; there is significant interdependence.

Many methods of classifying industrial products have been promulgated: with all, borderline cases are inevitable. A basic approach starts with raw materials and goes through to manufactured products and then related services. Products can be viewed differently according to their functions in diverse industries.

The nature of demand for industrial products is derived, i.e. it is significantly affected by end-use. Hence the need to research end-use markets and understand trends right down the demand chain.

Products may be custom-built ('specials') or standard; the latter are more prone to competitive pressures. The 'augmented product' concept offers valuable opportunities to industrial marketers to differentiate their products, even if they are basically 'commodities'.

Concentration factors, such as geographical considerations and the size of firms within industries, complicate industrial markets. Bargaining power may be increased because of high concentration.

Public sector organisations exercise very significant patronage in some industries, e.g. civil engineering and building supplies.

Special trading practices such as reciprocal trading, consortia, leasing, project management, licensing and joint ventures also characterise industrial markets.

REFERENCES

1. Briggs, Asa, *Victorian People*, Penguin, Harmondsworth, 1975.
2. Reader, K. S., *The Modern British Economy in Historical Perspective*, Longman, London, 1969.
3. Clark, Colin, *The Conditions of Economic Progress*, Macmillan, London, 1940.
4. 'The final frontier', *The Economist*, 20 February 1993.
5. Smith, Anthony D., *The Measurement and Interpretation of Service Output Changes*, National Economic Development Office, London, 1972.
6. Fuchs, Victor R., 'The growing importance of the service industries', Occasional Paper No. 96, National Bureau of Economic Research, New York, 1965.
7. Judd, Robert C., 'The case for redefining services', *Journal of Marketing*, vol. 28, January 1964.
8. 'Structural shifts in major OECD countries', in *Industrial Policy in OECD Countries: Annual Review, 1992*, OECD, Paris.
9. 'Wealth in services', *The Economist*, 20 February 1993.
10. Quinn, James B., and Gagnon, Christopher E., 'Will services follow manufacturing into decline?', *Harvard Business Review*, vol. 64, no. 6, 1986.

11. Goodhart, David, 'Just the job for the future', *Financial Times*, 8 January 1993.
12. 'Now you see it', *The Economist*, 19 December 1992.
13. Pessemier, Edgar A., *New Product Decisions*, McGraw-Hill, New York, 1966.
14. Industrial Marketing Research Association (IMRA), *Regulations*, Lichfield, 1969.
15. Pearce, F. T., *The Parameters of Research*, IMRA, Lichfield, 1966.
16. Kotler, Philip, *Marketing Management, Analysis and Control*, Prentice Hall, Englewood Cliffs, NJ, 1980.
17. Stanton, William J., *Fundamentals of Marketing*, McGraw-Hill, Kogakusha, 1978.
18. Marrian, Jacqueline, 'Marketing characteristics of industrial goods and buyers', in *The Marketing of Industrial Products*, ed. A. Wilson, Hutchinson, London, 1968.
19. McCarthy, E. Jerome, *Basic Marketing*, Richard D. Irwin, Homewood, Ill., 1975.
20. Hill, Richard M., Alexander, Ralph S., and Cross, James S., *Industrial Marketing*, Richard D. Irwin, Homewood, Ill., 1975.
21. Owen, Douglas, ' "Organising" for profit and growth', in *Long Range Planning for Marketing and Diversification*, ed. B. Taylor and G. Wills, Bradford University Press/Crosby/Lockwood, London, 1971.
22. MacLean, I., 'Structural classifications – structure and development', *IMRA Journal*, vol. 7, no. 4, November 1971.
23. Hakansson, Hakan (ed.), *International Marketing and Purchasing of Industrial Goods: An Interaction Approach*, Wiley, Chichester, 1983.
24. Eugster, Carl, 'Growth planning', in *Long Range Planning for Marketing and Diversification*, ed. B. Taylor and G. Wills, Bradford University Press/Crosby/Lockwood, London, 1971.
25. Stacey, Nicholas A., and Wilson, Aubrey, *Industrial Marketing Research*, Hutchinson, London, 1963.
26. Sahal, Devendra, 'Invention, innovation and economic evolution', *Technological Forecasting and Social Change*, vol. 23, 1983.
27. Drucker, Peter F., 'Our entrepreneurial economy', *Harvard Business Review*, vol. 62, no. 1, 1984.
28. Ray, George, 'Innovation in the long-cycle', *Lloyds Bank Review*, no. 135, January 1980.
29. Drucker, Peter F., *The Frontiers of Management*, Heinemann, London, 1987.
30. Mathias, Peter, *The First Industrial Nation: An economic history of Britain 1700–1914*, Methuen, London, 1983.
31. Brittan, Samuel, 'The economics of the Great Crash', *Financial Times*, 29 October 1987.
32. Levitt, Theodore M., 'Marketing success through differentiation – of anything!' *Harvard Business Review*, vol. 58, no. 1, 1980.
33. Cunningham, M. T., and Roberts, D. A., 'The role of customer service in industrial marketing', *European Journal of Marketing*, spring 1974.
34. Banting, Peter M., 'Customer service in industrial marketing: a comparative study', *European Journal of Marketing*, vol. 10, no. 3, 1976.
35. Leadbetter, Charles, 'Taking a hard look at developing soft skills', *Financial Times*, 14 January 1991.
36. Levitt, Theodore, *Marketing for Business Growth*, McGraw-Hill, New York, 1974.
37. Channon, Derek, 'Industrial structure', *Long Range Planning*, vol. 15, no. 5, 1982.
38. Aaronovitch, Sam, and Sawyer, Malcolm C., 'The concentration of British manufacturing', *Lloyds Bank Review*, no. 114, October 1974.
39. Dullforce, William, 'Volvo BM and Poclain agree joint marketing venture', *Financial Times*, 2 July 1975.

40. Genillard, Ariane, 'Skoda smoothes out the bumps', *Financial Times*, 23 September 1992.
41. Green, David, 'Rent-an-airline scoops in earnings abroad,' *Daily Telegraph*, 24 June 1976.
42. 'The marketing of a major contract', *Industrial Marketing Digest*, vol. 6, no. 2, 1981.
43. Reed, John, 'How Perkins changed gear', *Marketing*, 27 October 1983.

REVIEW AND DISCUSSION QUESTIONS

Q1 Identify and discuss: (a) the changes which have taken place between the primary, secondary and tertiary sectors over the past 20 years in the region in which you live; and (b) any alterations in the provision of services between the public and private sectors.

Q2 Compare and contrast the effects of price variations on demand levels for industrial and consumer products, citing two examples of each type of product.

Q3 Indicate whether demand is likely to become more vertical or more horizontal for the following organisational products: (a) hops; (b) exterior floodlighting equipment; and (c) office furniture.

Q4 Distinguish between core, formal and augmented features of the following products/services: (a) software package for bookings in the leisure industry; (b) oxygen tanks for hospitals; and (c) marketing consultancy services offered to firms in the agricultural machinery market.

Q5 Distinguish the impact of different concentration levels on the buyer–seller relationship in industrial markets.

Q6 After consulting business journals and other publications to which you have access, give two examples each of reciprocal trading, joint ventures and consortia, and discuss their relative advantages and disadvantages.

CHAPTER THREE

Buying behaviour

INTRODUCTION

The effectiveness of marketing management does not depend solely on being able to offer competitive ranges of products and services, backed up, perhaps, by extensive publicity campaigns. For success, knowledge of the many influences which affect buying preferences is called for.

This insight into factors which affect purchasing decisions should be comprehensive. Apart from technical and economic factors which, of course, are important, non-economic inputs are also significant. These latter factors are based on some of the concepts of sociology and psychology; their influence is often subtle and not easily identified. But this does not mean that they should be ignored or left largely to trial-and-error learning, with all its associated shortcomings.

In business negotiations, the interaction between buying and selling companies is at both corporate and individual levels. At the former level, contractual obligations are arranged, while at the latter, personal contacts are made and individual relationships established. This interaction[1] continues if both buyer and seller consider that they benefit from it; the relationship is essentially mutual and dynamic. Conflict may arise from time to time, but most industrial markets tend to have stable and long-established relationships.[2]

As observed in Chapter 1, business enterprises have three levels of activity: the physical level covering plant, tools and materials; the economic level reflecting the activities of making and distributing products; and the human level relating to the activities of individuals within organisations. The policy and tactics adopted by enterprises depend on the decisions made by individuals in their various professional roles.

Human behaviour is complex; that strange, mythical figure 'economic man', completely motivated by rationality, who has access to perfect knowledge about market conditions and who could buy freely, clearly does not relate closely to actual buying behaviour in organisations. The case for acquiring systematic knowledge of the social, psychological and cultural factors affecting buying behaviour has been argued elsewhere.[3]

The fundamental psychological factors of cognition, learning processes, interpersonal traits, attitudes, motivation and personality theories should be related to particular market situations. 'The interaction of these individual factors and the ways in which they affect buying behaviour in both personal and organisational areas deserve careful study.'[3] People are members of society; they form cultures and subcultures. Market enquiries should be extended to include assessment of these environmental factors. Organisational buyers do not live like hermits; they are influenced by the personal behaviour of their colleagues, by the trading practices of other enterprises, and by the standards of the society to which they belong.

It is unrealistic, therefore, to approach the study of buying behaviour – personal or organisational – without an appreciation of the multiplexity of buying motivations. A balanced view is necessary; explanations of buying behaviour should not go from the one extreme of regarding 'rational' economic factors as solely responsible, to the equally extreme view that emotional or 'irrational' influences entirely account for the purchase of products and services.

ORGANISATIONAL BUYING MOTIVATIONS

The products and services bought by organisational buyers are related to the objectives and needs of their organisations: thus, their buying behaviour will be influenced by these constraints. In industrial and commercial transactions, products and services will be acquired primarily because they will be expected to contribute to the overall profitability of an enterprise – enabling, for example, production to be carried out more efficiently, or methods of office administration to be made more cost-effective. In many cases, the products and services bought for industrial and commercial consumption will be similar to those purchased by consumers, e.g. paint, stationery, heating fuels and cars, but the *reasons* for purchase will be be different and so buying criteria may also be distinctive.

As already observed, in addition to industrial and commercial undertakings which form the private sector of the economy, a great deal of buying activity is undertaken by purchasing agents acting for the public corporations such as public transport, health and welfare authorities, local authorities and various government departments. The constraints on buying behaviour, although not in most cases related to profit generation, will reflect the objectives of these organisations.

Apart from profit, companies may also be motivated by social or legal obligations, particularly related to safety and welfare provisions for their workforce. In some cases, certain costs may be incurred by companies in order to promote favourable attitudes towards them – for example, buying sports facilities, endowing scholarships or providing special facilities for staff.

Although the primary motivation of commercial buyers and those in non-profit-making organisations may differ, they have identical responsibilities: to acquire goods and services for use in their organisations as distinct from personal consumption.

CONFLICT OF MOTIVATIONS

Buyers' professional activities may be tempered by the fundamental instinct they have for survival and for enhancing their careers. This powerful motivation for self-preservation and improvement reflects the philosophy of Thomas Hobbes[4] (1588–1679), who held that people are 'instinctively' orientated towards preserving their own well-being. Buying decisions involving considerable risk are likely to be influenced by personal attitudes; as David McClelland has observed: 'A great part of the efforts of business executives is directed towards minimising uncertainties.'[5]

Cyert and March,[6] in their behavioural theory of the firm, identify four classifications of buying determinants: individual, social (interpersonal), organisational (formal) and environmental. Within these four types of determinant, the interaction of 'task' and 'non-task' variables is discussed. The former relate to the so-called rational factors which affect buying decisions – price, quality, delivery, etc. – typified as 'hard data' in marketing research. Non-task variables refer to factors such as motivation, personal values or political, social and cultural activities which may intrude in certain buying decisions. These influences are generally described as 'soft data'.

Although task factors are of paramount importance in organisational buying, the influence of non-economic factors should never be ignored. Research by David T. Wilson[7] has suggested that the personality traits of purchasing agents may significantly affect their style of decision making.

Organisational buyers are exposed to the complex interplay of economic and non-economic factors; they are also vulnerable to some element of conflict between organisational demands and personal needs; and they have to function as part of the management team, mediating between suppliers and users of a wide range of goods and services.

COMPLEXITY OF DECISION MAKING

As experienced marketers know well, organisational buying processes are generally complex and involve several people, frequently from different departments. Over the years, several studies have been made of typical buying situations and the number of people involved in them. A pioneer study in 1958 by Dun and Bradstreet (see Alexander *et al.*[8]) revealed that in the average firm no fewer than nine people influenced the buying decision.

Research by Alexander, Cross and Cunningham[8] revealed that in 106 industrial firms three or more persons influenced buying processes in over 75 per cent of the companies studied. In a special investigation of British engineering firms, McGraw Hill[9] found that there were more than five buying influences in companies with 400–1,000 employees; in companies employing over 1,000, more than six people were involved in buying decisions. There is general agreement by these and other researchers that organisational buying almost always involves more than one individual.

In some very large and complex contracts, buying negotiations are likely to be sophisticated; special committees may be set up to consider suitable sources of supply. 'Approved' suppliers may be invited to tender for specific goods and services, and the general tendency is for arm's-length-dealing. Long-term agreements for the supply of capital equipment, for example, will be dealt with at top management level, where the advice of specialist managers and consultants will be carefully evaluated before commitments are made.

Industrial production techniques are also often complex and demand expert knowledge; these skills may contribute to sophisticated buying procedures in which the role of the actual buyer is considerably diminished.

THE BUYING CENTRE/DECISION-MAKING UNIT (DMU)

In 1950 the journal *Scientific American* made a notable study of the various influences on purchasing decisions over 11 major industries including chemicals. Its enquiries centred on the journal's readership, which is largely made up of scientific and technical staff, many of them employed in large companies. This research was updated in 1970 and expanded by Erickson[10] in 1978 when, however, the study was restricted to the chemical industry. There was generally a very good agreement between the 1970 and 1978 survey findings, which indicated the influence of various departments in buying decisions.

The purchasing department continues to play a key role in buying materials, components and equipment, especially when it comes to taking advantage of new price differentials, tracking new sources of supply and choosing suppliers.

A multinational research study[11] published in 1985 focused on one key element of industrial buying behaviour – the buying process itself – and was based on a large sample of respondents spread over Australia, Canada, the United Kingdom and the United States.

Questionnaires were mailed to randomly selected groups of purchasing managers in the pulp and paper, chemical and allied products industries; a response rate of about 40 per cent was achieved from a sample of 1,632.

The study confirmed that managers *do* differentiate between the various stages of the buying process, and responsibilities for these are assigned to different functional areas or departments within the company. Another important finding was that the industrial buying process is more concerned with *what* is purchased than with any national characteristics. The buyer–seller relationship is of paramount importance, and the various roles in buying appear to be much the same wherever business is being transacted. (The interaction model developed by the IMP Project Group is discussed later in this chapter.)

The earlier studies conducted by *Scientific American* led, in 1967, to the introduction of the term 'decision-making unit' to British marketing literature. *How British Industry Buys* was sponsored jointly by the Institute of Marketing and Industrial Market Research Ltd, and gave a wealth of data about the buying procedures of over 900 companies. This enquiry, conducted by Hugh Buckner, revealed the inadequacy of some marketing strategies because communication was not being made with the people in organisations who really made the decisions to buy specific types of product or service.

This important British pioneering research indicated that industrial purchasing was essentially a team effort involving 'groups of specialists each with a definite delegated task'.[12] Actual routines varied according to the types of product and the nature of the organisations concerned.

In 1972 Gordon Brand[13] added valuable new data which showed how decision-making units reached their purchasing decisions. A further step forward was taken in 1974 with the publication of 'How British industry buys, 1974',[14] which was sponsored by the *Financial Times* and based on research undertaken by Industrial Market Research Ltd. This updated the earlier research and also extended it into two new areas – industrial buying of private cars and commercial vehicles. Also covered were plant and equipment, materials and component parts; there was, in addition, a special study of the British construction industry's purchasing routines.

The findings of this survey confirmed that industrial purchasing is a complex operation, with the nature of products and the amount of expenditure largely controlling the levels of management involved.

In 1983 the *Financial Times*[15] commissioned the Cranfield School of Management to undertake further research into British industrial buying practices. The following sectors were studied: plant and equipment, commercial vehicles and trailers, company cars, materials, component parts, office equipment including microcomputers, and mainframe and/or minicomputers. A stratified random sample of 2,963 companies was drawn from Dun and Bradstreet's computerised list of Key British Enterprises, and a pilot study of 300 firms in the early part of 1983 was followed by the main survey over the period May to September 1983.

Questionnaires divided the decision-making process into four basic stages: initiation of a purchase; specification; commercial evaluation; and monitoring performance. For each of these stages in the buying process, executives were asked to indicate whether decisions were collective, individual, departmental or external.

Table 3.1 shows the dispersion of financial responsibility within the companies surveyed. It will be observed that few companies authorise staff below departmental manager status (apart from routine re-ordering procedures) to make significant financial commitments. Above £2,500 the majority of companies require specific director approval, and board sanction tends to be needed for larger sums with ultimate authority for expenditure in the range of £50,000 and above.

The responsibility for buying expenditures over £50,000 by size of firm is given in Table 3.2. It will be noted that, as might be expected, major buying propositions are decided at board level, although individual directors exercise fairly significant influence in small firms and in those employing from 500 upwards.

Purchasing policy in companies with several establishments was also surveyed. Table 3.3 reveals some distinct variations in buying policies: for example, capital equipment is more likely to be bought centrally than products of relatively continuous consumption such as materials and component parts. The research

TABLE 3.1 The structure of financial responsibility within companies

	Final authority to approve rests with:			
	Board (collectively) (%)	*Individual director (%)*	*Departmental manager (%)*	*Lower management clerical (%)*
For expenditure up to:				
£500	4	31	52	14
£2,500	18	54	24	4
£5,000	29	55	14	2
£50,000	70	25	4	1
Over £50,000	88	11	2	–

Source: 'How British industry buys, 1983'.[15]

TABLE 3.2 Buying expenditure over £50,000: responsibility by size of firm (employees)

No. of employees	*Board (collectively) (%)*	*Individual director (%)*	*Department manager (%)*	*Lower management clerical (%)*
Under 100	88	11	–	–
100–499	92	7	1	–
500–999	87	11	2	–
Over 1,000	80	14	6	–

Source: 'How British industry buys, 1983'.[15]

TABLE 3.3 Policy on purchasing in multiple establishment companies

	Plant equipment (%)	*Mater-ials (%)*	*Com-ponents (%)*	*Office equipment (%)*	*Commercial vehicles (%)*	*Private cars (%)*	*Com-puters (%)*
Centralised purchasing policy	68	56	48	57	81	86	87
Decentralised purchasing policy	27	40	47	38	17	12	11
No firm policy	5	4	5	5	2	2	2

Source: 'How British industry buys, 1983'.[15]

indicated, however, that very few companies admit to having no clearly defined buying policy related to specific products.

These researches indicate the importance of understanding the complex nature of organisations and their needs. In the case of plant and equipment, 'How British industry buys, 1983' showed that the production manager played a vital role in initiating the decision to expand existing capacity. This was particularly evident in larger companies. In smaller companies the managing director was significantly involved at this buying stage, and in companies with between 100 and 499 employees other directors were active. This detailed report includes 'buying clout charts' which indicate the buying responsibilities assumed by various members of the DMU; these data are also analysed by size and type of industry.

FIVE ROLES IN THE BUYING PROCESS

Five roles in the buying process have been identified as: gatekeeper; user; influencer; buyer; decider – they form what has been termed the 'buying centre'.[16] At times, these roles may be undertaken by the same person; often, however, different people are active in the various roles in specific buying situations. The influence of individual members of the buying team will also be likely to change according to the nature of the purchase under consideration, as the surveys into British industry revealed.

The *gatekeeper* in the buying team deserves special consideration by organisational suppliers. Their identities may also not be easily discovered. In some cases, they may be junior executives who collect data sheets on equipment and send out routine enquiries for standard supplies. With more expensive and infrequently purchased items, the gatekeeper's role may be filled by a senior technical expert. It is of tactical importance to know *who* the specific gatekeeper is and the degree of influence exercised over the purchase of particular types of goods.

In the purchase of a computer system, Pettigrew[17] noted that internal politics were important influences; in particular he observed how the gatekeeper can structure the outcome of buying processes by filtering and amending the flow of information to suit his or her own objectives.

Users in some organisations may have particular influence on the type of product and the origin of supply, especially with some technical supplies. Their recommendations may be considered as vital imputs in the buying process. Users of products may be groups of individuals, perhaps laboratory research teams whose expert knowledge and practical skill will be likely to weigh more heavily than considerations relating to price, discount terms, etc.

In one survey[18] it was found that the works manager may want a product to have long life; the safety officer, on the other hand, may want one that carries no risk, while the buyer may be looking for the cheapest product. In such cases there is a resultant clash of objectives; the shrewd marketer will segment a promotional campaign so that different appeals are made to the various specialists taking part in the purchase of his or her products.

Influencers may not be readily identified. Communication within organisations is likely to be informal as well as formal; informal and personal influence may be significant in suppliers. Personal influence in consumer buying behaviour has been researched at some length, based on Katz and Lazarfeld's[19] sociological research. In industrial markets, a survey of 58 purchasing agents and other executives involved in buying was undertaken by Professor Frederick E. Webster[20] of Dartmouth College in the USA. His findings supported beliefs which were already widely held about industrial buying behaviour.

Table 3.4 details the relative importance of sources of information available to the organisational buyers surveyed.

Webster found that informal communication in industrial markets may be much less frequent than in consumer markets. Buyers occasionally may telephone their counterparts in other firms to check urgently *where* to buy certain supplies, but seldom *what* to buy. The general reaction was to avoid providing information about newly purchased products which gave particular companies some competitive advantage. The well-known tendency of consumers to reduce post-purchase anxiety by discussing their purchases with other users appears to be absent from industrial markets.

Another important finding related to the role of the manufacturer's salesman who was regarded as a source of highly useful and reliable information (see Table 3.4). His influence was felt throughout the various stages of purchasing. His 'flexibility' as a communicator was regarded as particularly important; the right kind and amount of information could be provided by an experienced technical representative who was highly trusted by purchasing agents.

The vital role played by industrial sales forces is also confirmed by later research, which stresses that 'personal contacts are at the heart of the interaction between organisations and, in industrial markets in particular, serve as the medium through which communications in buying and selling take place'.[1] Multiple tasks are performed during the interactions between the negotiating parties: information exchange, assessment, negotiation, crisis insurance, and social and ego enhancement.

Opinion leadership – another marked factor affecting consumer buying – seemed to be largely ineffective with organisational supplies. Webster[20] found that in general companies felt the specific nature of their problems precluded the probability of other manufacturers having exactly the same experience; these would therefore be unlikely to be useful guides. The two respondent companies which acknowledged the value of opinion leadership shared similar views: that companies which were looked upon as opinion leaders were of large size, were committed to planned programmes of new product development, were financially successful and were characterised as 'growth' companies.

Table 3.4 shows that, at the 'awareness' stage, trade journals were marginally more important than salesmen.

Webster concluded that informal or word-of-mouth communication from *external* sources did not appear to be significant in the industries he researched; the key figure was the supplier's salesman. It should be noted that Webster focused on *inter-firm* dimensions of informal communications; he did not study *intra-firm* relationships. This aspect was researched by John A. Martilla, whose studies in three industrial markets showed that 'word-of-mouth communication *within* firms

TABLE 3.4 Percentage of respondents finding each source important, by stage in buying process

	Awareness	*Interest*	*Evaluation*	*Trial*	*Adoption*
Manufacturer's salesman	84	90	64	70	56
Trade journals	90	38	22	16	8
Buyers in other companies	18	22	28	16	8
Engineers in other companies	26	34	44	20	18
Trade associates	42	24	14	4	8
Trade shows	76	38	16	12	4

Notes:
1. Respondents were asked to indicate any source that was useful to them at each stage of the buying process.
2. No requirements were placed on the number of sources – it was possible for a respondent to indicate that all sources were important at all stages or that none was useful at any stage.
3. Out of a possible 30 responses (6 sources × 5 stages), the average respondent indicated 10.

Source: Webster.[20]

is an important influence in the later stages of the adoption process. Opinion leaders were found to be more heavily exposed to impersonal sources of information than other buying influences in the firm.'[21]

Martilla's research led him to state that, contrary to Webster's general findings, 'buying influentials' in the paper-converting markets also reported that they sought 'information and opinions about paper from persons in competing firms, in much the same way as within the firm'. Generalisations about buying behaviour – industrial or consumer – appear to be unwise; the nature of co-operation which exists even among competitors varies from industry to industry. 'Some industries are characterised by their attitude of friendly collaboration with competitors at trade federation level and through personal contacts at senior level.'

Martilla agreed with Webster in that industrial 'opinion leaders' were difficult to identify, but in paper-converting firms they 'appeared to have more exposure to publicity material and sample books than the other executives who took part in the buying team'.[21]

He suggested that, if this pattern of impersonal communication applied to other industrial supplies, substantial advertising campaigns might be advisable to bring new ranges of products and services to the attention of buying influentials, who had no direct contact with suppliers' sales staff.

The functions of buyer and decider are sometimes undertaken by the same executive. The specifier or decider may be discovered only after considerable research. A firm supplying components for air filtration equipment found that the vital link in the buying chain was, in certain cases, the section leader of the team of design draughtsmen who actually nominated the suppliers of specific components.

Firms generally prefer to draw their suppliers from companies which have established a reputation for quality and reliability. Professional judgement of the suitability of some prospective suppliers may well hinge on the estimation of, for example, the production engineer. The power of the buyer is therefore subject to considerable constraints in selecting some suppliers.

This aspect of buyer power will be discussed more fully later (Chapter 5), but it is interesting to note a survey[22] of industrial buying behaviour in high-technology laboratory instrumentation, which was centred on 54 companies based in the Transvaal in the latter half of 1985. From a series of personal interviews it was established that due to the technical nature and complexity of the products, technical staff played a dominant role in purchasing decisions, buying personnel having 'only a token administrative function'. Further, final selection was the responsibility of groups of two or three people; significant criteria affecting decisions were technical and sales service back-up and product reliability, while price was 'relatively unimportant'. The critical contribution of personal contact between buyer and seller was once more confirmed.

Johnson and Bonoma[23] attempted to evaluate the dimensions of interactivity within the buying centre in research based on 60 instances of buying involving capital equipment and services. They examined the following dimensions:

1. Lateral involvement: number of departments involved.
2. Vertical involvement: how many levels were involved.
3. Extensivity: total number of individuals involved.
4. Connectedness: degree to which members of the buying centre are communicating.
5. Centrality: of the purchasing managers.

They noted that the mean process time was about six months, with the longest extending over several years. They also noted that in the search for supplier of services the prime concern was the reputation of the vendor.

For equipment sales, bids were often called as a basis for negotiation, and much effort was necessary before a contract could be agreed. It was concluded that what is important to the seller company is the following:

1. The degree of lateral involvement, because it indicates the potential diversity of opinion within the buying centre.
2. The centrality, because it indicates the power of the purchasing manager.

Research should aim to identify members of the 'buying centre' and to evaluate their relative contributions to the decisions to buy particular types of product and service. The more insight which can be obtained into the buying procedures of an organisation, the more effectively can marketing strategies be developed. Market knowledge includes the acquisition of up-to-date information about the 'mechanics' of buying within prospective customers' organisations.

A more sophisticated planning operation is needed by organisational supply firms; the responsibilities of individual executives concerned with purchasing routines in specific organisations require expert valuation. Sales staff should not be left without adequate guidance in the critical task of locating those who are likely to contribute to particular buying decisions. Collective, departmental and individual areas of responsibility need to be identified, and the marketing programme should include a variety of tactical communications – personal and through advertising media – which will ensure that *all* who are likely to be of importance within customers' organisations are aware of the supplying companies' products and services and of the benefits which they offer.

It will readily be seen that organisational buying is complex in the buying procedures which relate to particular supplies, and that the interaction of the individuals concerned in the buying process compounds this complexity. Further, the scale of purchase is substantial and the repercussions on an organisation from purchasing particular quantities of some products may be far reaching. For instance, investment programmes involving the purchase of capital equipment will have significant effects on financial and production policies with the objective of increasing efficiency and giving a manufacturing company special competitive advantages in its markets. Social costs may also result from improvements in technological efficiency; the installation of modern equipment may result in problems in labour utilisation. The effects of organisational purchases are, therefore, widely diffused and often go to the heart of a business.

CHALLENGE TO THE BUYER'S AUTHORITY

The role and status of the buyer in large organisations are, to some extent, adversely affected by the influence of technological specialists who may have more real power in nominating suppliers than the buyer is able to exercise. Specialist buyers, as in steel or packaging, are appointed in certain instances where the volume of business transacted and the responsibilities of ensuring adequate supplies are very significant. In such instances, general buyers are able to exercise considerably more influence at senior management level than if they had to rely heavily on advice and guidance from managers in other departments.

To maintain status in the organisation, which some buyers may feel to be endangered, the professional buyer may seek to reassert authority through adopting – as George Strauss[24] has shown – a variety of techniques ranging from rigidly enforcing routine procedures to persuasive and co-operative tactics, with the objective of retaining the initiative in buying decisions. Strauss identified five techniques:

1. Rule-oriented tactics.
2. Rule-evading tactics.
3. Personal–political tactics.
4. Persuasion–educational tactics.
5. Organisational–interactional tactics.

Buyers who were characterised as 'expansionists' aimed to influence work-flow patterns by a flexible mixture of informal and formal tactics. They aimed to influence buying considerations at an early stage, so that they retained control of the operations. Success seemed to be governed by these factors: (1) the technology of an industry (complexity offered the greatest opportunities); (2) management philosophy (where relationships were unformed because of new management, particular benefits accrued to the buyer); and (3) education (this enabled greater use to be made of informal approaches, and also assisted in committee discussions).

EVALUATING THE RISK FACTOR IN ORGANISATIONAL BUYING

The rapid growth of new technologies and the marked development apparent in many industries have added to the complexities and difficulties of purchasing goods and services.

In the packaging industry, for example, progress has been accelerated by the exponential growth of chemical- and petroleum-based plastics, which have spawned a rich vocabulary of highly specialised descriptions far beyond the traditional and readily understood specifications of paper packaging. To add to this bewildering array of technical terminology, many new laminates incorporating paper and plastic are also offered to buyers of packaging.

Similarly, textiles buyers are confronted with an intimidating list of new fibres and materials sprung from the creative genuis of textile laboratories and presented with all the panache of modern merchandising. The breathless pace of the artificial fibre industry has imposed on buyers of synthetic fabrics completely new standards of quality. By comparison, the pre-war buyer who dealt almost exclusively in natural fibres must have had an idyllic existence.

Information about new types and ranges of raw materials, products and methods has cascaded on to the desks of industrial buyers over the past decade. Advertisements and editorial comment in trade journals provide a rich diet of data relating to new technologies and products. Technical representatives also add to the flow of knowledge, eager to give personally the latest information on their products.

Business executives are directly concerned with decision making under conditions of uncertainty. This involves risk of varying degrees, and buyers in particular will evaluate the type and extent of the risk associated with specific products and services. The ability to tolerate risk has been seen as related to the firm's size and liquidity, and the degree of self-confidence of its management. Large firms are generally able to absorb the risk of innovation and to profit from exploiting the market opportunities. Pilkingtons has scored world-wide success with the float glass process, but only after vast expenditure in research and development which was continued despite early disappointments.

Bauer[25] proposed the concept of 'perceived risk' in buying decisions, i.e. that risk is assessed differently according to the perceptions of individual buyers. Although Bauer's original research applied to consumer behaviour, the perceived risk model may usefully be related to industrial buying. Suppliers can help in reducing 'perceived risk' by the exchange of technical and other information with their customers and pospects, thus improving their credibility.[26] Cunningham and White,[27] in research on buying processes in the UK machine tools industry, found that 60 per cent of all machine purchases surveyed went to suppliers of which the buyer had previous experience; in the case of very large companies, this 'high inertia' was 80 per cent, but it fell to as low as 17 per cent with the smallest companies.

Knowledge and experience gained over the years help, of course, in reducing the element of risk in many buying situations. It is frequently possible to draw up 'decision rules', which will be useful when evaluating competitive offers. Decision rules economise on management time and effort, and reduce overall costs of administration. They also help to control the level of risk in buying. Bauer[25] hypothesised that consumers adopted risk-reducing strategies with certain products and tended to buy only well-known or advertised lines. In the industrial area, there is evidence that buyers tend to display similar characteristics when faced with buying decisions involving significant risk.

Where essential raw materials or component parts are bought in, risk and uncertainty will be considerable factors in industrial buying decisions. Acceptable standards of quality, service and price will be carefully drawn up and discussed with potential suppliers. It has already been noted that organisational buyers become heavily dependent on the efficiency of their suppliers. Levitt[28] has observed that the whole process of bargaining in industrial negotiation becomes increasingly sophisticated:

> Price will be an enormously important consideration but it will hardly exhaust the proposition. Ability to perform the logistics of tightly scheduled delivery will become fully as salient an issue as price . . . the thing people and companies buy is not just a tangible product, but a whole cluster of related benefits, services and values.

Professional buyers recognise that the true value of products is made up of many parts. The relative importance of these qualities should be assessed in relation to the needs of the organisation.

Seven critical factors were found to influence buyers in the British valve and pump industry in the choice of their suppliers of raw materials. These factors were delivery reliability, technical advice, test facilities, replacement guarantee, prompt quotation, ease of contact and willingness to supply range. These attributes helped to reduce the risk element in purchase decisions. A 'favourable impression' of suppliers resulted from their ability to satisfy buyers on 'quality, service and price in that order'.[29]

When assessing suppliers, a manufacturer of hi-fi equipment looks first at quality and then promised delivery dates; after these criteria have been satisfied, the manufacturer checks that the materials would be delivered in a form which facilitates processing; only then is price evaluated. The company demands high performance from its suppliers, and works closely with them to achieve and sustain acceptable standards of quality.[30]

As was observed earlier, buyers may seek to reduce delivery risks by distributing their business over several suppliers, so that in the event of a local strike or some other unexpected event their own production lines are not seriously in danger. 'Multiple sourcing' has become standard practice in many large firms.

However, as seen in the preceding chapters, JIT and synchronised supply systems are increasingly being adopted by car manufacturers in the UK and elsewhere. These innovative production and stockholding strategies clearly demand strict scheduling of deliveries of components from a few rigorously selected suppliers.

The element of risk in buying decisions could be considered along a continuum ranging from routine (low-risk) purchases at one extreme to novel (high-risk) purchases at the other end of the scale. In the centre would fall many industrial transactions where the hazards could reasonably be calculated sufficiently to allow decisions of tolerable risk to be made. The situation may be seen as:

Little or no risk	'Reasonable' risk	High risk
Routine purchases	Occasional purchases	Novel purchases; high-cost fixed assets

So-called 'occasional' purchases would include those where the buyer had sufficient knowledge of product specifications and market conditions to enable him or her to place business with tolerable risk. Although these types of product may not be bought very regularly, and would therefore not qualify to be classified as routine purchases, buyers will have gathered valuable experience and information over time which contribute towards keeping risk at a minimal level.

The 'high-risk' purchases include innovations in goods and services which may be radically different from established supplies. Innovation may relate to the intrinsic nature of a product, to its overall appearance and design, to the type of packaging used or, perhaps, to some new method of distribution. Even more fundamental innovation may be created by new technology, as in high-duty special alloys, electronic components and ballistic missiles.

The technological and entrepreneurial qualities required for successful innovation need the practical support of official and commercial organisations which are able and willing to place firm orders. In many cases this means that those who buy these types of product first are exposed to relatively high risk. Few firms will be willing to expose their production lines to this sort of risk by adopting new techniques or components without prolonged trial and evaluation. Only then will they be willing to go further, provided that the innovation offers them the firm prospect of improved profitability. However, the increasing competitiveness of modern industry is forcing managers to demand even higher standards of performance before it is worthwhile disrupting existing production methods by changing suppliers or adopting new versions of products.

Industrial buyers are, to some extent, in a dilemma regarding innovating products. They will not wish to retard the development of their own organisations but, at the same time, they will be reluctant to accept unduly heavy risk. Yet they will be conscious of their status within the management hierarchy and of the opportunities which should be used to enhance their careers. It has been seen that progressive buyers typified by Strauss[24] as 'expansionists' deliberately involved technical managers in discussions and decisions regarding supplies, and were skilled in using formal and informal approaches. In this way the corporate or organisation executives aim to steer a careful course between satisfying their personal needs for status and security, and the development of their companies as progressive organisations.

Mansfield's[31] research into the rate of diffusion of new products and the impact of risk which affected their adoption is noted in Chapter 7. As experience and information about an innovation accumulate, the risks associated with its introduction decrease and competitive pressures mount. Moreover, in cases where the profitability of an innovation is difficult to assess, the mere fact that a large proportion of a firm's competitors have adopted the innovation may act as a spur to that firm. Suppliers should obviously try to reduce the element of risk, as perceived by buyers, through imaginative marketing strategies, particularly where new products are being introduced. (See Chapters 5 and 6 for further consideration of risk.)

POST-DECISIONAL DISSONANCE

After it has been decided to purchase some product carrying above-average risk, buyers may experience a feeling of dissonance or discomfort about the wisdom of their action. This post-purchase evaluation takes place when selection had to be made from several alternatives. On later reflection, buyers may recall the strong points of the rejected alternative products and, at the same time, become more aware of some disadvantages of the product chosen. For example, equipment bought may have high productive potential, but spares may not be as readily available as some competitive model with lower output. The 'negative' feature of the product which has now been ordered may begin to cause nagging doubts, giving rise to post-decisional dissonance. This psychological tension will tend to be particularly intrusive where a major investment has been made and the commitment is likely to result in the acquisition of relatively permanent assets, such as machine tools.

The concept of post-decisional dissonance emanates from the 'theory of cognitive dissonance' propounded by Leon Festinger, professor of psychology at Stanford University (USA). The theory rests on two hypotheses:

1. The existence of dissonance, being psychologically uncomfortable, will motivate people to attempt to reduce the dissonance (disharmony; conflict) and to achieve consonance (agreement; equilibrium).
2. When dissonance occurs, people not only try to reduce it, but also avoid situations and information which would be likely to increase dissonance.

An individual strives towards consistency (consonance; agreement; equilibrium) within his or her cognitive structure (set of beliefs about people, products, events, etc.) and endeavours to reduce tension so as to make life pleasant. Dissonance (disharmony; frustration) is a state of psychological tension which may result from purchasing a product, particularly if it is an expensive one. 'The magnitude of post-decision dissonance is an increasing function of the general importance of the decision and of the relative attractiveness of the unchosen alternatives.'[32]

Although published studies refer almost exclusively to consumer products, the concept of dissonance would appear to have some significance in industrial buying behaviour. It is closely concerned with the risk factor in buying situations.

According to Festinger's theory, a buyer will tend to seek reassurance in many instances *after* purchase decisions are taken. Buyers may endeavour to reassure themselves by seeking information in support of their decision, and will avoid sources of information which could result in loss of confidence. They may even actively seek information which reflects disadvantageously on the alternative products. Because it is generally recognised that perception is selective, people tend to collect information congruent with their existing beliefs and attitudes. They constantly receive stimulus information which is interpreted personally in order to achieve internal harmony. Conflict causes tension; this results in psychological discomfort, which people dissipate by searching for evidence to confirm their earlier behaviour.

The reassurance theory of advertising recognises that buyers may suffer dissonance after purchasing certain types of product. Research in the United States connected with car advertising has suggested that advertising messages should be directed to existing owners of the advertised car as well as to potential new buyers:

> A great deal of advertising, contrary to what one might expect, is read after rather than before the car is bought, and serves to persuade the reader that he has been wise and practical. Cadillac is well aware of this and its advertisements constantly pat the owner on the back for his good taste and rationality.[33]

It is well known, of course, that people become more aware of advertisements (and other owners) when they have recently bought an important new product. But this phenomenon does not fully explain the decided interest which new buyers have in reading advertisements featuring their chosen product. (See Chapter 10 regarding corporate personality and risk.)

Buyers of office equipment, industrial plant and machinery, etc. do not shed their fundamental human characteristics when exercising their professional skills. It would be reasonable to surmise that dissonance theory could be applied to some aspects of organisational buying behaviour. As noted in Chapter 2, package deals involving the supply, installation and servicing of commercial and industrial equipment may be taken as evidence that buyers are interested in controlling risks and in reducing post-decisional dissonance doubts.

MODELS OF ORGANISATIONAL BUYER BEHAVIOUR

In attempting to understand the complexity of buying behaviour in organisational supplies, theoretical constructions of phenomena which are considered to be interrelated and significant in specific market situations are formed by researchers. These conceptual frameworks are termed 'models'. A model is, therefore,

> a set of assumptions about the factors which are relevant to a given situation and the relationships which exist between them. The term model is normally taken to mean a formal developed model in which the assumptions are stated explicitly and relevant conclusions have been drawn by formally deductive (usually mathematical) methods. Hopefully, the model has also been tested in various ways by adducing evidence in favour of the original assumptions or by testing conclusions drawn from the model.[34]

The purpose of a model is to clarify the relationships between the inputs, such as advertising, competitors' activities or the various motivations which influence purchase behaviour, and the outcomes or outputs (adoption or rejection of a specific product or service from a particular supply source).

In the process of analytical and creative thought that is involved in the development of a theoretical model, variables may be identified and tested for their relevance to a particular business problem, such as the marketing of a technical product or service to certain types of customer.

Buying models should be helpful in understanding current purchasing practices and in giving clues as to likely future behaviour. Because of the acknowledged complexity of industrial buying behaviour, simplistic models are clearly not valid; at the same time, it is obviously unrealistic to make positive projections based on very limited data. Yet some attempt must be made to understand how a market works; what makes buyers 'tick'; and what the likely trends in a market are going to mean for specific products. Based on valuable experience over years, most business people carry in their heads a fairly sound appreciation of the factors affecting demand for their products; setting these variables down more formally is a valuable step towards more sophisticated and profitable understanding of market behaviour.

Hague has declared that a businessman can hope to understand the situations facing him only if these can be analysed clearly and stated simply. 'Simplified representations of reality – models – are his only hope of drawing out what is essential and what is inessential to particular problems in a complex business world.'[35] But business problems, he warns, are hardly ever purely economic, purely human or purely technical; they are usually a mixture of the three.

Because trading conditions change – sometimes quite drastically, as most firms have found over the past decade or so – models need to be updated from time to time. A static model of a dynamic market environment is worse than no model at all.

Industrial buying behaviour models have been rather sparse; those that have been available have largely focused on various theories of motivation, which have been influenced considerably by empirical consumer research.

In the study of consumer supplies, theoretical models have been developed which fall into three broad classifications:

1. Subjective verbal or descriptive models.
2. Decision process or logical-flow models.
3. Behavioural models.

VERBAL (DESCRIPTIVE) MODELS

The first category of model is the simplest and probably the most subjective, but it can be useful in giving researchers a general picture of the way in which buyers typically approach problems of purchasing certain supplies. In free-style interviews, buyers are asked to describe their routine behaviour, which will probably be strongly influenced by personal knowledge and experience over several years. Their general buying behaviour may give an insight into how best to communicate with them. Are trade journals regularly consulted? What kind of discussion takes place inside an organisation before certain supplies are ordered? These enquiries are often useful in the early stages of designing marketing research strategies.

LOGICAL-FLOW (DECISION PROCESS) MODELS

Logical-flow (decision process) models project buying behaviour as a series of steps which lead to either purchase or final rejection of the supplies offered to some prospective customers. These stages start with recognition of a problem (i.e. a need), progress through a phase of search activities for solutions to the problem to the next stage of evaluation of alternative solutions (comparing competitive offers), through to the processes of buying (selection and nomination of supplier) and so to the last phase of post-purchase evaluation.

This relatively simple buying model can be elaborated at each of the stages outlined, and the rate of movement through these phases will vary according to the nature of the supplies under consideration.

In this connection, it may be helpful to recall the three broad areas of buying which were discussed in the section dealing with the impact of risk on buying behaviour. With routine stores, decision rules are likely to have been drawn up – formally or otherwise – which would enable fairly speedy progress through the various buying phases. With high-cost equipment or supplies novel to the purchasing organisation, more deliberation is likely, and so it will take longer for buying decisions to be taken.

The Marketing Science Institute (MSI) model, devised by Robinson, Faris and Wind[36] is an example of a logical-flow model related to industrial supplies (see Figure 3.1). This model analyses buying situations into three 'Buyclasses' and eight 'Buyphases'.

		BUYCLASSES		
		New task	Modified rebuy	Straight rebuy
B U Y P H A S E S	1. Anticipation or recognition of a problem (need) and a general solution			
	2. Determination of characteristics and quantity of needed item			
	3. Description of characteristics and quantity of needed item			
	4. Search for a qualification of potential sources			
	5. Acquisition and analysis of proposals			
	6. Evaluation of proposals and selection of supplier(s)			
	7. Selection of an order routine			
	8. Performance feedback and evaluation			

Notes:

1. The most complex buying situations occur in the upper-left portion of the BUYGRID matrix, when the largest number of decision-makers and buying influences are involved. Thus, a new task in its initial phase of problem recognition generally represents the greatest difficulty for management.
2. Clearly, a new task may entail policy questions and special studies, whereas a modified rebuy may be more routine and a straight rebuy essentially automatic.
3. As Buyphases are completed, moving from phase 1 through to phase 8, the process of 'creeping commitment' occurs and there is diminishing likelihood of new vendors gaining access to the buying situation.

FIGURE 3.1 The Buygrid analytic framework for industrial buying situations (Source: Robinson *et al.*[36])

The Buyphases follow a sequential flow which is applicable to the purchase of a wide variety of supplies. These phases are set against three alternative Buyclasses which are likely to modify buying practices considerably. As observed earlier, at different points in the buying sequence, inputs into the decision process may be made from several areas of functional management.

The activities of the decision-making unit/buying centre, discussed earlier in this chapter, could be related to the MSI model. The last phase, clearly, is associated with the impact of post-decisional dissonance and underlines the necessity for sales staff to accept, as part of their regular duties, the responsibility of reassuring customers who have committed themselves to purchasing certain supplies. Post-purchase evaluation, particularly of expensive equipment, will be thorough, and the likelihood of further business will depend on product performance and on the committed interest of a supplier in satisfying customers' needs. The provision of efficient technical advice and servicing arrangements should be viewed as critical inputs into the general marketing strategy. An excellent sales-service network is a powerful addition to the marketing mix, and may be the deciding factor when alternative suppliers are being evaluated (Buyphase 6).

The various phases of buying outlined in Figure 3.1 are unlikely to be self-contained; some degree of spillover will be most likely. The model is, after all, a theoretical concept and guide which should be interpreted in the light of a particular buying situation.

The MSI model cannot be fully accepted for several reasons. It fails to acknowledge the multiplexity of behavioural factors which may influence the inputs made by various executives to specific buying decisions. It could be assumed that such inputs are solely affected by economic considerations, and although clues are given as to the nature of the other inputs – social, psychological and cultural – the extent of their influence is not assessed. Also, the model lacks subtlety in not differentiating between the relative importance of purchases: for example, buying low-value products, for the first time, apparently entails considerably more sophisticated evaluation than replacement of expensive equipment or even the managing director's car.

Further, this model suggests that, in new task situations, buyers are motivated to reduce risks and so evaluate many alternatives. But research shows that 'certain industrial purchasers will, in fact, reduce *perceived* risk by pursuing precisely the opposite strategy, that is, only seriously considering known, preferred suppliers – referred to by Peters and Waterman as the IBM effect'.[37] For these reasons the MSI model is more a skeletal framework of buying bahaviour than a fully integrated and complete model of the decision processes in organisational buying.

BEHAVIOURAL MODELS

The third type of buying model – behavioural – recognises and seeks to formalise the many inputs (economic and behavioural) which at times make buying a complicated and difficult process. The actual nature of these various inputs and their relative importance should, of course, be identified from systematic marketing research.

In consumer buying, the Howard–Sheth model is a highly developed theoretical explanation which takes into account social, psychological, cultural and economic factors and relates them to the buying habits connected with particular kinds of product. This model is discussed in some detail in consumer marketing literature.[3]

Sheth's industrial buying behaviour model

Based on the general design and methodology of the Howard–Sheth consumer buying model, Sheth has developed a model of industrial buying behaviour in which he has attempted to integrate the multiple factors involved in buying goods and services for organisations as distinct from personal consumption. His integrated model is shown in Figure 3.2, where three aspects of buying behaviour

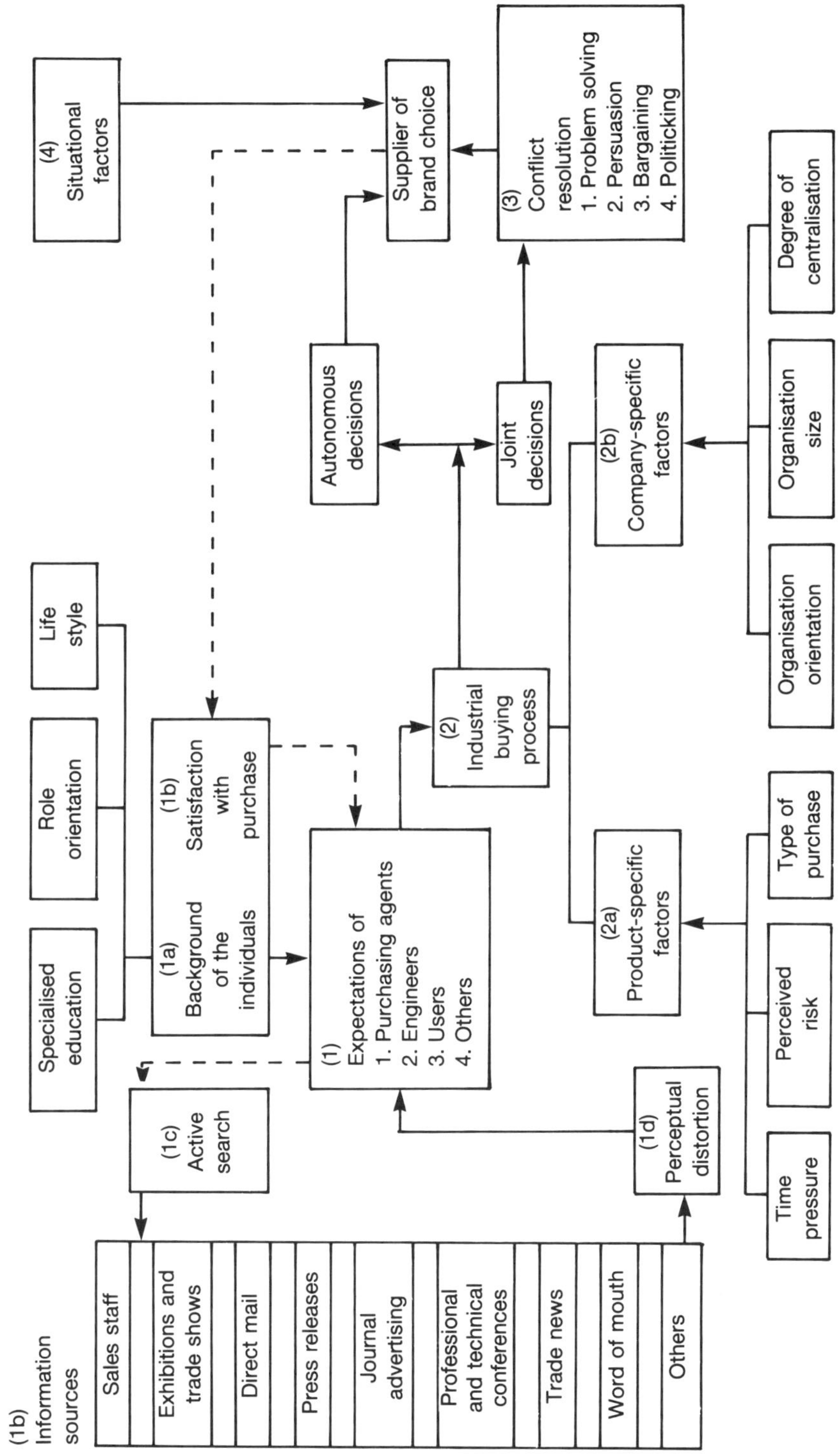

FIGURE 3.2 An integrative model of industrial buyer behaviour (Source: Sheth[38])

are clearly identified: (1) 'the psychological world of the individuals involved in organisational buying decisions'; (2) 'the conditions which precipitate joint decisions among these individuals'; and (3) 'the process of joint decision-making with the inevitable conflict among the decision-makers and its resolution by resorting to a variety of tactics'.[38]

Of the several psychological and social factors, 'expectations' about suppliers and brands are of prime importance; these expectations may well differ to some extent because, as has already been noted, organisational buying tends to be influenced by inputs from various departments. It would be necessary, therefore, for marketers to identify and understand the expectations of those who contribute to specific buying decisions.

Differing buying criteria may cause conflict: in general, users seek prompt delivery, satisfactory installation and efficient servicing arrangements; buyers pay particular attention to maximum price advantage and transport facilities; while engineers focus on standards of quality, performance and product standardisation.

Sheth contends that these different criteria arise principally from personal backgrounds, life styles, professional training, etc.; exposure to sources of information ranging from word-of-mouth to commercial advertising; the responsibility of buyers for 'active search'; the effects of perceptual distortion and retention of the various messages received by individual executives; and, finally, the degree of satisfaction with specific suppliers' products and services.

According to Sheth's model, six primary factors affect the nature of specific buying decisions. These fall into two categories: product or service-specific; and company-specific. The former category includes perceived risk, type of purchase, and time pressure, while the latter covers organisational orientation, organisation size and degree of centralisation. Sheth admits that, although there is considerable research evidence in general organisation behaviour to support these six factors, research is needed in industrial buying situations to determine their influence.

Although the process of joint decision making may, as observed earlier, lead to some element of conflict, this could have a catalytic influence in developing managerial effectiveness and improving the quality of decisions. Should buying conflicts degenerate into the 'tactics of lateral relationship' typified by Strauss[24] and outlined earlier in this chapter, then frustration and unstable decisions could result.

Finally, Sheth draws attention to the influence of 'ad hoc situational factors', such as temporary price controls, trade recessions, industry strikes and industrial mergers, which, as 'ample empirical evidence suggests', may particularly affect some industrial buying decisions.

Sheth's model describes many of the factors of organisational buying and articulates the complexity of industrial decision-making; these relationships are reflected in the integrated framwork. As with the Howard–Sheth consumer model, this industrial buying model requires systematic testing over a range of supplies and with particular kinds of organisation.

The theorised relationships which are believed to affect buying procedures may be considerably modified in practice. Sheth's model is not intended to be definitive;

it is valuable in offering a framework which, first of all, draws attention to the multiplex nature of organisational buying influences and, second, presents these factors in a systematic way. How far they relate to actual buying situations in particular organisations is a matter for objective investigation.

Webster and Wind's organizational buying behaviour model

Webster and Wind[39] have designed a comprehensive model of organizational buying behaviour (see Figure 3.3) which emphasises the contributions from several disciplines, such as individual, organisational and social psychology, sociology, government policies and economics. It incorporates the concept of the buying centre and the processes of intergroup behaviour, as discussed earlier. At the same time, Webster and Wind project the final buying decision as being influenced by four factors: (1) the general trading environment experienced by a company (as indicated in Figure 3.3); (2) the organization's internal environment – itself a complex of technological managerial and personal influences; (3) interpersonal influences as experienced in the buying centre or team; and (4) personal influences, at an individual level and as the outcome of the interplay of psychological phenomena such as cognitions, motivations, personality traits and learning processes.

While Webster and Wind's model is instructive in drawing attention, in a systematic way, to the multiple determinants of organisational buying procedures, it has limited value for professional marketing management, primarily because it tends to lack discrimination in discussing these several influences. Both the Howard and Sheth model and the Webster and Wind model have been described as 'useful schemas' which cannot be accepted as theories because 'they do not contain any precise explanation of the impact that one variable may be have on another'.[37] The latter model also fails to focus adequately on the critical relationships that develop between buyers and sellers; these are considered in some depth in the next section.

INTERACTION MODEL

This comparatively new approach to industrial marketing and purchasing underlines the interaction which takes place during negotiations, and is based on research by Hakansson and others who formed the IMP Project Group.[40] The research project studied industrial buying and selling behaviour in five European countries: France, Italy, Sweden, West Germany and the United Kingdom. Six research institutes were involved (in the United Kingdom, UMIST and the University of Bath). Both qualitative and quantitative data were collected from 900 'operative interviews'.

The theoretical base underlying the interaction model is derived from two sources: interorganisational theory and the new institutional economic theory. In addition, it is said to be directly related to evolutions in the literature of marketing, and particularly to the emphasis on intercompany relationships.

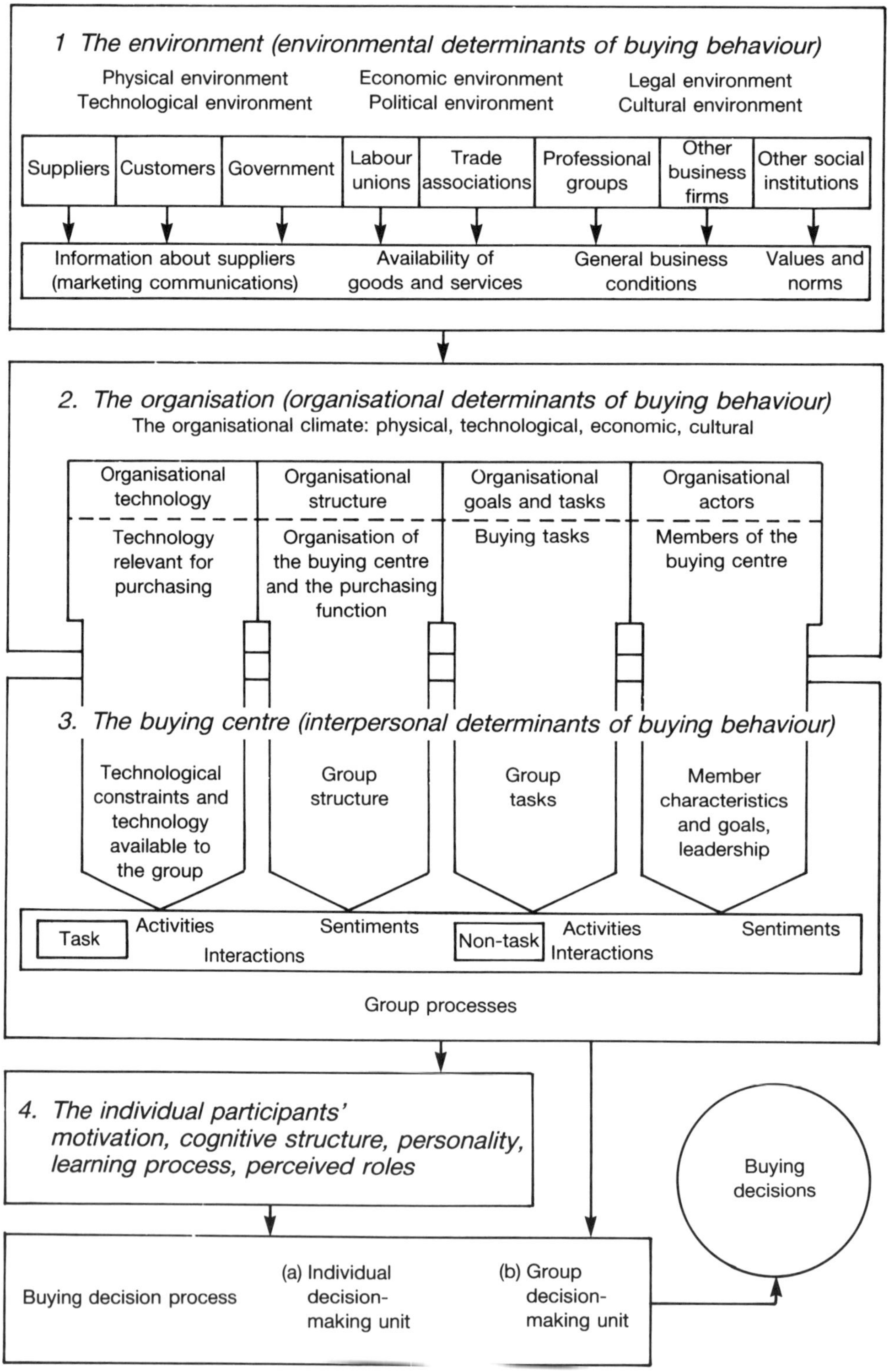

FIGURE 3.3 Webster and Wind's organisational buying behaviour model[39]

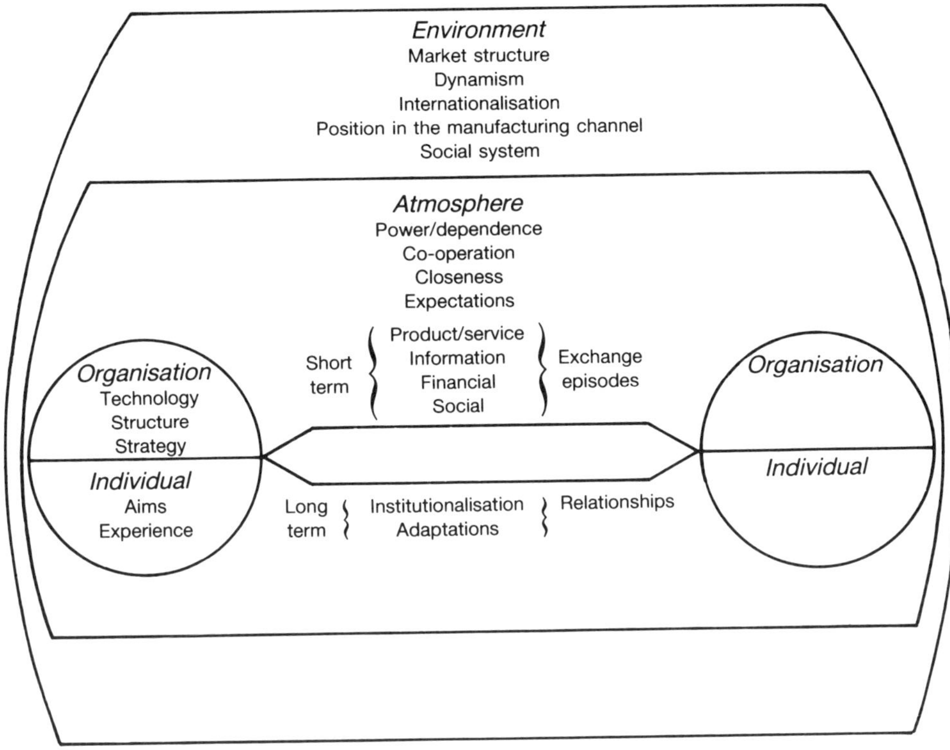

FIGURE 3.4 The interaction model of industrial marketing and purchasing (Source: Hakansson[40])

The marketing and purchasing of industrial goods and services is viewed as a process in which both parties take active roles within a certain environment. Four basic elements contribute to the interaction between buyers and sellers: (1) the interaction process; (2) the participants in the process; (3) the interaction environment; and (4) the atmosphere created by the interaction. The researchers believe that industrial marketing can 'only properly be analysed by examining both the buying and selling process'; 23 case studies are included in their detailed text to illustrate the central thesis.

The four sets of variables are shown in Figure 3.4. It will be seen that there are several subdivisions of these basic elements. For example, in the interaction process there are what are termed 'episodes' which may be 'individual' and refer to the placing or delivering of a particular order or to long-term relationships developed through contacts over time which lead to expectations of behaviour by both parties. These expectations eventually become institutionalised and may have much in common with the traditional behaviour which is observable in a particular industry.

EPISODES	RELATIONSHIPS: *Limited*	RELATIONSHIPS: *Extensive*
Simple	I	II
Complex	III	IV

FIGURE 3.5 Interaction process typology (Source: Hakansson[40])

The interaction process is governed by relationships and by episodes, as shown in Figure 3.5. Cell I of the matrix refers to situations characterised by simple problems and limited previous relationships between the two parties to a business transaction. According to Hakansson this is the 'classical' model of exchange situations, where the buyer can quite freely choose among existing alternatives; decision-making is relatively simple because of the nature of the problems involved. Marketers in these situations have very limited scope because 'almost everything is standardised'.[40]

Cell II (complex episodes/limited relationships) occurs where two companies are about to transact business for the first time. For example, in the buying and selling of major capital equipment, the relationship will be limited in duration while the actual negotiation is complex. Routine buying procedures are unlikely, so companies must establish mutually acceptable levels of behaviour at an early stage in the negotiations. Several people are likely to contribute to these types of negotiation, so it is important for suppliers to co-ordinate effectively the various inputs made by members of their staff. A positive 'atmosphere' can be developed over time, but it requires careful nurturing to ensure that, once established, it is maintained. This will benefit suppliers, because buyers will be loath to switch sources once they have established mutually sound relationships.

Cell III of the matrix (simple episodes/extensive relationships) occurs frequently in business transactions; firms will have established routines for solving problems which they do not need to resolve in detail, since they can rely on well-trusted relationships with their suppliers. In such situations, both parties need to be sensitive to changed circumstances that may result in 'episodes' becoming more complex than hitherto.

Cell IV (complex episodes/extensive relationships) may arise from a crisis or need for change in an established relationship. The need may have technical or commercial origins – as, for example, in product development or in changes of ownership.

The interaction approach towards buying and selling projects the relationship as formed by the actions of both parties 'in contrast to the more traditional view of marketing which analyses the *reaction* of an aggregate market to a seller's offering'.[40] Hence, it is claimed that industrial marketing and purchasing can properly be described as the 'management of buyer–seller relationships'. That business negotiation is essentially a dynamic process will hardly surprise experienced executives who, although they may not be able to articulate the theory, know full well the complexities involved in successful business deals. The interdependence of buyers and sellers in industrial product and service markets is well recognised in practice, although even long-established relationships and loyalties may be vulnerable to new levels of competition from, for instance, the newly industrialised countries.

Hakansson's theory is helpful in drawing attention to the need for executives – in both purchasing and marketing – to develop negotiating skills appropriate to specific products and market conditions. Both formal and informal contacts contribute to the establishment of relationships that can result in mutually satisfactory business transactions. Since the research enquiries covered several countries, it is perhaps not surprising that attitudes towards participation and authority were found to be 'quite different' in France and Germany compared with Sweden, although it was considered that more extensive research was needed before this cultural phenomenon could definitely be established.

ARM'S-LENGTH TRADING VERSUS ALLIANCES

The development of co-operative relationships between suppliers and their industrial customers, which underlies Hakansson's interaction model, has been studied by two American researchers, who aimed to discover the degree to which 'arm's-length' trading behaviour could be effectively replaced by 'alliances' which encouraged closer ties and newer types of working arrangement. From a random sample of 1,157 firms from three major SIC groups covering a variety of components, including fabricated metal parts, electronic subassemblies and finished components such as motors and power units, a final sample of 155 respondents completed a mail questionnaire related to a supplier who was well known to them, so that the nature and degree of close working relationships between buyers and sellers could be assessed.

The research findings appear to dispute the belief that closer relationships were 'a universally desirable idea'.[41] 'Bilateral governance' (the term used to describe close relationships) was stated to be 'useful only when specific assets and uncertainty evoke a need to protect and adopt'. It was also stated that selling is 'not simply the "flip side" of purchasing', and that safeguards are necessary to protect the interests of the negotiating parties. Buyers and sellers were said to have 'different incentives for close relationships, but their approaches to developing alliances may differ'.

These rather inconclusive findings, based on a relatively limited response rate of about 13 per cent, certainly sustain the researchers' recommendations for further research into this contemporary development, which reflects a more mature and pragmatic approach than the adversarial tactics characterising many business transactions.

KEY ROLE OF NEGOTIATION

Skilful negotiation is crucial for managerial effectiveness within organisations and also externally, with customers, suppliers, government departments, etc. Almost everything that a manager does involves some kind of negotiation: as Leonard Sayles says, 'trading, compromise, give and take are the order of the day' for successful managers who 'place great stress on negotiations as a way of life'.[42]

Negotiation, it has been said,[43] is characterised by the four Cs:

1. Common interests (something to negotiate for.)
2. Conflicting interests (something to negotiate about.)
3. Compromise (give and take on points.)
4. Criteria or objectives (determining the objectives or criteria for achievement).

These four characteristics neatly describe the essence of negotiation: both parties enter into a bargaining relationship, perhaps of buyer and seller, or between firms exploring potential opportunities for joint venture projects. These sessions should result in the establishment of mutual benefits based on trust, which is the foundation of satisfactory agreements. Both the short-term advantages and the likely long-term effects of such agreements need to be carefully evaluated during the various phases of negotiation.

Negotiation involves not only the exchange of factual information, but also the fostering of an acceptable emotional environment. Non-verbal communication, for instance, may be critical in influencing the progress of negotiations, as Michael Argyle[44] has indicated in developing the concept of bodily or non-verbal communication, related, in particular, to the social and cultural implications of certain bodily signals. Negotiators need to be aware of the effects of these non-verbal indicators (actions may speak louder than words) on those whom they are trying to influence. While words are the tools of communication – and it is important to understand the distinct cultural limitations of some words – non-verbal messages may frustrate the whole process of specific negotiations. Diplomatic skills strengthen technological presentations, and may help to reassure prospective customers, particularly in overseas business deals. These factors are discussed more fully elsewhere.[3]

Bargaining is an integral part of negotiation, and has been practised from time immemorial by merchants, industrialists, trade unionists, individuals and most certainly children; satisfactory long-term relationships are built up between negotiating parties who ensure that the terms of the agreement are fully understood and capable of being fulfilled by each of them.

SUMMARY

Organisational buying behaviour is complex: motivations are mixed and often conflict; decision-making is frequently shared, sometimes with as many as six people involved. The decision-making unit identifies five roles: gatekeeper, user, influencer, buyer and decider.

Risk is inevitable in buying; the evaluation and control of risk are important for successful buying. Dissonance is often felt after buying commitments are made.

Various models of organisational buying have been developed: subjective verbal (descriptive); decision process (logical-flow); and behavioural. Sheth's model is complicated and offers a systematic framework; this model requires objective testing. Hakansson *et al.* have produced an interaction model which emphasises the important role and processes of negotiation between buyers and sellers.

REFERENCES

1. Cunningham, Malcolm T. and Turnbull, Peter W., 'Interorganisational personal contact patterns', in *International Marketing and Purchasing of Industrial Goods: An interaction approach*, ed. H. Hakansson, Wiley, Chichester, 1983.
2. Drucker, Peter F., *The Practice of Management*, Heinemann, London, 1961.
3. Chisnall, Peter M., *Marketing: A behavioural analysis*, McGraw-Hill, Maidenhead, 1985.
4. Hobbes, Thomas, *Leviathan*, Routledge, London, 1887.
5. McClelland, D. C., *The Achieving Society*, Free Press, New York, 1961.
6. Cyert, Richard M. and March, James G., *A Behavioural Theory of the Firm*, Prentice-Hall, Englewood Cliffs, NJ, 1973.
7. Wilson, David T., 'Industrial buyers' decision-making styles', *Journal of Marketing Research*, vol. 8, no. 4, 1971.
8. Alexander, R. S., Cross, J. S., and Cunningham, R. M., *Industrial Marketing*, Richard D. Irwin, Homewood, Ill., 1961.
9. 'Special report on the buying and selling techniques in British engineering industry', McGraw-Hill, London, 1963.
10. Erickson, Robert A., and Gross, Andrew C., 'How industry buys – an update', *The Challenge of the Eighties*, Esomar, Brussels, September 1979.
11. Banting, Peter M., Ford, David, Gross, Andrew C., and Holmes, George, 'Generalisations from a cross-national study of the industrial buying process', *International Marketing Review*, vol. 2, no. 4, 1985.
12. Buckner, Hugh, *How British Industry Buys*, Hutchinson, London, 1967.
13. Brand, Gordon, *The Industrial Buying Decision*, Cassell, London, 1972.
14. 'How British industry buys, 1974', *Financial Times*, November 1974.
15. 'How British industry buys, 1983', *Financial Times*, January 1984.
16. Webster, Frederick E., jun. and Wind, Yoram, *Organisation Buying Behaviour*, Prentice Hall, Englewood Cliffs, NJ., 1972.
17. Pettigrew, A. W., 'Industrial purchasing as a political process', *European Journal of Marketing*, vol. 9, no. 1, 1975.
18. Fletcher, W., 'The diversity with the DMU', *Marketing*, December 1978.
19. Katz, Elihu, and Lazarsfeld, P. F., *Personal Influence*, The Free Press of Glencoe, 1955.
20. Webster, Frederick E., jun., 'Informal communications in industrial markets', *Journal of Marketing Research*, vol. 7, no. 2, 1970.

21. Martilla, John C., ' "Word-of-mouth", communication in the industrial adoption process', *Journal of Marketing Research*, vol. 8, no. 2, 1971.
22. Abratt, Russell, 'Industrial buying in high-tech markets', *Industrial Marketing Management*, vol. 15, 1986.
23. Johnston, W. J., and Bonoma, T. V., 'Purchase process for capital equipment and purchases', *Industrial Marketing Management*, vol. 10, 1981.
24. Strauss, George, 'Tactics of lateral relationship: the purchasing agent', *Administrative Quarterly*, Cornell, September 1962.
25. Bauer, Raymond A, 'Consumer behaviour as risk taking', in *Dynamic Marketing for a Changing World*, ed. R. S. Hancock, AMA, Chicago, 1960.
26. Cunningham, Malcolm T., and Homse, Elling, 'An interaction approach to marketing strategy', in *International Marketing and Purchasing of Industrial Goods: An interaction approach*, ed H. Hakansson, Wiley, Chichester, 1983.
27. Cunningham, M. T., and White, J. G., 'The behaviour of industrial buyers in the search for suppliers of machine tools', *Journal of Management Studies*, 1974.
28. Levitt, Theodore, 'The new markets – think before you leap', *Harvard Business Review*, vol. 47, no. 3, 1969.
29. Cunningham, M. T., and Roberts D. A., 'The role of customer service in industrial marketing', *European Journal of Marketing*, vol. 8, no. 1, 1974.
30. Waters, Richard, 'Price is not the only criterion', *Financial Times*, 2 June 1989.
31. Mansfield, Edwin, *Industrial Research and Technological Innovation*, W. W. Norton, New York, 1968.
32. Festinger, Leon, *A Theory of Cognitive Dissonance*, Stanford University Press, 1957.
33. Riesman, David, and Larrabee, Eric, 'Autos in America', in *Consumer Behaviour*, ed. Lincoln H. Clark, Harper, New York, 1958.
34. Rothman, James, *Consumer Research Handbook*, ed. R. Worcester, McGraw-Hill, Maidenhead, 1972.
35. Hague, D. C., *Managerial Economics: Analysis for business decisions*, Longman, London, 1977.
36. Robinson, Patrick J., Faris, Charles W., and Wind, Yoram, *Industrial Buying and Creative Marketing*, Allyn and Bacon, Boston, Mass., 1967.
37. Smith, David, and Bard, Mary, 'Everything you always wanted to know about industrial buying behaviour, but were afraid to ask – in case it made the research too expensive!', *Journal of the Market Research Society*, vol. 31, no. 3, 1989.
38. Sheth, Jagdish N., 'A model of industrial buyer behaviour', *Journal of Marketing*, vol. 37, no. 4, 1973.
39. Webster, F., and Wind, Y., 'A general model of understanding organizational buying behaviour', *Journal of Marketing*, vol. 36, no. 2, 1992.
40. Hakansson, Hakan (ed.), *International Marketing and Purchasing of Industrial Goods: An interaction approach*, Wiley, Chichester, 1983.
41. Heide, Jan B., and George John, 'Alliances in industrial purchasing: the determinants of joint action in buyer–supplier relationships', *Journal of Marketing Research*, vol. 28, 1990.
42. Sayles, Leonard, *Managerial Behavior*, McGraw-Hill, New York, 1964.
43. Kapoor, Ashok, 'MNC negotiations: characteristics and planning implications', *Columbia Journal of World Business*, vol. 9, no. 4, 1974.
44. Argyle, Michael, *Bodily Communication*, Methuen, London, 1975.

REVIEW AND DISCUSSION QUESTIONS

Q1 Which 'non-task' variables are likely to emerge in the following organisational purchase decisions: (a) the purchase of playground equipment by a local authority; (b) the purchase of copper rivets by a leading jeans manufacturer; and (c) the hiring of a market research agency by a charitable organisation?

Q2 Contrast the nature and also the relative importance of the buyer–seller relationships which are influential in consumer and also industrial markets.

Q3 In what ways do managers in organisations try to minimise both pre- and post-purchase risk in their decision-making?

Q4 Using either primary data from, for instance, systematic survey enquiries or personal experience, or secondary data derived, perhaps, from an article or professional report, or a combination of both methods, 'fill out' the variables in Sheth's decision model shown in Figure 3.2.

Q5 To what extent is Hakansson's interaction model an improvement on the more traditional industrial decision models, such as those of Sheth, and Webster and Wind?

Q6 Would you tend to agree or disagree with the statement that industrial purchasing decisions differ so fundamentally from individual consumer buying decisions that they deserve special attention by suppliers of goods and services? Give reasoned arguments to support your views.

CHAPTER FOUR

Market research

MARKET DECISIONS

One of the principal functions of management is to make decisions. Drucker has acutely observed:

> Whatever a manager does he does through making decisions . . . management is always a decision-making process . . . the important and difficult job is never to find the right answer, it is to find the right question. For there are few things as useless – if not dangerous – as the right answer to the wrong question . . . nor is it enough to find the right answer, more important and more difficult is it to make effective the course of action decided upon. Management is not concerned with knowledge for its own sake; it is concerned with performance.[1]

Marketing management has to accept responsibility for making complex decisions; these cover such factors as the nature of products, product mix, pricing policy, distribution strategy and promotional activities. In order to make decisions that are likely to lead to successful business, marketers need to do the following:

1. Assess the extent of their existing information about specific markets.
2. Relate this store of knowledge to the types of decision they have to make.
3. Specify the nature of additional information they will need before particular decisions can be made within an acceptable degree of risk (see Figure 4.1).

This sequential approach is, perhaps, deceptively simple: it is far from that in practice, as experienced marketing executives readily admit. For example, target markets must be closely defined so that relevant information is collected; almost every market can be divided into several submarkets or segments, each with its own characteristic features influencing demand and supply. (See Chapter 6 for further discussion.) Some markets, such as those for electronic products, are volatile because of the unremitting rate of technological innovation and competition from across the world. Others, like basic chemicals or sand and gravel, are commodity-type products which experience different market behaviour. In Chapter 5, the dynamics of market behaviour are considered within the framework of strategic planning, including comparative evaluations of corporate strengths and weaknesses (SWOT analysis), as indicated in the second stage of Figure 4.1.

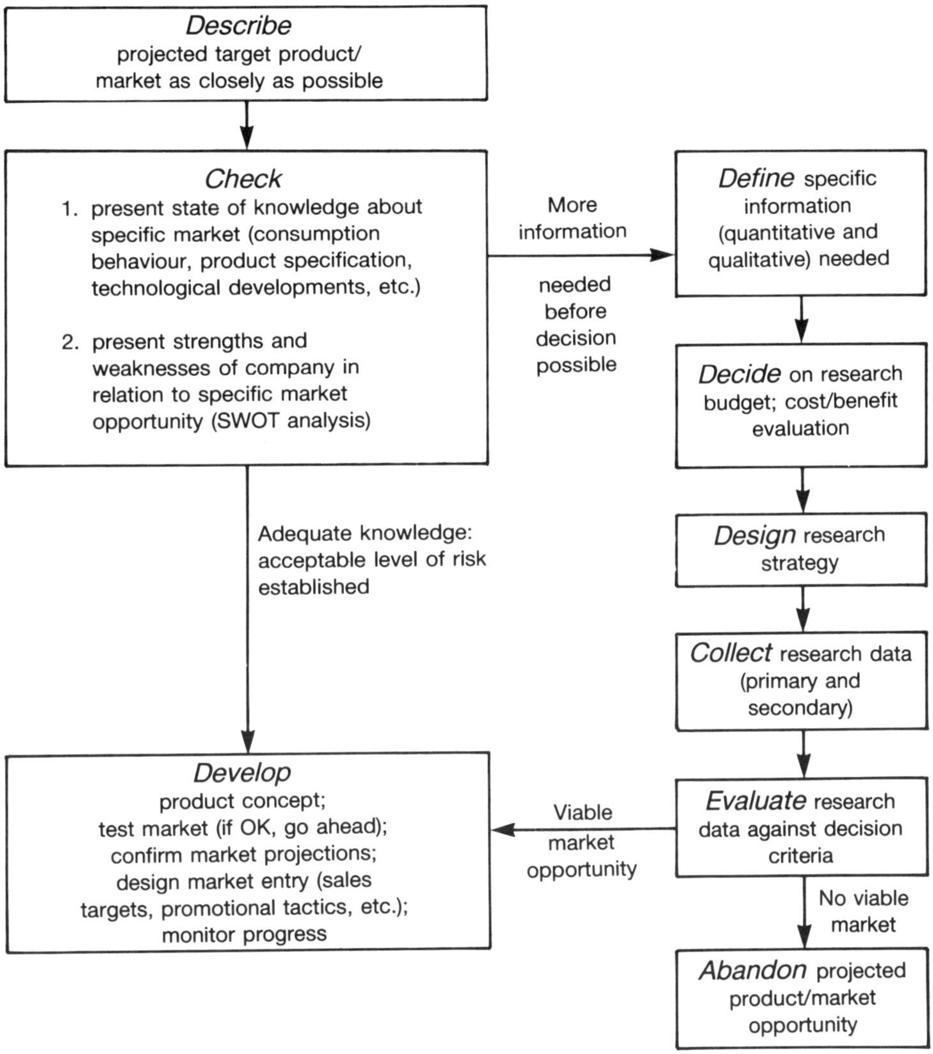

FIGURE 4.1 Outline scheme of marketing research related to product/market strategy

If knowledge about a specific market is considered to be adequate and the opportunities it promises have been related to corporate resources, then, as shown in Figure 4.1, the risks of market entry have to be evaluated in line with company policies and guidelines on rates of return on investment, profits, etc. Provided the levels of risk are acceptable and the prospective market opportunities remain attractive, the go-ahead may be given to commit resources to product development and eventual launch.

Nowadays, however, few companies are likely to feel confident enough to take on new ventures or expand significantly their present activities, without rigorous evaluations of the markets concerned. That is why industrial companies, in particular, are increasingly following the sequence of activities shown on the right-hand side of Figure 4.1.

Although their technologies and scales of operation may be very different, businesses today have common interests: for example, how to improve productivity, reduce costs, increase profits, expand market share, satisfy existing customers and win new ones – and achieve all these challenging tasks in an environment of fierce competition from home and overseas companies.

In Chapter 1, one of the four specific responsibilities of marketing management was recognised to be that of analysis: systematically monitoring markets, identifying and evaluating trends, probing new market needs, etc. These activities are necessary irrespective of the technologies or other special characteristics of organisations. No business is immune from the threat of failure arising from market ignorance.

Robert Schlaifer has described marketing as 'the place where the most money is risked on the least information'.[2] Admittedly, a substantial amount of advertising appears to be undertaken with more optimism than actual knowledge or reasoned argument about the likely pay-offs. In the majority of marketing problems, it is usually possible to collect data that will enable decisions to be based rather more firmly on fact. Information is the raw material of management productivity; marketing management should be alert to the need to acquire and use intelligently information about the markets in which they are operating or which they plan to enter.

NEED FOR DISCIPLINE IN DATA COLLECTION

Management information should not be gathered indiscriminately or viewed merely as a 'play safe' strategy. Russell Ackoff[3] has pointed out that many people demand more and more information when, in fact, they already have more paper coming into their offices than they can possibly read effectively. As the result of carefully analysing the type of decisions which executives had to make, Ackoff found that a very great number of these could have been taken quite reasonably with more limited and selective information.

Yet, paradoxically, there are occasions when executives are badly served with information: the symptoms shown are of malnutrition rather than of over-indulgence. The right kind of information is not always to hand at the time it is wanted; it not only needs to be available in adequate quantity, but it should also be relevant to the decisions under consideration. Robert Heller vigorously comments: 'Managers are to information as alcoholics are to booze. They consume enormous amounts, constantly crave more, but have great difficulty in digesting their existing intake.'[4]

Mr Harold Macmillan's (as he then was) famous observation about the value of official statistics to management of the British economy – that using them was like planning a train journey with last year's Bradshaw guide – could equally apply to the value of outdated management statistics. Inevitably, statistical and other data are historic, but with effective planning the time intervals between collection and presentation can be shortened.

In defining information needs, marketing management should not fall into the trap of demanding unlimited data. Levitt has stressed the difference between data and information. 'The enormous prodigality of the computer has so accelerated the process of data accumulation that we often actually know less than we did before. Great masses of data are disgorged . . . what is needed is discrimination in the case of data, not its sheer abundance.'[5] Data are useful only if relevant.

Marketing information does not necessarily have to be sophisticated or expensive to produce. Relatively simple but up-to-date information is preferable to sophisticated information which has lost most of its value because of the long time taken to collect and present it.

Before seeking information, marketing management should first of all define the nature of the problem facing them. This disciplined approach will help to clarify information needs and avoid wasteful use of management and other resources in acquiring data which may not be really relevant to the problem in hand. Too frequently, managers seem to be seeking solutions to problems, the nature of which they have never taken the trouble to identify and analyse. 'Instant solutions' are demanded for problems which themselves are never actually clarified. (The stages of market planning are discussed in the next chapter.)

Only by defining the problem can the constraints in certain marketing situations, for example, be known and research directed to these specific areas.

> Rolls Royce used for years to congratulate itself because it had half the world market for civil airliner engines. But this true fact concealed the vital information: What was the company's share of new business? The answer wasn't a half or even a quarter: Pratt and Whitney had been clobbering Rolls all over the airways, and failure to recognise that fact was as fatal to the company as deadly nightshade.[4]

CATEGORIES OF INFORMATION NEEDS

Information for marketing decision making could be usefully classified in three broad categories:

1. Information for strategic decisions (e.g. whether or not to enter a particular overseas market; or to diversify into new markets).
2. Information for tactical decisions (e.g. planning of sales territories).
3. Information to provide a 'data bank'; this will require periodic updating to ensure that it retains its usefulness (e.g. details of competitive products, market share analyses, VAT requirements).

Collection of information in any of these categories should be undertaken systematically and according to the nature of individual companies and the types of commercial or industrial activity in which they are engaged. As companies develop, new needs for information will tend to arise; hence, data should be reviewed from time to time and evaluated for their contribution towards the specific decisions now being undertaken by management. Some data may require to be improved in quality: for example, markets may have become highly segmented, and relatively superficial market assessments may be of little value as more sophisticated competition emerges.

IMPACT OF DYNAMIC ENVIRONMENT

The dynamic nature of many markets underlines the need for managers to keep their information up to date. Marketing information interprets the changing environment and its needs so that the right kinds of decision can be taken affecting production and marketing policies. As Kotler has pointed out:

> The relevant environment includes the *microenvironment*, specifically the economy, technology, law and culture, and the *task environment*, specifically buyers, channels, competitors and suppliers . . . A major task of an effective marketing information system is to provide speedy, accurate, and interpretive information to its decision makers.[6]

In order to develop effective strategies (see Chapters 5 and 6), professional marketers should undertake systematic scanning of the environment in which they are trading. This task is particularly important because the business environment is subject to so many changes; these trends are discussed further in Chapter 11. The intrinsic volatility of many markets, home and overseas, has of course, rendered the task of monitoring and evaluation difficult and, sometimes, daunting. But unless firms have acquired sound knowledge about the environments in which they operate, they are unlikely to be successful.

The extent and depth of environmental scanning will tend to vary according to the scale of a business and the complexity of its products and/or services. In general, information will be needed on demographic, sociocultural, political, technological and economic trends, which constitute essential elements of the trading environment and the background against which product, customer and competitor analyses are evaluated. In Chapter 5, Porter's well-known model of market forces encapsulates the argument for understanding what makes the market tick.

Analytical skills should be complemented and reinforced by creative interpretation of, perhaps, emerging environmental factors, such as the growth of the so-called green movement, with its zealous advocacy of anti pollution measures, the economic use of scarce resources, etc. (see Chapter 11).

TWO-WAY FLOW OF INFORMATION SYSTEMS

Marketing management information flows are two-way: from the organisation to the environment and from the environment or market to the organisation which seeks to service specific needs in that market (see Figure 4.2).

Marketing information should be gathered methodically, both from within the marketing organisation, using the accounting and financial control system, and from market sources. Many firms do not co-ordinate the information which is in the accounting department with the data needs of marketing management. At a relatively small extra cost, invoices and other financial records could be designed so that they provide useful analyses of sales by product type, region or territory.

Associated with the environment analysis referred to in the preceding section is the need for marketing management to obtain a fundamental understanding of the structure of the markets in which they trade. *Market structure* refers to the intrinsic nature and organisation of a specific market or market segment, i.e. whether it is relatively simple or complex. In the former case, only a few producers and buyers will be involved, as with specific supplies for atomic energy plants. Complex market structures arise where there are many buyers and the product has applications over several industries, e.g. zinc die castings. (Refer to Chapter 2 on derived demand, and also on vertical versus horizontal demand.) Other examples would be electrical components or supplies of fuel oil, which are likely to be sold to small users through a network of distributors, but sold direct in the case of large customers.

Another key aspect of market structure is the extent of concentration in certain industries, in terms of demand or buying power. If, as noted in Chapter 2, there are relatively few buyers, as in the case of aero-engineering, then their suppliers may experience extremely tough bargaining. But where there are many buyers, their bargaining powers are likely to be curtailed. (These points are discussed further in Chapter 5 on Porter's model.)

Concentration may also be present in the supply of some goods and services; high concentration characterises industries such as petrol refineries, pharmaceuticals and telecommunication equipment – as we saw in Chapter 2, the 80/20 rule is noticeable in such markets. Other industries, like joinery manufacture, are characterised by many small suppliers: that is, fragmentation exists. Many of these

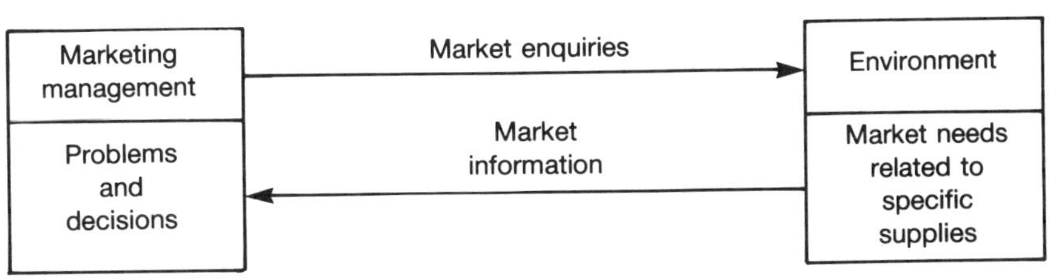

FIGURE 4.2 Two-way flow of marketing information system

small-scale firms will probably have strong regional sales but limited national coverage. They may also specialise in serving the needs of specific end-users, e.g. high-performance hydraulic fluids for automated production lines.

Analysis of market structures should, therefore, go beyond the macro market and break this down into significant sectors and subsectors, in order to obtain a real grasp of the nature of demand and supply. The trends of macro market demand may be distinctively different from those experienced in micro markets. (See Chapter 6 on market segmentation.)

A thorough understanding of the dynamics of an industry and its markets is essential in market research, and is particularly important in designing an effective sampling scheme, as will be seen later in this chapter. Considerable variability exists in industrial markets, and disciplined enquiries are necessary to ensure that later stages of the research are soundly based.

During the initial processes of investigating market structure, 'key players' – on both supply and demand sides – will be identified, evaluated and ranked in importance. These, as has been said before, should be analysed to the level of specific market segments, noting, for example, market shares held by competitors. Competitor-profiles could be developed relative to specific end-use markets and customers. Particular attention would focus on new entrants, perhaps from overseas companies seeking opportunities for profitable expansion. Buying behaviour in these market sectors would also be studied, on the guidelines given in the preceding chapter.

The rate of technological development and product innovation also need careful evaluation. Some industries, as noted already and as discussed relative to innovation in Chapter 7, experience dynamic technological growth and remorseless rates of obsolescence, while others seldom seem to depart from their traditional steady-state behaviour. For many years, certain industries, such as UK machine tools, could be characterised as the latter, but as Porter[7] points out, these firms lost out to Japanese competitors who revolutionised the design of machine tools by the application of electronics.

Delving into a market to establish its structure is a fascinating if somewhat exhausting experience; in developed economies, where quality, variety and performance are rigorously demanded, up-to-date knowledge of markets is as essential as technical excellence.

MISLEADING IMPRESSIONS OF THE RESEARCH FUNCTION

Robert Buzzell, in an article in the *Harvard Business Review*, expressed concern that 'the term "research" ever came to be used to describe the activities of most marketing research staff units'. He suggested that a much more appropriate designation would be 'marketing intelligence', since its function was analogous to military intelligence in warfare. 'Military intelligence personnel are not expected to develop a science of warfare. Their mission instead, is to obtain complete, accurate and current information.'[8] (Discussion of the particular responsibilities of researchers in marketing strategy recommendations will be found later in this chapter).

It could be argued, of course, that the label is of little consequence, that it is the function that matters. On the other hand, misleading descriptions can put people off products. 'Research' may suggest to some management esoteric enquiries undertaken in the cloistered calm of an academic institution far removed from the hurly-burly of commercial life. This view is enhanced by the academic aura which surrounds the function of learned research.

Marketing research has a very practical purpose: to provide reliable knowledge about specific aspects of marketing. It is nearer to the function of field intelligence than of the research laboratory. But its function is not just to provide intelligence or information, but to *interpret* data. To be of value, research into marketing should be objective; the opinions of executives and representatives may be based on years of experience in a particular industry, but they tend to be subjective views. Marketing research is scientific enquiry: 'Science may be at least partly defined in terms of the attitude of disinterest and impersonality one must take towards the outcome of scientific investigation . . . science deals with the unembroidered fact rather than with opinion and belief.'[9]

Marketing research can make a real contribution to the marketing of organisational supplies. By their training, scientists, engineers and technicians demand objective facts which are subjected to close scrutiny and analysis. This objective approach should not end at the laboratory or factory door: it should be extended to include objective analysis and interpretation of all those factors which are likely to affect the profitable marketing of industrial products. This is the key role of marketing research – and it can be applied to companies of all sizes.

OPTIMISING INTERNAL RECORDS

The incompatibility of data originating from various departments of an organisation may be frustrating. For example, if weekly or monthly statistics are kept by production, marketing and financial sections of a business, do they relate to the same bases? Some companies have special accounting periods which may not coincide with the records kept by the production management or by the marketing people. Personnel investigations with the Department of Trade were, in a particular instance, considerably frustrated 'because half the figures relating to staff were collected on a calendar month basis and the other half on a four week basis'.[10] A similar problem has been experienced with sales statistics and the financial records kept by a manufacturing firm.

In Chapter 1, the interface relationships of marketing management were discussed at some length. The collection and dissemination of information for managerial guidance should be designed so that full value can be derived from departmental statistics. Marketing management should become acquainted with the various statistical returns made, for example, by the production controller to the financial department. Stock records should be compared against market targets and actual sales performance. The profitability of an organisation may be increased if managers in all functional areas are more willing to exchange information and to perceive that a parochial use of statistics is a short-sighted policy which could damage general efficiency.

It was suggested earlier that an audit of information available within an organisation would be a worthwhile management exercise. It might reveal (and often has) that records of very similar nature are being kept by different sections; that duplication of this nature has grown up from either ignorance or managerial competitiveness; and that some of the information assiduously collected serves no real function. It might have been demanded some years ago when markets were different, but no one in authority had issued instructions to stop this routine production of data. From time to time, therefore, organisations might usefully check the application of the data, which, at today's staffing costs, entail considerable expense. Inadequacies may be discovered in the existing data because of changes in the environment, and this may require additional analysis: for example, expansion in overseas markets, formerly analysed by broad regional breakdown, may now require the collection of more elaborate data. Essentially, a marketing information system should be flexible to retain its value. Special data may be necessary to supplement routine information, so that specific marketing problems can be approached objectively.

DEFINITION OF MARKETING RESEARCH

Several attempts have been made to define marketing research in formal terms. At one time 'market research' and 'marketing research' tended to be used to describe particular activities – the former referring merely to enquiries into market size and related statistics, the latter covering a far fuller area of enquiries involving, for example, behavioural factors and advertising strategy as well as measurement of market demand. This pedantic distinction is now discarded and the terms are used indiscriminately.

In 1961 the American Marketing Association (AMA) defined marketing research as 'The systematic gathering, recording and analysing of data about problems relating to the marketing of goods and services'.[11] In 1962, the British Institute of Management (BIM) followed closely the AMA's definition: 'The objective gathering, recording and analysing of all facts about problems relating to the transfer and sales of goods and services from producer to consumer or user.'[12]

Kotler has drawn attention to marketing research's role as 'systematic problem analysis, model building and fact-finding for the purposes of improved decision making and control in the marketing of goods and services'.[6] This definition emphasises the end-purposes of marketing research activities.

The fact that market research has a strongly pragmatic value – to aid decision making – should make it especially attractive to industrialists. The reduction of uncertainty and the avoidance of potentially 'wrong' decisions are two very good reasons for using it. At the same time, and as two American researchers have emphasised, there is no point in doing research if the person who receives the resultant data is not in a position to do anything differently. 'Marketing research is committed to the principle of utility. In general, if research is not going to have an effect on decisions, it is an exercise in futility.'[13]

Marketing research related to industrial products has been defined by the Industrial Marketing Research Association (IMRA) as 'The systematic, objective and exhaustive search for and study of facts relevant to any problem in the field of industrial marketing.'[14]

These various definitions emphasise that marketing research involves objective analysis and fact-finding for marketing effectiveness related to supplies, either for consumption by individuals or to be used in production of other goods.

Far from being theoretical, marketing research applies in real-life conditions some of the techniques of scientific analysis to provide management with up-to-date marketing knowledge. It forms, therefore, the cornerstone of a successful marketing strategy; applying market research does not guarantee success, but it *will* narrow the field of uncertainty surrounding many marketing decisions. Marketing research is not an end in itself: it is not some kind of expensive peripheral activity which only organisations with substantial resources can indulge in. Decisions have to be made in organisations of all sizes; if they are based on accurate knowledge, it is reasonable to surmise that they are more likely to be sound than if they rely solely on managerial experience and inspiration, or what a salesperson said when he last visited the works. Marketing research should be regarded not as a luxury service, but as an essential method of acquiring facts which were not available beforehand.

Since market research has, therefore, the prime function of reducing risks in decision making related to the marketing of goods and services, the greater those risks, the more justification exists for investing in objective information. Small-scale, low-risk decisions obviously do not warrant the costs and time involved in extensive research, but strategic options that may have highly uncertain outcomes and result in the commitment of significant resources call for professional research enquiries. Figure 4.3 shows a typical relationship between investment in market information and the risk characteristics of the decision associated with different levels of information. After a time, the typical curve flattens out, indicating that beyond a certain limit it would no longer be advantageous to spend more money on research activities.

APPLICATIONS OF ORGANISATIONAL MARKET RESEARCH

In the past, market research has tended to be closely associated with consumer products. Studies of the effectiveness of research techniques have normally been confined to markets other than industrial, and the impression may have been

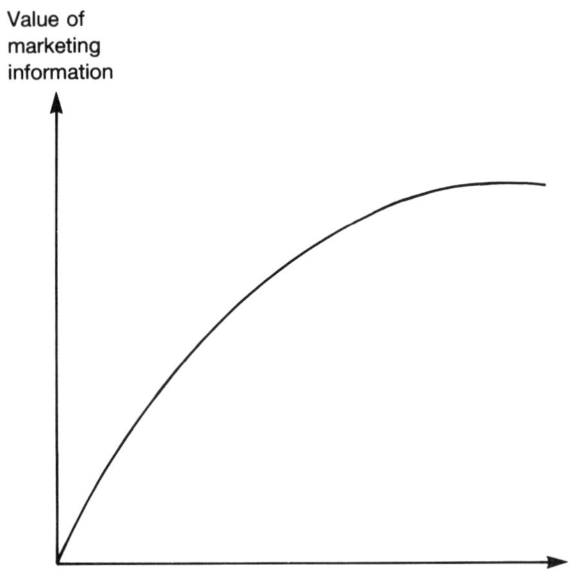

FIGURE 4.3 Typical relationship of market research information and risk in decision making

formed that the field of marketing research is limited to products which can be bought in supermarkets and other retail outlets. But this is to underestimate the value of marketing research to industrial markets. The problems of marketing industrial and technical products are certainly no less complex than those faced when devising the launch of a new soap powder or soft drink. Many industrial managers would say quite strongly that they face far more difficult problems which demand considerable technical knowledge, apart from commercial acumen and experience.

The diversity and complexity of industrial marketing decisions demand better knowledge. Information needs, it has been noted, fall into three broad classes: strategic, tactical and 'data bank'.

In organisational markets, technical and scientific factors add to the web of influences affecting buying preferences. The time-scales of consumer and industrial markets are, in general, vastly different.

Marketing management are responsible for identifying customers for their products and services, for evaluating their present needs and predicting their likely future needs. Marketers largely control the destinies of their companies, and it is no longer defensible that their decisions should be based on inspired guesswork or hunches. Objective, systematic research into market opportunities should become the first step in forming the marketing plan. Research should include economic and business analyses, technological evaluations, assessment of competitors' activities, analyses of political, social and other environmental factors – particularly where overseas trading is concerned – and an overall appreciation of the factors affecting or likely to affect a company's market.

Some of the fundamental knowledge needed for the development of effective industrial marketing strategies has been discussed in Chapter 2. This basic information will, no doubt, need to be added to before specific decisions can be made. As will be indicated later, the early stages of market research will be centred around the identification of available data.

INFORMATION FOR SERVICE INDUSTRIES

As well as physical products, industry and commerce are concerned with the marketing of services. These 'intangible' goods require expert marketing no less than tangible products.

As with products, the markets for services are dynamic, and so services should be designed to keep abreast of changing market needs. This entails market research to analyse and evaluate industrial and commercial trends. Research could indicate, for example, that specific markets for some services are relatively poorly catered for by present suppliers. It may suggest new areas for profitable marketing, or indicate where resources could be most usefully deployed. For instance, there is greater potential for home improvement loans in districts where there is a high rate of home ownership. Research should enable profiles to be developed of typical customers. With financial sources such as banks, clients may in fact have two profiles, one as borrowers and the other as lenders of funds.

It will be advantageous for service industries to identify key accounts through research, and to devise strategies to win this business by offering specialised services. With low-volume customers, package deals may be designed that will satisfy their needs and keep the costs of servicing them at acceptable levels.

> The case of a large European bank shows what can happen when individualised products are offered in the mass market, or poorly planned standard products introduced to a market that may not even recognise or appreciate its expensive features. A detailed analysis of the bank's economics uncovered differences in the cost–revenue structures of two important market segments: small individual customers accounted for 6 per cent of all revenue and 14 per cent of all costs, while small commercial customers accounted for 39 per cent of all revenue and only 15 per cent of all costs.[15]

Apart from feedback of 'hard data', service industries would benefit from a general appreciation of the service rendered (attitudes of staff, quality of service, accuracy of information, etc.). Some American banks are reported[16] to use 'professional shoppers' who are existing customers and also report anonymously to their bank on their perception of the overall standard of service. User-panels are not, of course, new to product marketing; perhaps service industries also could benefit from regular feedback from their clients.

Market research can be useful in designing effective methods of market communication as well, including media advertising. With financial services in particular, the location and appearance of offices is important in building an acceptable corporate image. The joint-stock banks have adopted corporate symbols which clearly distinguish their premises and give reassurance to clients, especially if they are away from their home town. Banks need to project an image of security, reliability, confidentiality, accessibility, financial expertise, etc.: hence the plan of corporate communications deserves special attention. In the past, joint-stock banks have tended to ignore market research or to use it in distinctly limited ways. The greater level of competition now evident in the financial sector of the economy suggests that banks, building societies and insurance companies should make more use of a well-established marketing tool. These enquiries should be comprehensive – not just limited to economic data – and cover psychological, social and cultural trends; these have been discussed in some depth in a specialist text.[17]

PUBLIC SECTOR SERVICES

Marketing research techniques can also be applied productively in the planning of non-profit-making activities such as the social services, public transport, education and health services. Unless reliable information is used at the design stage of these services, it is clear that public resources may be unwisely committed. To serve people's needs it is advisable to identify these as closely as possible; mere conjectures are not good enough. Objective research will also be of value in assessing the effectiveness of existing services and may identify new areas which could legitimately be the concern of public authorities. Far greater use of marketing research could, therefore, result in better utilisation of scarce resources and improved benefits to the community. In some directions, services may have become over-elaborated when relatively simple services may be adequate to meet the needs of particular sections of the community. There may be a need for new types of public service where a district is changing its character because of industrialisation or the arrival of immigrant populations.

That marketing research techniques used by profit-oriented firms are of use in the public sector, where primary motivations tend to be different, should not be regarded as a bizarre proposal.

> Research techniques by which profit-making firms measure the marketability of their products, and improve the effectiveness of their services, distribution and communications, are applicable to projects concerned with education, culture, health, environments and energy supply. New standards may thus evolve to help measure the effectiveness of such non-profit organisations in achieving goals that do not pertain directly to such economic goals as sales and profits.[18]

The needs of people deserve objective analysis; managerial accountability for the effective use of corporate resources applies equally in both sectors of the economy.

Planning is accepted as an important element of public administration. Marketing research is not confined to commercial investigations; it in fact evolved a substantial part of its methodology from the pioneer social investigations made, for example, by Bowley *et al.*[19] in the early part of this century. Since that time techniques have been refined and extended, and the strong link between marketing research practitioners and social investigation continues with several research agencies specialising in medical and social welfare investigations.

HIGH-TECHNOLOGY PRODUCTS

The trend in UK manufacturing is, as observed earlier, in the direction of the newer, high-technology products (with their related services), and so it is relevant to consider how marketing research can help in the development of this important sector of the economy.

Particularly useful examples of this application of market research are given in a paper by Cowell and Blois.[20] This has an interesting account of three cases of technologically advanced products and their marketing problems.

In a research institute a new technique had been developed that was able to detect minute vibrations in objects. An outside body was considering finance for the further developement of this project, but before committing themselves, they demanded that a survey should be conducted to ascertain (1) the potential markets for the applications of this technique; and (2) the outline specification of equipment acceptable to the markets identified in (1). Following systematic market enquiries, the level of market interest and the necessary guidelines for development of the technique were established.

In another case, a research institute was interested in buying some equipment that made it possible to examine complex molecular structures. Initial enquiries by a member of the scientific staff revealed that this specialised machine would have only limited use throughout the year by the institute, but that there was a 'large' market for its use by other organisations. As the result of an attractive offer by a potential supplier, the institute instructed its marketing manager to (1) check the validity of the physicist's market enquiries; and (2) collect some more information about the commercial viability of the potential purchase. Within the tight limitations of time and cost, this survey was able to establish that (1) the physicist's estimate of outsiders' usage of the equipment was too high; and (2) the type of service offered to potential users would cost more than originally believed because of the need for advisory services. In addition, the machine would rarely be fully loaded; and delay in filling the machine to achieve economic operation would clash with the market need, which was primarily for a 36-hour sample analysis service.

The third case concerned a company making a wide range of equipment for the engineering industry which was offered the opportunity of making a new design of a solid/solid batch separator. So far, only prototypes of this separator had been made and used by the designer.

The company wished to extend its product range and so asked consultants to investigate the market potential for this product. Estimates were needed of

(1) potential industries and users of the separator; (2) present and potential UK market in terms of units and value in these specific industries; and (3) state of competition.

The market researchers were provided with enough technical data to enable them to undertake the survey. The resultant research indicated that (1) criteria listed by a group of chemical engineers with known expertise in the use of separators did in practice influence the choice of separators; (2) after some aggregate value of market size had been obtained, it was evident that purchases fluctuated quite violently; and (3) the costs of market entry would be extremely high and involve concentrated efforts over a long period to provide acceptable proof of the separator's capabilities under operating conditions.

PLANNING MARKET RESEARCH

Marketing research can be conveniently divided into five steps which lead logically to the final survey report. These phases apply irrespective of the nature of the market – consumer, industrial or public service. Professional skill is needed at every stage of the research programme to ensure that the findings of the surveys are based on objective data which have been obtained from representative samples of a specific population (see Figure 4.4).

STAGE 1: RESEARCH BRIEF

This initial and crucial stage will decide the nature and direction of the entire research. It entails defining clearly and in specific terms the marketing problem to be investigated. With industrial products, market research objectives may be focused on the needs of particular customers for machines of special capacity or for specific formulations of chemicals. The extent of the product range, the likely demand for spares (and the resulting stock levels needed), the nature of sales-service support expected by some industries and the type and level of competition are a few of the problems which industrial marketing researchers continually tackle.

Before clear definition of the marketing problem is feasible, it may be necessary to make some exploratory enquiries in certain areas of the organisation, e.g. selling arrangements, publicity methods and pricing structure. This preliminary work should gain researchers valuable background knowledge and may in fact point to the real problem which has to be investigated. The marketing problem may relate closely to production methods, for example, and some degree of integrated research may be necessary.

At this critical briefing stage, both management and researchers should endeavour to obtain clear agreement on the objectives of the research. Management should be prepared to take researchers into their confidence and present them with an unvarnished picture of their organisation and the kind of marketing problems which face them. Marketing researchers have the duty to probe and ensure that

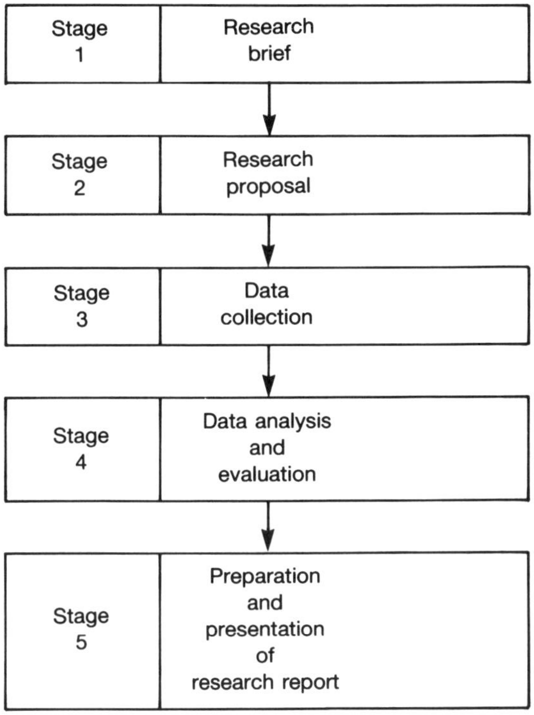

FIGURE 4.4 Five sequential stages of marketing research

they have been given adequate information on which to base a research strategy. The relationship between client and researcher is similar to that of barrister and professional client. Unless the briefing is throrough, misunderstandings and even catastrophe could result.

If the proposition put forward by a client seems unrealistic, a reputable marketing researcher will point out the constraints which, inevitably, govern the nature of research activities. Like all products and services, research costs money; it involves time and professional skills. Before a research brief is accepted, both parties should agree on the level of accuracy required, the date by which the research report will be available and the approximate price to be paid.

A great deal of thought, time and more care should be given, therefore, to the marketing research brief. Clients and researchers should be prepared to spend some time on defining the precise terms of reference which will guide the research programme. Slipshod thinking at this initial phase will set the whole research off course and probably cause deep annoyance to both parties later on.

STAGE 2: RESEARCH PROPOSAL

At this stage a research proposal or work plan should be developed which, by means of a simple model of the problem, will specify the data to be collected and the methodology to be adopted. It is important to check that the proposed research strategy will satisfy the objectives set out in the first phase. These objectives should be developed and refined into one or a series of working hypotheses which can be tested during the research programme. These hypotheses 'arise as a result of prior thinking about the subject, preliminary investigation of available data and material (including related studies), or advice and counsel of experts or interested parties. Like the formulation of the problem, such hypotheses are most useful when expressed in precise, clearly defined terms.'[21]

The contents of a research proposal will tend to vary according to the nature and scope of particular enquiries concerning products and services. As observed already, information on market structure will be of paramount importance and will provide the background to further aspects of the proposed research: for example, market size (including sector analyses), market trend, market shares (principal competitors rated for technological performance, pricing competitiveness, delivery and after-sales service, selling and promotional effectiveness, etc.), buying behaviour (including assessments of buying power), export market evaluations, and special trading constraints such as tariffs, quotas, legislation, technical standards and patents.

A research schedule should be drawn up giving timing for the various operations. This will take account of the methodology to be used (specific techniques of marketing research will be covered in the next section) and the time constraints imposed by the client.

A statement of cost should also be included together with terms of payment. In the case of fairly extensive research, payment of fees may be phased, perhaps an initial one-third due on placing the research contract, followed by an interim one-third half-way through the agreed time schedule, and a final one-third payment on presentation of the research report.

Staged payments are unlikely to be a feature of relatively short-term projects, where fees are usually due on completion of the research.

If, during the research, significant changes are made – perhaps involving extra dimensions of information or coverage of additional market sectors – the cost implications will need to be checked, and fees may have to be adjusted.

Experienced research users generally invite at least three survey firms to submit proposals; these may differ in terms of not only technical expertise but also financial cost. The former should be evaluated before considering the latter. How, for example, are the stated objectives of the research related to the proposed research methodologies, and what kinds of information will result from these activities? Will this information (both quantitative and qualitative) be adequate for the management decisions which are being considered? What degrees of accuracy are these data likely to possess? Only after these and similar questions have been satisfied should prices be compared. Research firms tend to develop specific professional expertise, sometimes related to industrial sectors which may be directly relevant to a client's needs. In such cases, expert research experience and knowledge may be available at competitive prices.

STAGE 3: COLLECTION OF DATA

The research programme having been agreed, the next stage is likely to occupy a considerable amount of time. The relative efficiencies of collecting data by alternative methods will have to be checked. Complementary data may be desirable in some types of market investigation. Sampling procedures need to be thoroughly planned to avoid some of the biases which make research such a precarious profession.

STAGE 4: ANALYSIS AND EVALUATION OF DATA

Every stage of the research programme is interrelated. It is no use applying sophisticated techniques of analysis and statistical tests of data at this stage if the original research design did not ensure that, for example, the sample methodology was soundly based.

Data are the raw material of the research programme; they have to be refined by means of tabulation, analysis and interpretation. During these processes, significant relationships between variables may be discovered; these require objective discussions and evaluation related to the problems which the survey has undertaken to study.

Systems of data storage and retrieval may also be incorporated in this stage of the research. Provision should be made to update information so that market knowledge on critical factors in buying behaviour retains its value for management decision making. New competitors may, for example, enter the home or an overseas market. Different distribution strategies may radically alter the nature of competition. A comparatively low-ranked competitor may be taken over by a large industrial group which is prepared to invest substantial funds in an aggressive bid for a larger market share.

Computers have revolutionised data processing, which, in a comparatively short period, has progressed from hand analysis to systems of mechanical tabulation, eventually to arrive at the speed, flexibility and diversity of modern computerised systems. The attractions of such a flexible and speedy system may contain dangers: a careful check is needed to avoid the GIGO effect (garbage in–garbage out).

Questionnaires can now be read mechanically and at great speed. Sophisticated analytical techniques such as factor analysis are no longer fairly tedious (if not prohibitive) methods of analysing certain kinds of data.

These improvements in the technical efficiency of research data processing are of direct benefit to clients. Speedier and more elaborate surveys are possible and at very economic cost.

STAGE 5: PREPARATION AND PRESENTATION OF RESEARCH REPORT

This stage completes the research programme; it deserves professional attention because faulty communication can undo a lot of the good work done earlier.

Researchers should develop their managerial expertise in presenting the findings of research surveys so that they are fully understood by clients.

> Interpretation of survey findings is a matter on which experts express strongly conflicting views. Some would have researchers give their own interpretation of the findings of surveys, while others, equally dogmatic, believe that researchers should limit themselves to reporting the facts discovered through the survey.[22]

The question of interpretation should be discussed at the time the research brief is agreed. Clients as well as researchers may have different views, so some clearly agreed policy is desirable. To discourage researchers from exercising their professional knowledge in the interpretation of a survey's findings would seem to be a rather short-sighted policy. They may be able to suggest alternative marketing strategies as a result of approaching problems with professional objectivity. For several months, the client's problems will have become the focus of intense commitment: it would be unproductive not to exploit this valuable source of creative managerial inputs.

In preparing a survey report, researchers 'should keep in mind those who will read it'.[22] Both the content and the style should be designed to satisfy the needs of particular readers. Clear, grammatical language should be used, with data shown attractively in tables and diagrams. The format, printing and binding are factors that can help considerably in making the contents of a report intelligible and acceptable.

Some industrial marketing research reports include substantial technical data which, in detail, may not be required by commercial management. In such cases, it is often advisable to prepare two editions: one which contains a detailed technological assessment, to be read exclusively by technical specialists; the other, intended principally for commercial management, covering technology in less depth and concentrating more on commercial implications of the marketing developments studied. Where separate reports are not desirable, care must be exercised to ensure that any technical terms used are defined so that the report can be understood without undue trouble.

Because delays may occur in production of the main report, clients may find it helpful to have a preliminary report which distils the research findings. In addition to the final written report, some clients invite researchers to discuss the survey findings, preferably after all involved have carefully studied it.

TECHNIQUES OF MARKET RESEARCH

An important part of research activity is to decide on the research strategy, the second step of the sequential stages shown in Figure 4.4. Research strategy covers the selection of suitable methods of survey, the nature of the research instruments, the sampling design and types of data to be collected (quantitative or qualitative or, ideally, both).

Data for marketing research can be obtained by several methods and from various sources. An effective research design 'is the overall operational pattern of framework of the project that stipulates what information is to be collected, from which sources, and by what procedures. If it is a good design, it will ensure that the information obtained is relevant to the research problem and that it was collected by objective and economical procedures.'[23]

SOURCES OF DATA

Marketing research data are derived from two main sources:

1. *Primary data*: these originate from field research which may use either one or a mixture of techniques such as observation, experimentation and questionnaires.
2. *Secondary data*: these result from existing information which may be available from internal records or from externally published sources.

SECONDARY DATA

Secondary data will be discussed first because, as Political and Economic Planning (PEP) observed many years ago: 'The answers to many problems often lie within the files of an organisation or in published material.'[24] This level of research, often known as desk research, has many advantages: it is economical, comparatively speedy and can be undertaken with complete confidentiality. Desk research should always be made full use of in any type of marketing research enquiry. It should be the first step to take in tackling a research problem; it may well provide adequate information for the decision which has to be taken. Only rarely is there no relevant information which can be culled fairly readily from internal records or from published sources.

The advantages of harnessing routine accounting and production records for marketing analyses were discussed earlier. There are many opportunities for making better use of internal records to give, for example, sales analysed by area, type of customer or industry. Much greater 'mileage' should be extracted from company delivery notes, invoices and other departmental records.

Where companies are selling products or services direct to users, as with most industrial marketing, it is possible to develop a fairly simple method of collecting market data which experienced representatives can operate successfully.

Kodak was reported[25] to use a system of 'customer indexes' based on survey cards filled in by representatives, giving basic information such as industry of a customer, particular application of supplies purchased, size of organisation and extent of use of competitive products. This customer profile is completed for every call made by a representative. At the end of a 'journey cycle', representatives return the survey cards, with the latest data recorded, to the sales office for incorporation in a master data file. These customer index cards are subsequently returned to representatives who will, as necessary, complete follow-up cards recording any changes in the customer profile and send these to head office so that the master records can be amended. Most of these records are fully computerised, which enables overall analyses of the current position of industrial sales to be made very quickly.

These customer indexes are also useful in designing territories, promotional activities, forecasting, etc. The great advantage of this method lies in its simplicity of collection and the fact that it is constantly being updated.

With a little ingenuity and cooperation from staff in various sections of an organisation, many internal records could provide data of value to the marketing department.

External secondary data are available from many sources: statistics and reports issued by governments, trade associations, academic institutions, etc. In the United Kingdom, the Central Statistical Office (CSO) acts as a co-ordinating organisation in guiding researchers to the appropriate source of statistics issued by individual government departments. The Business Statistics Office (BSO), Cardiff Road, Newport, Gwent, deals specifically with industrial and commercial data. Two very useful official publications, *Guide to Official Statistics* (HMSO) and *Regional Statistics* (HMSO), provide valuable guides to sources of statistical data for particular products and services.

All continental European countries operate central statistical offices which collect and publish annually statistics relating to those countries. Monthly statistics and also data dealing with specific industries may be available. Extra data, so far unpublished, may be obtainable on payment of a fee.

Official sources

Some examples of principal official sources of general reference for industrial marketing research are listed below:

- *Guide to Official Statistics*: a very useful starting point for identifying relevant sources of official information.
- *Annual Abstract of Statistics*: provides information on population, housing, manufactured goods, etc.
- *Monthly Digest of Statistics*: similar to the *AA*, but published at monthly intervals.
- *Abstract of Regional Statistics.*
- *Scottish Abstract of Statistics.*
- *Digest of Welsh Statistics.*
- *Digest of UK Energy Statistics*: published annually; gives details of production and demand for various UK energy fields. Reports of the nationalised energy industries provide additional statistical analyses.
- *Overseas Trade Statistics of the UK*: published monthly; gives detailed analyses of overseas trade statistics. Special analyses obtainable from HM Customs and Excise.

- *Housing and Construction Statistics*: published quarterly by the Department of the Environment.
- *Local Housing Statistics*: also published each quarter by the Department of the Environment.
- *Agricultural Statistics*.
- *Financial Statistics* (key monetary data).
- *Passenger Transport in Great Britain*: published annually by the Department of the Environment.
- *Highway Statistics*: another annual publication emanating from the Department of the Environment.
- *Social Trends*: valuable collection of key social statistics, published annually.
- *Annual Report of the Department of Health and Social Security*.
- *Economic Trends*: monthly review of the British economic situation. Quarterly data on the national income and balance of payments are also included.
- *Census of Population*: gives detailed analyses of the UK population, which may be particularly useful in some derived-demand markets.
- *Census of Distribution*: gives basic information on the structure of retail distribution; last taken in 1971 but superseded by annual sample enquiries from 1976.
- *Census of Production*: one of the most important sources of desk research for industrial marketers. The first Census of Production in the United Kingdom was taken in 1908 in respect of 1907. It originated from the controversy over tariffs: one of its main objectives was to ascertain the quantity and valued of different kinds of manufacturing output. Originally planned on a quinquennial basis (although this time interval was distorted by the two world wars), the Census has now been replaced by a simplified annual one, the first of which occurred in 1970. The new system of censuses offers information similar to the old quinquennial enquiries but by means of quarterly enquiries into sales coupled with a summary Census of Production each year. These quarterly enquiries will be supplemented by monthly enquiries, and detailed enquiries may also be extended into purchases of materials at three year intervals. Census results are published in the *Business Monitor* series, appearing as 110 individual industry reports together with a summary volume. Summary findings are published in the journal *British Business*.

  The Census covers production which is defined as 'industrial production, including construction, gas, electricity and water supply and mines and quarries'. Full details were required only from firms with over 25 employees; smaller firms provided summaries of their activities. From 1973 certain modifications were made to comply with the statistical requirements of the Statistical Office of the European Communities.

  The first change affected the coverage of the Census. Previously, Census returns had to be submitted, as noted above, by establishments employing 25 or more people except that in 13 industries, where small firms made an important contribution to total output, the coverage was extended to establishments with 11 or more employees. In the 1975 Census, all establishments employing 20 or more were asked to complete a questionnaire.

For those establishments employing 20–99 people, the 1973 Census questions were little different from those used in the Census for 1971 and 1972. New questions covered payments for outworkers and the cost of goods bought for merchanting; questions on transport costs were discontinued apart from a few industries.

Establishments with 100 or more employees were also asked these new questions, as well as questions on value added tax and the cost of non-industrial services.

To avoid identification of individual firms, Census report figures are sometimes amalgamated.

More extensive use has been made of sampling: for example the 1985 Census took a one in four sample of firms with 20–49 employees, and a one in two selection of those employing 50–99.

- *Department of Employment Gazette*: monthly publication giving details of employment in Britain.
- *British Business* (formerly known as the *Trade and Industry Journal*): weekly publication by the Department of Trade and Industry which gives valuable data on industrial and commercial trends, both home and overseas. Publishes industry reviews, trade fair guides, etc.
- *Bill of Entry*: Customs and Excise data.
- *Business Monitors*: give detailed information about many important industries. The P (production) series covers a wide sector of industrial activities. The SD (Service and Distribution) series covers shops, catering trades and instalment credit business of finance houses and retailers. The CA (Civil Aviation) series deals with airports, passengers, freight and airlines. Seven M (Miscellaneous) monitors include motor and vehicle registrations, cinemas, company finance, and acquisitions and mergers.

  In some instances, *Business Monitors'* data tend to be too broadly classified for the purposes of specific enquiries; this may arise because too detailed analyses could lead to identification of the sales of particular companies.

Non-governmental sources

Non-governmental sources of published data in Britain are plentiful; some of the principal sources are detailed below:

- *CBI Overseas Reports*: issued quarterly by the Confederation of British Industry.
- *Directories and Yearbooks*: there are very many of these types of publication, some specialising in certain industries and others of a more general nature. Of particular interest for industrial market research purposes are the following:

- *Kelly's*: the UK volume of *Manufacturers and Merchants* is useful for locating 100,000 industrial companies and telephone numbers; it contains industry lists by product classifications.
- *Kompass*: in four volumes, a valuable source for developing industrial samples, company profiles, etc.
- *Dun and Bradstreet*: publish several directories including *Guide to Key Enterprises, International Market Guide* and *British Middle Market Directory*. A major drawback is that these registers are based on companies, not establishments, so branch offices are omitted and subsidiary companies are not always recorded.
- *Extel Group*: publishes, as a subscription service, details of British and European companies.
- *Keynotes Reports*: give valuable data over many industries, and provide, for example, overviews, outlooks and forecasts for various sectors.
- *ICC (Inter Company Comparisons)*: present key comparative data.
- *CBD Directory of UK Associations* } list, under industry headings,
- *CBD Directory of European Associations* } relevant trade associations.
- *The Economist Group*: partly under the name of The Economist Intelligence Unit (EIU); publishes, on a regular basis, reports on certain industrial sectors, such as the automotive industry, as well as special reports on topics of current interest. As a result of a management buy-out in 1984, *The Corporate Intelligence Group* was set up. This publishes *ad hoc* surveys for clients as well as continuing surveys on off-highway equipment and industrial markets in North America and Western Europe.
- *Euromonitor*: publishes *Market Research Great Britain* each month.
- *BLA Group*: publishes *Market Assessment* bi-monthly, which covers many industrial product markets.
- *Mintel*: reports cover mostly consumer products and are available on subscription.
- *The press*: *The Economist*; the *Financial Times*; *The Times*; the *Daily Telegraph*; the *Guardian*; the *Sunday Times*; the *Observer*; the *Sunday Telegraph*; the *Independent*, etc.
- *Times Top 1000*: lists major British-based companies and multinational groups.
- *Gower Press*: publishes a valuable series of economic survey reports which relate to specific industries and markets both home and overseas.

On-line services have grown spectacularly over the past few years and give ready access to published information from virtually all over the world. Databases are of two types: (1) based on bibliographic sources, such as reports, or abstracts, from newspapers and other journals; and (2) numeric, consisting of statistical data on the economy, companies, international trade, etc. Examples of the first category are *Infoline Ltd*, which has many databases covering marketing and sales prospecting, finance and credit checking, business intelligence and news, and British Trademarks and British Standards; and *FT Profile*, operated by the Financial Times Business Research Centre, which offers a wide range of data on companies in the UK and abroad. Examples of the second category are *ICC Database* (see earlier listing) and the *Central Statistical Office (CSO)* which offers an extensive data coverage of, for example, population, manpower and industrial products. *Datastar* is one of a number of 'host' on-line services which holds both bibliographic and numeric databases from several sources, such as the *Financial Times*.

OneSource Information Services Inc., formerly Lotus OneSource, a division of Lotus Development Corporation, is a leading provider of CD-ROM information products. *OneSource* provides critical financial and market data together with business background information on public and private companies in the USA and world-wide, US commercial and savings banks and their holding companies, and US insurance companies. *OneSource* sales offices can be contacted in the USA on 1–800–554–5501; in the UK telephone (0784) 455445 for details of the extensive CD-ROM databases covering, for example, CD/Europa (60,000 companies throughout Europe), CD/Corporate: International Public Companies (over 10,000 companies world-wide) and CD/Corporate: UK Private+ (over 130,000 private and public companies in the UK).

On-line patents search is offered by the Patents Office, Newport, Gwent, covering extensive, specialised searches in patent literature at national and international levels. New product concepts can be checked against international technical trends and commercial developments.

The on-line British Standards database Standardline contains bibliographical and subject details of all current British Standards, their amendments and drafts for comment. Standardline uses a basic file structure set up by ISONET (the International Organisation for Standardisation world-wide network of national standards information centres). The most comprehensive source of standards information on-line is IHS (International Standards and Specification) available on the host Dialog.

On-line searching can provide almost instant information on very many topics, but, as always, discretion should be exercised to ensure that relevant data are being accessed. Guidance is obtainable from ASLIB (Association for Information Management) and the *Directory of Online Databases*, published by Cuadra Associates Inc.

On-line searches generally involve a computer access charge covering the time involved in the collection of specific information. To use on-line searches effectively, it would be advisable to train staff so that professional skills are acquired. While competition among on-line data suppliers has resulted in some price adjustments, the costs involved are still significant; full value should be derived through expert accessing.

Professional institutions and specialists

Professional institutions and specialists offering information on specific aspects of industrial markets include the following:

- ASLIB (Association for Information Management) 20–24 Old Street, London EC1V 9AP.
- Association of British Chambers of Commerce, 4 Westwood House, Westwood Business Park, Coventry CV4 8HS.
- British Standards Institution, Linford Wood, Milton Keynes MK14 6LE.
- Business Statistics Office (BSO), Cardiff Road, NP9 1XG.
- Central Office of Information (COI), Hercules Road, London SE1 7DU.
- Chartered Institute of Marketing, Moor Hall, Cookham SL6 9QH.
- Commission of the European Communities Press Information Office, 8 Storey's Gate, London SW1P 3AT.
- Companies House (Registrar of Companies), Crown Way, Maindy, Cardiff CF4 3UZ.
- Department of Trade and Industry, 66–74 Victoria Street, London SW1E 6SW (and also regional offices).
- Export Market Information Centre, 123 Victoria Street, London SW1E 6RB.
- Financial Times Business Research Centre, 1 Southwark Bridge Road, London, SE1.
- Institute of Management (formely BIM), Africa House, Kingsway, London WC2B 6BL.
- Institute of Practitioners in Advertising (IPA), Belgrave Square, London SW1X 8QS.
- Market Research Society, 15 Northburgh Street, London EC1V 0AH.
- National Insitute of Economic and Social Research, 2 Dean Tench Street, London SW1P 3H.
- Office of Population Censuses and Surveys, St Catherine's House, Kingsway, London WC2B 6JP.

Other sources

Specialist libraries such as the City Business Library, 55 Basinghall Street, London EC2V 5BX, and the libraries of London Business School, Manchester Business School and Warwick Business School are excellent sources of research data and offer, on a fee basis, to provide specific industrial and commercial data. Another valuable source is the Science Reference Library, 25 Southampton Buildings, Chancery Lane, London WC2A 1AW.

TV audience research reports are available from individual television contractors and also from specialist research agencies.

In addition to official data guides there are several commercially published guides to market data such as *Sources of UK Marketing Information* by Elizabeth Tupper and Gordon Wills (Benn, 1975), *Principal Sources of Marketing Information* by Christine Hull (Times Newspapers) and *Where to Find Business Information* (John Wiley, 1979). A particularly valuable reference text is *The Source Book* (Keynote Publications). *British Rate and Data Guide* (*BRAD*) and *Willings Press Guide* are useful sources of reference on media relevant to industrial and other sectors of the economy. It may also be useful to approach professional and trade journals, whose editorial staff may be willing to give valuable insights into the specific industries covered by them.

Study of some of these sources of published data may well result in enough information without extending research into field enquiries. Moreover, this stage of desk research will be very useful in developing the methodology of research because of the structural knowledge of particular industries which results from an intensive search.

OFFICIAL INDUSTRY CLASSIFICATION

Before considering primary sources of data, it will be advantageous to describe in general terms the basis of industry classification which is used in official statistics such as the Census of Production.

In the UK, the basic framework for analysing industrial activities is the Standard Industrial Classification (SIC). The SIC was first issued in 1948 to encourage uniformity in preparation of the UK official statistics for industry. As the result of experience in use and reflecting changes in the structure of British industry, the SIC was revised in 1958, in 1968 and again in 1980. The last edition is the present-day system of classification based on industries. This revision has tended to restrict the usefulness of some of the past data when analyses have been concerned with examining trends in certain industries over a fairly long period of time. The Central Statistical Office acknowledges that it has to face the problem of keeping a balance between the need to be up to date and the loss in comparability with past data. The CSO believes that change in industrial classification once in ten years is about right.

Concern has been expressed that, despite the growing significance of the service industries to the overall economy (see Chapter 2), the SIC provides far less information on service activities than it does for the manufacturing sector: 'in 1980, when the most recent (and major) revisions to the classification were concluded, service employment was more than double that of the manufacturing sector, and yet there are still only 102 service divisions, compared to 210 for manufacturing, a ratio of two to one'.[26]

The SIC has been described by the chief statistician of the Central Statistical Office as an empirical classification which is 'not derived in any way from theoretical ideas on how activities should be grouped or should necessarily be combined because products or processes are similar, or other notions. It does not try to reflect the way in which economic activities are found to exist in the UK.'[27]

Until the 1980 revision, SICs were divided into Minimum List Headings (MLHs) which progessively narrowed down industrial activities for the purposes of classification and measurement. However, while these breakdowns were often useful, specific products tended to be subsumed under fairly broad headings. In some cases it may be possible to obtain more relevant information from the Business Statistics Office.

The 1980 revision of the SIC was primarily designed to bring it more into line with the European Communities Statistical Office's activity classification, Nomenclature Générale des Activités Economiques dans les Communautés Européennes' (NACE), thus enabling statistical data across EC countries to be more readily compared as well as providing for analysis of UK industry and commerce.

Unlike previous SICs, the 1980 edition has a decimal structure. The full range of industrial activities is first divided into 10 broad divisions (indicated by single digits), which are then subdivided into 60 classes (two digits), further divided into 222 groups (three digits) and then into 334 activities (four digits). These are listed in detail elsewhere.[28] The full range of potential subdivisions is not necessarily followed in all cases; it depends on the diversity of the activities covered by a specific classification.

The general effect is to provide more detailed classification of economic activities, since there are 334 activity headings compared with 181 MLHs. For example, a distinction is drawn, wherever possible, between principals and agents in the distributive trades. In the financial area, a distinction is made between the insurance companies and insurance brokers or agents, and between banks, building societies and investment companies, and services such as stockbroking and foreign exchange dealing.

The CSO plans to publish reconciliations between the revised SIC and the 1968 edition (and vice versa), between the revised SIC and NACE and between the revised SIC and ISIC (International Standard Industrial Classification). Full details of the revised SIC are available from CSO.

Problems of unit of classification

Although the SIC is valuable, this basis for analysis may result in the total production of some important firms being included under one classification, whereas they may in fact produce considerable quantities of some other products which are important in those particular markets but represent only a relatively small proportion of their total output. Factory canteens run by companies would, for instance, be included in the turnover of the 'establishment'. However, there are exceptions to this 'blanket' measurement; where, at a particular address, two or more departments have distinctly different types of activity and completely separate records are available, each department may be treated as a separate establishment for purposes of official analysis. The unit of classification is the 'establishment', i.e. the whole of the production at a particular address of a farm, mine, factory or shop, classified according to main products on the basis of the SIC.

Care is needed in interpreting data from sources using the SIC: for example, establishments concerned chiefly with merchandising, broking, importing and exporting are analysed under distributive trades and not under the product classification to which their activities relate. Repairers of radio and television sets, watches and clocks, furniture, etc., are classified under distributive trades, whereas establishments concerned with repairing ships, locomotives, aircraft and most kinds of plant and machinery are entered under the respective manufacturing activity.

As noted already, statistical breakdowns by the SIC often tend to be too wide for specific industrial analyses. There is, for example, 'a tremendous difference between harvesting machinery and barn machinery. To classify these two as the same industry is quite unrealistic in many ways. They are influenced by totally different considerations; they require totally different production techniques; and they require totally different materials and components.'[29]

Researchers frequently encounter other examples of official classifications which do not contain homogeneous industrial activities.

The *International Standard Industrial Classification* (ISIC) was drawn up by the United Nations in 1948 in an attempt at standardisation of statistics between nations so that comparisons could be facilitated. It is 'a compromise of the classifications of a number of countries';[4] like the SIC, which it closely resembles, it was revised later. The ISIC is a valuable source of data for export marketers. The Standard Industrial Classification (SIC) and the Nomenclature Générale des Activités Economiques dans les Communautés Européennes (NACE) were derived from ISIC, principally by extending the analyses to further subdivisions and sectors.

The United Nations has published lists of principal products under each ISIC industry and also an international classification of goods and services, known as ICGS, which classifies into subgroups the products of each industry group. NACE is supported by the Nomenclature Commune des Produits Industriels (NIPRO); this gives detailed lists of products under each industry, but only for that section of NACE covering manufacturing industry.

US SIC

The SIC system was developed by the US Federal government to facilitate the collection and analysis of industrial data. Each major area of activity, known as a 'division', is assigned a two-digit classification code. Each division is divided into 'major groups' which, in turn, are subdivided into more than 150 three-digit 'industry groups'. At the next level of analysis they are further separated into four-digit 'specific industries'.

The basic reporting unit of the American SIC system, like the British, is the establishment. As with the other SIC systems, drawbacks occur, such as assigning the entire output of a multiproduct establishment to a single four-digit manufacturing industry, thus inflating returns for that industry as well as understating those of secondary industries to which part of a firm's output may contribute.

Directories of businesses

The BSO maintains registers of production firms for the purpose of conducting statistical enquiries which may be of significant value to industrial marketing researchers.

The Classified List of Manufacturing Businesses has been compiled from the BSO's register of UK manufacturing businesses. Contributors to the Census of Production from 1970 were asked if they were willing to have the name and address of their business included in an official classified list of businesses. The resultant list gives these details for each manufacturing local unit belonging to an establishment covered in the annual Census. In cases where a company has more than one manufacturing local unit, separate entries are made. Non-manufacturing units, in particular units which are offices, are omitted; hence the head office of a firm may not be listed.

The lists are arranged alphabetically within each MLH of the SIC; the 1989 edition included over 41,000 business addresses, about a quarter of those on the register, accounting for about 45 per cent of employment in manufacturing. The Classified List of Manufacturing Businesses is published in six volumes as *Business Monitor* PO 1007, and restricted to activity headings, but special geographical and alphabetical analyses in the form of computer print-outs may be purchased from the Business Statistics Office, Newport, Gwent.

The 1993 *UK Directory of Manufacturing Businesses* contains nearly 20,000 manufacturing units.

Overcoming statistical shortcomings

One ingenious method of overcoming statistical shortcomings is to

> derive market size by utilising other information. For instance, by developing a consumption factor for the product based on employment . . . The principle is quite straightforward: if there is a homogeneous industry classification then employment, for example, does become an extremely good measure of the importance of an industry because you are able to develop a relationship between employment and the use of your product in that industry.[29]

Oxygen consumption per employee in constructional steel work, for example, is 200 cubic feet per person, but in agricultural machinery it is only 10 cubic feet per person. This method could be used to calculate regional usage rates, and the relative impact of technical change on demand could be forecast. Other basic indicators of industrial activity could relate to power consumption, floor area, etc. The output of the British car industry affects the demand, for example, for machine tools, steel, petrol and many other commodities.

Statistical demand analysis attempts to discover the size and importance of real factors which affect demand for a product. Many industries make use of each other's forecasts in deriving their own. Thus, forward estimates for the production of steel, coal, cement, alkali and sulphuric acid are often taken as general predictors of a country's overall economic progress.[29] Sales of one product may be closely related (as with derived demand) to the sales pattern of other products: for example, the demand for f.h.p. motors may relate to sales of washing machines, dishwashers, refrigerators, etc.

> Sometimes a 'double tie' can be identified . . . for example, if a company manufacturing metal cans identifies a specific end-product market it may forecast the sales of its own product by using the tied indicator of the demand for tinned peas. But also the forecast of the market for the sales of cans for that

> specific product could be ascertained by considering the acreage of peas which are contracted for sowing by the leading canning companies.[30]

The effect of lead/lag indicators should be appreciated: 'changes in one variable do not necessarily have an immediate effect on the other: one may lead and the other lag.'[30] The number of cars sold affects the demand for steel, but this demand is lagged by about 18 months, hence providing an indicator of future activity in the steel industry. The wholesale price index generally leads the cost of living index by about three months.

It is sometimes possible to construct a model of market behaviour which assists market analyses and forecasting. Movements in demand may be correlated with economic indicators, but great care is needed to avoid spurious deductions. Total consumer disposable income, increases in birth rates, distribution of age groups in the population, etc. are useful in predicting likely trends in consumer product markets. In some industrial markets, Gross Domestic Fixed Capital Formation (GDFCF) could be a useful indicator in forecasting demand, for example, for air-conditioning equipment.

Monsanto, one of the three largest fibre producers in the United States, was reported to have developed a mathematical model for the US tyre market which is analysed by motor trade sectors (car original equipment, car replacement, truck) and further subdivided by type of tyre (cross-ply, belted cross-ply, radial). By this method, Monsanto 'are able to quantify the volume of fibre or steel used and so arrive at the expected future demand for each type of fibre'. In addition, Monsanto staff 'every quarter, and sometimes more frequently visit the five leading tyre manufacturers'[31] to present their latest market predictions and to obtain the views of these tyre executives, who are encouraged to take an active part in the discussions by supplying Monsanto with their own market predictions. These various inputs are fed into the computer and result in consensus forecasts.

Gordon Bolt[32] has described the effect of chain reaction in specific industrial products, portable compressors, which have basically four market segments: government departments, local authority and service authorities, contractors and plant hire. In times of economic stringency, the first market affected will be that of government departments, and within a few months local and service authorities will curb their purchasing; contractors will be affected within six to nine months as new projects are cut or postponed. But because some activities must continue, the plant hire segment tends to experience a considerable increase in business from three months after a national credit squeeze has been imposed.

A European steel firm used a mathematical model based on sales statistics to forecast market trends; inputs cover products, customers, factories and sales agents; a cement firm in Europe studied several correlations between the consumption of its products and the total national investment, both governmental and private sector. 'It found a close correlation exists between the demand for cement and the demand for electricity.'[33]

For several years, the American Can Company has forecast beer-can demand by correlating sales to 'income levels, number of drinking establishments per thousand persons, and age distribution of the population . . . Armour and Company has found that it can accurately predict the number of cattle to be slaughtered in future months by using such explanatory variables as range–grass conditions and steer–corn price ratios.'[33]

In attempting to relate lead/lag indicators or correlation factors, either simple or multiple, market analysts should proceed cautiously.

While model building 'is essential as a means of learning more about the relationship between economic variables . . . the complexity and scale of such an exercise limits the possibility of research to academic or government agencies'[34] or possibly also to large commercial organisations which can afford to invest funds in management ventures. There is, as Jones and Morrell pointed out, 'always a temptation for those who are skilled in statistical and economic techniques to try to wring more out of their raw material than it is capable of producing' and to become more absorbed in the elegance 'of their techniques than the validity of their conclusions.'[35]

This brief review of the alternative ways of analysing and estimating the demand for industrial products will show that marketing research requires an imaginative approach to sources of market data as well as judgement in selection and expertise in handling the resultant statistics.

PRIMARY DATA

This refers to data which are unique in the sense that they must be specially generated because of the inadequacy or, indeed, absence of secondary data.

Three main methods of collecting primary data, which are common to all types of market survey, are observation, experimentation and questionnaires.

Observation

Observational techniques may provide valuable marketing information. As a technique of marketing research, observation has been borrowed from anthropology, which has distrusted people's ability to verbalise their feelings or experiences accurately or completely. In studies of the pub-going and drinking habits of an industrial town in Lancashire in 1943, Mass-Observation (the firm founded by Tom Harrison, a pioneer in observational research methods) 'used personal interviews, observations and diaries kept by volunteer observers'.[36]

In industrial situations, observational techniques could be useful in checking the types of equipment used by different kinds of customer (origin of manufacture, capacity, etc.); or customary working behaviour could be studied to assist in the design of, for instance, safety factors in hand tools and workshop equipment. One large petrol company checked consumers' reactions to 'talking' petrol pumps (self-serve) by a team of 'spies' who watched, from a discreet observation post, the behaviour of motorists to the printed and broadcast instructions. As a result, they 'found it necessary to simplify both the equipment and instructions.'[37]

Paul Hague[38] has given an interesting account of the use of observation in initially assessing market shares of glass bottles for food packaging by a company planning to build a new factory to produce glass bottles. Teams of researchers visited supermarkets and noted manufacturers' identity marks on the base of bottled foods. This audit enabled all major suppliers of bottles to each food manufacturer to be identified, and also revealed the penetration of imported bottles into UK food manufacturers. This observational research tactic was followed by a series of personal interviews.

Another application of observational techniques recorded by Hague was connected with research into the information needs of transport and distribution managers. In response to conventional survey enquiries, they stated that they rarely used information to fulfil their duties. But from a later series of observations, it became apparent that several types of information, e.g. route planning data and pricing lists, were actually used.

The Honda Civic hatchback car was redesigned following observations on how people loaded their car boots. Philips also used observational techniques – two-way mirrors – to note shaving habits; this assisted the company in the design of a new electric shaver.[39]

Observation, like other methods of survey, is prone to bias. 'In making observations we each select, organise and interpret visual stimuli into a picture that is as meaningful and as coherent to us as we can make it. Which stimuli are selected and how they are organised and interpreted are highly dependent upon both the backgrounds and frames of reference of the observer.'[22] This technique is not, therefore, to be used indiscriminately: trained, professional observers are likely to perceive factors which an untrained, naive observer could easily overlook. But there is also a danger that a trained technician acting as an observer will see only factors which relate directly to technology; he or she may not appreciate that other influences, perhaps personal, may well account for the behaviour being observed. Observers should be briefed on all aspects of the action or event they are to observe.

Experimentation

Experimentation, in the strict scientific sense, refers to controlled experiments in constant environmental conditions, so that the effects of a particular variable or factor may be carefully studied and evaluated. This ideal testing environment is the very antithesis of the conditions which are experienced in the actual marketing of goods and services. Commercial transactions are complex and subject to many variables, several of which lie outside the control of the marketer. In consumer markets, considerable attempts have been made to gauge the likely reactions of consumers to new products, advertising campaigns, etc., through so-called laboratory tests and by phased marketing usually involving test-marketing campaigns. Experiments have also been undertaken in pricing, packaging and methods of distribution.

While the highly organised systems of test-marketing cannot apply to industrial supplies, there is some value in being prepared to evaluate alternative methods of approaching customers. In one sector of a market, for example, a different distribution policy using franchises might be adopted and carefully checked over a period of time. Pricing policies could be tested out in distinctive market areas, bearing in mind the level of competitive activity. Promotional campaigns could be varied in different market sectors and advertising media assessed for their effectiveness. From 'experimentation' of this nature, useful information may be acquired, although the dangers of broad generalisations should be avoided.

Questionnaires

Questionnaires are widely used in marketing surveys of all kinds; they can be administered by telephone or mail, or through personal interviewing.

Constructing a questionnaire is an expert task which should be undertaken with great care. 'The type of questionnaire obviously depends on the method of survey, and this will be dependent on the nature of the problem being investigated, the kind of population sampled, and the sample size.'[22]

Questionnaires may be (1) highly structured, with a series of formal questions designed to attract answers of limited response; or (2) unstructured, where formal questions are replaced by a freer style of investigation – an interviewer encourages conversation to develop, guiding it skilfully by means of an 'interviewing guide' or checklist of the main topics of enquiry. Generally, questionnaires are hybrid or semi-structured. Some flexibility in the overall design of questionnaires is desirable, but it is vital to keep firmly in mind the purpose of questionnaires: to attract valid and reliable information about defined areas of investigation.

Although unstructured questionnaires are frequently used in industrial surveys, it is important to realise that they place particular demands on interviewers to ensure that free responses are adequately recorded. Also, analysis of large numbers of these responses tends to present problems later in the research.

Direct questioning is not always productive, and less direct methods of investigation such as group discussions have been used effectively. This more subtle approach, which is discussed later, can provide valuable complementary knowledge to that gained from the more restricted scope of direct questioning.

As noted earlier (see pp. 121–2), the range of investigations will vary according to the objectives of specific surveys, but major areas of measurement are likely to be as follows:

1. *Consumption patterns*: identification of trends and underlying causes.
2. *Perceptions* of specific products/services; company image.
3. *Expectations* related to products/services; identification of benefits sought from purchase.
4. *Attitudes* towards suppliers, particular products/services, etc.
5. *Motivations* to buy (or avoid) products/services from certain suppliers; industrial buying processes; relative impact of economic, technological, psychosocial factors, etc.

6. *Media habits and influence* on selection of new suppliers, and awareness of economic trends in both home and overseas markets.
7. *Competitors' activities*: identification and classification of main competitors in specific market sectors.
8. *Classification of buyers*: related to end-use markets for specific types of product/service; classified by SIC, region, volume purchased, etc.

Industrial marketing surveys frequently use technical terms; it is important that these are correctly used because technical experts will soon grow tired of responding to badly drafted survey enquiries. It is also important that the questions asked are not likely to be misunderstood and so attract biased answers. Questions should be drafted and pilot-tested to ensure that their meanings are clear. As noted earlier, it is sometimes advisable to divide research enquiries into specific question areas relating to technical or financial aspects so that specialists can give replies to these questions more readily.

Interviewing

Interviewing is a crucially important function of market research; it involves social as well as technical skills – the psychological atmosphere of an interview is created by the interaction which takes place between respondent and interviewer. In a relatively short time, an interviewer has to motivate a respondent to participate in a survey, so the ability to establish, quickly, a good working relationship is vital to the success of the whole survey. This calls for a flexible approach to individual respondents who may range from the managing director down to factory chargehands or operatives. (See Chapter 3 on the decision-making unit.)

Interviewers have four general responsibilities: (1) to locate informants as specified in the sampling plan; (2) to translate these contacts into effective interviews; (3) to secure valid and reliable responses; and (4) to record responses accurately.

Interviewers should have expert knowledge of the industries which are being covered by the survey, or the intellectual ability to acquire sufficient information in a short period of intensive training.

Some organisations tend to rely on their sales staff to provide market information. It is argued that surveys are better undertaken by people who have an intimate knowledge of the product and the industry. But the fact remains that a hopeful seller is rarely able to adopt a completely objective view of the market in which he or she is active. Industrial research interviewing should not be regarded merely as an alternative occupation for members of the sales force; the problem of bias is too serious.

Professional interviewing skills are necessarily the most important factor in survey work; technical knowledge of a particular industry alone does not ensure successful interviews.

Telephone surveys

Telephone surveys may be especially useful in the early stages of designing a sample to establish, for example, whether a particular kind of machine is being used in the case of a 'user survey'. Some fairly simple questionnaires may also be suitable for this type of approach, but spontaneous answers to highly technical enquiries cannot be expected. On the other hand, with skilful research staff, some extremely valuable survey work can be satisfactorily undertaken by telephone. It is particularly important to organise such surveys efficiently: for example, a list of areas of questioning should be prepared beforehand, so that the interviewer covers the topic under survey adequately.

Some telephone contacts may well be selected, with their agreement, for personal extended interviews if their telephone responses indicate that they have unusually good information to provide for a specific research project. One of the most difficult aspects of telephone interviewing is, of course, ensuring that the right person is being approached. Some degree of tactful probing may be necessary to check that a willing talker on the telephone is in fact able to give valid and reliable information.

Other factors affecting the quality and efficiency of telephone surveying relate to the personal style of the interviewer. Without the added advantage of personal contact and, therefore, of being able to assess the likely reactions and behaviour of respondents, telephone interviewers need to develop their communication skills so that they can almost 'feel' the atmosphere of an interview and guide it to a successful outcome. A few people develop such skills to great effect; others can improve through good training.

Obviously, lists of representative firms or other organisations would have to be prepared in advance of telephoning; every care should be taken to make contacts which will result in a reliable sample of the specific population under survey. Stratification will assist in this important task.

Central telephone interviewing facilities are operated by several market research firms in the UK, and their services may be appropriate for certain types of industrial market research investigation.

Computer-assisted telephone interviewing (CATI) is a method of gathering survey data through linking computer technology and telecommunications, thus eradicating paper questionnaires. Various versions of CATI have been developed, which have a common basic procedure: an interviewer reads questions, which are displayed on a VDU, to the telephoned respondent, whose answers are recorded by keyboard. Although CATI can steer respondents through fairly complex sequences of questioning, it seems to be rather limited in its ability to handle open-ended (free-response) questions. An attractive feature of the system is that it results in almost instantaneous tabulation of survey enquiries.

A development of CATI is known as *computer-assisted personal interviewing* (CAPI), which occurs when researchers conducting face-to-face interviews input data on laptop computers, and feed the results via telephone to their survey organisations.

Mail surveys

Mail surveys are superficially attractive in terms of economy and speed. But realistic cost appraisal should be based on *all* the costs involved (printing, stationery, postage – including prepaid arrangements – and administration) and also related to the number of *effective* replies received. The valid reply rate may well double or treble the original crude estimate, apart from the problems of bias from non-reply and the doubts about the representativeness of those who have reponded.

If questionnaires are mailed, every care should be taken with presentation. Clearly-designed questionnaires with simple instructions to guide respondents should be accompanied by reply-paid facilities and a covering letter inviting co-operation in the survey. At least two follow-up shots are advisable, but it should be borne in mind that, inevitably, these tend to extend the period of the survey. Some cut-off point will need to be established or the client will never receive its report.

Since an interviewer will not be present to assist in interpreting survey questions (a useful though risky intervention because of possible bias), mail questionnaires require particularly careful drafting. Questions should be free of ambiguity, capable of being answered without excessive trouble, and reasonable in the type of information they request.

Response rates tend to be low with mail surveys unless the subject of enquiry is of vital professional interest. It may be possible to weight the answers from various sectors of a market and so overcome to some degree the handicap of low response. This will depend largely on adequate knowledge of the pattern of industrial structuring in a market; and this very information may, of course, depend on the outcome of the survey.

Some method of following up non-respondents is to be recommended; it may also be possible to check reasons for non-response either by telephone or personal enquiries. In some cases, a simple version of the original questionnaire may be accepted for completion.

QUALITATIVE RESEARCH

The scope of survey enquiries is likely, as we have seen, to cover quantitative and also qualitative factors affecting buying behaviour, such as attitudes, perceptions and motivations. Information about these qualitative aspects of consumption is often termed, rather pejoratively, 'soft' data and contrasted with 'hard' data originating from qualitative assessments. However, the latter are not necessarily superior to non-numeric data; together the two types of data bring insight into the complexities of markets and the many influences affecting demand.

Qualitative research is inherently unstructured, flexible and oblique; it has been applied, rather freely, to describe several kinds of marketing research, such as exploratory research, depth interviewing, group discussions and focus groups.

Group discussions

Consumer marketing researchers often organise discussions within, for example, a group of consumers: about their shopping habits. People tend to be influenced by the psychological atmosphere generated by a group, and their feelings may be expressed quite strongly. 'In the atmostphere of a group, individuals react to one another and the way in which they influnce personal attitudes can be studied. Sharp criticism of individual beliefs is frequently aroused, and the discussion generated among the group by their shared interest tends to become extremely frank.'[22] It has been reported, for example, that physicians, 'who are often difficult to interview alone, seem to be considerably more garrulous, frank, and at times argumentative when in a group with other physicians'.[40]

In industrial research, group discussions may be useful in obtaining the views of a body of professional buyers or users. British Oxygen adopts this technique for the following reasons:

1. To get a better understanding of markets.
2. To solve problems.
3. To get action from management.

'In technical markets, a group discussion amongst, say, engineers can bring out areas of interest that you did not know even existed . . . A greater understanding of attitudes and opinions is also obtained as members of the group are defending their views with people of an equal level and experience.'[41]

This process of material and frank exchange of ideas and experience should be initiated and guided by a group or discussion leader, who should not impose his or her own views, but should encourage discussion and keep it flowing in relevent channels. The proceedings could be recorded (with the approval of group members) or noted by an objective observer; preferably, both methods should be used.

The qualitative data from this kind of research should be expertly evaluated. They will add depth to more formal investigations, and could also most effectively indicate the real reasons why certain products or services have been successful. The 'Freudian slip' in group discussions may offer a valuable clue to market behaviour.

There is clearly scope for developing this branch of survey methodology in researching organisational supplies. Recruitment of representative groups is an important factor, and the actual place and time of meeting should be carefully planned.

A series of group discussions, organised by a specialist research firm, helped a high-quality food manufacturer which wanted to extend its business in the catering market. Discussants in these groups dealt vigorously with the usage of convenience foods and the general problems of catering; strong views were expressed about the methods used by market leaders to launch new products. The uninhibited responses of caterers of various sizes and from different segments of the catering industry resulted in valuable insights into market behaviour.[42]

Group discussions may involve between seven and nine people and last up to 1½ hours.

Brainstorming

Brainstorming has been described[43] as a specialised version of group discussions, aiming to foster the spontaneous development of ideas from participants. Criticism is banned; imaginative and constructive ideas are encouraged; efforts are devoted to generating new approaches to problems. Associated with this technique is the group problem-solving method known as *synectics*.

Depth interviewing

Depth interviewing is another qualitative research technique designed to collect sensitive information which may not be forthcoming in routine market research enquiries. In the relaxed atmosphere of a typical non-directive interview, which could last between 30 and 60 minutes, an experienced discussion leader explores, in a conversational style, motivations and attitudes related to some activity, such as safety practices, hygiene procedures and dealing with supply problems. Responses are usually recorded, with the agreement of participants, and evaluated later by expert analysts.

It should be added that there is little general agreement on what constitutes a depth interview; the term is usually used to indicate the study of one individual respondent's beliefs, opinions, attitudes, etc., but the approach is more generally used in group discussions, as outlined earlier.

Focus groups

These, and extended creativity groups (ECGs), are derivatives of group depth interviewing and have been used, for example, in horticultural and agricultural markets, and in studying the prescription habits of medical general practitioners. Some of these discussions may last several hours, and group moderators need to adapt their skills to the characteristics of particular groups, so that discussions develop constructively.

Continuous research

Most marketing research tends to be *ad hoc*: specific problems are the trigger for market investigation. This 'one-off' attitude to surveys overlooks the benefits of monitoring the market so as to spot emerging trends or changes in the overall structure of competition.

Popular forms of continuous or longitudinal research include panels, audits and tracking studies measuring brand and advertising awareness, etc.

Panels can be made up of individuals, households or firms from which comparative data are collected over regular periods of time. They suffer from two drawbacks: conditioning and wear-out. The first refers to the tendency for panel members' behaviour to become atypical over time, and is more likely to occur in consumer than industrial market research; the second relates to the fact that there is usually a drop-out factor. Panel losses may be offset to some extent by matching recruits to former members or, perhaps, by inflating the original size of the panel to allow for falling membership over time.

Some years ago, British Gas undertook continuous research[44] on fuel prices over sectors of industry. Industrial fuel users, selected by stratified random sample to be representative of industrial activities by region, were contacted each month to obtain data on current fuel prices, negotiations and 'offers'. Approximately 170 companies covering about 240 fuel contracts relating to about 1,600 industrial establishments were surveyed.

Co-operation was encouraged by offering, without charge, price data in respect of the fuel for which respondents provided price information. Competitive fuel prices with the respondent's own pricing data were supplied.

British Gas use this research data to construct their contract prices, which are market orientated. Marketing research showed that three possible situations of price/demand relationship apply whenever an industrial fuel is bought. These were classified as follows:

1. Load retention: price/demand relationship in which a customer using a fuel at present will remain using it.
2. New business: when new equipment is being installed involving a choice of fuel.
3. Changeover: point at which a customer using one fuel will change to another fuel.

From detailed analyses of these marketing relationships, British Gas designed a differential pricing scheme for the distinct market segments.

Omnibus surveys

This type of survey is undertaken on a regular basis by some leading research companies which offer clients the opportunity of buying questionnaire space. Different clients share the costs of an omnibus survey, which contains common classification questions plus questions covering aspects of marketing relevant to the needs of specific clients, perhaps buying frequency of particular products or price awareness. Most omnibus surveys are involved with consumer markets, but a few cover organisational markets. An example is Audience Selection's 'Key Directors Omnibus', based on a sample of telephone enquiries every quarter among 400 directors from the top 10 per cent of British businesses.

Omnibus surveys may be suitable for information needs that are fairly straightforward; they are relatively low cost and offer clients the advantage of speedy access to survey results.

Expert informants

It is frequently valuable to identify and contact recognised experts in the particular industries under survey; they are not necessarily in the largest firms. From a series of free-discussion interviews, an extremely good insight may be obtained on the structure and problems of a particular industry. A large paper group was reported[45] to approach marketing research by subdividing the market into homogeneous sectors and commencing enquiries in each sector with the best-informed sources known. The sample size is not predetermined; successive firms are interviewed until a stable answer pattern emerges.

INTEGRATED RESEARCH STRATEGY

An effective research strategy is not necessarily confined to one method of enquiry.

> It is not so much a question of which *method* is best, as which *set* of methods is likely to result in an objective research programme . . . Some leading American social scientists, who are particularly concerned with the limitations of research, have made a strong plea for 'triangulation' of research methods in order to reduce the effects of bias, especially reactive measurement errors.[46]

Reactive measurement effects may arise from respondents' personal reactions to being surveyed or from the nature of the investigator.

The basic methods of questionnaire and interviewing will remain generally popular, but researchers should be willing to consider alternative and complementary methodological strategies. This more creative approach will assist in reducing bias and also add a new dimension to survey findings.

SAMPLING METHODOLOGY

Sampling methodology is the foundation of an effective research design: it deserves special attention. Basically, a sample is a microcosm of the population or universe from which it is drawn, and can only be accepted as accurate within certain limits.[28] Samples should be representative in order that valid conclusions may be made about their populations – otherwise the whole research process is gravely flawed and the resultant data are very unreliable. Sampling offers many benefits: it saves time, money and effort – data are available far more readily and at much lower cost than from a census or complete enumeration.

In many organisational markets, the universe or population researched may be comparatively small, ranging from perhaps 20 organisations to a few hundred; examples are large computer installations, petrol refinery equipment, special printing inks, etc. However, other organisational markets are large and have many thousands of buyers – for example, office equipment, fork-lift trucks, or commercial and industrial insurance policies – and the total value of sales to such users may be larger than in some major consumer markets.

Frequently, however, an organisational market supplier deals with a very restricted number of customers in specific end-use markets, several of whom are likely to represent a substantial proportion of total turnover. (The incidence of concentration factors in organisational markets will be recalled from the discussion in Chapter 2.)

In forming an effective sample design for an organisational market, it is desirable – even imperative – to know the structure of the market or market sector on which the research will focus. This preliminary knowledge is indispensable, hence the value of consulting knowledgeable people connected with specific markets. Intensive desk research will augment these discussions. All this preparatory work should be undertaken thoroughly, so that the market research project is firmly based.

Sampling frames

Sampling frames (sources from which potential informants can be raised) may be developed from some of the sources listed earlier. As with the research strategy, more than one source will be needed to build up an adequate sampling frame. This can be a tedious job, but it is important that it is well done. Every aspect of the research programme contributes to the value of the eventual survey report.

Sampling frames should be evaluated against the following five criteria:[47]

1. *Adequacy*: a sampling frame should cover the target market or sector adequately for the purposes of the survey.
2. *Completeness*: unless the sampling frame is complete, significant firms may be missing; admittedly, it is often difficult to assess the completeness of a particular frame, but some commonsense checking may reveal serious omissions.
3. *No duplication*: multiple entries may occur, so alertness is recommended and some adjustments may have to be made.
4. *Accuracy*: many lists are notoriously unreliable, with out-of-date entries and careless editing.
5. *Convenience*: this refers to ease of access to a list, and its suitability for developing a valid sample. Lists should be studied to see whether stratification of entries is feasible.

Very few sampling frames fulfil these rigorous requirements, but they are useful guideliness for evaluating the quality of prospective frames.

Lists of customers should be reasonably reliable, but it is most unlikely that they represent every firm in a particular industry. For customer surveys such lists would be useful, but for general survey purposes they would be inadequate. In some industrial enquiries, it may be possible to buy specially developed direct-mail lists, but these should be very carefully vetted before being used as sampling frames.

Specialist directories (see pp. 128–9) provide valuable information for developing specific sampling frames. The membership lists of certain professional bodies, such as those covering chartered accountants, architects, civil engineers, etc., may be regarded as valid sampling frames; however, there are other institutions and associations which cannot claim to represent all firms or practitioners in the market sectors served by them.

Designing an effective sample

After a valid and reliable sampling frame has been acquired or developed, the next stage is to design an effective sample. At the risk of oversimplifying a highly sophisticated subject, it can be said that there are two main types of sample: (1) *random or probability*; and (2) *quota or non-probability*. With the former, each unit of a particular population (which term is used in a statistical sense and is by no means restricted to human populations) has a known chance of being selected in a sample drawn from it by random process. In the latter case, samples are chosen on a non-random basis, often by allocating quotas to different strata of a particular population.

Probability sampling is widely used by research bodies, by the UK Government Social Survey and by the American Bureau of the Census, because of its sound theoretical base. Non-probability or quota sampling, although lacking rigorous statistical acceptability, is in popular use: it is relatively speedy, economic and administratively simple. But it should be remembered that with random or probability samples, it is possible to estimate by statistical tests of significance the degree of accuracy of specific samples from a given population. With non-random samples it is not legitimate to use such tests. Since many market research surveys in organisational supply markets are not based on random samples, their findings cannot, unfortunately, be subjected to rigorous testing.

Where, as noted already, industries are highly concentrated and a skewed distribution of customers and prospects applies, it would clearly be incorrect to choose a random sampling technique, because the survey results would be unreliable if one or more of the main organisations were to be omitted from the sample selected. In such instances, *all* the major firms should be surveyed and a sample taken from other strata covering medium and small organisations.

Strict random sampling is, therefore, unusual in researching organisational markets, with some type of quota sampling generally being adopted: 'many industrial researchers do not pay much attention to sampling, preferring to fill their information gaps by a process of sequential interviewing until they are satisfied that they have obtained a reasonably representative view of the market'.[48] (For further definition of sampling techniques, see reference 22.)

Some companies sell to a very restricted number of customers, and it would be feasible to survey all of them, i.e. take a census. It would be important, however, to recognise that these particular customers may not always be fully representative of their industries. Once again, careful reflection is needed on the scope of a specific survey, before deciding on the sampling scheme.

Samples, both probability and non-probability, can be stratified; this refers to the division of a particular population into strata relevant to the needs of a survey. Typical examples in consumer surveys relate to age groups, gender and socioeconomic classifications; in industrial markets, strata might be related to size of firms, end-use sectors, geographical location, etc. Stratification factors should be carefully chosen: too many strata complicate the survey, may add little to the overall usefulness of its findings, and increase costs.

Pilot surveys may help in identifying feasible stratification factors for main surveys. Some strata may include firms which are prominent in their industries, and whose behaviour and opinions concerning the matters being surveyed would be of crucial importance to know fully. It may be desirable, therefore, to allocate a larger proportion of the sample to such strata; in effect, some degree of oversampling would occur, while less important sectors would be underrepresented in the sample.

Sample size

Sample size depends on the basic characteristics of the population being surveyed, the type of information required and, of course, the cost involved. Hence, samples may vary in size for several reasons. In theory, if a population were to be completely homogeneous throughout, a sample of one would adequately represent all the units in that population, but this is most unlikely. Where it is believed that certain characteristics are variously distributed, i.e. there is considerable heterogeneity, a large sample would be needed in order to assess these attributes accurately.

With probability sampling, it is feasible to calculate mathematically the size of a sample, provided that researchers determine with what accuracy the survey findings are needed. (Refer to specialist text, reference 22, for further coverage.) However, most surveys into organisational markets use non-probability sampling, and it has already been seen that this precludes the legitimate use of significance tests.

A pragmatic way of dealing with the problem of sample size in such situations would be to break the sample into subgroups or strata, as noted before, and then, working backwards, researchers could start from the smallest subgroup and gradually build up the size of the sample. It is very important that the smallest subgroup has sufficient sampling units to enable accurate estimates to be made of the defined characteristics of that particular stratum. The complexity of the information required will, of course, influence the size of individual strata.

In general, it should be noted that the larger the size of the sample, the greater its precision or reliability; though, as seen earlier, increases in costs and time taken for completion of the survey have to be borne in mind.

When computing sample sizes, it is advisable to be alert to the non-response factor, some degree of which will be unavoidable. So if a final sample of 240 is planned and non-response is estimated at 20 per cent, it would be wise to inflate the original sample figure to 300. According to sample theory, however, while this procedure preserves the number in the final sample, it does not reduce bias arising from non-response itself.

A useful example[49] of research methodology relates to a survey of the UK market for fork-lift trucks, which were known to have many applications. From previous surveys and various official statistics, a matrix of 13 business sectors (SIC groupings) and 7 size (employees) classifications was developed. Extra inputs came from Dun and Bradstreet, Market Location (a commercial firm specialising in listing and mapping industrial and commercial firms in the UK), and the survey organisation's own files.

Truck ownership was known to be comparatively low generally, and to vary widely across and within market sectors. Some type of disproportionate sampling was, therefore, considered necessary.

From previous studies of this market, it was feasible to compute an estimated penetration percentage for each cell in the matrix, and by applying these figures to the number of establishments, an estimate was derived of the number of 'truck-equipped establishments'. Sample quotas were allocated to each cell in proportion to its relative importance in the total truck-owning market. Each of the 10 Standard Regions of Great Britain was allocated separate quotas.

To safeguard the efficiency of the quota sampling scheme, lists of contacts were pre-selected and issued to interviewers on a controlled basis: replacement addresses were issued only when the initial set had been fully accounted for.

Finally, this fairly sophisticated sampling procedure was followed by structured interviews by a team of 21 telephone interviewers, who were mostly home-based; but in the case of very large establishments with many trucks, face-to-face interviewing took place, which enabled qualitative assessments to be made.

INDUSTRIAL MARKETING RESEARCH ASSOCIATION STUDY

Some years ago the Industrial Marketing Research Association, the professional British organisation of researchers specialising in this branch of market research, published the results of enquiries conducted to identify the principal characteristics of industrial firms using marketing research and the reasons they did so.

General interest in marketing research was found to extend over several industries, but the following, ranked by importance, were the major users:

- Chemicals and allied industries.
- Vehicles.
- Engineering and electrical goods.
- Construction.
- Food, drink and tobacco.
- Metal manufacture.

Companies using marketing research tended to be characterised more by financial and capital intensity than by number of employees.

The 10 principal functions of marketing research in those industries surveyed were 'positively identified', as indicated in Table 4.1. This pattern of research functions 'turns out to be similar to that of United States marketing research in general, although US firms practise research more consistently'. Table 4.1 reveals that there is little general interest in researching into promotional effectiveness or in psychological investigation of buying behaviour.

The relative importance of desk research is reflected in Table 4.2. With desk research, the most important source was stated to be the Census of Production.

Sampling frames tended to be raised internally and were used by about three-quarters of respondents. Sampling methods tended to be stratified; 'formal probability sampling is the exception'.[50] Larger companies were much more likely

TABLE 4.1 Top ten functions of industrial marketing research

Functions	*% regularly carrying out*
Sales forecasting	76
Analysis of market size	70
Trends in market size	61
Estimating demand for new products	51
Competitive position of comparing products	48
Determining characteristics of markets	43
Determining present uses of existing products	41
Studying economic factors affecting sales volume	38
General business forecasting	30
Evaluating proposed new products and services	30

Source: IMRA.[50]

TABLE 4.2 Survey information-gathering and evaluation methods

Method	*% using method*	*% ranking top*
Desk research	88	38
Expert informants	77	23
Own staff and records	79	22
Sample surveys	59	16
Other methods	25	1

Source: IMRA.[50]

to adopt a flexible approach to sampling; the report suggested that this relaxed attitude was feasible because they were already likely to possess considerable knowledge about their markets because of their high market shares. They were, therefore, prepared to let a picture gradually emerge as the fieldwork progressed.

CODE OF CONDUCT

A professional code of conduct has been developed jointly by the Industrial Marketing Research Association (IMRA) and the Market Research Society (MRS), to which individual members of these bodies are committed. The code has operated since 1954; the latest revision took place in 1983. At research company level, the Association of Market Survey Organisations (AMSO), which includes all the major research firms, has its own code of standards, related to corporate responsibilities; this is compatible with the IMRA/MRS code.

SUMMING UP

Systematic marketing research has been slow in developing in the marketing of non-consumer products and services. There is clearly plenty of scope for this vital tool of marketing management in the dynamic and competitive market environment, where reliable information is more than ever necessary for success.

Many years ago it was said that 'Some British industries do not make sufficient use of market research; they thus suffer from a removable uncertainty.'[51] Unfortunately, much the same could be said today, although there are growing numbers of industrial firms interested in knowing more about the benefits that market research could bring them.

SUMMARY

Effective marketing is based on sound market information: this is obtained through objective marketing research.

Markets are dynamic and information needs to be kept up to date. Organisations of all kinds can benefit from using marketing research; it helps to reduce the uncertainty or risk related to specific management decisions.

Five sequential stages in marketing research have been identified: brief, proposal, data collection, data analysis and evaluation, and preparation and presentation of final report. At all stages, professional objectivity must be maintained.

Two types of data, primary and secondary, are generally used in marketing research. Sources of secondary data should be identified and used before embarking on expensive field research (primary data collection).

Industrial and trade classifications assist in analysing market behaviour.

Specific research techniques include personal, postal, telephone, group and panel research. A carefully devised, integrated research design is important.

REFERENCES

1. Drucker, Peter F., *The Practice of Management*, Heinemann, London, 1955.
2. Schlaifer, Robert, *Probability and Statistics for Business Decisions*, McGraw-Hill, New York, 1959.
3. Ackoff, Russell L., 'Management misinformation systems', *Management Science*, 14 December 1967.
4. Heller, Robert, 'Why facts need figuring out', *Observer*, 20 April 1975.
5. Levitt, Theodore, *Marketing for Business Growth*, McGraw-Hill, New York, 1974.
6. Kotler, Philip, *Marketing Management: Analysis, planning and control*, Prentice Hall, Englewood Cliffs, NJ, 1980.
7. Porter, Michael E., *The Competitive Advantage of Nations*, Macmillan, London, 1990.
8. Buzzell, Robert D., 'Is marketing a science?', *Harvard Business Review*, vol. 41, no. 1, 1963.
9. Geldard, Frank A., *Fundamentals of Psychology*, Wiley, New York, 1963.
10. Easterfield, T. E., 'Operational research studies', *Accelerating Innovation*, Aslib, 1975.
11. American Marketing Association, *Report of the Definitions Committee*, AMA, Chicago, 1961.
12. British Institute of Management, 'Survey of marketing research in Great Britain', Information Summary No. 97, BIM, London, January 1962.
13. Aaker, David A, and Day, George S., 'Increasing the effectiveness of marketing research', *California Management Review*, vol. 23, no. 2, 1980.

14. Industrial Marketing Research Association, *Regulations*, IMRA, Lichfield, 1969.
15. Rosier, Jacques A., 'The coming crisis in bank management II', *The Bankers' Magazine*, August 1973.
16. Gaulton, John, 'Marketing and all that', *Journal of the Institute of Bankers*, December 1973.
17. Chisnall, Peter M., *Marketing: A behavioural analysis*, McGraw-Hill, Maidenhead, 1975.
18. Horne, Annette, Morgan, Judith and Page, Joanna, 'Where do we go from here?', *Journal of the Market Research Society*, vol. 16, no. 3, 1974.
19. Bowley, A. L., and Barnett-Hurst, A. R., *Livelihood and Poverty: A study in the economic conditions of working class households in Northampton, Warrington, Stanley and Reading*, Bell, London, 1915.
20. Cowell, D. W. and Blois, K. J., 'Conducting market research for high technology products', *Industrial Marketing Management*, vol. 6, 1977.
21. Ferber, Robert and Verdoorn, P. J., *Research Methods in Economics and Business*, The MacMillan Company, Toronto, 1969.
22. Chisnall, Peter M. *Marketing Research*, McGraw-Hill, Maidenhead, 1992.
23. Green, Paul E., and Tull, Donald S., *Research for Marketing Decisions*, Prentice Hall, Englewood Cliffs, N.J., 1975.
24. Political and Economic Planning. 'Sample surveys – Part One', *PEP Report No. 313*, vol. 16, PEP, London, May 1950.
25. Anderson, P. G., 'The industrial user and his marketing research needs', in *The Effective Use of Market Research*, ed. J. Aucamp, Staples Press, London, 1971.
26. Marshall, Neill, 'Producer services', in *Economic Activity and Land Use: The changing information base for local and regional studies*, ed. Michael J. Healey, Longman Scientific Technical, Harlow, 1991.
27. Green, R. W., 'Statistical classifications – structure and development: the government's viewpoint', *IMRA Journal*, vol. 7, no. 4, 1971.
28. Chisnall, Peter M., *The Essence of Marketing Research*, Prentice Hall, Hemel Hempstead, 1991.
29. MacLean, I., 'Statistical classifications – structure and development: an industrial marketing research viewpoint', *IMRA Journal*, vol. 7, no. 4, 1971.
30. Battersby, Albert, *Mathematics in Management*, Penguin, Harmondsworth, 1971.
31. Trafford, John, 'Monsanto's model for the tyre market', *Financial Times*, 16 May 1972.
32. Bolt, Gordon J., *Marketing and Sales Forecasting: A total approach*, Kegan Paul, London, 1971.
33. Teresi, S., 'Sales forecasting', *Management International Review*, vol. 6, no. 2, 1966.
34. Parker, George G. C., and Segura, Edilberto L., 'How to get a better forecast', *Harvard Business Review*, vol. 49, no. 2, 1971.
35. Jones, E. O., and Morrell, J. G., 'Environmental forecasting in British industry', *Journal of Management Studies* vol. 3, 1966.
36. MacFarlane-Smith, Joan, *Interviewing in Market and Social Research*, Routledge and Kegan Paul, London, 1972.
37. Courtenay, Edward, 'Talking pumps', *Sunday Telegraph*, 23 April 1972.
38. Hague, Paul, *The Industrial Market Research Handbook*, 3rd edn, Kogan Page, London, 1992.
39. Skapinker, Michael, 'Why people-watching is essential for product development', *Financial Times*, 2 February 1989.

40. Goldman, Alfred E., 'The group depth interview', *Journal of Marketing*, vol. 26, July 1962.
41. Ansell, A. E., 'The group depth interview', *Journal of Marketing*, vol. 26, July 1962.
42. Rayne-Davis, John, 'Interaction can yield more than interviewing', *Industrial Marketing Digest*, vol. 3, no. 3, 1978.
43. Sampson, Peter, 'Qualitative research and motivation research', in *Consumer Market Research Handbook*, ed. Robert Worcester and John Downham, Van Nostrand Reinhold, Wokingham, 1978.
44. Johnson, F. J., *Market Segmentation and Pricing Research in an Industrial Market*, Esomar, Hamburg, 1974.
45. Dening, James (ed.), 'Marketing industrial good', *Business Publications*, London, 1969.
46. Chisnall, Peter M., 'Multi-dimensional research – integrating research techniques', *Journal of Management Studies*, vol. 10, no. 2, 1973.
47. Yates, F., *Sampling Methods for Censuses and Surveys*, Griffin, London, 1953.
48. Hutchinson, Colin R., 'The practice of industrial marketing research in a changing environment', *IMRA Journal*, vol. 9, no. 2, 1974.
49. Atkin, Bryan, and Larsen, Tore Moritz, 'Problems of sampling, interviewing and grossing procedures for large-scale representative surveys in industrial market', in *Sampling Problems and Data Collection*, Esomar, Copenhagen, 1981.
50. Pearce, F. T., *Parameters of Research*, IMRA, Lichfield, 1966.
51. Carter, C. F., and Williams, B. R., *Investment in Innovation*, Oxford University Press, Oxford, 1958.

REVIEW AND DISCUSSION QUESTIONS

Q1 In the light of Chapters 3 and 4, what difficulties would you expect to encounter in conducting primary research on the DMU (decision-making unit) influences on the purchasing of office air-conditioning units?

Q2 Design a notional market research brief for consideration by the marketing director of a company supplying liquid handsoap which has experienced a 20 per cent decline in sales volume over the past three years.

Q3 Compile a report, based on secondary data, on the market in the UK, or in another country with which you are particularly familiar, for one of the following products/services: (a) factoring; (b) motor leasing; and (c) bitumen.

Q4 Outline some possible shortcomings of secondary data, and indicate ways in which industrial market researchers seek to overcome any such disadvantages.

Q5 What particular considerations should be borne in mind when using telephone, postal or personal questionnaires to gather information in industrial markets? Contrast the typical approaches used when researching consumer products.

Q6 Describe the role of sampling in developing an effective market research strategy for an industrial product/service of your choice. Indicate the sampling methodology you would recommend, and the rationale supporting it.

CHAPTER FIVE

Strategic planning I

NEED FOR METHODICAL APPROACH TO PROBLEMS

Management is essentially concerned with problem solving, decision making and organising finite resources to achieve identified objectives.

Being methodical implies adopting and following an effective method; it involves a disciplined and well co-ordinated effort. A methodical approach concentrates mental and physical energies; haphazard and erratic actions dissipate and eventually destroy these vital forces. Of course, the blind following of a routine, no matter how methodical, may sometimes result in failure and frustration. But this may be because the problem was wrongly diagnosed, or an inappropriate method of dealing with it was devised. Clear, objective thinking is necessary at the diagnostic stage and throughout the planning process.

Adopting a methodical approach does not mean that the same path is the way to success with different kinds of problem. What *is* important is a methodical *and* flexible approach, so that feasible solutions are offered for specific problems. One of the salient characteristics of a first-class manager is the flexibility of his or her reactions to problems. It should be remembered that new business opportunity is a dynamic situation, whereas most formal planning approaches are static.

As the operating environment becomes less stable and more difficult to predict, organisations should ensure that their strategies are adaptive to the changes which are taking place both inside and outside their businesses. From time to time, all organisations should review their basic operations to make sure that they are attuned to the changing environment and opportunities.

For example, the operating environment of the British Post Office Corporation has become increasingly competitive over the past decade or so. The 1969 Post Office Act transformed the Post Office from a Department of State into a state corporation that had to achieve a predetermined level of profits. The establishment of a marketing department in 1972 added to the keen commercial awareness and new professional skills which were needed to tackle, for instance, the fast-growing and aggressive competition in parcels traffic from several new market suppliers.

ROLE OF PLANNING

Planning attempts to control the factors which affect the outcome of decisions; actions are guided so that success is more likely to be achieved. 'To plan is to decide what to do before doing it. Like methods, plans can be specially made to fit circumstances or they can be ready-made for regular use in recurrent and familiar situations.'[1] In other words, a methodical approach can be custom-built or ready-made according to the nature of the problem involved.

As discussed earlier in this text, most organisations – whether they are primarily motivated by profits or by, for example, social welfare policies – are today immersed in dynamic environments. The whole fabric of society has changed so radically, bringing new expectations and demands with it, that organisations of all kinds can continue to be useful only if they react to the changing needs of their markets. In the specialised managerial function of marketing, flexibility is essential. Strategic planning is concerned with allocating the resources of an organisation in the most effective pattern of reaction to the identified needs of those whom it professes to serve.

Plans must be regularly assessed for their effectiveness, and systematic updating should be an accepted management discipline. W. W. Simmons has drawn attention to the fact that in their early days Communist planners made some of their greatest mistakes by not realising that their plans had to be subject to change if they were to continue to be relevant and effective.

> They tried to impose a fixed 5 year plan on changing conditions. Unfortunately, some American businesses are still making this mistake . . . Frequently, a well-constructed plan only six months old will be found to be very much out-of-date. Someone may claim it could not have been a good plan. In fact, it may have been the best possible plan. It is serving its purpose. Because of the plan, management now know what changes are necessary to improve future business.[2]

Export markets in particular (as discussed in Chapter 8) require careful planning a long time ahead of actual entry operations. The time lag is affected by the product type, its manufacturing complexities and the methods of distribution adopted. Exporting cannot be jumped into at the last moment; strategic planning should map the route along which companies travel to secure profitable overseas business. The contributions of marketing research, product design and development have been covered in earlier chapters. The integration of production and marketing plans, etc. are matters requiring adequate study before final decisions are made to enter particular markets.

Managers of successful companies have frequently pursued strategies of one kind or another without consciously analysing their actions. However, there is increasing evidence to support the development of formal strategic plans. This becomes particularly important when the tasks of operational management are delegated from the policy-forming centre and as businesses acquire wider interests. Kotler[3] points out that the development of strategies has two main benefits: (1) they facilitate the achievement of objectives; and (2) they require people to come together. This produces better understanding and awareness and a 'shared sense of opportunity, direction, significance and achievement'.

This identification of shared objectives is also stressed by another researcher,[4] who states that the need for an explicit strategy stems from two key attributes of an organisation: (1) that success hinges on people working together, thus mutually reinforcing corporate inputs; and (2) that these efforts have to be done in rapidly changing conditions.

CHARACTERISTICS OF AN EFFECTIVE PLAN

In 1949 a leading management scientist[5] listed four general features of an effective plan: unity, continuity, flexibility and precision. These characteristics are, of course, interdependent. Unity means that only one organisational plan should be operating at any one time; if more than one plan is put into action, confusion will result and organisational resources will be used inefficiently. Continuity refers to the linking of successive strategies over time so that long-term objectives are finally attained. Flexibility was discussed in the preceding section; in a dynamic environment it is courting disaster to adopt a static strategy. Precision demands disciplined methods of market measurement and forecasting. Without reliable data, plans cannot be formulated with reasonable chances of success. Measurability is also a link between planning and control; plans should be monitored for their tactical effectiveness.

Drucker has identified three elements in business planning, which 'is a continuous process of making present entrepreneurial decisions systematically and with best possible knowledge of their futurity, organising systematically the effort needed to carry out these decisions against expectations through organised feedback'.[6] This definition was observed by Ansoff[7] to contain three elements: making decisions systematically; preparing programmes for their implementation; and measuring actual performance against the programmes. Management planning requires, therefore, method, sustained effort, precise standards by which to evaluate performance and continuous monitoring to ensure that resources are being optimised. Without planning, chaos takes over and soon reduces any kind of organisation to a miserable shambles.

We live, as Mintzberg has reflected, in a society of organisations. 'We are born in organizations and are educated in organizations, so that we can later work in organizations. At the same time, organizations supply us and entertain us, they govern us and harass us (sometimes concurrently). Finally we are buried by organizations.'[8] Personal lives and professional activities involve and are involved in organisations. Inevitably, organisations need management; this imposes order, gives leadership, arranges resources, motivates endeavours and make decisions. To quote Mintzberg again: 'what distinguishes the formal organization from a random collection of people – a mob, an informal group – is the presence of some system of authority and administration'.

RELATIONSHIP BETWEEN MARKETING PLANS AND CORPORATE PLANS

Strategic planning is based on two concepts: market environment and strategic fit, i.e. the way in which a company organises its resources in order to secure an effective relationship with the markets in which it operates.

Kotler[3] feels that where a firm is marketing orientated, its entire organisation is welded together in one unified, coherent system which is directed towards a well-defined set of objectives. Unless an organisation has devised an effective strategy, it is open to buffeting from its competitors. As pithily expressed by Howard Perlmutter: 'Without a strategy, the organisation is like a ship without a rudder, going around in circles.'[9]

The relationship between marketing planning and corporate planning has been emphasised, although it is accepted that the value of integrated planning is 'more observed in theory than in practice'.[10] According to an experienced American senior executive,[11] marketing planning is the starting point for all corporate planning. Businesses exist because customers are willing to buy the goods and services offered to them, so planning for those markets is the basis for the extent and direction of all other corporate decisions.

The survival and growth of an organisation depend heavily on the quality of management planning. Some die-hard business people despise planning, preferring a 'seat-of-the-pants' approach to problem solving. Sometimes they are spectacularly successful, but more frequently, their disorganised efforts have led to catastrophe. 'General Eisenhower was reputed to have said, "In preparing for battle I have always found that plans are useless, but planning is indispensable." '[1]

SYSTEMATIC PLANNING

It would, of course, be naive to believe that planning can ever be perfect: it is an art as well as a technique. However, it is useful to consider it as a series of integrated events that lead sequentially from stated objectives. These steps in the planning process are as shown in Figure 5.1.

These main stages of planning will now be considered in more detail, so that the various elements which contribute to successful operations can be identified and assessed. Planning should not be viewed as a sterile exercise; if it is thought to be so, then this may be a reflection of a deteriorated management philosophy. Managers are not just people of action: they need to think ahead and to do so clearly. Planning clarifies the processes of thought, because the very act of writing down proposed courses of action is a powerful mental discipline which leads to more effective behaviour.

PLANNING STAGE 1: STATING CLEAR OBJECTIVES

The setting up of goals or objectives is the first step in the planning process. This foundation step should be carefully designed so that an effective structural plan

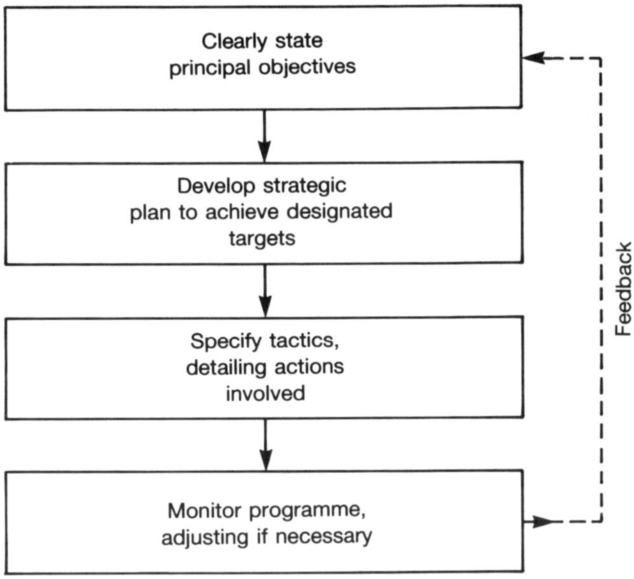

FIGURE 5.1 Four sequential stages of planning

develops. To guide efforts, objectives should be stated in specific terms related to the fundamental philosophies and policies of a particular organisation. 'Vague or undefined objectives lead to vague, undefined and unco-ordinated plans, and to decisions taken under pressure of circumstances leading to actions which are often incompatible.'[12]

Economists generally assume that firms aim to maximise profits. However, another view which is attracting support is that modern, large corporations managed by professionals may well pursue other objectives, such as organic growth. As a result, the traditional view of profit maximisation as a prime objective may be challenged by the behaviour of corporate management in certain firms. Risk-aversion policies, for instance, may well discourage professional managers from pursuing profit maximisation at all costs.

Bearing in mind these observations, two main types of organisational objective can be identified: primary and secondary.

As just mentioned, the traditional view was that the primary objective of a business could be presumed to be the generation of profit. However, other objectives may be desirable and affect profit-earning activities. These secondary objectives – which, as Ansoff[7] has observed, are not in any way inferior to the primary objective – are necessary if a company is to plan effectively for its future progress. In the short term, for instance, a profit maximisation policy may be affected by changes in economic conditions which demand some restructuring of corporate resources to meet new levels of competition. Survival or market share defence may, in fact, become primary objectives.

Quantified objectives set standards of performance against which progress can be measured. These can be one or more of the following typical marketing criteria: percentage share of defined market; ratio of profit on sales; total sales (home, export); contribution ratios, etc.

With refreshing directness, Drucker has reminded top management that their first responsibility is to ask themselves the question, ' "What is our business?" and to make sure that it is carefully studied and correctly answered . . . That the question is so rarely asked – at least in a clear and sharp form – and so rarely given adequate study and thought, is perhaps the most important single cause of business failure.'[13] The definition of a business (or non-profit-making organisation) should be derived from an examination of customers' needs, because through satisfying customers (or clients), organisations survive and prosper.

Organisations should set realistic objectives; these should be related to both short-term and long-term goals. Since marketing is concerned with the efficient use of corporate resources to meet specific market needs, these targets – short- or long-term – should be based on budgets which are tied in with levels of forecast demand.

Firms may be broadly classified as either reactive or proactive: the former receive stimuli from their markets and respond in some way – a largely passive posture in which entrepreneurial energy is at low ebb; the latter adopt a positive attitude to their markets, searching actively for new business opportunities, monitoring market trends and energetically pursuing likely business opportunities. These entrepreneurial firms aim to shape the environment to fit their resources. Such contrasting business styles will obviously affect the objectives set down by such firms and, of course, their overall trading performance.

DEVELOPMENT OF BASIC CORPORATE VALUES

Winning companies have well-defined corporate values which are known and supported by all who work in them. Customers, products and employees are all recognised to be vital ingredients for above-average corporate performance.

The staff involved in research and development at 3M regularly visit customers. J. C. Bamford, the leading British earth-moving equipment manufacturers with world-wide sales, have a well-articulated policy of quality and product improvement, with everyone in the company fully aware of these corporate objectives. All share the same corporate culture, which is expressed not only in positive attitudes towards customers, but also in high standards of behaviour. US research over a period of ten years found that companies that do better had 'excellent communications'.[14] Everyone knew the corporate goals and was encouraged to help to achieve them; successes were always recognised, while failure from time to time was tolerated.

In 1985 a survey[15] of senior executives in major European companies undertaken by the Management Centre, Europe, across ten countries and drawn from different industries, found that what gave these highly successful companies the edge on their competitors was the importance they attached to basic corporate values. As with comparable studies in the United States, there often seemed to be a rather curious inverse relationship between those companies which emphasised profitability as a primary corporate value and the actual profitability achieved. On the other hand, companies generally ranking customer satisfaction as the most important corporate value were highly profitable. It is important to note, however, that professed commitment to high corporate values needs to be translated into practice: strong declarations themselves may sound impressive, but implementation has to be effected by management at every level of organisation and expressed in many ways, such as high standards of customer service, good teamwork between executives in different departments as well as in the same section, keeping promised delivery dates, etc. Clearly, these duties should always be undertaken by those responsible for them, but too often such everyday tasks are just not well done.

CORPORATE MISSION STATEMENTS

Mission statements have tended to attract, sometimes deservedly, scepticism and even ridicule, leading to suggestions that a company, like the proverbial British public, may be in one of its periodic fits of morality. Portentous corporate announcements lack conviction and may even be counterproductive. Frequently associated with some of these affirmations of corporate mission are codes of ethics. (See Chapter 11.)

Most corporate mission statements, observes Ackoff with a somewhat sardonic eye, are worthless and generally consist of pious platitudes. 'They often formulate necessities as objectives; for example, "to achieve sufficient profit".'[16] A mission statement, he declares, should not be content to state what a firm *must* do in order to survive, but should indicate what it *chooses* to do in order to thrive. *Five criteria should be used to evaluate a mission statement*:

1. It should contain a statement of objectives that makes progress towards them measurable.
2. It should differentiate a company from other companies – 'it should establish the individuality, if not the uniqueness, of the firm'.
3. It should define the business that the company *wants* to be in, but may not be in at the present time – a 'unifying concept' should be sought which will expand corporate horizons and re-energise efforts.
4. It should be relevant to all the firm's stakeholders: customers, suppliers, shareholders, employees and the public, and state how the company intends to serve these various constituencies. Most mission statements are seriously deficient because they are addressed only to shareholders and managers, whereas *all* employees should feel that they are being involved.
5. It is of prime importance that a mission statement should be exciting and inspiring.

Ackoff recommends that if a company's mission statement fails any of the five criteria quoted, 'it should be redone'.[16]

In essence, mission statements should be written in crisp, easily understood language, which communicates a sense of corporate direction and effective leadership, and should motivate individuals at all levels of the organisation.

In its half-year report for 1992, BICC included this statement: 'We aim to meet the world's demand for power, communications, transport and building through leadership in cable making and construction. We are committed to total quality, technical excellence and customer satisfaction.' Another leading British industrial group, TI Group, announced in 1992 that 'TI's strategy is to be an international engineering group concentrating on specialised engineering business, operating in selected niches on a global basis.' While these corporate messages are valuable indicators of aims and strategic objectives, they do not fulfill all the criteria for effective mission statements given by Ackoff.

Andrew Campbell of the Ashridge Strategic Management Centre studied company mission statements and concluded that, on their own, they were of little value. 'There were, on the one hand, companies with a mission statement and nothing to look forward to but death in a few months' time.' He suggested that instead of trying to write mission statements, a company should formulate a sense of mission and persuade employees of its validity – a process that is likely to take years not months. Four aspects are seen to be critical:

1. Establish the purpose of the company and explain why it exists.
2. Define the business, its activities and its ambitions.
3. Describe how the company plans to treat its employees, customers and suppliers, i.e. the organisation's values.
4. Ensure that corporate promises are kept by, for example, providing managers with adequate training and resources so that agreed policies can be implemented.

Only when the mission is well established and understood should it be written down; in this way, the statement will be of real value and reflect the commitments made by employees throughout the organisation.

'People', says Campbell, 'are more motivated and work more intelligently if they believe in what they are doing and trust the organization they are working with. Psychologists and organizational behaviourists recognize that most people are searching for meaning in their life. If an organization can provide meaning for an employee on top of pay and conditions, it will inspire greater commitment and loyalty.'[17]

SITUATION (SWOT) ANALYSIS

A logical starting point in setting corporate objectives would be an objective audit of resources, identifying strengths and weaknesses of existing skills; technological, production, financial, administrative, marketing, etc. This SWOT (strengths, weaknesses, opportunities, threats) analysis focuses on the position of a company relative to its competitors.

The fundamental approach to this analysis should be undertaken as objectively as possible to ensure the validity of its findings. Since a company may well operate in several distinct markets with different levels of competition, product complexity, etc., specific analyses will be more realistic than generalised assessments. (See Chapter 6 on market segmentation.)

Competitors should be identified and ranked for their relative impact on proposed strategies. Threats may arise, for example, from technological developments or patent rights giving suppliers significant advantages in product design, manufacturing costs, etc. Other threats or constraints may emanate from legislation affecting product safety features and necessitating redesign of some products. In other cases, firms may have considerable research and development resources which enable them to become market leaders (see Chapter 7 on innovation).

On the other hand, opportunities often arise from the ability to react quickly to changing market needs and, perhaps, offer improved versions of earlier innovations. Some companies' strengths may lie particularly in having highly trained sales forces covering wide sectors of industry and commerce, as is the case with IBM.

Comparative strengths and weaknesses apply to all organisations, and to people as well. Associated with these factors are the concepts of the limiting factor and leverage, to which we shall return later.

In completing a SWOT analysis, certain assumptions will be made about future trends likely to influence market demand; probability judgements could be applied to these assumptions. The end result of this systematic approach will be a series of well-devised, objective statements which form the foundation of an effective marketing strategy.

Sir John Harvey-Jones, who led ICI with panache for several years, has strongly pragmatic views on business development: 'there is no point in deciding where your business is going until you have actually decided with great clarity where you are now. Like practically everything in business this is easier said than done'.[18]

Ansoff has observed that a large majority of corporate decisions have to be made within the framework of a limited total resource, no matter what size the organisation may be. There are alternative uses for scarce resources, and the objective 'is to produce a resource-allocation pattern which will offer the best potential for meeting the firm's objectives'.[7]

Financial audits are standard features of organisations of all types; with similar professional objectivity companies should carefully check the various factors that contribute to their marketing efficiency.

Marketing audits

Marketing audits are seen by Kotler[3] to have three diagnostic steps: (1) marketing environment review; (2) marketing system review; and (3) detailed marketing activity review. The first stage establishes the current and expected marketing environment of the organisation. The second stage reviews the internal marketing system as to its suitability for the emerging marketing environment. At the third stage a review is made of the main components of the specific marketing mix (see later discussion).

One way in which a marketing audit can benefit a business may derive from an internal audit of customers' accounts. For example, one company found that small orders represented 62 per cent of total orders received, but only 17 per cent of total value; by contrast, the biggest customers made up 10 per cent in value of total sales, although representing only 1 per cent of total orders. Clearly, changes were advisable in the direction of marketing efforts.

Companies may, for example, stipulate that orders should be of certain minimum size for direct shipment; smaller orders may be diverted to distributors. Standards may be laid down related to the frequency of visits by sales staff to specific types of customer, rated for new potential profitability; quantity discounts may be introduced to encourage the placing of larger orders at one time. Indiscriminate selling is not likely to result in maximum profitability; planned operations are necessary in today's highly competitive conditions.

It may sometimes be advisable to prune or rationalise product lines in order to increase marketing productivity. Most companies tend to list some products which do not really pay for their keep.

Sevin, who has undertaken notable research into marketing productivity analysis, has categorically stated: 'Manufacturers and wholesalers generally do not know reasonably accurately the dollar marketing costs and the dollar profit (or loss) contribution of each of their products, customers, sales territories and other segments of their business.' As the result of controlled market experiments, a company was able to eliminate 592 out of 635 unprofitable products, many of which, it was discerned, were viewed by their customers as not being substantially different from standard and profitable items in the product line. Subsequent to this rationalisation programme, Sevin reported that 'long run sales volume was increased and marketing costs were reduced substantially, while the dollar net profit contribution was increased by almost 24%'.[19]

The systematic analysis of product ranges by ranking the profit contribution of individual products or main types of product is a very useful exercise for marketing management in conjunction with financial colleagues.

Evaluating products by the contribution which they make to overheads and profitability is a realistic approach which acknowledges that it is frequently difficult, if not impossible, to allocate overheads over individual products scientifically in a multiproduct firm. As a result, overhead charges tend to be distributed more or less arbitrarily; different methods of allocation are likely to affect significantly the net profit ranking of individual products.

Table 5.1 lists main product groups by monthly sales volume, sales revenue and direct profit (defined as net selling price minus total variable costs). The last column on the right gives the cumulative gross contribution to profits. It will be observed that 80 per cent of the total contribution to profits is generated by about 46 per cent of the product groups. Further examination of this ranked list of product

TABLE 5.1 Analysis of profit contribution ranked by product groups

Product group units	*Sales vol. (£)*	*Sales revenue (£)*	*Direct profit (£)*	*% cumulative gross contribution*
A	108	9,900	4,844	13.5
B	454	10,229	3,734	23.9
C	308	7,937	2,887	32.0
D	144	6,614	2,757	39.7
E	420	6,934	2,621	47.0
F	51	4,952	2,455	53.9
G	28	4,088	2,356	60.4
H	351	5,520	2,204	66.6
I	325	4,262	1,751	71.5
J	59	4,226	1,731	76.3
K	182	3,825	1,360	80.1
L	78	3,117	1,236	83.5
M	132	2,617	1,053	86.5
N	29	2,083	946	89.1
O	140	2,354	940	91.8
P	76	1,895	657	93.6
Q	11	1,174	570	95.2
R	19	1,354	537	96.7
S	60	1,068	427	97.9
T	38	984	281	98.6
U	2	278	146	99.0
V	23	530	143	99.4
W	2	278	135	99.8
X	9	177	63	100.0
Total	3,049	86,396	35,834	

Source: Muir.[20]

performance will reveal the very marginal value to the business of some product groups; one-third of the product range renders only 5 per cent of the total profit contribution. Clearly, questions will have to be asked about the reason for continuing to sell certain product groups.

In some cases it may be possible for customers to accept substitutes from the main range, which may have been introduced since they were supplied with 'specials'. There may be valid reasons for leaving some of these 'marginal' products in the selling list: they may attract other, more profitable business, or it may be feasible to increase prices to offset their general low level of contribution. In some cases it may be more advantageous to buy-in certain products for which a firm experiences limited demand. This will enable it to maintain the attraction to customers of a comprehensive range of products without incurring diseconomies. There can be no hard-and-fast rules which generally apply. In the end analysis, marketing managements have the responsibility of ensuring the profitability of their companies and at the same time of satisfying, as far as reasonably possible, customers' needs. The temptation to be the world's supplier must, of course, be resisted.

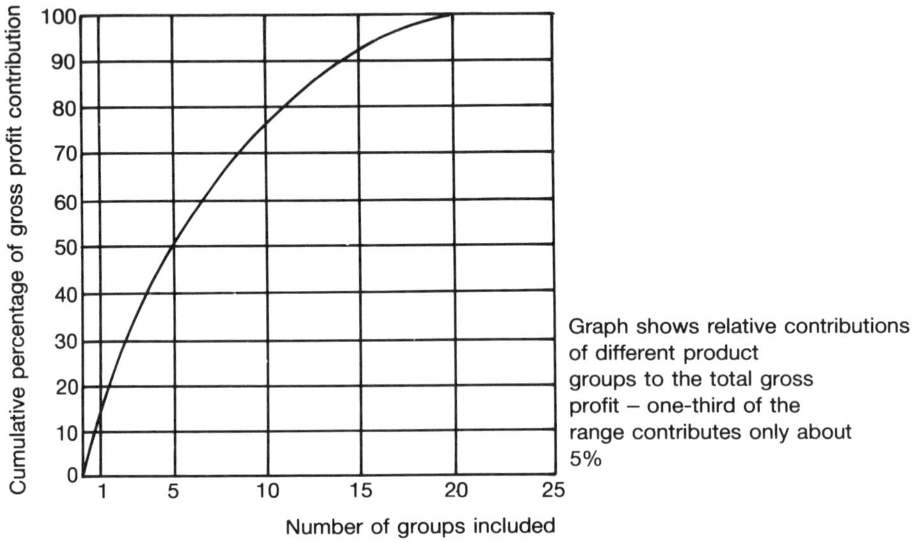

FIGURE 5.2 Cumulative gross profit contribution by product groups (Table 5.1) (Source: Muir[20])

The data in Table 5.1 are graphically represented by the asymptotic curve shown in Figure 5.2.

Imbalance can exist between sales and profits over various product ranges. One company discovered that almost 50 per cent of total profits were generated from just under 38 per cent of total turnover represented by one product group. Another product group accounted for 7.5 per cent of total sales but contributed only about 3 per cent of profits. While home market sales were nearly 43 per cent of total business, they contributed just under 30 per cent of operating profit. New marketing strategies were designed to remedy this potentially dangerous corporate situation.

LINKING MARKETING AUDIT AND MARKETING RESEARCH

Marketing research, as indicated in Chapter 4, provides objective and relevant data for marketing decision making. The characteristics of demand, market shares, buying behaviour, competitive activities and related factors will be collected from systematic market research and will assist in developing strategic objectives.

SIGNIFICANT CORPORATE INFLUENCES

Before attempting to fix corporate objectives, management should identify and evaluate likely obstacles or constraints which may exist in their organisations. Some of these may be overcome eventually, but in the short term, at least, they are likely to inhibit management objectives. It is advisable, therefore, to classify the nature of the constraints and to consider how, for instance, a phased programme within the scope of developing resources could be designed to attain specific corporate objectives.

Two specific factors are likely to be particularly influential in strategic planning:

1. The principle of the limiting factor.
2. Leverage.

The principle of the limiting factor

Even the largest organisations do not have unlimited resources; and one will show itself to be more critical than the others when, at a particular time, corporate opportunities are being considered.

Chester Barnard, an influential American management theorist and highly successful business executive, has referred to the principle of the limiting factor in solving corporate problems. 'The limiting factor is the one whose control, in the right form, at the right place and time, will establish a new system or set of conditions which meets the purpose.'[21]

Finance is, of course, always limited, but there may be occasions when finance is available but other factors inhibit its effective application. All organisations tend to have significant factors that influence their development; the identification and appreciation of these dominant planning components may reveal, for instance, unexpected competitive disadvantages. In marketing terms, the immediate limiting factor could relate to the level of distribution, which may be inadequate for national coverage; or, perhaps, to the technical knowledge of sales staff who may be expected to sell more sophisticated products. The existing design resources within a firm may be inadequate to meet new competition which has eaten its way into the market share held by the company.

A few years ago, the British Oxygen Company recognised that its limiting factor was the nature of demand for its products: this was essentially reactive and dependent on industrial activity. In addition, BOC products could not be economically transported more than 150–200 miles from point of production.

The invasion of the British market by Air Products faced BOC with an entirely new competitive situation; for years it had enjoyed a virtual monopoly in the British gas market. BOC was, in the words of the chairman of its industrial and medical cases group,[22] forced to start marketing gases, a task for which it was ill prepared. The defensive posture adopted against Air Products' aggressive marketing in the late 1960s was abandoned and BOC sought to regain ground by positive marketing not only of gases, but of the technological expertise and advice which it could offer to customers.

Another outcome of the changed market environment was that BOC vigorously pursued a policy of diversification, so that its activities now range across welding products, vacuum engineering, medical equipment, refrigeration equipment, frozen food retailing and specialised food distribution.

Leverage

In addition to limited resources, probably including one particularly influential limiting factor, organisations have – or should aim to have – distinctive competences which give them significant market advantages. McKinsey[10] studied the management practices of 37 companies. Among other findings, they concluded that the distinguishing characteristic shared by these companies was that they did one particular thing well. They had developed significant strength in one feature of their businesses which gave them a comparative advantage over their competitors. As Blois[23] observes, this concept is well known and understood, but one of the problems of applying it is that the features which result in this competence change over time in line with environmental changes. Hence, leverage should be viewed as a dynamic factor, particularly in volatile market conditions.

This concept of comparative advantage could be linked, perhaps, to the early nineteenth-century classical economic theory of international trade. The principle of comparative cost or advantage advanced by David Ricardo and others stressed that specialisation of production in which a country has special proficiency would be more beneficial to its economy.

Manufacturers (and distributors) should deliberately seek to develop recognised, distinctive abilities which are attractive to their customers. There are many ways in which 'leverage' can be developed: it may, for instance, relate to specific patents, or to superb after-sales service, or to efficient distribution arrangements including acceptable delivery times. Even in commodity product markets, leverage can be built into the deal – it is perhaps even more important for this to be done because of the nature of supply in these markets. (In Chapter 2, the concept of the augmented product was mentioned, particularly with reference to commodity products.)

For several decades, companies have been urged to develop *distinctive or core competences* which will give them competitive edge. This strategy has been termed 'the gospel of know-how',[24] and in following it, companies carefully nurture their core competences relative to technological developments and market demand. Core competences may be strengthened through licensing, joint ventures or subcontracting arrangements – facilities management is discussed later.

But in dynamic trading conditions, no company can feel secure for long; even giants like IBM, which dominated data processing by its aggressive marketing strategies over many years, have proved vulnerable to the actions of their competitors, technological advances and customers' buying preferences. As *The Economist* noted:

> IBM's prosperity had been built on its near-stranglehold on the market for large, main-frame computers, established in the late 1960s with a bold "bet-the-company" investment in a family of machines called the System 360. Like most

> of its much smaller rivals, IBM built its machines to proprietary standards, so that they did not work with those of other makers.[25]

Customers became 'locked in' to the IBM system. But after nearly 20 years of oligopoly profits, IBM was confronted with the challenge of the personal computer, which at first it ignored. Eventually, however, in 1981, IBM decided to enter the fray and 'hurriedly assembled its machines from off-the-shelf components, making it possible for hundreds of other firms to build machines to the same standards, and capable of running the same software'.[26]

The degree of standardisation of design and components, such as micro-processor chips, together with the ability to use the same readily accessible software, provided an open invitation to a horde of new entrants eager to supply the rapidly expanding market. In a comparatively short time, cut-throat competition characterised the personal computer (PC) market sector; prices tumbled, and customers began, at last, to assert their buying freedom. IBM's long-held technological hold over the computer industry was shattered. For 1992, the group reported a net loss of $4.97bn; the UK subsidiary incurred operating losses of £398m, plus a restructuring charge of £218m, resulting in a pre-tax loss of £616m.

Meanwhile, Microsoft, a small PC software company which in the early 1980s, and at IBM's invitation, had designed software for the PC that IBM was about to launch, was able to use this patronage to develop into becoming the prime supplier of PC systems software. Belatedly, IBM is attempting to re-assert itself in this market sector through extensive promotional campaigns.

In the no-holds-barred competitive environment of the vast computer industry, no company – except IBM – tries to compete in every segment. 'Every other firm concentrates on where it can be best. Intel, Compaq, Apple, Sun Microsystems and Microsoft have all thrived this past year, despite brutal price wars.'[27] (Market segmentation strategies are discussed in the next chapter.)

Facilities management

Associated with the theme of core competences is the concept of facilities management (FM).[28] This refers to the strategy of contracting out non-core activities, so that companies can concentrate their energies and resources on developing fully those aspects of their businesses which give them specific competitive advantages. The basic idea, like many managerial theories, is not new – for many years, organisations have used outside specialists to provide catering, cleaning, transport and security services – but the trend is growing for this principle to be applied to higher-level functions, such as computer networks installation and management, and accounting.

The demand for FM (or 'outsourcing', as it is sometimes known) is growing strongly, particularly for information technology functions in both the public sector and commercial companies. In 1992, for example,[28] Andersen Consulting Process Management Unit signed an initial five-year contract worth $89m with BP to run all the financial and accounting services for the group's North Sea oil joint venture operations. Many public authorities, like Berkshire County Council, have contracted out printing to specialist companies and secured significant cost benefits. In the USA, where FM is widely practised, the Federal Aviation Administration awarded a five-year multi-million dollar contract to cover the operation of computer services.

How far companies can shed 'peripheral' activities, reduce numbers of employees, and still retain a solid core of competence within their organisations, may be debated at length. As mentioned earlier, core competences may be enhanced through, for example, joint ventures and licensing, as well as subcontracting. The doctrines of core competences and corporate focus should not be viewed as irreconcilable; they can be harnessed to help organisations of many kinds to increase the efficiency of their operations, particularly in times of economic stress. Specialist suppliers and subcontractors will increasingly be perceived as partners in the businesses run by their client companies; joint prosperity will depend on the effectiveness with which they can contribute to the total value-added process. Much of this type of activity has existed for generations, but much closer working relationships are now necessary and are evident, for instance, in the manufacturing policies of Japanese car firms in the UK (see Chapters 1 and 2).

To succeed in the increasingly competitive conditions of modern markets, companies, it has been stated,[29] must become two things above all: (1) they must be *changed-based and adaptive* – typified as 'chameleons'; and (2) they must be *alliance- rather than fortress-minded*, both in their relations with other companies and also internally between different departments and disciplines – typified as 'collaborators'. The latter relates closely to the Harvard concept of the 'boundaryless' company, while the former resembles 'living with ambiguity and paradox', or 'just reconciling opposites'. However, in its avid pursuit of change, the chameleon company should certainly not abandon all the well-tested systems of management, or disaster will be likely to occur. The problem is said to be 'how to balance collaboration with the fashionable and important idea of core competences', to which these corporate typologies pay 'scant attention'.

MARKET DYNAMICS

Porter has stated that 'The essence of formulating competitive strategy is relating a company to its environment.'[30] Since companies operate within distinctive market conditions of supply and demand, it is vital to study the dynamics of market behaviour before attempting to devise a market strategy. 'Every industry has an underlying structure or set of fundamental economic and technical characteristics . . . the strategist must learn what makes the environment tick.'

Obviously, it is not always easy to define an industry absolutely; Porter takes a 'working definition' of an industry as a group of firms that are making products (or supplying services) that are close substitutes for each other.

He also observes that competition in an industry continually operates to drive down the rate of return on investment towards the 'competitive floor rate of

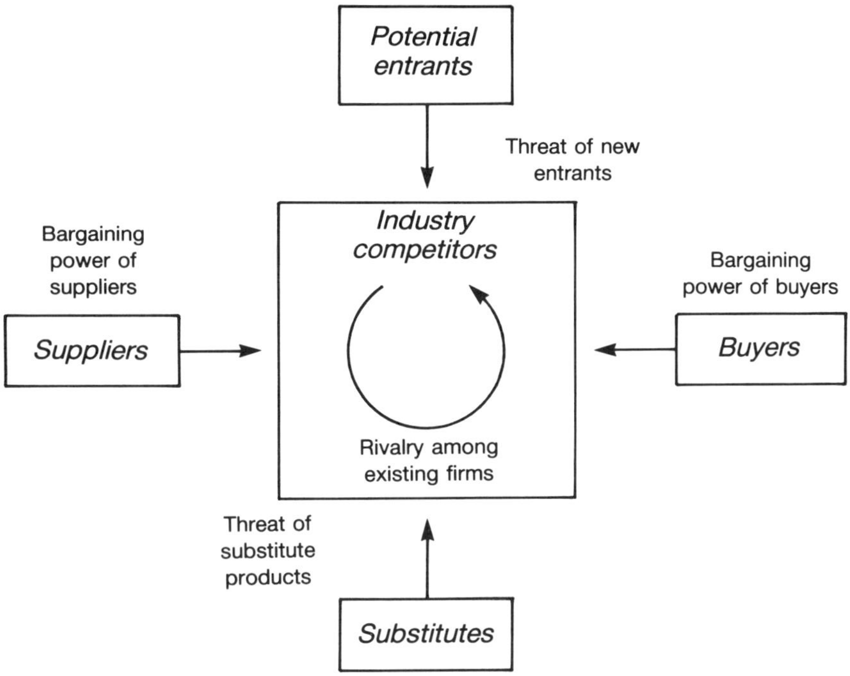

FIGURE 5.3 Forces driving industry competition (Source: Porter[31])

return', or to that which would be earned in the classical 'perfectly competitive' industry. This approximates to the yield on long-term government securities adjusted upwards for risk bearing.

Many experienced managers will already know a good deal about their industries, but even they can benefit from systematically updating their knowledge by objectively considering the five basic forces which determine the dynamics of demand and supply in their particular industrial and commercial sectors. This will lead to a thorough grasp of the relative strengths and weaknesses of their respective businesses. These five market forces are, briefly, as follows:

1. Threat of new entrants.
2. Bargaining power of buyers.
3. Bargaining power of suppliers.
4. Threat of substitute products/services.
5. Rivalry among existing firms. (See Figure 5.3.)

Every industry, as seen earlier, has its own structure, and the strength of each of the five competitive forces is a function of the underlying economic and technological factors which form that structure.[31]

The nature of these various influences and their effects on market behaviour will now be considered. Both product and service markets can be evaluated across the five basic factors listed above.

1. Threat of entry

A prospective new supplier brings an alternative source of supply to the market which may threaten existing suppliers' shares and profitability. Depending upon the corporate resources of the market entrant and the state of the market at that time, the overall profitability of the industry may be imperilled. If formidable barriers to entry exist and present suppliers are well managed, a newcomer will not pose a serious threat. The seriousness of the new market competition will depend on six major barriers to entry, as follows.

(a) *Economies of scale* refer to declines in unit costs of production (or other functions associated with a company's activities) as the absolute volume increases over a given period of time. If economies of scale exist within an industry, they will act as barriers to entry by forcing a new firm to enter on a large scale (in order to reap comparative benefits) and thus risk retaliation from the existing large-scale suppliers or, alternatively, to enter as a small-scale producer and accept the inherent cost disadvantages. Porter[30] notes that scale economies may be generally applicable over a business, or they may be highly specific. For instance, scale economies in production, research, marketing and service are probably the key barriers to entry in the mainframe computer industry, as Xerox and GE discovered to their cost; whereas, in television production, significant scale economies are limited to the manufacture of colour tubes and do not apply to the same extent to cabinets. Multiproduct businesses may be able to enjoy economies of scale by applying certain components across several types of product range, or by sharing selling and distribution costs.

Economies of scale are strongly evident[32] in pet food production in the United Kingdom, where the Mars Group, through its subsidiary Pedigree Petfoods, plays a dominant role. Many forays have been made by companies to challenge its supremacy, but the costs of entry are extraordinarily high. Pedigree has consistently invested heavily in production improvements, apart from high advertising expenditure.

(b) *Product differentiation* acts as an important barrier to entry because of brand identification and loyalty, built up from extensive advertising, customer service, unique design (perhaps patented), etc. Consumer product companies have aimed to develop particularly strong loyalty to their highly promoted brands. Industrial products do not have the same general market visibility, although in their market sectors, industrial and commercial firms should be able to develop strong customer allegiance through consistent attention to factors like quality and service. 'Image' building, discussed in Chapter 10, may be very beneficial in attracting orders across a range of products offered by a multiproduct firm.

Products can be differentiated intrinsically, i.e. by functional design, or they may be perceived to be different because of better appearance ('applied' design) or because of higher standards of sales service. Industrial as well as consumer goods and services should be assessed creatively for opportunities to differentiate them from the general run of goods on offer. (Refer to the extended discussion in Chapter 11.)

(c) *Capital requirements* may be significant barriers to entry if extensive investment in, for example, production, stocks, research and development is necessary in order to challenge existing suppliers. In capital-intensive industries, in particular, investment costs and the nature of risks may be distinctly limiting. Xerox chose to rent copiers rather than sell them outright, thus creating a formidable capital barrier to entry in this product market.

In the pharmaceuticals industry, barriers to entry are high because of the massive investment needed to finance the development, testing and marketing of new drugs by powerful groups such as Hoffman-Roche, Ciba-Geigy, Bayer, BASF, Abbott, Squibb, Glaxo, ICI, Smith Kline Beecham and Wellcome.

(d) *Access to distribution channels* – products of all types must be readily available to customers. Established firms are likely to have well-defined channels of distribution with which they may have particularly strong links because of efficient servicing. In other cases, a widespread network of exclusive distributors may prove very difficult for a newcomer to challenge or build up from scratch. Perhaps a non-traditional channel of distribution may offer new entrants an opportunity to develop their business.

In the late 1980s, the American tyre makers, Goodyear Tire and Rubber, experienced the full effects of the recession, but by the early 1990s it was on the way to recovery. This was helped by a slow recovery in the demand for tyres across the world, but also by a radical switch in Goodyear's distribution strategy. For years, the US tyre replacement market had been served by depots and independent dealers; this long-held tradition was overthrown when, in early 1992, Goodyear announced that it would be selling its tyres through Sears Roebuck, America's largest retail chain organization. The replacement market is three times larger than the original equipment sector, and offers better margins.[33]

(e) *Cost disadvantages independent of scale* – established firms may enjoy certain cost advantages that are not available to potential competitors, irrespective of their size and attainable economies of scale. Such advantages may derive from: (i) proprietary product technology; (ii) favourable access to raw materials such as mineral deposits; (iii) favourable locations, government subsidies applicable to existing firms; and (iv) a learning or experience curve (Porter[30] refers to the latter as a 'first cousin' of the former). In some businesses there is an observed tendency for unit costs to decline as experience in, for example, producing or marketing a product increases. (This concept will be discussed later in the chapter.)

(f) *Government policy* may limit or even prohibit entry to certain industries by imposing regulations related to the extraction of raw materials, safety and pollution standards, or by licensing and other controls related to particular activities, such as airline operations, banking, medical and nursing establishments.

Porter[30] stresses two important additional points about the threat of entry: (1) it changes as market conditions change, for example, the expiry of patents with Polaroid led to Kodak's sudden challenge in the instant photography market; on the other hand, the vastly increased economies of scale in the automobile industry have virtually prohibited new entry; (2) strategic decisions involving a large segment of an industry can significantly affect the threat of entry, as, for example, when the US recreational vehicle industry adopted vertical integration in order to lower costs.

2. Bargaining power of buyers

This requires very careful consideration in evaluating market behaviour. Buying power can be influenced by one or more of the following factors:

(a) relative buying power – large-volume buyers are particularly powerful where an industry has high fixed costs, as in chemicals (aspects of buying concentration have already been discussed in Chapter 2);

(b) where the product being bought represents a high proportion of an industry's costs (as with capital goods) and 'shopping around' is therefore likely;

(c) where products are largely undifferentiated, so alternative sources of supply can be easily to hand and switching costs are insignificant;

(d) where buyers may be able to threaten backward integration, as has happened in the automobile industry; 'tapered integration' – producing a proportion of their component needs themselves and buying the balance from outside suppliers – not only gives these manufacturers a very strong bargaining advantage, but also provides them with detailed knowledge of costs of producing these components;

(e) where the product supplied is an important element of the end product, buyers tend to be less price sensitive, as, for example, in components for oilfield equipment or medical instruments, where malfunction can have disastrous consequences.

Sellers may be able to improve their strategic bargaining position by selecting particular types of firm whose buyers exercise reduced power in the market for a specific product or service. Selective targeting of customers has been successfully adopted by two US firms – National Can and Crown Cork and Seal – which focus on segments of the can industry where they are able to offer differentiated products, minimise the threat of backward integration 'and otherwise mitigate the awesome power of their customers'.[30]

3. Bargaining power of suppliers

This arises by the threat to increase prices or reduce the quality of goods and services, thus squeezing maximum profitability from a particular industry, as happened when the chemical companies raised their prices to contract aerosol packagers.

The following conditions contribute to the power of suppliers in a given market:

(a) When a supplier industry is dominated by a few companies (oligopoly) and is more concentrated than the industry it is selling to;

(b) When the product being supplied is unique or at least differentiated, or if it has significant switching costs (buyers would be faced with considerable difficulties if they attempted to change suppliers);

(c) When a supplying industry does not have to cope with alternative products offered to a specific industry, as for example, when steel suppliers and aluminium suppliers competing for the same industry inhibit their respective bargaining powers;

(d) When suppliers may be able to threaten forward integration into their customers' industry;

(e) When an industry is not a relatively important customer of the supplier group – otherwise, supplying companies' fortunes will be closely linked with that industry and strong co-operation will be actively encouraged to ensure the continuity of customers' businesses; this may be reflected in reasonable pricing policies, assistance with R&D, etc.

4. Threat of substitute products/services

This limits the potential profits of an industry by imposing price ceilings which can be avoided by upgrading the product or differentiating it in some way so that it is distanced from potential substitutes. Suppliers of a specific product compete not only among themselves, but also against suppliers of acceptable substitute products. Natural fibres have experienced crushing competition from synthetic fibres; sugar producers have had to face large-scale production of high-fructose corn syrup; banks are facing increasing competition from building societies; life assurance sellers are also competing with unit trust marketers; plastics increasingly replace timber in window frames and doors; concrete roofing tiles decimated the clay roof tile industry, etc.

Substitute products that merit particular strategic attention are: those able to develop increasingly attractive price/performance characteristics relative to an industry's 'traditional' purchase; or those produced by industries earning high profits, when substitutes are rapidly adopted 'if some development increases competition in their industries and causes price reduction or performance improvement'.[30] Supplier firms in an industry may act jointly to counter the effects of substitutes, as, for example, the famous 'Woolmark' promotion has done for several years.

5. Rivalry among existing firms

This becomes more marked as an industry matures and little real growth is apparent. Rivalry among suppliers intensifies as profits are threatened and weaker companies go to the wall. Competitive tactics such as price cutting, increased promotional expenditure and product variations are widely practised in the fight for market share. Such activities will soon be noted by rival firms, which are likely to retaliate.

Where high fixed costs operate in an industry, suppliers may deliberately shave prices in order to keep production at economic levels. Lack of products differentiation – virtually 'commodity products' – is likely to result in low customer loyalty, price sensitivity and fierce competition.

High exit barriers arising, for example, from specialised assets may oblige supplier firms to 'dig in' and grimly fight for survival, in the hope that demand conditions will improve in the foreseeable future.

In some industries, for example chemicals and paper production, capacity is usually increased by large increments which, for the time being, often result in severe imbalance in the supply–demand position.

From time to time the nature and extent of rivalry in an industry will vary; hence individual firms should be flexible in their product strategies so that they maintain a competitively attractive position.

OVERVIEW

Porter's model of the competitive factors fashioning the structure and behaviour of an industry provides a readily accessible explanation which, although not containing anything with which an experienced marketing executive would not be fully familiar, gives a useful framework for strategic analyses.

From the evaluation of the structure of the industry in which a company operates and of the market or markets it supplies, a corporate planner should be able to identify his or her firm's relative strengths and weaknesses. The planner's next responsibility is to design effective plans of action so that the company can most effectively use its resources to achieve the agreed corporate objectives. Before this step is taken, however, it is necessary to incorporate the planned objectives into specific time periods.

TIME HORIZONS IN FORECASTING AND PLANNING

The nature of an organisation will affect the time horizons of its objectives. A component manufacturer will not have the same degree of forward planning as a supplier of petrochemical installations. In general, heavy industry and capital-intensive industries have long-term planning horizons and the life of the capital assets involved also tends to be longer than in many consumer product industries. Rank Xerox, for example, operates three-year planning periods.

It is usual to distinguish between short-range (3 months to 1 year), medium-range (1 to 5 years) and long-range forecasts (5 to 25 years). Short-term forecasting provides information to guide 'day-to-day operations within the limits of the resources currently available. It usually needs to be accompanied by estimates of the random fluctuations which the tactical decisions aim to reduce.'[34] Short-term forecasts are primarily concerned, therefore, with tactical planning. Medium-term forecasting acts as a check-point indicating whether or not progress is being maintained along long-term trend lines. Medium-term forecasts are valuable in checking on the optimum use of corporate resources. The third category of forecast, i.e. long-term, 'provides information for major strategic decisions: it is concerned with extending or reducing the limits of the resources'[34] mainly affecting capital expenditure. Clearly, the longer the time period, the greater the probability that new environmental factors will arise. 'For the generality of industries five years is the basic period forecast and in nearly every case a short-term view of from one to two years is incorporated in the forecast . . . in most cases the forecast forms part of an annual business plan, sometimes being subject to revision during the course of the year.'[35]

Some discrimination should be exercised in using the expressions 'short term', 'medium term' and 'long term', because perceptions will be influenced by the nature of particular industries. Battersby[34] has pointed out that the Post Office looks 40 years ahead; shipbuilders' short-term forecasts would be very different in the period covered from those of a consumer products manufacturer, whose market changes much more rapidly. Capital goods are not subject to the violent swings that often characterise consumer products such as fashion clothing. Lead time will also vary considerably across industries; specially skilled labour may require a training period extending over several months and even years, adding further to the complexity and uncertainty of long-term forecasting and planning.

Lord Weinstock, who has dominated GEC for many years, has characteristically strong views on corporate planning horizons: 'Five-year plans are usually not five-year plans at all because, even when people do take notice of them, they are almost invariably changed every year. So that is not a five-year plan, it is a one-year plan.' He feels that there is a danger that five-year or even three-year plans may well lead executives to think that they are able to have more control over the destiny of their companies than is actually the case. Such plans 'are apt to deflect people from reality'. GEC demands that all its planning activities should be 'infinitely flexible'; blind adherence to detailed plans is no substitute for business flair. As Lord Weinstock's deputy drily commented: 'People who have flair have a feeling whether they should do something or not, they don't have to pore over highly speculative figures for days.'[36]

FUNDAMENTAL QUESTIONS FOR CORPORATE PLANNERS

This initial phase of corporate planning should, if it is done thoroughly, include answers to the following fundamental questions:

1. What kind of organisation are we managing?
2. Why does our organisation exist?
3. What kinds of customer/client do we aim to serve?
4. What kinds of product/service do these customers need?
5. What are we particularly good at doing?
6. How does this strength relate to market needs?
7. What are our competitors doing?
8. What makes us different from our competitors?
9. What should we do to improve our market position in (a) the short term; (b) the long term?
10. What should we do to achieve these criteria?

PLANNING STAGE 2: DEVELOPMENT OF STRATEGIC PLAN

In stage 1, the objectives of the organisation will have been clearly stated in relation to its corporate resources. These objectives may be diverse, ranging from improved market performance leading to profitability (in the stringent economic environment of today, this may be secondary to corporate survival dependent upon adequate cash flows) to, as in the case of public sector education and welfare activities, more effective allocation of available services.

The term 'strategy' has become widely adopted in business circles, particularly related to the production and marketing of a great variety of goods and services. Academics have enthusiastically dedicated themselves to researching this impressively titled management function. Buzz words have abounded, while volumes on strategic management become weightier. Ambitious adoption may have obscured appreciation of its essential nature and purpose. Almost every business activity now tends to be labelled 'strategic', so a brief reflection on the origin and applications of strategy should help to indicate its specific value in developing the marketing performance of an organization.

In Mintzberg's view, one of the more important functions of management is to make strategy for their organisations, 'or at least oversee the process by which they and others make strategies'. He goes on to say that 'in a narrow sense, strategy-making deals with the positioning of an organization in market niches', but in a broader sense it refers to how the collective system called organisation establishes and, if necessary, changes its basic orientation. Further, strategy making is seen to be concerned with 'the complex issue of collective intention – how an organization composed of many people makes up *its* mind, so to speak'.[8]

But Mintzberg warns that 'like every theory, strategy is a simplification that necessarily distorts reality. Strategies and theories are not reality themselves, only representations (that is, abstractions) of reality in the minds of people'.[37] He concedes, however, that good strategies, like good theories, minimise the degree of distortion.

The concept of strategy as applied to management first occured in 1948 when Von Neumann and Morgenstern presented their now well-known business games theory. Antony Jay, in his stimulating text *Management and Machiavelli*, has suggested:

> The first transference you have to make when studying political history in management terms is to read 'economic conflict' for 'military conflict'. The difference between killing and selling may, objectively, be rather more than superficial, but not in the qualities they demand of those planning and executing the campaign.[38]

Military metaphors have been further pursued by Kotler and Singh,[39] who comment that Clausewitz saw war as a necessary means to pursue national self-interest, its objective being to vanquish the enemy by achieving unconditional surrender. On the other hand, Liddell Hart, the greatest twentieth-century military theorist, saw the objective of war to be a better state of peace and was severely critical of Clausewitz's theory of total annihilation.

In business terms, cut-throat competition can lead to ultimate defeat, so modern competitors rarely adopt the Clausewitzian objective. In the United States, this type of competition is inhibited by the anti-trust laws, apart from the generally unacceptable outcome of forcing utter defeat on competitors. Liddell Hart's doctrine may be a more appropriate guide for business people. Giant firms may well compromise on market shares, at least in the short term.

Peaceful coexistence may indeed be present in some markets and encourage firms to seek niches or segments where they can exercise comparative advantage. (Market segmentation strategies will be discussed in the next chapter.)

Attack strategies, based on the military model, should make use of the 'principle of mass', namely that superior contact power must be concentrated at the critical time and place for decisive action. Five possible strategies are identified as: frontal; flanking; encirclement; bypass; and guerrilla.

For pure frontal attack to succeed, an aggressor needs to have strength over competitors. Military dogma asserts that for frontal attack to be successful against a well-entrenched opponent or one controlling the 'high ground', the attacking force must deploy a 3:1 advantage in fire power.

A modified form of frontal attack is commonly used, such as cutting prices related to those of other suppliers. This could be effective provided the market leader does not retaliate and also that customers perceive good value in the cut-price product and are willing to buy it. Texas Instruments is quoted as being brilliantly successful in using the price weapon strategically; it invested heavily in R&D and moved very rapidly down the experience curve (see Chapter 6).

Flanking attacks concentrate on weak spots; an aggressor may act as if he will attack the strong side to tie up defenders' troops, but actually launch an attack at the side or rear. His limited resources limit an aggressor's use of force, so he uses subterfuge.

Encirclement – also called 'envelopment' – involves launching a grand offensive on several fronts so that the enemy must protect its front, sides and rear simultaneously. However, for this strategy to succeed the aggressor must have superior forces.

Bypass attack is analogous to peacetime political warfare ('cold war'). This might be reflected in commercial terms by diversifying into unrelated products and into new geographical markets for existing products. In these ways the main enemy is avoided and easier target markets are attacked, which enable the business base to be broadened. In the United States, Colgate had traditionally fought against Procter and Gamble until it was recognised that head-on battle was futile. The new strategy involved maintaining Colgate's lead abroad and bypassing Procter and Gamble at home by diversifying into markets where there was no Procter and Gamble presence. Several acquisitions in textiles, hospital products, cosmetics, sporting goods and food goods enabled Colgate to re-establish its business strength: in 1971 Colgate was underdog to Procter and Gamble in about half of its business, but by 1976 it either was comfortably placed or faced no competition at all from Procter and Gamble in 75 per cent of its business.

Guerrilla warfare consists of making small, intermittent attacks on different territories held by an opponent, with the aim of harassing and demoralising him and eventually securing concessions. In business terms this might be achieved, for example, through selective price cuts, intense promotional bursts of activity, and 'assorted legal actions against the opponent'[39] related to possible violations of anti-trust law, trademark infringement and deceptive trade practices. This pin-pricking strategy, although normally practised by a smaller firm against a larger one, and less expensive than the other strategies outlined, is not necessarily cheap in terms of resources. In the end it has to be backed by a stronger attack if the opponent is to be beaten.

Six defence strategies modelled on military engagements have been identified as: position defence ('fortified front line'); mobile defence ('defence in depth'); pre-emptive defence ('offensive defence'); 'flank-positioning' defence; 'counter-offensive' in defence; and 'hedgehog' defence ('strategic withdrawal').

Position defence is tied to a psychology of 'fortification'. The French Maginot Line and the German Siegfried Line were twentieth-century versions of the medieval fortresses, suggesting impregnability; but all failed in time.

In the business world, static defence is marketing myopia: the myth of the invincible product. Like frontal attack, it is one of the riskiest military strategies. 'Henry Ford's myopia about his Model T brought an enviably healthy company to the brink of financial ruin.'[39]

Mobile defence occurs when a firm attempts to stretch its domain over new territories that can serve as future centres for defence or counter-attack. Market expansion would be carefully controlled to avoid wasted efforts.

Pre-emptive defence ('offensive defence') assumes that prevention is better than cure; war, not peace, is considered to be the natural state of business. All the various attack strategies could be used in pre-emptive defence, the aim being to keep the competition always on the defensive.

'Flank positioning' defence occurs when a firm establishes a flanking 'position' as a hedge against some probable but uncertain event, or as a defensive corner overlooking a weak front. As in the military sphere, this strategy is of little value if it is so lightly held that it could easily be frustrated by a small force, while the main force passes by unmolested.

'Counter-offensive' in defence strategy is when the defender can respond to an attack by mobilising reserves and counter-attacking vigourosly by either head-on, flanking or pincer movement strategies. To do this effectively, a defender should identify a chink in the attacker's armour, namely a segment gap.

'Hedgehog' defence, or strategic withdrawal, occurs when a firm decides to consolidate its competitive strength and to concentrate resources at strategic points for counter-attack. This may involve rationalisation of product ranges and strategic withdrawal from fragmented market segments.

The various attack and defence strategies which have been outlined indicate some of the alternatives open to business planners. Since companies frequently borrow from the military strategists in describing their market behaviour, knowledge of certain martial theories may help in constructing marketing plans.

As observed earlier, managers, like Molière's prose-speaker, frequently adopt a business strategy of some kind without being consciously aware of its theoretical origin. With relatively small enterprises where personal ownership and management are not seperate functions, strategy is not formalised; the policy-maker is also responsible for the tasks of management. However, as the organisation develops, managerial responsibilities tend to become divorced from ownership, and specific aspects of management, such as marketing strategy, are delegated. The need for an explicit strategy then becomes apparent. In this case, a working plan, sometimes referred to as a mission statement, should set out clearly the marketing objectives of the company, and indicate the roles and responsibilities of individuals, who need to work closely and effectively together to ensure that the organisational goals are achieved.

Strategy is concerned with the broader aspects of organisational performance; it maps out the roads to be traversed – alternative routes will need to be studied – to reach the planned destination. The vehicles to be used are a tactical choice (the third stage of planning).

Two schools of thought in the development of a strategic plan have been identified as occupying different positions on a continuum: at one end is the 'rational–comprehensive method', while at the other end is the 'process of disjointed incrementalism'.[40]

The first method makes three basic assumptions: (1) that the goals and objectives of a company can be clearly identified and agreed upon; (2) that the strategic planner has access to complete information; and (3) that the selected strategy is rationally chosen by all members of the organisation.

The other method – disjointed incrementalism – directly challenges the views held by the rational–comprehensive approach. It proposes instead that it is virtually impossible for either an individual or an organisation to deal adequately with the complexity and conflict confronting them; it recognises that data, both internal and external, are frequently not available; and it accepts that individual members of an organisation tend to have different goals and objectives that cannot be dealt with satisfactorily by a single set of decisions.

This alternative approach to the development of corporate strategy involves a continuous process of choice between policies that differ only marginally from the status quo. Objectives are more implied than explicit, and gradually, through a series of decisions, a strategy appears.

Not surprisingly perhaps, the researchers agree that strategy in most cases is formed by a combination of the two contrasting approaches. 'Broad strategic decisions are based on partially formulated objectives and incomplete estimates of external and internal affairs'.[40] These broad strategies are then put into effect in a stepwise manner and modified from time to time in response to new information and pressures from members of the organisation.

Porter[30] perceives competitive strategy as taking offensive or defensive action in order to create a *defendable* position relative to the five competitive forces enumerated earlier in this chapter. This involves several potential approaches:

1. Positioning the firm strongly against competitors.
2. Influencing the balance of power by strategic moves, such as product innovation or large-scale capital investment.
3. Anticipating changes in market behaviour and adopting a proactive strategy.

Whatever strategic plan is devised, it is essential that marketing information is up to date and objective (see Chapter 4).

Virtually all strategies, according to Porter,[30] can be classified in one of three generic categories: (1) *overall cost leadership*; (2) *differentiation*; and (3) *focus*. The first refers to companies deliberately seeking to be the *lowest cost producers* in their industry, so enabling them to be price leaders. This position may be achieved through economies of scale (see the section on pricing, pp. 188–97), which are likely to be associated with the experience curve effect (refer to the marketing portfolio approach, pp. 233–61).

Differentiation, as the name suggests, involves efforts by companies to become identified by their customers and prospects with specific attributes of their products and services, such as quality, technical back-up services, effective distribution and speedy deliveries. These factors should, of course, be specifically related to market needs.

A focus strategy is based on effective market segmentation and targeting within well-defined sectors, as discussed in Chapter 6.

These three strategies are not, of course, exclusive, as Toyota and other companies dedicated to manufacturing excellence have demonstrated. Firms may adopt a variety of these according to the situations experienced in the specific markets in which they operate. Like all theories and their resultant typologies, crude applications should be avoided; sensitive interpretation is to be preferred.

FACETS OF MARKETING STRATEGY

Marketing strategy has several aspects: product range strategy; pricing; promotional activities and selling and distribution (place). Popularly known as the four Ps, these various marketing inputs together produce the *marketing mix* (see Figure 5.4); combinations of the inputs are needed to secure particular marketing objectives.

1. PRODUCT RANGE STRATEGY

Product planning

Product or service planning is strategic because the growth of an organisation

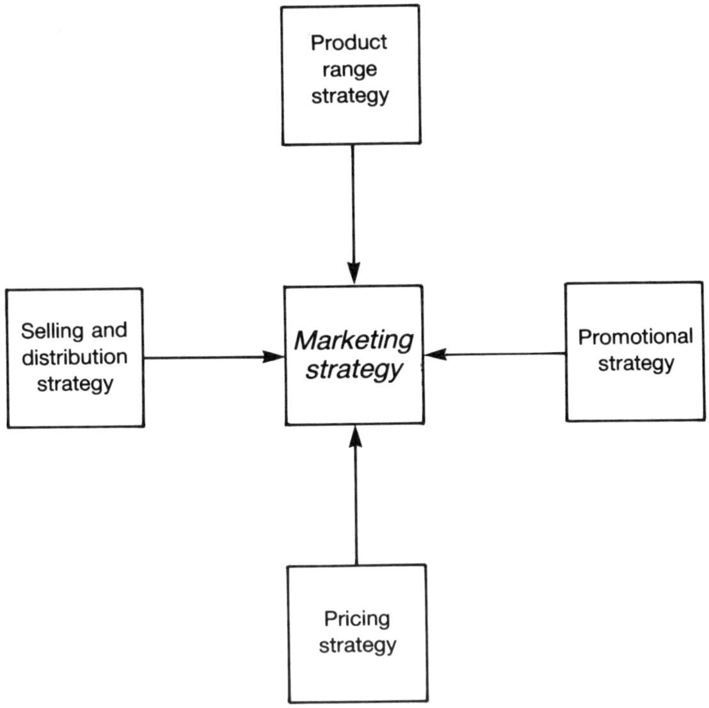

FIGURE 5.4 Facets of marketing strategy

depends largely on the development of new products or services, the elimination of outmoded or unprofitable lines, and the improvement of existing products/services to give better satisfaction to customers or clients. (In Chapter 7 the innovation of products is discussed in some detail.)

In 1957, Ansoff[41] projected a useful matrix (see Figure 5.5) to enable companies to assess their market efforts and growth opportunities. This basic matrix has since been developed and freely used by many researchers.

Option 1: Market penetration is based on existing products in existing markets with the objective of increasing business through more effective marketing. Three courses are feasible: (1) stimulate consumption of products; (2) take business from competitors; and (3) attract non-users to buy the product. Where markets are experiencing zero growth and purchasing frequency cannot be increased, a desperate fight for market shares will be evident.

Option 2: Market development focuses on selling existing products in new markets or market segments. This can be achieved by (1) opening up additional geographical markets (home or overseas); or (2) developing alternative versions of existing products to appeal to defined market segments not at present served.

Option 3: Product development produces a policy of product innovation for sale in current markets. This may involve intrinsically new types of product derived from technological inventions, or product adaptations and improvements.

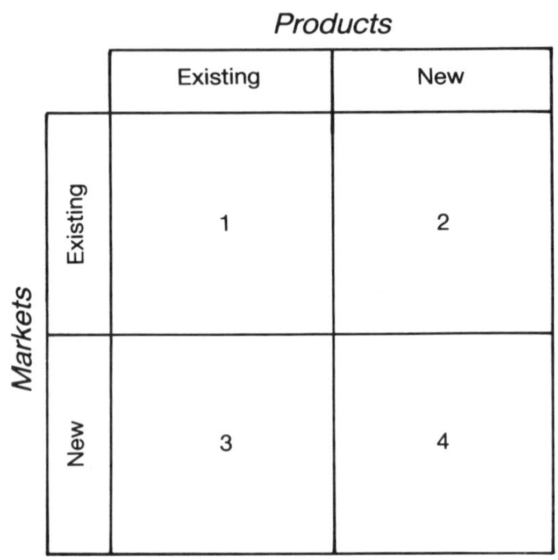

FIGURE 5.5 Product/market matrix (Source: Ansoff[41])

In 1992 Courtaulds, which had demerged its textiles operation two years earlier, announced improved profits and a dual-track strategy for growth based on a material called Tencel to be marketed globally. This innovatory artificial fibre is targeted at the high-quality cotton market; it does not need dry-cleaning and can be laundered like cotton. Sipko Huismans, Chief Executive of Courtaulds Textiles,[42] confessed that the group had made mistakes in the past, either because it had failed to understand the market or because it had underestimated the reaction of competitors. But he remained very optimistic about Tencel's market opportunities, which he intended the company to exploit itself rather than through setting up co-marketing agreements.

Option 4: Diversification entails both new products and new markets and is the most radical of the options outlined. This enterprising strategy compounds the risks to which a firm is likely to be exposed when it seeks to grow by a mix of both new products and new markets.

Kotler[3] outlines three broad types of diversification: concentric, horizontal and conglomerate. Concentric diversification occurs when a company adds new products or services which have technological and/or marketing synergies with current products and which, generally, will appeal to new customer groups. Horizontal diversification occurs when a company adds new products that are technologically unrelated to current products, but which could appeal to current customers. Conglomerate diversification occurs when a company markets new products that are unrelated to current experience, but which could appeal to new classes of customer.

Diversification – not putting all your eggs into one basket – is age-old advice to investors, but has often proved a dangerous policy for businesses to adopt. Over the past few years, companies have increasingly shed acquisitions which have frequently led them outside their corporate competences. The Prudential Corporation, one of Britain's leading life assurance companies, spent £230m on what proved to be a disastrous diversification into estate agency. In November 1990, it was announced that the Pru was 'going back to basics'. Other financial organisations have also abandoned their much-vaunted forays into extensive networks of estate agencies. They were, undoubtedly, unlucky in their timing, which closely coincided with a severe recession in the housing market, but a more critical factor was their lack of managerial skills at head office level to assimilate and develop these expensive diversifications, which proved to be intrinsically unrelated to their core businesses.

Porter critically observes that 'unrelated diversification almost inevitably detracts from focus, commitment, and sustained investment in the core industries'. He notes that in the USA and Britain, this form of diversification 'seems to have contributed to competitive problems', and draws attention to the fact that in continental Europe and Japan, 'many of the strongest international companies are either not diversified or have diversified into closely related businesses, often through internal development'.[31] It is the latter type of diversification which has been remarkably productive, and was used, for example, by Sandvik when it shifted from speciality steels to rock drills, and by Canon in its dramatic evolution from being a camera-making company into producing whole new ranges of office equipment, such as calculators and copiers.

There are, however, a few conglomerates which seem to be exceptions to the rule quoted above. Skilful operators like Hanson choose their acquisitions carefully and tend to concentrate on mature, low-technology, short-cycle businesses which are not very capital intensive. These are compatible with Hanson's hands-off parenting style.[43]

Product positioning

Product (or brand) positioning is a very useful concept in assessing marketing opportunities; it refers to the place occupied by a particular product in a given market. This evaluation should be comparative and assessed by measuring customers' (or consumers') perceptions and preferences for all products (or brands) of a type available in a specific market.

A 'perceptual map' could be designed showing how customers perceived competitive firms and/or comparative products along certain dimensions or attributes. Figure 5.6 maps six companies' perceived positions along the dimensions of quality and price. Where positions are mapped close to one another, it may be assumed that these companies are in fairly direct competition. Special computer programmes have been developed to generate perceptual maps, but considerable care needs to be exercised because of the degree of subjectivity associated with this positioning technique.

Positioning may relate to one or more features such as intrinsic design, suitability for special uses (e.g. under water), well-known firm or brand name,

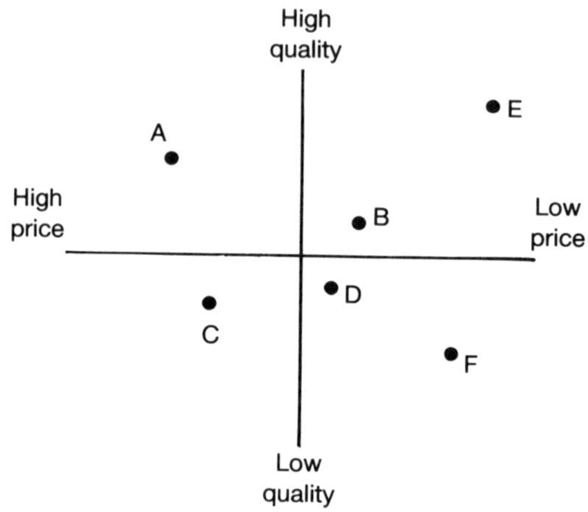

FIGURE 5.6 Two-dimensional perceptual map of six companies relative to specific product ranges

industry track record, or established name for technological innovation. In a study a few years ago of the UK car market, the relative positioning of the principal suppliers indicated quite distinctive market segments (see Figure 5.7).

Product positioning analysis enables marketing management to understand better the nature of competition relative to certain types of product and market. This comparative evaluation may give clues as to how products might be developed to coincide more closely with customers' perceived needs and to give suppliers a competitive edge. In some instances it may be feasible to reposition a product through more skilful promotion, by design modifications or by new channels of distribution. Strategic repositioning of products and/or services may be desirable from time to time as technological and other changes affect market demand.

Product portfolio

Businesses are most likely to have products and markets at various stages of development, and it is important that they should know of the relative distribution of sales and profits over these sectors. Innovation, discussed later, is crucial to corporate development. At the same time, risk is a significant factor in decisions regarding new products and new market ventures, particularly those where a company lacks significant technological or marketing experience.

A creative product strategy aims to build a balanced product range which optimises productive efficiency and marketing effectiveness. The product or service mix should be wide enough to attract and retain customers' interest; at the same time, firms should not aspire to be universal providers in these days of high-cost operations.

The portfolio method of market planning adopts the analytical approach of financial investment, which has the objective of spreading risk and the opportun-

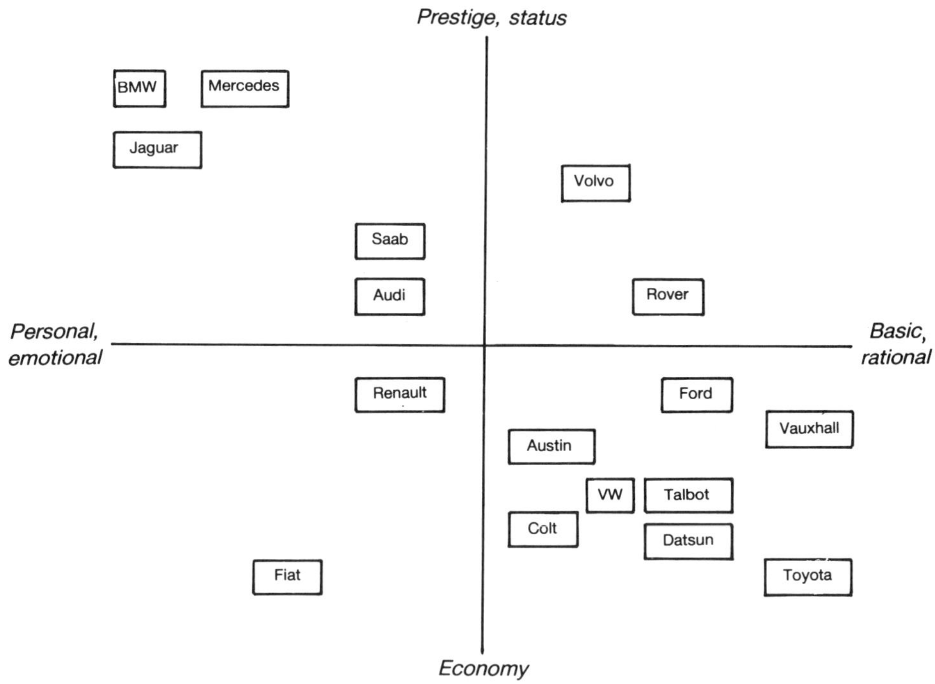

FIGURE 5.7 Perceptual map of UK car market

ities of profit across a balanced range of investments. Like an investment portfolio, different combinations of products and markets may be devised by companies according to their objectives, experience and resources. The product/market grid shown in Figure 5.5 can be further elaborated by developing profit projections for each of the cells which a company is operating in or planning to enter.

More attention will be given to portfolio planning in the next chapter. It might be enlightening here to recall Levitt's[44] reflection that most companies have products which can be classified in one of the following categories:

1. 'Yesterday's winners' – products, at one time profitable, which, because of declining demand or intensifying competition, now contribute little if anything to corporate earnings.
2. 'Today's providers' – these products are the backbone of corporate profitability, 'the milk cows on which all else feeds'.
3. 'Tomorrow's hopefuls' – these products are being developed or have been recently launched; as yet they are not self-supporting, but their sales performance so far suggests that they may become 'the milk cows of the future'.

An even more pungent classification described a typical product range as (1) killers; (2) fillers; and (3) thrillers. On reflection most companies would agree that on a contribution basis, their products qualify for inclusion in one of these categories.

2. PRICING STRATEGY

Pricing is a critical element in the overall marketing strategy: it is one of the most difficult tasks facing management. Price is only one of the variables which contribute to the marketing mix; it is interrelated with the other factors affecting buying decisions, such as product design, after-sales service and promotional efforts. Pricing cannot, therefore, be considered in isolation; it certainly should not be determined without a thorough appraisal of the contributions made by the other elements in the marketing strategy.

Pricing can be projected as an active, dynamic part of marketing strategy, planned to achieve certain corporate objectives; or it may play merely a subservient role in the marketing of goods and services. Some specific pricing objectives may relate to attracting quick cash flow without profit maximisation: keen pricing may be pursued in order to enhance market share; prices may be set to achieve minimum levels of return on investment; there may be cases where unusually high prices can be charged because of relative scarcity, product patents, technological supremacy, etc. Firms tend to have pricing strategies relative to specific market environments.

The problem of industrial pricing was the focus of a survey, *How British Industry Prices*,[45] published in 1975 and still very relevant. In most industrial companies, pricing appeared to be cost dominated and little influenced by marketing policy. There was little variation in pricing behaviour over the three types of industrial market covered – capital goods, components and materials. The vast majority of companies reported that prices were fixed in relation to costs either by adding a customary percentage to costs or by establishing a required gross profit margin. Only about one-fifth of respondent companies said that selling prices for at least some of their products were primarily affected by factors other than costs, but even then they tended to adopt mainly a defensive pricing posture and follow the general level of prices set by competitors.

The survey also found little evidence that discounts were used effectively to promote marketing objectives; the most common basis of discounts was customer classification rather than more directly sales-related factors such as quantity per order or volume bought over an agreed period. It seemed that the granting of discounts had degenerated into a routine activity which had little relevance to the actual volume of business transacted.

Only about one-third of the companies surveyed carried out any kind of formal investigation of price acceptability before setting prices. Likewise, the results of pricing decisions were hardly ever investigated apart from a few relatively elementary enquiries. In general, systematic marketing research involving pricing policies was rarely used.

Interaction of demand and supply on prices

Specific markets (or segments) have particular pricing problems; many influences operate, but it is possible to isolate some general factors. One which is significant refers to the relevant demand–supply position. The interaction of demand and supply and its impact on prices should be considered at three levels: (1) raw materials and bought-in component parts; (2) the nature of the demand for the industrial goods produced from these supplies; and (3) the nature of the demand for the products which are made from the industrial goods in (2).

Some of the principal factors affecting levels of demand (and prices) in organisational supplies were outlined in Chapter 2. Of particular importance is the fact that organisational buyers may be more sensitive to factors in the marketing mix other than merely price. Price is an indicator of quality as well as an economic label: the concept of value is subjective. Buckner's[46] research showed that price reductions below 1 per cent of existing market suppliers' prices caused virtually no change in choice of supplier. But price reductions of 1 to 9 per cent resulted in significant switching of supply sources; approximately 40 per cent of buyers said they would be prepared to change suppliers. Where price reductions were over 10 per cent, 14 per cent of buyers were reported to be willing to accept new suppliers; this indicates that if prices are reduced too much, suspicions about quality, for instance, tend to be aroused. Fewer sales may in fact result for the firm which attempts to expand its market share by severe price cutting.

Demand factors are usually responsible for setting price ceilings; cost factors form a floor (or several floors) for pricing in a market. But neither floor nor ceiling is necessarily static: they may be changed by promotional activities (lifting demand) or by a different allocation of costs (raising or lowering the floor). Competitive activities, technological developments, etc., may also intrude to affect pricing.

Trading structure and pricing strategy

Another important factor which influences prices relates to the trading structure in particular industries. In Chapter 2 the incidence of concentration factors was observed to affect buying behaviour and, particularly, bargaining power. Trading structures range from a situation where many firms of approximately the same size are active in a market which has minimal barriers to entry, to a monopolistic (or near-monopolistic) market situation where one or two very large firms dominate supply and entry to the market is extremely difficult. The majority of industries are characterised by a mixture of large, medium and small firms. Price competition is affected significantly by the balance which exists between the various sizes of firm. The more suppliers which exist within an industry with an equitable distribution of market shares, the more marked will be the tendency for price competition to be active.

Pricing decisions are complex and should thus be considered against the following factors:

1. Nature and extent of demand.
2. Competitors' activities (influenced by the trading structure).
3. Costs of production and marketing.

4. Pricing objectives (business policy).
5. Product life cycle (discussed in next chapter).

Effect on pricing policy of horizontal and vertical integration

Some companies have developed vertically integrated organisations in an effort to exercise some measure of control on market demand at several levels of production and distribution. Horizontal integration is aimed at reducing the level of competition at a specific level, e.g. manufacturing, with the objective of reducing costs and achieving higher profits through economies of scale, rationalisation of production, etc. The degree of integration and the level of price competition in an industry tend to be closely linked.

In a study of 1,649 US manufacturing processing units, Buzzell[47] found that because vertical integration requires managers to invest considerable capital in new operations, the strategy may not be productive from a cost/savings viewpoint. However, he also observed that integration strategies are often successful, both in terms of profitability and greater production innovation, especially for firms enjoying strong market positions.

Bid pricing

Public sector organisations are subject to statutory controls; these are likely to stipulate that certain supplies must be obtained through competitive tendering. Firms are invited by advertisement to quote for specific contracts, e.g. road construction, and sealed bids are deposited with the buying authority. It is customary for the lowest bid to be accepted, but in some cases a company which has made an attractive, though not necessarily the lowest, offer may be invited to negotiate further.

Sealed-bid pricing, as Kotler observes,[3] is a prime example of pricing based on expectations of how competitors will price rather than on a fixed ratio to a firm's costs or to demand. While a firm may be very interested in securing a particular contract, its bid cannot be less than marginal cost without damaging its business position. However, the higher its price is raised above marginal cost, the less likelihood there is that it will be successful in attracting the desired business.

Firms need to consider the probability of getting a contract at a particular bid price against the potential profit. A series of calculations at various price levels will indicate the expected profits and guide the final bid price (potential profit x probability = expected profit).

Price collusion

Companies may seek to reduce price competition and establish some control over markets by some form of collusion, generally unofficial. Legal sanctions usually apply against such trading practices.

Importance of identifying nature of costs

An efficient system of costing is vital for management pricing decisions. These costs should be clearly identified so that the nature of their impact is understood. Costs are the foundation of prices.

Basically, costs are usually divided into two general categories – fixed and variable. Fixed costs do not vary significantly with volume of output over a stated period of time (rent, salaries, insurance, etc.). Variable costs, as the name suggests, vary – often proportionately – according to changes in the volume of output (labour, power, raw materials, etc.). The critical factor is the relationship in the overall cost structure between these two main types of cost.

Another way of looking at costs is to classify them as either incremental or full. Incremental costs refer to the direct costs of labour, materials and supervision incurred if a particular order is taken and which would not arise otherwise. Full costs include the direct costs and also the apportioned overheads, such as administration and depreciation, which of course apply whether or not a specific order is booked.

When a business operates below capacity, the general tendency is to accept orders that will cover incremental costs and make a *contribution* to overheads. In the short term this policy is often sound, but it could be dangerous if it became extended indefinitely.

In the crisis conditions of world markets where prices of raw materials are subject to violent changes, up-to-date costing information is clearly more important than ever. Pricing in times of chronic inflation is a nightmare exercise for which no really satisfactory guidelines have yet emerged.

Costing may well become counterproductive if the system or data used are no longer valid; and some products, previously regarded as liabilities, may be capable of rendering acceptable returns, as Sir John Harvey-Jones indicates in his pragmatic text.[18] In another case,[48] a manufacturing company had decided to apply a 6 per cent price increase across the whole range of its products; but it first of all improved its costing system, which enabled production costs to be evaluated against specific products, and the impact of the proposed increase was examined in relation to competitors' products. It was discovered that two loss-making lines could not sustain any price increases; these were eliminated, cutting a loss of £47,000. Prices of the remaining products were adjusted in various ways, from decreases up to 30 per cent increases. As a result of this more enlightened approach, profits increased £70,000 over and above what would have been achieved by the 6 per cent increase.

Finally, profitability may be improved by increasing the volume of goods made and marketed, or by reducing costs and improving productivity. Cost-cutting, product rationalisation strategies are primarily defensive, although, in the short term at least, they may be the only viable approaches which could be adopted by companies threatened by more ambitious competitors. The alternative strategy of expanding production, which may lead to economies of scale, requires skilful evaluation of market trends, the development of an effective marketing programme, and shrewd assessment of the risks attached to this enterprising activity.

Basic approaches to pricing

(a) *Cost-oriented pricing*. Also known as cost-plus or mark-up pricing, cost-oriented pricing is very widely used; its simplicity is also its weakness, for little account is taken of market behaviour, i.e. customers' expectations or competitors' activities. Merely to add together the costs of raw materials, labour, overheads, etc. and then apply some traditional 'mark-up' percentage ignores not only the nature of demand, but also the nature of the costs involved.

As already observed, costs are generally classified as either fixed (indirect) or variable (direct). The cost-oriented basis of pricing can then be simply projected as follows:

$$\text{Price} = \text{Fixed (direct) costs} + \text{Variable (indirect) costs} \times \%\ \text{profit margin}$$

Businesses often calculate prices on some type of standard costing base, using a traditional formula developed from experience, as the following example typifies:

Direct (variable) costs	£	£
Materials	125	
Labour	75	200
Indirect (fixed) costs		
Overheads		
(50% of direct costs)		100
Total cost		300
Profit margin (25%)		75
Selling price		£375

While this pricing system seems quite easy, its efficiency depends on knowing, with a fair degree of accuracy, the total amount of overheads, and also having a reliable estimate or forecast of the total volume of sales of specific types of product or service for the trading year involved. So, it will readily be seen that sound estimates are the foundation of costs and resultant prices. If these prove unreliable, then prices will be radically wrong and the effect on the business could be catastrophic.

(b) *Break-even analysis*. Since costs are estimates and are affected by volume of projected sales, it would be wise to make an attempt to find out what is likely to happen if the relationship between fixed costs and variable costs changed over time because sales increased.

Break-even analysis can be used where products or services are of a uniform type and total overheads (indirect or fixed costs) and gross profit are known. For example:

$$\text{Break-even } (B/E) = \frac{\text{Overheads}}{\text{Gross profit (\%)}} \times 100$$

If overheads were £30,000 and gross profit margin was 25%, then B/E would be:

$$\frac{£30,000}{25} \times 100 = £120,000 \text{ annual sales}$$

or £10,000 monthly sales

At this level of sales, the business would be at a break-even point, i.e. making neither a profit nor a loss. However, it should be realised that the break-even point is affected by increases or decreases in gross margin, and increases or decreases in overheads (the latter are not likely to remain unaffected by inflation and other increases).

If total sales	=	£200,000
and *B/E* (as example)	=	£120,000
and gross profit margin	=	25%
then, profit (year)	=	£20,000 (i.e. 10% net profit on total sales)

In addition to the effects of the changes in overheads, reductions in variable costs, for example, can have the greatest impact on marginal profitability, i.e. reduce the level of sales at which the break-even point operates. This may be effected through improved product design, perhaps incorporating fewer components with resultant economies in production and assembly, or by production engineering improvements leading to more efficient, lower-cost production, or from marketing efficiencies such as more productive selling efforts.

$$\text{Let break-even point} = S \times \frac{FC}{C}$$

where *FC* refers to fixed costs
C is contribution
S refers to sales

Applying this formula to the figures in the previous example (as shown in Figure 5.8) gives:

$$B/E = \frac{£200{,}000 \times 30{,}000}{C}$$

C is calculated below and is derived from the equation $A-B$.

A	Total sales	=	£200,000
	Fixed costs	=	30,000
			170,000
	Profit	=	20,000

B Variable costs are, therefore, £150,000.

Since $C = A-B$, then by substitution

$$C = £200{,}000 - £150{,}000 = £50{,}000$$

Applying this to the formula given above:

$$B/E = £200{,}000 \times \frac{30{,}000}{50{,}000}$$

$$= £120{,}000 \text{ (as shown in the example and Figure 5.8)}$$

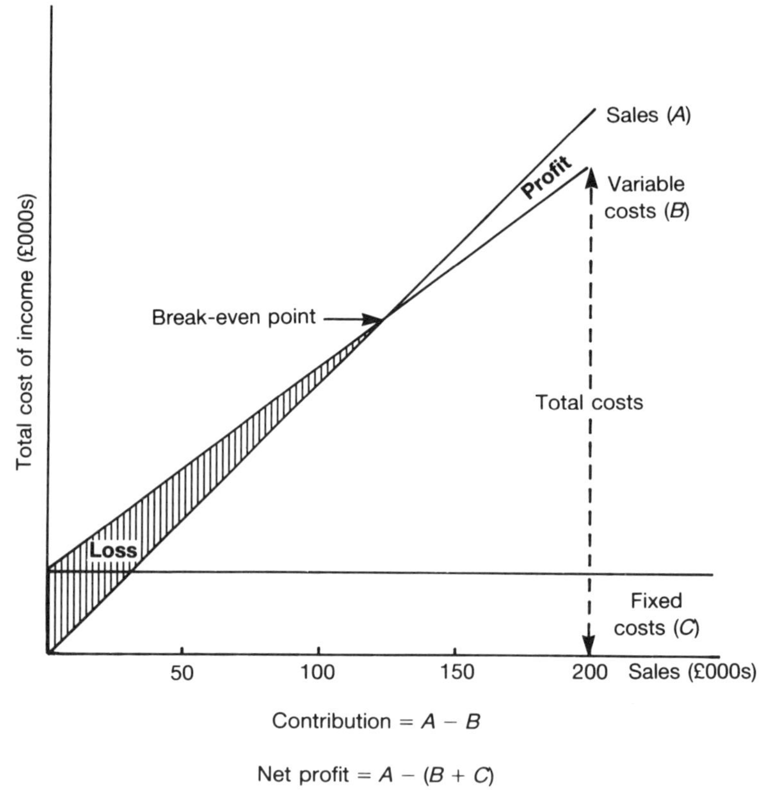

FIGURE 5.8 Break-even analysis

Now, if variable costs are reduced by, say, 5 per cent to £142,500, contribution will increase by £7,500 to £57,500 and break-even point will fall to:

$$£200{,}000 \times \frac{30{,}000}{57{,}500} = \text{approx. } £104{,}348$$

At the same time, overall profits have increased, it may be assumed, to £27,500, i.e. 13.75 per cent on sales, compared with the original 10 per cent.

Certain assumptions are incorporated into break-even analysis: for instance, that costs move linearly with output, and that variations in output have no effect on prices charged. With these points in mind and also because many markets are increasingly volatile with fierce price competition, static analysis like break-even should be approached warily. But used with care, it provides useful managerial evaluations, particularly on the relative effects of changes in costs on overall financial performance.

(c) 'Contribution' pricing. Another approach to pricing is worth attention; it is based on the principle of 'contribution', i.e. the amount that is left after total direct costs have been deducted from the selling price, and which *contributes to the overheads of a business*. As noted in break-even analysis:

Selling price − Total direct costs = Contribution to overheads.

The contribution basis of pricing has two special applications: (1) in cases of limited production capacity when decisions have to be made about volumes of specific products to be made; and (2) when decisions have to be made about accepting certain types of business – which may be below customary price levels.

When a business is operating below capacity, the general tendency is to accept orders that will cover direct costs and make a *contribution* to overheads. In the short term this policy is often sound, but it could be dangerous if it became extended indefinitely. When conditions have improved and full or near-maximum capacity is operating, only those orders which yield high, or the highest, contribution should be accepted. Again, it is very important to check costs before starting 'contribution' pricing. An example of the contribution approach to pricing is given below:

Sales		
1,000 units @ £10		£10,000
less Direct costs		
Materials @ £4 per unit	£4,000	
Labour @ £2 per unit	2,000	6,000
		£4,000
	=	£4 (this figure should be evaluated against total overheads)

Across total product range, different 'contributions' may emerge from analyses of costs, and prices could be adjusted up or down to ensure that overall profitability was maintained at an acceptable level.

(d) *Demand-oriented pricing.* As noted earlier, cost-oriented pricing is a narrow and incomplete approach to running a profitable business: more creative, demand-oriented pricing is needed. This acknowledges the fact that the demand for products and services influences prices. When demand is high, price may be set to take advantage of this market situation, although this may be only a temporary phase. Alternatively, prices may have to be 'trimmed', i.e. reduced, when demand falls significantly. Demand-oriented pricing requires a sound knowledge of demand trends and price sensitivities in each market segment in which a company operates or plans to do business. (Refer to Chapter 2 on elasticity of demand.)

(e) *Price discrimination.* This is a common type of demand-oriented pricing which may be effected on a customer basis (different levels of demand and relative buying power); or product differentiation may enable prices to be related to specific versions of products (as practised by Ford).

(f) *Market skimming.* Also known as 'prestige pricing' or 'creaming', this obviously depends on the novelty of the product (see Chapter 2 on elasticity of demand), its attributes and the likelihood of competition (e.g. compact discs).

(g) *Penetration pricing.* This is a deliberate policy of pricing low to attract maximum volume of sales quickly. As with prestige pricing, this strategy needs careful handling to avoid arousing a huge demand that could not be met from existing resources. Large volumes of sales may be counterproductive in terms of profits; chasing business at any price is a desperate tactic that is almost certain to end in disaster. No one buys price: they buy the expectation of benefits that will make their lives more pleasant, or their own businesses more profitable.

Positioning by price

As noted earlier, product (or brand) positioning is a very useful concept: it refers to the place occupied by a particular product in a given market. In addition to product design, packaging, promotion and methods of distribution, pricing can be used effectively to position a product relative to competitors' offerings. This suggests that some reliable information should be collected about competitors' products, pricing policies, etc. It can then be decided whether the product is marketed at the 'going rate' (*competitive parity*), lower than competitors (*competitive pricing*), or higher than competitors (*prestige pricing*).

Whatever pricing approach is adopted, the prospects of the business will be affected, so costs should be checked, competitors' likely reactions assessed, and the impact on sales evaluated at different levels. Competitive pricing in order to build up market share may well attract hostile reactions and start off a self-defeating price war.

Bear in mind that price conveys a message of quality; unless a product has unique attributes (and these are seldom unchallenged for long), it might be prudent to opt for the 'going rate', but to give special service back-up to customers. Most markets have price ranges for specific products; the skill lies in knowing the depth of this 'band of confidence' and positioning a product where it will benefit from being at the top end of this 'price band'.

In consumer markets, pioneer research into price sensitivities has been done by Gabor and Granger,[49] who, influenced by Jean Stoetzel of the Sorbonne, developed 'buy-response' curves related to specific types of product. Some leading marketing research firms have also developed special survey techniques related to pricing problems. (Buckner's research[46] on industrial price sensitivities was mentioned earlier in this chapter.)

Consistency of pricing in product range

Indiscriminate price reductions may adversely affect the total sales of a product range. Price reduction of a 'quality' product may shift sales from 'standard' lines of similar characteristics. The impact of price variations on sales of the total product range, and on its overall profitability, requires careful assessment. Pricing is, therefore, strategic in directing the profitable development of businesses.

Major factors affecting export pricing

Three major factors affect pricing in export trading: (1) changes in exchange rates; (2) changes in import duties; and (3) changes in transport, including insurance charges. The heavy fall in the trading value of the pound and the general uncertainty surrounding currency movements over recent years have added to the complexities of overseas trading, particularly export pricing strategies.

Exchange rate fluctuations have serious repercussions on profitability, especially where long-term trading commitments are involved – as in the supply of specially designed equipment or major contracts for the installation of textile or steel mills which take several years to complete. The country of destination and the strength of its currency clearly influence pricing decisions because it is less risky for an exporter to negotiate business in terms of a strong currency than the other way round.

Traditionally, British export business has been transacted in sterling, which was widely accepted as a dependable international currency. However, major British companies are now restructuring their export price lists. Overall, there are indications that sterling as a pricing base for British exporters, particularly those engaged in long-run business, is being abandoned in favour of quoting in currencies like the US dollar, the German Deutschmark or the Swiss franc.

The risks and actual costs involved in export business require objective analysis. There is a need, therefore, for systematic research into specific overseas markets to establish the nature of competition, the nature and level of demand, and the other important factors which are discussed in Chapter 8 dealing with international marketing.

The complexities of export pricing demand special and lengthy discussion which is outside the scope of this text. Essentially, management information for pricing to win overseas business should be developed methodically and, over time, regularly updated because of the complexity and dynamic nature of international markets.

PROMOTIONAL STRATEGY

Two facets of marketing stragety – product range and pricing – have been reviewed; the third input to the overall strategic plan relates to promotion. In Chapter 10 particular attention will be directed to the problems of corporate communications, including the promotion of organisational supplies and services. This chapter, which concentrates on strategic planning, is concerned with underlining the interdependence of the various inputs. Unfortunately, the promotional inputs to the overall strategic plan tend, in some firms, to be developed in relative isolation from the other contributory factors.

In organisational markets, promotional inputs to marketing strategy are often underrated and demoted to an inferior role. As a result, advertising agencies may be badly briefed, so that the resultant advertising campaigns do not seem to have direct relevance to overall marketing objectives. This myopic view of advertising is reflected in the low quality of a great deal of technical advertising, although over the past decade or so some industrial suppliers have greatly improved their standards of advertising. The leading management and professional journals now feature advertisements which are often extremely well designed – a refreshing distance from the flat-footed approach which generally stigmatised industrial, technical and professional promotional efforts.

Marketers of organisational supplies and services should be prepared to spend time and effort in planning promotional inputs that will reinforce the overall marketing strategy. A fully integrated plan is just as necessary in non-consumer markets as it is with chocolates, cosmetics or washing machines. (The logistics of planning advertising campaigns are discussed in Chapter 10.) Promotional strategies themselves depend on the effective linking of several variables: media, timing, intensity, etc. These demand professional skills which may partly be available within an organisation; more usually, however, they are drawn from the services of specialists advertising agencies. But as noted earlier, the essential point is for marketing management to ensure that promotional specialists work closely within the general marketing plan. While creative flair should not be stifled, marketing management have the final responsibility for developing an integrated and coherent marketing plan in which the various inputs are balanced effectively.

Of course, promotional activities are not solely concerned with tangible products. In the service industries (see Chapter 2), promotional policies play an important part in developing market demand. Not only in industrial services but also in the public sector, promotional activities have been most effective. There are several notable examples in the health and welfare services, e.g. the extremely successful 'immunisation' campaign which has played a large part in influencing parents to have their children safeguarded against diphtheria and other infectious diseases.

SELLING AND DISTRIBUTION (PLACE) STRATEGY

This fourth main input to the overall marketing strategic plan is particularly important in organisational markets. In Chapter 2 the logistics of supply affecting consumer and industrial products were compared. Selling is mainly affected by direct contact between manufacturers and their customers, many of whom are likely to be of considerable size. Channels of distribution, unlike most consumer products, are therefore relatively simple. Many products sold to organisational buyers are designed to meet their specific needs, and involve complicated technical specifications. Such products often require significant technical support services, which may be supplied direct or through specially appointed agents or distributors.

The critical role of the industrial sales person was noted in Chapter 3 to be particularly effective at the various stages of the sophisticated buying routines which characterise organisational markets.

Although direct selling is prevalent in industrial markets, industrial distributors, such as steel stockholders or builders' merchants, play important roles in certain product markets. IBM sells its computer systems direct to users, while Dow Chemicals uses a distributor–fabricator channel for its polyethylene foam.

Seton Healthcare, which dominates the UK market for elasticated tubular support bandages, switched its major marketing efforts from hospitals – where competitive contracting suppressed profits – to prescription products supplied to retail chemists and also the community care market. District nurses and health visitors, who tend to be easier to contact than GPs, are targeted by a direct sales force which includes several former nurses. These trained nurses are able to demonstrate products and give professional advice on specific applications. In the Netherlands, Seton has established a joint venture with its distributor to sell directly to the community care market; this could lead to considerable expansion across Europe for this enterprising company.

Distribution systems can be characterised generally as intensive or exclusive. The first category results in widespread availability of a product, such as basic raw materials. The second category deliberately limits distribution of specific products, as with appointed regional distributors of farm implements, etc. Between these two extreme distributive policies, selective distribution may be adopted; this gives adequate access to a market without the high costs of intensive distribution, and also allows the marketer more control over the final selling arrangements for his product.

Selling may be one of the many tasks of a salesperson whose responsibilities, according to Kotler,[3] may be analysed across six activities: prospecting, communicating, selling, servicing, information gathering and allocating. The actual mix of tasks will vary with the purchase decision process, company marketing strategy and the market conditions.

Of the various tasks listed, those of servicing, selling and prospecting are likely to be core responsibilities. With many industrial products, servicing may involve consultation on customers' problems in manufacture of their own goods, technical advice, arrangement of finance and expediting delivery.

Prospecting covers the search for new business, which, in some firms, may be supported by advertising to act as an introduction to the sales force (see Chapter 10). Other valuable support could be rendered by the sales office and the market research manager, who might be able to prepare lists of target customers for the salesperson to concentrate on. Through these kinds of back-up the salesperson would be able to increase his or her productivity and give more time to the principal task, namely selling.

Selling is a vital element of the marketing strategy and demands professional commitment, product knowledge, integrity and good organising ability. Levitt,[50] whose well-known article 'Marketing myopia' (published in the *Harvard Business Review* in 1960) stirred up debate about the function of marketing, later reviewed the impact of his missionary zeal. He felt that his astringent views had particularly influenced firms in 'the more technical industrial products and services' and had shown the need for clearly communicating product and service characteristics through face-to-face selling. However, precisely because these products are so complex, 'the situation produces salesmen who know the product more than they know the customer, who are more adept at explaining what they have and what it can do than learning what the customer's needs and problems are'. As a result, a narrow product orientation has developed instead of really trying to understand a customer's problems and offering feasible solutions within the capacity of the products or services marketed; sales staff tend 'to look in the mirror rather than out of the window'. Only their own production-oriented biases are reflected; what they should be looking at are customers' problems. (See also Chapters 2 and 10).

In Chapter 3, research studies on the complexity of industrial buying practices were noted: the DMU (decision-making unit) was seen to be a significant factor in the buying practices of industrial and economic organisations. In 1976, a research publication, *How British Industry Sells*,[51] focused on the *marketing* behaviour of industrial suppliers. Among its findings are the following useful insights:

1. Many companies might well profit from developing the consumer goods concept of key account sales staff.
2. Industrial sales staff might well be centred where business is, rather than nursing traditional territories.
3. Wide variations in selling costs (1 to 10 per cent) suggest that better use might be made of the time of sales staff. Although the average salesperson makes three or four calls a day there is no correlation between the frequency of calls and orders placed – the reverse, in fact, seems to apply.
4. Only in about 20 per cent of companies was the sales force under the direct control of the marketing director.
5. 26 per cent of companies do not set sales targets.
6. Selection and training procedures seem generally inadequate.

From the above, there appears to be plenty of scope for introducing higher standards of professional selling in industrial markets, particularly in view of the greatly increased competition and soaring costs since the date of this report.

Hakansson's research emphasised that industrial selling behaviour is concerned with establishing positive interaction between the two negotiating firms, and that this is not just the responsibility of the sales staff. 'Personal contacts between buyers and the technical and general management personnel were rated as highly as sales representatives as channels of communication.'[40] Teamwork is clearly involved in both successful buying and selling.

Industrial selling is, therefore, a complex activity: products and services are often highly technical and involve long-term contractual obligations; industries are frequently dominated by powerful firms, sometimes multinational in ownership and operations; technological developments in some fields, like electronics, are dynamic; available sources of business in the home market may be few – industrial restructuring has had widespread effects on suppliers to the older industries; and imported manufactured goods are more evident in the United Kingdom than ever before. This is a selective list of factors which contribute to the sophisticated nature of the industrial salesperson's job.

The various strategic inputs which make up the overall strategic plan should be well integrated. For instance, selling efforts should be synchronised with advertising campaigns; advertising copy should reflect some of the principal features of the sales presentation. Media, e.g. technical journals, should be carefully chosen for their effective coverage of specific types of industrial and other organisational sources of business.

The impact of effective distribution was experienced some years ago by a British firm of crane-makers, whose sales engineers used to sell pulley blocks singly. These blocks were subsequently packaged and distributed through merchants thus eliminating wasteful use of salespeople's time. The cost of one call by a sales engineer wiped out completely the profit on a pulley block. Export marketing of standard overhead travelling cranes was also reorganised. Because these cranes consist substantially of structural steel, which is bulky and costly to transport, export crane kits are made up of motors, winches, etc. From these components, cranes are expertly constructed in overseas markets.

Just as in consumer markets, industrial products and services will profit from creative ideas in marketing. Technical excellence supported by professional marketing leads to survival and growth, even in slow or no-growth markets.

The selling and distribution inputs into the overall marketing strategy for organisational products and services should, of course, be reviewed from time to time. Like consumer markets, environmental conditions change, sometimes radically, as when a new and aggressive competitor enters a market which has been quietly enjoyed for many years by a few indigenous suppliers. New strategic approaches may be necessary to counter such threats; the importance of efficient marketing intelligence (see Chapter 4) is obviously vital – it enables companies to adopt proactive policies rather than being forced into last-ditch, defensive responses. A survey[52] of 150 companies drawn from The Times 1000 revealed that only 20 per cent considered their marketing database to be the most important source of information when formulating strategy; almost 60 per cent did not use information about competitors when setting performance targets, preferring to base these on their own previous performance. Such introvert corporate planning hardly seems credible when competition is fierce in most markets.

Integrating industrial sales territories with effective systems of remuneration

The planning of profitable industrial sales territories should be linked with effective methods of motivating the sales force. This is not an easy task because of the complex nature of industrial markets, but it is one which should not be shirked.

Some years ago, a McKinsey survey found that half of about 100 executive incentive plans provided no more motivation than could be expected from straight salary remuneration although sales personnel were not specifically identified.

A *Harvard Business Review* survey[53] in 1980 clearly indicated the value of positive motivation schemes in industrial selling. The most important determinants of sales success related to: (1) task; (2) personality; (3) compensation; and (4) quality of management. Sales staff should be quite clear about their responsibilities because clarity of their sales task is strongly related to performance.

It is frequently argued that paying a straight salary provides sales staff with security and reduces worries about fluctuations in income. It is also simple in design and administration, and avoids questions of parity in pay across territories.

However, a straight salary lacks excitement and motivation for ambitious salespeople; generally these are quite willing to accept an element of commission. The design and implementation of sales incentive schemes tends to be time consuming and costly; it may also be counterproductive. But well-devised schemes have been shown to be highly productive (over a 10-year period, one US company grew at 15 per cent p.a.). A fully integrated scheme must be thoroughly tested and explained to sales staff.

Various sales force payment schemes will now be identified and reviewed.

1. Differential commissions

This scheme is related to specific products and marketing objectives: it encourages proportionately greater selling effort to specific products. There are alternative applications as follows:

(a) different rates of commission are applied to specific types of product;
(b) sales of specific products are 'weighted' according to certain criteria set by marketing and sales managers.

(i) *Example of differential commissions*

Product	*Monthly sales*	*Rates of commission*	*Monthly commission*
A	£12,000	1.0%	£120
B	£120,000	0.5%	£600
C	£18,000	2.0%	£360
D	£10,000	2.5%	£250
	£160,000	Total commission	£1,330

(ii) *Example of 'weighted' commissions*

Product	*Monthly sales*	*Rates of commission*	*Monthly commission*
A	£12,000	1.0%	£12,000
B	£120,000	0.2%	£24,000
C	£18,000	0.4%	£7,200
D	£10,000	2.0%	£20,000
	£160,000	Total	£63,200

£63,200 at, say, 2 per cent commission = £1,264

2. Base salary + planned extra compensation

The basis of this scheme could be 75% salary + 25% commission on sales. In this scheme planned extra compensation has two elements:

(a) specific commission rate for all sales up to 'expectation' level; plus
(b) 'accelerated commission rate' over the set level of expected sales.

The following approach is applied in the calculation of commission earnings plus salary:

1. Calculate 'sales expectation' for territory (potential related to specific products and markets), e.g. £1.8 million p.a. (£150,000 per month).
2. Formulate sales compensation package, e.g. £20,000 p.a.
3. Calculate base salary (75%), e.g. £15,000 p.a.
4. Planned extra compensation, e.g. £20,000 − £15,000 = £5,000.
5. Relate extra compensation to level of sales expectation (see 1),

   e.g. $\dfrac{£5{,}000}{£1.8 \text{ million}} = 0.0028$ or 0.28% on all sales

6. If sales in a particular month totalled, say, only £120,000, then earnings would be:

   £1,250 basic salary + £336 = £1,586

7. If sales surpassed 'expectation', the extra would qualify for an 'overexpectation payment' (dependent upon profitability of product mix, etc.) say, 1.5%.

   Hence, if sales exceeded planned expectation by £10,000 in any month, the sales person would earn an extra £150.
8. In addition, an extra bonus for new accounts opened (of minimum value) could be considered.
9. Sales could conceivably be expressed in EEU ('effective economic units' based on physical units, etc.).

3. Graduated commission

This approach is based on the following steps:

1. Calculation of break-even points or bases.
2. Previous sales year figures would be adjusted annually.
3. There would be no ceiling to earnings.
4. Volume bases would vary from territory to territory, and be determined by factors such as: sales potential; product mix; market trends; past history of sales in area; cost of sales; product service call frequency; extent of supervision.
5. Rates could be 1% → 3% → 5% →; feasible earnings would be calculated as if the new plan had operated during the previous six months.
6. Details of the scheme would be adjusted if only marginal effects on sales are experienced.
7. It is important to check that the volume and profitability of sales are projected carefully so that these outstrip extra selling costs.

4. Dual scheme

This scheme is similar in some respects to Scheme 2 and it has two elements:

(a) 'maintenance' commission;
(b) 'increased' commission.

(a) *Maintenance commission* would be paid on all sales in excess of a predetermined level of market penetration.

(b) *Increased commission* would be paid on volume in excess of agreed volume of sales, such as sales achieved by the sales representative (or predecessor) the previous year, on the average volume over previous years.

The following example illustrates this scheme.

Representatives A and B each have territories with annual volume potential of £2,000,000.

A's sales last year were only £300,000 (15% of potential), while B's sales were £600,000.

The reference penetration level has been calculated at 20% or £400,000, above which maintenance commission is payable.

B, at £600,000, is already 50% above the reference penetration level of £400,000.

A will have to increase volume by £100,000 (33⅓%) to achieve reference penetration level.

To illustrate the effects of this scheme, it may be assumed that:
A increases volume by 50% to £450,000
B increases volume by 10% to £660,000
with the following effects:

1. *Traditional commission* (4% on all sales in excess of last year)

   A: 4% × £150,000 (£450,000 − £300,000) = £6,000
   B: 4% × £60,000 (£660,000 − £600,000) = £2,400

2. *Dual commission* (4% as follows: (i) 2% on all sales in excess of 20% base penetration level; and (ii) 2% on sales in excess of last year's volume)

   A: (i) 2% × £50,000 (£450,000 − £400,000) = £1,000
   plus
   (ii) 2% × £150,000 (£450,000 − £300,000) = £3,000
   £4,000

   B: (i) 2% × £260,000 (£660,000 − £400,000) = £5,200
   plus
   (ii) 2% × £60,000 (£660,000 − £60,000) = £1,200
   £6,400

Under the traditional plan (1), B is penalised for his or her past successes; as result, this representative is underpaid in relation to the important share of business he or she is responsible for.

The alternative (2) rewards B equitably, and also encourages A's efforts.

This scheme also emphasises two important points when calculating remuneration packages for sales forces:

(a) It is as worthwhile to prevent erosion of market share as it is to pay to obtain increased share.
(b) An accelerated commission rate is correct in principle because of its motivational value, regardless of past performance.

However, a dual commission scheme tends to be easier said than done, and it will not work if territory potentials differ substantially. Also, success depends on the ability to generate a credible set of sales potential estimates for each territory (exact precision may not be feasible or even absolutely necessary). In addition, it is important to develop equitable transition procedures to ensure acceptability of the proposed new system.

Planning a sales incentive scheme

Effective sales incentive schemes deserve expert planning, which will cover the following stages and detailed inputs.

1. Define clearly sales/marketing objectives:
   (a) market/industries served;
   (b) industrial trends;
   (c) general economic trends;
   (d) nature of products offered;
   (e) nature and level of competition;
   (f) identification of buying motivations.
2. Define sales organisation tasks:
   (a) type of sales representatives;
   (b) training and development;
   (c) degree of autonomy;
   (d) extent of supervision;
   (e) role and responsibilities of sales force;
   (f) organisation of customer accounts – national/house accounts;
   (g) key target accounts.
3. Develop sales compensation package:
   (a) discuss at various levels of the sales organisation;
   (b) check options with the financial accountant.
4. Test proposed compensation package:
   (a) apply to past performance data;
   (b) check different levels and likely impact on earnings;
   (c) check if likely to lead to unacceptable erosion of differentials between representatives and management;
   (d) design overriding management bonus based on representatives' performance.
5. Communicate optional package to sales force:
   (a) brief sales management/supervisors;
   (b) supervisors to outline scheme to representatives;
   (c) supervisors to report reactions to senior management;
   (d) scheme to be adjusted if necessary.

6. Communicate final scheme at general sales meeting: offer a trial run (12 months) with quarterly reviews of progress.

Successful schemes are likely to have the following characteristics:

1. The scheme is equitable: mutually profitable.
2. It is based on market knowledge and accurate market assessments.
3. It is relatively easy to understand.
4. It is relatively simple to calculate and check progress.
5. It must encourage higher earnings based on extra effort.
6. It must protect sales representatives in cases of low-volume sales over which they do not have direct control, e.g. when factory deliveries break down.
7. Territories must be carefully planned.
8. The scheme must be supported at all levels of the sales organisation.
9. All levels of sales force should benefit.
10. Sales tasks must be clearly understood.

Finally, industrial sales representatives are usually mature, educated and technically qualified. They are, therefore, capable of assuming relatively sophisticated responsibilities which may extend to market investigation, new product development, etc. Their duties as *sales staff* should be made quite clear to ensure the success of any pay incentive scheme.

Territories should be analysed by industry, size of customer, etc., and target accounts identified. Call frequencies should be related to present (and prospective) market value.

PLANNING STAGE 3: SPECIFYING TACTICS

This third phase of the planning process spells out the tactical operations by means of which the strategic objectives are to be achieved. The precise boundaries of strategic and tactical decisions and operations tend to become rather blurred. Short-term goals and the related activities to achieve them are sometimes referred to as 'tactical', while the term 'strategic' is used to describe long-term corporate objectives and planned activities.

In fact, in Mintzberg's opinion 'there is good reason to drop the word "tactics" altogether and simply refer to issues as more or less "strategic", in other words, more or less "important" in some context, whether as intended before acting or as realised after it'.[54] 'Policy' is another label which Mintzberg finds misapplied: its usage 'is terribly confused' and 'reflects the fact that "policy" was the common word in the management literature before "strategy" replaced it in the 1960s'. The semantics are hardly helpful to those who prefer pragmatic knowledge to intellectual debate. Mintzberg quotes Rumelt's view[55] that 'one person's strategies are another's tactics – that what is strategic depends on where you sit', adding that it 'also depends *when* you sit; what seems tactical today may prove strategic tomorrow'.

However, for the purposes of discussion in this text, tactics are regarded as subservient to strategy; tactics are the tools or methods used to implement strategic decisions.

Tactical operations should detail the specific actions which it is considered will result in the target objectives being attained. These may refer to profit or to some other measure of efficiency, such as more effective allocation of public services. Areas of personal responsibility should be explicitly mapped out together with detailed schedules showing the time periods involved. The tactical programme should be divided into a series of phases with individual subsidiary goals. This will aid management in checking progress and will also be effective in motivating staff to attain goals that do not appear to be so remote as to lose their immediate appeal.

Marketing tactics (and their related targets) could be divided into four main phases: infiltration; consolidation; expansion; and domination. This systematic phasing would enable marketing management to allocate responsibilities for opening up, for example, key accounts in particular areas or industries. As a foothold is gained in a market, new tactics may be necessary to build up business and expand market share. Undoubtedly, competitive reactions are likely to become tougher and market growth will become increasingly difficult. The final phase – domination – may not, in fact, be feasible or even desirable. Although not dominating the total market, some suppliers may develop particularly profitable market sectors in which they are able to specialise and where they become major sources of supply. (See the discussion in Chapter 6 on market segmentation.)

PLANNING STAGE 4: MONITORING PLANNING PROGRAMMES

The last stage of planning is concerned with monitoring the tactical efficiencies of an organisational marketing plan. Beforehand, measures of performance will of course have been drawn up. Systematic reporting is an essential constituent of corporate planning. (See Chapter 1 on the 'control' factor in marketing management.)

Evaluating market trends and the relative performance of competitors will provide guidelines for the strategic repositioning of products and services. Regular checks on corporate image are also valuable in relationships with suppliers, customers, financial institutions and the trade unions.

Standards of performance are likely to involve cost/sales ratios, market share, territory quotas, product performance (relative efficiencies compared to competitors' products), etc. All these need to be expertly devised and critically monitored; this demands a sound database so that trend analyses can be readily developed.

Diagnostic analyses should be based on objective facts, so that deviations between planned and actual results can be carefully evaluated against national and global economic trends, technological developments, overall industry performance, etc. Apart from proficiency in statistical analyses, marketing management need to apply creative interpretation to the data.

This comprehensive approach should provide mangement with insights into the many and complex factors which have influenced demand for their products and services.

Cost-effectiveness is a basic discipline of managerial performance; in the marketing sphere of operations it is particularly necessary to ensure that strategies and tactics are professionally evaluated.

In Chapter 1, the four functions of marketing management were identified as analysis, planning, control and action. The analytical function was specifically covered in subsequent chapters; this chapter, so far, has concentrated on the remaining responsibilities which complete the sequence of professional marketing.

Like any other business activity, marketing incurs costs – hence the importance of control mechanisms to ensure that expenditure is productive in terms of the corporate objectives stated in the first phase of planning.

Marketing managers have four major control devices which they should use fully: (1) sales targets; (2) marketing budgets; (3) marketing audits; and (4) profit centres.

Aspects of these control systems have been discussed in this and preceding chapters. Sales targets or quotas, for example, should be related to specific products/services, the potential for which will have been formulated from market forecasting, including the use of data from systematic marketing research, as noted in Chapter 4. We have also seen how sales force payment systems could be integrated with territorial sales targets in order to motivate sales staff to maximise their selling efforts.

The overall order position requires regular checking. Four critical sets of information should be known for efficient marketing audits:

1. The opening order situation.
2. Orders received since the last audit.
3. Orders converted to sales since the last audit.
4. The closing order situation.

While the volumes and values of orders should be known, it is also necessary to be aware of the projected profitabily of such orders. (Refer to Sevin's analysis given earlier, pp. 164.)

The order position should be compared with the relevant sales targets, analysed into products/services, territories, etc. Value of sales relative to production, i.e. stocks held, should also be checked carefully so that effective ratios are maintained.

Performance standards have been mentioned already: they are vital to the whole process of monitoring and controlling marketing activities. These should be linked closely to overall and specific corporate objectives.

Profitability depends on a well-devised combination of product/service mix, market share and cost control. (Market share will be specifically discussed in the

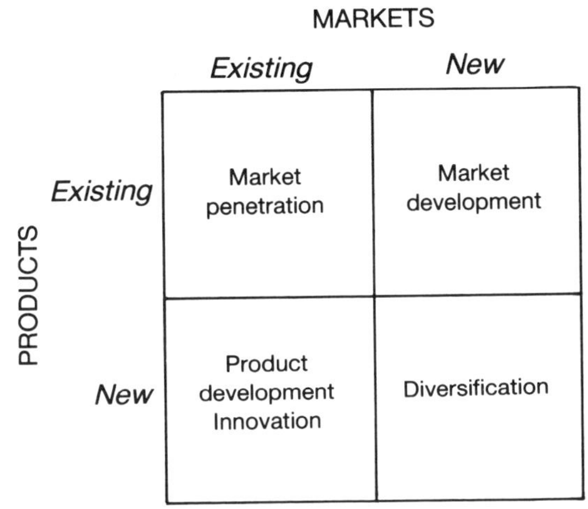

FIGURE 5.9 Alternative product/market strategies

next chapter.) Market share analysis focuses on sales performance relative to competitors, and is a lead indicator of corporate activity, but careful interpretation of the statistics is necessary when assessing relative performances. If, for example, a company's sales have fallen but its market share has remained more or less the same, it can be assumed that the whole industry is affected by similar environmental influences. But a more penetrating analysis should be made which might discover, for instance, that a new competitor had entered the market and was rapidly taking business away from traditional suppliers, perhaps because of improved technology, superior product design, etc.

Ansoff's product/market matrix[41] given earlier in this chapter provides an effective framework for monitoring marketing productivity. Against this strategic screen, answers should be sought for the following questions:

1. How much can sales of existing products be increased in present markets?
2. How much can sales of existing products be increased in new markets?
3. How much can sales of new products be achieved in present markets?
4. How much can sales of new products be achieved in new markets?

Answers are likely, as noted before, to involve a mix of marketing strategies, i.e. market penetration, market development, product innovation and diversification, as shown in Figure 5.9.

In the initial discussion of product portfolio – to be continued in the next chapter – it was stated that successful companies aim to have an effective distribution of products/services and markets, so that overall levels of profitability are maintained.

All businesses need new products and new customers if they are to survive and grow. Marketing and selling efforts should, therefore, be allocated to achieve specific targeted sales to both new and existing customers. Marketing management

PRODUCTS \ CUSTOMERS	*Existing*	*New*	
Existing	55%	25%	80%
New	10%	10%	20%
	65%	35%	

FIGURE 5.10 Allocation of targeted marketing and sales efforts

may devise guidelines, or even issue directives, related to markets and customers, on the basis of the example given in Figure 5.10, which indicates a feasible approach.

To achieve the projected sales in the four quadrants of the matrix, marketing costs will obviously be entailed. Apart from product development costs, such as R&D, new products will doubtless require relatively heavy marketing investment before they develop into profitable, main-line product ranges. Estimates of expenditure related to projected sales and profits should be drawn up for specific products, existing and new. The relationship between sales and profitability should be borne in mind. The following relationships tend to characterise particular business situations:

1. Increased sales with proportionately lower increases in costs.
2. Increased sales with decreasing costs.
3. Increased sales with constant costs.
4. Constant level of sales with decreasing costs.
5. Decreased sales with proportionately greater decrease in costs.

These alternatives need to be related to specific industries and their products/services. At different levels of output, for example, economies of scale may take effect and result in significantly lower unit costs, enabling price competitiveness to be a dominant feature of marketing strategies. Ranges of products may experience different profit/sales relationships. In some cases, marketing managers may judge that, beyond a certain level of sales, diseconomies in marketing efforts are likely to occur, making further expansion unprofitable.

In consultation with financial and production colleagues, marketing managers should attempt to evaluate the relationships between different levels of sales of specific products and the costs involved in achieving projected targets. Included in these analyses should be study of the impact that these plans will have on production and inventory costs. With new products, in particular, production lines need to be 'warmed up'. Phased marketing should be considered: a few key industries and customers might be targeted at first, followed by controlled expansion to other markets. In this way, production problems are minimised and extended delivery times avoided.

In some organisations, marketing departments may be organised as *profit centres*, which would be expected to produce, on a contribution basis, targeted surpluses after variable costs have been covered. Inside departments, this principle could be extended to product/market activities, such as overseas sales operations. This system could be productive provided costs have been fairly allocated and agreed between financial and marketing executives, but the operation of such a system should not become bureaucratic.

Finally, marketing managers should develop fully their analytical skills, recognising that marketing decisions are, in fact, also financial decisions, which may commit their companies to substantial investment costs and expose them to significant dimensions of risk. In Chapter 1, greater teamwork in organisations was recommended, especially between managers in different functions. Systematic monitoring of the effects of marketing strategies and tactics is imperative; 'flying blind' is a frightening concept in the hazardous conditions of modern markets.

SUMMARY

Strategic planning is vital for successful marketing; corporate resources are limited and should be effectively used. Market environment and strategic fit underlie strategic planning. Marketing planning is the starting point for all corporate planning.

Four steps in the planning process are identified as follows:

1. State objectives.
2. Develop relevant plan.
3. Specify tactics.
4. Establish monitoring system.

Situation analysis involves market audit, which has three diagnostic steps:

1. Marketing environment review.
2. Marketing system review.
3. Detailed marketing activity review.

Significant corporate influences are the limiting factor and leverage.

Porter's model of market dynamics notes five forces:

1. Threat of new entrants.
2. Bargaining power of buyers.

3. Bargaining power of suppliers.
4. Threat of substitute products/services.
5. Rivalry among existing suppliers.

From careful evaluation of these factors, a company can develop an effective marketing strategy.

Time horizons should be built into plans: the intervals involved will depend significantly on types of industry.

Four facets of marketing strategy (4 Ps) have been identified as: product, promotion, price and place (distribution).

A product/market matrix is useful in analysing market behaviour. Four options are open: market penetration; market development; product development; and diversification. Product (or brand) positioning refers to the place occupied by a particular product in a given market; this comparative evaluation should be based on research. Product portfolio planning aims to spread risks and opportunities of profit across a balanced range of products and markets.

Pricing is a critical input to marketing strategy and should be interrelated with the other inputs so that it contributes creatively to the total marketing effort.

Promotion – discussed further in Chapter 10 – is often badly handled in organisational markets: it deserves expert attention.

Selling and distribution – together forming the fourth element of overall marketing strategy – are significant factors for success. Selling in organisational markets is usually direct and often involves considerable technical knowledge and complex negotiation. Research-based information about customers' needs and buying behaviour is imperative.

The final stage of planning entails monitoring the tactical efficiencies of the marketing plan. Standards of performance (quotas, targets, etc.) should be devised. Professional marketing, as outlined in Chapter 1, has four responsibilities: analysis, planning, control and action, all of which demand attention.

REFERENCES

1. Jackson, K. F., *The Art of Solving Problems*, Heinemann, London, 1975.
2. Simmons, W. W., 'Practical planning', *Long Range Planning*, vol. 5, no. 2, 1972.
3. Kotler, Philip, *Marketing Management: Analysis, planning and control*, Prentice Hall, Englewood Cliffs, NJ, 1980.
4. Tilles, S., 'Making strategy explicit', in *Business Strategy*, ed. H. Igor Ansoff, Pelican, Harmondsworth, 1972.
5. Fayol, Henri, *General and Industrial Administration*, Pitman, New York, 1949.
6. Drucker, Peter F., 'Long-range planning: challenge to management science', *Management Science*, vol. 5, no. 3, 1959.
7. Ansoff, H. Igor, *Corporate Strategy*, Penguin, Harmondsworth, 1968.

8. Mintzberg, Henry, *Mintzberg on Management: Inside our strange world of organizations, Free Press, New York, 1989.*
9. *Perlmutter, Howard, 'The tortuous evolution of the multinational corporation', Columbia Journal of World Business*, vol. 4, no. 1, 1969.
10. Leontiades, Milton, 'The importance of integrating marketing planning with corporate planning', *Journal of Business Research*, vol. 11, November/December 1983.
11. Davidson, J. H., Foreword to *Offensive Marketing or How to Make Your Competitors Followers*, Cassell, London, 1972.
12. Hill, Colin, 'Introduction to planning and forecasting', *Management Accounting*, vol. 45, May 1967.
13. Drucker, Peter F., *The Practice of Management*, Heinemann, London, 1955.
14. Pilditch, James, 'Winning companies concentrate on their people and products', *The Times*, 4 July 1987.
15. Harmon, Frederick, and Jacobs, Gary, 'Enduring corporate success: the profile and the process', *Management Centre Europe Executive Report*, America Marketing Association International, 1986.
16. Ackoff, Russell L., *Management in Small Doses*, John Wiley, New York, 1986.
17. Skapinker, Michael, 'Mission accomplished or ignored?', *Financial Times*, 11 January 1989.
18. Harvey-Jones, Sir John, *Making it Happen*, Collins, London, 1988.
19. Sevin, Charles H., *Marketing Productivity Analysis*, McGraw-Hill, New York, 1965.
20. Muir, Andrew, 'Planning and product range', in *Long Range Planning for Marketing and Diversification*, ed. B. Taylor and G. Wills, Bradford University Press/Crosby/Lockwood, London, 1971.
21. Barnard, Chester, *Functions of the Executive*, Harvard University Press, Boston, Mass., 1938.
22. Leslie, Nicholas, 'The open society at BOC', ed. J. Ensor, *Financial Times*, 18 November 1975.
23. Blois, K. J., 'The manufacturing/marketing orientation and its information needs', *European Journal of Marketing*, vol. 14, no. 5/6, 1980.
24. Lloyd, Tom, and Sveiby Karl E., *Managing Knowhow*, Bloomsbury, London, 1987.
25. 'The toughest job in American business', *The Economist*, 16 January 1993.
26. 'Hardware and tear', *The Economist*, 19 December 1992.
27. 'To save Big Blue', *The Economist*, 16 January 1993.
28. Taylor, Paul, 'Management sees the benefits', *Financial Times*, 21 October 1992.
29. Lorenz, Christopher, 'Chameleons in their true colours', *Financial Times*, 7 February 1992.
30. Porter, M. E., *Competitive Strategy*, Macmillan, New York, 1980.
31. Porter, Michael E., *The Competitive Advantage of Nations*, Macmillan, London, 1990.
32. Rawsthorn, Alice, 'Barking up the wrong tree?', *Financial Times*, 16 July 1987.
33. Griffiths, John, 'Chairman pumps life into ailing tyre group', *Financial Times*, 30 September 1992.
34. Battersby, Albert, *Sales Forecasting*, Pelican, Harmondsworth, 1971.
35. Jones, E. O., and Morrell, J. G., 'Environmental forecasting in British industry', *Journal of Management Studies*, vol. 3, 1966.
36. Turner, Graham, 'GEC's pragmatic planners', *Long Range Planning*, vol. 18, no. 1, 1985.
37. Mintzberg, Henry, 'The strategy concept II: another look at why organizations need strategies', *California Management Review*, vol. 30, no. 1, 1987.
38. Jay, Antony, *Management and Machiavelli*, Penguin, Harmondsworth, 1967.

39. Kotler, Philip, and Singh, Ravi, 'Marketing warfare in the 1980s', *Journal of Business Strategy*, vol. 1, no. 3, 1981.
40. Hakansson, Hakan (ed.), *International Marketing and Purchasing of Industrial Goods*, Wiley, Chichester, 1982.
41. Ansoff, H. Igor, 'Strategies for diversification', *Harvard Business Review*, vol. 35, no. 5, 1957.
42. Abrahams, Paul, 'A future based on a dual-track strategy for growth', *Financial Times*, 21 May 1992.
43. Lorenz, Christopher, 'Why diversity is a dirty word in some circles', *Financial Times*, 11 September 1992.
44. Levitt, Theodore, 'Ideas for action', *Harvard Business Review*, vol. 52, no. 6, 1974.
45. Atkin, B., and Skinner, R. N., *How British Industry Prices*, Industrial Market Research, London, 1975.
46. Buckner, Hugh, *How British Industry Buys*, Hutchinson, London, 1967.
47. Buzzell, Robert D., 'Is vertical integration profitable?', *Harvard Business Review*, vol. 61, no. 1, 1983.
48. Speirs, Michael, 'How to manage value', *Management Today*, June 1985.
49. Gabor, A., and Granger, C., *The Attitudes of the Consumer to Prices ex Pricing Strategy*, Staple Press, London, 1969.
50. Levitt, Theodore, 'Marketing myopia: retrospective commentary', *Harvard Business Review*, vol. 53, no. 5, 1975.
51. *How British Industry Sells*, Industrial Market Research, London, 1976.
52. Holberton, Simon, 'Introvert strategies', *Financial Times*, 31 October 1990.
53. Doyle, Stephen X., and Shapiro, B. P., 'What counts most in instructing your sales force?', *Harvard Business Review*, vol. 58, no. 3, 1980.
54. Mintzberg, Henry, 'The strategy concept I: five Ps for strategy', *California Management Review*, vol. 30, no. 1, 1987.
55. Rumelt, R. P., 'Evaluation of strategy: theory and models', in *Strategic Management: A new view of business policy and planning*, ed. D. E. Schendel and C. W. Hofer, Little, Brown, Boston, Mass., 1979.

REVIEW AND DISCUSSION QUESTIONS

Q1 Compose a 'mission statement' for a firm (20 employees) currently marketing vulcanised rubber sheeting for supermarket check-out points and also for production lines.

Q2 Outline the principal features and considerations involved in developing a situational analysis in industrial markets.

Q3 Select a specific industrial sector and describe how each of Porter's five competitive forces currently operates in that market sector.

Q4 Porter claims that most strategies belong to one of three categories: overall cost leadership, differentiation and focus. Choose an industrial service area with which you are familiar, and identify three firms, each implementing one of these strategies.

Q5 What are the key differences between a cost-dominated as distinct from a market-oriented influence on industrial pricing policies?

Q6 A firm marketing a leading brand of drugs used in the treatment of high blood pressure distributes these through a national network of medical wholesalers. GPs are targeted directly by a sales force of 25 representatives. Evaluate the various sales force payment schemes available so that the company can achieve optimum marketing efficiency.

CHAPTER SIX

Strategic planning II

In this second chapter on strategic planning, discussion will focus on specific features such as market segmentation, product life-cycle analysis and the marketing portfolio approach. These aspects of market planning are more popularly related to consumer product markets, but in organisational markets – public as well as private sector – they also have useful applications.

MARKET SEGMENTATION STRATEGIES

Nearly every market can be divided into several submarkets which have significant characteristics affecting demand and supply. Often, the trend in the macro or global market is different from that observed in the micro or submarkets. The growth of specialised market segments has encouraged firms to make and supply goods and services which are closely related to the needs of particular kinds of customer. Instead of treating all customers the same, i.e. offering identical ranges of products and levels of service, objective market research enables groups or clusters of customers to be identified whose needs can be adequately met more through specific marketing attention.

A business executive should 'stop thinking of his customers as part of some massively homogeneous market. He must start thinking of them as numerous small islands of distinctiveness, each of which requires its own unique strategies in product policy, in promotional strategy, in pricing, in distribution methods, and in direct-selling techniques.'[1]

Market segmentation, as Wendell R. Smith[2] noted in 1956, has a disaggregative effect because it recognises several demand schedules for the supply of particular commodities or services. These differential responses are the *raison d'être* of market segmentation strategies.

Segmentation encourages the development of specialist firms which can cater for the needs of relatively small markets. Unlike the big manufacturer who has invested heavily in volume-production equipment designed to make a restricted range of products, enterprising small manufacturers can avoid headlong collision by concentrating on those sectors of global market demand which are relatively insignificant to the large-scale producer.

In cases where a market is markedly fragmented, a new entrant would be advised to focus on a relatively small segment, particularly if only limited resources are available. Kotler[3] terms this a 'niching strategy' and states that an ideal niche should have the following characteristics:

1. Sufficient size to be potentially profitable.
2. Growth potential.
3. Opportunities for an entrant company to exercise its superior competences (see the discussion of leverage in Chapter 5).
4. Customer goodwill.

Other characteristics favouring 'niching' would be patents and a measure of channel control.

As a practical example of successful market 'niching', *Fortune* magazine reported that for years 3M's strategy has been to avoid domination of a product market. Instead, it tries to find 'crevices' that others have missed and fill them in. 'We're a nickels-and-dimes company. We don't have many big ticket items.'[4]

BTR, the British conglomerate which ranked eleventh in the FT 500 Companies for 1992 and operates in consumer, construction, energy and electrical, industrial and transportation industries, includes companies like Dunlop, Newey and Eyre, Borg Warner and Graham Builders Merchants. Its chief executive has declared that 'BTR finds gaps in markets, niches which it can fill by supplying superior quality of service . . . BTR is marketing reliability. Its marketing stresses the reliability, availability and consistency of BTR products.'[5]

Dynamic segmentation has resulted in the British transport undertaking, BRS,[6] growing in real terms despite the general fall-off in demand for trucking in the United Kingdom. BRS has spearheaded its marketing efforts over the following closely identified segments: rental (short term, from one day upwards); contract hire (customer's livery is used even though BRS may supply driver, maintenance, finance and even management for an entire fleet); haulage (now only 10 per cent of BRS turnover); service (maintenance, rescue, etc.); and Transcard (charge card for transport operators). Selling and promotional efforts are specially tailored to these segments.

The fastest-growing segment is contract hire, so BRS is focusing one-third of its total sales and marketing expenditure on advertising and other promotional activities, and only two-thirds on its new sales force. This concentrated marketing expenditure is expected to have significant impact in an industry which has traditionally restricted its total marketing and sales costs to less than 5 per cent of turnover.

Sir John Harvey-Jones has endorsed niche marketing strategies for their growth potential: 'I believe real business growth will only be achieved by companies who are focused down extremely tightly into niche markets which they clearly understand.'[7] At the same time, he warned, companies must watch their financial management extremely carefully, and their financial strategy must go hand in hand with a business strategy.

Allied Colloids, based in Bradford with a turnover in 1992 of £254.5m and profits of £42.1m, makes a range of speciality chemicals such as water-absorbent polymers which have many industrial uses, including in the paper industry. These special types of chemical 'usually rely on the application of new ideas to solve customers' problems';[8] such products, which are virtually unknown to the average consumer, are made in small quantities and sold at relatively high prices.

Market niching strategies, states Tom Peters, are valid for the service sector as well as for manufacturing, and for large organisations as well as small or medium-sized businesses. New market niches should be developed by introducing new products and continuously updating existing products through differentiation and added values from quality and service. This policy, as research has shown, 'works as well in declining as in growing markets; the top differentiators in "mature" industries in the US (e.g. tyres and cigarettes) actually outperform the best differentiators in growth industries'.[9]

The Munich-based speciality car-maker BMW announced in 1992 that its strategy was to develop market niches and segments within those niches. All the activities of the company would be streamlined, so that efficiencies in production and marketing would make it possible to offer a wide range of product variations to appeal to particular types of customer, who are willing to pay premium prices for distinctive design and performance.

Perhaps this discussion of the exciting prospects for market niching should also include the sombre warning from Lord Weinstock, whose views on corporate planning were given in the preceding chapter, that niches can become tombs.

FACTORS AFFECTING FEASIBILITY OF MARKET SEGMENTATION

Four principal factors influence the opportunities for effectively segmenting markets: identification, measurability, accessibility and appropriateness.

The first factor – identification – is in the province of marketing research (see Chapters 4 and 5). As a result of objective enquiries, knowledge of market consumption behaviour should enable specific subsectors to be identified.

The second factor – measurability – relates to the estimation of subsector patterns of consumption. With some technical products, any accurate measurement of demand may be difficult because of the lack of specificity in published data. However, reasonable estimates may often be built up from systematic investigation.

The third factor – accessibility – refers to the ability of a company to direct its marketing efforts at a particular segment, which may, for example, require special technical selling expertise.

The final factor – appropriateness – relates to the suitability of specific segments for an individual company's resources and overall objectives.

These four factors are relevant to the sequential approach to segmentation which is given in Figure 6.1, the first four stages of which subsume the principles underlying effective market segmentation strategies. In following this sequential approach, Porter's model[10] of market dynamics, discussed in the proceding chapter, will doubtless be helpful, particularly in the second and third stages. End-use analysis (see Chapter 2) is also likely to be useful in these early stages. The final selection of target markets will follow from rigorous evaluation of market sector opportunities in terms of investment costs, sales and profitability over specific periods of time. Cost–benefit analyses may be applied when whittling down the number of opportunities which are likely to develop into long-life successes.

At the selection stage, some efforts may be made to rank the final market sectors which have emerged from this sequential analysis, and to allocate resources to these sectors according to their potential for earning specified rates of return over certain time periods. Only prospective market sectors which satisfy – with reasonable safety margins – corporate expectations would proceed to the stage of developing and implementing marketing strategies and tactics.

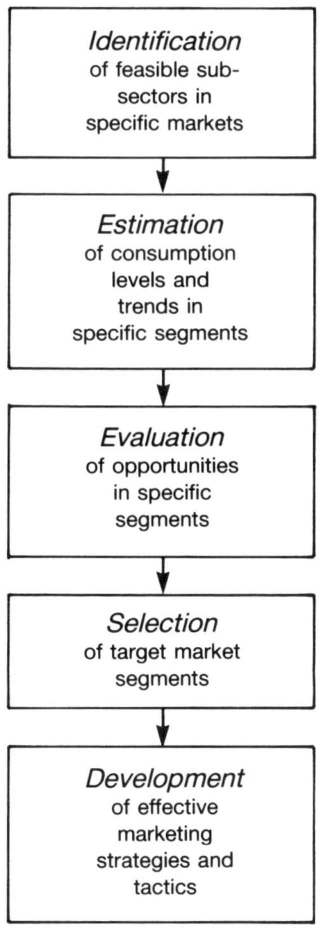

FIGURE 6.1 Sequential approach to market segmentation

BASES FOR MARKET SEGMENTATION

Various bases for segmenting markets have been adopted. In consumer markets, these have included socioeconomic groupings, geographical location, personality characteristics, usage rate, brand loyalty, buying motives and attitudes, family life cycle, ethnic/religious influences and professional mobility. Aspects of these diverse methods of analysing consumer buying behaviour are discussed in some detail elsewhere.[11]

In organisational supplies and services, the policy of market segmentation may be related to factors such as customer size, location, industry classification, usage rate, and nature of operations (commercial firm or public sector).

An interesting example of effective market segmentation relates to the UK car market. A particularly vital sector of this market for UK producers concerns the demand for company cars, which now represent over 70 per cent of new car registrations; in 1960 the figure was 20 per cent.

Another instance of profitable segmentation is the UK paint industry, which is dominated by a few relatively large firms, although many small and medium firms still exist. The UK market for paint can be segmented into decorative paints, used mainly on buildings, and industrial paints, used in manufactured products. The former segment has various subsectors according to the types of paint, which, while sharing common raw materials, differ significantly in their chemical make-up, related to specific market needs.

Demand for vehicle paints relates to automobile sales and to refinishing. Demand follows closely the levels of activity in the car and commercial vehicle markets.

General industrial paints have many applications: for example, coatings for drums and cans; aircraft finishes; and rolling stock. A specialised sector is concerned with marine coatings; these can again be divided into several subsectors – deck finishes, hull coatings, etc.

The paint industry could be clearly segmented, therefore, both by size of firm and by type of paint related to specific end-uses.

Creative use of market segmentation is made by Johnstone's Paints of Droylsden, Manchester. This fifth-generation family firm, which was taken over in 1989 by the French state-controlled oil and chemicals group, Elf Aquitaine, has its main business in trade decorative paints which are supplied in certain volumes and may require special skills in application. Despite intense competition led by the giants in the industry, Johnstone's has experienced organic growth through concentrating on giving its customers reliable products, competitively priced and backed by first-class service. 'Consistency matters enormously to trade painters. They notice if anything changes and they stick with you if things work right', says the chairman.[12] To ensure its stronghold in this defined market segment, Johnstone's has given detailed attention to both technological and commercial aspects its business, installing, for example, the latest mixing plant – a modern warehouse from which it distributes to 18 trade centres in the conurbations of Britain – and, ingeniously, extensively using square-section three-litre plastic pails, of which a pallet will hold 36 compared with only 27 round tins.

Another manufacturing company facing dominant competition in a commodity-product market also developed an effective production–marketing strategy. Avon Rubber in Wiltshire has struggled for decades against groups oversupplied with commodity-type tyres. Following radical restructuring affecting all sectors of its business, Avon diversified away from its traditional markets and targeted users needing specialist tyres. In addition, it augmented its other product areas such as industrial polymers. Its chief executive is reported to be 'confident that the culture of the company has changed and that its managers are both more disciplined and more dynamic'.[13] (See Chapter 5 on corporate values).

Over recent years, it has been ICI's declared policy to move away from low-priced commodity-type products like chemical fertilisers, to high-priced speciality chemicals, such as pharmaceuticals and agro-chemicals. These speciality products will be sold to carefully targeted markets in Europe, North America and the Far East. (Further discussion of ICI's business activities occurs in the section dealing with product portfolio planning.)

However, shifting from basic commodity-type products to specialised production and niche marketing requires skilful direction and management throughout a business. Economies of scale in production and generic marketing approaches are customary in undifferentiated-product firms. Entering specific segments and offering products tailored to certain customers' needs demand sets of attitudes and a degree of flexibility which are likely to be novel to many old established companies. Speciality markets require special treatment.

Boliet, a subsidiary of a large raw-material-based multinational firm with corporate headquarters in southern Europe, wanted to switch into a speciality chemicals market. The company concentrated on processing pine gum rosins, sold as raw material to manufacturers of paper, size and synthetic resins. Very little upgrading of the rosins took place, and the lack of growth and pressure on margins (only a few large customers) led to the decision to integrate forward by processing the rosins into polymerised rosin and stabilised rosin esters. These specialised chemicals, known as 'tactifiers', are vitally needed by adhesives manufacturers. Boliet believed that, although its gum-based products would not be of as high quality as competitors' products, they would be adequate for most applications and the company might be able to undercut market leaders.[14]

Analysis revealed that tactifier competitors could be classified according to raw material base: petroleum, hydrocarbon, polyterpenes, wood, tall oil and gum rosins; these influenced production costs and applications. The specialised nature and applications of these products resulted in complexity – many brands supplied by 13 leading competitors producing over 70 products.

Research identified six specific product variables influencing selection of brand and source: softening point, viscosity, colour stability, starting colour, tack and price. Four 'company variables' were: product range, service support, geographical coverage and reputation for reliability.

By means of factor and cluster analyses, these multiple and complex criteria were grouped into 12 segments, of which seven were judged by management to be feasible and four were particularly attractive. It was decided to focus on these latter segments for the first 18 months, with projected sales of 3 per cent specific market share or 19.2 per cent of the total market.

Detailed market positioning strategies were combined with the segmentation, and effective marketing mixes were devised. For competitive reasons results cannot be divulged, but it was reported that the company's strategy 'is having a significant effect on the market'.[14]

Industrial market segmentation focusing on 'benefits' sought by customers primarily in terms of product attributes and performance characteristics relates to the Champion Corporation, a very large US industrial equipment manufacturer with a substantial share in air compressors.[15] It supplied several types of compressor: reciprocating, rotary and centrifugal, each with various applications as measured by horsepower, pressure, size, lubrication, maintenance requirements, etc.

Competitors had developed skills in 'niche strategies'; price and service were important factors. The four largest companies accounted for about 40–5 per cent of unit sales; smaller firms with speciality products and overseas suppliers had significantly added to the general level of competition.

Company-owned or independent distributors were the traditional channels of distribution; these stocked spare parts and frequently offered service. This well-established barrier to entry was being attacked because some large-volume end-users threatened to buy direct from speciality and importing suppliers. As a result of this pressure, Champion decided to review its product line and marketing strategy. Based on multivariate analysis, sets of 'benefit packages' were derived which were then related to the ranges of compressors offered by Champion and its competitors. Some of these benefits were not capable of being met with the current or planned technological resources. Others were technologically feasible and suggested new product opportunities worth further study.

Benefit analyses were then constructed on the basis of benefits deliverable. From these approaches it was possible to distinguish between benefits sought and those which the firm could meet in the short to medium term. 'Technology gaps' were identified which could guide new product development.

The Bowater group decided in 1987 to reduce its traditional business interests in paper and packaging, and to concentrate more on higher-value-added products of greater profitability and growth potential. Three years later, it adopted the principle of 'critical mass' (refer to Chapter 8) in three sectors: health-care packaging, personal-care packaging and coated industrial films. Through the acquisition in 1992 of Cope Allman, a cosmetics and pharmaceuticals packaging group, and also of DRG Packaging, which supplies specialised packaging to the food and health-care markets, Bowater substantially covered the first two targeted sectors. In 1993 it bid for Speciality Coatings International, an American group involved in the precision coating of specialist films and papers used in the imaging, graphics and computer industries.

Bowater's well-devised industrial strategy is clearly based on careful evaluation of market trends in specific sectors which have prospects of high earnings.

At IBM UK, reorganisation of the corporate customers segment – which represents over 80 per cent of turnover – is reflected in moving from a geographical branch structure to one based on customers in nine identified sectors or end-use market segments: banking, insurance, retail, local government, national government, utilities, transport and communications, production and engineering, and one specifically for oil, pharmaceuticals and chemicals. The heads of these new business groupings have responsibilities covering: customers, market development, client operations (finding generic solutions that are applicable to sector customers), and high-level consultancy.

Mercedes-Benz, one of the most celebrated car-makers in the world, made a dramatic announcement[16] in January 1993: it intended to transform itself from a traditional maker of exclusive luxury cars into an exclusive full-line manufacturer offering high-quality vehicles in all segments of the market. These would include: a 'people carrier' or multipurpose vehicle to be made in Spain, which would compete with, for example, Renault's Espace and Chrysler's Voyager; a four-wheel-drive vehicle to challenge the Range Rover and Discovery, Chrysler's Grand Cherokee and Mitsubishi's Pajero/Montero/Shogun; and a small city car similar to Renault's Turingo.

Mercedes has had to accept that new environmental standards and stricter traffic requirements have made the traditional divisions of the car market – luxury, medium and small – less and less relevant. Instead of engineering exercising the most powerful influence in its production strategy, it realises that future market opportunities will primarily focus on 'vehicle concepts rather than around engine prestige value'.[17] Mercedes freely acknowledges that, with 1992 sales lower than the preceding year, it has to change to stay alive.

In following this strategy, it will revolutionise the whole of its business operations, including moving to a product development process based on 'target costing', a variant of the Japanese system known as 'market share pricing'. This leads to target pricing – a form of 'backward-cost' pricing, by which a firm aims to produce to a price determined either by market forces or by some other influence. In Mercedes' case, it will note what a customer would be willing to pay for a particular type of vehicle, calculate its profit margin, and then cost every component and process in an attempt to market at the perceived target price: a radical departure for a company that was content for years to offer the ultimate in auto-engineering without concern for costs.

Service markets can also be segmented: for example, airlines usually arrange seating according to price/quality segmentation criteria, and tickets are issued for first-class, business-class and economy-class travel. For many years, banks and insurance companies have segmented customers into two main market sectors, corporate and private, within a framework of geographical regions and districts, and industrial/commercial activities. Specialised banking services have been offered to the small and medium-sized business sector of the economy.

An interesting study[18] of effective segmentation of the building society market was undertaken some time ago, which revealed that, at the primary level, segmentation covered three distinct categories of people: (1) a building society's existing investors; (2) investors with accounts in other building societies; and (3) people who did not hold any building society investments. Within these primary segments it was possible to identify a secondary stage of segmentation, as follows:

1. *Bankers*: people who use the building society more or less as a bank; these have relatively low-average-value accounts and also high rates of withdrawals to deposits.
2. *Savers*: people who use their accounts to save up for particularly expensive items – e.g. holiday, house deposit – or retirement; they have higher-than-average balances and only withdraw infrequently.
3. *Investors*: an increasing number of more affluent customers who switch funds for differential gains; they tend to have larger accounts than the other categories and relatively few transactions, either withdrawal or deposit.

In order to gain an even clearer picture, however, a tertiary segmentation is required. This involves socioeconomic analyses of the primary and secondary segments: for example, husband/wife role in savings and the selection of savings medium; decision criteria for savings; and age and economic profile of key investor groups.

Another example[19] of significant segmentation in the service industry relates to retail banking, where it is proposed that customers can be classified according to their level of affluence:

1. *The very rich*: a small but important group with assets of £1 million or over, probably 50+, well travelled, reasonably sophisticated and expecting high levels of personal service.
2. *The rich*: a much larger group with assets around £100,000, likely to be males 45+.
3. *High net worth individuals* (HNWIs): a semi-mass market with investable assets of £15,000–£100,000.
4. *Medium net worth individuals* (MNWIs): the largest number of significant savers and most of the personal deposit market for both building societies and banks.

Each of these segments, with its characteristic habits and needs, requires particular marketing attention; the first segment quoted will obviously have very different ways of conducting their financial affairs from, say, the mass market represented by MNWIs.

Segmentation may also be applied to international marketing; one proposed[20] method of analysing world markets classified countries according to their gross national product per capita (see Chapter 8).

Segmentation of markets by industrial classification is quite widely used by marketing management. In Britain, the Standard Industrial Classification (SIC) forms the basic approach. (See Chapter 4 for detailed discussion of this official system of industrial classification.) A similar SIC of US industrial activity may also assist in specific market analyses and strategies (see Chapter 4). Because of individual variations in classification, it is, unfortunately, difficult to make direct comparisons between the SICs of individual countries.

As noted in Chapter 4, analyses of industrial activities based on SICs need to be approached with care. Despite the limitations arising from some degree of arbitrary classification, the SICs provide useful bases for market analyses. Further analyses of UK SIC data may, in some cases, be available from the Business Statistics Office.

New market sectors may develop as a product matures; new uses may be found for the same basic material. For example, nylon was first used industrially as warp knits in 1945; by 1948 it had been adopted for tyre cords; it was used in textured yarns by 1955; and by 1959 it had extended to carpet yarns. Pharmaceutical compounds have tended to extend from use in personal medical care to veterinary medicine.

Some manufacturers, such as those producing motor components or carpets, may segment their markets at the primary level according to the method of purchase, such as derived-demand customers (see Chapter 2), wholesale distributors, retail stockists or mail-order business. Further segmentation may occur because of customer size, location or other significant variables.

But it should be remembered that the objective of market segmentation is not to complicate operations. The essence of an effective marketing segmentation strategy is that it should result in increased market penetration and more efficient use of corporate resources; at the same time, customers' needs should be more fully satisfied.

PRODUCT LIFE CYCLE (PLC)

The concept of product life cycle and innovation strategy are directly associated. Products, in general, have limited lives during which they retain profit-earning capacity. The span of useful life varies considerably according to the nature of products, the rate of technological developments, the nature of demand and marketing management decisions.

Despite its many critics, the PLC concept has much to contribute towards the development of effective marketing strategies. Basically, the PLC theory states that products tend to follow a pattern similar to biological development: from birth to growth to maturity and then to eventual decline and death. This well-known cycle of finite life is, therefore, applied to the study of the demand for specific types of product: the number of phases suggested by various researchers has ranged between four and six. In Figure 6.2, five phases are given to represent the generalised concept of product life stages.

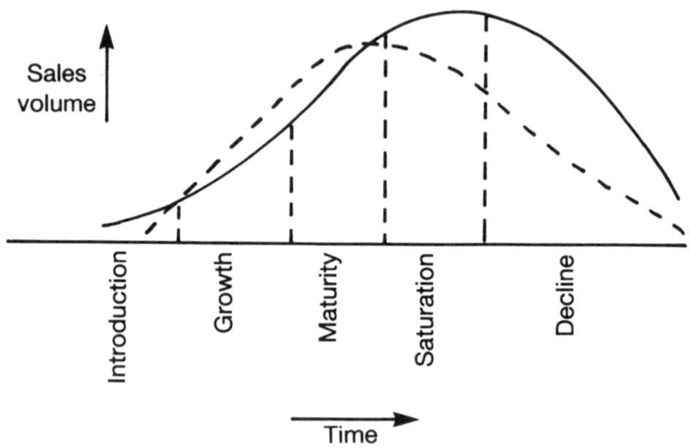

FIGURE 6.2 Generalised concept of product life cycle showing five sequential stages (dotted line refers to general trend of unit profits)

The pattern of growth and development reflected by the curve in Figure 6.2 is, of course, only a *general* tendency; individual products will tend to have characteristic market profiles over time. The period of growth will vary: some products, particularly in fast-moving consumer markets such as 'pop' records or fashion clothing, will experience volatile patterns of demand.

The length of profitable life as well as the duration of each stage of the demand curve will tend to vary significantly according to the types of product service involved. Further, some markets are now experiencing more rapid change, leading to product obsolescence, because of technological developments and the introduction of new competitive activities. Plastics, for example, have been widely adopted in furniture manufacture, encouraging the development of new moulded designs, upholstery coverings, etc.

Associated with the product life-cycle concept is that of the profit cycle (see Figure 6.2, dotted line). It will be observed that the profit cycle of a product does not follow the same curve as the sales volume trend. No profit may be earned in the introductory stage because of high development and promotion costs. Unit profits will tend to attain their peak performance during the growth stage until competition starts in earnest; they may then start to decline, although total profits may still be rising because of rising sales volume. Eventually, in the later stages of the product life cycle, the declining volume of sales, increased costs and heavy competition are likely to cut deeply into profit margins and overall profit targets. In the final stage of product obsolescence and decline, profits may be entirely eliminated (see Chapter 5 on the marketing audit).

PROBLEMS WITH PLC THEORY

The validity of the PLC and, in particular, the trend of the bell-shaped curve have been challenged by many researchers; at the same time, enthusiastic supporters of the theory have promoted it as a powerful management tool. Intuitively, the concept has almost immediate appeal; rationally, it is more difficult to accept it without considerable qualification.

Of the several problems associated with PLC, that of product definition is one of the more formidable. Three levels of product identification were distinguished by Polli and Cook[21] in connection with consumer goods: class, form and brand. Product class refers to substitutes that may be used to satisfy the same want (e.g. cigarettes); product form is a finer definition of product class (e.g. plain filter cigarettes); product brand is specific and unique.

Although it is by no means certain how products were defined in some researches, there appears to be general agreement that 'product form' offers the most appropriate basis for PLC studies.

Day[22] poses the question as to when a change in product is sufficiently distinct to justify a separate life-cycle analysis. He cites examples to demonstrate that PLCs summarise the effects of many concurrent forces in a product market; those acting together may help or hinder the rate of product sales growth. While it is important to identify and understand these influences, they may not dictate an entirely new PLC.

What exactly consititutes a new product has proved a rather difficult hurdle for researchers to overcome satisfactorily. 'Newness' appears to be largely subjective, and depends on customers' perceptions. Perhaps, as Rink and Swan[23] and others suggest, new products could be classified into several degrees of newness. They offer the following four-way classification of new products: the unquestionably new product; the partially new product; the major product change; and the minor product change. (See also Chapter 7 on categories of innovation.)

Another problem of the PLC concept is the difficulty of establishing the various stages of the life cycle, since these are, in practice, not clear-cut at a particular time. Distinguishing, for example, between the introduction and growth stages seems to rest largely on marketing decisions which influence diffusion. 'Whether the growth process is slow or rapid is not determined by some absolute principle, but is partially dependent upon specific circumstances, the marketing strategy adopted and the resources allocated to the product.'[24] It is suggested that, in this case, the simple solution would be to merge the first and second stages into a single 'growth' stage. The elusive nature of the boundaries between stages frequently mars the value of PLC as a reliable analytical tool.[22]

A further problem of the PLC theory relates, as mentioned earlier, to the nature of the trend curve. While a considerable number of researches with consumer products (mostly food) have supported the existence of the classic bell-shaped curve, Cox's research[25] into ethical pharmaceuticals found that six different types of curve were necessary to explain sales trends. On the other hand, Cunningham[26] found that the sales of automobile components, chemicals and general engineering products in the United Kingdom usually followed the general PLC trend.

Research focusing on about 100 industrial components marketed by a large midwestern manufacturer in the United States to the heavy-duty truck and farm

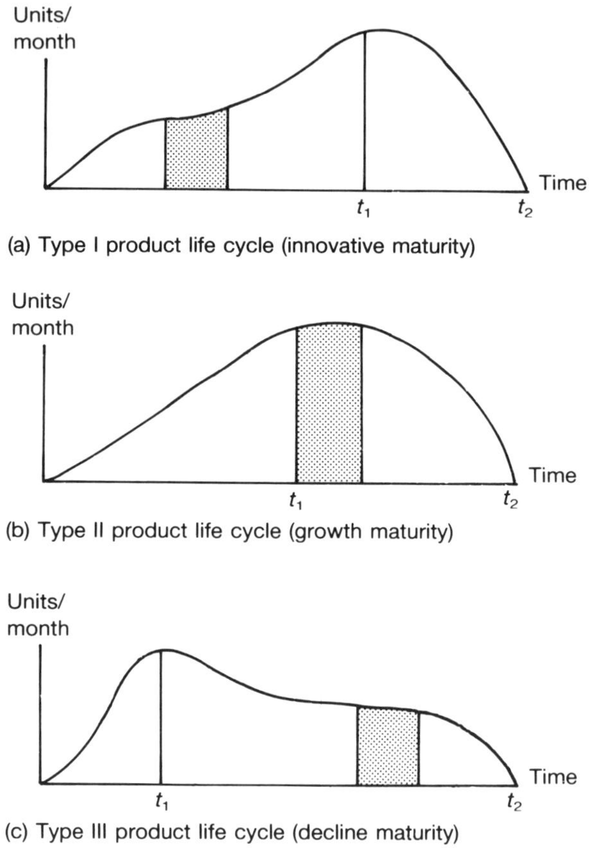

Note: t_1 = time between commercial birth and peak monthly sales
t_2 = time between commercial birth and commercial death

FIGURE 6.3 Three types of product life cycle for industrial components (Source: de Kluyver[27])

equipment industries over the period 1967–73 revealed that three types of PLC curve appear to exist. Type I relates to products perceived to be highly innovative (see Chapter 7 on discontinuous innovations): diffusion is fairly slow at first, indicating that a learning process is an important factor. Type II tends to conform to the more traditional PLC curve: growth is fairly rapid while decline is quite short (see Chapter 7 on Robertson's dynamically continuous innovations). The type III trend curve reflects very rapid growth followed by a long maturity phase which includes a decline prior to the eventual decline stage ('continuous innovations'). These curves are shown in Figure 6.3.

Projections from PLC historical data may also be problematical: for instance, what adjustments should be made where demand for some consumer durables and industrial materials may be particularly sensitive to economic conditions (as in derived demand – see Chapter 2)? More sophisticated approaches than mere extrapolations are obviously imperative; the present state of knowledge suggests that caution and common sense would be advisable qualities when markets are exposed to many variables, some of which cannot be controlled.

USING LIFE-CYCLE THEORY CREATIVELY

Life-cycle theory is particularly valuable in reminding management that innovation strategies are important to business survival and growth (see Chapter 7).

It is possible to extend the life cycle of a product by carefully planned improvements, as Rank Xerox did with its photocopying machines. Its policy of product improvement 'is really no more than the application of standard product life extension techniques' to 'equipment whose basic design is now several years old'.[20]

Other methods of extending the profitable life of products could be: (1) new uses for the product; (2) extended use by existing customers; (3) increased consumption (in present use) by existing customers; and (4) new customers. (See the product/market matrix discussed in Chapter 5.)

Although technical products, in general, do not have the volatility of consumer products, the concept of product life cycle should not be ignored. Sophisticated electronic control equipment, for instance, tends to experience rapid obsolescence.

> Not only are products maturing more rapidly, but product life cycles generally are growing shorter. For more than 15 years . . . the DC-3 held its place as the leading commercial airliner. But the DC-7, and later the turbo-prop Electra, were obsoleted in less than five years by the pure jet DC-8, the 707 and others like them. Today's complex military weapons systems, unlike the weapons of World War II, are obsolete almost before they leave the drawing board . . .[28]

In the textiles markets, natural fibres such as wool and cotton suffered a heavy setback when synthetic fibres were popularised. But the decline in natural fibre clothing was partially halted by subsequent technical developments which resulted in satisfactory mixed fibres used, for example, in wool-mix and cotton-mix outerwear. New technology has in fact developed another product life cycle for these traditional products. Unfortunately, many textile companies underestimated the original challenge of synthetic fibres and were unwilling to change their production and marketing policies. Inevitably, those which failed to respond to the new market needs were either absorbed by more enterprising competitors or forced out of business.

PRODUCT LIFE-CYCLE ANALYSIS

Companies could make more effective marketing decisions if they analysed the performance of their products/services against the concept of the life cycle. This would enable them to plan a balanced product mix and guide the allocation of marketing efforts. Often, companies continue to spend heavily on promotion when the product featured is in the decline stage and should have been replaced by an improved model some time ago.

Marketing management has two fundamental tasks related to product life-cycle theory:[28]

1. To reshape and control the life cycles of individual products/services.
2. To improve corporate profitability by ensuring that products are at different stages of development, so that the overall product mix is well balanced.

Life-cycle management matches corporate objectives with the projected market performance of products.

The following *programme in life-cycle analysis* (see Figure 6.4) has been proposed:

1. *Develop trend data* over a period of time sufficiently long to indicate trends (perhaps three to five years). These data should cover unit and value sales, profit margins, total profit contribution, return on invested capital, market share and price.
2. *Trace recent trends* in the number and nature of competitors. Market shares of competitive products should be analysed and objective evaluations made of competitors' activities, such as distribution strategies, promotional policies, pricing policies and design. These analyses should refer to specific market segments, as discussed earlier in this chapter.
3. *Analyse developments in short-term competitive strategies*, e.g. new products introduced, plans for expanded production, promotional plans announced.
4. *Develop or update historical information on life cycles of similar or related products* as a guide to likely trends of particular products now under survey.
5. *Project sales for the product over the next three to five years, based on the data collected.*
6. *Estimate an incremental profit ratio for the product during each of the projected years' sales.* Incremental profit ratio refers to the ratio of total direct costs (manufacturing, advertising, product development, sales, etc.) to pre-tax profits. This is expressed as a ratio, e.g. 4.8:1 or 6.3:1, and measures the number of pounds required to generate each additional pound of profit. The ratio improves (i.e. becomes lower) as the product enters its growth period; it begins to deteriorate (i.e. to rise) as the maturity stage is approached; and as obsolescence is reached, the ratio climbs more steeply.
7. *Estimate the number of profitable years remaining in the product's life cycle.* On the basis of all the information available, allocate the product's position in its life-cycle curve.

DEVELOPING PRODUCT LIFE-CYCLE PROFILES

When the analytical processes outlined above have been applied to the various products which make up a company's product range, the next task of marketing management is to develop a life-cycle profile of the total product line.

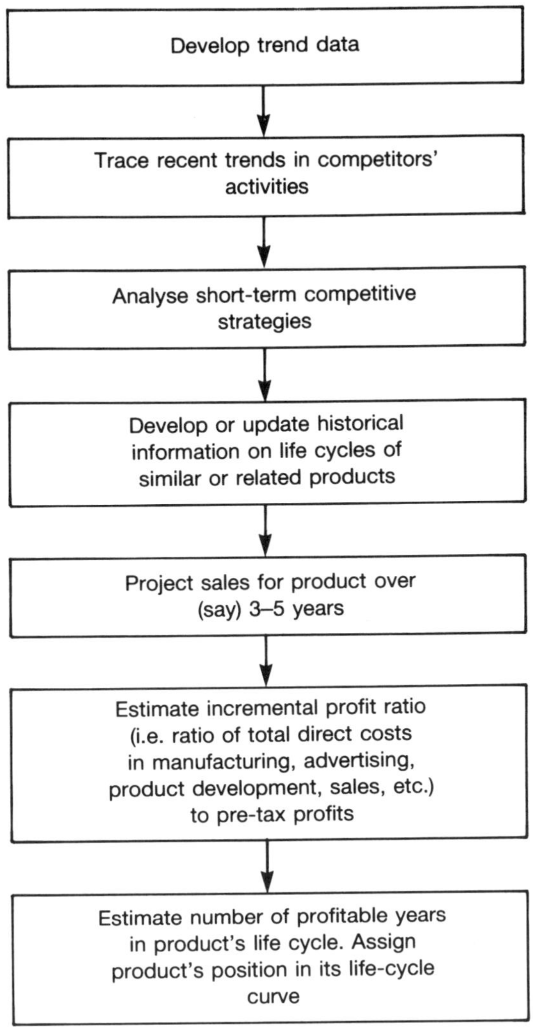

FIGURE 6.4 Typical steps in product life-cycle analysis (Source: based on Clifford[28])

The four stages involved in this analysis, given in Figure 6.5, are as follows:

1. *Determine the percentage of the company's sales and profits* which fall within each phase of the product life cycle.
2. *Calculate the change in life-cycle and profit profiles* over, say, the past five years; project these profiles over the next five years.
3. *Develop the target life-cycle profile* for the company; measure the company's present life-cycle profile against it. This target profile will guide marketing strategies. Factors affecting it will be industry trends (rate of technological development and product innovation); the average length of product life

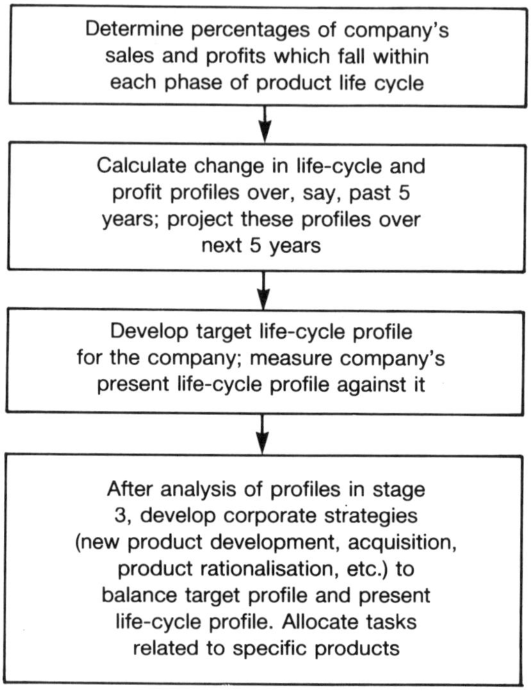

FIGURE 6.5 Typical steps in life-cycle profile of total product line (Source: based on Clifford[28])

cycles in the company's ranges; and corporate expansion and profitability objectives. If life cycles tend to be fairly short, clearly it will be necessary to have a high proportion of profitable products in the early stages of the sales curve.

4. *Develop corporate strategies* (new product programme, acquisition, product line rationalisation, etc.) to balance the target profile and the present life-cycle profile. Allocate tasks related to specific products.

RELEVANCE OF PRODUCT LIFE-CYCLE ANALYSIS TO ORGANISATIONAL MARKETING

As observed earlier, the concept of product life cycle has tended to be viewed as relevant to consumer products but to have limited, if any, validity for organisational marketing decisions. Obviously, theoretical concepts of this nature tend to deal in generalities, and application of their principles inevitably calls for an appreciation of the characteristics of specific markets. That the profitability of industrial companies is affected by changes in market needs, technological invention and innovation, and factors such as high labour costs, is clearly demonstrable. For instance, an electronics company whose products typically have limited life spans of about two years 'suddenly found itself with two products late in the growth phase, nine in the maturity or obsolescence phases – and none in introduction or early growth'.[28] Fortunately, the company realised its predicament in time and managed to survive by a crash programme of rapid development and through acquisition.

A packaging company also found, through product life-cycle analysis, that only 6 per cent of current sales were represented by products in the growth stage, compared with 25 per cent required in the target profile projected by the company planners. Two products were identified as obsolescent and were eliminated, reducing the total share of business represented by declining products from 15 per cent to 11 per cent – 'close to the 10 per cent the target profile called for'.[28] At the same time, new product and acquisition programmes were given priority in the overall corporate strategy.

Businesses of all kinds depend on an infusion of new products or services for corporate growth. Market strategies should be guided by the findings of analytical processes such as those of the product life-cycle profile. New products should not be introduced indiscriminately; the total product range should be evaluated and related to marketing profitability and market share (see the discussion in Chapter 5). Otherwise, there is the danger that new products could merely end up competing with existing profitable products in a company's range, while total market share is not expanded. Production and marketing costs will have been increased to no real corporate advantage.

MARKETING PORTFOLIO APPROACH

In Chapter 5, a brief reference was made to product portfolio planning, which, it was noted, derived from investment portfolio planning. Financial investment and product/market investment have much in common: both deal with finite resources that may be used in alternative ways to achieve agreed objectives. These goals may well vary over different types of investment and kinds of product/market. Capital appreciation may be the guiding principle with a particular stock- or shareholding; market share growth may be the dominant factor in management decisions in a specific product market.

In both financial investment and product marketing, certain criteria will determine the objectives of management. These criteria will largely determine the overall nature of the resultant mix of investments or product markets.

Industry leaders like Sir Christopher Hogg of Courtaulds are fully aware of the role of product portfolio planning, as the following extract from the group's 1992 report indicates:

> We have been looking to achieve consistently improving profits and dividends through a portfolio of businesses which have sufficient similarities for each to draw material benefits from being part of Courtaulds. To achieve the margins we want, we aim for these businesses to be amongst the strongest in their markets

> and to offer something different from their competitors. To underpin the growth in earnings we want, we look for the markets we serve to offer overall the prospect of sustained real sales growth, either inherently and/or from geographical expansion; and we also look to improve continuously our operational performance.[29]

GKN, known for generations as Guest, Keen and Nettlefolds, with steel and iron interests in South Wales and nuts and bolts in the industrial Midlands, has undergone a radical transformation of its traditional business activities since the 1980s. After extensive restructuring involving selling off more than half the companies which formed the group a few years ago, GKN has switched the emphasis of its business through the growth of industrial services, which include waste disposal, scaffolding, vending machines and distribution pallets, the last-named involving a pallet-pooling operation covering the movement of millions of wooden pallets in the UK and across continental Europe.

Up to 1980 the UK automotive industry was the principal source of GKN's turnover; in 1984 industrial services accounted for 20 per cent of group profits, but in about five years this figure doubled. Although the portfolio of its industrial activities has been fundamentally redistributed, GKN's automotive sector is still the main source of turnover and profits. The company has also sought to spread its risks by a strategy of internationalisation, with plants in Germany, France, Italy and Spain. In time, its pan-European approach will be extended to eastern Europe.

GKN's European automotive supplier business is built on closely working with its main customers in the design and development stages, bearing some of the costs itself. Its customers are supplied with subassemblies on a JIT delivery basis (in Chapter 1 the development of synchronised delivery systems was discussed).

It was reported that GKN's automotive subcontracting business 'is increasingly becoming akin to a service business with a growing emphasis on after-sales service and the development of close relations with customers'.[30]

Companies rarely make and sell just a single product to one market; the general tendency is to manufacture and market a range of products of various types and to offer them to a variety of markets. Complexity rather than simplicity characterises the majority of businesses; as a result, companies have to make key decisions related to the 'portfolio' of products and markets with which they are involved or plan to deal. The objective is to attain an optimal mix of products and markets.

Factors to be considered will include the modification or deletion of existing products, the addition of new products, the allocation of marketing resources to develop new markets and the rationalisation of customer lists. Unless marketing management evaluate their product and market activities *as a whole*, it is very likely that resources will be allocated in such ways that suboptimisations in performance occur. (See Chapter 5 on the marketing audit.)

Portfolio planning can be of particular help to diversified businesses with interests over several industries and markets. It can be used primarily as an analytical tool or, with greater benefit, extended to be a decisive factor in strategic management.

STEPS IN PORTFOLIO PLANNING

The following stages in implementing portfolio planning can be usefully identified.

1. Definition of SBU

Firms need to be redefined as strategic business units (SBUs); these may or may not coincide with operating units. The different businesses operated by a firm should be identified as economically distinct product/market segments; the resources used in these sectors should also be identified.

One of the difficulties of putting portfolio planning into practice is in the definition of SBUs or product/market groups. To some extent, judgement appears to be involved. Linneman and Thomas[31] state that the key to successful portfolio planning is proper SBU definition and they give the following guidelines in determining classifications of SBUs:

1. The SBU should be (or be capable of becoming) a 'stand-alone' business.
2. One manager should have accountability and control of the SBU's resources.
3. The SBU should have a distinct corporate role.
4. The SBU should have a clear market focus.
5. The SBU's businesses should be technologically related.
6. The SBU should be large enough to allow for scale and/or experience effects.
7. The SBU should make sense from a geographic standpoint.

As these authors wisely observe, there must be a compromise between a too broad and a too narrow interpretation of an SBU. Fragmentation only results in an unwieldy and unmanageable number of SBUs. Aggregating business activities crudely may, on the other hand, be equally counterproductive: a cardinal principle of the SBU concept is to focus on strategies for discrete businesses.

Aaker endorses this view in stating that, when strategies and competitors have a high degree of commonality across businesses, it makes sense to combine them in a single SBU. But where they differ significantly, it 'is probably more useful to use separate SBUs'. The size of businesses is another factor to consider: very large-scale operations may well be divided into two SBUs, 'even if the involved business strategies are similar'; but in the case of very small businesses, it may not be feasible to organise activities as separate SBUs.

Ideally, an SBU should have its own set of resources, including manufacturing, sales, distribution, engineering and accounting; in practice, however, 'efficiency demands that SBUs share some of these facilities and operations'.[32]

Nestlé, the Swiss multinational food group, underwent a fundamental strategic revolution in the early 1990s, resulting in the formation of seven SBUs, each with global strategic (but not tactical) responsibility for particular business activities, such as coffee and beverages, or food. Unlike its prime competitors, Unilever and Procter and Gamble, and industrial groups like ICI, Nestlé has been a late-comer to the concept of SBUs. In addition, the group has severely pruned its headquarters administration, which for many years imposed centralised control over almost every function of its business.

2. Evaluation of each SBU against matrix criteria

The various product portfolio models (discussed later) depend on a matrix or grid which basically classifies businesses by product/market attractiveness on one axis and by competitive position on the other. More sophisticated measurements are also associated with certain of these models, and rather ingenious descriptions are attached to individual cells of matrices.

The dimensions used in portfolio matrices can, for example, be based on market share and growth; or sector profitability and competitive position; or more complicated criteria such as brand (firm) and product category (industry) sales growth, market share and profitability.

Determination of valid and relevant criteria are clearly important if the portfolio analysis is to be useful to management. Whenever terms such as 'sales' are used, it is vital to define what is being measured: for instance, 'sales' could refer to the absolute level of a product's performance, to the rate of growth of those sales, to product *class* sales, to overall industry growth, to sales valued at current or constant prices, etc.

3. Development of SBU strategy

An effective marketing strategy is devised for each SBU, and progress is monitored regularly to ensure that corporate objectives are being achieved.

The three steps briefly outlined are by no means easy to ascend. While the theory of portfolio development is attractive, the more difficult task is to decide on the allocation of corporate resources that will result in an optimal overall result. Like investment portfolio development, knowledge, insight, experience, judgement and luck seem to contribute towards success (or failure). Many factors lie outside the control of both the financial investor and the professional marketer: risk is usually related to the prospects of attractive rewards. According to Wind it is more difficult to estimate the risk associated with most product portfolios than in the case of portfolios of securities. Also, 'whenever considering the product portfolio, the *sources of risk* (and their correlation) are also of considerable importance',[33] he cites a product portfolio in which all products are subjects to strong regulatory constraints as being generally less desirable than one with similar expected return but with diverse sources of risk (e.g. government and competitors).

Following the takeover of the US chemicals group Celanese in 1987, Hoechst, based in Frankfurt and ranking twentieth in the FT European Top 200 Companies listing, has developed further its strategy of business units within broad product divisions of its mammoth chemical interests. In the USA, the Hoechst Celanese Corporation has been founded; its mainly American management have significant scope for decision making, in line with Hoechst's general policy of decentralisation in order to re-energise its operations.

In July 1992, ICI announced that it intended to split its business into two industrial groups, by creating a separately quoted company called Zeneca. This radical de-merger, effective in June 1993, was confirmed at the board meeting held on 25 February 1993. Zeneca, the new bioscience group, covers pharmaceuticals, agrochemicals, seeds and specialities businesses, accounting for sales in 1992 of about £4bn and trading profit of £587m. The other group, which continues to trade as ICI, is responsible for paints, explosives, materials, industrial chemicals and regional activities with sales in 1992 of £8,383m and trading profit of £148m. This extensive range of products is likely to be pruned by disposals, while petrochemicals and chlor-alkali production will probably be integrated into joint ventures, in line with ICI's declared policy of focusing during the 1990s on areas where it can be successful globally: for instance, paints, explosives (in which, following acquisition of Atlas in the USA, ICI is the global leader) and specialised plastics.

Earlier, ICI had negotiated with Du Pont to swap its nylon interests for the latter's acrylic business and a cash settlement of $431m. However, this deal was blocked by the EC's merger task force on the grounds that it would give Du Pont 43 per cent of the market by value of nylon carpet fibre. In late 1992, the European Commission approved an alternative deal, which entailed Du Pont's transferring 12,000 tonnes of ICI's nylon fibre capacity to a competitor, thus reducing its market share to 38 per cent.

So ICI, which originated from the merger in 1926 of Britain's four leading chemical companies – Brunner Mond, Nobel, United Alkali and British Dyestuffs – as a defensive strategy against the newly formed German chemicals cartel IG Farben, has, like its former threatening competitor (which was split up by the Allies after the Second World War) been demerged. Christopher Lorenz points out, however, that the managerial logic behind ICI's de-merger is by no means peculiarly Anglo-Saxon: 'In common with Union Carbide in the US, France's Rhone Poulenc has already been moving in a similar direction through a string of divestments'.[34]

PRODUCT PORTFOLIO MODELS

At least four product portfolio models have been widely discussed and have attracted varying levels of support:

1. Boston Consulting Group (BCG) growth-share matrix.
2. McKinsey/GE business assessment array.
3. AD Little business profile matrix.
4. Shell International directional policy matrix.

These will now be described and compared.

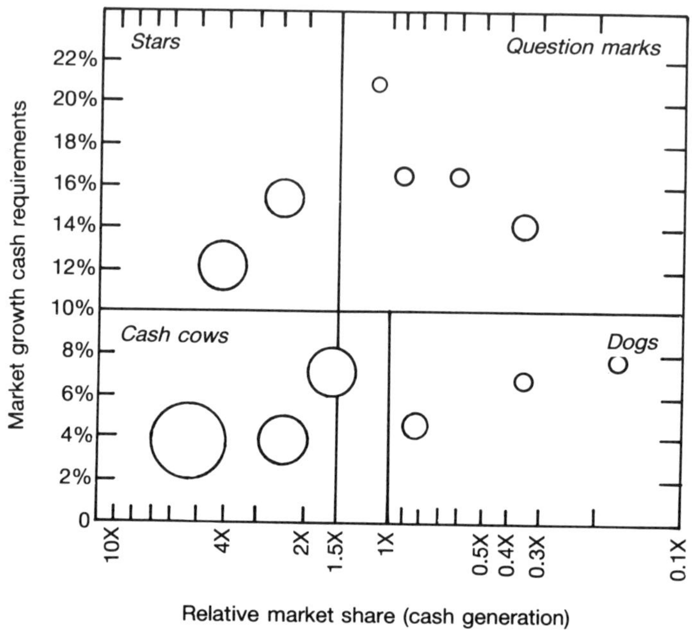

Note: Circle area is proportional to size of business concerned, e.g. turnover or assets

FIGURE 6.6 BCG portfolio model (Source: Hedley[35])

BOSTON CONSULTING GROUP (BCG) GROWTH-SHARE MATRIX

This popular matrix (see Figure 6.6) is based on the generation of cash flow as a measure of success and the allocation of cash to particular product groups. It uses market growth (vertical axis) and relative market share (horizontal axis) as the two definitive parameters. Relative market share measures individual market share relative to that of the largest competitor in a specific industry. Descriptive tags are attached to each sector of the matrix.

Disillusionment followed over-enthusiastic adoption of the BCG matrix in its early years, when it 'became clear that the model assumption did not always hold'.[32] However, it became evident in the 1980s that the value of such models lay in providing disciplined approaches to the internal analyses of business performance in specific sectors, and in suggesting feasible strategic options, rather than hard-and-fast directives.

The 2 × 2 matrix in Figure 6.6 shows relative competitive positions plotted on a logarithmic scale 'in order to be consistent with the experience curve effect, which implies that profit margin or rate of cash generation differences between competitors will tend to be related to the *ratio* of their relative competitive positions (market shares)'.[35]

This *experience curve effect* was noted by the Boston Consulting Group in research into firms' activities over 1968–70, and was studied over several countries.

As a function of accumulated experience, a process of learning takes place over time. According to BCG, value-added costs tend to decrease by 20–30 per cent each time accumulated production doubles.

Experience curves can be plotted on log–log scales and indicate the relationship between unit costs and *cumulative* volume; BCG found[36] that the performance of many tasks followed an 80 per cent curve, i.e. there was a 20 per cent reduction in hours for each doubling of performances.

Enis points out that BCG's experience analysis has two aspects: scale and learning. The first refers to the traditional concept of economies of scale which can result in lower costs per unit of production because fixed costs can be spread over more units. The second aspect of experience analysis is 'the fact that costs fall in a systematic relationship to cumulative production, i.e. the so-called learning curve'.[37]

As a firm gains experience over the various stages of developing, producing and marketing its products, many opportunities are presented for improving its performance, such as reducing costs or improving its technology. These benefits accrue from experience, though clearly firms in an industry tend to exploit their opportunities differently. A successful company competing in a given market segment will, as a result of experience effectively applied, have lower costs and still sell at the going price; it should, therefore, be able to enjoy a higher profitability than its competitors. However, the contribution which experience can make to the profitability of a firm is governed by an important factor, namely the transferability of such experience. In other words, where knowledge and technological skills are readily available in an industry, a new entrant may be able to outpace existing experienced firms by rapidly acquiring and utilising these resources.

The experience curve effect is particularly evident in continuous process manufacturing involving large-scale production of fairly standardised products/components. It is not as readily identifiable in the service industries. In mature industries, and also where value added is low, the impact of the experience curve is markedly less. Where the experience curve results in lower costs, price reductions in an industry tend to occur; these open up new applications for a product and so extend market opportunities, as happened in the case of the integrated circuit.

BCG portfolio strategy

Four principal strategies are related to the quadrants of the BCG matrix (see Figure 6.6).

1. *Stars: high market share, high market growth.* These products are market leaders and growing fast, but needing substantial amounts of cash to maintain their position. Eventually their rate of growth will slow down and they will become cash cows and major earners supporting other SBUs. Star businesses 'are frequently roughly in balance on net cash flow, and can be self-sustaining in growth terms'.[35] Sometimes, they may need heavy investment beyond their own cash generation potential, and low margins may also

be necessary at times to disengage competition. These products hold the company's future prosperity, so BCG advises the adoption of an aggressive marketing strategy.

2. *Cash cows: high market share, low market growth.* These products and businesses generate larger amounts of cash than are needed for their relatively low-growth market sector. They provide vital funds for investment elsewhere in the firm. Management should avoid expensive share-building activities, and carefully protect the profitability of these products.
3. *Dogs: low market share, low market growth.* Their poor competitive position results in poor profits while, at the same time, they frequently demand cash in excess of what they can earn just to keep a competitive position. Hence these types of product are also known as 'cash traps'. Although their investment may be relatively low, there is little hope that they will earn satisfactory levels of profit.
4. *Question marks/problem children: low market share, high market growth.* These products and businesses demand a great deal of cash just to survive; they generate little themselves because of low market shares. Management have to decide whether to spend a lot more and build these products into leaders, or withdraw them from the market.

Wind comments that companies may well find themselves with products or businesses in all four BCG categories, and so the portfolio concept calls for transfer of cash from cash cows to problem children, while the product or business flow is from problem children to stars and from stars to cash cows. These portfolio dynamics 'are based on the premise that high growth products require cash, while low growth products should provide cash'.[33]

Since discussion of the BCG portfolio approach involves market share as one of its parameters, a brief review of research into market-share profitability would seem to be appropriate.

Profit Impact of Marketing Strategies (PIMS)

During 1973 the Marketing Science Institute and the Harvard Business School researched the probability of 57 major North American corporations involving 620 individual businesses for the three-year period 1970–2. The research focused primarily on RoI (return on investment) because this is the performance measure most often used in strategic planning. It was recognised, however, that RoI results are often not entirely compatible between business because (for example) of variations between depreciation policies.

The research findings were that a positive correlation existed between market share and RoI (see Figure 6.7). On average, it was found that 'a difference of 10 per cent in market share is accompanied by a difference of about 5 points in pretax RoI'.

Explanations which were advanced for this included the impact of economies of scale, market power and the quality of management. 'Specifically, as market share

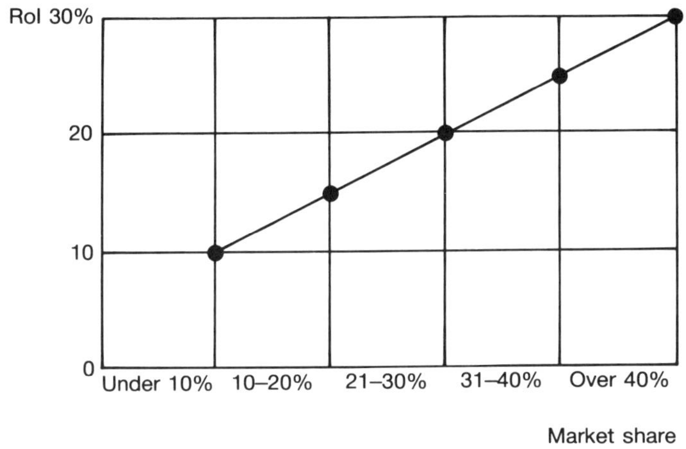

FIGURE 6.7 Relationship between market share and pre-tax RoI (Source: Buzzell *et al.*[38])

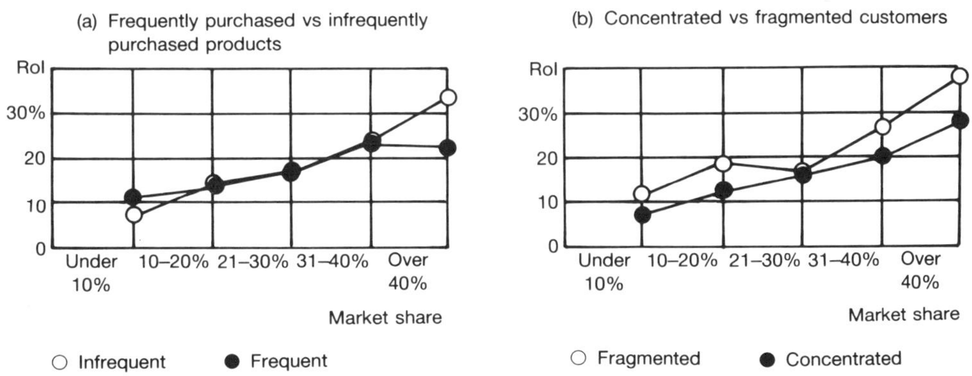

FIGURE 6.8 Industry variations in market share/RoI relationship (Source: Buzzell *et al.*[38])

increases, a business is likely to have a higher profit margin, a declining purchase-to-sales ratio, a decline in marketing costs as a percentage of sales, high quality and higher priced products.' Research data also showed that the advantages of large market shares are more significant for businesses which sell products that are 'purchased infrequently by a fragmented customer group' (see Figure 6.8).

Infrequently purchased products are generally durable, involve considerable expenditure, are frequently complex and are often difficult for buyers to evaluate. (See the discussion in Chapter 3 on the risk factor in buying.) Buyers may, therefore, be willing 'to pay a premium for assured quality'.

Frequently purchased products (typically bought at least once a month) tend to be of low unit value where the element of risk in buying from a relatively unknown supplier is not perceived to be great. This may encourage 'shopping around'.

A strong relationship was established between companies which had strong competitive positions in their primary product markets and high profitability. These companies included IBM, Gillette, Eastman Kodak and Xerox, 'as well as smaller more specialised corporations like Dr Scholl and Hartz Mountain (pet foods and accessories)'.[38]

The PIMS database has been considerably expanded over the years and now contains data from more than 450 firms covering 3,000 SBUs, some of which have been in the database virtually since its origination.

Why market share is profitable

The PIMS researchers advanced three 'possible reasons' why market share is profitable:

1. *Economies of scale*. These occur in buying, manufacturing, marketing and other cost components. 'A business with 40 per cent share of a given market is simply twice as big as one with 20 per cent of the same market . . .' This statement reflects the experience curve which was discussed earlier.
2. *Market power*. Economies of scale, as many economists have postulated, may be less important than the actual bargaining power of large-scale enterprises. Powerful concentrated buying strengthens bargaining against suppliers (see Chapter 2). Size, as Drucker has cogently argued, 'has a major impact on strategy, and strategy, in turn, has major impact on size'.[39] While the simplicity and size of a small organisation enable it to respond with flexibility to opportunities, the larger organisation, because of its resources, is able to undertake (for example) long-term research projects or promotional schemes which are outside the scope of smaller companies.
3. *Quality of management*. It was suggested that the 'simplest of all explanations' accounting for the market share/profitability relationship lies in the quality of management which is generally characteristic of market leaders.

These three explanations are not mutually exclusive: PIMS stresses the need to analyse and identify the relationships and impact of these variables on particular businesses.

Why do profit margins on sales increase so sharply with market share?

PIMS research discovered that three significant factors influenced profitability related to market shares.

The biggest single difference in costs, as related to market share, referred to the purchase-to-sales ratio. Research showed that for large-scale businesses (over 40 per cent market share) purchases represent only 33 per cent of sales, compared with 45 per cent for businesses with market shares under 10 per cent. Low purchase-to-sales ratio goes hand in hand with a high level of vertical integration. Although a greater extent of vertical integration 'ought to result in a rising level of manufacturing costs', research did not show this, perhaps 'because, despite the increase in vertical integration, costs are offset by increased efficiency'. But, in addition, economies of scale in buying may be effective. There was no evidence that large-scale firms charge higher prices, although it was admitted that the measures adopted were 'rather crude'.

The second contributory factor referred to the tendency, as market share increased, for the marketing costs-to-sales ratio to decline. Research indicated an average 2 per cent saving in marketing costs to sales between the smallest and largest firms surveyed. This reflects the ability of larger undertakings to spread fixed marketing costs more widely, to use more efficient promotional media and to adopt more effective selling tactics.

The third factor affecting profitability was observed to depend on the ability of market leaders 'to develop unique marketing strategies and to have higher prices for their higher-quality products' than their smaller competitors. Market leaders tend to market 'significantly higher-quality products and services' than those with lower market shares. They also spend considerably higher sums on R&D relative to sales (2.6 per cent for market share under 10 per cent; 3.55 per cent for market share over 40 per cent). Such firms as Eastman Kodak, IBM and Procter and Gamble are typically market leaders whose marketing strategies are highly innovative.

Types of market-share strategy

PIMS researchers stressed that, because of the strong relationship of market share to profitability, top management had the responsibility of establishing market share objectives. The following broad groups of market-share strategies were identified:

1. Building.
2. Holding.
3. Harvesting.

to which Kotler[3] and others have added:

4. Divesting.

1. *Building strategies* are based on planned efforts to increase market share through new products and other systematic marketing schemes. Market-share building, as noted earlier, may be pursued in cases where the present market position and objective analysis of corporate resources suggest that potential for expansion exists. This aggressive share-building strategy, inevitably, carries risks which require expert evaluation.

Only about 20 per cent of the businesses surveyed by PIMS enjoyed market-share gains of two points or more from 1970 to 1972; these successes were, as might be expected, mostly among relatively new businesses.

Before they launch an agressive market-share-building strategy, PIMS proposes that companies should be prepared to answer the following questions:

(a) Are there adequate financial resources?
(b) If the drive for market share is not successful, will the company remain viable?
(c) Will market targets be capable of being achieved within the constraints imposed, e.g. monopoly?

2. *Holding strategies* are designed to maintain the existing market share held by a company: preserving the status quo. This cautious policy may be followed because further expansion of market share has been judged to be too costly. 'For established businesses in advanced economies – which is to say, for the majority of businesses in advanced economies – holding is undoubtedly the most common strategic goal with respect to market share.'

PIMS researchers acknowledged that, because competitive conditions in markets vary so much, useful generalisations about methods of securing and maintaining profitable market shares are difficult to make. As observed earlier, however, some broad relationships were found to exist between RoI and competitive behaviour. Large-market-share firms earn high rates of return when they charge premium prices – usually accompanied by premium quality. In addition, RoI is usually greater for large-share businesses when they spend more than their major competitors on marketing and R&D. But for small-share firms, the most profitable holding strategy tends to be just the opposite: RoI is highest when prices are somewhat below the average of those charged by market leaders, and when marketing and R&D expenses are relatively low.

3. *Harvesting strategies* involve deliberate policies of allowing market shares to fall to secure higher short-term earnings and increased cash flows. This type of disinvestment decision is often dictated more by necessity than by strategic choice.

PIMS research reveals that only large firms are, in general, able to follow this strategy successfully. 'Market leaders enjoyed rates of return about ¾ point higher when they allowed market share to decline over 1970–2.' It was not possible to measure definitively the profitability of harvesting because in many cases market share were reduced by intensified competition, rising costs, etc. Nevertheless, it is apparent that following a deliberate harvesting strategy 'affects profits diametrically differently from "building" . . .'

4. *Divesting strategies* are aimed at selling or liquidating the business because other business opportunities offer prospects of better growth and profitability. In BCG matrix terms, this strategy might be applied to dogs and question marks/ problem children.

In addition to divestment or harvest strategies, Harrigan and Porter propose that leadership and niche should be included among the strategies for decline, 'which vary greatly, not only in their goals but also in their implications for investment, and managers can pursue them individually or, in some cases, sequentially'.[40]

Leadership strategy is followed by a firm which tries to reap above-average profitability by remaining one of the few companies in a declining industry. Having obtained this position, the company will usually switch to a holding or controlled harvesting strategy. It is then, in theory, able to become more profitable (taking the investment into account) because it can exert more control over the process of decline. There are obvious risks attached to this policy.

Niche strategy in a declining industry involves identifying a segment that will either maintain stable demand or decay slowly and which, at the same time, has market conditions allowing for high returns. A company choosing this exit strategy moves quickly, obtains a strong position in this segment and disinvests from other sectors.

Harrigan and Porter reported that companies that are most objective about managing the decline process are also participants in the substitute industry: they view decline as a potential opportunity for profit.

Low-market-share-strategies

The case for high market share has so often been emphasised that, as Woo and Cooper[41] assert, 'conventional wisdom has it that companies with low market shares are doomed to marginal profits, at best, while market share leaders show the best returns on investment'. If this view is accepted uncritically, the strategic alternatives facing such companies would seem to be either to fight hard and build up market shares or to leave the market. However, it is contended that companies in industries with slow growth and few product changes, and those making frequently purchased products, are among businesses that prosper with low market share. Likewise, low-share businesses that follow a specific focused competitive strategy, often emphasising quality and cost, appear to do best.

In 1978 Hammermesh and associates researched three US companies which had low market shares: Burroughs Corporation, Crown Cork and Seal Co. Inc. and the Union Camp Corporation. All these earn 'quite respectable returns on their equity, have healthy profit margins and continue to maintain strong sales year after year'. The only thing these companies had in common was low market share; their market environments were extremely different. But it was found that their strategies shared four characteristics: creative market segmentation, efficient use of R&D, strictly controlled growth ('think small') and strong leadership.

Careful segmentation is vital for a low-share company which 'must compete in the segments where its own strengths will be most highly valued and where its large competitors will be most unlikely to compete'. Crown Cork and Seal, for example, chose to concentrate on two product segments – metal cans for hard-to-hold products like beer and soft drinks, and aerosol cans. Because transport costs are a high proportion of total costs, Crown Cork built small single-product plants near its customers instead of large and possibly more efficient multiproduct plants some distance away.

These two market segments have both shown disproportionate growth; they also need expert skills in container design and production. Crown Cork is also in a strong position because it is the largest supplier of filling equipment to the soft-drink and brewing industries. Growth segments needing special expertise have resulted in profitable marketing opportunities for this low-market-share supplier.

An example of the efficient use of R&D is given by Union Camp, whose chairman declares that the company does little basic research like Du Pont, but is good at improving processes, developing improved and some new products, and helping to build new manufacturing capabilities.

Burroughs' R&D is concentrated on 'truly innovative products'; its chairman is directly interested in this activity and 'exerts tremendous pressure on his engineers'.

Low-share companies also strictly control their expansion; Burroughs' growth is limited to 15 per cent per annum. In the rapidly growing computer industry, where General Electric and RCA found the pursuit of market share too costly, Burroughs has been content with slowly gaining modest increases in market share.

Another important factor is that low-market-share companies, unlike many of their larger competitors, are not on the whole diversified. If they diversify, they tend to enter closely related areas of business.

The final characteristic of these companies is the 'pervasive influence of the chief executive'. For example, the chairman of Union Camp retains responsibility for sales and marketing.

Hammermesh[42] admits that low-market-share businesses face serious obstacles to success, such as small research budgets, few economies of scale in production, limited public and customer recognition and difficulties in attracting capital and ambitious employees. Also, previous research has indicated that on average the RoI in low-share businesses is much less than in businesses with high market shares.

Extended research into low-market-share firms was undertaken by Woo and Cooper, who studied 40 businesses taken from a total of 649 domestic manufacturing firms over the period 1972–5. These low-share businesses were selected on the criteria of a pre-tax RoI of at least 20 per cent and market shares not exceeding 20 per cent of the combined share of their three largest competitors. Because of the nature of the PIMS database, from which these firms originated, most of them were divisions of large corporations rather than 'free-standing' small businesses.

The findings of this research showed the following:

1. *Profitable low-market-share businesses exist in low-growth markets* (the names of the companies and their industry segments could not be revealed but the researchers were able to establish characteristics, as reflected by 13 different factors).
2. *Their products do not change often* – a stable market environment is the principal factor. 'Low market growth, infrequent product and process changes, high value added, and high purchase frequency all contribute to more predictable and less turbulent environments.' Such markets are not likely to attract new entrants.

3. *Most products are standardised and few extra services are offered* – 'contrary to expectations, 72.5 per cent of successful low-share performers competed in markets characterised by standard products'.
4. *Most make industrial components or supplies* – small businesses can forge strong links with their customers by understanding their needs in terms of performance, service and cost.
5. *More than half of the low-share businesses studied offered products and supplies that are frequently purchased*, and for which customers 'tend to rely more on experience and less on the brand name of market leaders for indications of reliability and performance'. Such suppliers had comparatively low working capital ratios, because 'high purchase frequency usually tends to faster turnover of inventory and receivables'.
6. *Over 80 per cent of profitable low-share businesses were in industries with high-value-added products*. These industries are less prone to forward integration by suppliers or backward integration by customers. Also, many opportunities exist for product differentiation.[41]

In summary, low-market-share businesses that are well managed may well be profitable, provided they have carefully thought through their market opportunities related to their limited resources. Selective focus is the leading feature for a successful strategy: particular market segments are identified and customer needs closely studied – product quality, price and service are crucial factors. Strict control is kept over R&D and marketing costs and the width of the product line.

The various basic market-share strategies which have been reviewed do not offer ready-made solutions to specific marketing problems. Instead, they point to possible alternative ways of approaching particular market situations after carefully evaluating the costs and benefits which accompany them. Companies may vary their market-share strategies in line with market opportunities, the level of competitive activities and the general economic environment. From time to time, firms will probably find it necessary to modify their market posture; in today's business conditions a flexible policy may be advisable.

Critics of the market-share concept

The concept of market share is theoretically tidy and impressive, but it has attracted critics who point out that markets can be defined in many ways and the resultant market-share measurements can be quite different. It is not always easy to measure a firm's market share because information on a specific market is inadequate or unobtainable.

In other cases, as Majaro[43] points out, all the variables measured indicate a constant market share; this is distinctly observable in oligopolistic industries such as cement, where a very small number of manufacturers dominate the market and where price leadership is strong.

Also, markets should be described in 'a marketing-orientated way'; a high-quality producer of, say, carpets should not be directly compared in market-share terms with a firm marketing lower-quality products. Like must be compared with like, otherwise market share analysis loses credibility; so precise definitions of markets are important before PIMS becomes really useful to a company in a specific industry and market sector.

Day has noted that the influence of market share is most apparent with high-value-added products, where there are significant barriers to entry and the competition consists of a few large, diversified firms with the attendant large overheads, e.g. plastics, major appliances, automobiles and semi-conductors. However, even in these industries there are factors that may distort market behaviour, such as the following:

1. A competitor may have significant, patented technology.
2. The principal component of a product may be supplied by a firm with inherent cost advantage because of an integrated process.
3. Acquisitions or licensing can result in access to significant experience (learning curve) or the benefit of lower costs through off-shore production or component sourcing.
4. Profitability may be highly sensitive to the rate of capacity utilisation, irrespective of size of plant.

In Day's opinion there are many situations where the relationship between profitability and market share is very tenuous. He states that there is, however, specific evidence from PIMS research that the value of market share is not as significant for consumer goods as for industrial products. 'The reasons are not well understood, but probably reflect differences in buying behaviour, the importance of product differentiation and the tendency for proliferation of marginally different brands in these categories.'[44]

Porter was particularly astringent in his comments on the popular portfolio approach in an interview with Christopher Lorenz of the *Financial Times*:

> The fundamental difficulty with BCG was that it tried to create one logic and strategy that provided the ultimate solution to any problem. It tried to take all the richness of competition, to say that the only important thing happening in any industry was the inexorable decline of cost, and that there was only one thing a company could do: capture that advantage by getting ahead of the 'experience curve'.[45]

From this belief sprang the delusion that the only way to success was to achieve massive scale and market leadership, or else clear out. But, as Porter pointed out, there are 'an infinite number of possible strategies, even in the same industry'.

His views are equally strong about the 'hackneyed four-box diagram' known as the BCG portfolio matrix. He prefers to develop a highly complex map of corporate activities called 'the value chain', made of contributions from the various specialised activities of a company such as technology, human resource management and purchasing. When a company has defined precisely which activities result in a competitive edge, it should organise itself to develop this leverage (see Chapter 5).

Reflecting on his seminal text *Competitive Strategy*[10] (already referred to in Chapter 5), Porter concedes that his original views now need some revision inasmuch as 'companies should not just concentrate on either cost or differentiation'. They should always aim to achieve an effective balance and blend of these and other inputs. Precepts tend to be simple; their interpretation should not, however, be simplistic.

Modern design and production technologies, efficient cost control and well-planned marketing may, in fact, enable companies to offer variety and quality at highly competitive prices. In retail distribution, for example, the British department store group John Lewis Partnership (JLP) has built up an enviable reputation based on quality, service and also keen pricing ('never knowingly undersold').

Peters points out that, for a decade after establishing the PIMS database, its originators argued that market share was the 'prime begetter of profits'. But 'reanalysis of the data led to a startling and more robust conclusion'. While high market share brings high profit, *sustainable* market share depends mostly on leadership in what the PIMS researchers call 'relative perceived product or service quality', i.e. product attributes relative to competitive products as perceived by customers. Peters draws attention to the fact that PIMS researchers now state that relative quality is the most important single factor affecting an SBU's long-term performance. Superior ratings on relative perceived quality enable firms to 'outearn those in the bottom third by a two-to-one margin'.[9]

Peters stresses that 'this conclusion' is largely independent of sector activity (service versus manufacturing; consumer versus industrial), geography (North America versus Europe), or market trajectory (low growth versus high growth; low inflation versus high inflation). Further discussion of the impact of quality on business occurs in Chapter 11.

As noted earlier, care is needed with definitions of the measures used in portfolio analysis, particularly where market share is concerned. How is the product market or market sector defined? What level of geographic division is exercised?

> What is meaningful for a manufacturer of industrial equipment facing dominant local competition in each of the national markets in the EEC? Because the company is in each market it has a 5 per cent of the total EEC market, while the larger regional competitor has 9 per cent. In this case the choice of a regional rather than national market definition was dictated by the *trend* to similarity of product requirements throughout the EEC and the consequent feasibility of a single manufacturing facility to serve several countries.[44]

Market share at *any* price is likely to lead to corporate suicide. Sooner or later the sales curve will flatten out, while profit contributions will reach a maximum and then start to deteriorate. Gains in market share will be at increasingly heavy costs, so that to grab an extra percentage of the total market demand may not be justifiable in profit terms.

Strategies to increase market shares should, therefore, take note of *all* the factors which will influence profitable development. An efficient system of costing is clearly demanded or the chase after increasing market share may end in frustration. Most companies, as Sevin[46] has pointed out, are multiproduct firms which lack sophisticated analytical techniques for determining and allocating marketing costs and net profit contributions. In real-life market conditions the complexity of business operations, compounded by the lack of really adequate management information, renders it difficult if not impossible to indicate precisely the relationships between market share and profitability. It should be borne in mind that developing a market share entails a long-term investment in time and money and may well cut back profits in the immediate and middle future.

Market-share analysis is concerned with establishing the relative size of a firm's business in comparison with its competitors in a given market segment. This approach is the logical step forward from market segmentation analysis, which is the foundation of an effective marketing strategy. The profitable exploitation of market opportunities stems from objective market research and the identification of potentially valuable market segments which are relevant to the resources of a particular company. In these selected market sectors a firm should plan to secure effective market shares, carefully monitoring its overall progress and profitability.

MCKINSEY/GE BUSINESS ASSESSMENT ARRAY

This sophisticated business screen consists of a nine-cell portfolio matrix with the horizontal axis representing industry attractiveness (market dimension) and the vertical axis representing business strengths (product dimension) of the strategic business unit (see Figure 6.9). It was developed in the USA by General Electric planners from portfolio approaches used by the consulting firm of McKinsey.

Industry attractiveness is based on rating of factors such as market growth rate, market size, profit margin, competitive intensity, cyclicality, seasonability and scale economies. According to applied weighting, a particular industry is classified as high, medium or low in overall industry attractiveness.

Business strength or the ability to compete in a specific industry recognises that certain competences will be necessary. SWOT analysis, as noted in Chapter 5, is applied in the assessment procedures.

The following factors are weighted: relative market share, price competitiveness, product quality, knowledge of customer/market, sales effectiveness and geography.

Three 'zones' – known as green (go), amber (caution) and red (stop) – indicate respectively: invest and grow; maintain share rather than increase or decrease it; and harvest or divest.

This stop–caution–go screen would be helpful in guiding investment decisions and, obviously, would require regular review. Kotler[3] states that many companies first classify their business using the BCG approach and then go into greater detail with a GE screen.

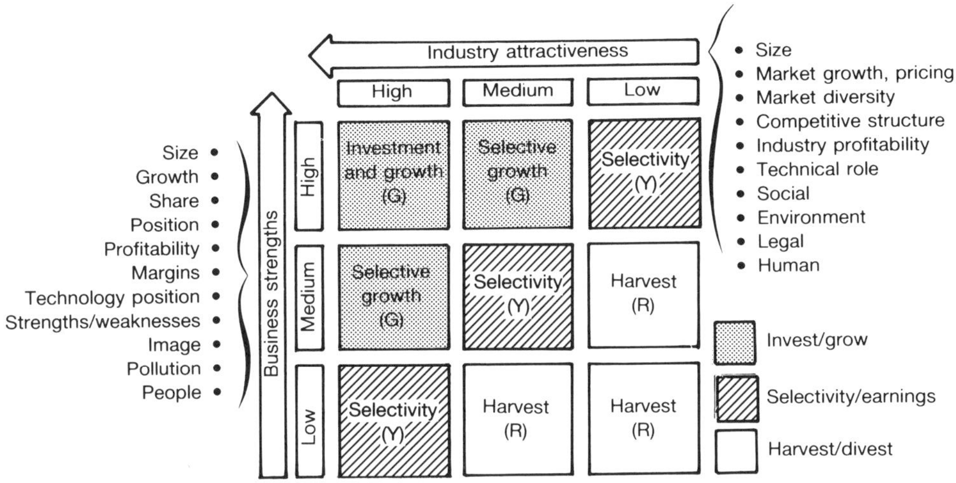

FIGURE 6.9 McKinsey/GE business screen (Source: reprinted, by permission of the publisher, from *Corporate Planning Techniques and Applications*, ed. R. J. Allio and M. W. Pennington, p. 214. © 1979 AMACON, a division of American Management Association, New York. All rights reserved.)

Aaker[32] cautions that, although the GE screen is 'much richer and more broadly applicable than the BCG matrix', its measures can also be 'more subjective and ambiguous', especially across business units: for example, in the selection and weighting of factors. Also, like the BCG matrix, results are significantly influenced by definitions of product markets.

AD LITTLE BUSINESS PROFILE MATRIX

This has two basic dimensions: competitive position (vertical axis) and stage of industry maturity (horizontal axis) (see Figure 6.10).

The four stages of industry maturity follow a theme similar to that of the product life-cycle stages. Competitive position has five stages: weak, tentative, favourable, strong and dominant. Wind[33] points out that the data used are primarily historical, and, as with the BCG, the correlates of the dimensions are not explicit. It offers little advantage over the BCG, which it closely resembles.

SHELL INTERNATIONAL DIRECTIONAL POLICY MATRIX (DPM)

This also has two basic dimensions: profitability prospects (horizontal axis) and competitive capabilities (vertical axis) (see Figure 6.11).

The profitability dimension has three classifications: unattractive, average and attractive. Profitability is determined by market growth. The competitive dimension

		STAGE OF INDUSTRY MATURITY			
		Embryonic	*Growth*	*Maturity*	*Ageing*
COMPETITIVE POSITION	*Dominant*				
	Strong				
	Favourable				
	Tentative				
	Weak				

FIGURE 6.10 AD Little business profile matrix (Source: Wind[33])

		PROSPECTS FOR SECTOR PROFITABILITY		
		Unattractive	*Average*	*Attractive*
COMPANY'S COMPETITIVE CAPABILITIES	*Weak*	Disinvest	Phased withdrawal Custodial	Double or quit
	Average	Phased withdrawal	Custodial Growth	Try harder
	Strong	Cash generation	Growth Leader	Leader

FIGURE 6.11 Shell International directional policy matrix (Source: Seidl[47])

has the same three classifications; it measures the relative competitive strength of the business or product:

> The prospects for a business can be evaluated for different scenarios and will establish a range of positions along the horizontal axis; the appraisal of its competitive ability will put it in a position along the vertical line. Between them, these assessments define a limited range of logical positions in the overall decision grid. These positions, in turn, can point to possible strategies for which more detailed study appears to be justified.[47]

The strategy recommendations contained in the nine cells of the matrix and the categories of product are not dissimilar to the BCG approach. Like the BCG matrix, there is considerable subjectivity in selecting criteria and in evaluating business units, although, of course, the DPM is more specific and quantitative.

Shell[47] stresses that whatever strategy is eventually selected, the aim is that it should be resilient, i.e. viable in a wide range of possible futures. Hence, each strategy ideally should be tested against all scenarios; the results in all of these should be acceptable – no disasters should result.

The Shell portfolio of investments is analysed each year against the updated scenarios. The analysis tries to judge the mix of different businesses, the mix of countries, to examine where there are opportunities which one might be missing, when the business is unbalanced or vulnerable to risk, and what the internal strengths and weaknesses are.

Shell completes its analysis by a technique known as 'vulnerability analysis', developed from modern decision theory and derived from the subjective yet informed appraisal of a number of experts whose estimates are quantified and the potential impact calculated.

OTHER PORTFOLIO MODELS

In addition to the four basic product/market portfolio approaches, Wind[33] has developed a *model based on risk/return*, i.e. based on the two fundamental assumptions of portfolio analysis: expected return and degree of risk involved.

Other portfolio approaches have set the various stages of the product life cycle against stages of market development. For example, Enis[37] has designed a *product/market matching matrix* with four stages of the PLC on the vertical axis and four stages of market behaviour on the horizontal axis (See Figure 6.12).

It will be seen that strategic guidance is given related to the nature of market development (new, expanding, stable and contracting) and the phase of product life (introduction, growth, maturity and decline). Also, there are three major areas of strategic activity: market development, market extension and market exploitation. As the result of various marketing-mix decision, strategic decisions involving building, holding or harvesting will be reflected in the relevant areas of the matrix.

Enis observes that the traditional PLC discussion essentially assumes that PLC stage and market stage are synonymous. In this case, the position would be termed 'market development' and the trend as indicated in Figure 6.12. However, 'marketers should consider the possibility that the market-development stage and the PLC stage are not synchronised'.[37] Aggressive marketing might push the PLC ahead of market stage: for example, a product introduced into one market is brought into a new market, or a mature or even declining product is offered to an expanding or stable market. Enis instances the products of industrialised countries, such as chemical pesticides or jet aircraft, offered to developing countries. In such cases 'market extension' occurs (see Figure 6.12).

Enis says that a less admired but perhaps more common situation arises when a particular product lags behind the market stage. For example, a firm may introduce its brand of tyres, toothpaste or turbine generators into markets already covered by competitors; this is referred to in Figure 6.12 as market exploitation.

Barksdale and Harris[24] have developed an *integrated portfolio model incorporating the BCG and PLC approaches* (see Figure 6.13).

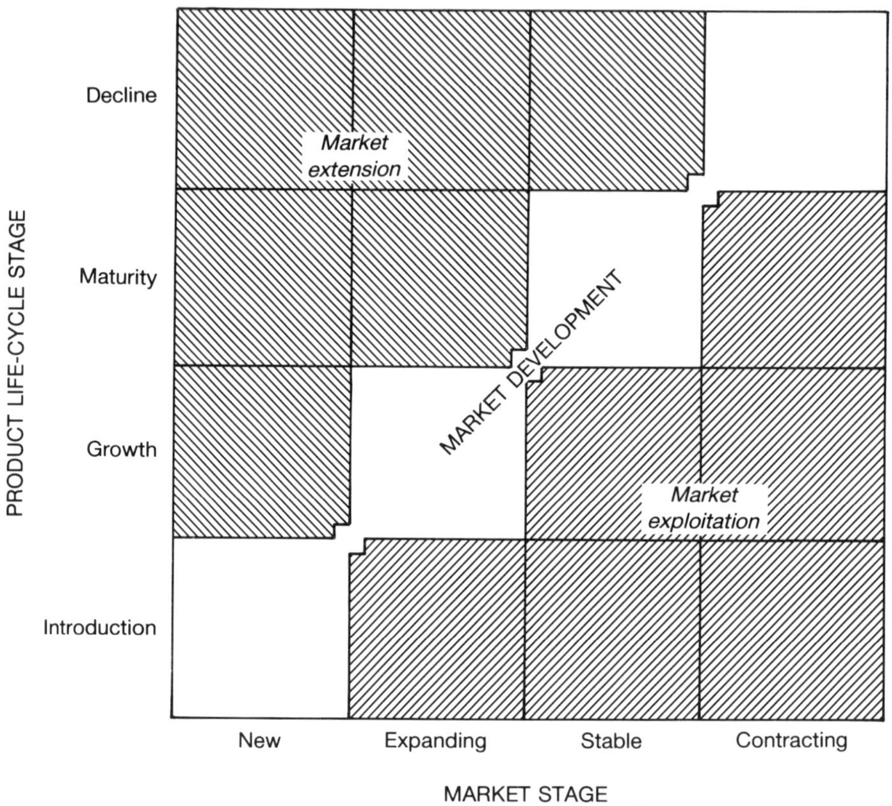

FIGURE 6.12 Product/market matching matrix (Source: Enis[37])

These researchers declare that the BCG matrix, as at present formulated, is incomplete for two reasons: (1) it ignores products that are new to the world; and (2) it overlooks products with negative rates of growth. 'In other words, the product portfolio matrix concentrates on the growth and maturity stages of the product life cycle.'

Following the practice of attaching names to identify products in different cells of the matrix, Barksdale and Harris label pioneering products 'infants', while products with high shares of declining markets are described as 'war horses' and those with low shares of declining markets are 'dodos' (see Figures 6.13 and 6.14).

This 'extended hybrid model' recognises the importance of both the pioneering and decline stages of the PLC in strategic appraisals. The eight-cell matrix in Figure 6.13 is made up of the customary four BCG categories plus the new classifications mentioned above.

In a declining market 'cash cows' become 'war horses'; these successful veteran products still hold strong market positions and, if efficiently managed, can be significant cash generators. General Foods' Maxwell House coffee is given as an excellent example of a 'war horse'. For years it has been a leading brand of instant

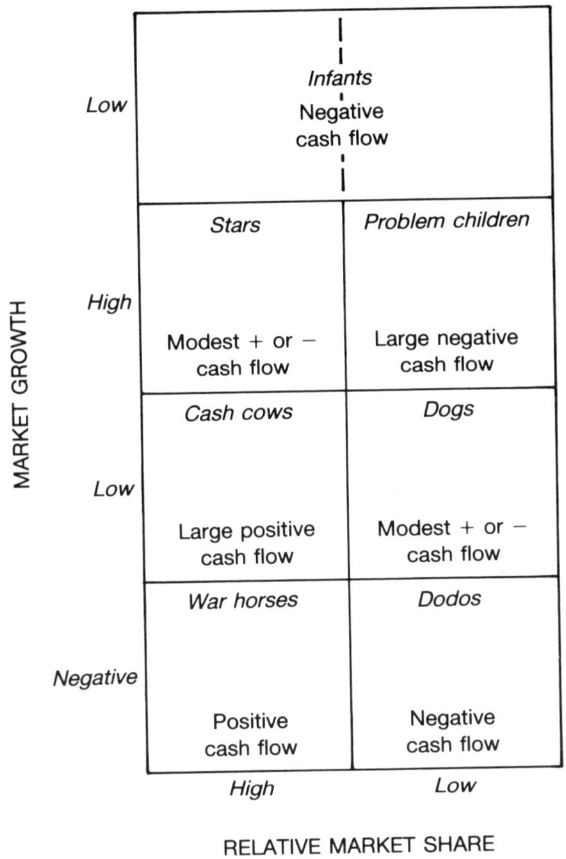

FIGURE 6.13 Product life-cycle portfolio matrix (Source: Barksdale and Harris[24])

coffee; although the market is declining, Maxwell House remains a viable successful brand.

'Dodos' (products with low shares of declining markets) offer little prospect of growth or cash generation; normally they are removed from the product portfolio, but there are occasions when, as the result of competitors' withdrawal, it may be profitable for a firm to remain in a declining market. Nuclear reactors are given as an example of this type of product. The US market is rapidly declining because of government regulations, public opinion and accelerating cost.

'Infants' are innovative products that must be marketed expertly. They do not generate profits for some time if, indeed, ever; meanwhile they consume large amounts of cash. The British electronic home information system, Prestel, is a typical example of this type of pioneering market activity.

Barksdale and Harris admit that their expanded matrix does not overcome the problems involved in defining products and markets, or eliminate the ambiguity

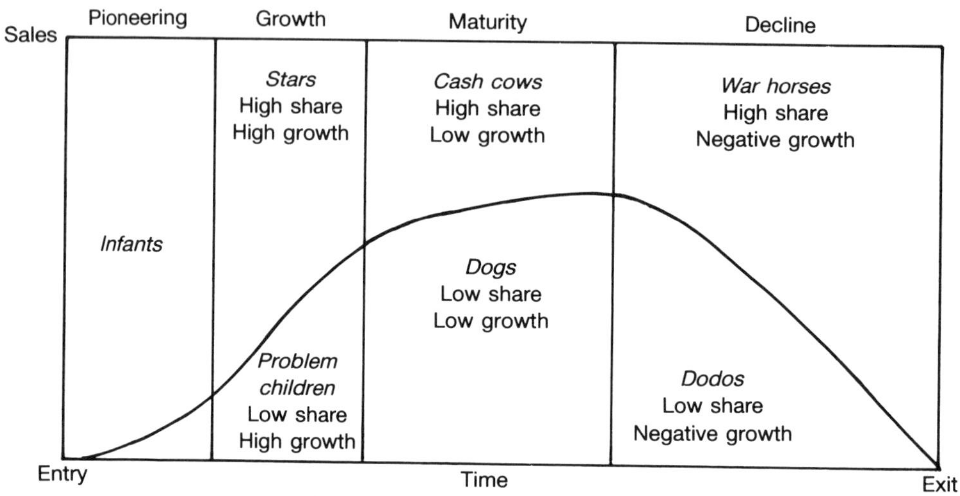

FIGURE 6.14 Combined PLC/product portfolio concepts (Source: Barksdale and Harris[24])

encountered in defining rates of growth. But their approach does claim to offer a stronger and more comprehensive framework for strategic decision making.

A further interesting and creative approach to product/market analysis is given by Campbell and Cunningham,[48] who conducted a two-year study involving 63 customers of a leading company in the packaging industry. Data covering 167 trading relationships in 10 market segments were collected. The analyses involved three stages:

1. A life-cycle classification of customer relationships. Only customers for one product or relatively homogeneous product group should be entered in the same analysis chart. Separate analyses are necessary where several different products are involved (see Figure 6.15).
2. A customer/competitor chart which allows management to evaluate their competitive position in each market segment (see Figure 6.16). Separate charts should be prepared for different products. Examination of competitors' trading activities should be useful in designing effective strategies.
3. Identification of key customers and individual analysis of the most important ones. These are then grouped into a customer portfolio similar to the growth/share matrix (see Figure 6.17). The horizontal axis refers to the competitive position of the supplier company; the vertical axis relates to the growth rate of the customer's market. 'Competitive position is measured by the share the supplier holds of the customer's purchases relative to the share held by the largest competitor.'[48] Examination of Figure 6.17 reveals, for instance, that the company has one key customer in cell 4 whose market is growing steadily and where the company's share of purchases is relatively high. But there are

Criteria for classification of customers	Customer categories			
	Tomorrow's customers	Today's special customers	Today's regular customers	Yesterday's customers
Sales volume	Low	High	Average	Low
Use of strategic resources*	High	High	Average	Low
Age of relationship	New	Old	Average	Old
Supplier's share of customer's purchases	Low	High	Average	Low
Profitability of customer to supplier	Low	High	Average	Low

* The technical, marketing and production resources devoted to developing future business rather than maintaining existing business.

FIGURE 6.15 Life-cycle classification of customer relationships (Source: Campbell and Cunningham[48])

some less optimistic business situations, such as cell 3, which require further investigation.

In cases where a very large customer represents a high proportion of sales, a more detailed breakdown splits the customer into a 'series of subcustomers'. As Figure 6.18 shows, the largest customer is made up of four separate businesses; these have been classified along the horizontal axis using the same categories as Figure 6.15. On the vertical axis, the growth rate of purchases has the same dimensions as in Figure 6.17. Analysis of Figure 6.18 shows that there is a small but developing business for product 1; a slow-growing but specialised business for product 2; a large and steadily developing business for product 3; and a slightly declining demand for product 4.

This three-stage customer analysis applied to a specific industrial market sequentially refines and focuses the market evaluation. It adapts the well-known marketing concepts of PLC, segmentation and portfolio analysis.

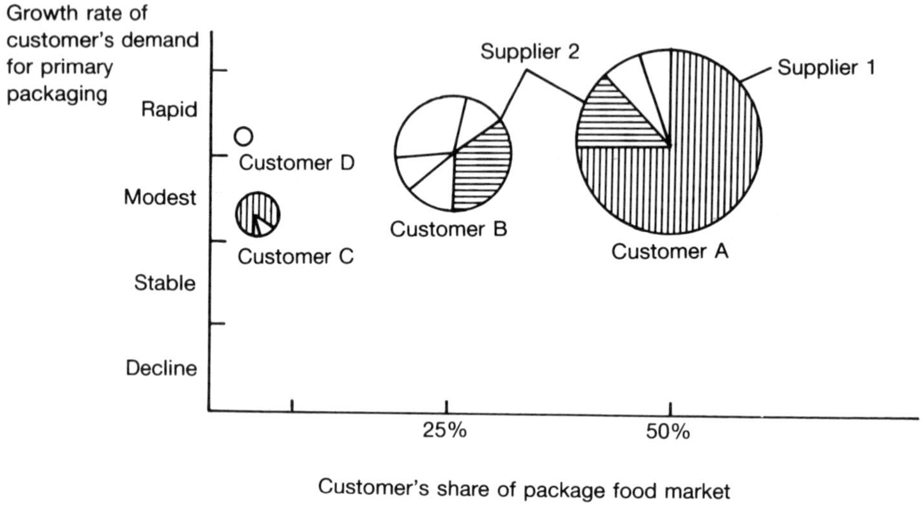

Note: Size of circle is size of customer's purchases of primary packaging and pie slice is size of each competitor's share.

FIGURE 6.16 Customer/competitor analysis (Source: Campbell and Cunningham[48])

OVERVIEW

Portfolio frameworks are intended to supplement, not supplant, managerial judgement. They should be used sensitively and with an understanding of their limitations. Wind and others have warned against viewing portfolio analyses, 'despite their attractiveness, as a ready cure for any ailment . . . If a prescription ignores any relevant dimensions or the projected position of the business under alternative scenarios, it will be quite misleading.'[49]

The four principal portfolio models that have been discussed are based on a matrix, one axis of which represents the relative market share or similar characteristic of a firm's strength, while the other axis relates to industry or market attractiveness. Some of these models use composite dimensions (e.g. McKinsey/GE) consisting of several objective and subjective factors to describe each axis. Others, like the BCG, have a single measurable criterion for each axis. Because managerial judgement largely forms the basis for the inclusion of many factors in composite dimensions attached to portfolio analyses, considerable care is needed in interpreting the resultant information. Before portfolio dimensions are imposed, a company's trading environment and resources should be thoroughly studied. As Wind suggests, a tailor-made approach may be desirable.

HBR SURVEY OF PORTFOLIO PLANNING

In 1979 a survey of *Fortune*'s '1000' companies was sponsored by the *Harvard Business Review* to evaluate strategic portfolio planning practices. It was found

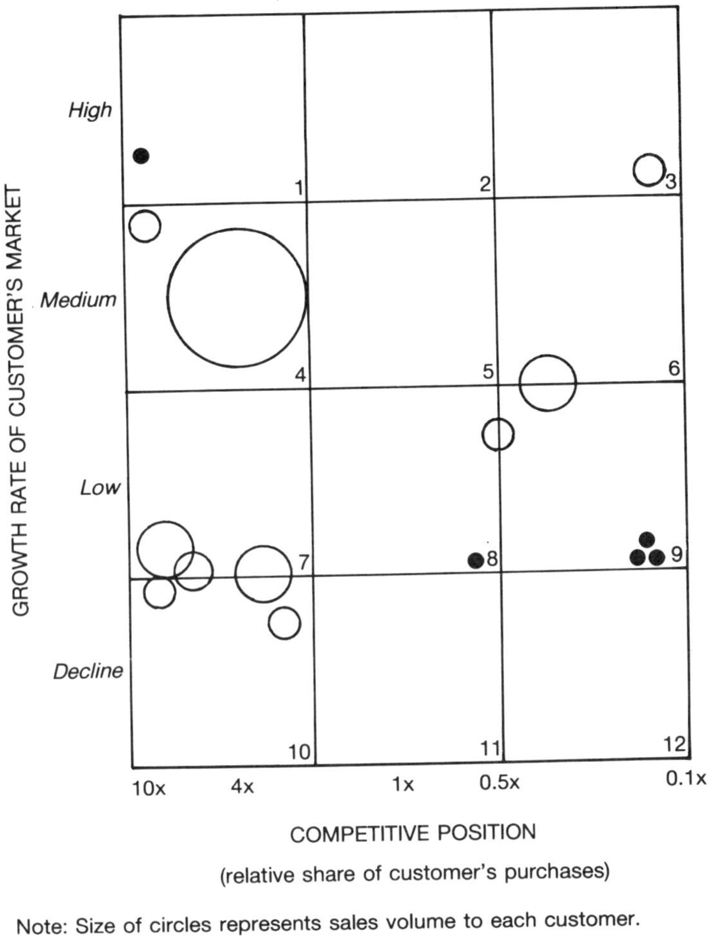

FIGURE 6.17 Key customers portfolio (Source: Campbell and Cunningham[48])

that portfolio models help managers to strengthen their planning processes and solve the problems of managing diversified industrial organisations. However, it was also found that the secret to success was not just in the analytical techniques that make up portfolio planning theory, but also occurred in meeting the administrative challenges of incorporating the theory into management practice.

The more serious limitations of portfolio planning were identified as: (1) portfolio planning takes a great deal of time and companies 'often get stuck' trying to implement it; (2) if portfolio planning is regarded merely as an analytical planning tool, a company will fail to reap benefits; (3) in implementing portfolio planning companies often focus on inappropriate factors, e.g. cost efficiency instead of organisational responsiveness; and (4) portfolio planning seems unable to 'successfully address the issue of new business generation'.[50]

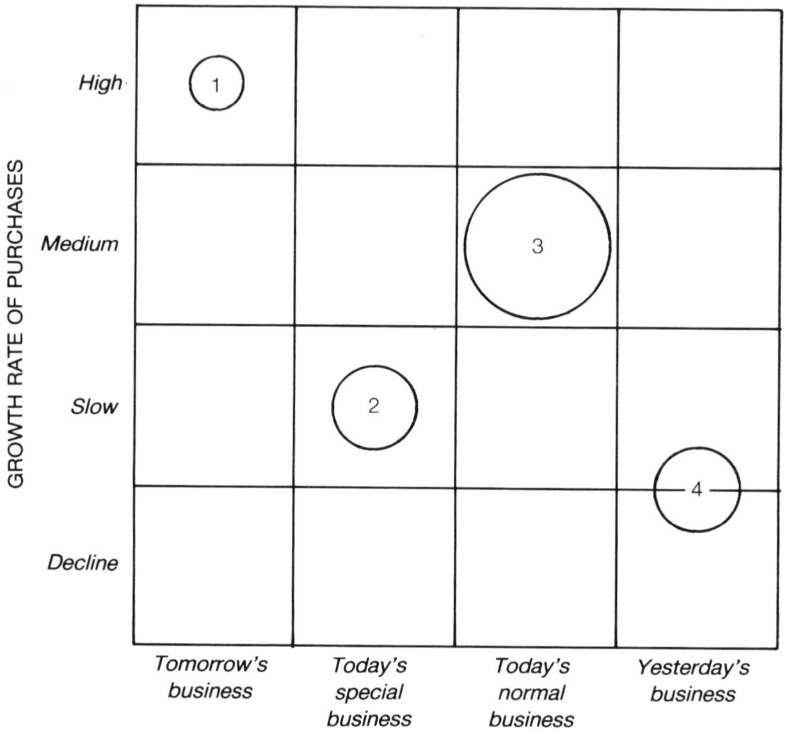

Note: Size of circles represents the volume of customer's purchases. Numbers refer to the different products of the supplier company sold to the customer.

FIGURE 6.18 Analysis of a key customer (Source: Campbell and Cunningham[48])

Despite the above difficulties, corporate managers supported portfolio planning largely because the approach: (1) promotes significant improvements in the quality of both business and corporate strategies; (2) results in selective allocation of resources; (3) provides a framework for adapting overall planning to the needs of each business; and (4) greatly increases companies' strategic control.

In most companies, portfolio planning is 'triggered by a performance crisis and the need to allocate resources selectively in a capital-constrained environment'. In major companies, the theory has been rapidly accepted as a useful management tool, although a great deal of 'ill focused' debate has been centred around the analytical techniques – which grid to use – and not enough attention has been given to the core issue of how a company can best 'define an SBU and assign a strategic mission to it'.

In 1979, 36 per cent of *Fortune*'s '1000' and 45 per cent of *Fortune*'s '500' industrial companies had introduced portfolio planning to some extent, and each year during the following five years another 25 to 30 firms used this approach.

According to the survey, 70 per cent of all organisations commenced portfolio planning by comprehensively re-examining the definition of each of their businesses. 'In 75 per cent of these, the re-evaluation led to the classification of SBUs as sometimes or usually different from operating units. The larger the company, the more likely it is to have SBUs that do not coincide with operating units.'[50] However, the resultant SBUs are usually aggregations of existing operating units or segments of single units.

Some of the companies surveyed were found to have reached the process portfolio planning stage very quickly; others had many attempts without success.

Portfolio planning is here to stay because it can provide these critical benefits to management: (1) the generation of good strategies because of analysis of competitive activities; (2) the promotion of more selective resource allocation trade-offs; and (3) the major contribution it makes to the management process. 'The essence of managing diversity is the creation in each business of a pattern of influence that corresponds to the nature of the business, its competitive position and its strategic mission.'[49]

Finally, portfolio planning should not be left as 'an elegant theory'; it must be implemented, and the findings of the survey indicate that this is happening widely.

SCENARIO ANALYSIS

Traditional forecasting and planning approaches are based, it has been alleged,[51] on the assumption that tomorrow's world will be much the same as today's; this inference expressly ignores the likelihood of changes, some of which may be drastic and have far-reaching effects, as the energy crises of the 1970s had in the UK. Ansoff observes that 'when the oil-producing nations united and suddenly produced a major discontinuity in the world petroleum prices, many firms around the world were using extrapolation-based long-range planning to anticipate the future. Understandably, no advanced indications of the surprise were given in forecasts used by these firms.'[52] In 1970, in fact, the US Cabinet Task Force on Oil reported: 'We do not predict a substantial price rise in world oil markets over the coming decade.'[53] With hindsight – hypothetically the most reliable input into forecasting – this considered opinion appears disastrously defective.

Corporate decisions tend to be made on the basis of information from specialised sectors of management: research and development, technical, financial, production, sales and marketing, etc. When attitudes appeared to be more stable and behaviour patterns more readily predictable, various inputs from management specialists seemed to be adequate. Today, however, such information would be incomplete without data about social, cultural, political and environmental factors affecting the consumption of a diverse range of goods and services.[54] Marked shifts in values have been noted by analysts such as Gordon Rattray Taylor,[53] who has defined values as end states, i.e. ways of life and patterns of behaviour; concepts such as security, honesty, freedom, piety and justice.

Scenario analysis enables management to expand their personal and professional horizons and to project their minds imaginatively and constructively when planning for the future. A scenario, as Aaker sees it, 'is an alternative view of the future environment that is usually prompted by an alternative possible answer to a strategic question or by a prospective future event or trend'.[32] The process of scenario building gives management the chance to consider, in some depth, the uncertainties facing a business and the factors likely to contribute to the threats and opportunities which may lie ahead.

Sets of scenarios may be generated related to technological, economic, psycho-social, political and ecological trends: for instance, the likely impact of political and economic developments in eastern Europe or China; the extent to which Japanese firms will continue to challenge specific industries, like cars and electronics; the potential effects on present members of the EC of its further extension; the impact of demographic trends on patterns of consumption related to specific industries and their products and services; the extent to which multinational corporations will develop further their global interests and the likely effects on investment policies and employment opportunities; the likely trends in US trade policies over the next few years; political developments in Africa and Asia and their effects on supplies of strategic materials; and the degree to which perceived new environmental hazards may be identified in the near future, and the kinds of industry that may be affected.

The range of issues is obviously very wide, and some discretion is needed to isolate those which are most likely to become salient within certain periods of time, perhaps up to five years, ten years, and so on. Because of the speed of modern communications, the intrusive nature of the mass media and the growing expertise of lobbyists, issues can quickly come into prominence and present companies with problems, as the chemical industry has found to its cost.

Scenarios have been developed by consumer research groups such as SRI International, with life-style segmentation typologies, and also by large corporations like Royal Dutch/Shell. In planning for the 1980s, for example, Shell used two alternative scenarios: 'The World of Internal Contradictions' (WIC), and 'Business Expansion' (BE). The former propounded slow growth in an environment of social stress; the latter, more optimistic view, was that although trade cycles would no longer be predictable, and there would generally be a perplexing, uneasy environment, healthy growth could be achieved in the long term, provided that strong political leadership, more enterprising industrial policies and more closely integrated systems of international trading were pursued. Which of these scenarios came nearest to reality may now be debated with the benefit of retrospective analysis.

Applied Futures Ltd, which is linked with the International Research Institute on Social Change (RISC) projects scenarios on a 15–20-year time span, which include quantitative, technological and qualitative data covering social and political trends. Taylor Nelson's 'Monitor' service is now operated by Applied Futures.

The SRI International approach to scenario building is based on 60,000 interviews every year through its network of 17 research organisations across the world. From analyses of the resultant data, a sociocultural map is developed which presents the relationships between the influences underlying trends in values, social behaviour, etc.

SRI has adopted an eight-step procedure in developing scenarios, as follows:[55]

1. Analysis of key company decisions and strategic interests
↓
2. Identification of key factors directly influencing decisions
↓
3. Identification of key environmental forces influencing key decision factors
↓
4. Extensive analysis of each identified environmental force
↓
5. Definition of 'scenario logics', i.e. organising themes, principles or assumptions that provide each scenario with logical foundation
↓
6. Elaboration of selected scenarios, combining scenario logics with environmental analyses
↓
7. Analysis of implications of each scenario for key decision factors identified in step 2
↓
8. Analysis of implications of scenarios for corporate decisions and strategies

This eight-step plan outlines the sequence of activities from initial analysis of key decisions and strategic interests to final analysis of the implications of specific scenarios for corporate decisions and strategies. In this process, probabilities may be attached to the incidence of certain factors, and the resultant scenarios may be viewed as 'pessimistic', 'optimistic' or 'most likely'. Projections of these different scenarios should be helpful in assessing, for example, opportunities for new products or services, or for developing sales in certain overseas markets.

In studies of the future oil environment, Shell has used the scenario approach, and analysed in depth the key environmental factors likely to influence its business. The Henley Centre, which has established a strong reputation for its forecasting services, constantly audits factors which are likely to develop into trends in consumption affecting the businesses of its clients.

Within the past decade, the free enterprise system has spread across the former centralised economies with varying degrees of success. How far state ownership and control of industry and commerce will be replaced by private enterprise poses many questions for firms seeking to transact business in these countries. With what success will the implacable political ideologies of many generations give way to democracy, free enterprise and personal freedom? These and many other problems are studied by scenario analysts.

At a Market Research Society seminar in June 1989, Joop de Vries of Shell International[56] revealed that his group felt it necessary, every two years, to update its view of the world; in doing so, the company was able to spot changes and to assesss how it had adjusted to these influences. Shell has 'always had a high-growth scenario which people thought a good thing'; the second scenario, however, looks at developing countries, and includes 'the very worrying demographic trends'; and a third scenario paints 'a picture of industry and the world [that] is profoundly different'. It questions the nature and purpose of companies and the ways in which they manage their resources and conduct their businesses. What kinds of structure will be effective in modern organisations? Hierarchical relationships may wane, as groups of professionals engaged in specialist activities become more widely evident in the knowledge-based industries which are a marked feature of developed economies.

Scenario analysis can be directly helpful in the development of strategic plans; it endeavours to give insight into the complex and uncertain environment of modern markets, so that decision making can take place within acceptable parameters of risk. Related to this process of analysis and evaluation is the technique of sensitivity analysis, which is concerned with generating likely outcomes from selected changes in the specific variables controlled by management. In the case of marketing, such factors are probably levels of pricing, advertising, etc. Spreadsheet software programs are popularly used in such analyses.

SUMMARY

Specific features of strategic market planning are market segmentation, product life-cycle analysis; the marketing portfolio approach; and scenario analysis.

Market segmentation recognises that nearly every main market can be divided into several micro or submarkets, according to certain characteristics of demand and supply. Effective segmentation is influenced by four factors: (1) identification; (2) measurability; (3) accessibility; and (4) appropriateness. Organisational markets may be segmented by customer size, location, industry classification, usage rate, nature of operation, etc.

Product life-cycle theory and innovative strategy are closely linked. Despite many critics, PLC had much to contribute: it emphasises that products have limited lives in which to earn profits. More than one PLC curve may be evident in certain markets. Marketing strategists should use PLC analytically and creatively by developing PLC profiles of the various products in their product ranges and by planning, in good time, for 'new blood' products.

Marketing portfolio analysis is critical to ensure that a balanced range of products and markets is achieved. Portfolio planning entails identification of strategic business units (SBUs). Four popular portfolio models have been developed: Boston Consulting Group (BCG); McKinsey/GE; AD Little; and Shell. Barksdale and Harris have developed an integrated PLC/portfolio matrix.

Four broad groups of market-share strategies are: building, holding, harvesting and divesting. Low market shares may be profitable in certain cases; expert handling is needed to ensure profitability.

Portfolio frameworks supplement managerial judgement: they do not supplant it. Before portfolio dimensions are imposed, thorough study of a firm's trading environment and resources must be made.

Scenario analysis is a technique for identifying key environmental factors which may be influential in specific markets, and may affect patterns of demand for many kinds of product and service. It enables management to develop alternative views of prospective events and trends, and attempts to reduce the risks and uncertainties of strategic planning.

REFERENCES

1. Levitt, Theodore, *Marketing for Business Growth*, McGraw-Hill, New York, 1974.
2. Smith, Wendell R, 'Product differentiation and market segmentation as alternative marketing strategies', *Journal of Marketing*, vol. 21, July 1956.
3. Kotler, Philip, *Marketing Management: Analysis, planning and control*, Prentice Hall, Englewood Cliffs, NJ, 1980.
4. Smith, Lee, 'The lures and limits of innovation', *Fortune*, 20 October 1980.
5. 'The simple successes of BTR', *Marketing Business*, August 1989.
6. Price, Roy, 'How BRS segments its markets', *Industrial Marketing Digest*, vol. 9, no. 1, 1984.
7. Harvey-Jones, Sir John, 'Niche markets and sound strategy', *Quarterly Enterprise Digest*, 31, London, September 1992.
8. Marsh, Peter, 'Specialities key to chemical industry recovery', *Financial Times*, 16 March 1988.
9. Peters, Tom, *Thriving on Chaos*, Macmillan, London, 1988.
10. Porter, Michael E., *Competitive Strategy*, Macmillan, New York, 1980.
11. Chisnall, Peter M., *Marketing: A behavioural analysis*, McGraw-Hill, Maidenhead, 1985.
12. Fazey, Ian Hamilton, 'Family planning for the young ones', *Financial Times*, 12 March 1987.
13. Rawsthorn, Alice, 'Reviving punctured fortunes', *Financial Times*, 13 July 1987.
14. Doyle, Peter and Saunders, John, 'Market segmentation and positioning in specialized industrial markets', *Journal of Marketing*, vol. 49, spring 1985.
15. De Kluyver, Cornelis A., and Whitlark, David B., 'Benefit segmentation for industrial products', *Industrial Marketing Management*, vol. 15, 1986.
16. Done, Kevin, 'Mercedes steers in direction of a less luxurious future', *Financial Times*, 27 January 1993.
17. Done, Kevin, 'Mercedes-Benz slaughters a sacred cow', *Financial Times*, 27 January 1993.
18. Doyle, Peter and Newbould, Gerald D., 'Advertising management for building societies', *Advertising Quarterly*, no. 42, winter 1974/5.
19. Channon, Derek, 'Through the eyes of the customers', *Banking World*, November 1987.
20. Hughes, Michael, 'Increasing penetration in industrial markets', in *Long Range Planning for Marketing and Diversification*, ed. B. Taylor and G. Wills, Bradford University Press/Crosby/Lockwood, London, 1971.

21. Polli, Rolando and Cook, Victor, 'Validity of the product life cycle', *Journal of Business*, vol. 42, no. 4, 1969.
22. Day, George, S., 'The product life cycle: analysis and applications issues', *Journal of Marketing*, no. 45, fall 1981.
23. Rink, David R, and Swan, John E., 'Product life cycle research: a literature review', *Journal of Business Research*, vol. 7, no. 3, 1979.
24. Barksdale, Hiram C., and Harris, Clyde E. jun., 'Portfolio analysis and the product life cycle', *Long Range Planning*, vol. 15, no. 6, 1982.
25. Cox, W. E., 'Product life cycles as marketing models', *Journal of Business*, October 1967.
26. Cunningham, M. T., 'The application of product life cycles to corporate strategy: some research findings', *Marketing*, spring 1969.
27. De Kluyver, Cornelius A., 'Innovation and industrial product life cycles', *California Management Review*, vol. 20, no. 1, 1977.
28. Clifford, Donald K. jun., 'Managing the product life cycle', *European Business*, July 1969.
29. Hogg, Sir Christopher, Chairman's Statement, Group Report, Courtaulds, May 1992.
30. Leadbeater, Charles, 'GKN: a multi-cultural challenge', *Financial Times*, 24 August 1990.
31. Linneman, Robert E., and Thomas, Michael J., 'A commonsense approach to portfolio planning', *Long Range Planning*, vol. 15, no. 2, 1982.
32. Aaker, David A., *Strategic Market Management*, John Wiley, New York, 1992.
33. Wind, Yoram J., *Product Policy: Concepts, methods and strategy*, Addison-Wesley, Reading, Mass., 1982.
34. Lorenz, Christopher, 'Shaking off the heavy brigade', *Financial Times*, 26 February 1993.
35. Hedley, Barry, 'Strategy and the "business portfolio" ', *Long Range Planning*, vol. 10, no. 1, 1977.
36. Boston Consulting Group, *Perspectives on Experience*, BCG, Boston, Mass., 1972.
37. Enis, Ben M., 'GE, PIMS, BCG and the PLC', *Business*, vol. 30, no. 3, 1980.
38. Buzzell, Robert, D., Bradley, T. Gale, and Sutton, Ralph G. M., 'Market share – a key to profitability', *Harvard Business Review*, vol. 53, no. 1, 1975.
39. Drucker, Peter F., *Management: Tasks, responsibilities, practices*, Harper and Row, New York, 1974.
40. Harrigan, Kathryn Rudic, and Porter, Michael E., 'End-game strategies for declining industries', *Harvard Business Review*, vol. 61, no. 4, 1983.
41. Woo, Carolyn Y., and Cooper, Arnold C., 'The surprising case for low market share', *Harvard Business Review*, vol. 60, no. 6, 1982.
42. Hammermesh, R. G., Anderson, M. J. jun., and Harris, J. E., 'Strategies for low market share businesses', *Harvard Business Review*, vol. 56, no. 3, 1978.
43. Majaro, Simon, 'Market share: deception or diagnosis?', *Marketing*, March 1977.
44. Day, George S., 'Diagnosing the product portfolio', *Journal of Marketing*, vol. 41, no. 2, 1977.
45. Porter, M. E. (interview with Christopher Lorenz), 'The man who put cash cows out to grass', *Financial Times*, 20 March 1987.
46. Sevin, Charles H., *Marketing Productivity Analysis*, McGraw-Hill, New York, 1965.
47. Seidl, R. L., 'How useful is corporate planning today?', Corporate Finance Conference, 10 October 1979, Shell Group Planning Division, Shell International Petroleum Co.

48. Campbell, N. C. G., and Cunningham, M. T., 'Customer analysis for strategy development in industrial markets', *Strategic Management Journal*, vol. 4, October/December 1983.
49. Wind, Yoram, and Mahajan, Vijay, 'Designing products and business portfolios', *Harvard Business Review*, vol. 59, no. 1, 1981.
50. Haspeslagh, Philippe, 'Portfolio planning: uses and limits', *Harvard Business Review*, vol. 60, no. 1, 1982.
51. Wack, Pieere, 'Scenarios: shooting the Rapids', *Harvard Business Review*, vol. 63, no. 6, 1985.
52. Ansoff, H. Igor, *Implanting Strategic Management*, Prentice Hall, Englewood Cliffs, NJ, 1984.
53. Taylor, Gordon Rattery, 'Prediction and social change: the need for a basis in theory', *Futures*, vol. 9, no. 5, 1977.
54. Zentner, Rene D., 'Application of survey research in corporate decision-making', in *Attitude Research enters the 80s*, ed. Richard W. Olshavsky, American Marketing Association, Chicago, 1980.
55. Huss, William R. and Honton, E. J., 'Alternative methods for developing business scenarios', *Technological Forecasting and Social Change*, vol. 31, 1987.
56. de Vries, Joop, 'What is futurology?: political, societal and global scenarios and how they are used', *Proceedings of Market Research Society Seminar*, 15 June 1989.

REVIEW AND DISCUSSION QUESTIONS

Q1 Outline the similarities and differences between the various bases for segmentation used in consumer and industrial marketing strategies.

Q2 Suggest feasible segmentation variables for the following industrial concerns: (a) shop-fittings manufacturer; (b) management database firm; and (c) corporate incentive travel agency.

Q3 In what ways might an awareness of the PLC (product life-cycle) concept benefit managers in organisational markets? Discuss how, in practice, such products might feasibly be located on the PLC curve.

Q4 Explain why the industrial product life cycle and the profit cycle, though related, should be treated separately.

Q5 Using the BCG portfolio model, analyse the performance of an industrial organisation which is well known to you, or one to which you have access through contacts and/or published data.

Q6 Evaluate the various criticisms of market-share strategies covered in this chapter; state your case objectively and also creatively.

CHAPTER SEVEN

Innovation strategy

INTRODUCTION

Successful innovation is one of the most challenging problems facing business management, and marketing management in particular. Innovation is not just one action; it is a complex process of interrelated actions requiring expert integration and control. Many contributions are made to a successful programme of innovation related to products or services. These inputs originate from research and development, production, personnel services, purchasing and financial areas of management, which, allied to the marketing function, take an organisation along the road to a profitable innovation.

The interface relationships of marketing were reviewed in the opening chapter of this book. To succeed in innovation, communications and close working arrangements between the various functional management areas are essential. Innovation is risky enough without its problems being magnified by internal misunderstandings and inefficiencies. Ingenious ideas are not enough in themselves to generate new life into an organisation; they need to be translated into products and services that will be sought after because of the benefits conferred on people who adopt them. The management of innovation cannot be shirked; without effective teamwork even a stimulating concept can result in commercial disaster.

In Chapter 5, it was emphasised that all businesses need new products and services in order to survive and grow in a competitive world. But, as Levitt has indicated:

> Though innovation is a necessity of business life, it is unnatural. It requires abandoning what's familiar and has been mastered for the unfamiliar and untried. Understandably, innovation does not happen automatically or easily. The only thing that's automatic is inertia – remaining with the accustomed and the comfortable.[1]

Innovation acts like a catalyst in industry and commerce: it invigorates efforts and brings new opportunities for profitable expansion. It harnesses inventive genius to specific applications in the fields of medicine, information technology, petrochemicals, biotechnology, agriculture, microtechnology, etc. There is, as the President of the Massachusetts Institute of Technology once said,[2] an urgent need for continuous innovation, both to improve the quality of life and to further economic development.

Portfolio planning, discussed in Chapters 5 and 6, has demonstrated that successful businesses spread their risks across product/service ranges and markets; marketing strategies allocate resources and efforts to achieve specific targets, as shown in Figure 5.10, where, for instance, new products are projected as 20 per cent of total sales. This is clearly an ambitious target that is only feasible when a company has committed itself to a programme of perennial innovation.

RELATIONSHIP BETWEEN INNOVATION AND INVENTION

The theoretical distinction between innovation and invention has been discussed by various leading management writers. Schumpeter regarded the process of innovation as quite distinct from that of invention. He maintained that invention could exist either independently of, or combined with, innovation. In his view, although most innovations can be traced to some conquest in the realm of either theoretical or practical knowledge that has occurred in the immediate or the remote past, there are many which cannot. It is possible to innovate 'without anything we should identify as invention, and invention does not necessarily enhance innovation, but produces of itself . . . no economically relevant effect at all'.[3]

Mansfield[4] applied the term 'innovation' to applied invention, and stated that economists have traditionally argued that an invention has little or no economic significance until it is applied commercially. He felt that successful innovation lay in exploiting an invention fully. To Rogers, innovation was 'an idea perceived as new by the individual. It really matters little so far as human behaviour is concerned, whether or not an idea is "objectively" new as measured by the amount of time elapsed since its first use or discovery. It is the newness of the idea to the individual that determines his reactions to it.'[5]

The Report of the Central Advisory Council for Science and Technology (1968), while acknowledging that technological innovation could be variously defined, confined its use in the report to denote generally

> the technical, industrial and commercial steps which lead to the marketing of new manufactured products and to the commercial use of new technical processes and equipment. At one extreme, innovation can imply simply investment in new manufacturing equipment or any technical measures to improve methods of production; at the other it might mean the whole sequence of scientific research, market research, invention, development, design, tooling, first productions and marketing of a new product.[6]

Project Sappho, the study of industrial innovation conducted at the University of Sussex, qualified innovation as 'a complex sequence of events, involving scientific research as well as technological development, management, production and selling'.[7] Like the Central Advisory Council Report, Sappho researchers viewed innovation as involving 'the commercial application of previous inventive work and experimental development'.

Peter Carl Goldmark,[8] a Hungarian physicist who worked for CBS, had over 150 inventions to his credit, including the first practical long-playing record. He believed that a great deal of basic technology went begging for want of someone to take the step towards innovation: an inventive idea without development is useless.

European industrial policy, it has been declared, depends on a healthy electronics sector, yet most EC funding has focused on expanding R&D, emphasising the need for collaborative projects while failing to face the fact that 'one of European manufacturers' biggest traditional weaknesses' lies in the 'belief that laboratory breakthroughs can substitute for efficient manufacturing and aggressive marketing'.[9] Meanwhile, the Japanese have concentrated their technical resources on product development and production engineering, astutely 'fine-tuning' their products to market needs.

Scientific breakthroughs do not automatically confer industrial leadership, as Dr Ralph Gomory,[10] for many years IBM's top researcher and technologist, has observed. Where industries have attained certain degrees of scale, competition, he contends, is mostly concerned with designing better versions of existing products and/or improving the present processes of manufacture.

According to Akio Morita, the legendary founder of the Sony Corporation, businesses need three types of creativity: (1) technological or inventive; (2) product planning; and (3) marketing. To be productive, the first input must be closely integrated with the two other inputs. However, although Sony's Walkman radio was a highly successful innovation, the company stopped making word processors in 1993 because the highly competitive market conditions rendered this product unprofitable.

For several years, Sir Clive Sinclair has fascinated the public with his prolific inventions: the revolutionary pocket calculator, the digital watch, the ill-fated C5 electric tricycle, the highly popular home computer and, more recently, the Zike electrically powered bicycle. He freely admits that he sees himself as an inventor rather than an entrepreneur or scientist; to being restless and finding it difficult to get down to the managerial discipline of running a business: 'I am not a professional manager by training or inclination.'[11]

To summarise, innovation depends on inventions, but invention needs to be harnessed to commercial activities before it can contribute to the growth of an organisation. Innovation may involve fundamentally new inventions – for example, those based on the petrochemicals and electronics industries – or it could refer to improvements in existing products. The commercial objectives, however, are likely to be the same: increased profitability through improved market share, expanded market opportunities, greater competitive advantages, etc.

PRAGMATIC APPROACH OF EARLY INDUSTRIAL INNOVATION

Many of the historic innovations in Britain's textile, pottery and metal industries sprang, however, from the outstanding inventive genius of individuals like Hargreaves, Arkwright, Trevithick, Maudslay and Spode. Through their forceful personalities, these industrial pioneers – some of whom had limited theoretical knowledge – finally won acceptance for their revolutionary new methods of production. Their successes depended less on formal scientific education than on persistent experimentation in practical working conditions. For example, Goodyear, who was successful in the vulcanisation of rubber, had no pretensions to chemical knowledge and found that chemists, who had failed to rid rubber of its stickiness, were unable to help him in his persistent efforts. However, as Jewkes[12] observed, he was encouraged by reflecting that what is hidden and unknown and cannot be discovered by scientific research will most likely be discovered accidentally, if at all, through sheer persistent effort. This he did with so much success that the US Commissioner of Patents wrote in his report of 1858 that Goodyear had made himself so much a master of rubber that nothing escaped his attention.

Good fortune appears to influence research success from time to time: serendipity (a term originated in 1754 by Horace Walpole in his fairy-tale 'Three Princes of Serendip' who 'were always making discoveries, by accident and sagacity, of things they were not in quest of') has accounted for some remarkable scientific and technological discoveries, e.g. the discovery of penicillin, floating soap and aniline dyes. The last were discovered in 1856 by W. H. Perkin when a student at the Royal College of Chemistry. He experimented with compounds discovered by Faraday and Hoffmann and, in trying to synthesise quinine, discovered mauve, the first aniline dye.

This fortuitous invention, as Jewkes notes, seems almost the rule in chemistry, but rarely occurs in mechanical engineering. A chemist might well, accidentally, come upon some new and surprising property in a known compound. But it seems most unlikely that an engineer grouping together 'pieces of metal with one idea in mind . . . discovers that he has stumbled upon a device of a kind that he had not been seeking'.

In 1947 John Bardeen, Walter Brattain and William Shockley, in Bell Telephone Laboratories at Murray Hill, south of New York, first demonstrated the 'transistor effect' which over the next few years led to the revolutionary new industry of microelectronics. Up to that time, the cumbersome and fragile vacuum tube was the basic technology behind radio, television, radar, medical equipment, etc. However, 'solid state' technology, as the transistor was termed, was largely the result of an accidental event. In the course of experiments, Brattain 'altered conditions slightly and was astounded to find the current flowing the wrong way'. This phenomenon was at once explained by his team-mates. 'In today's parlance, Brattain had contrived accidentally to inject "holes" into his germanium crystal – and hence to draw a flow of electrons (current) out.' Working feverishly, the trio made an amplifier and organised their first telephone demonstration of the transistor effect. But pioneering publicity of this remarkable invention largely failed to attract the attention of the media: 'Even the *New York Times* buried the story in a few brief sentences at the back of the paper.'[13]

Drucker states that innovative companies are aware that the target market for a successful new idea is usually unexpected. 'In developing dynamite, Alfred Nobel was trying to find a better military explosive. But dynamite is too unstable to be used in bombs and shells; instead it was used for removing rocks and replaced the pick and shovel in mining, railroad building, and construction.'[14]

As the result of fundamental research into the behaviour of chemicals at very high pressure, ICI invented polythene, which, at first, was thought to be primarily useful as a very superior insulant. Its applications, in fact, proved to be diverse: packaging, household products, cold water piping, etc.

Invention, as Burns and Stalker have observed in their penetrating analysis of the problems of managing innovation, 'was seen as the product of genius, wayward, uncontrollable, often amateurish; or if not of genius, then of accident and sudden inspiration . . . In nineteenth century Britain the archetypal formula for the process of innovation was enshrined in the fantasy of Watt and the kettle.'[15]

Indeed, as some American researchers have vividly commented:

> A common conception of the inventor . . . is that of a solitary drudge, perhaps a bit gone in the head, toiling away in a basement workshop. Living on dreams and borrowed capital, he produces gadgets of dubious worth and is fondly tolerated by society as a harmless and even entertaining aberration . . . Like most stereotypes, this one has a grain of truth in it. The world of invention does have its eccentrics, its seekers after perpetual motion, antigravity, death rays and the like . . . But you will also meet inventors who don't remotely fit the mould . . .[8]

The originators of some of today's popular products are often surprising: Gillette was originally a travelling salesman in corks; the joint inventors of Kodachrome were musicians; Carlson, the inventor of Xerography, was a patent lawyer; and the automatic dialling system was invented by Almon B. Strowger, a Kansas City undertaker.

When industry was still largely craft-based and men and their masters worked closely together, this unorganised approach to invention and innovation seemed to be sufficient. Even then, business opportunities were not always seized. 'Swan, a chemist, made experimental incandescent lamps in 1860 which employed the same high-resistance conductor, carbonised paper, as was used in the first commercial lamps marketed 20 years later . . . it was Edison who . . . first developed the lamp and formed an independent concern to manufacture it.'[15]

The apathy of industrial firms towards new product concepts has been critically noted:[12] RCA resisted Armstrong's ideas of frequency modulation; the Sulzer loom was offered to and rejected by the leading European textile manufacturers; the established aircraft companies did not think that the retractable undercarriage had any future; in 1925 the Marconi Company told Baird that it had no interest at all in television; and the invention of the gyro compass failed to receive the backing of the navigational equipment manufacturers.

When Paul Eisler, a brilliant inventor, showed the prototype of the printed circuit to Plessey, it was rejected because it was perceived as a threat to the jobs of women workers on production lines, wiring and assembling electrical circuits.

ORGANISATIONAL CONSTRAINTS ON INNOVATION

The institutional environment of modern industry and commerce has tended to impose new constraints on innovative strategies. The haphazard though often successful pursuit of new technologies and their derived products can no longer be tolerated, particularly when the survival and growth of large corporate undertakings are at stake.

In an economic and social environment which has changed, and is still changing radically, product and service innovation is an increasingly important competitive strategy. Technological obsolescence has taken its toll of many products, and the pace of competition has shortened lead time and the resulting pay-off period. Data[16] on 500 innovations in major industrialised countries over the period 1953–73 and across a broad spectrum of industry show that 13 per cent of these products had to be withdrawn from the market and less than two-thirds of the significant innovations achieved financial profitability. Only 46 per cent of the products generated repeat business; 42 per cent became standard products. It was found that, with the exception of the United Kingdom, these innovations were also helpful in attracting new customers (53 per cent) and in penetrating new markets.

Innovation strategies clearly contain a strong degree of risk; this may be compounded of financial, physical, social or psychological elements. Pressure of competition, the expectations of customers and society in general, and corporate growth spur entrepreneurial activities. The Institute of Mechanical Engineers has noted that major factors detracting from a higher rate of innovation in the United Kingdom are as follows:

1. Lack of enterprise and motivation among senior management.
2. Lack of appreciation of marketing techniques in middle and lower engineering management.
3. Shortage of production engineers.
4. Shortage of skilled workers.

This strongly pragmatic view is reflected in a quotation from their report:

> Good design is characterised by simplicity, and innovation must not be confused with complication. The prime requirements in the product are quality, reliability and delivery on time. These considerations should take precedence over advanced products . . . There is no lack in British industry of novel ideas, but

industry does lack the environment and encouragement needed for their successful application.[17]

Eric Von Hippel[18] and his colleagues at the Massachusetts Institute of Technology found in their extensive study of industrial innovation that users were the principal source of innovation in scientific instruments, equipment for making semi-conductors and printed circuit boards (PCB), and pultrosion equipment (a process for making fibre-reinforced plastic products of constant cross-section used in demanding structural applications). Most of the innovative users of scientific instruments were individual researchers in universities, whereas big electronic companies, such as IBM, GE and AT&T, were largely responsible for innovations in the areas of semiconductors and PCB manufacturing equipment. But in the case of tractor shovel, engineering thermoplastics and plastic additives, almost all innovations emanated from manufacturers. Some 90 per cent of innovations in pultrosion equipment were originated by users, typically small and medium-sized companies with no R&D facilities or staff formally trained in plastics technology.

Innovation by suppliers was generally less evident, but the researchers found certain kinds of industrial equipment, such as that used in thermoplastic resins, where suppliers of components and materials were significant innovators, together with manufacturers and users.

The three main sources of innovation – users, manufactures and suppliers – vary because, as von Hippel explains, innovation is an economic event and the most likely source of innovation depends on the likely distribution of innovation-related rents (or temporary profits) in the *precise* category of product, process or service being considered.

Research and development costs are frequently significant factors in innovation, as in the case of the Bridgestone Corporation of Japan, which developed an RCOT (Rolling Contour Optimisation Theory) radical tyre for the consumer market. This fundamentally different design offers less rolling resistance at speeds, reduced tyre noise, significant braking facilities and noticeable fuel efficiency. But such research-based products involve a hefty R&D investment – in Bridgestone's case, £133m in 1987.[19]

INDUSTRIAL GROWTH AND INNOVATION

With characteristic directness, Drucker reminds management that innovation is a slow process. Many companies owe their present-day leadership to the 'activity of a generation that went to its reward 25 or so years ago. Many companies that are unknown to the public will be leaders in their industry tomorrow because of their innovations today.'[20] The successful company, says Drucker, is in constant danger of reclining in smugness, living off the accumulated innovative activities of an earlier generation.

Products which are today commonplace were unknown[21] at the onset of this century: aeroplanes; radio and television equipment; navigational aids; radar;

diesel engines for road, rail and sea transport; forklift trucks; gas turbines; combine harvesters; synthetic fibres; silicones; antibiotics; synthetic detergents; fluorescent lamps; radioactive isotopes for industrial use; electronic computers and other electronic devices, etc.

It has been observed[22] that a clustering of innovations in one technology may lead to inventions in many others; a 'distinct bunching' seems to occur with far-reaching effects, as applications of new technologies, like solid state, have shown. New industries and extensions of old industries, such as chemicals and transport, have developed from technical innovation. Nuclear energy, space travel, satellite communication systems, supersonic air travel, laser technology and the myriad products of the pharmaceutical and synthetic fibres industries are now established features of advanced economies.

Mansfield, in his notable investigations into technological innovation, observed that successful innovators in steel and petroleum grew more rapidly in the 5–10-year period after innovation occurred than other firms of comparable initial size. The average growth rate was often more than twice that of the others: 'The average effect of a successful innovation was to raise a firm's annual growth rate by 4–13 per cent, depending on the time interval and the industry.'[4] As may be expected, the impact of a successful innovation on the growth of a small firm was much greater than on a large firm.

In industries such as electronics, new product opportunities have been exploited by successful companies which, like Philips, have grown consistently over a long period of time. But the dynamic technology which characterises these markets has meant that producers are brought to maturity at a fast and ever-quickening rate. The rapid technological growth which resulted from the two world wars was developed even further by the 'race to the moon'. In its meteoric progress, the electronics industry has been responsible for a profusion of inventions starting with the unsophisticated radio sets of the early 1900s, moving to radar detection systems and microwaves, and then to television, transistorised equipment and guided missiles, as well as electronic computers.

This breathless pace of innovation has had far-reaching effects in industrial, medical and social life. Perhaps that minuscule product, the transistor, has done more to revolutionise communications than any other single product of the past three decades. This advance was followed in 1961 by the first integrated circuit, which was developed very rapidly; in 1965 one chip could accommodate 10 transistors; 15 years later the number of transistors on one chip had grown to the astronomic figure of 100,000. Today, many thousands of transistors, resistors and diodes can be put on to one minuscule, low-cost chip.

One of the world's largest makers of chips for Teletext (Ceefax, Oracle, etc.) – the Mullard subsidiary of Philips – has reflected on the dynamic nature of its industry:

> We're now involved in the bulk manufacture of something which is very clever, only it has to be in extremely high volume production – millions of chips a year.

> Development is so rapid that we have had to devise a new way of coordinating the various engineering functions. There has to be much closer coordination between the various specialists in design, development and production. It costs a minimum of £3–4 million to set up a production facility and its expected lifespan is only four years. For such levels of risk, professional management skills are imperative.[23]

The remorseless pressure on innovation and profit making is also evident in 3M's corporate plans, which, as discussed in *Fortune*,[24] stipulate that 25 per cent of sales must be derived from products that did not exist five years before. Each of 3M's ten divisions is expected to hit this ambitious target.

3M, says Tom Peters, does better at making small starts than any other large firm he has encountered; despite its size, no project is too small for consideration. 'Unlike large-scale projects, small starts in small markets can be modified or abandoned quickly.'[25]

LEADERS AND FOLLOWERS

Strategic change in many industries, as Ansoff has emphasised, is so rapid that firms must continually survey their markets in search of new opportunities.

> For firms which have no provisions for response to strategic challenges and which refuse to anticipate it, the awareness of the problem usually comes through a traumatic experience, such as a drastic drop in sales or earnings, a product breakthrough by competition, a continued failure to meet profit objectives or a 'sweep of the new broom' triggered by change in top management.[26]

Firms, according to Ansoff, may be classified as either reactors, planners or entrepreneurs. 'Reactors' wait for problems to occur before trying to solve them; 'planners' attempt to anticipate problems; and 'entrepreneurs' deliberately anticipate both problems and opportunities. This latter and more enterprising type of management does not wait for a specific trigger but is constantly researching for strategic market opportunities so that profitable growth can be maintained.

Mature industries appear to have an innate resistance to new technology and to the challenge and change it may bring with it. Often there appears to be an almost insuperable barrier of resistance and even hostility, which may at last be overcome by the persistence and apparent market success of innovating firms. Finally, and almost reluctantly, the majority of firms in such industries adopt the role of followers.

Over three decades ago, Carter and Williams[27] found 'no great difficulty' in classifying firms according to the 'degree of technical progressiveness' achieved by them. These classifications were as follows:

1. 'Those which are in the forefront of discovery in applied science and technology, quick to master new ideas and to perceive the relevance of work in neighbouring fields.'
2. 'Those which are quite uninterested in science and technology, and are perfectly content to continue with traditional methods without even examining the alternatives.'
3. 'A large middle group, neither outstanding leaders in technology nor wholly uninterested in it.'

Technical progressiveness was seen, from research, to be related 'to the general quality of the firm; and attention to other aspects of its general quality – for instance, to management efficiency or to salesmanship and market research – helps to create the conditions for technical progress'. Category 1 firms are clearly entrepreneurial and quick to spot market opportunities, whereas group 2 are complacent and their lack of entrepreneurial energy is disturbing; the third group appear to be the large 'middle wedge' who are certainly not leaders, but who may be reluctant followers.

Companies which, at an early stage, moved into industries such as dyestuffs or detergents have been able to maintain their leadership for decades. Competitive advantage, states Porter, has been built on economies of scale, 'learning curve' economics (see Chapter 6), strong brand recognition, well-established customer relationships, ready access to prime sources of raw materials, etc. Although innovatory products may be copied, the other competitive advantages 'may well be more sustainable'.[28]

Leadership in innovation may also come from those who are, in some way, 'outsiders' to an industry. Uninhibited by traditional norms and practices, these energetic and enterprising entrants are willing to challenge, experiment and apply specialist skills acquired in other industries to the development of new processes and products.

A striking example of entrepreneurial leadership in high technology is Oxford Instruments, whose management are reported to have actually made the decision to go into superconducting magnets when returning from a US conference at which the technological breakthrough had been announced.[29] These high-power magnets which work only at extremely low temperatures are applied in a range of sophisticated equipment such as body scanners. Sir Martin Wood, the dynamic entrepreneur with a distinguished academic research career, started this highly innovative firm from the garage of his home in Oxford. Any high-tech entrepreneur should be aware, he says, of his own strengths and weaknesses. He lays no claim to the title of managing director or chief executive; he deliberately lets the business be run 'by the bright, highly motivated scientists and engineers the firm tries to recruit'.[30] He sees his job as spotting opportunities and trying to enthuse people to take them up.

In Drucker's robust phrasing: 'Innovative companies talk of work and self discipline . . . Above all, the innovative company organizes itself to abandon the old, the obsolete, the no longer productive ... and it prefers to abandon its obsolete products itself rather than have them made obsolete by competition'.[14]

DIFFUSION OF INNOVATION

One of the astonishing things about earlier innovations and the patterns of diffusion has been the size of the gap which has sometimes extended between knowledge and action, between invention and innovation, between innovation as 'best practice' technique and the diffusion of innovation to become 'representative' technique. Coke and smelted iron, Mathias notes,[31] had a time-lag between innovation and diffusion from 1709 to 1760 and later.

Mansfield's research into the diffusion of new industrial products led him to observe that the speed with which a particular firm adopted a new technique appeared to be directly related to the firm's size and the potential profitability it offered. In general, there appeared to be a definite 'bandwagon' or 'contagion' effect which influenced the spread of a new process or product through an industry. Perceived risk was reduced as more firms used the innovation, while the fact that a large proportion of a firm's competitors had now adopted it also significantly influenced individual decisions. (See also Chapter 2 and 3.) However, Mansfield warned against the facile assumption that particular firms are consistently leaders or followers. 'According to our findings, there is a very good chance that these firms will be relatively slow to introduce the next innovation that comes along.'[4]

Ozanne and Churchill's study[32] of the industrial adoption process was based on the five stages of adoption outlined by Rogers:[5] awareness, interest, evaluation, trial and adoption/rejection. They surveyed 90 'decision-makers' in 39 midwestern US industrial firms about the adoption of a new automatic machine tool ($35,000–$70,000) which, although not radically innovative, had certain readily observable improvements. Respondents were analysed across several criteria.

Five factors affecting adoption of an industrial innovation were identified:

1. Activating factors – 'changes in a company's external or internal environment that may set in motion the industrial adoption process'.
2. Purchase-directing factors – 'factors which influenced choice of a particular supplier of an innovation'.
3. Duration of the industrial adoption process.
4. Alternatives considered.
5. Use of information.

The researchers concluded that the industrial adoption process is extremely complicated and far more complex than individual buying behaviour.

Webster[33] has also emphasised that the communication and diffusion processes of industrial innovation are 'somewhat different' from consumer markets 'because of the unique features of industrial markets' (see the extended discussion on the complexity of organisational buying behaviour in Chapters 2 and 3).

The acceptance and diffusion of some novel and technically advanced products may be impeded unless marketers ensure that potential customers receive adequate 'education' in the uses and technical features of such innovations. This task may be shared between a firm's technical design staff and marketing management.

Research into the diffusion of new capital equipment focused on the British flour-milling industry in a survey reported in 1972. 'This industry was chosen because it had undergone very many changes over the years and was the first industry to adopt any form of automation, when in 1785 the industry introduced the first fully integrated handling and processing scheme.'[34] This receptivity to technological change had continued to characterise the flour-milling industry, which was also comparatively compact: 'The entire flour output of the UK and Eire is manufactured by approximately 140 mills covering a wide range of capacities.' Hence, low-cost research was feasible.

Following a series of unstructured interviews, five innovations were selected as representing significant technological improvements in flour milling: pneumatic conveying; bulk flour outloading bins; bulk flour silos; short surface milling system; and reverse jet filter dust collector.

During the research study, the initial introduction of an innovation was checked by reference to the machine record books in the various companies surveyed. The sample was stratified according to ownership, i.e. 'group' mills and independent mills.

From Table 7.1 it will be observed that pneumatic conveying and short surface milling systems diffused through the independent mills at a faster rate than in the group mills. The researchers suggested that this quicker pace may be due to the urgent need of independent millers to adopt new processes which will ensure their survival. On the other hand, bulk flour outloading and bulk flour silos have been more readily adopted by the group mills, presumably because these innovations are connected with economies of scale and involve substantial capital outlays which they can sustain. The reverse jet filter also diffused more rapidly through the group mills, aided perhaps by production trials which could be arranged conveniently in one mill of a group.

TABLE 7.1 UK flour-milling industry's adoption of selected technological innovations

Innovation	*Number of years taken to adopt innovations by 25% and 50% of sample*					
	Group mills		*Independent mills*		*Total mills*	
	25%	*50%*	*25%*	*50%*	*25%*	*50%*
Pneumatics	12	–	12	18	12	19
Bulk outloading	8	16	11	15	9	15
Flour silo	6	16	15	20	11	16
Short surface	12	–	11	12	11	–
Reverse jet filter	4	7	6	9	4	8

Source: Allen and Hayward.[34]

TABLE 7.2 UK flour-milling industry's adoption of five selected innovations

No. of innovations adopted		*Group mills*	*Independent mills*	*Total mills*
0	Laggards	2	5	7*
1		5	6*	11
2	Medians	13	10	23
3		21	6	27
4	Innovators	9	10	19
5		8	16	24
Total		58	53	111

* Up to 15 sacks capacity.

Source: Allen and Hayward.[34]

The number of innovations adopted by each mill was surveyed, and it will be seen from Table 7.2 that the independent mills led in adoption of all five innovations. Smaller-capacity mills clearly lagged in utilising innovation methods of production.

The rate of diffusion of new technological ideas within an industry such as flour milling is affected, therefore, by the structure of the industry and by the level of competition within it. Processes of adoption are also likely to be accelerated by the simplified decision making of smaller companies, whose management are probably more keenly aware of the pressing need to be responsive to production and marketing innovations.

Diffusion of a product may also be strongly affected by differing technical standards, as happened with video-cassette recorders, when Philips' VHS and Sony's Betamax systems were in head-on competition, until the latter eventually withdrew from this market. This dramatic event simplified decision making by consumers and the market rapidly expanded.

High-definition television (HDTV) is another innovation where technical standards will play a key role in the adoption and diffusion of the final product. Apart from the complex issues of an effective design, the problems of adoption will have to be tackled: television stations, programme-makers and equipment suppliers will be involved in heavy investment. But programme-makers will be reluctant to incur massive expenditure unless their programmes are demanded by broadcasting companies. In turn, these will want to have the reassurance that large numbers of viewers have HDTV sets in their homes. Meanwhile, American and European groups have been battling to secure a foothold in the market for this latest technical innovation in television systems. The outcome will be uncertain until millions of viewers are finally convinced that HDTV is really worth its projected high cost.

MULTICOUNTRY RESEARCH ON DIFFUSION

The National Institute of Economic and Social Research has studied the diffusion of new technologies across industrial companies for over 30 years. Its first report[35] was published in 1969 and analysed the introduction and diffusion of selected post-war industrial innovations in several countries. In 1983 the NIESR's second report[36] covered six technologies: the basic oxygen process, which in the 1970s became the dominant method of steel-making; continuous casting; tunnel kilns for use in brick production; shuttleless looms in the cotton-type weaving industry; the float process of manufacturing flat glass; and numerically controlled machine tools.

Of the six technologies studied, the two steel technologies as well as float-glass were characterised as 'revolutionary' and have changed entirely the respective manufacturing processes. While the tunnel kiln was a significant step in brick-making, it did not have the same kind of fundamental effect which was observed in the three 'revolutionary' innovations.

A third report by NIESR,[37] published in 1988, updated earlier research findings, and extended the scope of research to include 'two important new technologies, robots and flexible manufacturing systems (FMS), that are at a relatively early stage of their dissemination'. These new 'high-tech' technologies could be included among the 'revolutionary' innovations noted earlier.

An important factor in the diffusion of all the original six plus the two new additional innovations is related to the opportunity of trying them out on a limited basis, i.e. divisibility. (See the section on factors affecting the acceptance of innovations, pp. 282–3). The four technologies based on steel, glass and brick manufacture, and those involving robotics and FMS, are intrinsically indivisible and involve widespread changes in production processes, the building of new plant, etc. So diffusion has depended on major decisions to make heavy investment in order to adopt these innovations. On the other hand, shuttleless looms and numerically controlled machine tools have diffused at a faster rate because of their divisibility and consequent lower risk in trial and adoption. Small-scale trials can be undertaken without major investment and fundamental restructuring of manufacturing processes; adoption can be gradual, as distinct from the sweeping changes experienced in the indivisible technologies.

Major innovations therefore take a long time to diffuse: the basic oxygen process of steel-making took nearly 20 years to reach saturation in western Europe and Japan, and by 1986 only about 4 per cent of crude steel in the USA was made in the old open hearth and Bessemer and Thomas systems. The diffusion of continuous steel casting in the 1980s was spectacular, but on the whole it is less advanced than the new methods of steel-making just mentioned. Tunnel kilns used in brick-making achieved around 80 per cent adoption in the UK, and significantly higher diffusion (90 per cent) in Germany, France and Italy. The float-glass process had almost entirely replaced the old method of making plate glass by the mid-1980s: 'in 1986 there were four times as many float plants world-wide as there had been 15 years earlier'.[37] In the OECD countries, it was reported that the float technique had achieved about 90 per cent diffusion, but in the developing countries as well as in the centrally planned economies the diffusion rate was much lower, particularly for making sheet glass. The disadvantages of large-scale float-glass plants for countries with limited domestic markets has been overcome, to some extent, by the introduction of smaller-capacity plants.

Shuttleless looms have experienced quickening rates of diffusion in the cotton-type weaving industry: in the decade up to 1986, over 90 per cent of all new looms installed in Europe were of this advanced type – in 1986, in fact, this figure had risen to almost 100 per cent. Expansion in Asia and Africa is also significant: for example, 52 per cent in Asia (85 per cent in Japan) and 91 per cent in Africa.

Numerically controlled machine tools (NCMTs) have also developed strongly: between 1980 and 1985 world production of NCMTs more than doubled, and it is reported that the scope for further diffusion is 'very large'; this will be aided by the roles played by NCMTs in the new technologies of robotics and flexible manufacturing systems (FMS). Over the period 1982–5, the number of robots increased fivefold in Japan, France and Italy, trebled in the USA, the UK, Germany, Belgium and Sweden, and was 'probably similar' in other countries. The number of FMSs doubled during 1984–6 in Japan, Germany and the USA, and is likely to have progressed similarly elsewhere.

NIESR also researched the validity of the belief that diffusion followed an S-curve, and reported that 'the figures do not provide much concrete evidence for the exclusive validity of any very regular S-curves, but they definitely support the rational expectation of *some kind* of an S-curve'. Slopes were observed to be different for each technology, and the turning points in growth also differed. The researchers advised caution in the use of an S-curve assumption and proposed that 'an equally good, indeed better, representation is that the *whole* wave of the technology, from birth through maximum use to death, might follow the bell shape of a normal distribution curve, although the right-hand side of the curve may fall more steeply'.

NIESR's third report stated that it takes a relatively long time to reach the first 10 per cent of diffusion in any major geographical area; after this point has been reached, the diffusion rate is rapid until about 70 per cent is attained, but then the pace slows down. This is seen in the time path of diffusion for all four of the 'indivisible' technologies researched by NIESR over several decades.

The process of technological advance is inherently dynamic; the rate of adoption of new technologies fundamentally affects the ability of countries and firms to compete in world markets. In its first report, NIESR established that during the 1950s and 1960s, while Sweden and the UK led in introducing new technologies, others – particularly Germany – were able to achieve a faster rate of adoption. But NIESR's second and third reports revealed that Japan and Sweden gave new technologies the 'quickest and widest acceptance, while the UK appears to have moved nearer to the leading countries'.

BEHAVIOURAL FACTORS INFLUENCING INNOVATION

Detailed discussion of the behavioural factors which influence the diffusion of innovations may be found in another text,[38] which is particularly concerned with the psychological and sociological aspects of marketing. In marketing of organisational supplies and services, management would benefit from acquiring an understanding of the non-economic factors that affect buying behaviour. Adoption of innovations is not confined to commercial goods and services, so management in the public sector – involved, perhaps, in health, education or other social services – should also base their strategies on an appreciation of the fundamentals of human behaviour which considerably influence decisions to try innovatory products or services. Myths, fears and fables often inhibit the adoption of new ideas, as an attitude study which was concerned with the fluoridation of water revealed some years ago in the United States. 'Some people voted against it for a variety of bizarre reasons which they had persuaded themselves were facts. Fluoridation was said to be "rat poison", to cause hardening of the arteries, premature ageing, loss of memory and nymphomania; it also ruined batteries, radiators and lawns.'[15]

Another example[22] of the problems in the acceptance of innovation in some communities concerns the apparently simple hand-pumps used at wells in Indian villages. Following extensive drought in the 1960s, large power-driven drilling rigs were used to drill deep bore-holes; by 1975, of the 150,000 installed as many as two-thirds had broken down, sometimes within three or four weeks of installation. Design and manufacturing faults were identified and corrected, but breakdowns continued. Only then was it realised that the problem was not just one of engineering; servicing arrangements were inadequately organised. Moreover, in many villages nobody felt any personal responsibility for looking after the pumps. When all these contributory factors were tackled, pump performance improved.

Diffusion, as an American researcher[39] has noted, is a complex social phenomenon involving both economic and non-economic factors. The latter cannot be ignored if successful marketing is to be the outcome of, perhaps, years of research and development. Mansfield has proposed that economic variables may, in fact, be 'less important than the more elusive and essentially non-economic factors, such as the personality attributes, interest, training and other features of top and middle management, which will play a deciding role in determining how quickly a firm introduces an innovation'.[4]

A practical example of the need to take note of non-economic factors to ensure acceptance and diffusion of new technologies and products was experienced by ICI,[40] which designed a laser detector to give early warning of any escape of inflammable or toxic gases from process plants. This sophisticated device was mounted in a tower 40 metres from the ground and continuously swept an area a little larger than a football pitch with its beams. ICI reported that not the least of the problems it encountered was to convince plant operators that they could pass safely through the laser beams, as well as to assure safety officers that there was no danger of the lasers igniting a leak of gas.

Those who are the first to adopt new products or services deserve the special interest of marketing management. Cultural, social and psychological factors may not always be immediately apparent, but they may, nevertheless, exercise very profound influences on buying preferences.

PRINCIPLES AFFECTING ACCEPTANCE OF INNOVATION

Five important principles affect the acceptance of innovations in general and have been identified as follows:[5]

1. *Relative advantage.* This should be assessed from the *user's* viewpoint, hence the need to undertake systematic market research to establish customers' needs, levels of satisfaction with existing products/services, and expectations. As already noted, products should have attributes which give them competitive advantages. These may be a mix of technological, economic, financial or psychological benefits: for example, lower production costs resulting from the use of a new type of machine tool, attractive leasing arrangements covering the installation of a new computer system, enhanced safety features on certain new equipment, the reassurance of buying from a recognised source of supply, or special servicing and training schemes related to new equipment.

As seen in Chapter 1, products can be readily augmented so that they offer a constellation of competitive features and customer benefits.

2. *Compatability.* This concerns the need to understand the likely impact of new products/services on customers' beliefs, values, attitudes and experiences. For example, production engineers may, traditionally, lay great stress on sturdily built testing machines, whereas new technologies, such as lasers, have entirely different design parameters.

3. *Complexity.* This relates to the extent to which an innovation can readily be understood by users and providers: for instance, highly sophisticated technologies demand specific professional expertise, which may entail special training programmes for users' staff. Provision of such programmes should be part of the marketing strategy of suppliers, otherwise adoption of innovations will probably be noticeably retarded. Generally, the less complex an innovation is, the more likely it is to be adopted and diffuse rapidly.

4. *Divisibility.* The significance of this factor has already been noted in the NIESR research reports quoted earlier, when it was seen to influence the adoption rates of new technologies. In many consumer markets, small or trial-size packs can be bought, but in industrial markets it is generally far less easy to try out new products, particularly those involving extensive restructuring of production plants, or the installation of computerised control systems. In such cases, suppliers should do all they can to overcome this inherent disadvantage, perhaps by 'using their users', i.e. developing such good relationships with existing customers that they are willing to allow prospective users to observe specific systems in actual use. Incentives may also be offered to firms which are early adopters of innovatory products. In some cases, it may be feasible to phase in the introduction of new industrial processes or products, perhaps by jointly supporting pilot plant developments.

5. *Communicability.* This refers to the success with which the results of an innovation are communicated and readily observed by adopters, and also those who have yet to be convinced of the advantages of changing their present buying

behaviour. For example, a new process plant may result in improved productivity – maintenance of higher-quality production, significantly reduced reject rates, marked cost economies, an enhanced safety-at-work record, etc. In due course, the effects should also be apparent in larger market share, improved profitability, etc.

However, the benefits of some innovations may not be so readily discernible, as happened in the case of pre-emergent weedkillers which are sprayed on to fields before weeds appear. Difficulties were experienced in convincing farmers of the potential value of such products; this affected the rate of adoption, which was slow, because there was virtually no immediate evidence (by means of dead foliage) that the treatment was effective. Only after some early adopters used these innovative products, and found that they actually worked, did diffusion take place. (Refer to Mansfield's research, described on p. 278.)

CATEGORIES OF INNOVATION

The nature of innovations was briefly referred to earlier; some methods of classifying innovations will now be considered. Difficulties immediately arise in defining what is meant by innovation and its related prior activity, invention.

> We speak of the development of some revolutionary idea, such as the jet engine or the Wankel rotary piston engine, meaning the building of one machine which established the fact that results can be obtained by the new principle. At the other extreme we speak of the development of a new aircraft design, which of itself embodies no radical innovation, meaning the systematic testing and modifying in numerous minor ways of the design to satisfy standards of performance and safety for the special conditions which the aircraft will encounter, and, between the extremes, of course, there are to be found innumerable intermediate conditions.[12]

Radical, earth-shattering innovations are generally rather rare events: the Polaroid camera or the Xerox dry-copying process are unique examples of inventive genius linked with shrewd marketing policies. Generally, however, inventive advance and technological change are built up from a number of relatively small, incremental improvements. These do not usually attract the headlines, but the contribution to commercial success of many of these modest innovations may be substantial. The managing director of Philips Electrical Ltd has commented:

> Innovations are a continuing occurrence in our everyday business life – and they are mostly minor in nature . . . all these changes are ongoing, and they are vital to the continued success of our business. Each minor innovation may have only a minor impact on its own, but if we put these innovations together over time, they are very important for an industry and for the position of an individual company within it.[41]

Sir John Harvey-Jones has asserted that, while 'big leaps forward are much more satisfying than small incremental changes', making money from them is problematical. 'It is the small innovations, targeted directly to someone's needs, that produce the quick and generous pay-back.'[42]

The case for incremental innovation is also argued strongly by Peters: 'In fact, research concludes that most landmark products (called "technological guideposts" in engineering and science-based firms) do not involve breakthroughs. Instead, they are the culmination of many changes, each small, which eventually lead to wholesale user adoption of the product.'[25]

Porter takes a similar view: 'Much innovation, in practice, is rather mundane and incremental rather than radical. It depends more on a cumulation of small insights and advances that on major technological breakthroughs.'[28]

NIESR[37] also referred to the significance of incremental innovation. For example, the two steel technologies which it researched would not have been operating so widely without extensive technical development of the initial innovation; the float-glass process was originally restricted to thick plate glass and was only later extended to the production of thinner window glass; many changes took place to shuttleless looms which enabled them to handle fabrics of diverse colours and structures; and speedy development of the control mechanism resulted in NCMTs becoming almost universally acceptable.

The vital contribution of what may be termed 'sequential innovation' is, therefore, supported by several researchers and writers including Mathias,[31] who notes that every major innovation is developed not only on basic advances by the famous, but also on innumerable smaller developments made by the unknown. In addition, the distinction between new products and product enhancements is often so small that it is rare for something entirely new to be developed without the idea, at least, originating in some earlier product. It has been noted[43] that even the pocket calculator had its origins in the mechanical adding machines and calculators of almost a generation ago. However, microtechnology has radically transformed the product so that it bears little resemblance to its forebears.

Profit-earning products sometimes originate from an idea picked up almost at random, developed and improved, and then expertly marketed.

Innovations tend to spread over a continuum: from technology-led at one extremity to marketing-led at the other pole, plus, as a senior executive[44] of British Telecommunications states, a third dimension related to commercial objectives. These three forces have influenced the development of BT's businesses and specific services such as Prestel, which, after a troublesome start-up, is now attracting wider patronage.

In his fascinating study of industrial innovation, Langrish produced four models of the innovation process based on the linear sequence of events which 'most writers on innovation have either clearly stated or implicitly assumed'. These start either with a discovery or, at the other extreme, with some kind of need that requires to be satisfied. Langrish identified within each of these two subdivisions two types of model:

1. *Discovery push*:
(a) 'science discovers, technology applies' model;
(b) 'technological discovery' model, e.g. Pilkington's float-glass process.
2. *Need pull*:
(a) 'customer need' model – this may emanate from the direct request of a customer or result from systematic marketing research;
b) 'management by objective' model, e.g. the need to lower manufacturing costs may encourage research into new and more economic processes.

Langrish's research, based on a sample of 51 innovations, established that an average of three new ideas was necessary for each innovation. In some fields, such as high magnetic solenoid superconductors, the number was actually very much higher: 18. However, Langrish confessed the difficulty he and his associates experienced in fitting innovations which had attracted the Queen's Award into any one of his four models in 'a clear and unambiguous manner'.[45]

According to Ferrari,[46] successful technical innovation is almost always the result of a synthesis between interpretation of market requirements ('market pull') and recognition of technical possibilities ('technology push').

Major innovations, in the view of Philips Electrical, 'arise more from technological push than consumer pull'.[41] There is a danger that such innovations may result in systems or products that have no easily developed market. Philips emphasises that companies must avoid situations where R&D develop products without reference to marketing feasibility. This can be achieved only by developing strong links between R&D, production and marketing. Successful innovation is essentially a team job. (See Chapter 1 on the interface relationships of management.)

In Stonier's view, 'market pull' is being displaced by 'technology push': there has been a shift from empirical knowledge (often derived from developing technology) leading science to theoretical science shaping technology. Advances in chemistry lead to the synthesis of new compounds in search of a use. Solid-state physics sets the stage for the transistor, which then evolves into the microprocessor. The miracle chip looks for new markets. In 1971 the first pocket calculator, costing $240, appeared in the USA. Before the end of the decade, pocket calculators jumped across the Atlantic so that in the UK on average each household possessed one.[47] Nowadays, this innovation is virtually a commodity product, freely available, relatively low priced and considered indispensable by millions of users.

With technological advances and manufacturing and marketing skills, prices inevitably collapse, as Alan Sugar has shown dramatically with microcomputers in the UK.

Drucker, in a reflective paper on challenges facing executives, has drawn attention to one of the earliest research managers, the German–American physicist Charles Protens Steinmetz, who worked for General Electric Company in Schenectady, New York, in the earlier part of this century. He and his project teams were motivated by 'technology-driven' applications of research, which resulted, for example, in new products like fractional horsepower motors. The relationship between science and technology in research was radically redefined by Steinmetz, who 'identified the new theorotical science needed to accomplish the desired technological results and then organised the appropriate "pure" research to obtain the needed knowledge'.[48]

Rothwell[49] has typified innovations as being along a continuum: at one end are *evolutionary* innovations which are incremental in nature; at the opposite end are *revolutionary* innovations which are radical in their culture and impact. In his research focused on the textile machinery market, Rothwell concluded that, while the short-term prosperity of textile machinery companies can often be assured through product improvement innovation ('evolutionary'), in most markets more radical innovation ('revolutionary') has been necessary to ensure firms' long-term survival.

A truly revolutionary innovation was Paul Eisler's printed circuit. This led to miniaturisation, the integrated circuit or silicon chip, and low-cost mass production of electronic circuitry. Other dramatic, revolutionary innovations include the jet engine, the Xerox dry-copying system, and the float-glass process. (Refer also to the NIESR research given earlier, pp. 280–2). But as we have seen, the more usual mode of innovations tends to be evolutionary or incremental: products and processes are improved by many small advances in technology which together help to give companies sustained competitive advantages.

Myers and Marquis's[50] report on factors affecting US technological innovation over the period 1963–7 classified innovations in manufacturing firms as either *defensive* or *offensive*. Defensive innovation aims to preserve market share and the present rate of corporate growth. 'It may be in response to competition, or to changes in market demands for quality, reliability, design, safety, etc., or to price erosion of its products or to increased costs of materials, or labour, or to changes in government regulatory actions and tariffs.' Offensive innovation is a deliberate policy of opening up new markets or enlarging existing markets by a planned series of new products/services. It is likely, of course, that individual companies are engaged in a mix of innovation strategies across particular markets.

Another method[51] of categorising *fundamental innovations* is into: (1) *characteristic innovations*, which give rise to new socioeconomic activities or industries; and (2) *generic innovations*, which not only lay the basis of new socioeconomic activities, but also cut across several new and old industries. For example, 'both the catalytic cracking process and internal combustion engine were fundamental technical breakthroughs but the former was a characteristic innovation, whereas the latter was generic'. Although these types of innovation clearly overlap, they are nevertheless conceptually distinct. What distinguishes them is the magnitude of the ripple effect; generic innovations tend to have more of a global effect, while characteristic ones are more local in their effects. Generic innovations give rise to a cluster of interrelated innovations: for example, steam power led to numerous other innovations.

An earlier classification[52] of innovations placed them in three basic groups – continuous, dynamically continuous and discontinuous:

1. A *continuous innovation* involves merely the modification of a product rather than the dramatic introduction of a totally new product. As noted earlier, incremental improvements form a very considerable part of innovation strategies. These products are so similar to existing products that consumers' behaviour does not need to be changed if these new products are to be adopted.
2. A *dynamically continuous innovation* involves more disruption than the first category, although not fundamentally changing established patterns of behaviour.
3. A *discontinuous innovation* refers to new products which have led to significant changes in ways of living and production processes: radio and television, long-playing records, ball-point pens, the jet engine, synthetic fibres, stainless steel, antibiotics, tungsten carbide tools, photo typesetting, etc. These types of product innovation result in significant alterations in consumers' behaviour as and when adopted; they diffuse slowly because their use generally requires changes in values and habits – for example, dehydrated foods were relatively slow in becoming widely accepted because of original concern about their nutritional value.

Interactive electronic home shopping systems are being vigorously developed among Chicago households by Telaction, a wholly owned subsidiary of the US retail chain J. C. Penney.[53] Access to what is termed the 'electronic shopping mall' is through an ordinary cable TV channel. Customers can browse through the mall or shop by product category, request more information about any particular item and listen to a detailed voice-over description. Purchase is effected by dialling a local telephone number and obtaining a personal identification number (PIN) from one of the live operators. Telaction has patented its process in 26 countries; the system, it is said, astutely combines two favourite pastimes, shopping and TV watching. How far this 'distance shopping' will diffuse is yet to be seen. Perhaps it will, in time, have industrial buying applications. It certainly calls for some radical changes in shopping, which is acknowledged to be a social as well as an economic transaction.

It may be possible to collate these basic groups of inovations with Langrish's models. Pilkington's float-glass process, for instance, would probably fall into the category of a 'discontinuous' innovation; Langrish classified this particular product as related to 'discovery push' and as a 'technological discovery'. Stainless steel would also follow this pattern of classification.

In this category of innovation, high risk appears to be inevitable. Float-glass, an invention which has been commercially exploited with great success, experienced several crises in its development. The first production plant, set up in May 1957 'continued to turn out nothing but unsatisfactory glass for a period of 14 months'.[12] Pilkington persisted, and in July 1958 'the first square foot of good glass was produced'. Even then difficulties were not at an end, and it was only after many more months of intensive work and enormous investment that the float-glass process became commercially viable.

Jewkes makes the salient point that the basic concept of floating molten glass over molten tin had, in fact, been patented in the early 1900s, but it had never been exploited. Commercialisation waited for a company with substantial resources, whose top management were willing to take high risks in the belief that market opportunities were now waiting to be seized.

Another example[40] of the shrewd commercialisation of invention relates to Alfred Nobel, who was not only a successful inventor but also an astute businessman. In 1863 he improved on Sobrero's invention of nitroglycerine so that it could be detonated in a controlled way by means of a percussion cap. Later inventions led to dynamite and gelignite. Nobel perceived that lucrative industrial applications were ready for exploitation in blasting for railways, roads, bridges, etc., in the rapidly developing industrial countries. He took out foreign patents and established manufacturing operations which, in time, spread over five continents. To finance and manage this vast enterprise, he developed effective local partners. In essence, Nobel founded the first multinational industrial business, and skilfully controlled the risks of developing new markets.

Entrepreneurial spirit was also displayed when the decision to market the Xerox 914 copier was taken. When this innovatory machine was first planned, Xerox invited 'the three most reputable consulting firms to make separate independent studies as to market opportunities and potential'.[54] Two consultants advised against marketing it; the third saw some vague chance of success, but limited market potential of about 8,000 placements being achieved in about six years. Xerox's president and his associates refused to accept these dismal projections because the forecasts took very little note of a consumer learning curve: that 'people would learn to want copies of written materials once quality copies became easily available'. With this latent demand in mind, Xerox boldly launched the 914 copier in 1961; within three years over 80,000 units were marketed.

As noted earlier, the dry-process photocopying method was originated by Chester Carlson, a patent lawyer whose ingenuity and persistence eventually resulted in the process which Xerox was able to develop so spectacularly. But Carlson's path to success was not easy: for three years he researched his ideas at the New York Technical Library until, in 1937, he filed his first patent. Production was delayed until 1946, when a small company, the Haloid Corporation (later to be known as Xerox) decided to commercialise the revolutionary process.

Marketing of new products frequently calls for imagination, as is illustrated by the way in which General Motors overcame the US railways' reluctance to replace their steam locomotives by the newly developed diesel locomotives. These had been designed and produced in anticipation of a potential demand but without any guaranteed sales. By lending a diesel locomotive to a railroad for use in its switching yard, the manufacturers eventually obtained widespread use for long-distance trains.

New inventions offer industry new opportunities to develop but, inevitably, there has to be a time for assimilation so that the resultant innovations can be turned into profit-making products. This critical problem was cogently described by the chairman of Bayer AG, the third largest (by sales turnover) of Germany's chemical companies:

> It is true that 30 years ago there was a lot of innovation in some areas, such as fibres. In order to produce new fibres, new dyestuffs, new plastic materials, new machines were needed. New materials in one field cause innovation in other fields. But after a time, innovation halts. You have to digest what you have. It is possible at that stage for the smaller companies and, when your patents run out, companies in other countries, to start manufacturing the same products without the burden of research and development and other overhead costs . . . Then the only solution is more innovation. This is more difficult each time because of the ever-increasing costs of research. But it is absolutely necessary.[55]

MODEL OF TECHNOLOGICAL INNOVATION

The process of technological innovation has been formalised by Myers and Marquis[50] as a series of stages, although they, in common with other leading researchers, have stressed that the linear sequence shown in Figure 7.1 will not always occur.

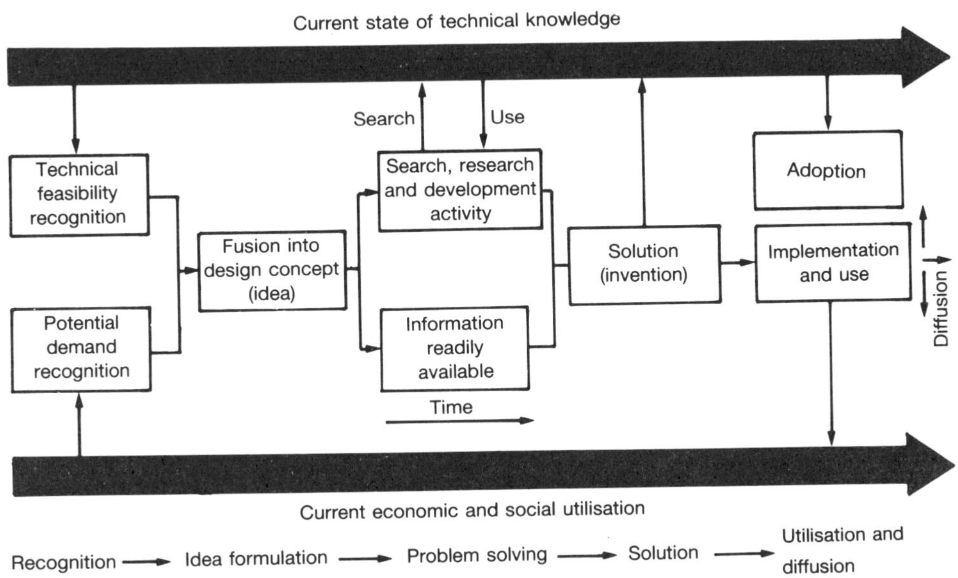

FIGURE 7.1 The process of technical innovation (Source: Myers and Marquis[50])

The starting point for successful innovations recognises the interaction of market demand and the technical resources available at a particular time. The nature of demand needs to be identified as either existing or potential; the latter category may call for considerable effort in promoting a new method of production. 'The idea for an innovation consists of the fusion of a recognised demand and a recognised technical feasibility into a design concept ... If a technical advance alone is considered, it may or may not result in a solution for which there will be a demand.'[50]

Levitt has argued: 'Ideation is relatively abundant. It is implementation that is scarce.'[54] Ideas, no matter how brilliant, must be brought down to earth and considered within the environmental constraints in which a company has to develop its marketing strategy. The design concept is, therefore, the point from which, having identified certain market needs, there should follow an intensive process of problem solving. This critical stage of innovation will no doubt unearth many problems and may even result in abandonment of the proposal. Information will be needed, some of which may be readily available; but in some cases special investigations into technical and commercial aspects will have to be initiated.

Eventually, a feasible technical solution may be forthcoming – or 'a solution to a modified problem with somewhat different objectives'.[50] But even then, the process of innovation is not complete: the final stage will decide the actual ability of a company to satisfy the needs of its customers. In this stage, considerable manufacturing start-up costs and marketing expenses will be incurred. The earlier technical uncertainties will now largely be replaced by the problems of marketing, including those involved in the vital processes of adoption and diffusion within periods of time which are commercially realistic.

The costs involved in this ultimate stage of the innovation process are typified by the estimates made by the US Department of Commerce, Panel on Innovation and Invention (see Figure 7.2). The data in Figure 7.2 indicate that start-up costs represent a major proportion of the development and implementation costs of innovation. Jewkes has pointed out: 'The more extensive the scale on which the new product must initially be manufactured, the more formidable may be the task of development.'[12] Where both technical complexity and dynamic competition are present, a company is confronted with exceedingly difficult problems related to the scale of investment in innovative products.

NEW PRODUCT STRATEGIES

Johnson and Jones[56] have classified new products in terms of product objectives defined in two dimensions: increasing market newness and increasing technological newness (see Figure 7.3).

Although this matrix dates back to 1957, it still provides a very useful framework for analysing innovations and developing suitable marketing strategies.

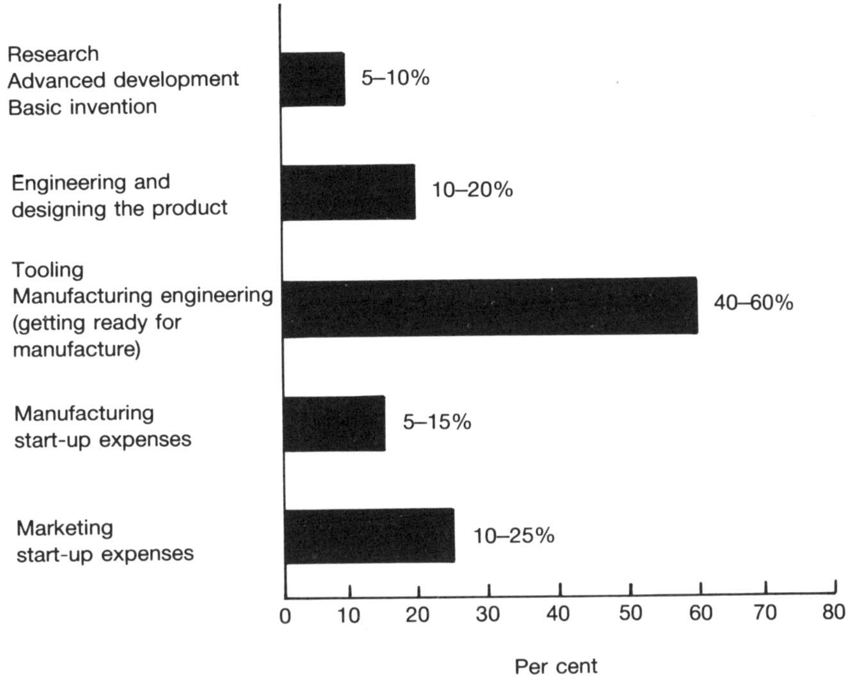

FIGURE 7.2 Typical distribution of costs in successful product innovations (Source: Department of Commerce, *Technological Innovation*, 1967, quoted in Myers and Marquis[50])

The choices open to a company may be noted from Figure 7.3 to involve the following:

1. No change (sometimes referred to as 'masterly inactivity').
2. Stay in the same market, but endeavour to improve market share by a policy of reformation (product modification) or replacement (product innovation).
3. Stimulate demand for present products in existing markets by remerchandising, by planned improvements and by widening the line of products.
4. Identify and expand into new market segments involving, perhaps, product modification and/or diversification.

The PIMS research[56] identified three broad groups of market-share strategies (building, holding, harvesting) which could usefully be considered in conjunction with the classifications of new product strategies outlined in Figure 7.3.

A building strategy is adopted by companies which seek to develop by planned innovation in design, production, marketing and distribution methods. Such organisations aim to be industry leaders. This aggressive or 'offensive' marketing strategy, as observed earlier, carries with it risks which are frequently very substantial (see Chapters 2, 3 and 6).

Increasing technological newness →

↓ *Increasing market newness*

Product objectives	*No technological change*	*Improved technology* To utilise more fully the company's present scientific knowledge and production skills.	*New technology* To acquire scientific knowledge and production skills new to the company.
No market change		*Reformulation* To maintain an optimum balance of cost, quality and availability in the formulas of present company products. Example: use of oxidised microcrystaline waxes in Glo-Coat (1946).	*Replacement* To seek new and better ingredients of formulation for present company products in technology not now employed by the company. Example: development of synthetic resin as a replacement for shellac in Glo-Coat (1950).
Strengthened market To exploit more fully the existing markets for the present company products.	*Remerchandising* To increase sales to consumers of types now served by the company. Example: use of dripless spout can for emulsion waxes (1955).	*Improved product* To improve present products for greater utility and merchandisability to consumers. Example: combination of auto paste wax and cleaner into one-step 'J. Wax' (1956).	*Product line extension* To broaden the line of products offered to present consumers through new technology. Example: development of a general-purpose floor cleaner 'Emerel' in maintenance product line (1953).
New market To increase the number of types of consumer served by the company.	*New uses* To find new classes of consumer that can utilise present company products. Example: sale of paste wax to furniture manufacturers for Coul Board wax (1945).	*Market extension* To reach new classes of consumer by modifying present products. Example: wax-based coolants and drawing compounds for industrial machining operations (1951).	*Diversification* To add to the classes of consumer served by developing new technical knowledge. Example: development of 'Raid' dual-purpose insecticide (1955).

FIGURE 7.3 New products classified by product objectives (Source: Johnson and Jones[56])

Some firms prefer, however, a less adventurous programme of innovation; they adopt an imitative strategy as market followers who are content to 'wait and see'. They monitor the progress of new products marketed by 'leaders' and prepare to come quickly into a market when it begins to show symptoms of real growth. This follow-the-leader strategy may enable them to improve products and also to avoid some of the mistakes made by market pioneers. Although the initiative may have been taken by a more enterprising firm, some large concerns, because of their immense resources and experience, are able to catch up when they eventually decide to invade a market with a new product. This was certainly the case when Gillette finally decided that stainless steel razor blades pioneered by Wilkinson were seriously challenging the market share held by its traditional type of blades. A sleeping giant, when finally aroused, has enormous muscle power in a market.

'Imitation is not only more abundant than innovation, but actually a much more prevalent road to business growth and profits. IBM got into computers as an imitator; Texas Instruments into transistors . . . Holiday Inns into motels.'[57]

The imitative product strategy may well be associated with the PIMS 'holding' marketing share strategy which seeks to defend and preserve a company's position.

Being 'second to market' was seen by the National Institute Economic Review to have definite attractions in its report on the electronic capital goods market:

> The performance of the first laboratory prototypes and early commercial deliveries almost always leaves a great deal to be desired, so that the scope for improvement is very great. For this reason, some entrepreneurs have followed a deliberate policy of being *second* with a new development rather than first. Success in such a policy often requires a greater capacity for moving fast with new developments once the time is considered ripe.[58]

Judgement is clearly a necessary attribute of successful business managers and this will rest on the assessment of risk associated with specific ventures.

Some companies may seek to extend their market opportunities through acquisition of firms which have complementary product ranges or special technological knowledge (see Figure 7.3). This strategy of innovation may be productive, but there are often considerable personal and organisational problems which tend to impede market progress.

An innovative strategy may be founded on developing new uses for a product (see bottom middle-left of Figure 7.3). For example, it has been noted[39] that Teflon was originally developed as a corrosion-resistant material which could withstand high temperatures; it was adopted initially for specific industrial purposes, such as low-friction bearings, and rollers for desks and drawers. Only later was the potential of this product recognised for consumer products, such as Teflon-coated woodwork. This product now has diverse uses across industrial, commercial and consumer markets. (See also Chapter 6 on market segmentation strategies.)

The innovative strategy to be followed by an individual company cannot be quoted like a set of rules. As with market-share strategy (of which it is an intrinsic part), there are usually several alternative methods of 'innovation' open to careful

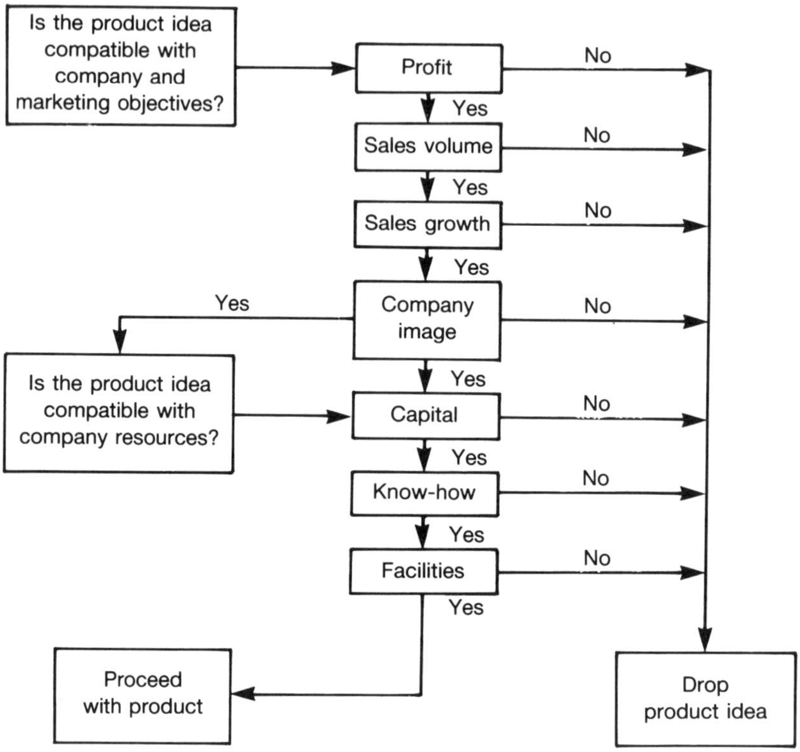

FIGURE 7.4 A simple decision model to assess the viability of a new product design (Source: derived from Design Council[57])

evaluation. The most feasible solution may not necessarily be the ideal one, but at least it should have the virtues of realism.

DECISION MODEL APPROACH TO NEW PRODUCTS

The viability of a new product could be analysed against the framework of a simple decision model, as shown in Figure 7.4.[57] A checklist or logical decision model is often extremely useful in assessing potential marketing prospects for a new product or service. The example in Figure 7.4 may, of course, be further elaborated to meet specific corporate needs.

SUCCESS AND FAILURE IN INNOVATION

It is clear that innovation thrives where the managerial techniques of planning are applied in the various stages of developing new products/services. Pessemier[59] has proposed six steps (see Figure 7.5) in new product development.

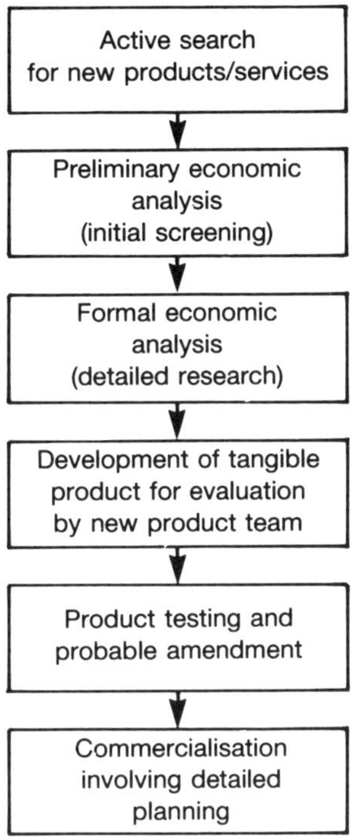

FIGURE 7.5 Outline steps in new product programme (Source: Pessemier[59])

Marketing research (see Chapters 4 and 9) has an active part in new product observing people's behaviour in the home market or in export markets, and with consumer products and those used in factory processes. Markets of all types need to be closely monitored to ensure that trends are evaluated in time for corporate policies to be formed and put into effect.

The head of R&D at Sharp, the Japanese consumer electronics group, has declared: 'In the past, we could see market needs very clearly. But from now on, they will become more diversified. We must do more in-depth studies of what consumers really want. Research must be focused. We must explore potential needs hidden below the surface.'[60] Sony has also admitted that in the past its products were technology driven in the expectation that new ideas would catch on with consumers. 'Market research was often neglected on the grounds that consumers would have not a sensible opinion about an entirely new product.'[61] Now the company accepts that consumers' needs must be studied more, if innovations are to succeed. Peters, in fact, has asserted that, at one time, Sony 'proudly turned its back on market research and produced "user-friendly" designs by gut instinct'.[25]

The Central Advisory Council for Science and Technology has stressed that

> any firm; or indeed any country, engaged in world trade in advanced industrial products, must repeatedly modernise its manufacturing processes and introduce

> new or updated products if it is not to lose markets and go out of business because of competition from advances elsewhere. Hence the constant need for market awareness and for technological innovation.[6]

Management should not only be effective technically, but should also be market orientated, and direct links should exist between R&D and the organisation as a whole. Realistic programmes of innovation should take account of production capacity and market size together with the costs involved in product development.

Project Sappho, which was concerned with investigating factors influencing successful industrial innovations, identified two marketing factors which directly affected the likelihood of success: 'Successful innovators understood user needs better than less successful innovators, and successful innovators pay more attention to marketing than less successful innovators.'[7]

Four 'outstanding groups of success factors' were classified by Sappho in the following ranked order: the organisation and its market; the characteristics of the business innovator in the firm; the quality of research and development; and the efficiency of the firm's internal and external communication networks.

REASONS FOR NEW PRODUCT FAILURES

Innovation and risk are inseparable; products may fail for many reasons, perhaps because they are 'before their time' (like Harry Ferguson's pioneering work on four-wheel-drive vehicles) or, as seen earlier, because their adoption may demand extensive reorganisation or too radical a change in traditional habits.

Andrew Robertson has analysed the case studies in Sappho to see 'what had led the less successful innovating firms into error'. He found that four firms had made no inquiries of potential users, six had made too few enquiries, two had ignored the results of their enquiries, two had misinterpreted the answers they received, six were committed to preconceived designs, and three failed to understand the working environment to which their instrument (all three were instrument-makers) would be subjected. These were all errors which successful innovators avoided by keeping closely in touch with their customers during the period of product development. For example, one instrument firm demonstrated working models of its new design to a select group of potential users with whom they maintained close contact, consulting them about cost estimates and pricing problems.

Eleven of the 34 firms had undertaken no marketing research or had neglected to apply the findings of any research done. Seven put too little effort into marketing, five largely neglected user education, while seven suffered from environmental factors which were beyond their control, such as the emergence of cheap substitute products. The need for educating users was reflected by the company that attempted to market an advanced analytical device which required skilled operation and maintenance. An adequate manual was not provided; 'in the words of one frustrated analytical chemist who could not get the results he wanted from the machine, the makers should have supplied an electronics engineer to keep it in working order'.

Robertson summarises the root causes of these failures as the neglect of marketing research and preconceived ideas about market needs.

Apart from the high rates of failure – between 60 per cent and 90 per cent – of industrial innovations, products that failed to achieve expected market share or profit projections overran cost estimates more than successful ones. It seems that 'there is no natural cut-off point in the failure sequence such as is provided by the break-even point in the successful sequence.'[62]

In the USA, extensive research into industrial product failures was undertaken by Celantone and Cooper,[63] who grouped these into six basic categories:

1. *The better mousetrap no one wanted* (28 per cent of failures): products which, although possessing certain unique features, were not able to attract the interest of sufficient numbers of buyers; such products frequently originated from technical R&D without guidance from market research or sales staff.
2. *Me-too product experiencing head-on competition* (24 per cent of failures): imitative products which lacked any unique features or competitive edge.
3. *Competitive one-upmanship* (13 per cent of failures): products which soon suffered from, for example, inadequate market analysis, or poorly devised market entry, and were easy prey for more professional competitors.
4. *Environmental ignorance* (7 per cent of failures): products which were developed without adequate knowledge of the changes in economic, social, technological or other environmental factors affecting consumption patterns.
5. *Technological dog-product* (15 per cent of failures): products which earned this pejorative label because they were fundamentally flawed in design, concept, delivery or capability.
6. *Price crunch* (13 per cent of failures): products priced at levels above the values placed on them by customers, whose perceptions are likely to be influenced by comparative evaluations of competing products. This type of failure may be due to poor market knowledge (including competitor analysis), inefficient methods of production, inadequate costing systems, unrealistic pricing assumptions, etc.

These six categories are unlikely to be discrete, and various elements of their underlying influences may contribute to specific product failures. Fundamental deficiencies, however, seem to be related closely to insufficient basic knowledge of market needs, which results in products/services being developed with little prospect of being able to satisfy the dynamic expectations of specific types of customer. Some of the prime causes of failure, such as categories 1 and 2, seem to be almost elementary mistakes which should not really have occurred.

Canadian research in 1985 on the criteria for successful innovation focused on 125 industrial firms; of the 203 products analysed, 123 were declared to be successful. Lengthy personal interviews were conducted with the managers most familiar with these products in order to establish the key factors for success.

Three independent and strong dimensions were found to feature in successful product innovations: (1) meeting financial objectives, e.g. sales and profit targets; (2) opening up new opportunities for the firm leading to attractive ventures; and (3) market impact, e.g. products that achieve high market shares in domestic and overseas markets. Product advantage was, not surprisingly, a quality which was particularly influential in market performance.

Of factors that appeared to have relatively limited or little consequence for successful innovation, low price was noted: 'it was not as effective as some experts believe' as a market entry strategy. On the other hand, products that reduced customers' total costs were more likely to be acceptable.[64]

Product innovation in 61 small electrical engineering companies in Yorkshire was found to be the most influential factor in determining their financial success.[65] Thirteen companies had actually been set up to manufacture new products, while a further 15 had diversified into new products. These new products ranged from minute telecommunication equipment (bugging devices) to outside broadcast sound-mixing desks. It was significant that none of the 10 least successful companies had developed new products.

One of the benefits of dedication to new product generation was that small-business owners were alert to marketing problems and, as a result, were often able to devise more effective marketing policies than firms trading in established markets.

PROJECT TEAMS AND SUCCESSFUL INNOVATION

It was observed earlier that the days of the talented, sometimes amateurish, inventor who worked isolated from industrial and commercial pressures seem to have gone for good.

After carefully studying the source of over 80 inventions made during the nineteenth and twentieth centuries, Jewkes[12] concluded that more than half of the cases could be ranked as individual inventions in the sense that much of the pioneering work was carried through by men working on their own behalf. Where inventors were employed in institutes, these organisations allowed the individuals to follow their own ideas without hindrance.

However, the fact that inventions require expensive development before they are commercially viable innovations has, inevitably, led to project teams whose members have a variety of talents, including managerial ability. According to a leading US source, independent inventors are giving way to scientist inventors who work for universities, companies and government. This trend has been accelerated by 'the remorseless advance of technology, and its high risks and need for substantial capital investment'. Du Pont wistfully figures that it takes the lifetime of two highly paid researchers to yield a single major commercial development. But the pay-off from a single successful process or product may be worth lifetimes of work. 'A chemist named Wallace Carothers puttered fruitlessly in Du Pont labs for more than six years.' He was trying to make fibre-forming polymers and had experimented with polyesters, but had given them up because of their low melting points. He then turned his attention to a different set of compounds – polyamides – and invented nylon. It took about 15 years, and involved the work of some 50 different scientists, before Du Pont was able to market Crolyn magnetic computer and video tape in June 1967.[8]

As ICI sees it, 'inventors are individuals whose essential purpose is to create problems – by introducing something new'. These problems are then often solved by other innovators working as a group, who have the task of developing the concept into a marketable product. Innovation, it is emphasised, 'is essentially about people, illogicality, climate, excitement; dull people cannot invent . . . enthusiasm and personal attributes are linked with scientific logic and judgement – and more illogicality'.[40]

The products which are successfully innovated today tend to be the result of teamwork in large research-orientated organisations. Myers and Marquis have emphasised: 'The management of innovation is a corporate-wide task, and is too important to be left to any one specialised functional department.'[50]

In the USA, Xerox operates an innovation board of marketing, production and R&D executives who jointly discuss and evaluate new product ventures. NCR has 'show and tell' meetings, where executives from manufacturing, marketing and R&D openly discuss new business opportunities.[66]

The former director of research for Royal Dutch Shell advocates the 'one–three–nine principle' in developing innovations: for every three inventors, one supporting colleague to keep them informed of the latest scientific developments, plus a further three colleagues for every inventor to develop concepts into marketable products or processes. 'Incidentally, I suspect that in Japan the 1:3:9 approach to invention is much more widely accepted than elsewhere, which perhaps explains Japanese successes in the field of technological innovation'.[67]

John Deere, the American agricultural and construction equipment manufacturer, facing tough competition at home and abroad, has discovered how flexible, team-based operations can be used effectively in the development of innovations. The various divisions of this large company had traditionally enjoyed a great deal of autonomy; this rigid structure was challenged by the introduction of project teams, drawn from different departments, and composed of product engineers (designers), manufacturing engineers, etc., to constitute what is virtually 'integrated engineering'. This has speeded up the development of new products, such as a 'backhoe' loader-digger. (In Chapter 1, the British construction equipment firm of JCB was noted to have adopted fully fledged multidisciplinary teams in developing new products.)

Peters[25] has urged that 'adversaries should be turned into partners' in order to cultivate productive relationships between the different functional areas of activity within companies, between suppliers and the firm, and between the firm and its distributors and customers. In this way, innovations will be fostered and mutual respect and trust engendered.

After painstaking research, ICI[40] developed new alumina fibres into a marketable product, Saffil®, capable of withstanding temperatures up to 1600 °C and, unlike asbestos, biologically safe. A New Ventures Group was set up to conduct research, assess potential uses for this innovation and organise marketing distribution.

Jewkes has wisely observed that the working groups even in a large industrial research laboratory are normally small; the real moving spirits are few and the rest are pedestrian, although useful of course as team members. Because knowledge has become so specialised, researchers tend inevitably to focus on limited fields. Teamwork is essential, although it carries with it 'a countervailing loss of power'. Einstein, however, was said to have commented: 'I am a horse for single harness, and not cut out for landau or team work.'[12]

PRODUCT CHAMPIONS

Because of the danger that potentially good innovative ideas may never survive the built-in inertia or the devastating screening processes operated in some large organisations, some researchers, among them Schon,[68] have proposed that *product champions* should have the task of promoting feasible new ideas in their organisations. This role could be coupled with that of innovation manager or project team leader, who would have freedom of access to executives throughout the firm.

Sappho found that a product champion fulfilled a useful role where he or she was also the business innovator, but it did not subscribe to the 'somewhat romantic view that the product champion can overcome the defects of an unsuitable organisation or a weak business innovator'. Merely dispensing job titles is not enough to bring success; senior management should show their whole-hearted commitment to organised innovation by giving project leaders adequate authority to accomplish their difficult task. Sappho researchers observed that firms which modified their organisations and gave greater freedom to innovators performed 'slightly better'.[7]

In the development of float-glass, mentioned already, Sir Alistair Pilkington assumed the vital role of product champion, when the project was considered to be a big financial gamble. In addition to his team's dogged perseverance, the entrepreneurial chairman of the board, Harry Pilkington, collaborated closely in what proved to be a highly successful innovation.[38]

As noted before, the transistor was the result of outstanding teamwork directed by Walter Brattain and William Shockley of Bell Telephone Laboratories.

Peters views the product/project champion as someone special: 'a dreamer and also a scrounging pragmatist', who takes on tasks with high risks but gives them total dedication. Such a person, he says, 'is almost a sure bet to be egotistical, impatient, and disruptive'.[25]

INFORMALITY MAY LEAD TO SUCCESSFUL INNOVATIONS

Informal methods of working have, of course, had their successes, often outstanding, as in the case of the IBM disc memory unit which was developed secretly in one of the IBM laboratories without the sanction of management because of budget difficulties. Whittle, the jet engine pioneer,

> struggled along without any encouragement either from the Air Ministry or from aero-engineering firms and, in 1935, he actually allowed his patent to lapse. After 1935 he obtained limited backing from a London finance house and he was able to devote all his time to his research, although still an Air Force officer . . . when the first jet aircraft flew successfully in Great Britain in May 1941, it could be said to be the product of Whittle's genius and the help of a small, but highly enthusiastic and extremely devoted group of collaborators.[38]

Aaker[66] has referred to major new business ventures which many large companies, such as Xerox, develop into separate entrepreneurial units; these are often termed 'skunkworks'. See the later discussion of Peters and Waterman's text: *In Search of Excellence*.

EXPLOITING INNOVATION

Invention and innovation, as we have seen, are closely related but distinct functions; without the latter, the former is likely to have no economic effectiveness. Successful innovation exploits fully the fruits of invention. But the processes of invention and innovation often carry high risk, heavy investment and uncertain pay-off periods. Delay is likely to result in loss of market leadership and give competitors the opportunity to snatch business by introducing new products directly targeted at specific market segments.

Various methods of exploiting innovation are used, including buying in innovations, joint ventures and alliances, licensing deals, technology transfer, intrapreneurship, etc.

BUYING IN INNOVATIONS

Because of the enormously high cost of innovation, there is a growing trend by large organisations to buy in feasible innovations. This may be effected by taking over a firm with a successful record of innovatory products; by merging with another company in the hope of achieving synergistic benefits; by obtaining the rights of manufacture and marketing by licence deal; or by buying developed products or product ideas from inventors and/or product brokers.

Among the most successful product ideas bought by the Borg Warner Corporation were those that resulted in the automatic overdrive and the Schneider torque converter. The General Foods Corporation purchased from Birds Eye the rights to its invention of deep freezing methods.

Langrish[45] and his colleagues observed that analysis of the origins of 25 important process and product innovations by Du Pont, a US firm noted for its technical progressiveness, revealed that only 10 of them were based on discoveries attributable to Du Pont's own staff.

As noted earlier, Du Pont invented nylon and also developed it; the company did not discover terylene but, as Dacron®, it developed it. ICI developed both nylon and terylene but discovered neither, although it did discover and develop polyethylene.

British and American pharmaceutical companies were said to have taken no part in the crucial discoveries connected with penicillin, and 'it was difficult enough to persuade them to take part at the pilot plant stage even when the chemotherapeutic virtues of penicillin had been placed beyond doubt'.[12]

Conventional wisdom – or professional myopia – have proved difficult barriers for inventors to crash through. New scientific discoveries have frequently been ridiculed by those who have held the reins of power in research applications. Before the invention of the transistor, some scientists said[12] that there was nothing more to be discovered in that field.

JOINT VENTURES AND ALLIANCES

Companies, as indicated in Chapter 8, may have complementary resources, such as technological strengths which could be matched effectively by marketing skills. In this way, many overseas business ventures are developed relatively quickly and within acceptable levels of risk for the participating companies. This may be particularly important in cases where the product life cycle is judged to be short, and new versions of the product are in the course of development.

Joint ventures can be instrumental in keeping motivation high among the participants, especially when one of the companies has been battling for years with the problems of technical development. Hewlett-Packard is reported[66] to be involved in hundreds of joint ventures and alliances with firms having unique access to customers, foreign markets, technologies and software systems.

Joint venture companies may also be generated from collaboration between venture capital corporations and scientific and academic institutions. For example, the finance corporation Investors in Industry, known as 3i, participated in 1986 in a joint venture with Research Corporation Ltd (REL), and the Imperial College of Science, Technology and Medicine (London). IMPEL, in which the majority shareholding is held by the academic partner and the finance is provided by means of equity and a line of credit, has established a successful record in exploiting consultancy, contract research, technology transfer, etc.[69]

Ciba-Geigy entered into a joint venture with the Olin Corporation of Stamford, Connecticut, in 1991, to develop microelectronic materials. Each company has a 50 per cent stake, amounting to $70m, in the venture, which combines R&D,

production and marketing of photoresists and polyamides used in making semiconductors.[70]

JCB, the construction equipment company based in Staffordshire, announced in 1991 a joint venture with Sumitomo Construction Machinery (SCM) of Japan, by which Japanese-designed crawler excavators, suitably modified for the European market, are made at JCB's plant. JCB has a 51 per cent stake in this venture, which gives it ready access to the growing market for a product range dropped from the company's sales lists some time ago.

LICENSING DEALS

These, as noted in Chapter 8, are popular in global marketing strategies, as Pilkingtons have ably demonstrated. In a licensing deal, 'the rights to implement an innovation are transferred for value to a third party who will make, use or sell the invention'. It is viewed as a good route provided there is strong patent protection combined with a reasonable product life-time, and the resources to monitor effectively possible infringements of the patents involved. It has been proposed that 'the best security may lie in a trade secret rather than a published patent to which competitors can have relatively easy access'.[69]

Several types of licensing arrangement exist; it is vital that both licensor and licensee fully understand and agree the terms of such agreements.

Porter takes a decidely vigilant view of 'alliances', which term he uses to encompass joint ventures, licences and 'various other kinds of interfirm relationships which are particularly common in automobiles, aircraft, robotics, pharmaceuticals, etc.' While alliances offer economies of scale, and access to technologies, marketing skills and other valuable resources, they may also bring disadvantages: differing and conflicting objectives 'are just the start'. Partners may, in time, transmute into challenging competitors, as 'Japananese firms have demonstrated in countless industries'. Alliances are generally considered by Porter to be inherently unstable and transitional in nature, and mostly to be found in second-tier competitors or companies striving to catch up in increasingly challenging markets. In his considered opinion, global leaders seldom rely on alliances to provide them with the assets and skills vital for competitive advantage in their industries.[28]

TECHNOLOGY TRANSFER

As observed before, joint ventures and licensing arrangements not only involve industrial firms, but also occur between venture capital organisations and academic institutions, when intellectual property and technological expertise are exploited.

British Technology group (BTG), formed by the merger in 1981 of the National Enterprise Board and the National Research Development Corporation, was originally a state-owned technology transfer organisation; it played a pioneering role in commercialising scientific research in UK universities – for example, magnetic resonance imaging, cephalosporin antibiotics, and a glass cement filling for dentistry. Up to 1986, BTG exercised a virtual monopoly on patents for British academics, but this was withdrawn by the Government when universities, such as Imperial College, were encouraged to make their own technology transfer arrangements. Commercial venture capital groups have also developed linkages in academia. BTG's record of fighting for the protection of patent rights is impressive: it includes legal action against the Pentagon related to the 'hovercraft' principle, which resulted in a settlement of £3.7 million.

In March 1992, BTG was privatised by means of a management and employee buy-out backed by CINVen, Europe's second largest venture capital company, and also 10 other institutional investors and 11 British universities. BTG employees hold just over 30 per cent of the new company's equity. The newly constituted company plans to develop further links with universities in the UK and abroad, and to expand internationally in commercial and industrial sectors. For instance, licences were negotiated in 1991–2 with Ericsson Radio Systems AB of Sweden for the broad-band linear amplifier used in radio communication systems, with Kolbenschimdt AG of Germany for use of the Mitchell VET variable valve timing system in automobiles, and with Sokkia Co. Ltd of Japan to manufacture laser surveying equipment for the construction industry.

INTRAPRENEURSHIP

Large industrial companies sometimes seem unable to cope with energetic members of their staff who want to exercise their innovative talents, which is how the concept of intrapreneurship came into being. This may take the form of a small company specifically set up to exploit commercially certain technologies and skills which are believed to have significant market potential. A few years ago, Pilkingtons combined four separate energy-related centres of expertise in a small company – Pilkington Energy Advisers Ltd (PEAL) – to offer a comprehensive energy consultancy service. Earlier attempts to organise and develop energy-related skills in the Pilkington group had not been successful because of the absence of a 'champion'. PEAL was given operational freedom, but remained within the group.

LEAD TIME AND INNOVATION

Lead time is one of the most critical factors in innovation. The Central Advisory Council for Science and Technology reported on the tendency for firms and countries to overcome long lead times and heavy development costs 'by buying-in other people's technological knowledge and by concentrating on the commercial application of important inventions and innovations'.[6]

Examples of significant innovations resulting from 'outside' inventors have just been given. Another notable example refers to the ICI Plant Protection Division[40] which, in the mid-1970s, searched for a suitable post-emergence herbicide to control grass weeds. This was part of its consistent research programme during which about 10,000 different chemical compounds active against major crop pests are screened each year. Work was stopped on a compound of its own when ICI's toxicological studies revealed that it might not meet the safety standards in crop protection. After 2½ years of complex negotiations, an agreement was reached with a Japanese chemical company for rights to a suitable compound which had been synthesised by that company. This enabled ICI to produce Fusilade®, which was first marketed in 1981 in Central America and Romania. Later, clearance was obtained virtually world-wide, and so within seven years of first hearing about a potential active ingredient ICI had been able to launch a major new crop protection product. Success was achieved through the efficient co-operation of many innovative scientists and technologists.

The importance of the close working together of many specialists has already been discussed, but reiteration of this critical aspect of successful innovation is worthwhile. Not only must technical experts be of high calibre in their respective fields, but commercial management must also be equally effective. In the National Institute Economic Report on the electronic capital goods market, particular stress was laid on the need for high-quality management in all aspects of an innovating company's operations:

> Where this management talent was missing or where it did not obtain adequate finance, good inventors failed to make the transition to commercial success. This was the case with Forest in radio (and hundreds of other radio firms in the 1920s), with Fransworth in television, and with Zuse and several other firms in computers. Good R&D is a necessary condition for success in this industry, but it is not a *sufficient* condition.[58]

Honda has stated that it needed ten years to transfer its technology to its US assembly plant, and it will take much longer to establish a fully fledged American development facility. A Honda executive is reported to have said: 'The key is people. It can't be done by textbooks. It has to be done face-to-face.'[60]

IN SEARCH OF EXCELLENCE

Over the winter of 1979–80, two experienced American management consultants[71] set out to probe the secrets of successful business management. Supported mainly by McKinsey, they studied in depth the management techniques of a carefully selected sample of 62 US companies which had acknowledged reputations for innovativeness and excellent corporate performance. Although the sample was never intended to be perfectly representative of US industry as a whole, it was held to reflect a fairly broad spectrum and included high technology, consumer goods, general industrial goods, services, project management and resource-based companies.

The research focused principally on big companies and was concerned with finding out how they managed to survive, prosper and keep an innovative edge. Specific financial criteria applicable to excellent performance were selected; these related to measures of growth and long-term wealth creation over 20 years; the other three were measures of return on capital and sales.

The findings of this extensive research, later published in the highly popular text *In Search of Excellence*, showed that successfully managed innovative companies were characterised by eight attributes. Although these are generally regarded as basic business skills and part of conventional wisdom, the outstanding companies were 'above all, brilliant on the basics'. In other words, they fulfilled what are often described as the ordinary responsibilities of management extraordinarily well. These eight attributes were as follows:

1. *Bias for action* – getting on with the job; tackling problems quickly in small, mixed groups.
2. *Close to the customer* – learning about customers' needs, and through regular contacts picking up ideas for new products.
3. *Autonomy and entrepreneurship* – innovation is fostered right through these highly successful companies; people are encouraged to be creative, to take risks and to give good ideas a chance.
4. *Productivity through people* – everyone in these outstanding companies is treated with respect: they are seen as important contributors to corporate success; managers are genuinely interested in helping members of their staff to improve their performance through training, leadership and motivation.
5. *Hands-on, value driven* – companies that perform outstandingly well are clear about their corporate values; they know what they stand for, and their leaders are able to create 'exciting environments through personal attention, persistence and direct intervention – far down the line'. 'Excellent companies' have corporate leaders who demonstrate their total commitment to values that are clearly communicated; they are not content to leave these as abstract conceptions, but see to it that detailed plans of action will ensure that ideas are put into practice.
6. *Stick to the knitting* – or, to use another homely expression, outstanding companies, like successful cobblers, stick to their lasts. Companies that expand by either acquisition or internal diversification are most successful when they stick close to their core skills, as 3M did with coating and bonding technology. The next most likely to be successful are those companies that diversify into related fields. The least successful, generally, are those companies that diversify very widely. Growth in top performing companies has mostly been home grown; the few acquisitions made have been small businesses that could easily be assimilated without altering overall corporate values. Step-by-step diversification policies keep risks to manageable proportions.
7. *Simple form, lean staff* – the structures and systems of excellent companies are 'elegantly simple'; top-level corporate staff are frequently fewer than 100.
8. *Simultaneous loose–light properties* – rigid control alongside corporate values of autonomy, entrepreneurship and innovation right down to the

> factory floor. Shared values include the need for disciplined feed-back; customer problem solving is an obsession at all levels of these highly successful businesses.

The third factor – autonomy and entrepreneurship – demands extended discussion in a chapter dealing with innovation strategy. It is observed by these researchers that 'the most disencouraging fact of big corporate life is the loss of what got them big in the first place: innovation'.[71] However, the companies with enviable track records had the ability 'to be big and yet to act small at the same time'. Many of them even encouraged 'skunk works' – groups of eight or ten enthusiasts working more or less entirely on their own in a kind of meaningful muddle.

For this fanatical activity to be productive, 'champions' are vital (see pp. 302–3). Such champions should essentially be volunteers who are fired by the prospects of developing a new product or process. In a review of its last 50 or so successful and unsuccessful new product introductions, Texas Instruments found that failures were *always* associated with the absence of a *volunteer* champion. The experiences of other large companies such as IBM and GE also emphasised the importance of the role of champions.

Three primary roles in the 'championing system' were identified from this research study:

1. The *product champion* who believes in the project and who is likely to be a 'loner, egotistical or cranky'.
2. The *executive champion*, invariably an ex-product champion who knows all about the problems of husbanding an idea and protecting it from the corporate threat to smother it at birth.
3. The *godfather*, likely to be 'an ageing leader who provides the model for championing'.

It is stressed that champions are pioneers and are, therefore, easily identifiable targets, particularly when innovations fail as many inevitably do. But the companies that consistently support their champions reap rewards in successful innovation. Persistent effort must be encouraged; innovation has to work against very high odds, and the laws of probability clearly favour those companies which are prepared to make many attempts – 'innovation success is a numbers game'. Regular experimentation, shared values, customer orientation and quick and easy communication were important factors in the excellence of the companies surveyed.

The precepts laid down with evangelical fervour by Peters and Waterman seemed 'solid and convincing'[72] when they were first promulgated; the corporate examples were equally impressive. But some of the idols were later seen to have feet of clay; many of the companies had 'either stumbled or . . . actually lapsed into serious decline'[72] only about five years after *In Search of Excellence* appeared. One of the co-authors – Tom Peters – admitted in 1989 that the era of sustainable excellence was over: 'if excellence is to be applicable in the future, it required wholesale redefinition'. The excellent firms of tomorrow, he now declares, 'will cherish impermanence – thrive on chaos'.[25] This verbal agility reflects, perhaps, the transience of popular prescriptions for business. But it should not be the excuse for sweeping away with a dismissive gesture the inherent common sense of many of the eight 'attributes' which were said to characterise successful companies. For example, 'keeping close to the customer' – listening and diagnosing problems – led to a Japanese company redesigning some of its chain saws so that they would not operate if the oil got too low. This avoided damage caused by DIY users, and was requested by rental firms.[73]

The importance of corporate values – the fifth attribute – also remains valid; the benefits of well-defined values were mentioned in Chapter 5. Other attributes, such as entrepreneurship, have been covered at length in this chapter. The precept of 'sticking to the knitting' is evident in the widespread shedding by many companies of peripheral trading activities, in attempts to solve corporate problems by reorientating their energies.

SUMMARY

Innovation is vital for corporate growth; it is risky and often expensive, but without the systematic introduction of new products a firm's future is imperilled.

Innovation and invention are not the same: the former applies the fruits of invention so that profits are earned. Innovation depends on invention, either inside the firm or through licensing and other arrangements. Many companies owe their present-day leadership to consistent programmes of invention and innovation. New, dynamic technologies have accelerated the pace of change; products like electronics quickly become outdated.

Industrial innovation is frequently difficult due to internal organisational factors and also because of the complexity of buying behaviour. Methods of diffusion deserve special attention.

Various classifications of innovation have been applied, e.g. evolutionary, revolutionary, continuous, dynamically continuous and discontinuous. Incremental or sequential innovations often appear to be evident.

Behavioural factors influence the rate of adoption of innovations.

An imitative or follow-my-leader strategy is frequently attractive to firms; this reduces risk and may enable greatly improved versions of products to be marketed when the demand has been 'warmed up'.

A decision model approach to innovation (linked to market research) is helpful in assessing market prospects.

Project teams and product champions have contributed notably to innovation successes. On the other hand, informality and serendipity have also played quite significant roles in successful invention and innovation.

Lead time is critical: this encourages firms to buy-in product concepts.

Successful firms are characterised by the whole-hearted commitment of all who work in them to the development and commercialisation of new products.

REFERENCES

1. Levitt, Theodore, *Thinking about Management*, Free Press, New York, 1991.
2. Wiesner, Jerome B., 'Is innovation in decline?', *McKinsey Quarterly*, winter 1979.
3. Schumpeter, Joseph A., *Business Cycles*, McGraw-Hill, New York, 1939.
4. Mansfield, Edwin, *Industrial Research and Technological Innovation*, Longmans Green, London, 1969.
5. Rogers, Everett M., *Diffusion of Innovation*, Free Press, New York, 1983.
6. Central Advisory Council for Science and Technology, *Technoligical Innovation in Britain*, HMSO, London, 1968.
7. Science Policy Research Unit, University of Sussex (Project Sappho) *Success and Failure in Industrial Innovation*, Centre for the Study of Industrial Innovation, London, February 1972.
8. Blundell, William E. (ed.), *The Innovators: How today's inventors shape your life tomorrow*, Dow Jones, Princeton, NJ, 1968.
9. Jonquières, Guy de, and Cane, Alan, 'National champions become laggards', *Financial Times*, 29 April 1991.
10. Lorenz, Christopher, 'In praise of the corporate tortoise', *Financial Times*, 7 November 1989.
11. Mgadzah, Ray, 'Sinclair set to reveal latest brainwaves', *Sunday Telegraph*, 25 February 1990.
12. Jewkes, John, Sawers, David, and Stillerman, Richard, *The Sources of Invention*, Macmillan, London, 1969.
13. Fishlock, David, 'Ma Bell's Christmas gift to mankind', *Financial Times*, 23 December 1987.
14. Drucker, Peter F., *Frontiers of Management*, Heinemann, London, 1986.
15. Burns, Tom, and Stalker, G. M., *The Management of Innovation*, Tavistock Publications, London, 1966.
16. Chakrabarti, Alok K, 'Industrial product innovation: an international comparison', *Industrial Marketing Management*, vol. 7, no. 4, 1978.
17. Report to Advisory Council for Applied Research and Development, *Industrial Innovation*, Institute of Mechanical Engineers, October 1979.
18. von Hippel, Eric, *The Sources of Innovation*, Oxford University Press, Oxford, 1988.
19. Garner, Roy, 'Reshaping the rules of tyre development', *Financial Times*, 2 June 1988.
20. Drucker, Peter F., *The Practice of Management*, Heinemann, London, 1955.
21. Parsons, S. A. T., *The Framework of Innovation*, Macmillan, London, 1968.
22. Pacey, Arnold, *The Culture of Technology*, Blackwell, Oxford, 1983.
23. Fennell, David, 'Racing ahead with the microchip', *Daily Telegraph*, 26 August 1982.
24. Smith, Lee, 'The lures and limits of innovation', *Fortune*, 20 October 1980.
25. Peters, Tom, *Thriving on Chaos*, Macmillan, London, 1987.
26. Ansoff, H. Igor, *Corporate Strategy*, Penguin, Harmondsworth, 1968.
27. Carter, C. F., and Williams, B. R., 'The characteristics of technically progressive firms', *Journal of Industrial Economics*, March 1959.
28. Porter, Michael E., *The Competitive Advantage of Nations*, Macmillan, London, 1990.
29. Cornell, David, *The Management of Growth in High Technology Companies*, Deloitte Haskins and Sells High Technology Group, October 1985.

30. Marsh, Peter, 'Evangelist of industrial innovation', *Financial Times*, 11 February 1987.
31. Mathias, Peter, *The First Industrial Nation: An economic history of Britain 1700–1914*, Methuen, London, 1983.
32. Ozanne, Urban B., and Churchill, Gilbert A. jun., 'Five dimensions of the industrial buying process', *Journal of Marketing Research*, vol. 8, no. 3, 1971.
33. Webster, Frederick E. jun., 'Communication and diffusion processes in industrial markets', *European Journal of Marketing*, vol. 5, no. 4, 1971.
34. Allen, D. H., and Hayward, George, 'Innovations in the capital equipment area: their effects on diffusion', *Business Graduate*, vol. 2, no. 3, 1972.
35. Ray, G. F., 'The diffusion of new technology – a study of ten processes in nine industries', *National Institute Economic Review*, no. 48, May 1969.
36. Ray, George F., 'The diffusion of mature technologies', *National Institute Economic Review*, no. 106, November 1983.
37. Ray, G. F., 'The diffusion of innovations: an update', *National Institute Economic Review*, no. 126, November 1988.
38. Chisnall, Peter M., *Marketing: A behavioural analysis*, McGraw-Hill, Maidenhead, 1985.
39. Warner, Kenneth E., 'The need for some innovative concepts of innovation: an examination of research on the diffusion of innovations', *Policy Sciences*, vol. 5, 1974.
40. Imperial Chemical Industries PLC, *The Innovators*, ICI, London, 1983.
41. Stewart-Clark, Sir John, 'Market assessment', in *Management of Innovation*, ed. Terry Bishop, Design Council, London, 1975.
42. Harvey-Jones, Sir John, *Getting it Together*, Heinemann, London, 1991.
43. Jones, Trevor (ed.), *Micro Electronics and Society*, Open University Press, Milton Keynes, 1980.
44. Hooper, Richard, 'Prestel – anatomy of an innovation', *ESRC Newsletter*, no. 55, June 1985.
45. Langrish, J., Gibbons, M., Evans, W. G., and Jevons, F. R., *Wealth from Knowledge: Studies of innovation in industry*, Macmillan, London, 1972.
46. Ferrari, Achille, 'Innovation: myths and realities', *Industrial Marketing Management*, vol. 2, 1973.
47. Stonier, Tom, *The Wealth of Information: A profile of the post-industrial economy*, Thames, Methuen, London, 1983.
48. Drucker, Peter F., 'Social innovation – management's new dimension', *Long Range Planning*, vol. 20, no. 6, 1987.
49. Rothwell, Roy, 'The role of technical change in international competitiveness: the case of the textile machinery industry', *Management Decisions*, vol. 15, no. 6, 1980.
50. Myers, Summer, and Marquis, Donald G., 'Successful industrial innovations: a study of factors underlying innovations in selected firms', National Science Foundation (NSF 69–17), 1969.
51. Shal, Devendra, 'Invention, innovation and economic evaluation', *Technological Forecasting and Socail Change*, vol. 23, 1983.
52. Robertson, Thomas S., 'The process of innovations, and the diffusion of innovations,' *Journal of Marketing*, vol. 3, January 1967.
53. Hargreaves, Deborah, 'Shopping from the Chicago armchair,' *Financial Times*, 25 November 1987.
54. Levitt, Theodore, *Marketing for Business Growth*, McGraw-Hill, New York, 1974.
55. 'Bayer's formulation for product innovation', *International Management*, February 1978.

56. Johnson, Samuel C., and Jones, Conrad, 'How to organise for new products', *Harvard Business Review*, vol. 35, no. 3, 1957.
57. Majaro, Simon, 'A market strategy for Europe', *Designing for European Markets: A management guide*, ed. John E. Blake, Design Council, London, 1972.
58. Freeman, C., 'Research and development in electronic capital goods', *National Institute Economic Review*, no. 34, November 1965.
59. Pessemier, Edgar A., *New Product Decisions*, McGraw-Hill, New York, 1966.
60. Jonquières, Guy de, 'Industry hits a cultural barrier', *Financial Times*, 5 December 1990.
61. Butler, Steven, 'Sony's lean manufacturing machine', *Financial Times*, 10 December 1992.
62. Robertson, Andrew, 'The marketing factor in successful industrial innovation', *Industrial Marketing Management*, vol. 2, 1973.
63. Celantone, R. J., and Cooper, R. G. 'A typology of industrial new product failures', in B. A. Greenberg and D. N. Bellenger, eds., *Proceedings, AMA Educators' Conference*, Series 41, American Marketing Association, Chicago, 1977.
64. Cooper, R. G., and Kleinschmidt, E. J., 'Success factors in product innovation', *Industrial Marketing Management*, vol. 16, 1987.
65. Foley, Paul, 'The innovative advantage', *Financial Times*, 10 March 1987.
66. Aaker, David A., *Strategic Market Management*, John Wiley, New York, 1992.
67. Beckers, Harry L., 'Commentary', in *Milestones in Management: An essential reader*, ed. Henry M. Strage, Blackwell, Oxford, 1992.
68. Schon, Donald A., 'Champions for radical new inventions', *Harvard Business Review*, vol. 41, no. 2, 1963.
69. Desforges, Charles D., 'Investing in innovation', in *3i Technology Forecast*, 3i Group plc, London, 1990.
70. Dullforce, William, 'Ciba-Geigy and Olin Corp to set up chip venture', *Financial Times*, 8 January 1991.
71. Peters, Thomas J., and Waterman, Robert H. jun., *In Search of Excellence: Lessons from America's best-run companies*, Harper and Row, New York, 1982.
72. Lorenz, Christopher, 'Excellence: how not to singe your wings', *Financial Times*, 25 January 1991.
73. Magrath, A. J., 'People productivity: marketing's most valuable asset', *Journal of Business Strategy*, July/August, 1988.

REVIEW AND DISCUSSION QUESTIONS

Q1 How useful is the distinction between inventions and innovations in industrial markets? Identify recent examples of each to illustrate your answer.

Q2 Some authors have suggested that the industrial adoption process is more complex than adoption by individuals. What are your views about this?

Q3 In this chapter, five principles were said to determine the acceptability of innovations and their diffusion. Apply these criteria to explain the acceptance of cellular telephones by sales managers for use by their sales forces in, for example, the United Kingdom.

Q4 Industrial innovations have been classified generically as: continuous, dynamically continuous, and discontinuous. Apply this approach to the following innovations, and give reasons underlying your selection: (a) personalised plastic photocopying cards for employees; (b) portable fibre-glass pigsties for free-range pig producers; and (c) computerised portable personal organisers for executives.

Q5 From your overall reading of this chapter, how would you advise a manager anxious to know if she can create an environment in her firm that will promote industrial innovation?

Q6 What exactly is a 'product champion'? What role does this person play in the development of innovations in industrial organisations?

CHAPTER EIGHT

International strategy I

THE CHALLENGE TO BRITAIN'S INDUSTRIAL SUPREMACY

In Chapter 2 it was noted that Britain was once known as the 'workshop of the world' and dominated world manufacturing, but that in the mid-Victorian years this industrial supremacy was increasingly challenged. The close of the nineteenth century witnessed a fierce struggle for overseas trade between Britain, the United States and Germany. Aided by protectionist trading, the last two countries had developed their basic industries and were now challenging the long-held superiority of British industrialists in world markets.

Through the Edwardian period and down to the time of the First World War, British products and services were behind the strength of the gold sovereign in trading exchanges. But the inevitable depredations of two world wars altered the pattern of world trading considerably.

The pattern of British export trade underwent a radical change after the First World War: textiles such as cotton piece goods halved their market share, while vehicles and machinery increased their market shares twofold; chemicals also experienced a significant increase – about one third – although coal exports fell.

For generations, Britain – the first nation in the world to experience large-scale industrialisation – had pioneered production processes in ship building, coal mining, textiles and the metal industries. British industrial leadership was virtually unchallenged. These days have now gone for ever.

Today, technologies are widely dispersed over the world. Competition is world-wide and increasing in intensity as countries which were formerly important export markets for British goods have developed politically and economically, and have largely adopted policies of self-sufficiency. The British Empire has dissolved, and with it have gone the trading privileges which were held to be the prerogatives of British industrialists and merchants. British goods and services are now exposed to the harsh climate of 'open' markets; old trading loyalties have been affected by the abrasive atmosphere of world economic conditions.

Technological expertise has contributed significantly to the growth of international business:

> Relatively small countries have indeed been able to establish very important positions in specific technologies which are of great importance to *all* countries

> . . . The most important post-war advance in steel-making occurred in Austria, Switzerland leads in pharmaceuticals and pesticides; Japan in some branches of electrical technology . . . The most recent studies appear to point clearly to a strong trend towards the fast development of trade in high technology products rather than in conventional products, showing that the newest trends are indeed the strongest.[1]

For many years after the Second World War, British industrialists had not troubled to develop their market overseas – they had slipped into the relatively easy habit of trading principally in the home market, where a sellers' market was in full swing. Production could be disposed of profitably and without undue effort.

In a report dated May 1950, PEP stated quite bluntly: 'For most exporters overseas trading is a residual interest, of much less importance to the company's progress than the home market. In addition, the standard of export marketing practice is rudimentary.'[2] This attitude contrast strongly with business activities in today's difficult trading environment; more and more companies are finding that exporting has become vital for their continued prosperity.

Twenty-five years later, despite the acknowledged urgency, the Royal Society of Arts issued a research report[3] on export performance, the findings of which closely echoed the PEP report. The research studied the export performance of 122 British companies with annual turnovers ranging from just under £5 million to over £50 million and accounting for about 25 per cent of total UK exports of manufactured products.

The findings are disconcerting: a general lack of a professional marketing approach to overseas markets and a curious lack of managerial logic in planning market strategies. One company exported to a total of 164 countries, but 90 per cent of export sales were with only 10 of these countries; the rest were expensive to service, but because the export sales director had spent 25 years in developing them, he would not consider rationalising his marketing efforts by axing some of these peripheral markets.

Most of the companies researched were surprised to discover that a remarkably large proportion of their exports were derived from a very limited number of countries, often fewer than six. The 'lowest overall return of profits on capital' appeared to be earned by companies which exported to the largest number of countries. Concentration on selected markets leads to increased opportunities and builds up market share.

Half the companies surveyed reported that exports were more profitable than home sales. About 40 per cent obtained higher prices in most overseas markets, 45 per cent occasionally were able to secure higher prices overseas and about 10 per cent could not.

Selective targeting enables small companies, in particular, to build up really worthwhile export business; there is no sense in trying to be the world's supplier if corporate resources cannot sustain the efforts needed for this herculean task.

PRINCIPLE OF CRITICAL MASS

Critical mass, a term borrowed from nuclear physics, refers – as Drucker[4] has noted – to the smallest fraction which is big enough to alter the nature and behaviour of the whole. The principle of critical mass is often advanced as vital to the profitable exploitation of markets, wherever they may be. Briefly, a company needs to attain a minimum level of size – achieve 'critical mass' – if it is to be effective in competitive environments. Instead of dissipating limited resources (as the BETRO report[3] observed of many British firms), companies should aim to obtain a significant position in carefully targeted markets. This view was also supported by a NEDO paper[5] on Britain's export performance, which recommended concentration on key markets: exporters tended to spread their efforts too widely and hence failed to build competitive strength in such scattered markets.

This lack of critical mass has also been observed of

> many US manufacturers [who] still try to find shortcuts around the evaluations and management attention that profitable business necessitates. For example, one communications equipment manufacturer took the approach of trying to sell its products through agents in 50 countries, rather than perform the analyses required to determine which handful of markets offered the best long-term potential and warranted more significant investment. As a result, the company never developed a really strong position in any of these markets and eventually lost out to more targeted competitors . . .[6]

Leading industrial groups are fully aware of the power of critical mass in world markets as the following examples illustrate. In 1992 ICI and Du Pont negotiated a 'swap deal' involving their nylon and acrylic businesses, resulting in Du Pont becoming the largest manufacturer of nylon in Europe with plants in the UK, Germany and the Netherlands. ICI's part of the bargain released it from a cyclical fringe business with profits continually under pressure from Far Eastern low-cost competition and world-wide production overcapacity, and gave the company a strong production base for acrylics in the USA.

The following year was marked by another large-scale exchange deal, when ICI traded its polypropylene business with turnover of £135m, for BASF of Germany's £60m acrylic operations in Europe. The deal enabled ICI to relinquish its loss-making European polypropylene activities and strengthen its position in the steadily growing acrylics market. In turn, BASF became the second largest polypropylene producer in Europe and secured critical mass in this market.

INTERNATIONAL MARKETING

International marketing is not merely a sophisticated way of describing 'export selling' – it is far more fundamental and reflects attitudes, orientation and behaviour towards securing profitable business overseas.

> International marketing is the performance of business activities that direct the flow of a company's goods and services to consumers or users in more than one nation. The only difference between domestic marketing and international marketing is that the activities that take place are in more than one country . . .[7]

In Michael Brooke's forceful phrasing:

> A successful international firm is one that has effective international marketing. To many this is a self-evident proposition, but sceptics have cast doubts on it. A good invention can be a substitute for any amount of inefficiency, while luck helps, but a world spread normally comes through effective marketing.[8]

For many firms, international marketing is virtually routine practice, and they have acquired impressive skills in negotiating business overseas. Some, as will be seen later, are large multinational or transnational organisations, but many exporting companies are small and medium-sized businesses headed by talented entrepreneurs, who have developed products or services specifically designed to meet the needs of target markets. The scale of their operations will obviously differ from, for example, the mammoth organisations quoted in the discussion of 'critical mass', but the principles of marketing remain irrespective of the scale of business operations. Product specialisation and market niching strategies (see Chapter 6) can be used in harness to open up profitable opportunities for small firms in export markets.

In an unfamiliar environment, marketing does not lose its value as a vital management activity. The overseas market of a particular company remains, of course, the home market of national and competing firms. Sir John Harvey-Jones has stressed the international nature of the competition faced by ICI in its own home market, where Dow, Du Pont, Hoechst, Badische, Bayer and Ciba-Geigy operate through subsidiary companies. In the same way, he concedes, ICI has companies in the United States, Germany and Switzerland: 'None of us has our own patch to ourselves, and we meet, fight and compete in nearly every country in the world.'[9] Successful operations by a foreign supplier will depend on its attitudes towards its customers, wherever they may be living.

Keegan has stated that 'in an increasing number of companies the concept of "foreign" is breaking down because of the growing involvement of corporate headquarters in the company's marketing program, irrespective of location'. To IBM, for instance, 'there is no such thing as a "foreign" market in the psychological sense – there are markets in different parts of the world, at different stages of development, with different characteristics . . . IBM knows as much about the French market for data processing equipment as it knows about the US market.'[10]

The mechanics of marketing can be adapted to the particular environmental differences of overseas markets. Involvement with customers' problems, wherever they may arise, is a function of successful marketing. In organisational markets, this will largely depend on the ability of suppliers to offer feasible solutions to problems such as the quality of alloy steels used in production. Solutions are being sought not just from home-based firms; competition is now across the continents of the world.

DECISIONS FOR PROSPECTIVE EXPORTERS

Marketing management wishing to enter or extend the sales of their products or services overseas are faced with these questions:

1. Whether – should overseas markets be developed?
2. Where – what markets should be selected for development?
3. When – at what time should these markets be tackled?
4. How – what market strategy or strategies should be adopted?

These points should be considered in relation to the company's overrall marketing strategy, and opportunities (and attendant risks) should be studied. It is sound policy for a company to spread its risks so that it does not become too dependent on one or two large markets which could, through political or economic upheavals, suddenly decline: for example the US protectionist policy of 1971 placed some British firms in difficult situations almost overnight. (See also Chapter 6 on product porfolio planning.)

All this points to the fact that would-be exporters should not be content with a few superficial ideas about the markets they propose to enter. Systematic research thoroughly planned and carried out by experts will provide factual data relating to the economic, social, psychological and cultural factors which are likely to affect the acceptance of a new product and the progressive sales planned.

The specific needs of identified types of customer should be analysed and related to the resources (financial, productive, marketing and administrative) of the prospective supplying firm. This calls for systematic marketing research in order to obtain objective and reliable data, both qualitative and quantitative. (See Chapter 9 for discussion.)

MOTIVATIONS INFLUENCING INTERNATIONAL TRADING

The principle of *comparative advantage* or comparative cost was developed in the nineteenth century by some of the leading British classical economists as an explanation of international trading. This theory postulated that each nation tends to specialise in the production of those goods and services in which it is comparatively most efficient, exporting them and importing those goods which they could produce less advantageously. At the macro level of economic activity, this theory of international business maximises, it is claimed, output from world resources. It is related to the basic economic techniques of mass production specialisation of output and division of labour. Without such concentration of resources and specialisation of efforts, the rapid industrialisation of the western economies would not have been feasible.

The principle of *absolute cost advantage* referred to the situation where a product could be produced distinctly more cheaply in a specific country than in another country. The first country was described as having an absolute cost advantage. This differential could be eroded by technological developments and the industrialisation of countries which formerly depended, for example, on Britain for supplies of certain kinds of machine tool.

However, these theories do not fully explain the pattern of contemporary world trade. Other motivations exist at the micro level which cause companies to seek business overseas.

BUSINESS MOTIVATIONS

An individual company is not directly affected by the theory of comparative advantage: self-interest is the prime motivation of individuals and trading organisations – direct conflict with national interests may well arise. Business people may consider, in fact, that they suffer from some of the trading policies laid down by governments. Perhaps it is only to be expected 'that the attitudes of governments on the one hand and businessmen on the other should, at times, be strongly ambivalent. Governments are under numerous pressures, internal and external, while businessmen can hardly be expected to support with enthusiasm measures which do not benefit them fairly directly . . .'[1]

Motivations such as economies of scale are likely to influence business decisions to expand markets overseas. As a Unilever chairman observed:

> The economies of scale in research and specialised central services owe their importance to a very simple principle. Knowledge has no marginal cost. It costs no more to use it in the 70 countries in which we operate than in one. It is this principle which makes Unilever economically viable.[11]

The opportunity to increase profitability, particularly when home market prices are depressed or controlled by government intervention, has forced many managements increasingly to look overseas for continued profitability and growth.

Manufacturers considering export business for the first time should evaluate carefully several factors before committing themselves. They will need to know, for example, the nature of the demand for their kind of products in specific overseas markets – is it likely to be regular and progressive? Does the manufacturer have the resources (financial, production, etc.) to meet the anticipated extra demand generated from export activities? Pricing policies will be of signified importance. Could prices in export markets be fixed to equal those obtainable in the home market after allowing for the extra costs involved in overseas selling? Alternatively, would export sales, even at prices somewhat below home market prices, be of value in contributing to overall profitability?

Although motivations at the macro and micro levels may differ to some extent, in multinational business organisations the theory of comparative advantage tends to become more evident.

Kotler[12] states that two factors draw a firm towards a strategy of international market development: (1) *push* – because of the lack of home market opportunities; and (2) *pull* – by increasing opportunities for its products abroad.

1. *Identify export motivations*
   e.g. Surplus production capacity
   Need to find new growth markets
   Unique product/technical knowledge
   Strong competitive advantage
   Economies of scale

2. *Audit corporate resources*
   e.g. Knowledge and experience of exporting
   Special staff skills
   Corporate strengths and weaknesses

3. *Analyse specific product markets*
   e.g. Nature of demand
   Buying behaviour
   Competitive activities
   Channels of distribution
   Media availability

FIGURE 8.1 Steps in evaluation of export opportunities

Companies which are contemplating exporting might well find the sequential approach given in Figure 8.1 a useful guide; this develops logically from identification of basic motivations to audit of resources and then to analyses of specific market opportunities. These steps follow the general guidelines given in Chapter 6 on overall market planning.

A firm, according to Porter,[13] may exercise two types of competitive advantage: low relative cost or differentiation. It may be able to produce a comparable product at lower cost or a comparable product with *enhanced value* that will justify a premium price. The essence is to provide customers with greater buyer value than competitors. Porter states that every firm is engaged in 'value activities', creating a value chain which includes all the technological and commercial inputs necessary to supply products that are attractive to specific types of customer (see also Chapter 6). This concept is related, of course, to that of the augmented product, discussed in Chapter 1.

TYPICAL PHASES IN DEVELOPMENT OF OVERSEAS BUSINESS

Some companies almost stumble into exporting; much to their surprise, and even alarm, they suddenly find themselves faced with an unsolicited enquiry from abroad. Others have become involved through merging with a business that already had overseas activities. In some cases, personal links have resulted in business being developed with certain countries. From the accidental to the planned approach

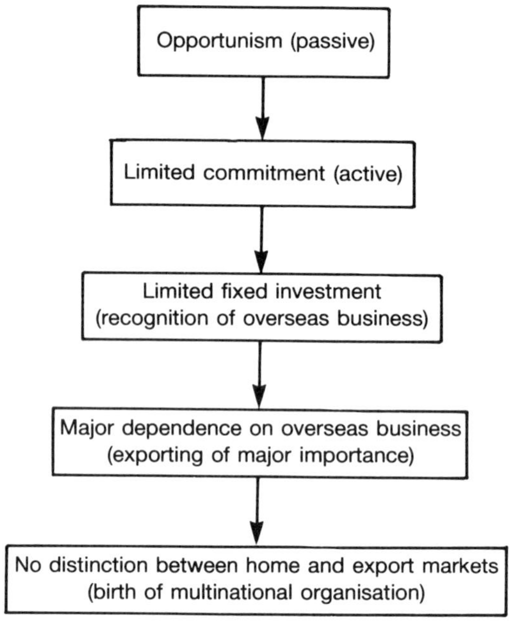

FIGURE 8.2 Phases in development of overseas business

there are clearly many events which may trigger off overseas marketing, but even today many companies prefer to adopt a passive attitude or, if they go abroad, tend to take up a defensive posture. Positive dynamic marketing often appears to be sadly lacking in many firms, which seem to have little real conception of the need to tackle market opportunities in a systematic, planned way. Their lack of success does not surprise experienced, professional export managers, who know that infiltration and exploitation of overseas markets demand standards of management and personal qualities which are far from common.

Five phases in the evolutionary process affecting companies engaged in international business have been identified.[1] Shown in Figure 8.2, these range from accidental to planned market operations and reflect different levels of behaviour and commitment:

1. Opportunism (passive).
2. Limited commitment (active).
3. Limited fixed investment (recognition of overseas business).
4. Major dependence on overseas business (exporting of major importance).
5. No distinction between home and export markets (birth of multinational organisation).

These phases will be discussed in turn.

1. *Opportunism* is connected with the accidental entry into exporting just discussed. The opportunity presented by a chance enquiry could, perhaps, be

developed by enterprising management; luck is really nothing more than being ready to seize suitable opportunities and turn them to advantage. Often a relatively small company dealing almost exclusively with home market customers receives an overseas enquiry about one of its products which has been noticed in the home market by an overseas business visitor. This may set in motion a whole series of policy and tactical decisions affecting product range, pricing, production policy, etc. The alertness of management to new market opportunities does not depend on high technical competence: it calls for some of the instinctive flair for business without which corporate resources are sterile.

Airedale International Air Conditioning of Leeds expanded its US business by responding to demands from American customers which led to the modification of an office air conditioner for use in school classrooms. This system is being further adapted for use in telephone exchanges.

2. *Limited commitment*, the second stage of corporate commitment to exporting, reflects the willingness of management to consider particular overseas markets because of the success, perhaps, of the opportunistic policy. These markets may be chosen because they are geographically accessible; because they appear to have cultural and social characteristics similar to existing markets; or because the degree of risk involved in entering them is acceptable. At this stage of exporting, products and pricing are likely to be the same as with 'opportunistic' exporting; there will be no long-term fixed investment, production being limited to marginal capacity. This stage is important, however, because it marks the transition from 'passive' to 'active' exporting.

3. *Limited fixed investment* occurs when the promise of increased export business leads to greater commitment by the exporter – extra capacity is allocated to export orders, which are increasingly recognised as an important contribution to the overall trading policy. Products are developed and pricing policies carefully devised to secure effective penetration of selected markets. There is a tendency to follow marginal pricing and, in general, an increasing commitment to overseas trade.

4. *Major dependence on overseas business* reflects top management's wholehearted commitment to exporting. Board-level directives will now activate management to concentrate more of their time on overseas trading problems. Pricing and product policies will tend to rank equal with domestic business. An overseas division may be set up which will quickly assume significance in corporate activities. Such a firm is not in exporting for fun, but to earn specific rates of return on its capital and other resources. There are likely to be some management casualties during this period of dynamic reorientation.

5. *No distinction between home and export markets*, the final evolutionary stage, heralds the birth of the multinational organisation which views the world as its oyster. Strategic business opportunities are assessed across entire continents and involve diverse cultures and global strategy. 'Capital may be held outside the country of origin, the shares may be quoted on all the principal stock exchanges and dividends declared in a currency not that of the country of origin . . .'[1]

The purest global strategy is said[13] to occur when an organisation concentrates as many activities as possible in one country, serves the world from this home base and tightly co-ordinates those activities that must, by their nature, be performed near the buyer. This was the strategy followed by Toyota and many other Japanese firms in the 1960s and 1970s. However, global strategies vary considerably in practice; Xerox used to concentrate R&D in the United States but disperse other activities, although these were closely co-ordinated, while the brand marketing strategy and servicing procedures were standardised across the world. A quite different global strategy was adopted by Canon, whose primary production and service activities were concentrated in Japan. However, provided the Canon brand was always used, considerable discretion was given to local marketing subsidiaries.

This ultimate stage in the transition from 'accidental' overseas involvement to long-term corporate commitment has had a significant influence on the pattern of world trading. It has not just affected economic policies, but extended into social, political and other environmental factors. More large organisations are becoming international both in philosophy and in scope of operations. For a continually growing number of firms, the entire world is considered a market-place for their products. Rather than asking 'Where in our country should a new plant be built or a new market developed?' more firms are asking: 'Where in the *world* should a new product be made or sold?'[7] Trading horizons have developed far beyond the traditional perspectives held for many years by business firms.

This more enterprising view of world markets ('The world is our oyster') has influenced the supply side as well as the marketing policy. Firms may seek suppliers from regions which have not been traditionally regarded as sources for particular kinds of goods. This liberalising of trading attitudes and behaviour should not be overlooked by firms which have tended to regard access to certain markets, and to some customers, as almost a trading right.

STRATEGIC APPROACHES

As has been observed already, the principles of marketing are universal, so the theoretical approaches to, for example, strategic market planning are also relevant when considering exporting opportunities.

Basic concepts such as *SWOT analysis* (see Chapter 5) are clearly useful in the preliminary stages of developing exporting strategies. SWOT analysis, which should be undertaken rigorously and objectively, may reveal, for instance, that a company enjoys a distinct leverage in its present operations, resulting from technological excellence, marketing skills, etc. Limiting factors may also come to light which may, in the short term at least, inhibit overseas development.

Market segmentation is another fundamental strategic approach which has wide application (see Chapter 6), and this will be discussed further in Chapter 9. Du Pont's approach in Europe has 'stressed the different customer segments to which products are sold rather than regional or product divisions'.[14] Broad business

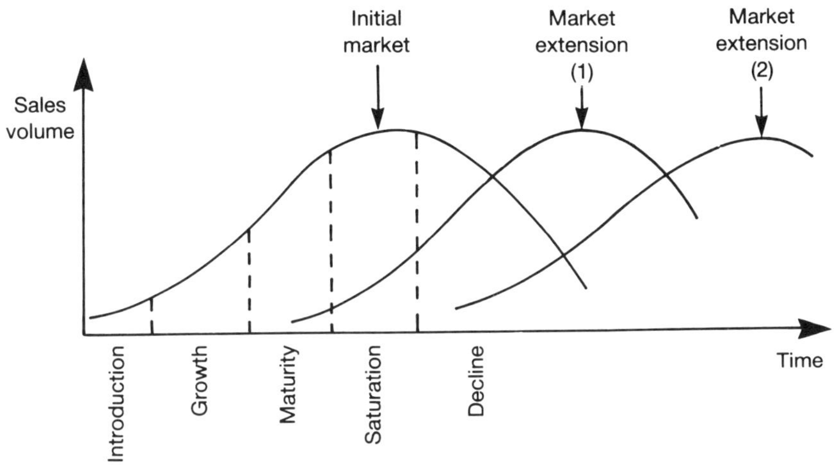

FIGURE 8.3 Product life cycle/market life cycle applied to international markets

groups that cover a variety of products have been developed, such as a general automotive marketing group with representatives from product divisions concerned with fibres used, for example, in car seats, and also with engineering plastics for car bodies and engine components.

Product life-cycle (PLC) theory (see Chapter 6) can be usefully adapted for purposes of international marketing. Leontiades has emphasised that the most useful feature of PLC is that it draws attention to impending change: 'the future will be different from the past and rarely predictable as a straight-line projection of it, though essential similarities may exist'. It also alerts management to the strategic importance of timing: 'the right strategy for one phase of the life cycle may be inappropriate at another stage'. Probably, however, the most important contribution PLC makes to international strategy is that 'it provides another basis for inter-country comparisons'.[15]

Related to PLC is the concept of MLC – *market life cycle* – which, as shown in Figure 8.3, proposes that a firm may extend its markets overseas in line with product innovations and improvements, which may render earlier versions unacceptable to more sophisticated markets. Because not all markets are likely to be at the same stage of development, opportunities may exist for extending the profitable life of some products in specific overseas regions.

As mentioned in Chapter 6, considerable care is needed in evaluating the PLC, the validity of which has been challenged by many researchers; the actual shape of the trend curve has popularly been that of the normal curve, whereas different profiles have been found to exist in specific markets.

Associated with PLC/MLC is the *market portfolio* approach, involving product porfolio planning (see Chapter 6 for an extended discussion) and its 'partner', market portfolio planning. Leontiades says that because multinationals can allocate their resources across different countries, this gives rise to a number of specific portfolio strategies. 'Any company that chooses where its international resources shall be deployed and how much shall be invested in businesses in different parts of the world faces a portfolio planning situation.'[15]

Various product portfolio models have already been examined (see Chapter 6). These, in particular the McKinsey/GE Business Screen and Shell's International Directional Policy Matrix, offer highly relevant approaches for evaluating international business prospects. For example, countries could be rated for their attractiveness along the horizontal axis of Figure 6.9, and evaluated against the vertical axis indicating a company's ability to compete in specific locations. Values of 1–3 could be assigned to the relative positions, and the resultant scores would, initially at least, indicate areas in which further market research should be undertaken.

Figure 8.4 outlines a *portfolio screen* relative to a company's competitive strengths viewed against the attractiveness of a specific market location. Scores less than, say, four might be taken as indicating that entry into that particular market was not advisable; this would be in contrast to high scores along the horizontal axis and equally high scores on the vertical axis, which might even result in a total score of nine in exceptional cases. (Factors influencing market attractiveness are considered in Chapter 9, dealing with market research.)

The *market dynamics model*, as projected by Porter[16] and discussed in Chapter 5, is also valuable in assessing the feasibility of investing or expanding in specific industries overseas, or, perhaps, of entering into trading alliances of various kinds (joint ventures etc. are discussed later). The disciplined approach inherent in this competitive analysis results in a fundamental grasp of the dynamics of market behaviour.

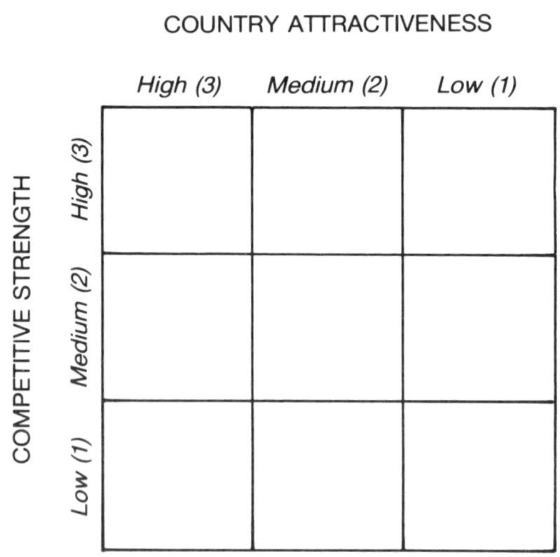

FIGURE 8.4 Company/market portfolio screen

Generic strategy categories were also discussed in Chapter 5, when it was seen that, according to Porter, the following three categories can be identified: (1) overall cost leadership; (2) differentiation; and (3) focus. The latter is based on effective market segmentation, enabling marketing efforts to be focused on well-defined market targets.

Overall cost leadership strategy has, as Keegan observes,[10] attracted a great deal of attention over recent years largely because of the experience curve concept (see Chapter 6). Price leadership may be feasible through economies of scale and trigger off large-scale realignment of corporate activities, as noted in the case of ICI's 'swap deals'.

Differentiation strategies are followed by companies which endeavour to make their products/services stand out from their competitors in specific markets, perhaps through product attributes, such as unique design features, technical back-up services, etc. In export markets, in particular, a differentiation strategy is likely to provide effective entry into profitable market niches.

A focusing strategy is based on well-devised market segmentation, enabling marketing efforts to be directed on to clearly defined customer groups.

It was pointed out earlier that these three strategies are not, of course, exclusive, and, in practice, elements from all three are likely to be used in developing a profitable overall strategy. Strategies may well be varied to meet the conditions of specific market locations: for example, the nature of competition, the sophistication of market behaviour, and legal and other constraints.

MARKET ENTRY STRATEGIES

In the section dealing with phases in the development of overseas business, an evolutionary process often appeared to characterise the way in which companies became involved in overseas activities.

Market entry may, however, adopt a more formal planning approach, as proposed by Leontiades,[15] who identifies *four generic national market entry strategies*: (1) skim; (2) penetration; (3) dumping; and (4) explore.

The first of these has the objective of a high rate of return consistent with a low commitment of corporate resources; limited and readily accessible market segments are targeted and exploited through a variety of tactics, such as direct exporting, licensing and agencies. (This approach is similar to the limited commitment stage noted earlier.)

The second strategy is used by companies which plan to secure a significant and increasing share of specific markets, and are prepared to commit substantial corporate resources to build up a long-term business overseas, perhaps through direct investment. (This approach relates to the limited fixed investment stage observed in Figure 8.2.) This penetration strategy is reflected in pricing policies which are influenced by the prospects of sales growth, although short-term profitability may be unlikely.

The third strategy – dumping – may be used by some companies faced with production overcapacity, subject to observance of rules against illegal dumping (defined by GATT as selling products at prices lower than those normally charged in a domestic market or country of origin, after allowing for transportation, local taxes, etc.). The US definition tends to be rather more stringent, and refers to dumping as unfair trade practices – unfair price cutting having for its objective the injury, destruction or prevention of the establishment of American industry. Dumping is a short-term strategy which is inherently opportunistic and unlikely to lead to the establishment of long-term profitable business.

The nature of the fourth strategy is exploratory: it enables companies to gain knowledge at first hand of the environmental conditions and buying behaviour of certain overseas markets. Contacts can be made and opportunities for further commitments carefully assessed for their likely long-term prospects. At this stage, market share, sales and profitability are secondary to the main purpose of this strategy, i.e. to learn as much as possible about major competitors and prospective customers, and to evaluate the influence of statutory and other factors on market behaviour.

The choice of entry strategy is, therefore, an important decision and will be determined largely by the logistics of overseas operations, which will be reviewed later in this chapter.

Companies planning to enter overseas markets have to decide on the nature of the products to be offered. Will these be standard versions of existing ranges already sold in the home market? Will they be adapted versions of such products? Or will specially designed products have to be developed in order to compete successfully? (See Chapters 5 and 6 on product policy and portfolio planning.)

Clearly, products identical or similar to those already in production for the home market will result in economies of scale and also allow for rapid entry into chosen export markets. However, the likelihood of acceptance by foreign customers requires careful research; standard products may, of course, be acceptable provided certain modifications are incorporated to comply with particular national and industrial specifications. Again, market research should be undertaken to provide guidance about the type of adaptation that may be necessary.

There may be other attractive overseas opportunities that can be catered for only by specially designed products. Such opportunities should be expertly assessed in terms of both potential business and also the costs involved – research and development, start-up production costs, marketing skills, etc.

Apart from matching products to markets, communication methods will also need to be appropriate to specific market environments. The decisions involved are shown schematically in Figure 8.5.

The top-left cell of the matrix (straight extension) is obviously the simplest strategy and the lowest immediate risk to the marketer; a typical successful example has been Pepsi-Cola.

The lower-left cell (communication adaptation) is also a fairly low-risk venture,

PRODUCTS

COMMUNICATIONS	*No product change*	*Adapt product*	*Develop new product*
No communication change	Straight extension	Product adaptation	Product invention
Adapt communications	Communication adaptation	Dual adaptation	

FIGURE 8.5 Product/communications strategies (Source: Keegan[17])

where only the methods of promotion, e.g. advertising copy, are modified to suit national markets.

The top-middle cell (product adaptation) and the lower-middle cell (dual adaptation) entail more fundamental changes than those just considered. Petrol, for example, may require reformulation for different altitudes; engineering products may be modified to comply, for example, with safety standards in particular countries. The extra costs will have to be set against the prospects of profit; in any case, modifications are likely to be significantly less than developing entirely new products, such as indicated in the far-right cell of the matrix (product invention). On the other hand, this latter strategy, although relatively costly, may well pay off provided that the market is thoroughly investigated and the company has resources suitable for this innovative strategy.

The various product/communications strategies are already associated with degrees of risk, and the development of an appropriate risk policy will be considered in the section on risk management (pp. 333–5).

GLOBAL STRATEGIES

Companies following global strategies scan the world for business opportunities to which they can apply their resources, skills and experience. They seek to develop competitive advantages which are not available to competitors who restrict their activities to the domestic market or, perhaps, limit their export activities to a very limited number of countries.

Some years ago, Levitt wrote in a notable article in the *Harvard Business Review*: 'A powerful force drives the world toward a converging commonality, and that force is technology . . . Almost everyone, everywhere, wants all the things they've heard about, seen or experienced via the new technologies.'[18]

Companies which follow high-share strategies in international business operations are, Leontiades states,[15] usually the giants of their industries: Shell, IBM, ICI, Electrolux and Du Pont. A high degree of standardisation of products generally characterises their operations; production facilities are organised across countries to achieve optimum unit costs; and mass-marketing techniques are widely used.

Porter[19] draws attention to the fact that there is no one type of global strategy – there are many ways of competing globally and these involve decisions about location, co-ordination of activities, etc. The best pattern, it is said, depends on the particular industry, and sectors of an industry may well differ in the degree of globalisation and the strategy adopted. (See the discussion of phases in international business on pp. 321–4 and of multinational and transnational companies on pp. 330–3.)

A global strategy may, as Aaker observes,[20] involve 'one or more motivations in addition to simply wanting to invest in attractive foreign markets'. For example, as noted already, scale economies can occur from product standardisation, and ready access may be had to low-cost labour/raw materials or supplies of components, etc., and also to important national markets, perhaps overcoming trade barriers such as tariffs or quotas.

MULTINATIONAL TRADING

Large overseas trading corporations are not, of course, phenomena exclusive to this century. Chartered companies such as the Hudson Bay Company and the East India Company originally governed as well as exploited commercially the then undeveloped lands of Africa and Asia, and large tracts of North America.

Ulrich Wiechmann has defined a multinational company as one that operated subsidiaries in a number of different nation states, which often have vastly differing political, cultural, economic and legal environments. He identifies the key problem of top management as that of 'tying together the business activities of the far-flung subsidiaries'.[21] This central task had to be undertaken actively so that a multinational marketing policy was developed.

Three factors have been noted as accounting for the rapid increase in multinational trading:

1. It has been the norm rather than otherwise for a firm to manufacture in more than one country.
2. Foreign investment is no longer exclusively or even principally of European origin.
3. The multinational company is acquiring a cosmopolitan appearance.[22]

Multinational companies are very large and have extensive corporate resources; these significant resources are available, often at no or low cost, to their subsidiaries, which, as a result, are able to behave extremely competitively in their respective markets.

Of the world's top 50 industrial groupings, as listed by *The Times*, five out of the top seven positions are occupied by Japanese *sogo shosha* ('general' or 'integrated' trading companies); within these the constituent companies continue their manufacturing activities independently, with their shares separately quoted. The *sogo shosha* acts as the commercial house for its member companies. This listing reflects the dramatic growth of these mammoth Japanese organisations, which have changed completely the ranking of the largest global companies.

Petroleum companies still figure prominently among the multinationals. Their significance in the world economy has grown substantially over the past decade; it has also earned them some harsh criticism. The oil companies' activities are closely linked with the political power exercised by countries which have emerged to challenge the whole structure of western economic and social life. Their operations involve networks of commercial, technological and political commitments which have developed in complexity, particularly since the dramatic emergence of OPEC. Wherever international companies exploit indigeneous basic raw materials, political and cultural reactions become highly sensitive.

Many of the large food and household societies consumer goods firms have developed multinationally 'as the tastes of industrial societies grow more alike and personal incomes are high enough'.[23] Unilever, Corn Products and Nestlé are typical of companies which originated from exploiting a particular process related to specific new materials. From this base they then extended their product ranges and markets until they have become large, transnational organisations.

International business negotiations are affected considerably by the relationships between the multinational firms and governments of the countries in which they operate. Developing countries are benefiting from the immense investment programmes of these giant organisations; there is often an uneasy balance between the demands of commercial policies and the expectations of governments in host countries. Political events may sometimes radically change, if not entirely destroy, the functioning of multinationals in certain countries.

Although multinational corporations may be able to enjoy the benefits of economies of scale, the ability to raise funds at most advantageous rates and to shift funds to secure most favourable rates of return, they are also particularly prone to risk compounded of many variables, several of which will lie outside their control. This may encourage them to pursue a policy of risk minimising, a cautious approach to trading likely to inhibit managerial initiative and corporate innovativeness (see Chapter 7).

TRANSNATIONAL TRADING

This term has been used by Bartlett and Ghoshal[24] to describe trading organisations which aim to achieve a flexible balance between centralisation and decentralisation, avoiding the rigidity of bureaucratic, inflexible policies which, inevitably, frustrate enterprising managers. This more liberalised corporate behaviour is based on careful evaluation of the most effective method of operating in specific market situations. Economic realities, observes Drucker,[25] are forcing multinationals to adopt a transnational system.

Whirlpool, the world's largest white goods manufacturer, announced[26] in July 1993 that it was setting up an Asian headquarters in Singapore; there are already subsidiaries in several Asian countries, including a Hong Kong office planning its

Chinese strategy. The new Singapore office will have product development staff, who will design white goods for the many diverse markets in Asia. Whirlpool plans to evolve in Asia by expanding its manufacturing facilities through a network of wholly owned subsidiaries, alliances and joint ventures.

Many large companies with global interests, such as Unilever, Monsanto, Sony, and Procter and Gamble are developing flexible, integrated networks of virtually independent operations across their overseas markets. Bartlett and Ghoshal have warned,[24] however, against indiscriminate adoption of the transnational structure: it should be used only by companies operating in highly complex business environments, where 'global', 'multinational' and 'local' structures are inappropriate. Transnational structures are best suited, it is said, to industries such as computers, telecommunications, cars and pharmaceuticals and photographic equipment; they are least suitable in metals, textiles, printing and publishing.[27] As observed before, in connection with various management structures and strategies, simplistic application of theoretical concepts is likely to lead to disappointing experiences. (See further discussion on pp. 355–60.)

THIRD WORLD MULTINATIONALS

An arresting article in the *Harvard Business Review* entitled 'Rise of the Third World multinationals'[28] drew attention to this fast-growing phenomenon in world trading. It is time to reconsider the prevailing image of the developing countries; while Third World multinationalism is still in its early days, the potential for growth is impressive. There are, it is alleged, three kinds of economic soil in which Third World multinational operations are taking root:

1. *Resource-rich* developing countries, mostly OPEC.
2. *Labour-rich* industrialising countries of limited natural resources and narrow domestic markets, e.g. Singapore, Hong Kong, China and Korea. These countries 'have evolved from basic trading nations to more complex, production-based economies'. In the 1960s, many satellite plants from developed countries were set up in these distant parts of the world: Hewlett-Packard, Fairchild, Philips, etc. However, by the 1970s the more enterprising developing countries 'became net exporters of labour, products and ideas'.
3. *Market-rich*, rapidly expanding industrialising countries, such as Brazil, Mexico, the Philippines, Argentina, Venezuela and Turkey.

Although significant differences exist between these three broad categories of Third World multinationals, they have a common advantage: 'governments that are manifestly pro-business and committed to enterprise growth'. Two other factors are seen to be effective in helping to accelerate the growth of business: (1) Third World solidarity; and (2) access to technology.

On the other hand, there are certain impediments to expansion. These are perceived to be: (1) low level of demand in general in developed countries which are essential customers of the Third World; (2) rising protectionism; (3) growing public debt; and (4) the widening gap between rich and poor.

The growth of Third World multinational business is also the focus of a research article in *Multinational Info.*[29] The authors state that, by and large, the Third World multinational companies (MNCs) specialise in more mature technologies, are well behind the frontiers of technological advance and are weak in marketing skills. Joint ventures offer them opportunities to extend their production and other skills. The newly industrialised countries (NICs) which have developed a new version of multinational trading will grow to 'challenge traditional MNCs in some areas'.

Of the four newly industrialised economies (NIEs) of East Asia – South Korea, Taiwan, Hong Kong and Singapore – Porter has commented that the first-named has achieved international status in a range of moderately advanced industries, and a 'group of Korean multinationals has emerged with the beginnings of global strategies'.[19] American and European multinationals have invested heavily in these countries: for example, Du Pont committed $240m in 1992 to setting up a pigments plant in Taiwan; Hewlett-Packard has assembly plants in Singapore; and Philips has traditionally been one of the largest western multinationals in East Asia – Singapore is, increasingly, not only a production base but also a design and development centre for other parts of South-East Asia.

It is interesting to note, however, that Du Pont decided to invest $300m in modernising its US polyester plants partly in response to a challenge from Nan Ya, a Taiwan-based company that is building a polyester plant in South Carolina.[30]

MANAGERIAL IMPLICATIONS OF OVERSEAS BUSINESS

RISK POLICIES

The five sequential stages of exporting which have been outlined are necessarily associated with varying degrees of risk.

The development of organisations brings management face to face with new problems as well as extending the area of existing problems. Decision making becomes more complex and is likely to take more time; the effects of these decisions are likely to be felt more widely and their implementation is likely to take longer. Exporting generally involves management in higher risks than their home market trading. A paradoxical situation exists in that one of the fundamental reasons for exporting is to spread corporate risks across diverse markets; and yet, inevitably, a considerable degree of risk is involved in operating in overseas markets. Decision making – a basic activity of management – entails acceptance of risk of some kind.

Taking acceptable levels of risks is what business is about, says Sir John Harvey-Jones. Companies that take no risk disappear, while those that take unacceptable risk clearly also disappear. 'The problem, therefore, is invariably to minimise the risk that can be minimised while taking quite high levels of risk in areas which cannot.'[9]

Aspects of risk in industrial buying behaviour were discussed in Chapter 3, when perception was observed to be effective in evaluating the nature of specific types of risk. The ability to tolerate risk has been seen to be related to a firm's size and liquidity, and to the degree of self-confidence of its management. The extent of 'tolerable' risk is also affected by the nature of a business; some are intrinsically high-risk, others are low-risk enterprises. Research-intensive businesses such as aeronautics and pharmaceuticals or the extractive industries such as oil drilling have a 'natural' acceptance of high risk. Nut and bolt manufacturers, on the other hand, do not operate in these parameters of risk; demand for their products may fluctuate but the rate of innovation is low, plant is unlikely to become rapidly obsolescent and vast sums are not at risk in research and development.

Product and market portfolio planning, discussed in Chapters 5 and 6 and earlier in this chapter, is based on the assessment of market opportunities related to the risks which are inevitably involved in exploiting them. Like any investment decision, financial risk is a key problem in international business ventures, and it is compounded because of the complex environment of world trading. Foreign exchange risk, for example, is an inseparable and major element of risk which has to be expertly assessed and managed, perhaps by stipulating payment in a specific currency, such as US dollars, or by hedging, where a firm enters into a contract to buy or sell, at an agreed rate, an amount of currency to be delivered at a specified future date.

Risk evaluation should be based on systematic market research (see Chapter 9) and also objective assessments of potential profitability. Such evaluations could use the approach given in Figure 8.4, in connection with company/market portfolio screening.

Attractive overseas opportunities should, therefore, be objectively assessed against the risks inherent in specific markets. Douglas and Craig[31] suggest that risks might be assessed on factors such as the number of expropriations, rates of inflation and foreign exchange risk; opportunities could be based on indicators such as GNP per capita, growth of GNP, and population size and density. In addition, costs of market entry and development require expert attention; costs of energy, labour, distribution and media are likely to vary over different territories. Many companies, accustomed to home trading for many years and then faced with developing export markets, should accept that they need to learn almost from scratch about the factors affecting profitable operations overseas; otherwise they may become involved in ventures of distinctly unacceptable risk. Management need to have up-to-date information and exercise judgement based on evaluation of these facts, bearing in mind the complexity of factors such as economic, sociocultural and politicolegal which will most certainly affect business development.

Successful overseas operations will depend considerably on the development of a carefully conceived risk policy. Marketing is a profit-earning function: it is not concerned merely with booking impressive orders, as the Rolls-Royce RB211 débâcle unmistakably showed some years ago.

In formulating marketing strategies – for home or overseas activities – companies should *develop an articulated risk policy*. Three kinds of risk policy have been classified:[2]

1. Risk avoidance (reduction of vulnerability).
2. Risk minimising (drawing up of 'risk profiles' of market opportunities).
3. Risk bearing (planned dispersion of risk through licensing, joint ventures, consortia, etc.).

Risk policies need to be established to control the element of risk involved in marketing goods and services overseas.

Risk management is a policy followed by Richard Branson of the Virgin Group; this means not risking a company's core business and understanding the nature and extent of the 'downside risk'. He advocates designing deals so that flexibility is not sacrificed and there is a way out if performance fails to come up to expectations. 'The development of the Group has been through a linked series of investments, which I gather the business schools call vertical integration, but which I just call common sense.'[32]

Another example of 'common sense' was the advice on managing risk given by the founder of Gore Tex, as quoted by Tom Peters.[33] Anything could be tried, as long as it was above the 'waterline', i.e. it 'would not affect the basic integrity of the organisation'. Peters adds that, while he cannot provide precise guidance on where the waterline should be placed, the advice is worth keeping in mind.

LOGISTICS OF OVERSEAS OPERATIONS

Two vital areas of management are involved in the logistic planning of overseas operations: production and distribution.

Production can be arranged in several ways; the most effective method will depend on several factors, e.g. the type of product, accessibility of raw materials, sources of supply of component parts, type of labour required for successful operation, amount of capital demanded for production facilities, degree of technical and other expert knowledge available at head office, and state of development of the organisation.

Cars produced by the large multinational firms, mostly American owned, are designed for global sales and are made in regional factories, drawing components and supplies from the most economical sources of specialised production, thus ensuring economies of scale.

Increasingly, firms are making foreign market investment through a mixture of strategies which may include exclusively owned production facilities, joint ventures, licensing deals and consortia.

The risks attached to specific strategies should be carefully evaluated; as indicated in Chapter 7, Porter[19] considers that, while 'alliances' are widely adopted and offer various advantages, they also tend to have disadvantages because of their inherently unstable and transitional nature.

PRODUCTION STRATEGIES

The following methods of production may, therefore, be considered suitable under particular conditions, dependent on the nature and resources of the trading organisation and the environment of the market overseas. Various strategies may be effective over different markets, so an exporting company may well have a variety of strategic approaches over world markets (see Figure 8.6):

1. Direct export, e.g. production at a home-based factory from which overseas markets are directly supplied.
2. Licensing arrangements, e.g. Pilkington's float-glass is made under licence by many foreign glass manufacturers.
3. Build a new factory overseas and develop strong national coverage, e.g. Philips' electronic equipment.
4. Joint venture with a foreign company, e.g. Du Pont.
5. Consortia or groups.

Home-based production

The type of product may largely determine its place of production. Large items of capital equipment demanding expert technical knowledge and manufacturing skills may be bought fairly infrequently, and it would tend to be uneconomic to set up highly specialised plant in more than one major area. Where direct exporting is adopted, manufacturers have the advantage of being able to have full control of the product eventually marketed. Specifications, qualities and service remain the prerogative and responsibility of the home-based organisation.

Apart from home-based production of completely finished products some manufacturers, e.g. British car producers, export their products in kit form for assembly abroad. This substantial trade is to accommodate foreign insistence on incorporating locally made parts in cars sold in their countries, and to overcome

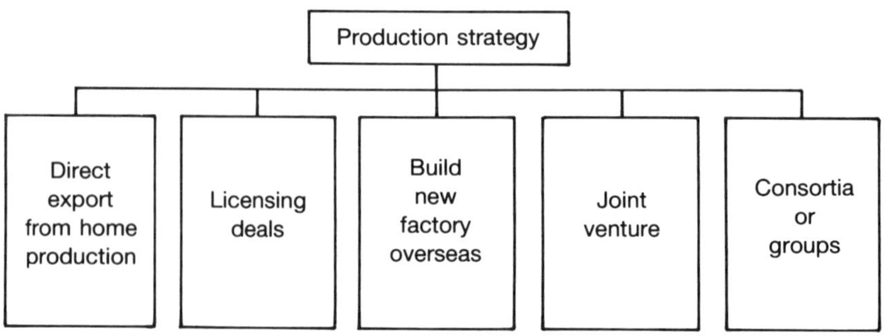

FIGURE 8.6 Production strategies for overseas trading

trade barriers against fully assembled vehicles. Land Rover vehicles, for instance, are supplied in assembly kits to several overseas centres, including Brazil. BMW has assembly arrangements covering some of its models in Thailand, Uruguay, Malaysia, Indonesia and, from 1994, Vietnam.

JCB, the well-known British construction equipment firm, whose basic corporate values have been mentioned in Chapter 5, spent three years and £4m in developing the Robot, a versatile skid-steer loader for this fast-growing sector of the European market. It will face head-on competition from the Melroe Bobcat manufactured by Clark Equipment of the USA, which has about 50 per cent market share, but it aims to capture 10 per cent of this market in about three years. This new product/market strategy is considered by JCB to be a much more effective way of building sales than attempting to achieve a 5 per cent increase in backhoe loaders, where the company is European market leader with a 40 per cent share.[34]

Generally, direct exporting has some distinct strategic advantages: a company's assets are protected from exposure to foreign political risk, and it is unhampered by capital investment in an overseas market, whose environment may become unfavourable.[15]

Licensing

This may be attractive to some manufacturers as an overseas production and marketing strategy; it may be very effective in minimising risks by avoiding the need to make heavy investment in capital and labour. Many licensing arrangements tend to be found among smaller companies which lack resources to exploit markets by themselves. Exceptions such as Pilkingtons occur, and it is possible only to generalise. Pilkingtons, whose float-glass process had 100 relevant UK patents by 1972 and corresponding patents in 50 other countries, is an outstanding example of successful licensing.

Nippon Sheet Glass, Japan's second largest glass-maker, which has a Pilkington float-glass licence and is also involved with Pilkingtons in joint ventures in Mexico, South Korea, Taiwan and Kentucky, in 1989 bought 20 per cent of Libbey-Owens-Ford, the main US subsidiary of Pilkingtons, from the parent company at a cost of $235m.

In their race to 'catch up' with the western economies, 'Japanese companies obtained over 2,500 licences to exploit foreign technologies'.[35] A similar pattern is being followed by the eastern European countries. In the Middle East, imported technologies are significantly simpler, while in the developing countries as a whole there are opportunities for licensing 'often almost forgotten' technologies.

A licence deal is usually a strategy adopted to reduce the time normally taken to plan and develop a product, apart from the risks involved in starting from scratch. In addition, some existing products may already be protected by patents in specific markets, and the only effective method of marketing in these areas would be to acquire a manufacturing or patent licence. It would be advisable to enquire fully into territorial restrictions, degree of exclusive use in specific markets, access to technical services of sponsoring company, precise financial commitment involved, i.e. initial downpayments and subsequent royalties, and options relating to future developments affecting the products now under licence. With a view to long-term development, a company may refuse to license in a market which is regarded as having important potential opportunities.

Patent protection associated with licensing deals offers reliable opportunities to enterprising manufacturers to increase profitability. Philips licenses electronics companies to make compact discs or CD players for a fee of $25,000 with a royalty of three US cents on each disk pressed and a small percentage on the factory price of each player produced. The patent licence contains no know-how, which can cost up to $1 million for vital turnkey technology.[36]

The plastics and petrochemical industries have been developed world-wide through effective international licensing agreements.

Thorn EMI, the UK entertainment and electronics group, signed a licensing agreement in 1992 with a Japanese electronics manufacturer to commercialise its new type of ferro electric liquid crystal displays (LCDs) for flat-screen televisions and portable computers. This innovation has cost 'several millions pounds' over the past few years, and it is hoped that royalties from this and other licensing deals will help to repay the heavy research costs. Even more remarkable is the fact that EMI does not actually make television sets or computer displays, and has no plans to do so in the future.

An important aspect of EMI's central research laboratories, with a staff of 230 including 165 scientists and engineers, is concerned with developing technology which can be profitably exploited through licensing deals. EMI states that it is concentrating on 'taking the technology leaps, rather than grinding through the production engineering work, which is best done by manufacturers'.[37]

A significant Anglo-Indian licensing agreement was signed in 1992 between Bridgeport Machines, a Leicester-based machine tool builder, and Batliboi, an Indian industrial conglomerate, under which Bridgeport horizontal machining centres will be made under licence. Collaboration of this kind was said[38] to be the key to the Indian market, which has been very difficult for western suppliers to enter.

A particularly interesting example of effective licensing arrangements was that of Associated Engineering (later the AE Group), the largest manufacturer of engine components in the world, which negotiated a licensing agreement with the Nippon Piston Ring Company enabling the Japanese to manufacture piston rings and valve seat inserts for car engines by the powdered metal (sintering) process. Brico Engineering, a subsidiary of Associated Engineering, had been successfully manufacturing the components by this method for some years, whereas its international competitors were, at that time, still in the prototype stage of development. The improved technical performance of sintered parts is demonstrated in the ability to withstand increasing wear and tear.

This was the second licensing agreement which AE had negotiated with a Japanese company. Some time previously another group subsidiary, Glacier Metals, entered into a licensing arrangement relating to the production of thin wall bearings in Japan.

Licence deals may involve service industries as well as tangible products. *Franchising* is like licensing, but is generally discussed in connection with the service industries.

Bass, the biggest British brewing group, which ranked fifty-seventh in the 1993 FT European Top 500 companies, achieved global prominence in the hotel industry through a deal giving it the ownership and franchise rights of the Holiday Inns brand name. This involves a franchise system, in the USA, of nearly 1,400 hotels with over a quarter of a million rooms, management of 121 hotels, and ownership of about 50. Through an earlier deal, Bass secured rights to the Holiday Inn name outside the USA, and in 1989 was running more than 150 hotels under this famous brand name.

As with licensing, franchising calls for careful research to identify suitable potential franchisees, while marketing plans should ensure that adequate control is exercised over this fast-growing trading development. Franchising has spread rapidly from the United States; well-known names such as Hertz, Avis and McDonald's typify this form of business activity.

Licensing may have drawbacks when companies seek to change their overseas production/marketing strategies. It also entails risks of its own: for example, royalties may be withheld or not paid at all for various reasons, often dubious; the territorial constraints may be disregarded and enforcement of the original licence terms may not be feasible. Clearly, the granting of licences requires expert legal and commercial advice. Leontiades[15] considers that a major drawback of licensing is the technological foothold it provides to potential future competitors.

Apart from direct licensing, a company may make arrangements, known as *contract manufacturing*, for manufacture of some of its products by an overseas firm, but retain marketing responsibilities itself. Kotler[12] notes that this strategy has been used by Sears Roebuck in opening up department stores in Mexico and Spain, and arranging for approved local manufacturers to produce some of the products they sell. Procter and Gamble has adopted contract manufacturing of soap in order to enter the Italian market; this strategy enabled it to challenge Colgate and Unilever, who were already firmly established with their own production resources. One of the drawbacks of contract manufacturing is control over the quality and efficiency of the production processes undertaken by a local manufacturer.

Building a new factory overseas

To set up manufacturing facilities in an overseas market requires considerable capital expenditure and long-term investment; these risks should be undertaken only after very thorough research into all the factors affecting production, e.g. recruitment and training of a suitable workforce, employment policies in the countries under study, and political and other constraints on development by non-national organisations. Leading industrial groups such as ICI, Philips Electrical and

Michelin have for several years supplied many overseas markets from factories in those countries.

In some instances the national origin of the trading organisation has tended to become of minor interest to customers, and the products made in these satellite factories are accepted as belonging entirely to the countries in which they are produced. As a matter of business policy, large international organisations frequently prefer to emphasise their national links in order to build up strong brand loyalty among their overseas customers.

Some types of product attract custom by virtue of the fact that they originate from specific regions. Scotch whisky, English bone china and Sheffield cutlery are held by many to be superior to indigenious products, and manufacturers need to reflect carefully on the effect on their sales if they were to supply certain markets from internal sources.

It is unlikely that factories will be dispersed over several overseas markets by relatively young companies. This phase in overseas production/marketing strategy tends to be confined to mature organisations with substantial experience in export trading and which possess technical and commercial expertise of unusual quality.

The inviting prospect of new business or the threat of losing a valuable market may be powerful motivations for companies to set up manufacturing plants overseas. In addition, of course, factors such as lower labour costs, transport charges, ease of recruiting suitable types of labour skills and tariff barriers are likely to be influential. The cost of transporting liquid ammonia 'was such as to preclude its export to distant countries, and it was necessary to manufacture it locally if a place in the market was sought'.[1]

Foreign direct investment (FDI) intrinsically involves greater risks than, for instance, direct exporting, because a company's geographical flexibility is significantly reduced, some of its assets are exposed to political risk, and lines of communication between centralised marketing and market-based production will be extended. Also, financial risks are greater because a company may not be able to repatriate profits resulting from operations in a specific country; high rates of inflation, such as in Latin America, may be another disadvantage.

Since the 1980s, there has been a rapid growth in the UK and also across the west side of the Atlantic in Japanese FDI. In Europe, the UK and Germany have received a large share of Japanese manufacturing investments, significantly in greenfield sites. In the UK, the Japanese car manufacturers Honda, Nissan and Toyota have set up car assembly plants and are developing full-scale production facilities. Some degree of controversy has been aroused by the nature and strategies of such activities, although two economists[39] from the Royal Institute of International Affairs believe that Japanese FDI has had a generally positive effect on host economies, augmenting the benefits of trade and stimulating technology transfer and the development of managerial skills.

Nissan has declared that it aims to establish a fully integrated motor vehicle operation in Europe, covering design, manufacturing, sales, service and marketing research functions.

Multinationals like Ford have dispersed their production plants and R&D activities for several years. For example, the Mondeo car, introduced in January 1993 to replace the Sierra in Europe, and the Tempo/Mercury Topaz in North America in 1994, will have its four-cylinder engines made in Bridgend in the UK, Cologne in Germany, and Chihuahua in Mexico for North America. A top-of-the-range aluminium V6 engine will be made at Cleveland, Ohio, for both the US- and European-produced cars; manual transmissions will be made at Halewood, Merseyside, and also at Cologne; an electronically controlled, four-speed automatic gearbox will be made in the USA. Following world-wide scanning, component suppliers, which have been radically reduced to only 200, have been selected to serve both European and North American plants. Ford states: 'A global company can concentrate its resources where they will be used most efficiently.'[40]

In April 1993, Mercedes announced that it intended to build a four-wheel-drive sports utility vehicle in the USA; as mentioned in Chapter 6, the company is reformulating its strategies in light of severe competitive pressures. In opening a production base overseas, Mercedes is following the path taken last year by its rivals BMW. The move will enable it to retaliate against Japanese car-makers who have secured significant sales in the US luxury car market. However, the proposed new vehicle is planned to extend Mercedes' range into premium-priced as distinct from its traditional luxury market segments.

GKN, the British industrial and services group, whose strategy of internationalisation was noted in Chapter 6, is expanding its US production activities, which will be operated by its American subsidiary, GKN Automotive. Since 1976 this company has grown to be the main independent North American producer of constant-velocity joints and driveshaft sets, supplying Ford and Chrysler as well as Japanese 'transplants' operated by Toyota, Honda and Mazda.[41]

Earlier it was seen that other multinationals, like Du Pont and Philips, have extensive manufacturing investments in various parts of the world, particularly in low-cost centres such as East Asia.

Probably the world's most highly organised multinational food company is Nestlé, the Swiss-controlled organisation with 300 factories dispersed over 70 countries. From their headquarters at Vevey, on the shores of Lake Geneva, Nestlé top management continuously monitor their global commercial strategies. The enlargement of the EC and world-wide realignments of currencies, together with the growing pressure on large corporations by their financial institutions and their investors to reveal more information about their trading operations, have all contributed to Nestlé's strategic appraisals.

In furthering a policy of diversification away from milk-based foods, Nestlé has had to abandon another of its corporate faiths – 100 per cent ownership of operating subsidiaries – and it is increasingly becoming involved in partial takeovers; this in turn has led to the need for increased disclosure about its financial affairs. As Nestlé continues its strategy of diversification and part-ownership, it will be interesting to study the repercussions on its traditional methods of capital structure and management. As indicated in Chapter 6, Nestlé instituted a fundamental reorganisation of its business operations in the early 1990s, setting up seven strategic business units (SBUs), each with global strategic responsibility for specific beverages or foods.

Bata, the world's largest shoe manufacturers, owns 40 factories and 6,300 shoe shops in 69 countries, and also tanneries and rubber-processing plants in several foreign locations. Before the Nazi occupation of his homeland, Czechoslovakia, Thomas Bata transferred the family business to Canada. Following overthrow of the Communist regime in 1989, Bata has been actively rebuilding his former industrial activities in eastern Europe.

Porter[19] states that the choice of concentrating or dispersing activities will ultimately be fashioned by the nature of particular activities and may also differ among segments in the same industry. Swedish firms like SKF and Electrolux tend to have highly dispersed and extensive FDI activities, operating through relatively autonomous foreign subsidiaries, which enables them to relate closely to market needs. Consumer packaged products, telecommunications and many services also typically adopt dispersed global strategies.

Joint ventures

International direct investment may also follow the route of joint ventures, referred to in Chapter 7 on innovation strategies, and in Chapter 2, where Volkswagen, for example, was noted to be developing east European links.

Large organisations may agree to combine their substantial resources in specific ventures in the belief that these will result in more effective infiltration and expansion in chosen markets. Joint ventures represent a major option for reducing capital investment and risk, and offer the decided advantages of acquiring intimate local knowledge of markets, government regulations, etc., when one of the partners is a national of the country where business operations are being conducted.

Equity held by a company can range from 10 to 90 per cent, but most companies fall between 25 and 75 per cent. In certain overseas markets, such as Mexico, India and Sri Lanka, joint venture operations are the only permissible entry strategy.[31]

Firms may have complementary resources: for example, specialised technology plus marketing skills may result from effective joint venture operations. This was the reason why 'the 170 US companies with widest international spread chose the joint venture form for nearly one-third of their 3,400 entries into foreign manufacturing between 1900 and 1967'.[42]

The three most important contributions made by overseas joint venture partners, as perceived by the managers of 80 of the 170 US companies surveyed, were: (1) general knowledge about the local environment; (2) local general managers; and (3) marketing personnel. Other advantages were related to the provision of local capital, access to local raw materials and production, and technical research and development skills.

Joint ventures are reported almost every day, and agreements range over many industries and countries, as the following examples indicate. In 1992, Perkins of the UK and Volva Penta of Sweden agreed to collaborate in the development, manufacture and marketing of a new range of small diesels for boats. An earlier Volvo joint deal, in 1989, was with Ssangyong Motor to produce a Volvo model in South Korea and to develop a new car jointly.

Ford agreed, in March 1993, to set up a $90m joint venture with the Yafeng Accessories Factory of Shanghai to produce plastic car parts for China's rapidly expanding automobile industry. In the late 1980s, Caterpillar Tractor, the world's largest construction equipment manufacturers, formed a highly successful joint venture with Mitsubishi Heavy Industries to make hydraulic excavators.

IBM entered into a joint venture with the Brazilian company SID to produce microcomputers; this agreement, in 1991, was particularly notable because it was the first time that the Brazilian Government had authorised joint ventures, and also because it was IBM's first joint venture in the world to make one of its own principal lines. As part of its restructuring programme, IBM is also developing a network of international alliances with partners in Europe and Asia: in 1992, for instance, it agreed to collaborate with Sony to promote Sony's standard for CD-based multimedia technology.

Oxford Instruments' (see Chapter 7) body scanner business has benefited significantly from a joint venture with Siemens of Germany. Eurocopter, a Franco-German helicopter manufacturer, announced in January 1993 a joint venture, valued at FFr550m, with three Russian companies to develop and market a 30-seat 14-tonne civil helicopter.

Du Pont, the mammoth US chemical group, announced in 1974 a major investment programme on worldwide expansion, of which Europe was to receive a substantial share: 'An $80m joint venture with Société des Usines Chimiques Rhône-Poulenc to build and operate a 100,000 tons a year adiponitrile plant in France.' This first European joint venture for Du Pont has encouraged further links of this nature. The Chairman of Du Pont acknowledged the dangers of diversification: 'We have learned that being good in the chemical business does not necessarily mean you are good in the pharmaceuticals business. To put it bluntly, we have laid an egg.'[43]

In January 1991, Du Pont established a joint venture between its pharmaceuticals business and Merck, the biggest US drugs company, to form Du Pont Merck Pharmaceuticals, with the objective of increasing the scale of economies of its existing operations. Another Du Pont joint venture was with Mitsui, the Japanese trading house, to penetrate further the Asian-Pacific market. The new company, Du Pont MBK Alliance, formed in 1992, was projected as matching Du Pont's product development skills with Mitsui's extensive regional branch network.

In an effort to stem fierce Asian competition in the USA and to rebuild its market status, in 1990 Smith Corona, the US typewriter manufacturers, joined with Acer, the largest producer of personal computers in Taiwan, so that it could extend its product range and attract new business.

GKN's international business expansion has been noted already; joint ventures will increasingly feature in its entry strategies in markets such as Mexico and Taiwan.

Whirlpool, whose East Asian activities have been referred to earlier, also plans to extend its eastern European activities: for instance, in 1992 it formed a joint venture with the Tatramat company of Czechoslovakia to make and sell washing machines and market other domestic appliances. In Hungary, a Whirlpool wholly owned subsidiary is another element of its overall drive to exploit markets in these developing regions.

Sun Life Assurance of the UK announced that it was planning, in 1993, to enter into a joint venture with the Life Assurance Company of India (LIC), the state insurance monopoly, to market unit-linked life assurance.

Other joint venture operations have involved, for instance, Michelin, the French tyre group, which has linked with Siam Cement, Thailand's biggest industrial conglomerate, to build a car tyre factory in the new industrial port complex about 100 miles from Bangkok.[44] This new joint venture, Michelin Siam Company – which will be controlled by the French group – forms part of its strategy to gain access to and expand in the Far Eastern market. It enables Michelin, for example, to overcome the problem of heavy duties on cars and tyres imported into Thailand.

In 1988, Michelin established a joint venture with Okamoto Industries to make tyres in Japan. Michelin will have a 51 per cent controlling interest in this new venture, Michelin Okamoto Tire, which will market both Michelin and its own Riken brands in the domestic market and the latter in export markets.

In September 1987, Colgate Palmolive made a 50/50 joint venture with Henkel of West Germany in Cotelle, a French company which makes bleaches, soaps, household cleaners, dishwasher detergents and fabric softeners. The last two product groups were allocated to the Germans, while the remainder were taken over by Colgate. From this venture, Colgate was able to gain access to new packaging technology which can be exploited in other markets.

Colgate considers that its French company now has a 'good strategic balance', but that in the UK and Germany it still lacks critical mass. Alliances of various kinds feature strongly in its strategic planning. In Turkey, for example, it has a manufacturing partnership, and in Scandinavia, Portugal and the Far East, American Home Products lines are marketed alongside Colgate's own.[45]

Alcatel NV, based in the Netherlands and with operating headquarters in Brussels, was set up in January 1987 as a joint venture covering the global telecommunications activities of Compagnie Générale d'Electricité (CGE) and the ITT Corporation. ITT sold its remaining 30 per cent stake to Alcatel in 1992.

In a treaty between the United Kingdom and France ratified on 29 July 1987, Eurotunnel PLC undertook to develop, finance, construct and operate the Channel Tunnel. A dramatic joint venture operation was entered into by ten major companies to construct the Channel Tunnel by May 1993. Eurotunnel appointed an independent organisation, known as the Maître d'Oeuvre, to monitor the design, development and construction of the contract and to advise on technical and other matters. The Maître d'Oeuvre is itself a joint venture between two firms of consulting engineers with two subconsultants. This gigantic and challenging enterprise, with its almost insatiable appetite for capital, opened to goods traffic in mid-1994, and it is planned to extend to passenger traffic in the near future.

A particularly interesting use of the joint venture is evident in developing business in China. Equity joint ventures are the links most favoured by the Chinese, but these are not regarded by foreign companies as attractive because of the low rates of return – even below those that the Japanese are prepared to accept. However, 'the major characteristics of Japanese strategy in China are their willingness to bide their time, take risks and accept low initial profits'.[46] They carefully select the nature and extent of the joint venture they are preparing to invest in: 59 per cent has been in the service sector, contrasting markedly with US figures of 30 per cent service and 70 per cent manufacturing industries.

China is a potentially attractive target market for telecommunications equipment manufacturers who are anxious to open up new demand for modern digital exchanges. Three firms – Alcatel, Siemens of Germany, and NEC of Japan – already have joint ventures to make exchanges in China, while ATT of the USA is planning to follow suit. The Chinese Government stipulates that technology transfer should be part of these deals.[47]

As might be expected, not all joint ventures are successful or survive for long. Chrysler and Renault abandoned, in 1990, a $500m joint venture to produce a four-wheel-drive leisure utility vehicle. Among the reasons was disagreement about vehicle concepts, an unworkable management structure, and problems over the use of the former Renault plant in Spain.

In 1990 Philips and Du Pont agreed to terminate a four-year-old joint venture to make compact discs; Philips acquired the consumer side of the business, and the professional side – which had shown disappointing growth – was sold. Philips also withdrew from another joint venture in 1990 – with AT&T, with whom it had a six-year agreement covering switching equipment for national telephone networks, and in which its residual stake was only 15 per cent.

A further joint venture withdrawal by Philips occurred in 1991, when it sold its remaining 47 per cent stake in a European white goods venture with its US partner, Whirlpool. In 1988 Philips had sold an initial 53 per cent stake to Whirlpool, with both companies having options to sell or buy the balance in the early 1990s. Philips plans to concentrate on its core activities of lighting and electronics, while Whirlpool's corporate theme is globalisation.

In 1987 Michelin entered into a joint venture with Wuon Poong, the third largest South Korean tyre-makers; this prospered until the Korean partner experienced financial problems and was taken over by Woosung, a diversified conglomerate which lacked, however, Michelin's commitment to quality production. As a result, the joint venture was dissolved and Michelin received payment for its 50 per cent stake.

After four years, Mazda and Ford agreed, in 1993, to end negotiations to set up joint venture operations in Europe, because of Ford's concerns about the potential profitability of the proposed collaboration.

Lorenz has suggested that many of the alliances made by international companies are not true joint ventures in the sense that the partners have well-balanced, complementary resources and skills, but are rather what has been termed 'competitive collaboration', where one partner actually intends to disarm the other:

> Many alliances between Japanese and Western companies in the electronics industry over the past decade have been of this type, with the Japanese using the partnership to secure long-term access to Western markets in competition with their partners, while the Western side makes only short-term gains, through the supply of products, components or technologies.[48]

Joint ventures may, in general, benefit both parties, but there is sometimes a clash of policies, which is inclined to be felt particularly by minority interests. This has tended to make companies rather cautious in their attitudes towards joint working arrangements. The problems of joint ventures are reflected in the fact that 'nearly 35 per cent of all the joint ventures that American companies have entered into with European companies in Europe have ended either in divorce, usually with the American company taking over, or in a significant shift of power, to a majority holding in favour of the American partner'.[42] It has also been established that one-third of the 30 joint ventures in the United States entered into by 45 European companies no longer exist; they are now fully American-owned European subsidiaries.

This research[42] has identified the following predictors of the probable viability of joint ventures, in this case between US firms and European partners:

1. The strategies of the enterprises concerned, particularly related to the degree to which their product lines may be diversified or not.
2. The organisational structure of the companies involved, particularly of the company from the investing country.
3. The degree to which the investing partner feels its head office staff are able to predict and, therefore, plan and control, the outcome of the marketing and production activities of the joint venture subsidiary.

The following variables were not regarded as significant by the companies surveyed:

1. The 'cultural distance' between the US firm and the country of its European partners.
2. The industry of either the parent or foreign joint venture subsidiary.
3. The degree to which conflicts or problems in joint ventures were over such matters as slowness of decision-making, the desire to integrate accounting systems, etc.

The terms of a joint venture should be carefully drafted. As with licensing arrangements, it is clearly advisable to have expert legal and commercial consultations before joint venture commitments are undertaken. Division of ownership may create conflicting loyalties among individual executives in member companies constituting the joint venture.

Consortia or groups

A consortium or group of companies involved in multinational business operations may be effective in certain industries. Some large civil engineering contracts (as noted in Chapter 2) are often won by an association of construction companies; these may be entirely British or include foreign companies. Some contracts are of such scale that they demand resources beyond the scope of even the largest contractors, so companies like Costain and Taylor Woodrow team up on multi-million pound projects such as civil engineering contracts in the Middle East. In 1976 Tarmac, a leading British construction group, was reported[49] to have secured, in conjunction with Asman Ahmed Osman & Co., the Arab contractors, a contract for a tunnel under the Suez Canal.

Porter[19] has observed that Korea and other Asian countries have become competitive in relatively simple civil construction projects such as schools and apartments, but their low-labour-cost advantage is being nullified by competitors from developed economies such as Italy, which when involved in international contracts, source their labour locally at cheap rates. The Korean construction industry is, therefore, declining because of its inability to tackle sophisticated projects, the loss of its low-cost base and the general depressed demand for construction work in the Middle East.

Consortia are likely to develop as effective methods of securing valuable export business, particularly where political factors may be significant in the allocation of large-scale contracts. The provision of project management services is developing fast to meet the increasing trend towards consortia working. Clearly, the overall design and co-ordination of the various inputs into a large civil engineering contract call for expert project management involving not only technical problems but diverse cultural reactions. As a US management consultant has observed: 'Ramadan is a month-long Arab fasting period. Although employees are required to come to work [construction] output historically falls to under 25 per cent of US levels during that month.'[50]

DISTRIBUTION STRATEGIES

As with production, companies seeking to expand into international marketing have several alternative, and sometimes complementary, methods of distribution in overseas markets. The general principles of these various methods will be reviewed, but individual arrangements will obviously be made after thorough market knowledge had been obtained.

Earlier in this chapter, it was seen that companies following the path of international trading often go through an evolutionary process, during which they gradually acquire knowledge about specific market opportunities. With growing

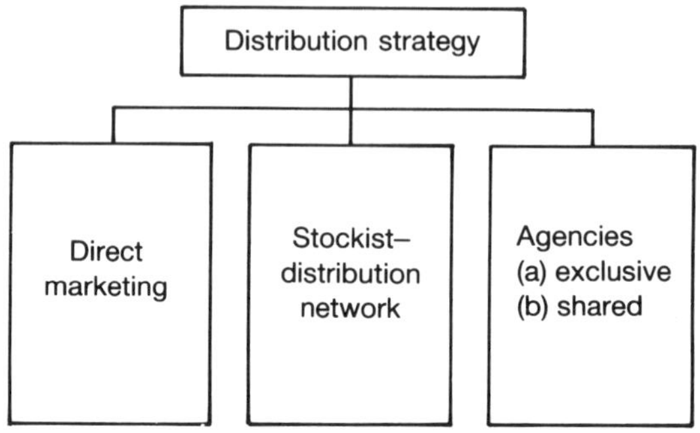

FIGURE 8.7 Distribution strategies for overseas trading

confidence, they then feel able to expand their commitments in terms of both production and distribution. It would be most unusual and certainly unwise for a firm which has no experience in overseas trading to attempt to implement an inflexible, detailed plan of operations. Instead, prospective exporters should – as they would in their domestic markets – carefully consider the reasons why a certain market might be entered and then develop a set of clear objectives (see Chapters 5 and 6).

Among the decisions then to be taken is the important one of how products will reach customers. Unless the channels of distribution are appropriate for the type of product and are efficiently operated, even intrinsically good products can end up as failures. So much of the overall success of an export drive depends on effective methods of distribution, it is worth spending a considerable amount of time and effort in evaluating alternative ways of ensuring that the channel eventually selected will make its full contribution to the marketing mix. Carelessly chosen methods of distribution may seriously damage the reputation of suppliers and also involve them in expensive litigation, if they seek to terminate agreements with distributors.

Methods of distribution may be one or a mix of the following (see Figure 8.7):

1. Direct marketing.
2. Stockist–distributor network.
3. Agencies:
   (a) exclusive;
   (b) shared.

Direct production and direct marketing strategies frequently go hand in hand. They tend to give greater effective control over export operations, but the costs involved should always be assessed carefully. Many medium and smaller companies would be unable to absorb the extra overheads involved in setting up, for example, a specialised staff to deal with export orders and enquiries. The alternative may be to use the services of export merchants who will supply, on a professional basis, expert knowledge and administrative facilities to exporters. With consumer products, direct selling operations may include setting up an exclusive network of retail distributors in large stores situated in major cities and towns. This type of selective marketing has been adopted for many years by some leading manufacturers of furniture, tableware and textiles.

An alternative distribution strategy may involve appointing local distributors who would be expected to hold reasonable stocks of a range of products for quick local delivery.

AEG, the mammoth electrical group of which 80 per cent is now owned by Daimler-Benz, radically reorganised its distribution methods in 1987. In line with the ethos of the European single market, the network of national warehouses was closed down, and deliveries of washing machines and other electrical products were made directly from Germany to customers across Europe. The result was considerable cost savings.

It is important for exporters to appreciate the status and role of distributors. Normally, they would buy the products which are specified in their agreements with the exporting firms, import these goods and pay all import charges and duties, warehouse expenses and selling costs. Commission is usually not included in their remuneration, which is based on the difference between the gross costs of the goods imported and the prices at which these goods are sold to their customers. In certain cases, a distributor may have to sell at schedule prices approved by the principal and commission may then be paid. Distributors are normally concerned with consumer products including durable such as cars; capital investment products and industrial supplies are generally too costly and bulky for distributive stockholding purposes.

A commission agency, as distinct from a distributor, obtains orders for its principal, which ships and invoices direct to the customers involved. For this service the agency receives an agreed rate of commission. In some cases an agency may buy on its own behalf as a distributor, but this option would need to be agreed.

The appointment of agents, exclusive or shared, should not be undertaken casually. Exhaustive enquiries should be made about the commercial standing of prospective agents, and their terms of appointment require very careful drafting regarding details such as remuneration, products to be sold, prices and discount structure, methods of promotion, provision of after-sales service where applicable, and other significant aspects of satisfactory commercial operations. Where agents are also selling products made by other companies, the agreement normally excludes them from selling goods which may reduce the likelihood of success with the products mentioned in the agreement.

The territory covered should be defined clearly, particularly where an extensive national area may be divided between several agents. It is also necessary to obtain agreement about the method of dealing with the commission payable, enquiries and orders which may emanate from the agency's territory without its active intervention, as in the case of visiting foreign buyers, trade buying missions, etc.

The duration of an agency agreement should be mutually agreed; also the method of determination which is acceptable to both parties. Certain events such as bankruptcy, liquidation or merger may be held to give either party a right to determine an agency agreement. It is important, therefore, to stipulate the nature of such events and the system of law to which the contract is to be subject. There may be cases where an agency agreement has to recognise the law of a particular overseas country, so exporters would be advised to examine the legal implications very carefully before committing themselves.

The British Overseas Trade Board and the Department of Trade and Industry offer British firms assistance in identifying suitable agents, and may provide a short list of prospects. However, it is the responsibility of companies to meet these potential agents, preferably in their own territories, and to assess their suitability for the specific marketing tasks to be undertaken.

Manufacturers may prefer to open up their own sales offices in major centres to control the marketing operation. Companies may sometimes find it advantageous to 'buy their way in' to a market by purchasing one or more distributors. However, this strategy needs careful handling as it could build up general trade resistance. Some industrial companies, such as Massey Ferguson and the various motor vehicle manufacturers, have world-wide networks of dealers with exclusive selling rights in defined geographical areas.

As firms develop international marketing skills, it is likely that they will want to have more control over their overseas operations. In accordance with the evolutionary principle noted already, subsidiary companies may be set up in major export markets, replacing partly or entirely agency networks. Further developments, such as overseas manufacture and joint ventures, will be likely to affect distributive arrangements. For example, where production bases are dispersed over several countries and supply, perhaps, specific versions of products to suit national and regional tastes, distribution will be decentralised.

Market behaviour is dynamic, so from time to time it would be advisable to check thoroughly the efficiency of existing methods of distribution, carefully comparing and contrasting the practices of competitors.

Products requiring installation or after-sales servicing, sophisticated equipment or bulky products will probably be handled direct by exporters. In some cases, distributors may be trained to take responsibility for providing installation and post-sales service, but special attention should be given to the contents and direction of such programmes, because the exporting company's reputation will be at stake. If systems of installation and servicing are inefficient, the prospects of expanding overseas will be severely diminished – and rightly so!

BARTER – AN OLD SYSTEM IN A NEW ENVIRONMENT

Barter, one of the oldest kinds of trading known to man, was widespread in the 1920s when war-stricken Europe was trying to revive international trade. In the depression years of the 1930s barter deals were again popular; Hitler's Germany was a notable user.

Nowadays, barter deals are tending to increase because of the market opportunities they offer that otherwise would be closed to traditional methods of financing deals.

Some countries with chronic balance of payments deficits and consequent shortages of foreign exchange impose priorities on the imports allowed into their countries. Would-be importers face these alternatives: manufacturing within the market, abandoning the prospective market, or evolving some suitable scheme of barter with products which are in excess supply. The barter transaction rests on the fact that the prospective importing nation cannot sell the excess goods itself for hard currencies. The bartering firm has to sell or use profitably the goods acquired by barter.

Barter was widely used by Communist countries, but its use has not been limited to them or even to the less developed countries with balance of payments deficits. For example, Ford of Britain has bartered cars for coffee (Colombia), cranes (Norway), toilet seats (Finland), potatoes (Spain) and cotton (Sudan). Companies which are not generally accustomed to the complexities of bartering often rely on specialised intermediaries to sell the goods they receive in exchange for their exports.

Some years ago in order to sell their products in the then USSR, the Pepsi Company made a barter agreement which involved it in becoming the sole agent for Russian vodka in the United States. The British subsidiary of Gillette has extended its sales in eastern Europe by extensive bartering arrangements made through a special London agency.

Occidental Petroleum entered into a 20-year agreement, valued at $20bn, to ship superphosphoric acid to the then USSR in exchange for ammonia urea and potash which, in fact, could be used by Occidental in its operations.[7] In 1992, Pepsi agreed to set up 100 Pizza Hut restaurants in the Ukraine in exchange for ships.[51]

Barter, or countertrading as it is often called, appears to be growing in trade with Latin American countries, particularly Brazil. Some deals can become unusually complex. A London-based agency arranged for the sale of British pharmaceuticals and vehicles to Ecuador in exchange for bananas, which had to be transhipped via a Mediterranean port for eventual sale in Egypt. It was discovered that western shipping lines would not handle the fruit, and a Soviet fleet had to be signed up; all this resulted in a month's intensive work for the agency involved.[52]

In 1984 Nigeria completed a $1bn barter deal with Brazil. This involved 40,000 barrels of oil a day in exchange for the equivalent value in goods.

Because bartering is different from normal trading, and also owing to its complexity, it may well be less profitable than regular export sales, which leads most firms to regard it as a necessary evil or a last resort. In tackling contemporary problems in overseas markets a firm should, however, adopt a more positive approach. If a company has unlimited market opportunities in non-barter transactions, it would be advisable to pursue these without getting involved in barter deals. But if the firm has more productive capacity than market opportunities, and if the future pattern of trading is likely to have to extend to numerous countries with balance of payments deficits and exchange restrictions, top management will need to decide how to optimise their profits.

In reacting positively to barter opportunities, a firm should evaluate the costs and benefits of the operation and set up an effective method of dealing with this new-style trading. Some of the factors to be carefully evaluated are as follows:

1. Possibility of a lower return on some barter deals than with normal trading.
2. Risk in handling unfamiliar products.
3. Probable extension of payment time.
4. Possibility of conflict with firm's hard-currency markets.
5. Long and complex negotiations with buying countries, many of which may lack business expertise.

Barter can also offer benefits, as in the following cases:

1. The use of excess productive capacity to cover variable costs and to make a contribution towards fixed costs and total profits.
2. Maintenance of exports and employment when these are important both to the firm and to the national economy (these factors affected Ford of Britain).
3. Entry into otherwise closed markets.
4. Attracting goodwill of overseas governments, which could lead to extended business later on normal trading terms.
5. Possible development of new and economic sources of supply for raw materials or component parts.

Barter dealing requires a systematic approach. The first step would be to establish a market intelligence system to identify and evaluate opportunities. (Export marketing research is discussed in Chapter 9.) Special negotiating expertise would have to be developed or acquired from professional agencies. Instead of relying entirely on intermediaries, a firm may develop its own barter organisation, authorised by top management to deal in a wide range of exchange commodities. Ford of Britain, for example, appointed an executive as 'special transactions manager'.

Chrysler has been involved in barter deals on numerous occasions. In one instance, a Middle Eastern country had no foreign exchange but had a surplus of hazelnuts. The government wanted to exchange trucks for hazelnuts. Chrysler was able to locate an import house that would buy 100 tons at a discount. The nuts were shipped to the import house; on receipt, the importer paid the money into an account against which several trucks were sold.

Another case involved Colombia, which at that time, was experiencing low coffee prices and a serious shortage of foreign exchange. A farm group had a surplus potato crop and wanted to buy trucks. Chrysler contacted several US brokers, then learned that the existence of a potato disease in Latin America meant that the US Department of Agriculture would not allow the potatoes to be imported. Not daunted, Chrysler turned to Europe and finally located a buyer in France, which, in turn, sold the potatoes to a manufacturer of industrial alcohol.

Kaiser Industries accepted from Colombia a bulk consignment of coffee in exchange for 1,000 jeeps. The coffee 'was traded in Europe for sugar, then the sugar for pig iron, and finally, the pig iron for US dollars'.[7]

Countertrading is not encouraged by western governments, the European Community and the General Agreement on Tariffs and Trade (GATT) because it tends to undermine open, cash-based multilateral trade.[53]

SWITCH TRADING

This is a more complex method of accomplishing results similar to barter trading. Many countries have bilateral trade and payments agreements. Because the bilateral trade seldom balances exactly, these accounts usually contain a supply of non-convertible currencies. The nation with these balances does not need them to buy more goods from the bilateral trading partner, and it cannot use them elsewhere because they are inconvertible. Thus the nation may be quite willing to transfer these credits to a third country, even at a discount, to obtain useful goods.

An international firm may be able to sell its exports to such a third country through a specialist in switch trading. These specialists are located primarily in Austria and Switzerland. The criteria for evaluating switch trading are generally the same as apply to barter transactions.

Switch trading is complicated and usually involves three or more parties, one from each of the countries with bilateral trading agreements with one or more of the other countries involved in a particular transaction. Clearly, this exporting strategy requires extremely careful planning and execution.

LEASING IN INTERNATIONAL MARKETS

Aspects of leasing equipment were considered in Chapter 2, when it was noted that leasing is an important marketing strategy which is developing considerably. Although more prevalent in the United States than elsewhere, leasing is growing rapidly in foreign markets. It is offsetting the immediate impact of escalating prices of capital equipment, which, together with the problems of generating sufficient profits to invest in new machinery, have made this marketing strategy remarkably effective.

Clark Equipment Company in the United States has a subsidiary, Clark Rental Corporation, which leases fork-lift trucks with marked success. The Prudential Insurance Co. of America has invested $7 million as part-owners of a new venture, TAW International Leasing, which plans to operate across the African continent leasing industrial equipment.[7] In the UK, equipment used in civil engineering contracts is often obtained through leasing agreements; this is particularly attractive to relatively small firms.

In Europe, leasing has become popular and is growing at a fast pace. Expensive equipment can be used without capital investment and for a relatively low annual cost. Under leasing contracts, service and maintenance clauses may be further benefits to the lessee. In countries with shortages of skilled mechanics and technicians, this back-up service is a strong inducement to negotiate a lease.

Leasing opens up new opportunities in world markets. It also encourages the use of new types of equipment, the adoption of which may be slow because of the perceived risk in innovation.

When inflation is rife in a particular overseas market, leasing agreements need to be drafted with special care; otherwise, as the contract period extends, heavy losses could be incurred by the supplying company. Another hazard could be in the entire loss of leased equipment because of political upheavals in some areas.

Many leasing arrangements provide users with the option of purchase after a period of time and on agreed terms. This flexible policy allows users to generate funds from the equipment before they are faced with an investment option.

Leasing as an overseas marketing strategy is likely to represent an increasing proportion of the income of industrial firms from export activities. Since it involves industrial exporters in substantial investment in equipment and in the logistics of servicing, very thorough evaluation of market opportunities is strongly advisable before making this necessarily long-term commitment in specific market areas.

SPAN OF INTERNATIONAL MARKETING STRATEGIES

International marketing strategies range, therefore, across a continuum from direct exporting from a home-based factory to sophisticated systems of supranational marketing by which large international undertakings, such as Ford, divide their marketing activities into 'zones', with a distribution network controlled by the 'zone' company. This global approach to marketing, frequently also involving zoned production of specific types or variations of products, is the ultimate expression of highly specialised mass production and distribution strategies.

NEED FOR FLEXIBILITY IN ORGANISATION

The determination of strategies suitable for companies to adopt is the crucial responsibility of senior management. Within industries, companies operate to secure advantage over their competitors in chosen markets. It follows that the dynamics of those industries and the nature of the business environment affect the style of individual companies' operational strategies (see Porter's model, Chapter 5).

The types of organisation – production and marketing – should not be regarded as fixed for all time. As markets and technologies develop, new organisational structures may be advisable to enable companies to take advantage of changing environments in world markets. Further, it is unlikely that a standard strategy would be acceptable and successful in all markets. Whatever approach is used, rigidity should be avoided and remote control should not be allowed to frustrate marketing opportunities.

Companies marketing over many countries face a variety of problems, some of which will be complex, particularly where political, fiscal and social variables appear to be in a state of almost continuous change. Reappraisals of particular marketing strategies may be necessary because of these changes. Marketing management decisions are likely to be taken nearer to the actual area of operations, where the advantages of close working knowledge of the environment will be of enormous help in maintaining a flexible marketing posture.

From a survey of 42 British industrial companies marketing in west European countries, five generic market entry strategies were identified:[54]

1. Technical innovation – the development and offer of specifically designed products backed by high quality and service.
2. Product adaptation – product modified to some degree to minimise customer inconvenience and conform to specifications, again supported by reliable delivery and other services.
3. Availability and security – emphasis on risk reduction and reliability through efficient service back-up.
4. Low price – offering lower initial price than competitors, backed by acceptable quality and delivery.
5. Total adaptation and conformity – offer of a product package matching the competition in all respects.

Each of these strategies must be evaluated for its relevance to the resources of a business and to its ability to exploit specific market opportunities successfully – bearing in mind, of course, the nature of competition.

BASIC BEHAVIOURAL PATTERNS OF INTERNATIONAL COMPANIES

Two basic approaches adopted by companies with international sales organisations were identified in the *Harvard Business Review*[55] a few years ago; they remain useful in studying typical patterns of organisational behaviour. It will be seen from Figure 8.8 that these organisational features may be viewed as extremes of a continuum and are characterised as 'centrist' and 'non-centrist'. These two extreme approaches to the management of international sales have their distinctive attractions and also disadvantages.

The 'centrist' approach allows head office to continue to have strong control over management policies, methods of operation, costs, etc., but it weakens management initiative in overseas areas which are modelled on the home-based organisation. It tends to breed inflexibility and, eventually, inability to respond effectively to the needs of different markets. Hostility between local management and head office staff may also be a danger of this rigid system of management.

The 'non-centrist' management philosophy recognises the need for flexibility in dealing with the diverse problems encountered in international trading. Immediate

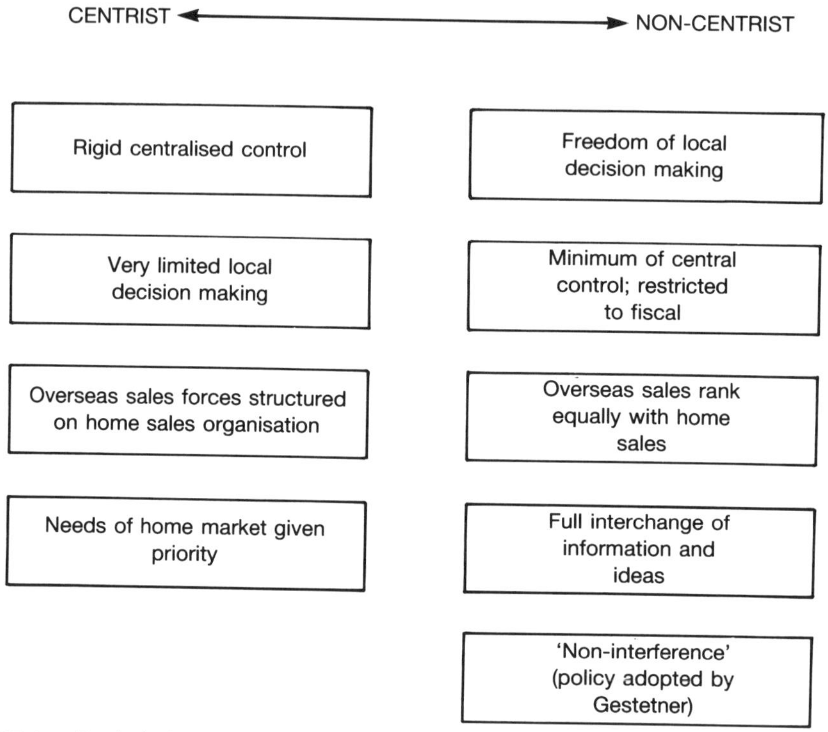

FIGURE 8.8 Basic behaviour patterns of international companies (Source: Gestetner[55])

on-the-spot management decisions can be made to take advantage of changes in local conditions. Of course, there are some drawbacks. Lack of centralised control could lead to wasted managerial time in 'reinventing the wheel' when central policy could have dictated solutions based on other areas. Local management may grow to resent any type of head office intervention, and locally evolved decisions may lack the perspective of a less personally involved evaluation made at head office.

> In general, controlling a non-centrist company is a much more contradictory procedure than controlling a centralist company. Whereas the centrist's whole being is bound up with control mechanisms, the non-centrist constantly walks a tightrope between allowing the local office freedom of action within certain bounds and safeguarding a financial investment from which a fair return must come – between avoiding corporate anarchy and giving the freedom to develop, create and relate to local circumstances.[55]

Companies with a large home market generally tend to adopt a centrist policy, largely because management assume that policies which have been successful domestically will be equally effective in other areas. Where companies have only a limited home market, management tend to be more alert to opportunities in other markets and are more willing to adapt their strategy.

International trading 'is more in the blood of businessmen in the small countries', which often based their trade on the old colonial markets. Until recently, however, 'there has been no tradition of international trading in the United States'[55] because of its self-sufficiency in raw materials and internal development. Although this self-sufficiency no longer exists, the huge US home market generally encourages the development of a centrist policy, whereas European organisations tend to be non-centrist.

Perlmutter's view[56] is that an organisation's policy is determined by the attitudes of its managers. He has suggested three models of international management: *ethnocentric, polycentric* and *geocentric.*

The first two relate to the typical development observable in large companies which have substantial overseas business. In *ethnocentric* organisations, decision making is highly centralised and detailed; day-to-day control is exercised from head office in London, New York or elsewhere. The *polycentric* style evolves from realising that there are sound reasons why many management decisions should be taken in the actual markets; local personnel are acknowledged to be more likely to know at first hand about the effects of certain management decisions than executives in distant headquarters. The needs of local communities may, for example, be given more attention, and hostile reactions avoided. This loosening of direct, central authority will tend to be offset by greater attention to systematic financial reporting. The major automobile groups have various degrees of polycentricity, which is occasionally modified by direct intervention from corporate headquarters.

Geocentrism means having a truly world-wide approach; staff regardless of nationality are moved freely across international subsidiaries. In this idealised concept of transglobal trading, research and development would be organised on an international basis, with the resultant findings made freely available to all subsidiary companies. The corporate creed is 'internationalism' built on the foundations of the free movement of staff and knowledge within constituent companies of a multinational group. Whether this idealistic approach would earn the whole-hearted support of some senior management is open doubt.

This scheme was subsequently modified by introducing *regiocentrism*, which, as distinct from *geocentrism*, acknowledges the importance of regional variations in buying behaviour and develops specific products and strategies to satisfy such demands. Geocentrism, on the other hand, is primarily concerned with standardisation of products, although some local variations may be feasible.[57]

Critics[58] of this typology, while conceding that it is conceptually useful, comment that it is difficult to distinguish accurately between the various types of corporate behaviour pattern. There may be far more than just the four basic typologies and, in any case, structures and systems are dynamic in international firms.

Stopford[59] states that the attitudes and assumptions of senior executives greatly influence styles of management, which vary considerably. However, there are 'certain common denominators' which distinguish Americans from their European colleagues, and these reflect the divergent cultures and philosophies. Foreign nationals may not share the attitudes and assumptions of senior executives in the parent company. Recently, there have been major changes in the domestic and foreign structures of many European firms, and subsidiaries have been adapting the US techniques to suit their particular way of doing business.

Rigid criteria of organisational behaviour may have had more chance of success some years ago when market environments were less competitive; more flexible and innovative structures now seem to be evident.

A middle path may be the most effective international management policy, which, while encouraging local initiative and developing managerial talent, safeguards the overall profitability of the organisation by a degree of intervention necessitating, for example, head office sanction of structural changes to local companies or the appointment of key personnel.

Three types of personality among national managers have been identified:[23] the *strategist*, who is best able to grasp the issues and put forward an integrated planning proposal; the *politician*, who has particular ability to influence people; and the *executive*, who is the highly motivated decision-maker. How far these attributes are necessary or desirable in overseas marketing positions is not clear; but it would seem that managers would generally be more effective if they were to develop a balanced blend of these distinct qualities. In particular, the need to be responsive to market changes – which are social as well as economic – should be a prime managerial objective. A new type of international manager needs to be developed who can move easily across cultural and national boundaries and develop the company's business activities without offending sensitive areas of human behaviour.

The management styles of 16 large-scale UK companies, including British Petroleum, Courtaulds, ICI, BTR, GEC and Hanson, were researched[60] over a three-year period; wide variations were discovered. While some senior managers believed that corporate headquarters should be deeply involved in the detailed strategy of each individual business, others thought that while corporate headquarters made suggestions, managers of businesses in the group should have freedom to get on with their jobs – provided they achieved set targets.

In general, three broad categories of company emerged: (1) strategic planning companies like BP, BOC, Cadbury Schweppes, Lex, STC and United Biscuits; (2) financial control companies like Hanson Trust, BTR, Ferranti, GEC and Tarmac; and (3) strategic control companies such as Courtaulds, ICI, Imperial Group, Plessey and Vickers.

It was found that each of these corporate styles had its advantages and disadvantages. Strategic planners have shown consistent growth of profits in recent years as well as impressive organic development; financial control companies have had even better financial performance than corporate planners, but have tended to grow largely by acquisition; and strategic control companies, though also performing well, have not been successful in their attempts to set their managers a mix of strategic and financial goals.

Porter[19] has asserted that excessive organisational structure is a principal cause of slow corporate response to changed circumstances. He advocates that: (1) management layers should be radically reduced; (2) most 'support' staff – in accounting, personnel, purchasing, etc. – should be 'assigned to the field, reporting to site [line] managers'; and (3) there should be a 'wider span of control at the organisation's front line', i.e. a radical cut in the number of supervisors. He declares that most big firms, and even many small and medium sized ones, have far too many middle managers: no more than five layers of management are said to be necessary, irrespective of the size of businesses.

Companies must aim to be fast moving, flexible and flat or flattish at the top, if they are to prosper in the 1990s. Organisations should replace vertical (hierarchical) structures with horizontal, 'reverse-pyramid' structures which encourage co-operation across functional boundaries. These flatter, networking organisations are seen to be vitally necessary to tackle the powerful challenges of modern markets, both domestic and foreign.

In 1984 the AT&T group, which for generations had exercised a monopoly in national telephone operations in the USA – known popularly as Ma Bell – became the focus of an anti-trust legal battle. The result was that AT&T had to relinquish its local telephone operations, which were split into seven separate businesses – the so-called Baby Bells. From this traumatic experience, AT&T emerged as the largest long-distance telecommunications operator in the USA with ambitions to become a global competitor in the telecommunications, computer and video industries.

AT&T's chairman, Mr Bob Allen, has reorganised the massive organisation into 20 separate product areas, each responsible, as a profit centre, for its own product development, pricing and marketing strategies. Decisions affecting, for example, market entry strategies, have been decentralised, and are shared by executives with close knowledge of customer needs.

The takeover of NCR has added impetus to AT&T's international strategy; this was demonstrated in 1992 by two deals in eastern Europe, one involving the modernisation of the Ukraine's telecommunication system, and the other relating to an investment in Poland's equipment businesses.[61]

When Mr Jack Welch took charge of the General Electric Company of the USA in 1980, he made some far-sweeping changes; management layers were scrapped, as were 350 strategic business units into which the group had been divided since the late 1960s (see Chapter 6). In addition, an extensive programme of corporate disposals and acquisitions was implemented, with the avowed intention of ensuring that all GE's businesses were global in scope and either first or second in their sectors.

Cross-fertilisation between divisions of the company is actively encouraged; top executives are moved freely from one GE business to another. Welch's process of 'work-out' aims 'to inject right down the line the attitudes of a small, fast-moving entrepreneurial business and continuously to improve GE's productivity by seeking much greater involvement by the workforce and customers in the way the business is run'.[62]

Another large US group, Hewlett-Packard (HP), attempted an organisational transmutation in 1990, when it announced that it was moving the international headquarters of its personal computer group to Grenoble in the French Alps. It transpired, however, that while only the group head plus the financial controller were being relocated, the move was significant because it made HP one of the first US multinationals to transfer key HQ posts outside the USA. The move has been described by the group head as a 'return to the decentralised way HP used to be managed . . . The heavy group superstructure above the product, manufacturing and marketing structure, created a lot of confusion.'[63] As a result of the reorganisation, the previous unitary structure of HP was replaced by manageable divisions, each with 'leaner' group management consisting of a group head and four global executives specifically covering finance, marketing, quality and manufacturing.

Corporate styles of management may need to change from time to time as industries develop and new levels of competition emerge. Many other factors are also likely to influence the structure and responsibilities of management in multinational corporations. It would be well to bear in mind Drucker's[4] incisive view that it is the essence of modern organisation to make individual strengths and knowledge productive and to make individual weaknesses irrelevant.

EXECUTIVE OPPORTUNITIES AND CHALLENGES

Although modern travel encourages head office staff to visit overseas markets regularly, and on special missions, constant intervention will not develop in local marketing staff their personal responsibility for the success of the agreed marketing strategy in their area. Overseas staff should be selected not only for their technical knowledge, but also for their commercial abilities. If the right people are appointed, they should be given the opportunity of developing management judgement in their particular sphere of operations. Tactical decisions should largely be left to them, within, of course, the framework of the company's policy.

The examples of corporate restructuring outlined in the previous section have indicated the trend towards 'flatter' organisations in multinational companies. Responsibilities for management decision making are, increasingly, being given to those who are directly involved in specific market sectors.

The plea for executive freedom at local levels of operation was made some twenty years ago in *Long Range Planning*:

> I believe that a sound approach to long range planning requires that the talents of these managers be used in a broader sense to help the chief executive of the total group to identify and select the strategies open to him. It is possible to gain considerable benefit by allowing a measure of subsidiary participation in the shaping of the future of the group. This is a process which, for example, is well developed in the Swiss-based pharmaceutical and chemical company, Sandoz AG of Basle.

> All strategic planning systems should be designed to encourage flair, an acceptance of the challenge of change and to nurture that all too scarce commodity, management talent.[4]

In the very aggressive atmosphere of most markets today, executives responsible for the success of overseas business may, as the result of corporate restructuring, be able to exercise their talents more freely, even if their professional risks are certainly greater. But as Antony Jay in *Management and Machiavelli* acutely observed: 'Men grow to the stature to which they are stretched when they are young, and the ones who are not stretched will fail to grow; some actually will be diminished.' He also notes that the Romans never appointed a man to be governor of a province unless he was fully trained and up to the job; great care was taken in ensuring that he 'knew all about Rome and Roman government and the Roman army before he went out'.[65]

A programme of corporate acculturation is a creative approach which should be adopted by companies planning to appoint staff to overseas posts. This will ensure that those who negotiate face to face with overseas customers are not only well trained in product knowledge, but also fully aware of their companies' corporate values (see Chapter 5).

Negotiating skills, which are complex and involve psychological and cultural factors (as mentioned in Chapter 3), are particularly important in developing international business. Insensitivity to cultural norms, for example, may easily frustrate business deals, as has unfortunately been the experience of some companies. With joint ventures, in particular, the clash of cultures is sometimes the root cause of failure. Douglas Lamont of Northwestern University Kellogg School of Management has noted: 'US–Japanese joint ventures tend to be much more difficult than US–British or US–German joint ventures, because the Japanese and the Americans have two different "mis-histories" about themselves, and these two sets of assumptions about what is correct in business can lead them astray.'[66]

Keegan has stressed that foreigners, especially Americans, should recognise that

> the Japanese have a custom of being silent for what seems to Westerners as an excessively long time. The Westerner should not become excited or feel a compulsion to speak during these periods of silence because it often results in a concession on a disputed point by the Westerner when he simply tries to keep the conversation going.[10]

(Further consideration of the ways in which cultural factors influence overseas business is given in Chapter 9.)

In Chapter 3, Hakansson's interaction model[67] of buying behaviour, which was based on research in five European countries, projected the marketing and purchasing of industrial goods and services as largely dependent on the development of a satisfactory interaction between buyers and sellers. This dynamic process is influenced by the distinct expectations which both parties have; these are likely to be affected by their national cultures and personal attributes, and the goals of their organisations.

Gordon Shenton of the Lyon Graduate School of Business has emphasised that, unlike 'Japanese or American management, or indeed with Italian and Spanish management', European management is not monocultural: 'it is rooted in cultural diversity.' This distinctive character should 'give a considerable edge to the best European management in the global field because it is not a skill which the Japanese or the Americans acquire easily'. Cross-cultural skills include the ability to decode professional and personal behaviour, and also entail the willingness to learn, on a continuing basis, 'how people function and what the rules of the game are for them'.[68]

The acquisition of cross-cultural skills should not be confined to marketing staff: increasingly, as Shenton states, the entire way of running a business can be affected. The successful European company will be staffed by people who, irrespective of their work function, will be part of a learning organisation which is alert to the opportunities offered by dynamic markets.

Exporting calls for a flexible approach to the way in which a business is run; it may be a shattering experience for a manufacturer which has enjoyed, for many years, a strong brand image in its home market, to find, when it ventures abroad, that it is trading not only in a different environment but without the benefit of an acceptable brand name. It may be necessary to pioneer sales abroad – and this calls for an entirely different orientation towards the potential customer. Some marketing executives seem to find difficulty in changing their personal attitudes, which have perhaps been formed from years of brand leadership in the home market. Unless they are willing to face this problem honestly, success is unlikely.

EXPORT PERFORMANCE RESEARCH

Research[3] undertaken under the auspices of the Royal Society of Arts identified specific determinants of export success. The need to concentrate on fewer markets and to develop these in depth was referred to earlier in the discussion of the principle of critical mass (p. 317).

Another crucial factor related to staffing, where it was found that British companies' export staffs are small in relation to the numbers employed on home sales, and are also small in comparison with the number of countries they have to cover. The Japanese appear to be far more realistic, reversing the ratio of home and export sales staff.

BETRO considered that two historic reasons may have led to the low staffing ratios in export selling:

1. The relatively low level of interest in exports (until 1965, British exports of manufactured goods never exceeded 12 per cent of the total).
2. Export was largely on a 'residual' basis after home market needs had been satisfied. A further cause could relate to the general tendency for overseas

countries to be handled *en bloc*, whereas the home market would be subdivided into individual sales territories enabling sales efforts to be directed more effectively.

Although over recent years most companies have given a higher priority to export marketing, sales personnel have increased by only about a quarter, and a disproportionate allocation of selling resources over home and export markets is apparent.

BETRO reported that there are 'many companies where the entire export effort revolves around one man (including a number exporting 50–80 per cent of their production). The physical task of keeping in touch with customers was clearly extremely difficult, and their report emphasised that regular personal contacts with overseas customers were vital to success in competitive markets. BETRO found that 'even the giant companies are short of adequate manpower to deploy in the most profitable markets.'[3]

Another important factor contributing to exporting success related to the selection of agents. British companies placed more stress on sound financial status and adequate technical qualifications than on marketing strength; the Germans and French tended to reverse the order of these criteria.

Only about a third of British companies set targets for their agents, but those which did achieved higher sales. There was also some feeling that French and German companies demanded a higher performance from their agents than did British companies, which often failed to integrate agents into their marketing strategies. Close working arrangements between companies and agents generally proved to be very successful.

BETRO also studied the impact of methods of costing and pricing policy on export performance. It was recommended that the professional expertise of accountants could be improved by a keener awareness of and closer involvement in problems of exporting, particularly price determination. Marketing management should be prepared to discuss fully these problems with their financial colleagues, and should acquire, for example, knowledge of the cost structure of their products. The allocation of these costs over home and export markets should be carefully examined for its effect on total corporate profitability.

In the earlier discussion on concentrating on key markets, the NEDO paper[5] identified significant factors affecting the UK's export performance. In addition to market targeting, other significant factors were isolated. They are, briefly: many companies devote insufficient effort to increasing competitiveness in non-price terms (design, development of new products, after-sales service, etc); many companies treat exporting as a marginal activity; there is a tendency to lose share more rapidly in large, fast-growing markets; products made are not those required by large, faster-growing economies (the United Kingdom is being forced into smaller, slower-growing markets); and there is an inability to supply the goods when needed.

An earlier NEDO report[69] had also emphasised the need for the United

Kingdom to produce higher-added-value products, and to get away from mere price-comparison products. 'Price is one of a number of characteristics of manufactured products upon which market share depends; and firms often competition less easily matched when it extends to non-price factors.' The report stated that the British engineering industry tended to turn out products of lower unit value than Germany or France, and to import relatively higher-added-value products.

Although NEDO was dissolved by the Conservative Government in 1993, these reports, admittedly written some years ago, contain findings and comment which are, unfortunately, echoed by various surveys of more recent date. For instance, in 1992 Gallup[70] undertook a survey for the DTI of purchasing officers in Japanese companies. This revealed, among other findings, that although British goods scored 'quite highly for quality and reliability', they were 'seen as relatively weak on back-up service, delivery on time and technological innovation'. One computer software executive's strong advice was that British companies 'had better understand the internal affairs in Japan and then think of marketing methods suited to it'. More than half of respondents felt that it was important for companies who wished to deal direct with Japanese buyers to conduct business in the Japanese language. It was also necessary for catalogues and other sales literature to be written in Japanese.

FOREIGN LANGUAGE PROFICIENCY

The importance of foreign language proficiency has just been mentioned, but further discussion is merited because it is time that lack of this ability was fully recognised as seriously handicapping British export performance.

A BETRO report[71] on this topic, published in 1979, stated that about 60 per cent of the 200 leading British exporters (Queen's Award Winners) regarded foreign language ability as of 'considerable advantage' to their sales force. Only about 62 per cent of export directors and 57 per cent of sales managers in manufacturing industry had 'some linguistic ability', but as few as 30 per cent of all export personnel and 42 per cent of export salespeople had some foreign language facility.

A survey published in 1992 by Korn/Ferry International, the executive search firm, revealed that fewer than one in five boardroom directors of leading British companies speak a foreign language, and two-thirds have never worked abroad. Some 84 per cent of the 581 directors of the 179 UK listed companies which participated in the survey spoke no foreign language; 14 per cent spoke one foreign language; and 2½ per cent spoke three or more. Even with firms which generated over half of their business overseas in 1991, the same low level of foreign language ability applied.[72]

Cunningham has drawn attention to the 'significance of "cultural distance" which managers know or perceive to exist between their country and various export markets'.[73] While geographical distance is readily recognised, cultural distance

– which refers to language, business protocols, social values etc. – tends to attract lower levels of interest.

As a medium of communication, language is a salient element of negotiation. Language is a key to understanding the cultural beliefs and values which influence people's behaviour in their various roles, including business negotiation. Cultural sensitivities are often subtle and not easily discerned, but export executives who have acquired a reasonable grasp of the language of the country in which they seek business are also likely to have developed valuable insights into the cultural and social environment.

SUMMARY

International marketing demands systematic planning, starting with well-designed marketing research. Companies should identify their export motivations, audit corporate resources, and relate these to identified market opportunities.

Five phases in entry to international marketing have been noted as: opportunism; limited commitment; limited fixed investment; major dependence on overseas business; and no distinction between home and export markets.

Strategic approaches are based on the general principles of marketing and involve, for example, market segmentation, product market life cycle, and product/market portfolio. Four generic market entry strategies were given as: skim, penetration, dumping and explore. Global strategies scan the world for business opportunities.

Multinational corporations operate subsidiaries in a number of different nation states; oil companies figure prominently. International business negotiations are affected considerably by relationships between multinational firms and the governments of the countries concerned. Third World multinationals are growing fast. Transnational trading is concerned with achieving a flexible balance between centralisation and decentralisation.

Risk policies in relation to export opportunities should be drawn up. Three kinds of risk policy have been classified thus: risk avoidance, risk minimising and risk bearing.

Product/communication strategies should be devised according to specific market conditions.

Production and distribution strategies should also be related to market opportunities: options for production include direct exporting, licensing, overseas manufacture, joint ventures, consortia or groups; methods of distribution may involve direct marketing, stockist–distributor networks or agencies (exclusive or shared). Barter, switch-trading and leasing are other options which may be suitable for certain deals.

The style of control of international sales may be across a continuum: centrist–non-centrist. Another approach suggests four models of international management:

ethnocentric, polycentric, regiocentric and geocentric. How far it is possible in practice to distinguish accurately betwee these various models is unclear.

A programme of corporate acculturation may be helpful to some multinational companies to ensure that managers are so knowledgeable about corporate objectives and philosophy that they can operate successfully wherever their sphere of activities takes them.

BETRO research identified exporting success as specifically related to concentration on key markets, the ratio of home and export sales staff, the selection and management of agents, and the need for accountants and marketers to work closely together, particularly in price determination.

NEDO emphasised that exporting success was also linked to 'non-price competitiveness' and the development of higher-added-value products.

Lack of proficiency in foreign languages impedes progress in overseas negotiations.

REFERENCES

1. Wormald, Avison, *International Business*, Pan Books, London, 1973.
2. Political and Economic Planning, 'Sample surveys – Part One', *PEP Report No. 313*, vol. 16, May 1950.
3. Royal Society of Arts, 'Concentration on key markets,' BETRO Report, 1975.
4. Drucker, Peter F., 'Social innovation – management's new dimension', *Long Range Planning*, vol. 20, no. 6, 1987.
5. Cornell, David, 'UK's performance in export markets', National Economic Development Office, Discussion Paper No. 6, January 1980.
6. Attiyeh, Robert S., and Wenner, David L., 'Critical mass: key to export profits', *Business Horizons*, December 1979.
7. Cateora, Philip R., and Hess, John M., *International Marketing*, Richard D. Irwin, Homewood, Ill., 1987.
8. Brooke, Michael Z., *International Management: A review of strategies and operations*, Hutchinson, London, 1986.
9. Harvey-Jones, Sir John, *Making it Happen*, Collins, London, 1988.
10. Keegan, Warren J., *Global Marketing Management*, Prentice Hall, Englewood Cliffs, NJ, 1989.
11. Unilever Company Report, 1972.
12. Kotler, Philip, *Marketing Management: Analysis, planning and control*, Prentice Hall, Englewood Cliffs, NJ, 1980.
13. Porter, Michael E., 'Changing patterns of international competition', *California Management Review*, vol. 28, no. 2, 1986.
14. Marsh, Peter, 'Marketing higher value niches', *Financial Times*, 22 January 1990.
15. Leontiades, James C., *Multinational Corporate Strategy*, Lexington Books, D. C. Heath, Lexington, Mass., 1985.
16. Porter, Michael E., *Competitive Strategy*, Macmillan, New York, 1980.
17. Keegan, Warren J., 'Multinational product planning: strategic alternatives', *Journal of Marketing*, January 1983.
18. Levitt, Theodore, 'The globalization of markets', *Harvard Business Review*, vol. 61, no. 3, 1983.

19. Porter, Michael E., *The Competitive Advantage of Nations*, Macmillan, London, 1990.
20. Aaker, David A., *Strategic Market Management*, John Wiley, New York, 1992.
21. Wiechmann, Ulrich, 'Integrating multinational marketing activities', *Columbia Journal of World Business*, vol. 9, no. 4, 1974.
22. Brooke, Michael Z., and Remmers, H. Lee, *The Strategy of Multinational Enterprise*, Longman, London, 1972.
23. Barto, Roig, 'The role of the national manager in a multinational company', in *The Multinational Company in Europe*, ed. Michael Z. Brooke and H. Lee Rommers, Longman, London, 1972.
24. Bartlett, Christopher A., and Sumantra Ghoshal, *Managing Across Borders*, Hutchinson, London, 1989.
25. Drucker, Peter F., *The Frontiers of Management*, Heinemann, London, 1986.
26. Baxter, Andrew, 'Whirlpool plans Asian expansion based in Singapore', *Financial Times*, 19 February 1993.
27. Lorenz, Christopher, 'The transnational's identity crisis', *Financial Times*, 19 March 1993.
28. Heenan, David A., and Keegan, Warren J., 'Rise of the Third World multinationals', *Harvard Business Review* vol. 57 no. 1, 1979.
29. Lall, Sanjaya, Chen, Edward, Katz, Jorge, Kosacoff, Bernado, and Villela, Annibal, 'The new multinationals: the spread of the Third World enterprises', *Multinational Info.*, no.4, February 1984.
30. Friedman, Alan, 'Shaken to the core', *Financial Times*, 18 August 1992.
31. Douglas, Susan P., and Craig, C. Samuel, *International Marketing Research*, Prentice Hall, Englewood Cliffs, NJ, 1983.
32. Branson, Richard, 'Risk taking', *Journal of General Management* vol. 11, no. 2. 1985.
33. Peters, Tom, *Thriving on Chaos*, Macmillan, London, 1987.
34. Baxter, Andrew, 'JCB moves into European compact loader market', *Financial Times*, 28 January 1993.
35. Ford, David and Ryan, Chris, 'The marketing of technology', *European Journal of Marketing*, vol. 11, no. 6, 1980.
36. Fox, Barry, 'A lynch pin for licensing', *Financial Times*, 10 March 1987.
37. Cookson, Clive, 'A licence to print money', *Financial Times*, 4 June 1992.
38. Baxter, Andrew, 'UK machine-tool maker in Indian licensing deal', *Financial Times*, 21 October 1992.
39. Thomsen, Stephen, and Nicolaides, Phedon, *The Evolution of Japanese Direct Investment in Europe: Death of a transistor salesman*, Harvester Wheatsheaf, Hemel Hempstead, 1991.
40. Done, Kevin, 'A model to smash the mould', *Financial Times*, 6 January 1993.
41. Griffiths, John, 'GKN to expand US production', *Financial Times*, 14 January 1993.
42. Franko, Lawrence G., 'The art of choosing an American joint-venture partner', in *The Multinational Company in Europe*, ed. Michael Z. Brooke and H. Lee Remmers, Longman, London, 1972.
43. Dafter, Ray, 'Du Pont in $1,000m Europe sales plan', *Financial Times*, 29 April 1974.
44. Betts, Paul, 'Michelin in venture to build Thai tyre plant', *Financial Times*, 17 December 1987.
45. Parkes, Christopher, 'Where partnership is no soft soap,' *Financial Times*, 7 December 1987.

46. Campbell, Nigel, 'Japanese business strategy in China,' *Long Range Planning*, vol. 20, no. 5, 1987.
47. 'Alcatel in China: the biggest prize', *The Economist*, 16 January 1993.
48. Lorenz, Christopher, 'Why joint ventures can end in tears', *Financial Times*, 16 January 1989.
49. Harris, Derek, 'Tarmac in £50m deal for Suez Canal', *The Times*, 17 March 1976.
50. Rand, Edward J., 'Learning to do business in the Middle East,' *The Conference Board Record*, vol. 13, no. 2, 1976.
51. Griffiths, Andrew, 'Runaway prices drain Ukraine', *Daily Telegraph*, 7 December 1992.
52. Vines, Steven, 'Trading minus the money', *Observer*, 18 December 1983.
53. Imeson, Michael, 'Swap shop', *Marketing Business*, April 1993.
54. Cunningham, M. T., 'The British approach in Europe', in *Strategies for International Industrial Marketing: The management of customer relations in Europe*, ed. P. W. Turnbull and Jean-Paul Valla, Croom Helm, London, 1986.
55. Gestetner, David, 'Strategy in managing international sales,' *Harvard Business Review*, vol. 52, no. 5, 1974.
56. Perlmutter, Howard, 'The tortuous evolution of the multinational corporation', *Columbia Journal of World Business*, vol. 4, no. 1, 1969.
57. Chakravarthy, B. S., and Perlmutter, Howard V., 'Strategic planning for a global business', *Columbia Journal of World Business*, summer, 1985.
58. Froggatt, J. David, 'Problems of resource allocation in an international corporation', in *The Multinational Company in Europe*, ed. Michael Z. Brooke and H. Lee Remmers, Longman, London, 1972.
59. Stopford, John R, 'Organising the multinational firm: can the Americans learn from the Europeans?' in *The Multinational Company in Europe*, ed. Michael Z. Brooke and H. Lee Remmers, Longman, London, 1972.
60. Skapinker, Michael, 'Do headquarters earn their keep?', *Financial Times*, 2 October 1987.
61. Dickson, Martin, 'A window on the world', *Financial Times*, 26 January 1993.
62. Dickson, Martin, 'Why GE encourages lèse majesté', *Financial Times*, 5 October 1990.
63. Lorenz, Christopher, 'Hewlett-Packard finds a strategy in its pragmatism', *Financial Times*, 8 April 1991.
64. Hussey, D. E., 'Strategic planning for international business', *Long Range Planning*, vol. 5, no. 2, 1972.
65. Jay, Antony, *Management and Machiavelli*, Penguin, Harmondsworth, 1967.
66. Durr, Barbara, 'Plagued by cultural gaps', *Financial Times*, 22 February 1991.
67. Hakansson, Hakan (ed.), *International Marketing and Purchasing of Industrial Goods: An interaction approach*, Wiley, Chichester, 1983.
68. Shenton, Gordon, 'Towards a definition of European management', *EFMD Quarterly*, summer 1992, European Foundation for Management Development, Brussels.
69. Stout, David, *International Price Competitiveness, Non-Price Factors and Export Performance*, National Economic Development Office, London, 1977.
70. Heald, Gordon, 'Finding a place in the rising sun', *Research Plus*, November 1992, Market Research Society, London.
71. BETRO Trust, *Languages and Export Performance*, Royal Society of Arts, London, 1979.
72. Taylor, Paul, 'Boardroom language gap revealed', *Financial Times*, 9 July 1992.

73. Cunningham, Malcolm T., 'The British approach to Europe', in *Strategies for International Industrial Marketing*, ed. Peter W. Turnbull and Jean-Paul Valla, Croom Helm, London, 1987.

REVIEW AND DISCUSSION QUESTIONS

Q1 In what ways do companies which are committed to exporting benefit?

Q2 How would you differentiate between a transnational and a multinational trading organisation?

Q3 Discuss the role which risk plays in export marketing decisions, and give some examples of effective methods of managing this critical factor.

Q4 Direct exporting, licensing, overseas production, joint ventures and consortia represent the main production strategy options open to industrial exporters. Outline briefly the benefits and drawbacks of each strategy.

Q5 Two generic patterns of organisational behaviour are given in Figure 8.8. In the same section of this chapter, Perlmutter's three export management styles were also noted. Select an exporting company which is well known to you, either professionally or through study, and identify the behavioural pattern and style of management.

Q6 In your considered opinion, what is the nature of the relationship between the organisational structure in exporting firms and their success in foreign markets? Support your views with at least two industrial examples.

CHAPTER NINE

International strategy II

RESEARCHING OVERSEAS MARKETS

Manufacturers are likely to know less about overseas markets than their own home markets where they may have been in business for many years. There are likely to be greater areas of uncertainty – 'grey' areas of undetermined risk that require evaluation before viable management decisions can be made.

Marketing research in the home market (see Chapters 4, 5 and 6) was seen to be fulfilling an important role in developing marketing strategies. The need for objective information is even more urgent for overseas marketing programmes. Basically, the type of information needed is similar, although it is often more difficult to obtain reliable data about certain export markets. A multistage research operation seeks to obtain general guides and then to isolate and investigate significant market behaviour and trends. The first step therefore involves a macro-analysis to identify countries or areas which appear to offer potentially attractive opportunities for market development (see Figure 9.1).

This initial screening will be undertaken by means of desk research. It will entail examination of environmental factors, political and legal constraints to entry and operation, and trading blocs; broad estimates will be made of total market size, past trends and probable future developments; figures relating to per capita income, GNP and similar economic data will also be collected.

As a result of this preliminary analysis and appraisal, it should be possible to obtain some general guides as to the areas which are most likely to be of interest to a prospective exporting company. It may be feasible to classify market opportunities by groupings or clusters suitable for commercial operations. These may be ranked according to their prospects of market cultivation. The degree of homogeneity existing within identified clusters or groups of markets needs careful investigation. It would be naive to assume that national boundaries are necessarily the controlling factors in the adoption and popularity of some products. Asa Briggs referred to the Common Market and future trends as follows:

> The younger generation are already far more 'integrated' than any generation before – through fashion, through entertainment, through education, above all through travel. Yet there will remain differences, some of which will not correspond to national boundaries and will rather reflect subcultures and economic subgroups – with religion continuing in some sense to influence the

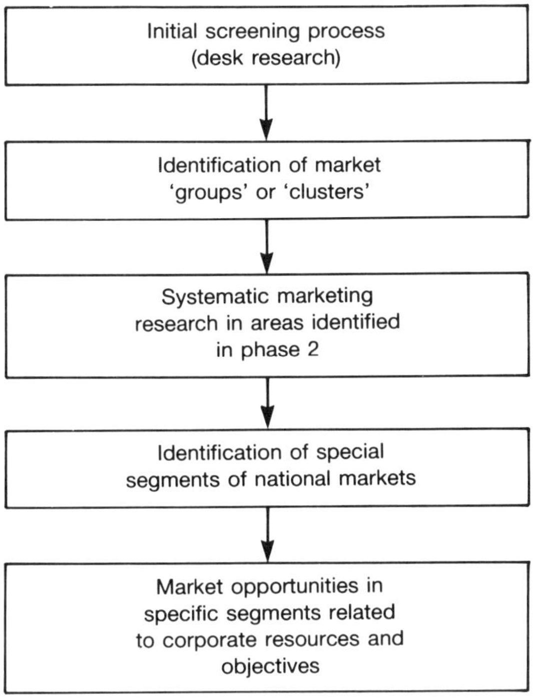

FIGURE 9.1 Multiphase research for international markets

> first and with the latter including not only pockets of poverty but occupational groupings. There is room for more long-term studies of constants and variables which would add a different dimension to market research. Europe may be integrated, but it will never in my view become completely 'homogenised'. It will always have variety, which is the essence of its inheritance, and the variety will be expressed in attitudes as much as in local circumstances.[1]

Paul Hague[2] draws attention to the fact that, while there are about 150 nation states in the world, each offering, in theory, some potential for exporters, only a quarter of these are of 'sufficient size, political disposition or state of economic development to warrant study except in special circumstances'. Listing the importance of commercial regions of the world in terms of percentage of global GNP and percentage of population, he identifies 'key countries': for example, Western Europe (Benelux, France, Germany, the Netherlands, Italy, Spain, Sweden and the UK) accounts for 30 per cent of global GNP and 8 per cent of global population; Anglo America (Canada and the USA) for 24 per cent global GNP, 6 per cent population; South-East Asia (China, Hong Kong, India, Japan, Korea) for 18 per cent global GNP, 55 per cent population; South America (Argentina,

Brazil, Venezuela) for 3 per cent global GNP, 5 per cent population; Caribbean America (Cuba, Mexico) for 2 per cent GNP, 3 per cent population. From this short listing, it will be seen that, while the first two clusters contain only 14 per cent of the world's population, they account for over half of global GNP. If the third cluster – South-East Asia – is included, the percentage of global population rises sharply to around 69 per cent, but, at the same time, the percentage of global GNP runs to over 72 per cent.

After initial screening, the second step consists of intensive research into the areas which the earlier filtering process has indicated to be of potential value. Depth knowledge will be sought of buying behaviour and all those factors affecting purchase of the products under survey. This is where the application of segmentation analysis proves to be of vital interest to marketers.

Data collected during this multistage research are analysed, interpreted and related to the resources and objectives of prospective exporters. Specialised segments of national markets may be revealed that will offer manufacturers profitable outlets for their production capacities.

International marketing strategy will be based on the systematic research programme outlined. How far it may be possible to use a standardised strategy will depend on the type of product, the characteristics of the markets involved and the availability, for instance, of comparable advertising media. Products may have a strong international appeal to certain age groups: for example, the promotion of Pepsi-Cola has deliberately fostered an international image. But it would be dangerous to assume that standardisation of products and methods of presentation across world markets is the answer to successful exporting.

Graham Turner, in his penetrating analysis of British industry, referred to the increasing tendency of big US corporations to take more heed of what their overseas executives say about new products. He instanced IBM which, for several years, was content to design its computers for the US market; if by chance these also suited European needs, the company was delighted. As the result of past mistakes, IBM now pays attention to what Europe says. In Kodak, much the same process has been taking place. In the past, products were developed to suit the needs of the US market; the overseas companies commonly took parts from the US model and it was launched in Europe six months later. 'Although the Instamatic was developed in the US, the European companies were closely consulted and the camera was manufactured simultaneously in Rochester, London and Stuttgart.'[3]

In a review of the changes in the global trading environment and their implications for international marketing strategies, Terpstra notes three major forces which, he declares, will be influential for the rest of this century. These dominant factors are: (1) continuing integration of the world economy; (2) technological change, already evident in the money markets with shattering repercussions; and (3) a more globalised competitive environment as the result of the first two factors.

These influences will be evident in several directions, e.g. product design and development, shortened life cycles and further globalisation of products. 'When

Procter and Gamble developed its new liquid Tide detergent, it drew on special skills and conditions in both its Japanese and European labs as well as work done in corporate headquarters in Cincinnati.'[4] Internationalisation of R&D will be stimulated by the availability of research talent in relatively low-cost centres in various parts of the world such as India, Israel, the Philippines and Taiwan. Vastly improved global communications systems will enable, for example, staff in different countries not only to talk but also to view diagrams and data.

The trend towards more globalised trading is apparent within many large organisations now fighting world competition; several examples of alliances of various kinds involving large multinational groups were given in Chapter 8. In addition, world-class companies such as Kodak are adopting much more adventurous business strategies:

> The pace of technological change is so fast that Kodak recognises that it is unlikely that it will make every breakthrough in-house, no matter how much it spends on R&D. For this reason, Kodak has become a kind of super venture capitalist. Hardly a week passes that a new link has been forged with small, bright companies operating on the frontiers in such fields as information technology, electronics and bio-technology.[5]

Terpstra[4] also sees major developments in marketing research and advertising services to meet the demands of international clients. Scanning of world markets will become of even greater importance. Sir John Harvey-Jones[6] has referred to the fact that there is now more and more information available on a world basis about competitive strengths. A study of the patenting profiles of competitors reveals with great clarity, he says, the direction of their technical thrust.

Levitt, in a vigorous analysis of world trading, avers that consumers are becoming 'homogenised' – more and more alike – despite deep-rooted cultural differences. 'The modern global corporation contrasts powerfully with the ageing multinational corporation. Instead of adapting to superficial and even entrenched differences within and between nations, it will seek sensibly to force suitably standardised products and practices on the entire globe.' He pursues this controversial theme: 'The global company will shape the vectors of technology and globalisation into its great strategic fecundity', heralding a 'new commercial reality' exploiting fully economies of scale throughout the business. Cars, electronic equipment, western fashion clothing, cosmetics, pop music, Coke and digital watches already flood world markets from massive production centres. He sweeps aside arguments for distinct cultural preferences – 'vestiges of the past' – but at the same time, he modifies his argument by saying that he does not advocate 'the systematic disregard of local or national differences. But a company's sensitivity to such differences does not require that it ignore the possibilities of doing things differently or better.'[7] (This contentious subject will be referred to again in the discussion of cultural influences, pp. 377–81).

SCOPE OF INVESTIGATIONS FOR OVERSEAS MARKETING

The theory of market segmentation underlies successful marketing, wherever it is practised. Market segmentation analysis provides data about buyers which enable products to be developed and offered to satisfy identified needs – economic, physical, social or psychological, or a mix of all these variables. In home markets, popular methods of market segmentation (see Chapter 6) are based on age, sex, social class, personality, brand loyalty, attitudes towards products and the extent of use of particular products.

International marketing analyses may also take note of these demographic and other data, but, in addition, special attention would be given to environmental factors such as cultural and social patterns and the state of technological development (see Figure 9.2), which analyses in the home market tend to treat as basic, everyday knowledge. Different patterns of behaviour in some overseas markets may mean that products which are perfectly acceptable in a different environment may not be successful when offered without any attempt at modifying the flavouring, consistency, packaging or, perhaps, the method of distribution to

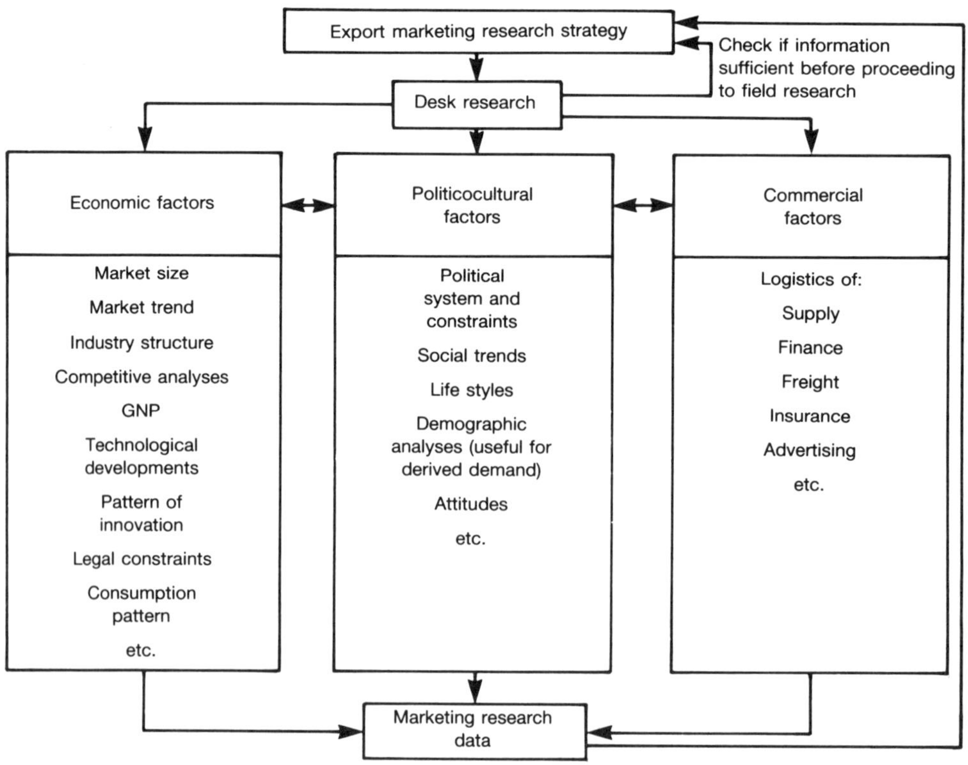

FIGURE 9.2 Scope of export marketing research

suit national preferences and habits. For instance, a US recipe of condensed soup was not successful when introduced to British consumers because they were unaccustomed to diluting the contents of prepared soups and, at first sight, the new product compared unfavourably in price. In addition, the colour and flavour differed strongly from their established buying habits and expectations. The golden rule for success is to take nothing for granted.

Melitta Werke Benz and Sohn is a diversified group spread over 105 countries and 71 companies, of which 33 are in Germany. Its products include household foil, electrical appliances, food and catering supplies. Melitta's guiding principle is: 'as much standardisation as necessary, as much differentiation as possible,'[8] with an increasing trend towards standardisation. Market entry strategy is not standardised, but other marketing activities such as planning and control, and product and branding decisions, are increasingly so. However, sales force and distribution strategies and tactics remain differentiated by market.

The US white goods corporation Whirlpool is busily engaged in developing its European business, and has declared that, while it is 'looking at more commonality, more standardisation, and a more common marketing approach', it is also important to bear in mind that 'globalisation should not become a buzz-word . . . there are still local distinctions'.[9]

SIZE AND EXTENT OF MARKET

As stated earlier, although population size is obviously of interest, it may not necessarily indicate the potential value of a particular export market. Some countries like Switzerland and Sweden, though small, have high purchasing power and are likely to be good customers for luxury products or those having strong design appeal. The ranges of products and services demanded in 'economies of affluence' are likely to be more sophisticated and complex than in less developed countries. Transport, entertainment and educational services will be highly organised and, in turn, will generate demand for supplies. Housing will be of a better standard in developed economies, and there will be greater opportunities for investment and the creation of further wealth.

The social and demographic structure of the population may be significant: for example, population trends, available educational facilities, welfare services, etc., may affect the adoption of certain types of product. A growing community with increased spending power and rising standards of living will be likely to offer valuable opportunities to enterprising marketers.

CATEGORIES OF COUNTRIES

Various definitions have been used to classify the comparative economic development of countries; these are commonly based on gross national product, per capita income, and the relative distribution of the sources of economic activity, from labour-intensive, agriculture-based countries to low-labour-density, capital-intensive mass production and the sophisticated technologies based on electronics, laser applications, etc., to the dominance of the service industries, as discussed in Chapter 2.

It was suggested, for example, some 20 years ago, that countries should be ranked for market opportunities by gross national product per capita. By adopting this method of classification three main segments of world markets emerge:

1. Industrialised countries (ICs).
2. Developing countries (DCs)
3. Less developed countries (LDCs).

It was proposed that multinational corporations should direct their marketing efforts towards the DC segment, 'which covers 19 per cent of the world's population and accounts for 32 per cent of the world's income. Countries in this sector also 'have a high growth rate of income (7.2 per cent) and limited population growth (1.5 per cent)'. Income per capita has, therefore, increased at a net rate of 5.7 per cent per year, compared with a growth rate of income per capita for ICs of under 3.5 per cent during the same period of time. It is claimed that total world income is experiencing a fundamental change in its dispersion; the developing countries are claiming a greater share of global income.[10]

The LDCs also deserve special consideration by marketing strategists; in these countries live about two-thirds of the world's population, but at present they account for less than 15 per cent of the world's income. However, LDCs offer enormously valuable potential markets because many of them are experiencing rapid economic development. 'During the UN's development decade of the 1960s, no fewer than 12 LDCs began to emerge from stagnation.'[10] Growth of per capita income is at least 4.5 per cent in Korea, the Republic of China, Thailand, Iran, Saudi Arabia, Zambia and the Ivory Coast. Per capita GNP of the Latin American countries as a whole increased at an annual rate of 3.5 per cent over 1968–71. Population growth has slowed down in the LDCs; this trend is likely to become more marked as industrialisation increases and control methods are more widely practised.

The highly developed and long established economies of the ICs do not, in general, reflect the same dynamic growth as the less mature economies. 'The average annual real growth of GNP (3.2 per cent) experienced by the US between 1967 and 1972 was the lowest of all OECD countries except Britain.'[7] It is suggested that market growth in the future lies with the DCs and, in the longer term, the LDCs. These growing economies will surge forward in the world league, eventually to attain the comparative affluence which the older economies achieved only after many generations of industrialised activities.

Keegan classifies global markets into five categories based on gross national product per capita, and while admitting that a degree of arbitrariness is present, he proposes that countries in these categories have similar characteristics, which enable them to be considered together for reasons of global strategic planning. These five categories are as follows:

1. *Pre-industrial countries*: these are agriculture based and have limited industrialisation, high birth rates, low literacy, heavy reliance on foreign aid, and political instability; they are concentrated in Africa south of the Sahara. Such countries are viewed as limited markets for all products, and are not likely to offer competitive threats in the foreseeable future.
2. *Less developed countries*: these are at the early stages of industrialisation with a higher GNP per capita than the first category of countries, but are still relative newcomers to industrial activities. Production is largely for local needs, and is limited to standardised products, or mature products for export.
3. *Developing countries*: these are moving rapidly from agricultural economies to industrialisation, but they still retain low labour costs. There are high rates of literacy and advanced education is notable.
4. *Industrialised countries*: sophisticated infrastructure, high levels of education, rising wages, etc., prepare these countries to move to post-industrial or advanced status.
5. *Advanced countries*: also known as post-industrial countries, these differ from category 4 mainly because the sources of innovation are 'derived increasingly from the codification of theoretical knowledge rather than from "random" inventions'. The service sector is also an important constituent of advanced economies, which are essentially knowledge-based, information-technology societies, where intellectual creativity is stimulated and developed through ready access to the full range of sophisticated computer packages, etc.[11]

In the volatile economic, political and social conditions of the last decade of the twentieth century, countries are changing their relative positions, sometimes, as noted in Chapter 8, through joint ventures and other forms of trading alliance. Several of the less developed countries have acquired political and business skills in negotiating advantageously with international companies which seek to set up manufacturing bases or to exploit their mineral wealth.

CULTURAL INFLUENCES

Research in international marketing operations should provide cultural guidelines. Without this fundamental appreciation marketers are ill equipped, despite an imposing portfolio of economic data, to attract overseas business. 'Superficially, modern cities over the world tend to look alike – the modern "superculture" . . . built upon the culture of airports, throughways, skyscrapers and artificial fertilisers, birth control and universities',[12] but beneath the surface, cultural shackles may not be loosened as easily as old buildings are demolished.

Cultural development within markets deserves special attention. It has been argued that there is nothing common about the Common Market, for example. The European Community is not a cultural entity which has identical patterns of thought, attitudes and behaviour throughout. Mark Abrams has in fact described three Europes: the 'new Europe' of big cities like Paris, London, Hamburg, Stockholm and their conurbations, together with areas of high-density population such as Switzerland and north-west Italy; the 'emerging Europe' of his second classification, which is composed of such areas as the semi-urbanised hinterlands of southern France, northern Italy and south-west Germany; and his third grouping, termed 'old Europe', which refers to the 'marginal' farming lands to be found in parts of Spain, Portugal and the north-west of Scotland.

Despite the EC there are vast cultural differences throughout Europe, reflected in traditional behaviour and attitudes and in at least 11 languages – without noting the many local or regional variations which exist, expressing subcultural value systems.

The EC cannot realistically be perceived as an entity. Parts of it are highly industrialised, with large cities and towns which, for generations, have been accustomed to comparatively advanced systems of transport, education and health facilities, etc., while in other regions the pace of life is vastly different and economic activity is still relatively elementary.

Latin America too is a variegated collection of societies, cultures and economies, with no particular region in a country representative of that country, let alone the whole of this very extensive land mass, whose inhabitants total about one-tenth of the world's population.

A market analysis of countries based purely on geographical contiguity is arbitrary and misleading. For example, the Middle East is defined geographically in many ways; it includes very different cultures, economies and market prospects. In popular terms, this vast area is considered to be synonymous with 'Arab'; but Iran, for example, 'one of the most dynamically growing industrial countries in the Middle East, is non-Arab with the Farsi language'.[13] It is also important to realise that Arab countries extend far into Africa and include Sudan and Somalia; and that Israel also comes within this developing region.

> It is necessary to distinguish between the countries still predominantly agricultural and possessing natural resources other than oil (e.g. Egypt), countries not so endowed but also producing oil (Iran), countries producing oil but with few other resources (Abu Dhabi), and finally those countries endowed with poor resources of any description where the pattern of life still has changed very little (South Yemen).[14]

Prospective exporters need to differentiate the trading orientations of countries like Saudi Arabia which encourage private sector activities, from the socialist states, notably Iraq, Algeria and Syria, where major developments are in the public sector and private sector activities are not regarded favourably. For example, almost 90 per cent of Iraq's imports are in the hands of state trading organisations which buy direct from foreign manufactureres; 90 per cent of Algeria's exports and 75 per cent of its imports are handled by the public sector; 70 per cent of Syria's imports are controlled by state agencies.

The McKinsey Quarterly[15] has drawn attention to the classification of OPEC countries made by Hollis Chenery of the World Bank. He identified three groups within the OPEC countries based on their absorptive capacities, resources and likely future policies.

Group 1 consists of five countries that have only 4 per cent of population but 50 per cent of the output of the OPEC group. Of these, Saudi Arabia, Kuwait and Abu Dhabi could continue to produce at today's level for the next 50 years, but they find it hard to absorb all their oil revenues for internal economic development.

Group 2 – Algeria, Iran, Iraq and Venezuela – represents about 25 per cent of total OPEC population and 30 per cent of total output. Their oil reserves are definitely limited and are likely to run out before the year 2000. Their policies are based on maximising present revenues, which are taken up by massive productive investment internally.

Group 3 – Nigeria and Indonesia – accounts for only 10 per cent of total output but 70 per cent of OPEC population. Their oil revenues will be easily absorbed; there will be no problems of accumulating significant financial surpluses.

This comparative analysis again illustrates the dangers of superficial classification; the OPEC classification itself is an insufficient guide to marketing strategies.

International Flavors and Fragrances Inc. produce flavours and fragrances which are marketed internationally to industries for use in their own consumer products such as foods and drinks, soaps and cosmetics. The chairman of IFF has emphasised the need for exporters to developing countries to understand human motivation and behaviour: 'that value systems change with cultures'. The 'small luxury of a flavoured drink or smoke, bright colour, or a perfumed soap or detergent' is attractive even where malnutrition may be evident. 'People in the developing countries are not automatons who will follow motivations to do what is best for them by someone else's value system.' Marketers should not attempt to impose their own sets of values; they must be sensitively aware of the cultural differences which affect consumption habits. Small details can affect sales: in many developing countries the best packaging is the kind that can be reused as a household container. 'Added value, not throwaway, is what people in these countires prefer.'[16]

Purchase decisions are clearly influenced by cultural patterns of behaviour. The status of women in society will be of significant interest, for instance, to manufacturers of domestic labour-saving equipment. A few years ago Singer found that in selling sewing machines in Middle Eastern countries, the husband rather than the wife had to be approached with the argument that the ownership of a sewing machine would make his wife more efficient and useful, and not merely save her personal trouble and time.

In a report to shareholders, the Unilever chairman commented that the price of success in multinational trading is 'endless readiness to adapt':

> We must recognise that the Irish like a different flavour in margarine from the English, that in the UK we can build up our own distribution of frozen food

direct to the shop but in Germany we also use the existing wholesaler distribution, that in Switzerland fabrics may be washed in an automatic washing machine at 85 °C which in Portugal will be washed by hand at 40 °C. The price of ignorance is loss. In Spain, for instance, we did not appreciate the role of the barman in the beer market, or the difference between the requirements of the small farmer in north-west Spain for animal feed and those of the very much bigger farmer in England. For each country, for each segment of the market, we must formulate our package of knowledge afresh.[17]

Small things often account for disturbing variations in sales, particularly in overseas markets. A British company which had exported successfully to New Zealand for several years found that a substantial fall in sales was not attributable to any fundamental dissatisfaction with its products, but was caused by an accidental change in the legend from 'Made in England' to 'British Made' on a newly designed package. 'The New Zealand consumer had thought that he was buying something produced in Hong Kong, since some products made in the Crown Colony are labelled "British Made".'[16]

An article in the *Harvard Business Review* has emphasised the 'widely differing assumptions' which affect the management behaviour of Japanese and Americans; these diverge particularly in their attitude towards individuality and self-sufficiency. In the US culture, a rugged sense of the pioneer spirit which opened up new territories has been tempered by, and often appears to be in conflict with, the other strong cultural factor – the emphasis of the US Constitution on the equality of man.

But in a large American organisation, the consequence of equality can be impersonalisation; in the effort to treat all men equally, all men are often treated the same. As one Japanese executive observed, 'You Americans treat each other like IBM cards – the only difference is where the punch holes are.'

But the Japanese, on the other hand, views himself far less as an individual than he does as a part of his family or work group. His achievements as an independent are not as important to him as his role in furthering the well-being of people associated with him . . . The Japanese are interested in fitting in with the group; in achieving harmonious relationships.[18]

These observations, based on a research study at Stanford University, were reflected in several work situations. The growth of Japanese banks was considered to be due only partly to patronage by the subsidiaries of Japanese companies on the West Coast. It was thought to be attributable more to the 'aggressiveness and *esprit de corps* that the Japanese staff instils in fellow managers and workers'. This sense of corporate responsibility is fostered by the systematic training of staff in a diverse range of duties, which gives the bank unusual flexibility in staffing arrangements and also relieves employees of the tedium of being restricted solely to one function of banking.

In Chapters 3, 5 and 8, the importance of psychological and cultural factors in negotiation, particularly for overseas business, was noted. The fact that the basic psychological processes such as cognition, learning, motivation and attitudes are experienced by everyone could, it is argued, lead to the supposition that customer response over different countries will tend to be similar. But this simplistic approach does not explain, for example, why a Frenchman does not satisfy his hunger with a hamburger as the American tends to, or 'why should use of a status appeal in Africa not be equally as effective as in Europe?'[19]

Sommer Allibert, the French plastic processing group which has developed from a small enterprise employing about 70 people to a multinational group with 8,000 employees, has always had a European approach and, more recently, has adopted a global strategy. Two-thirds of its sales are of consumer products such as plastic floor and wall coverings, garden furniture and bathroom equipment. The rest, accounting for one-third of turnover, are industrial products, particularly plastic coverings for the car industry including carpets, boot linings, dashboards and headrests.

There were, according to Sommer Allibert in 1987, huge differences in, for example, the French and West German markets for its consumer products. 'West Germany puts quality before price, while price tends to come before quality everywhere south of the River Loire.'[20] Colour is another distinguishing characteristic: the British like completely different colours for their wall and floor coverings from the French, which results, of course, in higher production costs.

The highly concentrated nature of European car production has put new pressures on component suppliers, which are expected to invest heavily in R&D and locate themselves near these huge manufacturing plants. 'Europeanisation' is also growing as a result of some car-makers offering firms like Sommer Allibert opportunities to work with them in bases outside France, e.g. Spain, leading to considerable investment in component production.

It is interesting to note that Sommer Allibert has, wherever possible, tried to be identified as a local company in its various locations, and recognises the need to provide special facilities for language training to develop greater mobility between its French and foreign management.

Although basic drives and psychological needs are universal, environmental factors such as cultural or subcultural inhibitions affect the responses made, for example, to advertising campaigns.

COMMERCIAL FACTORS

Feasibility studies need to be undertaken to evaluate the most efficient methods of transporting products to overseas markets (container shipments; roll on–roll off; air freight). Air freight of exports has increased significantly and is particularly important for goods of high value and low bulk.

Speed of delivery may be a very important factor in dynamic markets such as fashion clothing. Costs of stockholding overseas can be reduced; equipment can be installed and productive within a very short time of leaving suppliers' premises. The use of capital is economised because air freight speeds up delivery. Take, for instance:

> a manufacturer shipping parts to a factory abroad for use on his assembly line or as spares for existing equipment. On a straight comparison of air versus surface charges, he would pay say £10,000 more for air freight than for sea, every year. But because the surface journey might take several weeks he has to commit perhaps £130,000 of his capital to stock in transit. If he used air freight he could invest this money, and even at 10 per cent this would earn £13,000 a year. By using air freight he would thus save something of the order of £3,000 on his real distribution costs.[21]

Other benefits include lower costs of packing (an important factor with some sophisticated and fragile products) and, generally, more favourable insurance premiums because of the shorter transit times.

Marketing researchers should, therefore, examine thoroughly the alternative methods of transport available. Evaluation of costs should be comprehensive and bear in mind some of the points just discussed. This 'total distribution cost' approach may suggest a more flexible freight strategy which balances up the needs of individual customers with the full costs of using specific means of transport.

Advertising

Commercial investigations should also cover the availability of media for advertising purposes and the costs involved. Present methods used by competitors should be identified and assessed for effectiveness.

In the United Kingdom, people are avid newspaper readers; they are well served by a variety of national 'dailies', Sunday newspapers and regional morning and evening papers, as well as hundreds of special-interest magazines. This market saturation makes the UK unique in press media: the same intensive pattern should not be assumed in overseas countries.

In the United States, for instance, only the *Wall Street Journal* can claim to have any sort of national distribution as a newspaper; a national press, as known in the UK, does not exist. There are about 1,750 daily newspapers, but they have restricted circulation areas – although some of the larger newspapers, such as the *Washington Post*, have extensive syndication services.

There are also striking differences in Europe: France has no national newspapers on the British model; Belgian papers have small circulations and several would have to be used for a national coverage; in West Germany, only three papers could be classified as national.

Consumer and technical journals are widely available in most western countries. In addition, there is a growing range of 'international' journals such as *The Economist* and *Time. The Readers' Digest* publishes 30 local editions.

Rank Xerox recognises the need to maintain an awareness of the international media: 'Customers particularly in the major account areas no longer sit still within the confines of a national boundary.'[22] Rank estimates that an average 60 per cent of business people in most major markets can be covered by a modest schedule of five publications; national media, like business people, readily cross boundaries.

Commercial television is widespread in overseas markets, though some countries still do not allow it to operate. 'Intermittent' advertising on the British system, with the television company supplying the programme, is more customary in the Commonwealth. Sponsored programmes, after the US pattern, are evident in many Far East markets and in South American countries. Most major countries have some form of sponsored radio programmes.

Cinema advertising has declined in advanced economies, but in some remote markets, where the cinema continues to provide mass entertainment on the scale which was customary in western countries, advertising in this medium may be very effective.

Poster advertising campaigns have been affected by various legislatory constraints in western countries.

The media available in an overseas market should, therefore, be carefully analysed for their effectiveness in selling specific types of product or service. Campaigns may well be linked to special export events sponsored by overseas trade missions, and may involve local agents and distributors.

The trade, technical and professional press is highly organised in advanced economies. Technical publications are of two kinds: (1) vertical, for specific industries or types of occupation; and (2) horizontal, which typically contains articles of a more general nature, appealing to managers over a range of industries. Professional publications cater, as the name suggests, for the information needs of specific professions, such as accountants, architects, lawyers and medical practioners.

The European Business Readership Survey (EBRS) publishes, every two years, information on the reading habits of European executives. This extensive survey, available on-line and organised by RSL–Research Services of Harrow, Middlesex, is augmented by its Pan-European Survey (PES), and in Asia by the Asian Businessman Readership Survey (ABRS).

Leading European business publications include the *Financial Times*, *The Economist*, the German daily *Frankfurter Allgemeine*, the weekly *Der Spiegel*, and the monthlies *International Management* and *Euromoney*.

Multinational media are not just applicable to advertising consumer products, but are widely adopted for promoting business equipment and services. Research should, therefore, evaluate the effect of multinational media across, for example, several national boundaries in Europe. Local advertising campaigns could be effectively complemented by multinational advertising, which is particulary effective in reaching those in higher management.

A highly experienced senior advertising executive believes that a consistent international image is a rather overrated factor. Apart from some luxury products appealing to the 'jet set', identical branding pulls no weight. 'Does it influence the German housewife in her buying choice to know that one brand of margarine is also available in France? Even assuming she knows.'[23] A nice point, but could the same be said of a textile machine made by a well-known company supplying several countries?

Languages

The languages which are in commercial use in particular markets need identification, e.g. in Switzerland, where French, German and Italian are spoken, and Belgium, where French and Flemish are in daily use. In South Africa, when it is necessary to use Afrikaans, the wording of research questions will be affected by the limited vocabulary of that language. It cannot be assumed that the Spanish and Portuguese spoken in the Americas, and the French and Dutch spoken in Mauritius and Indonesia are necessarily the same as is spoken in the mother country. Differences exist even between the precise meanings of some English words as used by Americans and as understood by Englishmen and women. Margaret Mead has commented upon different meanings which the word 'compromise' carries for an Englishman and an American.

> For Britain the word 'compromise' is a good word, and one may speak approvingly of any arrangement which has been termed a compromise, including, very often, one in which the other side has gained more than 50 per cent of the points at issue . . . Where, in Britain, to compromise means to work out a good solution, in America it usually means to work out a bad one, a solution in which all the points of importance (to both sides) are lost.[24]

To quote Sir John Harvey-Jones again: 'Perhaps the biggest area of misunderstanding here is in our approach to our American customers and competitors, where we are lulled into complacency by our similar language.'[6] This is well reflected by the decision to drop the word 'pub' in British Tourist Authority advertising in America, and replace it with 'inn', because the former word had been adopted by downmarket American bars.

The barriers to success imposed by lack of foreign language proficiency among exporters was noted in Chapter 8. This problem has been discussed in relation to Japan, where 'three characteristics of the spoken language – its ambiguity, its numerous homonyms and its grammatical structure – exert a strong influence'.[25] Regarding the first characteristic, it has been emphasised that 'speakers favour indirect statements that feel out another person's moods and attitudes'. The ambiguity of Japanese, it is said, allows speakers the opportunity to avoid uttering 'no'. Instead a Japanese who does not actually want a product might say: 'Your product is not uninteresting to us, it is possible that we could consider it.' A westerner might easily mistake this response for interest; but to the Japanese it is an acceptable, indirect way of indicating lack of interest.

The second characteristic – homonyms (defined as a word of the same spelling or sound as another, but with different meaning, e.g. Pole) – often gives rise to misunderstandings. 'For example, the Japanese word, hai, which means "yes", is also used to mean "I understand" or "keep going".' Also, the existence of homonyms in Japanese may distort meanings when product names are translated from English into Japanese: for example, 'The name Esso was a great handicap to that company in Japan because it means stalled car.'

The third characteristic – grammatical structure – has numerous pitfalls because of the very many differences between English grammar and Japanese grammar. Although these are too complex to discuss in a satisfactory way in this text, an example will illustrate the inherent problems: 'in English, the structure of verbs changes to indicate the difference between present and future tense'.[25] In Japanese, this change does not occur and can cause misunderstandings between buyers and sellers. There is, for instance, no grammatical distinction in Japanese between 'I am providing service' and 'I will provide service', so a customer might 'interpret a promise to provide service at present as a commitment to provide service at some time in the future'.

Unspoken communication is, as already observed in Chapter 8, of particular significance in negotiating with the Japanese, who are accustomed to assessing the body language of those with whom they are negotiating. Japanese negotiations typically 'involve long periods of silence, particularly when there is an impasse'. Europeans should be sensitive to these cultural norms – 'the Japanese feel that men who talk too much are untrustworthy'.[25] Also, the gestures with which the Japanese greet visitors are different from those customary in the West, where handshaking is widely acceptable, whereas in Japan it is customary to bow and shake hands or merely bow – the seller, incidentally, always bows lower than the buyer.

The formality of Japanese customs was creatively encapsulated by Tom Peters: 'The Japanese aesthetic sense is centuries old. Within the Toyota or Sony Walkman lie the modern outcroppings of the tea ceremony.'[26]

Innovative research by Nigel Holden[27] into the relationship between language, proficiency and performance in overseas markets led him to suggest that firms whose attitudes and behaviour are strongly characterised by Anglocentric orientation towards their overseas customers are likely to be relatively inexpert at interpreting, and anticipating, differences in the sociocultural environment of export markets.

Further linguistic differences occur inside national boundaries. Regional variations are largely appreciated in the home market, but they tend to be overlooked in overseas markets. Subcultural influences may be important factors in certain regions, so research should include an examination of these related to particular types of supply.

POLITICAL INFLUENCES

Careful examination should be made of the likely impact on trade of political developments in countries envisaged as export markets. Trade is more likely to develop where political stability is evident. Economic and political factors are often inextricably linked; devaluation, floating rates of exchange, political strategies aimed at maintaining balances of power, etc.: all these are sophisticated influences which make international trading complex, difficult and exciting.

Risk evaluation was recommended in Chapter 8; it is clearly a salient factor in developing international business. To a considerable extent, risk is relative to the resources and experience of specific businesses, and it was suggested earlier that companies could assess their corporate risks on the lines of porfolio screening.

The ability to identify and evaluate the political environment of particular countries is very desirable in researching overseas markets. If, as *The Economist* comments, the EC's single-market programme is supposed to remove barriers to trade between its member countries, why does Ford have factories in Britain, Belgium, Spain and Germany? It might be expected that the company would consolidate where the costs proved the lowest; however, the 'biggest reason may well be risk diversification. If there is a strike in Belgium, or a rise in German wage rates, or 20% devaluation of sterling, then a spread of plants gives Ford the chance to cover a risk or exploit an opportunity.'[28]

As discussed earlier, the growth of mammoth trading organisations – the multinationals – has focused attention, some of it harshly critical, on the influence of big business on the political, social and economic environment in many countries. Multinational companies have injected vast sums in technological development and have contributed to the growth of national economies, not only directly but through the multiplier effect, which has generated substantial wealth. Critics of multinational companies draw attention to the power they are alleged to have to transfer production across national borders; the economic and social consequences of such disinvestment is particularly disliked by the trade unions. But this freedom is largely mythical as any radical business move of this nature would be in collision with government policies and would alienate public opinion.

The multinational firms tend to develop highly sensitive political antennae which are even more vital in expanding economic and political structures such as the European Community. The liberalisation of industry and trade and of opportunities for employment which is embodied in the Treaty of Rome depends on the most effective use of the resources of several countries. Within member countries national business firms, while retaining a considerable degree of managerial autonomy, frequently have the backing of the immense financial and other resources that are available to subsidiaries of multinational corporations.

Political intervention in business affairs will emanate from national governments and increasingly be at a federal level in Europe. Industrial activities will take place within a far more complex environment. Regulations concerning safety, food and drugs, packaging, etc., should be included in any marketing research study.

'INTERMEDIATE TECHNOLOGY'

Marketing research enquiries may not always be concerned with sophisticated market behaviour; customers have different needs. 'Backward invention' may be the answer to supplying certain markets. Intermediate Technology Development

Group (ITDG), a non-profit British enterprise founded by Dr Ernst Schumacher in 1965, publishes a catalogue of unsophisticated equipment specifically to meet the urgent needs of developing countries.

To meet the needs of the many millions of women in the world who still scrub their clothes by hand, an inexpensive manual washing device was developed. A small Yorkshire firm sold a licence to a company in Pakistan, so that it could make animal-drawn reapers and mowers which were urgently needed in this market. Wind pumps have been very successful in extracting vital supplies of water from many hundreds of feet below the surface of some of the driest regions of Africa. Micro-hydro systems, which use water to generate electricity, are now widely used in the remote areas of developing countries and have 'changed lives – not least because they allow people to read at night'.[29]

Combine-harvesters may not be the answer to agricultural problems in some developing countries; hand or animal-hauled machinery may, as was found in Nigeria, be far more useful. Marketing researchers should remember that products and services are useful only if they solve customers' problems; simple technology may not be inappropriate in some markets. It is futile to supply sophisticated harvesting equipment which is too complicated for some communities to use or to be capable of servicing.

In 1985 the Design Centre in London organised a special exhibition 'Design for Need', which focused on the innovative work of the ITDG and showed 20 examples of low-cost equipment, including a 26-foot-long kit boat for village fishermen in South India. Fibreglass was found to be too expensive for this product so the designers chose plywood as the principal material and used a 'stitch and glue' building technique which is popular with boat enthusiasts in Europe. Other examples of ITDG's ingenuity relate to small-scale hydroelectric designs, solar kilns for drying timber and load-carrying tricycles.[30]

The capital-intensive, sophisticated production methods of developed economies cannot be translated to a totally different economic and social environment without fundamental side effects. Development programmes should not be planned in isolation; a comprehensive appreciation of problems should avoid the social and cultural tragedies which have arisen from premature and indiscriminate mechanisation.

Companies may find that valuable markets exist in developing countries for products for which home demand has fallen because of the introduction of radical technological innovations. Product life-cycle theory, discussed in Chapter 6, could be applied to export opportunities. In some cases cheaper, relatively simple machinery which is near the 'decline' stage of the product life cycle may be just right for the needs of certain overseas markets. Where labour is plentiful, low machine productivity may not be disadvantageous: 'horses for courses' seems to be a relevant guide when evaluating potential markets.

RESEARCH METHODS FOR OVERSEAS MARKETING

DESK RESEARCH

As mentioned in Chapter 3 when dealing with general aspects of marketing research, desk research is an essential first step, and it is particularly important in export research. This type of research should be fully exploited before considering field research. It may well provide sufficient information for the particular decision which has to be made. It saves time and money, and is particularly valuable in giving a depth knowledge of markets.

A good grasp of statistical data concerning overseas economies is essential. Clearly, in some areas there is a shortage of reliable and readily available information. However, a great deal of desk research can be done in the United Kingdom, where extremely valuable information is freely available from government and other sources.

*Export Market Information Centre (EMIC)**

The resources of EMIC include the following:

1. *Foreign statistical publications*: produced by both national statistical offices and international organisations covering a range of topics including trade, production, prices, employment, population and other economic data. EMIC can also undertake some searching of selected trade statistics on-line.
2. *Foreign trade directories*: including telephone directories from most countries and specialised directories covering particular sectors of industry. Please note that UK directories are *not* available.
3. *National development plans*: these are issued by many countries and most are available for loan to exporters.
4. *Mail-order catalogues.*
5. *British Overseas Trade Information System (BOTIS).* BOTIS is the DTI's own database for exporters for information on products and markets, overseas contacts, export opportunities and promotional events. This includes:
   (a) the Product Data Store (PDS) – a computerised microfilm database of product and industry information on overseas markets. Sources include unique market reports researched by British Embassy staff. Coverage varies from country to country, but falls within three broad areas of interest: market size, market structure and market share.
   (b) the Overseas Contacts Service (OCS) – details of potential agents, distributors, importers, retailers and others supplied by British Embassies.

* (Formerly the Statistics and Market Intelligence Library), Department of Trade and Industry, 1–19 Victoria Street, London SW1H 0ET. Tel: 071-215 5444/5445, fax: 071-215 4231, tlx: 8811074 DTHQ G.

Also available are EMIC publications (PU), Promotional Events (PE), and Export Intelligence (EI).

Coin and cash card operated photocopying and operator services are available for personal visitors to the Centre, subject to copyright regulations. The Centre is open to the public for reference only from 9.30 a.m. to 5.30 p.m. (last admissions at 5 p.m.), Monday to Friday. Students are admitted by appointment only.

Export Intelligence Service (EIS)

This service sends export-related information to interested subscribing companies, trade associations and other similar organisations. Its main objective is to secure export orders for British companies by bringing individual export opportunities to their attention. It also supplies market information such as changes in tariff rates and import regulations. Each subscriber is profiled to receive only those notices which are personally relevant by commodity, overseas market and type of notice.

Most of the information is provided by the commercial sections of UK diplomatic posts overseas and is also gathered from the World Bank and the European Community. This information is edited, classified and checked by the EIS, part of the Department of Trade and Industry.

Under the Government's Export Initiative, the marketing and distribution of the EIS has been contracted out to Export Opportunities Ltd, part of the Export Network Group, which provides a one-stop, dial-up information and trading service. In addition to first-class post, information can also be sent by telex, fax, and electronic mail via Prestel, One-to-One, Telecom Gold or Mercury 7500.

A modest fee is charged for each notice according to the method of service used. All charges are payable in advance; full details are available from: Export Opportunities Ltd., Export House, 87a Wembley Hill Road, Wembley, Middlesex A9 8BU (081-900 1313).

Other services (see also Chapter 2)

British Business (formerly *Trade and Industry Journal*), published weekly, gives a wealth of information covering overseas markets, tariff charges, import regulations and overseas trade missions. Special market surveys, details of trade fairs and exhibitions, and other vital export data are given. It is a remarkable source of reliable and up-to-date information over world markets.

Hints to Businessmen is published by the Department of Trade and Industry. This series of booklets, covering almost every export market, gives a quick overall view of countries, their trading customs, travel facilities, economic conditions, etc.

Other useful publication include the *Overseas Trade Bulletin*, issued fortnightly by the Confederation of British Industry. The overseas Directorate of the CBI is divided into special geographical areas with a network of overseas representatives and contacts.

Economic surveys and reports published by the United Nations and foreign governments are available through HMSO.

Valuable information on export markets can also be obtained from: European Community Information Office, 8 Storey's Gate, London SWIP 3AT. Tel: 071-222 8122: and EC/EFTA Information Unit, 1 Victoria Street, London SW1.

Export and import statistics, as summarised in the monthly overseas trade statistics of the UK, can be obtained from: Statistical Office (Bill of Entry Section), HM Customs and Excise, 27 Victoria Avenue, Southend-on-Sea, Essex.

Other sources of data

- Central Office of Information (COI), Hercules Road, London SE1 (Publicity unit working jointly with the British Overseas Trade Board to promote British exports).
- Foreign embassies in London.
- British Export Houses Association.
- *CBI Overseas Reports*: issued quarterly by the Confederation of British Industry.
- Frost and Sullivan, 4 Grosvenor Gardens, London SW1W ODH: publishes industrial and consumer reports covering many markets.
- Institute of Export (publishes *Export*).
- Institute of Packaging.
- Institute of Directors.
- Institute of Practitioners in Advertising (IPA).
- London World Trade Centre, St Katherine's Dock, London E1.
- British joint-stock banks, merchant banks and special overseas banks with London offices (e.g. Lloyds Economic Reports: Barclays Overseas Survey).
- OECD: *Foreign Trade Statistics Bulletin* (Series A, *Overall Trade by Countries*, Series B, *Trade by Commodities Analytical Abstracts*, Series C, *Trade by Commodities Market Summaries*); *OECD Economic Outlook*; *Main Economic Indicators*; *National Accounts of OECD Countries 1960–1970*; *OECD Financial Statistics*; *Industrial Product Historical Statistics.*
- IMF: *International Financial Statistics.*
- Economist Intelligence Unit (EIU): publishes a range of periodicals/reports on European markets, and also a valuable series of country reports covering 180 countries.
- Euromonitor: publishes *Market Research Europe* and a range of European directories and other reports.
- *The Economist, The Times, Guardian, Financial Times, Daily Telegraph, Independent*; quality Sunday papers.
- Chambers of Commerce, particularly London Chamber of Commerce, 69 Cannon Street, London EC4N 5AB.
- International Chamber of Commerce, 38 Cours Albert, 75 Paris.
- International Trade Centre, UNCTAD GATT, United Nations, CH-1211 Geneva 10, Switzerland.
- Leading commercial libraries.

- Trade associations.
- Academic institutions.
- *International Directory of Published Market Research*: published by the British Overseas Trade Board (in association with Research and Financial Management Ltd).
- United Nations: *Yearbook of International Trade Statistics*; *World Trade Annual* (5 volumes); *Commodity Trade Statistics*; *World Economic Survey*; *Yearbook of National Accounts Statistics*.
- On-line services such as *Kompass* and *Key Note*: Extensive coverage of data about overseas companies.
- The Patents Office: its on-line patent search service offers valuable, specific services to exporters.
- Export Credits Guarantee Department (ECGD): provides extemely valuable assistance to British exporters through insurance against the major financial risks involved in exporting. Rates vary according to individual markets and the risks involved. Details are obtainable from Export Credits Guarantee Department, Aldermanbury House, Aldermanbury, London EC2, and regional offices.

  In December 1991, the Department of Trade and Industry announced that ECGD's short-term credit insurance business had been sold to the Dutch credit insurance company, NCM, for £70m. The medium- and long-term export credit provisions would continue to be handled by ECGD.

Professional organisations

Professional advice on export marketing research is obtainable from the following organisations:

- Business and Industrial Group (BIG) was formed under the auspices of the Market Research Society to continue some of the well-established activities of the Industrial Market Research Association (IMRA), which ceased operations in 1993.
- Chartered Institute of Marketing: publishes the *Marketing Surveys Index*.
- European Association for Industrial Marketing Research (EVAF): this can supply a comprehensive list of consultants or companies in western Europe who are able to undertake industrial marketing research.
- European Society for Market and Opinion Research (ESOMAR): holds annual congresses and special seminars in European cities; papers are read on many aspects of marketing and opinion research.
- Market Research Society, 15 Northburgh Street, London EC1V 0AH: publishes a yearbook giving details of organisations providing overseas (and other) research services; also publishes *International Directory of Market Research Organizations*, and *Country Notes* offering background information on a wide range of countries in western Europe, the Far East and North America.

- British Standards Institution, Linford Wood, Milton Keynes MK14 6LE: provides British exporters with information about technical requirements related to specific engineering, industrial and technological products. It publishes *INSTEP* (*International News on Standards and Exporting*) quarterly, listing standards, regulations, codes of practice and approval systems. A BSI database is available on-line (see Chapter 4). Technical Help to Exporters (THE) is a service managed by BSI under contract to the DTI. BSI also offers technical translations, mainly focusing on English translations of foreign standards and regulations.

When the examination of basic data suggests that a particular market may be of value to a marketer, the next step is to make a personal visit to that market. Discussions can be held with potential buyers and distributors and with embassy officials.

Because marketing is concerned with fitting products to markets, the proposed product should be carefully examined in relation to the special requirements of individual overseas markets. Some factors will have special significance for certain products: the impact of duties and taxes, trade quotas, food and drug legislation, safety regulations, (e.g. electrical appliance safety standards, American car safety regulations), labelling and packaging regulations, climatic conditions, etc.

PRIMARY RESEARCH

It would be useful to refer again to Chapter 4, particularly the section dealing with the stages of the marketing research process and also that covering the principal techniques involved in systematic research. Wherever marketing research is undertaken, the same disciplines should be applied: professional objectivity and the exercise of relevant skills apply equally to home and overseas market investigations. Admittedly, it is frequently more difficult to obtain reliable, objective data about some export markets, but perseverance is one of the hallmarks of the professional researcher.

Some of the techniques discussed in Chapter 4, such as interviewing, may have to be modified to conform to the social, cultural and commercial norms of specific countries. The first step – as already recommended – is to acquire a thorough grasp of the salient features of the market(s) which it is planned to enter: desk research, discussions with official and industrial experts, visits to trade fairs, etc. all help to build up that essential database. Tom Peters has said that we are all familiar with MIS (management information system), but how about CIS (customer information system)? 'This consists of formal market research and customer surveys . . . and of calling a couple of customers a week.'[26]

Caution should be exercised in consulting statistical data, the quality of which varies greatly according to the sources involved. Researchers need to be vigilant and attempt to assess data for validity and reliability.

Sampling

Sampling tends to be more complicated in overseas marketing research. It may be difficult, even impossible, to obtain reliable sampling frames for random sampling techniques. But sampling for industrial marketing research purposes is helped by acquiring a thorough understanding of market structure and the dynamics of a particular industry. Where industries are highly concentrated, it would, as we have seen, be incorrect to choose a random sample because one or more large organisations might be omitted from the survey. Strict random sampling is therefore unusual, and some type of non-random or quota sampling is generally adopted. Stratification assists in the process of designing such samples; end-use analysis offers a feasible method of building up a sample of industrial firms.

Experienced judgement may have to be the basis for constructing a sample in countries where social and economic data are sparse. The accepted practice of marketing research cannot always be directly transferred to some overseas markets, and data may have to be collected by less formalised methods. Free samples, small gifts and free lottery tickets have been used to attract co-operation in some economically under-developed countries.

Questionnaires

Questionnaires, it has been seen, may be highly structured, unstructured or, generally, semi-structured. They can be administered in various ways: face to face, by mail, by telephone, or through some form of computer linkage. Group discussions are often productive in technical enquiries as well as consumer surveys. These diverse methods have their advantages and also limitations; the selection of a suitable technique should be rigorously approached, carefully considering its relevance and likelihood of success. It is often advisable to use a 'mix of methods', according to the sophistication of specific markets: for example, a series of personal interviews might be very usefully augmented by a number of group discussions.

Drafting an effective questionnaire is a far more difficult task than most people realise; some guidelines are given in a specialist text,[31] and also in Chapter 4. Hague's *Industrial Market Research Handbook*[2] is another source of professional assistance, based on many years of practical experience.

Questionnaires for overseas research need particular care in drafting. Literal translation would obviously be totally wrong; and expert local knowledge in drafting questionnaires is vital to ensure that they will be acceptable and effective. In some cases pictorial methods, e.g. the barometer, have been particularly valuable in assessing consumer response, and some ingenuity should be used in designing suitable diagrams.

Interviewing

Interviewing skills are crucial to the success of any market survey; in overseas markets the task is even more onerous. Industrial, technical and commercial enquiries impose formidable responsibilities on interviewers, who may be working hundreds of miles from base. On their professionalism rests so much of the quality of the research findings. Objectivity – the core of sound research – must be maintained throughout an interview so, as stated in Chapter 4, market research should not be viewed as 'something which the sales force can do when they have the time'. This does not mean, of course, that export sales staff should not report market trends, competitors' activities, etc. However, such information, although valuable, is likely to have some element of subjectivity, which is inimical to professional marketing research practice.

Several UK-based market research firms offer telephone interviewing services from their offices to many parts of the world, especially Europe. These centralised services can quickly and confidentially contact leading buyers and users of specific types of product and service. Multilingual interviewers can readily overcome the customary problems associated with asking questions and recording responses given in the language of a specific country or region.

These initial enquiries may occasionally be sufficient for a company's decision-making needs, but it is usually necessary to organise some face-to-face interviews to ensure that management are provided with adequate information.

RESEARCH FINDINGS

As stated in Chapter 4, the communication of research findings demands professional attention, and some guidelines have already been given in this chapter and elsewhere.[2, 31] As far as overseas research is concerned, reports should indicate clearly the precise territory covered by the survey and the types of industrial and other activities involved. Special care should be taken to offer insight into the political, economic and sociocultural factors which may influence market behaviour.

PRINCIPAL METHODS OF ORGANISING RESEARCH

Research for export marketing can be undertaken in various ways. A brief outline of the principal methods will now be considered:

1. *Using own staff or importing agents*:
   (a) the first objection to this method is probably lack of objectivity; sales staff are usually incapable of giving an unbiased estimate of their products' likelihood of success;
   (b) the second objection is that the agents may have other interests which prevent them from giving an objective assessment of the market;
   (c) research is a specialist's job which requires particular training and experience;
   (d) this method may be the only feasible way of researching in some 'backward' markets.
2. *Using research agencies in overseas markets*:
   (a) selection of these can be difficult and risky;

   (b) where several markets are involved, multiple agencies may have to be used to cover the whole export programme;
   (c) a big advantage is that national research organisations should possess intimate knowledge of their own home market.
3. *Using a UK-based marketing research organisation plus the services of a locally based research firm*:
   (a) this method is used by many UK and US companies, which find it very effective;
   (b) it could be useful where manufacturers have no trained research staff (often the case in smaller companies).
4. *Using the services of a consortium of research agencies*:
   (a) superficially attractive, but member firms may vary considerably in the quality of their services;
   (b) closely related to this method is that of an international research organisation linked with advertising agencies over principal markets; this is generally effective.

It is largely a matter of policy whether marketing research is controlled centrally or otherwise. Large companies may have central direction of research with localised research units reporting back at regular intervals. Some systematic 'monitoring' of market movements is obviously desirable, and continuous research at an agreed level should be practised. Deeper research is undertaken on particular projects as the need arises, and as the monitoring system reveals potential market opportunities.

Leading research agencies offer special facilities for overseas research. For example, Gallup's London office will organise multicountry research 'irrespective of the number of countries involved'. The enquiry is piloted in the United Kingdom and the revised final questionnaire is then sent to the other interested countries for translation and further piloting if this is considered desirable.

Translated questionnaires, together with any comments, are returned to London where retranslation into English takes place. These are then checked against the original questionnaire and if any divergencies have occured, corrections are made. Any changes to take account of local conditions in particular markets are made at this stage, and the translations are then agreed with clients.

The analysis required by clients is compared with the questionnaire to ensure that the correct type of data results.

Coding instructions, to agreed standards, are given by London to affiliate research companies. Punching and tabulation are also controlled by London, and processing is by computer in the United Kingdom.

Whatever system is used, sponsors and researchers must work closely together. As with research in the home market, objectives of the survey must be clearly defined and agreed, particular attention being given to geographical limitations or other market boundaries. Instructions to investigate the European market might refer solely, for example, to the EC countries. Europe is not, as observed earlier, merely one community; parts of it are highly industrialised with large populations and substantial spending power. Other parts are still developing, and in some areas the level of economic activity is low. Research into these markets should be objective and thorough; broad generalisations about national characteristics are not adequate to identify valuable marketing opportunities.

GOVERNMENT ASSISTANCE IN THE UNITED KINGDOM

Initially known as the British Export Board, the British Overseas Trade Board (BOTB) was formed in January 1972 to take over the work of the British National Export Council and also some of the activities formerly carried on by the export services branch of the Department of Trade and Industry. The BOTB is concerned with giving directions for the development of British export activities and establishing priorities in those areas.

The Export Marketing Research Scheme was introduced by the Department of Trade and Industry (at that time the Board of Trade) in July 1969 to assist British industry, on a selective basis, in overseas marketing research; it is now administered for the BOTB by the Association of British Chambers of Commerce, 4 Westwood House, Westwood Business Park, Coventry CV4 8HS. Companies (excluding divisions of companies) with fewer than 200 employees, and UK trade associations, are eligible to apply for help under this scheme.

This service provides British exporters with professional consultancy advice and financial support for undertaking overseas marketing research, subject to the following conditions: the research proposal must be officially approved; it should be carried out by a professionally qualified market researcher; it should be concerned with genuine market research and not just to cover a salesperson's visit; a copy of the resultant report should be submitted to the BOTB; the country under focus should *not* be within the EC; the company should expressly intend to export goods made in the UK, as opposed to those sourced from elsewhere.

Four types of support are offered: (1) up to half of the specific costs associated with in-house marketing research conducted by a qualified member of staff; (2) up to half the cost of professional consultants' fees; (3) up to one-third of the cost of buying published marketing research reports; (4) up to 75 per cent of the costs for trade associations which commission research, or carry it out in-house, on behalf of members.

Certain activities will *not* be officially supported; these include general background research which is not part of a specific project, sales or promotional trips, attendance at trade fairs, research carried out entirely in the UK, and research conducted wholly or mostly on a group visit or trade mission. Advice in specific cases will be given by the scheme's administrators.

The BOTB issues a quarterly newsletter and other publications to encourage the promotion of interest in overseas markets. In co-operation with the Central Office of Information (COI) and other official bodies, the BOTB endeavours to publicise

British goods and services in overseas markets. The BBC External Services and the London-based overseas press correspondents are kept closely informed of British industrial and commercial achievements.

The BOTB also operates an Overseas Visitors' Bureau which organises and funds the visits of overseas buyers to the UK; in addition, the BOTB assists business visitors who come to the UK in the normal course of their own business. Commercial officers of the BOTB study, in depth, particular sectors of industry, so that overseas visitors can be given reliable information about sources of supply. The regional offices of the BOTB ensure that close personal contacts are maintained with local industries.

USING MARKETING TO DEVELOP EFFECTIVE EXPORT STRATEGIES

When the collection and evaluation of marketing research data has been completed, management should have a clear and comprehensive understanding of the opportunities and risks associated with specific export markets. In considering these prospects, various assumptions will be made about, for instance, the likely direction of market trends, competitors' strategies, government intervention, and the availability of corporate resources. Inevitably, a degree of uncertainty surrounds business ventures, particularly those involving new products and/or new markets. A well-tried technique for gauging the probable impact of changes in market variables on critical performance criteria such as cash flow, break-even analysis and overall profitability is *sensitivity analysis*.

A popular approach to sensitivity analysis is to project assumptions about the effects of market variables at three levels: 'optimistic', 'pessimistic' and 'most likely'; the resultant values will indicate the feasibility of alternative strategies.

At this stage, it would be advisable to ensure that satisfactory answers could be given to the salient questions listed in the checklist given below:

1. What are your exporting objectives?
2. Have you formally investigated overseas markets?
3. Which market (or markets) appear to be most promising?
4. What is the basis of your evaluation of market opportunities?
5. Have you researched these particular markets *in depth*?
6. What is the state of competition within these markets? (Prepare comparative data giving *your* anticipated market position.)
7. Are you fully aware of the relevant technical standards, legal requirements, tariffs or other barriers which might affect market entry?
8. Will your product(s) require redesign or modification to conform with the expectations of prospective markets?
9. What strategy do you plan to adopt in order to enter these markets?
10. How do you intend to (a) sell; (b) promote; (c) package; (d) transport; (e) finance your operations?

11. Have you carefully drawn up forecasts of prospective sales in these specific markets?
12. Have you adequate production facilities to meet anticipated demand?
13. How will these anticipated sales contribute to your overall profitability (a) in the short term; (b) in the long term?
14. Have you the right type of staff to market successfully overseas?
15. What market position do you plan to hold in (a) 5 years; (b) 10 years?

Answers to these questions should be based on objective analyses, and should be stated in quantitative terms wherever possible. Qualitative assessments should not be neglected and should be used to qualify and give depth to analyses.

SUMMARY

Like home markets, export markets need to be professionally researched: the need is even greater, since market knowledge is likely to be rather less complete.

Multiphased research, starting with desk research, will assist in screening markets for further detailed investigation. Economic, political, cultural, social and commercial factors should be included in this organised research.

Desk research facilities are extensive and should be fully exploited; there are many sources of export knowledge and assistance.

Groups or clusters of markets may be identified; these might be ranked for their prospective market opportunities. Intensive research into selected areas or market clusters may suggest that specialised segments exist which are worth cultivation.

Prospective exporters have to find sound answers to the following questions: whether, where, when and how? Hence the need for systematic market research. Finding effective commercial answers to these apparently simple questions is by no means easy. Sampling, for instance, tends to be more difficult than in the United Kingdom; the quality of published statistical data is likely to vary considerably; and questionnaires require expert drafting, bearing in mind that literal translation would clearly be quite wrong.

Professional advice is obtainable from the Market Research Society, EVAF, BSI, ITC and other bodies.

REFERENCES

1. Briggs, Asa; 'What kind of Europe – old or new?', *Advertising Quarterly*, no. 33, autumn 1972.
2. Hague, Paul, *The Industrial Market Research Handbook*, Kogan Page, London, 1992.
3. Turner, Graham, *Business in Britain*, Pelican, London, 1971.
4. Terpstra, Vern, 'The evolution of international marketing', *International Marketing Review*, vol. 4, no. 2, 1987.

5. Aris, Stephen, 'How can a big company strip down for action?', *Quarterly Enterprise Digest*, no. 19, May 1989, 3i plc, London.
6. Harvey-Jones, Sir John, *Making it Happen*, Collins, London, 1985.
7. Levitt, Theodore, *The Marketing Imagination*, Free Press, New York, 1983.
8. Olfermann, Joachim, 'Standardisation versus differentiation: a case study of marketing strategies', *European Management Journal*, vol. 5, no. 4, 1987.
9. Tait, Nikki, 'Waiting to see what comes out in the wash', *Financial Times*, 16 September 1991.
10. Weber, John G., 'Worldwide strategies for market segmentation', *Columbia Journal of World Business*, vol. 9, no. 4, 1974.
11. Keegan, Warren J., *Global Marketing Management*, Prentice Hall, Englewood Cliffs, NJ, 1989.
12. Limerick, Lord, 'A Mecca for exporters', *Industrial Management*, March 1975.
13. Upshaw, Douglas N., 'Organising to sell to Middle East Markets', *Conference Board Record*, vol. 13, no. 2, 1976.
14. Walter, Henry G. jun., 'Marketing in developing countries', *Columbia Journal of World Business*, vol. 9, no. 4, 1974.
15. Strange, Henry M., and Wood, Peter M., 'Facts behind the Middle East myths', *The McKinsey Quarterly*, summer 1975.
16. Hillman, Dan, 'Designs on the market', *Guardian*, 20 May 1974.
17. Unilever Company Report, 1972.
18. Johnson, Richard Tanner, and Duchi, Wilbain G., 'Made in America (under Japanese management)', *Harvard Business Review*, vol. 52, no. 5, 1974.
19. Sinclair, Craig, 'Technological change = social change', *Industrial Marketing Management*, vol. 2, 1973.
20. Betts, Paul, 'Why Sommer Allibert thinks of variations on a theme', *Financial Times*, 21 October 1987.
21. Martin, Frank, 'Air freight for exports', *Trade and Industry*, 30 January 1975.
22. O'Neill, Harry J., 'More on multi-national marketing', *Admap*, May 1976.
23. Robbins, Kenneth L., 'Does standardisation work in international marketing?' *European Management Journal*, vol. 15, no. 4, 1987.
24. Mead, Margaret, 'The application of anthropological techniques to cross-national communication', *Trans. New York Academy of Science*, Series II, vol. 9, no. 4, 1947.
25. Shane, Scott, 'Language and marketing in Japan', *International Journal of Advertising*, vol. 7, no. 2, 1988.
26. Peters, Tom, *Thriving on Chaos*, Macmillan, London, 1987.
27. Holden, Nigel J., 'The development of the concept of communication competence in relation to firms' interactions in overseas markets', unpublished Ph.D. thesis, Manchester Business School, University of Manchester, January 1986.
28. 'Multinationals survey', *The Economist*, 27 March 1993.
29. Madeley, John, 'Small solutions to big problems', *Financial Times*, 28 January 1991.
30. Madeley, John, 'Making it easier for the needy', *Financial Times*, 12 October 1985.
31. Chisnall, Peter M., *Marketing Research*, McGraw-Hill, Maidenhead, 1992.

REVIEW AND DISCUSSION QUESTIONS

Q1 Do you agree with the opinion quoted in this chapter that the Common Market is not, in fact, a *common* market? Develop your argument – either for or against this view – in the light of contemporary trends in Europe.

Q2 Describe the factors which should be taken into account when choosing between a standardised and a localised industrial export campaign.

Q3 Various definitions have been used to classify the relative stages of economic development of countries. Identify some of the salient measures currently used, and give examples of countries in specific stages of economic and social growth.

Q4 Discuss the significance of foreign language proficiency when exporting firms are attempting to open up new markets, as well as maintaining sound business relationships with their existing overseas customers. Relate your answer to countries where English is not widely understood.

Q5 Political influences have been noted as factors likely to affect exporting success, particularly in certain countries. Outline the possible political influences likely to impact on the operations of a firm exporting cranes for the construction industry to less developed countries.

Q6 What kinds of problem will probably be faced by managers who have to undertake primary industrial market research in prospective overseas markets?

CHAPTER TEN

Communications strategy

MYTHS AND MISCONCEPTIONS

The theoretical concept of the perfect market, at one time popular with classical economists, was based on certain assumptions. It was postulated, for example, that products and services of a type were homogenous, so buying preferences could not be based on differentiation in design or quality; large numbers of buyers and sellers were involved, hence no one firm could influence market prices and no discrimination existed; close and easy contact existed between suppliers and their customers; new firms were able, without difficulty, to enter an industry; and everyone had access to the same level of ideal information on market supplies. In these Utopian conditions that fictional character 'economic man' was held to be motivated in all his activities by purely economic considerations. This curious, completely rational being fitted neatly into the artificial environment projected by the early classical economists.

In such an 'ideal' economic situation, advertising was not needed because 'perfect' information was shared equally and no differences existed between generic products or services. It was the age of reason, not of emotion: rational choice determined buying behaviour.

Of course, the absurdity of these oversimplified and distorted economic theories is clear today. Modern business environments are complex and far removed from those primitive projections of economic life. Competitive activities involving product design, price, promotion, servicing, etc., characterise industrial economies. The market-place is a riotous assembly of suppliers shoving hard against each other to attract the attention of customers.

Across the developed world, levels of competition are rising inexorably; the pace of trading has accelerated; strategic alliances between powerful industrial and commercial groups (see Chapter 8) have added to the intensity of global competition. Modern transport systems and methods of communication have shrunk continents; satellites now serve the business and entertainment needs of millions. The advertising industry has proliferated in developed economies, and exploits virtually every conceivable opportunity for presenting persuasive communications to targeted audiences: television, press and magazines, cinema, radio, posters, exhibitions, etc., are all used with professional expertise.

Sophisticated skills in presentation have been acquired by the advertising industry, which, despite its critics, continues to play a dominant role in everyday life. Earlier, it had attracted the unfavourable attention of economists who, like Alfred Marshall, distinguished between 'constructive' or informative advertising and 'combative' or competitive advertising. The former was considered to be useful, whereas the latter was held to be a wasteful use of resources, even though output may have been increased and costs reduced. Marshall contended that these economies would have occurred without advertising. The debate about the economies of advertising continues; it is an area in which opinions are more plentiful than facts.

ORGANISATIONS OF ALL TYPES NEED TO COMMUNICATE

In the real world of industrial and commercial competition, organisations of all types and sizes attempt to communicate with their customers – past, present and potential. Not only profit-orientated organisations are engaged in the process of communication; health, education, welfare and charity organisations, for example, need to inform and motivate their patients, clients and donors, as well as society at large. Organisations are diverse, with their activities ranging over commercial, cultural, political and social objectives. But whatever their motivation, organisations must establish links with those they seek to serve; and they do this by some form of communication.

Organisations can choose to communicate with their customers and clients in several ways: through personal selling, public relations campaigns, exhibitions and various kinds of advertising. The promotional mix is to be determined according to criteria such as the nature of the product, relative market share and the nature of the market environment. The responsibilities of communicating with present and potential customers should be carefully considered against available resources, such as the size of the sales force, frequency of sales calls, competitive behaviour and advertising budget.

Advertising should help to make the sales force more effective and it should, therefore, be planned in an integrated way, i.e. making sure that advertising efforts are closely linked with sales objectives and the activities of the sales force. Unless advertising plans are fully meshed with the other elements of marketing strategy, frustration and wastage are almost inevitable. Sometimes it seems as if companies develop their advertising schemes in virtual isolation from their selling operations; it should be remembered that advertising is primarily an alternative and complementary method of selling products and services. It seldom, if ever, does the whole of this task, particularly in industrial markets. Market communications, whether personal or otherwise, demand clear thinking and expert planning. (See Chapter 5 on marketing strategy and promotional input.)

David Lowe Watson, supporting Bauer's concept of communications as 'a transactional process in which both audience and communicator take important initiative',[2] has suggested that the advertising process should be viewed as 'part of a network of relationships, linking the buyer, the seller and the product advertised'.[1] This concept of total communication and interrelationship should motivate transmitters to give reliable and useful information, which, in turn, would attract receivers to give their messages more favourable attention. There are indications that this more professional attitude to communication is influencing the publicity programmes of some large organisations. (The trend towards greater corporate responsibility in advertising and other functions of management is reviewed in Chapter 11.)

COMMUNICATIONS STRATEGY

In Chapter 5 a methodical approach to achieving organisational objectives was recommended; this entails developing a strategy. A marketing strategy was seen to have several components, to be combined in different 'mixes' according to the needs of specific markets. Of these various inputs to the overall marketing strategy, the promotional or communications strategy is an essential element. Communication objectives should be devised which are directly related to the general marketing objectives.

This strategic plan of communications should be comprehensive and should exploit fully all the diverse types of medium available in modern communities. These, as mentioned earlier, will include media advertising, editorial publicity, public relations campaigns, personal selling and 'word-of-mouth' informal communication.

Organisations, like individuals, are not islands: they need the support of their customers and the backing of their workpeople. They also prosper when they attract favourable public attitudes, as the enlightened communication policies of firms like ICI and Marks and Spencer have shown over several years.

A company must take account of the cultural and social environment in which it operates; the role of the commercial firm in society is increasingly debated and challenged; more stringent legal constraints, organised lobbying and social pressures have forced companies to expand their corporate responsibilities. Companies should ensure that they have well-managed communication links with government departments, local authorities, trade associations, consumer representative organisations, and schools and colleges.

Tracking surveys, such as the MORI Corporate Image Survey, provide companies with regular and objective assessments of public attitudes towards business and industry in general, specific industries, and interests salient to their clients. Since 1975, ICI has investigated the effects of its plants on local communities; these activities have not only raised awareness, but also improved the company's image.

WORD-OF-MOUTH COMMUNICATION AND OPINION LEADERSHIP

Not all communication is direct or dependent solely on advertising personally viewed. Word-of-mouth communication – informal communication – may be an effective though largely covert method of influencing attitudes and behaviour. Personal influence may modify or even entirely frustrate the persuasive effects of advertising campaigns. This type of subtle communication embodies group affiliations and opinion leadership.

> When we speak of studying communications, we must immediately face up to the transmission of ideas. We have, in the past, tended to think of idea communication as primarily a function of the printed word – or certainly of the formal mass and selective media, since radio and television have become so important. Perhaps we have given an over-emphasis to this formal mode of transmission of ideas – or at least not understood the level at which it works . . .[3]

This quotation is from the foreword to *Personal Influence*, in which Elihu Katz and Paul Lazarsfeld[4] presented their pioneer studies of how ideas are transmitted through the various levels of society. The buying behaviour of 800 women in Decatur, Illinois, was researched in the areas of movies, fashion, public affairs and food shopping. Personal influence was found to be a significant factor, 'although the fact that a woman is a leader in one area has no bearing on the likehood that she will be a leader in another'.

The concept of opinion leadership leading to a 'two-step flow of communication' was first formulated by Lazarsfeld, Berelson and Gaudet in their researches in connection with the 1940 US elections. They hypothesised that 'ideas often flow *from* radio and print to the opinion leaders and *from* them to the less active sections of the population'. Lazarsfeld and his associates found that friends, co-workers and relatives influenced personal voting decisions. 'Common observations and many community studies show that in every area and for every public issue there are certain people who are most concerned about the issue as well as most articulate about it. We call them the "opinion leaders".'[5]

Ernest Dichter, one of the progenitors of motivation research in the USA, drew attention some years ago to the power of word-of-mouth advertising;[6] customers are very often the best salespeople for the products which have given them satisfactory performance. They tend to welcome opportunities to give their opinions about specific products; it is gratifying to be regarded as a reliable source of advice, based on actual experience with specific products or services. At the same time, they are able to feel reassured about their own judgement and the decisions that follow from their typical approach to problems. Although Dichter's article was based on extensive consumer research, the principles of his findings have more general application and may usefully be considered in relation to industrial products and services.

Katz and Lazarsfeld,[4] in their Decatur study, showed that opinion leaders are more likely to be exposed to the mass media than those they later influence. Opinion leaders are seen as vital links in the chain of communication; they mediate between primary sources of information and the mass audience. Figure 10.1 is a radically simplified model of the gradual dissemination of information based on a 'trickle-down' theory of communication.

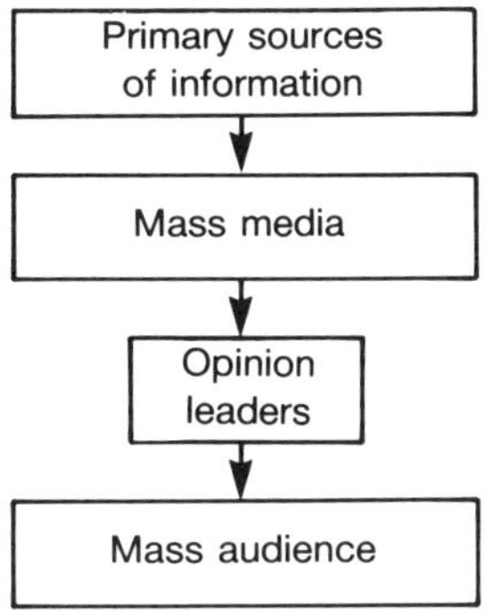

FIGURE 10.1 Simplified model of filtered communications

The identification of opinion leaders in specific areas of human activity, including the buying of goods and services, presents practical problems. It may be possible, through marketing research, to identify particular firms and individuals in certain industries whose managerial behaviour suggests that they regard themselves as innovators (see Chapter 7). As mentioned in Chapter 4, it is often possible, when researching industrial markets, to locate recognised experts who will be regarded within their industries as leading sources of information.

REFERENCE GROUPS

Herbert Hyman[7] originated the term 'reference group' in 1942: 'The concept says in effect that man's behaviour is influenced in different ways and in varying degrees by other people . . . an unrealised truism which has long been recognised.'[8] Later, Hyman felt that more attention should be given 'to the reference *individual* who had tended to be overlooked in the development of the group theory'.[9] He stressed that *both* concepts were influential; in buying certain products, 'influentials' or 'opinion leadership' were active.

Opinion leadership and communications strategy

Since 1968 the US Continental Can Company has undertaken regular research into the characteristics of opinion leaders in developing its communications strategy. It found that leaders were 'involved to a greater degree in organisations';[10] they had higher levels of aspiration, and were of higher socioeconomic groups than non-leaders.

Opinion leadership is a phenomenon which appears to be well established, although in practice the nature and extent of the influence wielded by industrial and community leaders is not easy to assess. Opinion leaders are not generalised; specific spheres of influence seem to fall within the scope of certain individuals. The diffusion of innovations – political, social or involving the choice of new products and services – was observed in Chapter 7 to depend on a relatively small proportion of people who are early adopters. In the field of communications, such individuals, acting through their social and professional contacts, may act as catalysts in developing public opinion. (For further discussion, see reference 2.)

Those who have such opinions and attitudes will consider them to be valid; perception is rarely objective. People tend to distort information through a process of selective attention, perception and recall.

> Not all marketing communications will be significant for all individuals; people tend to select from the myriad stimuli to which they are exposed those which appear to be relevant to their needs. Information, for example, will be filtered through the mesh of personal interests, attitudes, motivational structure, social background and cultural influences.[11]

With organisational buying, the relevance of information will also be concerned with specific needs, such as equipping a new warehouse or factory. Favourable or helpful communications are more likely to be perceived than neutral or hostile messages. 'And the more interested people are in the subject, the more likely is such selective attention.'[12]

Herbert Krugman, who for years was manager of corporate public opinion at the GE Company of the USA, has strongly urged that 'we should not speak of captive audiences "watching" TV advertising but also of active audiences "monitoring" the advertising and distributing their attention selectively, with closer attention to involving commercials, with less to the others, and preserving a certain economy of effort, i.e. by limiting their attention'.[13]

Multiple target audiences for corporate communications

There are several target audiences for corporate communications; these are likely to need different kinds of information. The tasks of communicating corporate policies should be drawn up with the needs of particular audiences firmly in mind. These will range from organisational buyers (and other members of the 'buying team') to trade distributors or agents, to raw materials and component suppliers, to 'opinion leaders' in industrial, financial and government circles, to members of staff (at all levels), and, perhaps, eventually to the final consumers of the product. Additionally, staff recruitment will be affected by the 'visibility' of an organisation.

Stock exchange confidence assists in the long-term financing of companies seeking to attract investment in, for example, new share issues. It is important that financial journalists should be kept informed of corporate plans, new product developments, improved manufacturing facilities, strategic alliances, etc.

Leading market and opinion research organisations, such as Gallup or MORI, undertake special studies of MPs, business and financial journalists, editors of specialist journals, trade unions and other centres of opinion leadership.

The boundaries of corporate communications are wide and expanding rapidly; top management should ensure that not only customers but all who, in various ways, are affected by the behaviour of their companies receive accurate and relevant information about the products and services offered and the policies pursued by them in, for example, employment, customer care or environmental issues.

MODEL OF MARKETING COMMUNICATIONS

It has already been observed that communications are influenced by several factors which lie outside the direct control of those who project messages for various reasons to target audiences. A more detailed appreciation of these behavioural influences is presented in another text;[11] a general understanding would, however, assist in developing insight into the complexities of strategic communications.

Figure 10.2 outlines the four principal phases of marketing communications. Briefly, these concern four aspects: *who; what; how; to whom.*

The communication process is originated by the sender – in marketing terms, the supplier of a product or service of some kind. From this source, messages are directed to selected markets through media of various types; these may be personal or impersonal. The final phase of the model refers to the customers or consumers (personal or corporate) with whom it is intended to communicate.

But, as already noted, the sequential flow of communications outlined in Figure 10.1 is not a simple process. Apart from the influence of personal factors such as subjective perception, a 'noise' factor affects communications (see Figure 10.2). This may modify or even radically change the whole nature of specific messages. Sources of external 'noise' may related to the activities of competitors who launch a special version of their equipment which directly challenges the product at present being promoted. Customers' attention will probably be diverted; the reception of the advertising campaign is likely to be distorted. Other sources of 'noise' could originate from political, social or economic disturbances which may lead to fundamental changes in organisational behaviour. Investment plans, for example, may be severely curtailed because of a sudden fall in world demand for the raw

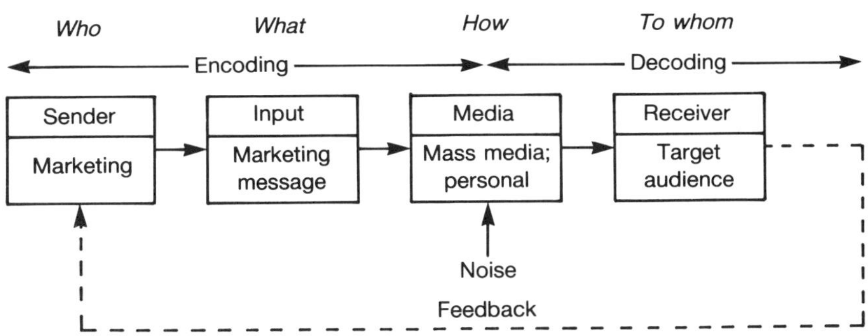

FIGURE 10.2 Outline model of marketing communications

materials or finished products marketed by certain sectors of industry. Stringent financial measures will supervene in management decisions. Many of these factors will not be controllable by the communicator, whose messages may, in a changed environment, be discarded or given very marginal attention.

Occasionally the 'noise' factor may act to the communicator's advantage, as in the case of rumoured shortages of certain basic materials. Buyers may be alerted by these rumours to stock up; they may, therefore, deliberately scan the technical press for sources of supply and be particularly receptive to advertising messages.

Two other factors influence the flow of communications between transmitters and receivers: these are 'encoding' and 'decoding'. The former relates to the communicator's message, which he or she has designed to give, in their opinion, certain information to their audience (customers, in the case of marketing management). A marketer may, unfortunately, misunderstand the needs of his or her market; the maketer's messages may be unhelpful because they are not relevant or only partially so. The encoding factor reflects the sensitivity which a marketer has developed to the changing needs of his or her customers.

The decoding factor concerns the reception of communication by the target audience. As discussed earlier, perception is seldom objective.

Because communication involves many factors, some of which cannot be governed by the communicator, a feedback mechanism is vital in order to monitor the effectiveness of, for example, particular advertisements so that maximum advantage can be taken of the various opportunities available for marketing communications. Often, the feedback system is neglected; vast sums are spent on advertising campaigns, but comparatively little expenditure or effort is directed towards measuring the effectiveness of particular promotions.

Feedback information may indicate that advertising, for example, is being misdirected because the medium used is not influential with certain members of the buying team. The complexity of organisational buying was observed, in Chapter 3, to present suppliers with special problems in communication. Advertisements in a particular campaign are likely to appear in several types of journal to ensure that *all* who contribute to the buying decision are exposed to information about the products or services offered by a company.

Personal as well as impersonal communications contribute to the overall marketing communications strategy. Hence, feedback should not be confined to the messages transmitted via the mass media. Webster's research[14] into industrial buying behaviour (quoted in Chapter 3) indicated the important role of the manufacturer's salesperson as a source of reliable and relevant information. It would seem logical for marketing management to train their representatives to be effective communicators, and to assess their performance in this critical function of negotiation.

Communication is a social process; people are both transmitters and receivers of messages of various kinds. Interaction takes place which develops attitudes and may lead to positive behaviour, e.g. the purchase of a promoted product. Feedback information may include: volume of sales in specific industries or areas; changes in buying attitudes; competitive strategies; or the perceived efficiency of the sales-servicing arrangements. There are many aspects of marketing which, as discussed in Chapter 5, call for a systematic flow of information to guide management decisions. Marketing research techniques may be most usefully applied to the evaluation of promotional efforts. (See Chapters 4 and 5.)

MAJOR DECISIONS IN MARKETING COMMUNICATIONS

Four main areas of decision in developing an effective scheme of communications may be summarised as follows:

1. To whom to say it.
2. What to say.
3. How to say it.
4. Where to say it.

The first stage is to define, as accurately as possible, the target audience: 'To whom to say it'. Senders aim to transmit messages to particular people – target audiences. The extent to which all potential buyers of a particular product or service are reached depends on the accuracy with which they were originally defined and on the effectiveness with which certain media cover these markets.

The next step, 'What to say', is termed communications policy; it is the primary stage which is advisably related to objective data from marketing research. Organisations will have diverse objectives and different needs for communicating with their public. At various stages in corporate growth, messages may change in their content or style. Whatever variation occurs, it is crucially important that these messages should reflect the overall corporate objectives and form an integral part of the marketing strategy.

The third step, 'How to say it', refers to the creative presentations of communications, particularly advertising. Ideas have to be translated into effective 'copy'. Research will aid in identifying the nature of particular audiences and their communication needs. With industrial and commercial supplies, the complexity of buying has added to the problems of effective communication. In overseas markets in particular, research will give guidance about the influence of cultural factors in communication.

The final stage, 'Where to say it', involves the selection of suitable media of communication, the timing of specific messages, the frequency of communication with specific audiences and the relative costs of alternative methods. If advertising, for example, fails to project the right message to the intended audience and at the desired time, it is badly conceived and planned.

These four areas of decision-making in communications are, of course, interrelated. They have been separately discussed merely to identify the elements of an effective scheme of communications.

PLANNING COMMUNICATIONS STRATEGIES

That systematic planning contributes to marketing success was discussed at some length in Chapter 5; the benefits of planning also apply to communications strategy and tactics. Figure 10.3 outlines a planned approach which should encourage management to develop expertise in this function of marketing.

The sequential processes shown in Figure 10.3 should be considered in conjunction with the areas of decision making just discussed, when the need for marketing research data became clear. As Berelson and Steiner have observed: 'Communications that are thought to represent some particular interest or characteristic of the audience are more influential on opinion than general undifferentiated sources. Thus, communications directed to particular audiences are more effective than those directed to the public at large.'[12] Communications designed with particular kinds of people in mind are more likely to appeal than those which are so general that no one feels personally involved. Communications aimed at some vague stereotyped customer or client are hardly likely to stimulate strong personal interest.

Specific types of communication strategy and tactics should be related to the significant characteristics of submarkets, which were reviewed in Chapter 6 in the section dealing with market segmentation.

Communication objectives, like general corporate objectives, may be classified as (1) long term; and (2) short term. In organisational markets, immediate reaction to advertising, for example, is most unlikely. Companies generally have several objectives in mind when communicating with their markets; these should be articulated because this will help in planning an effective communications strategy.

A highly specific advertising objective is the purpose of 'awareness advertising'[15] by multinationals of some products which may be prohibited either from being imported into certain countries or from being made locally. In some instances, local availability may be imminent and the market is being prepared for entry, but a significant role of awareness advertising relates to products that are not likely to be locally available in the foreseeable future. Brand awareness may be developed and information given about where a product may be bought, indicating that it is backed by efficient service agents.

In Chapter 3, post-decisional dissonance, based on Festinger's theory of cognitive dissonance, was discussed. The reduction of dissonance or post-purchase anxiety may be one of the objectives of an advertising campaign. Major purchases of durable goods – including industrial supplies – may lead to nagging doubts about some aspects of the business deal, perhaps because of the innovative nature of equipment that was purchased or a new source of supply that was involved. Research has revealed that buyers of consumer products have tended to seek confirmation of their purchasing behaviour. It would not be fanciful to suggest that the industrial buyer may experience similar feelings.

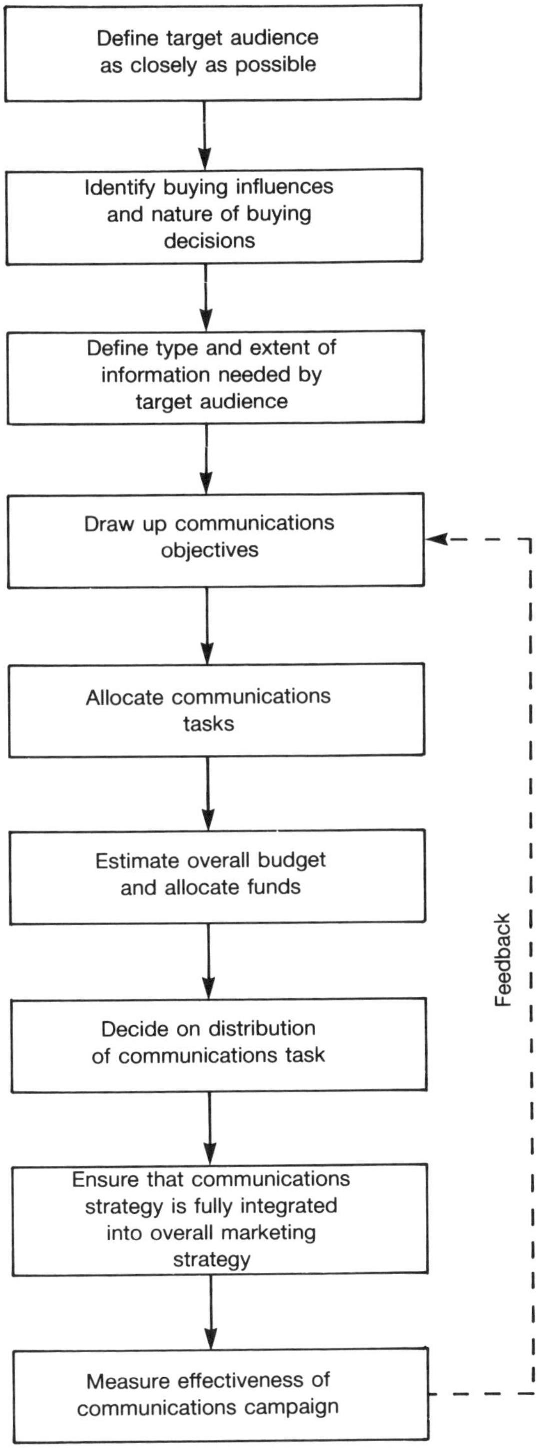

FIGURE 10.3 Planned sequence of communications strategy

Although the prime objective of advertising is generally to achieve sales, other motivations exist and, in the case of 'reassurance advertising', may contribute significantly to the overall success of a company.

THE CHALLENGE OF CORPORATE COMMUNICATIONS

Business, particularly big business, is the target today for almost incessant criticism. It is the sitting duck at which politicians, economists, sociologists and the public at large delight to snipe. Some of this criticism has been earned, but in many cases it is founded more on ignorance and fear than fact.

Multinational firms, in particular, have attracted unfavourable attention; they have been viewed as the bogeymen of modern industry and commerce. Their mammoth size and multifarious activities have appeared to many spectators to be threats to society itself, apart from suspicions about the vast economic power which they exercise across the world. Earlier it was observed that in certain countries an uneasy relationship tends to exist between some mammoth businesses and the governments of those countries.

Organisations of many kinds are getting bigger and on a scale which seems to be limitless. Asa Briggs[16] has observed that it is because the organisations are so big and seem so powerful that dissent can be so strident, rebellion so prevalent and so contagious. Reactions are often articulate and well organised, as with the consumerist movement which, in a few years, has grown from the level of a cottage industry to a sophisticated system of highly organised lobbying.

Infiltration of the policies of large industries into the personal lives of millions has aroused public antipathy on a scale previously unknown. More enlightened managements have correctly interpreted these trends and have taken steps to improve, among other things, their processes of communication both within their organisations and with the environment in which they operate.

Companies should not wait for some corporate misbehaviour – either real or imaginary – before they communicate with their customers and with the public at large. If they fail to give facts about their activities, then the field is wide open for conjecture, rumour and even hostile reaction. Perception, as discussed earlier, is seldom objective: fragments of information are often put together in a fairly haphazard manner, while the gaps in knowledge tend to be filled in by a mix of past experience, hearsay and, most likely, prejudice. Time is limited; the search for complete, objective knowledge is unlikely to be conducted by most people, including industrial buyers. Perhaps it would be well to recall Schumacher's wise words: 'We often notice the existence of more or less fixed ideas in other people's minds – ideas *with which* they think without being aware of doing so. We then call them prejudices, which is logically quite correct because they have merely seeped into the mind and are in no way the result of judgement . . .'[17]

Experienced marketers like ICI know full well the advantages of keeping a favourable market image. For many years, its famous 'Pathfinders' campaign significantly affected public attitudes, as research showed. Then, in September 1987, ICI launched an international advertising campaign, part of a £7 million corporate effort based on extensive market research, to project the group as 'world class'. The famous ICI roundel was 'updated' to project a modern dynamic organisation. More recently, ICI underwent a radical reorganisation involving a split into two separately quoted corporate entities. This massive restructuring attracted the attention of the world media, and aroused considerable speculation about the group's future prospects.

In an era of well-organised and articulate lobbying against perceived industrial and commercial malpractices, no company can afford to neglect the quality and quantity of its communications with customers and people at large. But clever promotional campaigns will not cover up an unattractive public face if this has devolved from unacceptable corporate behaviour.

It might be as well to close this section with some penetrating observations by Enoch Powell about public reaction to advertising:

> The professional politician can sympathise with the professional advertiser. They inhabit similar dog-houses. In the public mind advertising stands suspect of deception, and fearless loyalty to the unvarnished truth is not generally supposed to be the first qualification for success in it. I suppose the practitioner in advertising comes to accept, as one of the inconveniences incident to his profession, this low public estimation of his veracity and sincerity.[18]

THE FAMILIARITY PRINCIPLE

The familiarity principle ('Something that is known inspires more confidence than something that is unknown'), enunciated by Alfred Politz[19] about consumer product branding, is not without significance in organisational supplies and services markets. Uncertainty about the quality of products offered by a relatively unknown supplier will deter buyers, who will (as the discussion in Chapter 3 suggests) adopt, consciously or otherwise, risk policies in selecting sources of supply. Consistent and well-devised promotional campaigns will help to break down the barrier of suspicion which frequently makes it extremely difficult to enter new markets.

An illustration of the effect of familiarity on public opinion has been given by Robert Worcester[20] (see Figure 10.4). It will be seen that, based on nearly 2,000 consumer interviews, companies that are well known are also well thought of. That, as Worcester says, 'favourability increases with familiarity' was also confirmed in a study of 32 companies in 1983 (see Figure 10.5), which indicates that there is 'an almost straight-line relationship between how *well* a company is known and how favourably it is regarded'.[21]

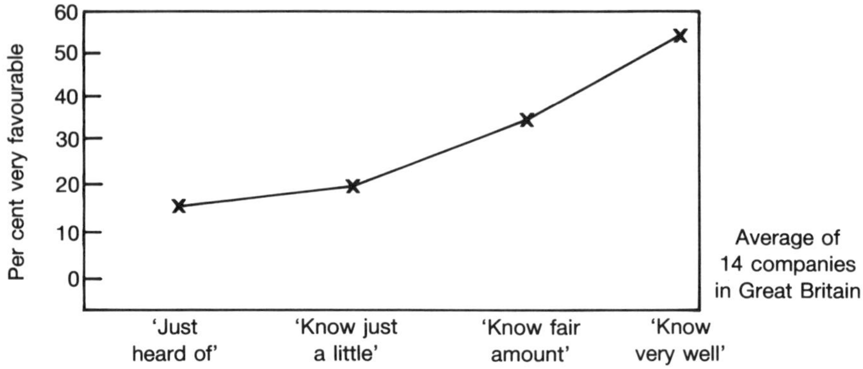

FIGURE 10.4 Effect of personal knowledge on attitudes to British companies (Source: Worcester.[20] Market & Opinion Research International, 1991 interviews. 'National probability sample of all adults in Great Britain, cooperative corporate image study', autumn 1969.)

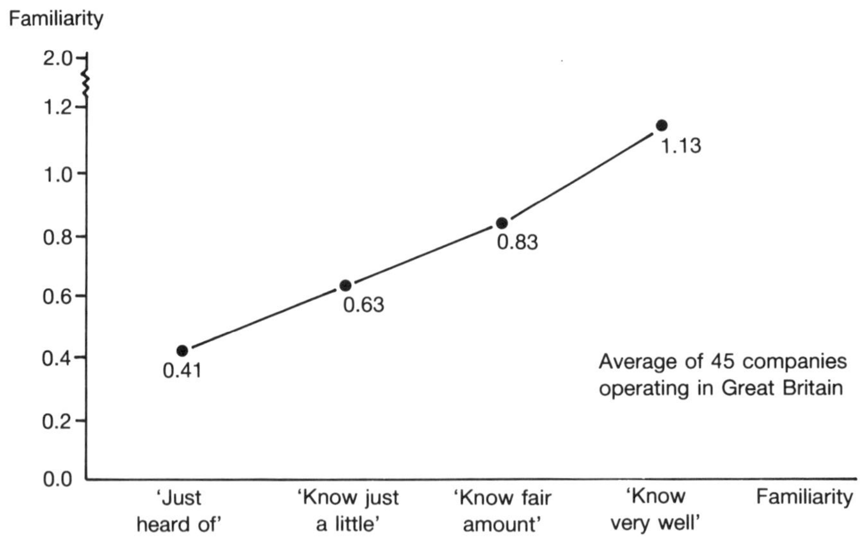

FIGURE 10.5 Companies are *usually* highly regarded by those who know them best (Source: MORI)

CORPORATE PERSONALITY

'An organisation is an entity, with a personality which it has acquired as the result of past behaviour and of the messages which it has given to those it serves, and also to members of its staff.'[11] This corporate image and reputation will influence the reactions of customers, potential as well as existing, and affect its development and prosperity. Further, this corporate personality may be based on subjective beliefs and attitudes which may appear to management to be biased and irrational.

Two kinds of belief and attitude are likely to exist: general and/or specific. The latter will be concerned with particular aspects of an organisation which are of significant interest to individuals. From these specific views an overall impression will be developed.

'Image' is how others – customers, present and potential, suppliers and also government agencies – see an organisation. They may not necessarily have had direct experience of that company or its products but, from hearsay as well as special knowledge, perhaps, they have gained an impression – formed a mental picture or image – of that company.

> A strong corporate image influences the predisposition to buy a company's products, speak favourably of it, believe its statements, apply for a job with it, and the like. It is important for industrial goods companies with listed shares. It is important to companies . . . and other organisations . . . seeking highly technical staff in a tight staff availability situation.[20]

Peter Hutton, a widely experienced marketing researcher, has shrewdly observed that 'most companies pay very little attention to their image in the world outside them and yet, in quite a large proportion of cases, the customers of those companies are quite strongly influenced by their own view – their image – of their suppliers'.[22]

Virtually everything a company does communicates the type of organisation it is: the quality of its products and services, pricing and general trading policies, promotional activities, personnel relations, after-sales service, etc. all contribute positively or otherwise to its overall corporate image.

Hutton identifies 'four levels of corporate image' which surround products (see Figure 10.6). The outer level refers to significant sociocultural influences which affect opinions and attitudes towards corporate activities. The next level relates to perceptions about specific economic activities, such as the chemicals industry or the insurance market, in which companies operate. The third level covers particular companies such as Ford, Rank-Xerox and IBM. At this level many key contacts are made with a wide range of people and organisations, like investors, employees, suppliers and competitors. The 'brand level' obviously relates to well-known branded products, although the names of the companies which own them may not be readily recalled. At the centre of the diagram is the product itself, whose performance decides the future of the company. These various 'levels' of corporate image are not, of course, independent, but are interrelated and affect the overall impression gained of a particular company.

Courtaulds was reported to have spent £1 million over nearly two years in developing a semi-abstract symbol known as the C mark, and in a co-ordinated campaign to improve the way in which the constituent companies (more than 70 main subsidiaries in 26 countries) handled their dealings with customers. 'We looked at basic factors, like how long we took to answer telephones. Our

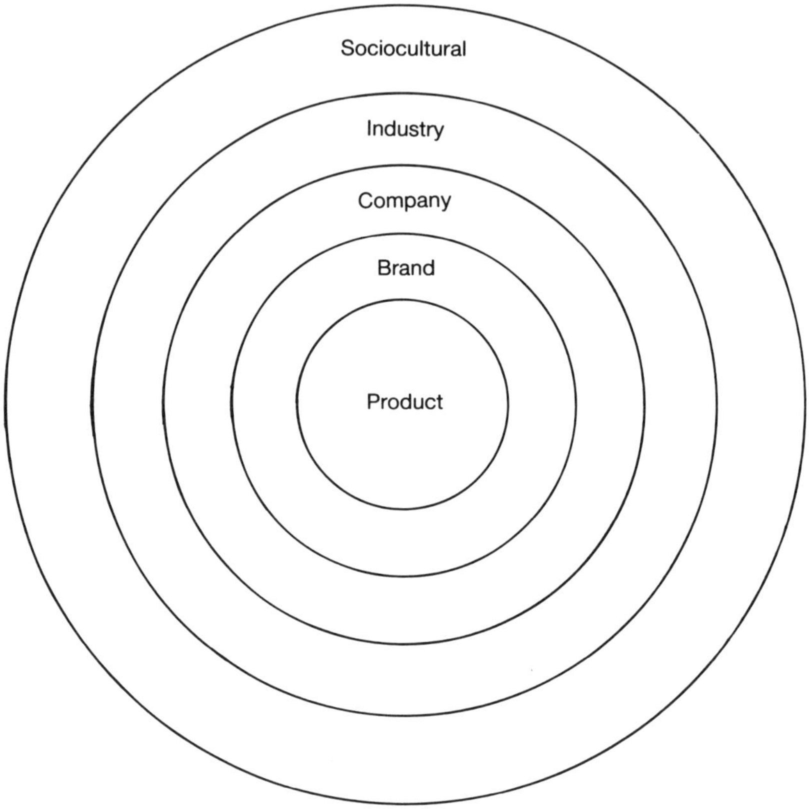

FIGURE 10.6 Levels of corporate image (Source: Hutton[22])

environment needed tidying up. Our reception area didn't say anything about who we were. Things that are totally typical of UK industry but tend to be handled differently in, say, the US or Japan.'[23]

A design consultancy service interviewed in depth more than 200 people drawn from top management, opinion formers and major customers, and their perceptions about Courtaulds and its business prospects were analysed. 'One of the things that came out was that there was terrific underlying desire for a central culture.'[23] Sir Christopher Hogg, chairman of the group, has declared that he wants the new logo to be like Rolls-Royce and symbolic of the high quality in products and services that customers can expect from Courtaulds. The new identity will not be promoted through an extensive corporate advertising campaign; companies will use it as and when they do targeted advertising.

One of the most recognisable and award-winning symbols is the Woolmark launched by the International Wool Secretariat and funded by sheep farmers in Australia and New Zealand in order to promote sales of wool. In 1987 a new advertising campaign was planned to refocus the Woolmark logo and target it at rather younger buyers of fashion clothing. Consumers, primarily women, were encouraged to perceive wool as a quality product with aesthetic appeal. Ready identification of the natural fibre is, of course, crucial to success at the point of puchase.

In 1989 the International Wool Secretariat launched its first pan-European advertising campaign across 16 countries using the theme 'Love from Woolmark', translated into 12 languages. This, and later campaigns, have formed part of IWS's centralised attempts to encourage European customers to choose wool for casual clothing and to enhance its appeal among younger age groups.[24]

Wally Olins, chairman of Wolff Olins, is one of the leading designers of corporate logos; he has declared that corporate identity is not a new concept, but a new name for an old idea: 'everything from a new nation to a new religion has chosen signs and symbols to express identity.'[25]

Famous logos are to be seen everywhere: television advertisements, printed media, posters, cinema and neon signs all make full use of the instant recognition which is the curious power of Shell, Esso and ICI symbols, even where literacy is low. Canada Dry, Mercedes, TWA, British Airways, the banks – the list is endless and spans the globe – all know about the pulling power of design and jealously guard their individual logos.

In common with typographical design, time takes its toll and logos tend to age. In 1989, British Petroleum's green and yellow shield, familiar to generations of motorists, was subtly redesigned to communicate the impression of a dynamic, growing company. As noted earlier, ICI also had its famous roundel redesigned. When the Prudential Assurance Company commissioned Wolff Olins to researchits corporate image, this resulted in a radically new logo which was derived from the traditional images of Prudence, reflecting wisdom, foresight and related attributes.

Wolff Olins was also responsible for the new corporate identity of BT, formerly known as British Telecom. Working closely with a steering group of BT's senior managers, a design team spent several months talking to BT's customers, competitors and employees, and in late 1990 BT finally approved the abbreviation of its corporate name and the now well-recognised figurative symbol of the piper, described by Wally Olins as 'a symbol of joyous communication through the ages'.[26]

Corporate identity and logo designs tend to arouse strong feelings, particularly criticism of the high costs associated with some recent large-scale corporate renewal programmes, as well as reservations about the intrinsic merits of the logos which eventually emerge from the frenetic activities of the design specialists.

In 1990 a study[27] was published, based on research by MORI, of the attitudes held by European chief executives and main board directors about issues related to corporate identity. The research focused on 243 of Europe's largest companies spread over Austria, France, Scandinavia, Spain, the UK and (West) Germany. Of the pan-European corporate identities which were most admired, Mercedes headed the list, which included Nestlé, Philips and Shell.

Across the countries surveyed, some variability existed in perceptions about the main aims of a corporate identity programme. For example, in France corporate identity was perceived primarily as a tool for communicating with people outside the company, such as customers, while in Germany and Austria particular stress was placed on internal communications. The Spanish took a more abstract view: corporate identity should express the culture of a company. In the UK, the tendency was to associate corporate identity activities closely with advertising and other aspects of overall marketing strategy.

WHY ADVERTISE?

Before advertising or any other form of promotion is considered, some very fundamental questions should be asked: these can be slotted into the phases of developing a communications strategy outlined in Figure 10.3. One simple question could well be the first to be asked: '*Why* advertise?' If a logical and coherent answer is not forthcoming, then no commitments should be made.

The use of corporate funds, whether in the public or private sector of the economy, carries with it the managerial responsibility for careful investigation and allocation of scarce resources. Production managers are expected to put forward factual information about the improved qualities or increased rates of production which could result from investing large sums of money in new equipment. Marketing managers should be prepared to state an equally sound case for the heavy costs incurred in their sphere of operations, particularly those related to promotional expenditure.

SUPPORTING THE SALES EFFORT

A significant function of the advertising of industrial products is to support the selling effort. Some years ago McGraw-Hill, in promotional campaigns for its business publications, featured a rather belligerent buyer who greeted some salespeople as follows:

- I don't know who you are.
- I don't know your company's product.
- I don't know what your company stands for.
- I don't know your company's customers.
- I don't know your company's record.
- I don't know your company's reputation.
- Now – what is it you wanted to sell me?

This rather discouraging reception is not just a copywriter's fertile imagination let loose, as Morrill's intensive research into the effectiveness of advertising of industrial products clearly showed. Morrill's extended study covered 1,000 advertising schedules of 26 different product lines in 90 product markets at 30,000 different buying locations. The products included 'a basic chemical sold in quantity to a tight market of 500 processors'; of the three major manufacturers, only the leader advertised. Also covered were three manufacturers 'who all make a low-priced electrical device used in all kinds of industrial plants' where competition is very keen.

Morrill admitted that two particular difficulties arose when researching the impact of industrial advertising:

1. 'It is impossible to assume the familiar principle that "what is recalled is effective" and then question buyers about what advertising they remember.' Buyers may recall advertisements, for example, that were not relevant to buying decisions, which are, in any case, complex. Recall may also be biased because 'a company executive tends to continue to read the advertising' of his or her present suppliers rather than of competing suppliers.
2. 'It is difficult to isolate the creative qualities of an advertising campaign from all the other elements that go into it . . .'

For these reasons, Morrill and his associates concentrated research on the *extent* of advertising in a particular campaign and the buyer's exposure to it. 'If we can show that these correlate with levels of sales – if more advertising and more exposure mean more sales, and less of both mean fewer sales – then we shall score a base hit . . .'[28]

Morrill's research indicated that industrial advertising effects 'are profound – and profoundly useful to know about'. They can be summarised as follows:

1. The buyer's opinion of the manufacturer who advertises is improved; 'this means a larger share of the market for the manufacturer'.
2. Advertising acts as a valuable introduction to prospective customers; costs of selling are reduced.
3. Lack of frequency of advertising is the single most common cause of promotional failure. Of several hundred failures studied, more than 90 per cent ran fewer than five pages of advertising in one magazine over 12 months. In general, five pages per year were needed to render a programme effective.
4. With adequate frequency, most industrial advertising appears extremely worthwhile. The total cost of selling to target audiences often falls by 10–30 per cent.
5. In a well-advertised market, the non-advertiser selling costs may actually increase by 20–40 per cent.
6. Companies can certainly sell without advertising, but planned advertising increases profitability.
7. Salespeople are made more effective; costs of advertising are outweighed by increased sales and profitability.

That there are plenty of industrial firms experiencing the value of advertising has been well documented by the US journal *Sales Management* over several years. Similarly, Webster's research,[14] detailed in Chapter 3, supported the important role of the trade press at the 'awareness' stage of the industrial buying process.

Some few years ago, a particularly interesting, and still relevant, market study[29] was made of machine-tool buyers in Chicago; these were contacted by telephone, and a total of 159 calls resulted in 92 completed interviews. Chicago was chosen as offering a representative sample because of its high concentration of machine tools and a large number of firms in the four SICs selected for coverage. Following this initial phase of research, a mail survey among US manufacturers and marketers of machine tools was carried out; 144 usable questionnaires were returned, representing 55.6 per cent of the membership of the National Machine Tool Builders' Association.

The objective of the study was to assess the degree to which industrial buyers and marketers have the same perception of the relative usefulness of alternative channels of market communication.

Buyers of machine tools regarded advertising in trade magazines as the most important source of information about products and services (37 per cent); salespeople followed in second ranking (27 per cent). Although statistical tests indicated a relatively low significant difference, the results showed that buyers consider advertising *at least* as important as personal salespeople in keeping them well informed.

Industrial marketers of machine tools considered that salespeople were by far the most important sources of communication with customers and prospects. This appears to reinforce the generally held view of the prime importance of personal selling in industrial marketing strategies.

INDUSTRIAL SELLING EXPERTISE

In Chapter 5 the selling and distribution input into overall marketing strategy was discussed, and it was noted that, while direct selling is prevalent in industrial markets, some merchanting activities also play important roles. Industrial selling generally is complex, not only because many of the products and services demand considerable technical knowledge, but also on account of the nature of organisational buying practices which, as seen in Chapter 3, may entail complex decision making in which important contributions are made by specialised functions of management, such as production or finance.

In some cases, industrial selling is characterised by long-term contracts and also sophisticated logistics of supply to meet the demands of JIT (just-in-time) deliveries (see Chapters 1 and 3). Very close relationships are likely to be established between a company and a few carefully selected suppliers, which in turn, have their own networks of sub-suppliers. As seen earlier, this type of industrial selling has evolved into partnership sourcing, as pioneered by IBM, HP and other larger corporations in the USA, and is now attracting the increasing interest of British industry.

A further complicating factor in industrial selling relates to the concentration of buying power in industries such as chemicals, brewing, telecommunications and electronics, as indicated in Chapter 2. Some of these industries are dominated by multinational groups which have immense muscle-power in negotiations. Selling to such organisations frequently means engaging in a series of technical and commercial presentations to groups of professionals who are, themselves, likely to be experienced negotiators.

Although personal selling is regarded as a vital input into industrial marketing, the ever-increasing costs of maintaining a direct sales force demand that selling effectiveness should be ensured. Costs per call – which include prospective as well as actual customers – continue to rise sharply. Greater attention should be given to identifying target markets and firms within those markets. In the United Kingdom, Market Location of Royal Leamington Spa offers a research-based service that is aimed at providing specific target clusters of user industries.

Professional selling skills should be developed in industrial sales forces. Elements of such skill include thorough knowledge of products and their applications in specific industries; the ability to diagnose customers' problems and to offer acceptable solutions in terms of the products being offered for sale; a sound grasp of the essential nature of customers' technologies and business operations; perceptive and sensitive insights into human behaviour (see Chapter 3); and highly developed negotiating skills, including knowledge of the buying practices of specific companies. Such a demanding set of criteria would seem to call for a paragon, not just a salesperson.

Negotiating skills – which are complex and involve psychological and cultural factors as well as technical know-how – should be fully developed by industrial marketing and sales staff. In international business, in particular, insensitivity to cultural norms (see Chapter 8) may easily frustrate business deals. For example, joint ventures often appear to fail because of the clash of culture – national and corporate – which results almost inevitably from differing expectations, perceptions, attitudes and cultural values.

Hakansson's interaction model of buying behaviour, discussed in Chapter 3, projected the marketing and purchasing of industrial goods and services as largely dependent on the development of satisfactory interaction between buyers and sellers. This dynamic process is influenced by the distinct expectations of the negotiating parties; these, it was found from research, were likely to be affected by national cultures, personal attributes and the goals of the organisations involved in the business negotiations.

The successful outcome of negotiation depends substantially, therefore, not only on the exchange of factual information about specific products and services, but also on the fostering of an acceptable emotional environment in which mutual respect and trust are engendered. As observed in Chapter 9, non-verbal communication may be a decisive factor in influencing the progress of negotiations. While bargaining is an integral part of the process of negotiation, and verbal communication plays a major role, experienced negotiators fully realise that communication essentially has to be two-way, and they are prepared to listen as well as to talk. In this way, they build up an atmosphere in which dialogue can develop between customers and themselves. This is far more likely to result in mutually advantageous, long-term relationships than attempting to dominate discussions by imposing a virtually non-stop monologue on reluctant listeners.

For their part, companies should stimulate and direct their sales forces through effective motivation (pay and promotional prospects, training programmes, job satisfaction, etc.) and by setting sales quotas or targets that bear realistic relationships to the prospects of given territories. In some large industrial organisations, representatives virtually assume the role and responsibilities of area marketing managers; they should be fully briefed about the overall objectives of their organisation.

In Chapter 5, various sales force payment schemes were identified and assessed for their relative effectiveness in motivating industrial sales operations, and it might be useful at this stage to refer back to this discussion.

ADVERTISING MEDIA FOR ORGANISATIONAL COMMUNICATIONS

Most industrial and commercial publicity (as well as that undertaken by official organisations) is through printed media of various kinds. In Britain there is a highly diversified range of publications, from the mass dailies through to esoteric quarterly journals, catering for the information needs of people at all levels of society. Details of these journals are contained in directories such as *British Rate and Data* (*BRAD*), *Willings Press Guide* and the *Newspaper Press Directory*.

A very useful and comprehensive guide to media planning, regulations, agencies, etc. in Europe (EC and EEA – European Economic Area) is *The Handbook of European Advertising* by Roger Bennett (published by Kogan Page). Another useful reference source is *The European Directory of Trade and Business Journals* (published by Euromonitor Publications). This gives information on the main European journals covering western European markets and industries. There is detailed information on over 2,000 main business and trade journals, mostly related to consumer goods and services, but UK listings include 'trade' entries covering, for example, brewing, baking and corporate finance.

THREE TYPES OF CIRCULATION OF TRADE PRESS

Trade and technical publications use three general methods of circulation: paid circulation (by post to subscribers, or over the counter); controlled circulation (mailed free to selected individuals); and professional circulation (to members of an institute).

Some controversial views have been expressed on the value of controlled circulation publications, although these have tended to grow considerably and now represent a major proportion of British trade publishing. They usually operate a readership reply service, and are produced to high professional standards. Their proliferation, and the fact that they involve no personal commitment or cost, may reduce their effectiveness.

Professionally circulated journals tend to be read with a degree of personal identification and involvement which adds significance to their announcements, including advertisements.

The relatively small circulations of some trade publications may involve advertisers in costs out of balance with the benefits likely to accrue. Preferably, circulation figures should be authenticated, as with ABC (Audit Bureau of Circulations) independent checks. Audited circulation figures are now quoted by certain leading technical journals. It may be more advantageous for industrial advertisers to use the national press on some occasions.

> A manufacturer of automatic vending machines wanted to appeal directly to top management and create an awareness at that level of its automatic catering service. The media list included the *Financial Times* as well as management and industrial journals. The manufacturers discovered subsequently that 75 per cent of the enquiries received came from the *Financial Times*. Part of this response, furthermore, may have uncovered market areas unsuspected by the advertiser, thanks to the breadth of coverage.[30]

TWO MAJOR CATEGORIES OF TRADE PRESS

Two major categories of the trade, technical and professional press were noted in the preceding chapter as horizontal or vertical.

Horizontal journals have a broad approach to the industry or profession they cater for. *Management Today*, for example, spans the problems of business management at a senior level. It features advertisements offering managerial services applicable to industry in general: travel, finance, insurance, credit cards, etc.

Vertical journals have a narrower field of operations: they aim to serve specific industries or professions, narrowing even to particular functions within those areas. These journals may be particularly useful in communicating with highly segmented markets. Some, like *Farmers' Weekly*, have six-figure circulations, whereas *Optics and Laser Technology* has a specialised circulation of just over 1,000.

EXPERT ADVICE NEEDED FOR EFFECTIVE MEDIA SELECTION

The nature of technical publications is clearly significant in selecting effective media. Organisational suppliers should make themselves aware of the different publications which cover their markets, and assess the value of individual journals. Specialist advertising agencies can offer expert advice in the selection of media, the timing of advertisements, and the integration of national press and trade press publicity. To ensure that industrial or technical advertising is seen by as many buyers as possible, copies of the publication (or 'pulls' of the advertisements) could be mailed to a selected list of customers and prospects. A reply-paid card could be included with a covering letter inviting attention to the products or services featured.

As noted in Chapter 9, the Central Office of Information (COI), the British Overseas Trade Board (BOTB) and the BBC External Services offer exporters expert advice and opportunities for publicising British products and services in overseas markets.

EDITORIAL COMMENT

In designing a communications strategy, the influence of editorial comment should never be ignored. Press releases, giving adequate information on new products, mergers, export achievements, etc., should be systematically organised either within companies or by professional public relations agencies. Many companies prepare 'press kits' which contain, for example, relevant statistics, photographs suitable for reproduction, and news about policies and specific achievements. Some distribute these after formal press conferences addressed by a senior member of the board of directors. Details of forthcoming promotional plans may be revealed. Members of the press may be invited to visit production plant and, at the company's expense, may obtain first-hand knowledge of overseas operations.

INTEGRATED SCHEME OF CORPORATE COMMUNICATIONS

All these activities are part of the scheme of corporate communications; they require careful planning and direction to ensure that publicity efforts are synchronised. Individual corporate communication problems should be analysed, so that the most effective combination of communication media may be devised. A favourable corporate image is developed only by systematic and sustained effort in the expert management of communications.

BUDGETING FOR EFFECTIVE COMMUNICATIONS

As with all products or services, costs are incurred in corporate communications. In commercial practice there are five main methods of estimating expenditure on publicity:

1. What can be afforded.
2. Percentage of sales, current or anticipated.
3. Comparative parity.
4. Objective and task.
5. Residual.

Usually, companies tend to be influenced by a mixture of these approaches to budgeting. 'Objective and task' is the most logical way of dealing with the problem (see below). Although it is not as widely practised as it deserves to be, several large US firms now use this method.

The first method rests on a subjective estimate of the value of publicity; it is arbitrary. It disregards the long-range investment of corporate communications. Essentially a play-safe strategy, it can lead to wasteful spending.

The percentage of sales method is widely used; this leads to heavy advertising when sales are high and light advertising when sales fall, which, it could be argued, is just the reverse of what should actually happen. Boom demand tends to be intensified while a slump may become even more pronounced. Fixed advertising/sales ratios may mean that too much or too little is being spent over particular time periods.

Comparative parity – or taking note of what comparable organisations spend on publicity – could equally lead to wasteful expenditure. This method assumes that competitors, for example, allocate their funds in an effective manner, and there may be no proof that they are more successful in their efforts. The costs of securing increased market share, as noted in Chapter 6, may be out of all proportion to the benefits to the organisation. It is clearly useful to know what competitors are spending on their corporate communications, but more sophisticated analyses are necessary before decisions to follow them are taken. For example, the distribution of market shares related to promotional expenditures should be carefully researched. Further, the 'promotional mix' of leading competitors should be identified and some assessment made of their overall marketing strategies.

'Objective and task' entails defining clearly the objectives of corporate communications. (See Chapter 5 and earlier discussion in this chapter.) These tasks should relate to specific targets: market-share growth, levels of awareness, changes of attitude, percentage increase in sales, distribution coverage, etc. With new products in particular, it is obviously important to make sure that promotional plans are carefully devised so that, for example, the right level and amount of information is provided to decision-makers to encourage the adoption of these innovations.

The costs of achieving certain objectives should, of course, be realistic. This approach encourages the development of managerial responsibility in the allocation of promotional funds, as well as acting as a useful framework of analysis on which to build the overall budget. In general, it is the recommended route to effective budgeting.

The residual method of funding promotional activities is the least satisfactory approach because it takes no account of the objectives of the communications strategy. It suggests a half-hearted interest in corporate communications and could frustrate the development of effective long-term plans.

Advertising ratios vary considerably over industries, with particularly strong relationships between sales and advertising in fast-moving consumer goods such as toiletries (about 15 per cent) and detergents (over 10 per cent). In industrial products and services markets, however, much lower ratios are apparent – the overall industrial ratio is just over 1 per cent. Considerable advertising expenditures relate to the public sector services covering health, social welfare and education; other compaigns are aimed to save energy, to recruit for the armed forces, etc. – apart from government aid to industry and commerce through various marketing schemes in overseas countries.

SYNCHRONISING ADVERTISING AND PRODUCT LIFE-CYCLE STRATEGIES

Products and services, as noted earlier, pass through a process of market development until diminishing returns eventually set in: the terminal stage of decline has been reached. This phenomenon appears to relate particularly to consumer products, although technological developments have resulted in many industrial products ageing, perhaps prematurely.

Communications strategies should be linked closely with the various phases at which specific products are identified in their life cycles (see Figure 10.7). In the early stages of introduction and growth, relatively heavy promotional costs may be incurred. These may be viewed as part of the development costs of new products, and as an investment recoverable over a period of one to five years. If products are protected by patents, it may be possible to spread promotional costs over several years, but with the high attrition rate which affects so many new products, the temptation to take too optimistic a view of a free run should be resisted. Patents can often be circumvented and, in any case, other innovations are likely to be marketed before long.

As a product or service approaches maturity, promotional expenditures tend to fall, and advertising is generally held at a sufficient level to extract full value (profit) as the decline stage is reached. 'Milking' the product entails maintaining demand at a level which does not tie up corporate resources that could be deployed more profitably elsewhere, e.g. in the development and marketing of new products. Overall corporate profitability is likely to be increased if the rate of decline is slowed down by carefully controlling promotional efforts.

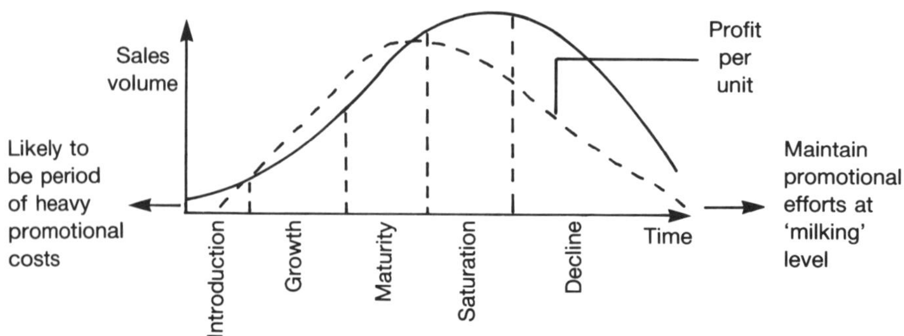

FIGURE 10.7 General relationship of product life cycle and promotional costs

In general, therefore, the intensity and content of advertising will differ according to the stage reached in a product's life cycle. Content, for example, will probably change its principal emphasis from information to persuasion and finally to 'reminder' as a product matures.

If, during the life cycle, it is decided to restyle a product, then extra promotional efforts are likely to be involved to stimulate demand. This frequently occurs with household products: superficially, these seem little changed from a generation or more ago, but they have in fact passed through several metamorphoses. The demand curve is then lifted and the product life may be extended, in some cases, for years. (See Chapters 5 and 6 on strategic planning, particularly PLC and portfolio analysis.)

LIMITED POWER OF ADVERTISING

Advertising is popularly thought to have almost unlimited power; to be some kind of brainwashing activity in which the viewer is a helpless captive. By the sheer brute force of heavy promotion, it is claimed that people can be 'forced to buy almost anything'. These fallacies are refuted by briefly examining a few classic examples of extensive promotional campaigns which failed to achieve their targets.

On 18 March 1971, Du Pont announced the withdrawal of Corfam® after losses amounting to \$250 million had been incurred. This shoe-leather substitute had been developed in the 1930s, but further activities were postponed because of the Second World War. By 1953 three departments of Du Pont were again involved in Corfam, and in 1962 a venture manager was appointed. In 1964, after extensive research and market tests, this novel product was launched and over one million pairs of shoes were sold. By 1968 over 40 million pairs of shoes were being sold in the United States alone; sales growth doubled each year until 1969, when it seemed as if a plateau had been reached.

The European Corfam campaign was not as successful as had been planned, and the Belgian finishing plant was closed down. Despite Du Pont's colossal expenditure on R&D and marketing (including heavy advertising), Corfam did not recover its investment costs in the six years it was on sale.

Significant factors which accounted for this marketing failure were partly technological and partly behavioural. During the period of Corfam's market growth, PVC became extremely popular because of its cheapness. Corfam was very durable but relatively expensive. Younger consumers increasingly preferred cheap 'throw-away' shoes, regardless of comfort, permeability and other quality attributes which Du Pont's researchers had painstakingly analysed.

Another example of the restricted power of advertising relates to part-works publications (magazines which are published in a planned series to form a comprehensive treatment of a particular subject). In 1975 Marshall Cavendish, one of the leading firms in part-works publishing, wrote off a projected 98-part weekly colour magazine about modern history, *Post-War World*, after only three issues.

About £100,000 had been spent on press, television and radio advertising, as well as £50,000 in production costs. Projected sales had been estimated at 250,000, but fewer than 100,000 copies were actually bought. The publishers ordered an immediate investigation into this 'extraordinary and unprecedented failure ... investigators are expected to find that there is little interest in that "depressed period of history" among the British public.'[31]

The British Eggs Authority once spent £150,000 (more than 10 per cent of its annual budget) on a special advertising campaign featuring National Egg Week. 'Hardly any extra eggs were sold, producers believe.'[32] People are not likely to change their consumption habits, particularly those related to food, in direct response to advertisements no matter how ingenious the promotional bombardment.

Advertising is only part of the marketing effort; it cannot force people to buy. A generation ago, tea bags were promoted widely in the UK but no significant sales resulted. Today, this product is very successful because of changed social habits, increased disposable incomes, etc. Slowly, the product overcame its original 'American' image and infiltrated into the supermarkets through being adopted widely in the catering trade.

Advertising is not a solo performer in corporate communications, nor can it sustain for long inferior products or poor service. Many advertising campaigns have been ineffectual because either the goods have not been up to expectations or they have not been delivered in time.

RESEARCH ON ADVERTISING OBJECTIVES

To obtain a clearer picture of how UK and continental companies developed their advertising strategies, and particularly how they set and evaluated their objectives, Urwick Orr and Partners researched leading firms. The number of companies using fairly sophisticated mathematical models was small, 'and even these companies were not entirely clear about what precisely they were trying to measure'. Although most consumer product firms declared that they practised advertising by objectives, such objectives were frequently expressed in elementary terms. The majority of companies marketing industrial goods admitted to having no advertising objectives at all. Banks and hire-purchase companies' advertising budgets were increasing, 'but none could point to clearly defined goals'.[33]

Even 'progressive' firms which had formulated clear advertising objectives tended to measure the effectiveness of their campaigns by irrelevant methods. One company, for instance, used psychological depth interviews to measure attitude changes, although its survey response stated its advertising objective to be 'informing the public of a product's availability'.

In general, the findings of this professional survey are not very reassuring. It is time that advertising objectives were more rigorously set, and that relevant and effective methods of assessing the impact of campaigns were developed.

Some years ago, Donald Marschner[34] investigated and analysed the advertising policies and practices of nine major oil companies in the United States which were all marketing nationally branded petroleum products. His purpose was to review the extent to which this sector of industry had adopted the practices recommended by the DAGMAR concept (Defining Advertising Goals – Measuring Advertising Results), which was a popular flow-model of advertising developed previously by Colley.[35] It should perhaps be noted that, in common with other linear models, DAGMAR theory oversimplifies the effects of advertising – fuller discussion occurs elsewhere.[11] According to Marschner:

> Traditionally, oil companies have been huge advertisers. Several of them spend between $10 and $25 million annually on advertising and sales promotion . . . nevertheless, advertising is a relatively unimportant ingredient in the typical gasoline marketing mix, simply because successful marketing depends upon doing a lot of other jobs well, too. The typical large oil company ploughs back only 1 per cent or 1½ per cent of its sales dollars into advertising.[34]

Nine major oil companies answered a lengthy questionnaire covering all aspects of advertising management. Marschner reported that the companies 'which accepted the DAGMAR theory in the early 1960s appear to be more successful than those which did not'. Eight criteria were used in this assessment: adequacy of research funds; isolation of advertising goals; goal determination in measurable terms; establishment of bench-marks in advance; advance agreement to use objective judgement; adequacy of survey methods; advertising director's attitude; and top management's attitude.

Marschner noted that there was some evidence 'to support the observation that usually advertising management seems to take its cue from top management, and that where the proper climate for objectivity has been decreed by the powers-that-be, better advertising is frequently the outcome'. Perhaps there is scope for more communication *within* organisations, so that the benefits of managerial functions like financial budgeting are more widely known and appreciated.

SUMMARY

A well-devised communications strategy contributes significantly to marketing success. Corporate personality attaches to all types of organisations; they need the support of their customers, workpeople, suppliers and the public at large. The familiarity principle applies to organisations as well as product brands.

An outline communication model has four aspects: *who*; *what*; *how*; *where*. Encoding, decoding and noise factors affect the transmission and reception of market messages. Word of mouth and opinion leadership may help or hinder a firm's marketing communications.

Major decisions to take are: to whom to say it; what to say; how to say it; and where to say it. Planning is necessary at each stage, and feedback should be organised to check that communication objectives have been achieved.

Market communications should be linked with sales efforts to ensure the economic use of marketing resources. Advertising expenditure, for example, should be related to product life-cycle stages.

REFERENCES

1. Bauer, R. A. 'The initiative of the audience', *Journal of Advertising Research*, vol. 3, no. 2, 1963.
2. Watson, David Lowe, 'Advertising and the buyer/seller relationship', *Admap*, August 1968.
3. Roper, Elmo, Foreword to Elihu Katz and Paul, F. Lazarsfeld, *Personal Influence*, Free Press, New York, 1955.
4. Katz, Elihu, and Lazarsfeld, Paul F., *Personal Influence*, Free Press, New York, 1955.
5. Lazarsfeld, Paul F., Berelson, Bernard, and Gaudet, Hazel, *The People's Choice*, Columbia, New York, 1948.
6. Dichter, Ernest, 'How word-of-mouth advertising works', *Harvard Business Review*, vol. 44, no. 6, 1966.
7. Hyman, Herbert H., 'The psychology of status', *Archives of Psychology*, no. 269, 1942.
8. Bourne, Francis S., 'Group influence in marketing and public relations', in *Some Applications of Behavioural Research*, ed. Rensis Likert and Samuel P. Hayes jun., UNESCO, 1959.
9. Hyman, Herbert H., 'Reflections on reference groups', *Public Opinion Quarterly*, fall 1960.
10. Fenton, James S., and Leggatt, Thomas R. 'A new way to find opinion leaders', *Journal of Advertising Research*, vol. 11, no. 22, 1971.
11. Chisnall, Peter M., *Marketing: A behavioural analysis*, McGraw-Hill, Maidenhead, 1985.
12. Berelson, Bernard, and Steiner, Gary A., *Human Behaviour: An inventory of scientific findings*, Harcourt, Brace and World, New York, 1964.
13. Krugman, Herbert H., 'Point of view: limits of attention to advertising', *Journal of Advertising Research*, October/November 1988.
14. Webster, Frederick E. jun., 'Informal communications in industrial markets', *Journal of Market Research*, vol. 7, no. 2, 1970.
15. Rau, Pradeep A., 'Awareness advertising and international market segmentation', *International Journal of Advertising*, vol. 6, no. 2, 1987.
16. Briggs, Asa, 'What kind of Europe – old or new?', *Advertising Quarterly*, no. 33, autumn 1972.
17. Schumacher, E. F., *Small is Beautiful: A Study of Economics as if people mattered*, Harper and Row, London, 1973.
18. Powell, Enoch, 'Truth, politics and persuasion', *Advertising*, no. 67, spring 1981.
19. Politz, Alfred, 'The dilemma of creative advertising', *Journal of Marketing*, vol. 25, no. 2, 1960.
20. Worcester, Robert, 'Corporate image research', in *Consumer Market Research Handbook*, McGraw-Hill, Maidenhead, 1973.
21. Worcester, Robert M., 'Corporate image research' in *Consumer Market Research Handbook*, ed. Robert Worcester and John Downham, Elsevier on behalf of ESOMAR, Amsterdam, 1986.
22. Hutton, Peter, 'Corporate image', in *Researching Business Markets*, ed. Ken Sutherland, IMRA, Kogan Page, London, 1991.

23. Gofton, Ken, 'A badge for the giant', *Marketing*, 24 September 1987.
24. Rawsthorn, Alice, 'Turning people on to wool', *Financial Times*, 26 January 1989.
25. Olins, Wally, *Corporate Identity: Making business strategy visible*, Thames and Hudson, London, 1989.
26. Rawsthorn, Alice, 'BT blows its new trumpet', *Financial Times*, 21 March 1991.
27. Rawsthorn, Alice, 'Mercedes wins in corporate identity', *Financial Times*, 15 March 1990.
28. Morrill, John E, 'Industrial advertising pays off', *Harvard Business Review*, vol. 48, no. 2, 1970.
29. Patti, Charles H., 'Buyer information sources in the capital equipment industry', *Industrial Marketing Management*, vol. 6, 1977.
30. Dening, James, *Marketing of Industrial Goods*, Business Publications Ltd, London, 1968.
31. 'Magazine – "A monumental failure" ', *Daily Telegraph*, 25 March 1975.
32. 'Egg Week a "fiasco" ', *Sunday Telegraph*, 17 March 1974.
33. Majaro, Simon, 'Advertising by objectives', *Management Today*, January 1970.
34. Marschner, Donald C., 'DAGMAR revisited – 8 years later', *Journal of Advertising Research*, vol. 11, no. 2, 1971.
35. Colley, Russell H., *Defining Advertising Goals for Measured Advertising Results*, Association of National Advertisers Inc., New York, 1961.

REVIEW AND DISCUSSION QUESTIONS

Q1 Suggest ways in which opinion leadership may function differently in consumer and industrial markets. How might a marketer of photocopying equipment make use of opinion leadership to develop sales in highly competitive markets?

Q2 Describe the nature and influence of 'noise' in communications strategies, and give an example of the impact of this phenomenon on the overall marketing objectives of company in an industry of your choice.

Q3 'Corporate image' is said to be influential in the successful development of an organisation. What exactly does this sometimes rather misused term mean, and in what ways can an industrial company build up a favourable image among its customers and society at large?

Q4 Choose any advertisement promoting industrial products or services which you have encountered recently, and evaluate it by the following criteria: (a) Is it clear who is being addressed? (b) Is what is being said clear? (c) Is the message conveyed persuasively? (d) Is the advertisement featured in the most appropriate medium? (This evaluation might be more effectively done on a comparative basis with advertisements from competing firms.)

Q5 What would you say are the principal differences between advertisements aimed at industrial managers and those designed to attract the interest of consumers? Give two examples of each to illustrate your opinions.

Q6 Describe the relationship between advertising and the product life cycle related to industrial goods and services.

CHAPTER ELEVEN

Strategic challenges

DYNAMIC CHANGES AND CHALLENGES

In the preceding chapters, the strategic problems and prospects facing organisations in the last decade of the twentieth century have been discussed within the framework of marketing theory and practice. Challenge and change are on all sides: the unification of Germany in 1990, followed by sensational political upheavals in eastern Europe, and the disintegration of the Soviet Empire have led to attempts to introduce more liberal political policies and some of the elements of market-orientated economics. Social, cultural and political values based on Marxist ideologies and Communist political systems have undergone fundamental reorientation; changes have been radical and far-reaching in their effects on individuals as well as organisations.

From this maelstrom, new norms of behaviour, both personal and corporate, are emerging; trading relationships with the western economies are being improved and developed, sometimes through joint venture operations. This has already happened with the German Volkswagen group's 31 per cent stake in the Czech Automobilova, which will be increased to a 70 per cent stake by 1996. VW plans to modernise Skoda's plants, introduce new models and build up sales to the West.

Another notable example of the industrial regeneration of central and eastern Europe relates to the Swiss–Swedish electrical engineering group Asea Brown Boveri, which has acquired about 20 companies and arranged joint ventures in Poland, the Czech Republic, Hungary, Croatia, Romania, Estonia and Russia. These companies, mostly former state monopolies, employ about 20,000 people, and ABB plans to double the scale of its operations in five years. Substantial programmes of capital investment and retraining of personnel are being implemented.

In 1991, Unilever bought Pollena Bydgaszcz, a large Polish detergents producer, renamed it Lever Polksa, and started a fundamental restructuring of the business, expanding its output and product ranges. This operation was stated to be 'the flagship of a plan to establish a local manufacturing and sales network in Eastern Europe on a scale equalled by few, if any, competitors'.[1]

The transformation from central planning to free-market activities is unlikely to be easy, and countries will doubtless progress at different rates. But there are already signs that the three most advanced central European countries – Hungary, Poland and the Czech Republic – which signed agreements with the EC effective on

1 March 1992, will take the lead in rebuilding trading links. Signatories to the EC Agreement (which later included Romania and Bulgaria) have committed themselves to industrial free trade, to be achieved within 10 years. However, in principle, EC countries will dismantle their barriers in five years or so.

All these historic events add to the turbulence of contemporary society and to the problems of developing satisfactory long-term business relationships. Nearly 20 years ago, it was said[2] that industrial societies can exist only in a state of dynamic equilibrium, continuously adapting to a manufactured world, and to a natural world that is changing as a result of people's actions – for example, in using up scarce natural resources. Essentially, a technologically based society has to be dynamic, and to ensure economic progress continued innovation is imperative: this is bound to bring with it changes of many kinds – new technologies, new kinds of organisation and new relationships – which are part of a learning system.

Business firms, declared Donald Schön some years back, are striking examples of learning systems: they have been 'the primary vehicles for the diffusion of innovations and therefore, in a major sense, agents of social learning for society at large'.[3] They have also been 'unsurpassed' in their ability to evolve creatively and to meet rapidly the demands of changing environments.

A learning company's strategy is essentially dynamic; it is constantly alert to new technologies, evaluating how these might enable it to offer customers better satisfaction. Unless firms are willing, as Schön advocated, to become learning organisations, they will certainly soon lose touch with their markets and suffer terminal decline.

Porter has stressed that the creation of competitive advantage is the name of the game; the companies he surveyed 'were caught up in a never-ending process of seeking out new advantages and struggling with rivals to protect them'.[4] Marketing strategists, in particular, should be fully aware of the changes which have taken place in both general and specific terms; these are likely to include economic, technological, social and psychological factors. They need, as Ansoff[5] recommends, to have wide-open 'windows of perception' on the market environments in which they trade. Vigilance is the password to success in markets, whether home or overseas. Customers are more knowledgeable and demanding; loyalty has largely eroded; suppliers are ruthlessly discarded if they fail to satisfy rising expectations; bargaining is sharper and more generally practised.

REGIONALISM

According to Drucker, internationalism is no longer Utopia: 'it is already on the horizon – but barely so. Regionalism is reality'.[6] The marked trend towards this was 'triggered by the European Community – but it will not be confined to it.' A new era of world trade based on groups of countries whose economies are bound closely together for mutual advantage has already opened. The EC, Drucker observes, started as a 'common market', 'a purely economic organisation, but it has assumed more and more political functions'. It has taken jurisdiction over many of the activities – business, social and personal – of the populations within its boundaries. Mergers, acquisitions, social legislation, professional qualifications, etc. fall within its extensive authority.

About 30 years ago, it was said, somewhat sardonically, that Europe was at sixes and sevens: the six member countries which then formed the European Economic Community (EEC), and the seven countries which made up the membership of the European Free Trade Association (EFTA). A brief account will be given of these early years of European economic groupings so that the evolutionary process, which is still active, can be readily appreciated.

EUROPEAN FREE TRADE ASSOCIATION (EFTA)

A customs union of western European countries was established in 1960, as a British initiative and in open rivalry to the European Economic Community. The original seven members were Austria, Denmark, Norway, Portugal, Sweden, Switzerland and the United Kingdom. Unlike the EEC, EFTA was unencumbered by political aspirations, agriculture was excluded, and individual members were free to pursue tariff policies towards the trade of non-member countries. The UK was able to keep its Commonwealth trading links affecting, for example, New Zealand's exports of butter and lamb. Free trade between EFTA members was achieved by the end of 1966, and all tariffs between EFTA and EEC countries were finally abolished in 1984. The UK, which had tended to regard EFTA membership as a negotiating ploy prior to membership of the Common Market, left EFTA and joined the EEC in 1973; Denmark took a similar decision. The remaining EFTA countries, augmented by Finland, have applied for membership of the European Community (EC) (see below).

EUROPEAN ECONOMIC COMMUNITY (EEC)

Popularly known as the Common Market, this organisation sprang from a grand vision of post-war Europe by Monet and Schumann, who, after the failure of the European Defence Community (EDC) scheme, sought to relaunch a European movement. In 1951 the European Coal and Steel Community (ECSC) was set up, the founder members being Belgium, France, Italy, Luxembourg, the Netherlands and West Germany. This innovative organisation's primary objective was the removal of internal barriers in the coal, coke, steel, pig-iron and scrap-iron businesses; it was later to play a major role in the reorganisation of the European coal and steel industries. The European Economic Community (EEC) together with the European Energy Community (Euratom) originated in treaties signed in Rome on 25 March 1957, the founder members being France, West Germany, Italy, the Netherlands, Belgium and Luxembourg. Since 1967 the ECSC, the EEC and Euratom have shared one European Commission and one European Council.

The interim goal of the Treaty of Rome was the establishment of a common market which imposed a greater degree of control over the trading policies of its members than the EFTA customs union did with its member countries. Common or harmonised policies in, for example, agriculture, transport, energy and indirect taxation were prominent features of the treaty. The elimination of non-tariff barriers (NTBs) was another important element of trade liberalisation policies. NTBs, which originate from many sources, are mostly directly applicable to manufacturing industry: physical barriers (e.g. customs checks); non-harmonisation of technical standards; variations in fiscal policies; and government procurement policies. The removal of technical barriers should have widespread benefits for those marketing industrial goods and services, in particular.

More ambitiously, the Treaty of Rome aimed at complete political union, a common currency and exchange rate mechanism, and the setting up of the European Court of Justice, and the European Parliament.

The Common Agricultural Policy (CAP) is the largest – and most controversial – single activity of the EEC and absorbs almost 70 per cent of its annual budget.

In 1973, as already noted, Denmark and the UK joined the EEC, which by 1987 had grown to 12 member countries: the original founding six plus Denmark, Greece, Ireland, Portugal, Spain and the UK. These countries, whose populations total over 340 million, represent the largest unified market in the developed world.

EUROPEAN COMMUNITY (EC)

In 1987 the Single European Act (SEA) was ratified by all member states of the EEC. Essentially a modification of the Treaty of Rome, it aimed to simplify and extend decision-making responsibilities and processes which had become unduly burdensome and time consuming. Differing product standards between member countries, the widespread diversity of export documentation, and differences in value added tax rates contributed significantly to the need for extensive and radical action. Well over 90 per cent of the internal barriers to the free flow of goods, services and capital had been eliminated by 1993, as the result of European legislation, although as *The Economist* acutely observed: 'Unfortunately, most governments find it easier to pass laws than to respect their letter or spirit.'[7] It is apparent that there is still much to be done before national interests are willingly abandoned in pursuit of the avowed goal of complete European integration.

EUROPE: A SINGLE MARKET

Further significant steps along the road to European unity were taken with the formal launch of the single European market on 1 January 1993. Two historic treaties had been signed in 1991. The first was the Maastricht Agreement, which established a *European Union* consisting of (a) the European Community, based on a revised Treaty of Rome and including provisions for economic and monetary union (EMU); (b) foreign and security policy; and (c) justice and home affairs. One of Maastricht's central objectives is the creation of a common European citizenship with the rights to unrestricted travel across the boundaries of member states.

Peter Sutherland, a former EC Commissioner for Competition, has stressed that 'EC membership entails the unambiguous rejection of unfettered national sovereignty and this was absolutely clear at the date of accession by the UK in 1973. The principle of the supremacy of Community law was established clearly in the 1960s . . .'[8] A perceptive critic has also commented that

> The political aspirations of the high priests of European integration are apparent in the names they use: the Brussels-based organisation started out as the European Economic Community; it then became simply the European Community, and now in the Maastricht Treaty is renamed simply the European Union. Yet the title which best matches its most unquestionable achievements is the unofficial name long used by most ordinary people: the Common Market . . . [The] antithesis between high politics and pragmatic trade liberalisation has been the most consistent theme in the running policy debate between the members of the Community, and it has regularly pitted the UK against the original Six.[9]

EUROPEAN ECONOMIC AREA (EEA)

The other notable agreement in 1991 brought the remaining members of EFTA to collaborate closely with the EC in the formation of the European Economic Area. This significant move means that 19 countries with a total population of 376 million will form a vast free-trade zone, stretching from Greece into the Arctic Circle. However, delay occurred in implementing the EEA because of Swiss voters' 'fears that it would bring a dilution of their prosperity and stability'.[10]

Under the EEA, the EFTA countries have to accept all EC regulations issued since the foundation of the Common Market in 1957. However, in some cases, such as pollution laws, individual members like Sweden already impose more stringent requirements: these are likely to influence the EC to adopt stricter laws. The EEA will give EFTA countries open access to the hugely enlarged European market; as noted already, they have applied for full membership of the EC.

EC Association Agreements, giving free access to the EC for most industrial goods and tariff reductions for most foodstuffs have been signed with Turkey (1963), Malta (1970), Cyprus (1987), Andorra (1991) and San Marino (1992).

EC POLICY-MAKING PROCEDURES

The Commission may send *proposals* – recommendations for action – to the Council of Ministers for consultation with a number of representative EC organisations, after which they may result in one of the following:

1. *Regulations*: in essence these are laws which are immediately enforceable throughout the EC without reference to national legislative bodies.

2. *Directives*: these are legally binding, but unlike Regulations, leave it to member states to decide how and when these aims are to be achieved.
3. *Decisions*: these are specific to member states, any legal entity or even an individual, and are legally binding. They relate primarily to competition policy.
4. *Resolutions*: these may relate to an opinion given to the European Parliament, or serve as a request for action. While not legally binding, they exercise considerable political influence.

THE CHALLENGES OF THE SINGLE MARKET

The dismantlement of internal barriers to trade in the EC presents managements with new opportunities for expansion; it also increases the level of competition, not just overseas but also in the home market. Industries will undergo further rationalisation in the face of dynamic international trading activities (see Chapter 8).

Europe is still in a period of transition and, although much has been accomplished, the EC has to tackle the tasks of assimilating many more countries and of influencing and managing this pan-European economic, political and social regeneration.

The single market does not mean that customers are going to shed their national characteristics and personal traits; free entry to markets also does not mean that customers will necessarily be willing to switch from established sources of supply. Marketers will need to be alert, well informed and shrewd, skilful negotiators. The impact of the single market will not be felt equally over industries or countries; it will offer particularly attractive opportunities for technologically advanced industries, such as electronics and other products and services with high value-added content.

Renault and Volvo responded to the competitive challenges and opportunities of the single market by steadily building up an alliance over three years. Following an agreement to exchange shareholdings in 1990, a joint car and truck research centre was set up in France; after this notable step, joint purchasing committees for both cars and trucks were established, and an agreement was made to exchange some car engines – this saved Renault massive development costs. In their marketing activities, the two organisations partially merged their French car and light commercial vehicles sales divisions in the early 1990s. However, the marked decline and fierce competition of the European car market led Renault and Volvo to consider converting their close working association into a merger, which was announced in September 1993.

The 50/50 alliance between would-be equals emerged as a 65/35 merger in Renault's favour,[11] and would have resulted in the sixth largest car-maker in the world and the second largest in Europe. While each company would have retained its own trademarks and brands, significant scale economies were planned by the newly created company, Renault–Volvo Automotive. The merger would have included all of Renault's operations, but only the automotive operations of Volvo, which would have continued to have marine, aero-engine and food interests. But this ambitious restructuring was suddenly abandoned because the Swedish institutions came out strongly against the Renault deal; opposition also came from Volvo's small shareholders and a growing number of Volvo's own staff. Pehr Gyllenhammer, the dynamic and long-standing chief of Volvo resigned, together with four of his fellow directors.

In February, 1994, Renault sold over half its equity holding in the Volvo parent company, their reduced stake having voting rights of 8.76%. They have also retained a 45% holding in Volvo's truck operations and 25% in Volvo's car operations. Further unravelling of the alliance involved dissolution of the joint purchasing and quality control initiatives, which had been prominent features of the merger strategy. It seems that the two companies will continue to collaborate commercially in their joint interests, without the structure of a formal alliance, as projected earlier.

In January 1993, 3M, the US multinational, instigated a fundamental restructuring of its European organisation in order to exploit fully the opportunities offered by the single market. Two principal and comcomitant steps have been involved in this reorganisation: (1) most strategic and operational responsibilities have been switched from 3M's national subsidiaries to 19 product divisions ('Business Centres') which have Europe-wide responsibility; and (2) the remaining geographic responsibilities, mostly concerned with support services such as staff development, information technology and finance, have been transferred from the smaller countries to several of 10 new European 'regions'. Three of these cover France, Germany and Italy, while the Nordic, Iberian and central European countries are now combined, as are the UK and Ireland.

A significant characteristic of this reorganisation is that regional heads rank equally with the managing directors of the European Business Centres (EBCs). This is deliberately designed to ensure that geographic managers retain their influence with EBCs, and that their expert knowledge of national preferences among their customers will be recognised when marketing strategies and tactics are being planned.

3M's 19 product divisions are dispersed over EBCs based in five countries: Belgium (where its long-established European head office is sited), France, Germany, Italy and the UK. This dispersal policy also applies within many EBCs, and inside the 33 smaller European Business Units which are integral parts of them. In the UK, for instance, the pharmaceutical EBC is based in Loughborough, and abrasive technologies, personal and environmental protection products, and photocolour systems EBCs are at Bracknell. In Germany, the telecom systems EBC is at Hamburg, while in Italy, EBCs covering printing and medical imaging systems are located in Milan.

The locations of these various EBCs and their constituent Business Units were decided by 3M on a pragmatic basis: for example, where there was already a big manufacturing facility, the relevant EBC would be located there.

3M's radical realignment of its European activities was originally projected to take up to five years. However, because of the enthusiasm of senior staff to implement the new system quickly, ensuring that they were able to build up effective new teams, it was completed in only 14 months.[12]

Courtaulds, the coatings and fibres group, announced in May 1993 that it was merging its European viscose and acrylic fibres activities with Hoechst, the German chemicals organisation. The joint venture, in which Courtaulds will be a majority stakeholder, was planned to consolidate Courtaulds' plants at Grimsby and Barcelona with the German group's activities and make them Europe's number two in the manufacture of acrylic fibres.

The British specialist engineering group TI formed a joint venture in June 1993 between its Dowty Aerospace division and Messier–Bugatti of France, which would result in the combined businesses having over one-third of the global market for medium and heavy aircraft landing gear. Plants will operate in the US, the UK and France, and the new venture will be known as Messier–Dowty, with TI having management control.

In 1990, ICI overhauled its European management structure in preparation for the single European market, and set up in individual countries 15 'national companies' – wholly owned ICI subsidiaries – together with a new organisation, ICI Europe, based in Brussels, which would be supported by six regional centres. About 18 months later, this extensive network was quietly closed down. Apparently, ICI recognised that it had overrated the potential demand from multinational customers for cross-border European sales co-ordination across its various businesses. Further, the U-turn acknowledges the need for ICI, in common with other multinationals, to simplify its structures and streamline its decision-making procedures.

American industry, typified by AT&T, the telecommunications group, is increasingly alert to global opportunities, and in May 1993 launched 'Worldsource', a set of customised international business telecoms services in direct challenge, for example, to BT. 'Worldsource' aims to create a network of partnerships with operators across the world, and has already established links in Japan, Singapore, Canada and Korea. AT&T plans to spend £230m over the next five years in developing 'Worldsource' in Europe, possibly in association with Mercury, BT's principal competitor in the UK. Already, AT&T has attracted significant interest from influential organisations.

The Japanese have been particularly vigilant about opportunities in Europe, and are already actively engaged in building up strong industrial roots. Sony, for instance, aims to achieve European self-sufficiency in colour televisions as part of its strategy of increasing production and overseas research to match the strength of its foreign sales – eight manufacturing plants in Europe make a variety of audio and video products.[13]

While the Japanese generally expect that the EC will become more protectionist, they are not too disturbed because they aim to be 'insiders'. 'The EC will become a hard shell for outsiders, so we will have to be inside', says Mr Okuhana of Toshiba.[13] Companies like Canon have also declared that their policy is to make their European activities self-sufficient in time to exploit fully the new and lucrative opportunities in Europe.

EASTERN EUROPE

After generations of centralised control, poor standards of management, low levels of productivity, comparatively little innovation, and totally inadequate investment, the countries of eastern Europe face formidable problems as they seek to catch up with the market-led economies of the West.

> There is a fierce debate about how best to reform the economies of eastern Europe and the former Soviet Union. But the goals are less often questioned; few doubt the importance of establishing a functioning market system in which industry responds to the demands of consumers rather than vice versa. The collapse of state communism, moreover, has helped undermine confidence in large bureaucracies everywhere.[14]

Extensive industrial restructuring and infrastructure development will be necessary so that these newly freed countries of eastern Europe can re-establish their economies. The nations of post-Communist Europe have started their long and arduous trek to political, social and economic freedom, and they will need encouragement and practical help from the EC and the USA in order to achieve their ambitious goals. Already, industrial growth is evident: for example, in Poland in the third quarter of 1992, industrial output increased by 7.7 per cent compared with the same period in 1991; most of this significant improvement was contributed by the private sector, which accounts for over 40 per cent of GDP and nearly 60 per cent of the labour force.[15]

Most of the countries of eastern Europe are keen to attract funds to build up SMEs (small and medium-sized enterprises), particularly those concerned with consumer products, electronics and other activities with export potential. Privatisation plans and legislation are being prepared so that ownership of the state enterprises can be passed to private investors.

Poland, the Czech Republic and Hungary (Visegrad countries) have EC Association Agreements which cover: (1) full trade liberalisation by 1999; (2) laws and rules modelled on the EC; and (3) moves towards free flow of workers, services and capital.

In January 1993, Czecholovakia experienced what has been termed a 'velvet divorce', which dissolved the federal state in a disciplined, peaceful manner and gave birth to the two independent states of the Czech Republic and Slovakia. The Czechs have seized the opportunity to accelerate privatisation and develop further business within the EC, particularly with their neighbours, Germany and Austria. Slovakia, with its less flexible industrial and commercial base, does not appear to exercise similar entrepreneurial energy. As noted earlier, the former Communist-controlled countries are attracting direct investment from major western European and Americal industry groups.

Paul Hague has wisely pointed out that eastern Europe has never been easy to research, 'requiring special language skills and people with an understanding of the formerly state-run economies'.[16] One of the related problems is the difficulty of collecting reliable central statistics.

Mini-regions may conceivably emerge;[6] some, in fact, have already done so: for example, a *Turkish Region* in central Asia and centred on Turkey; and a *Baltic Region*, to include the newly liberated countries of Lithuania, Latvia and Estonia, together with their Scandinavian neighbours, particularly Finland and Sweden. Perhaps in what was the USSR, another economic grouping might arise – so much will depend on political developments in these areas.

PACIFIC BASIN COUNTRIES

In his text on global marketing strategies, Keegan comments on the rapid rise of the countries of the Pacific Basin, especially Japan, which have outstripped the average growth across the world. 'For marketers, this means that markets *and* competition in the Pacific Basin are growing and developing more rapidly than in other parts of the world. The Japanese market, for instance, is today roughly one-half the size of the US market.'[17] While the public is generally well aware of the presence of consumer products, such as videos, televisions and motor-cycles, which originate from these countries, they are less likely to realise the extent to which several industrial market sectors are now being strongly challenged by products from these low-labour-cost economies.

In Chapter 8, it was noted that of the newly industrialised economies (NIEs) of East Asia – South Korea, Taiwan, Hong Kong and Singapore – the first-named had already attained international status in a range of moderately advanced industries; American and European multinationals have made significant investment in these strategic centres of production.

The Economist has drawn attention to the fact that the NIEs of Asia are hungry for petrochemicals and plastics: 'Already eleven non-communist countries of Asia's Pacific Rim (Japan, South Korea, Taiwan, Hong Kong, Australia and the six ASEAN countries) account for a third of the world's demand, and are expected to consume 40% by 2000.'[15] However, each Asian government is planning to build up local production centres to cope with this dramatic increase in demand. It has been claimed that, by the end of this century, gross national product of the Asian economies will be greater than Europe's and as big as North America's.

Like Porter, Peters identifies South Korea as having the greatest potential for achieving advanced status and developing national advantage in a range of important industries. He states that 'one of the most striking and important attributes of this nation is its commitment to education, reflected in a high degree of literacy and a high average level of education.'[18] The extensive system of higher education is generously supported officially and also by Korean companies.

Japanese industrial growth has been the focus of innumerable studies; the meteoric rise of Japan to become one of the world's leading industrial and commercial nations has fascinated and, at the same time, disturbed many of those who have closely observed its economic progress over the past few decades. There are, says Peters, two schools of thought about the so-called Japanese miracle: economists attribute success to consistent, conservative macroeconomic policy, while the explanations offered by sociologists and management theorists are in terms of group cohesion, life-time employment and other behavioural factors, including family traditions.

While both approaches have undoubtedly contributed to Japanese success, other more novel explanations should perhaps be considered, such as the 'unique, age-old Japanese passion for smallness, in a world where the advantages of smallness seem to be fast eclipsing the once generally perceived value of giantism'.[18] This deeply rooted Japanese trait has had significant economic consequences: for example, Sony's pioneering dedication to miniaturisation has resulted in its highly successful ranges of tape recorders, radios and VCRs. Although, as Peters comments, it was a US firm that invented the transistor and initially supplied transistors to Sony, it was the latter which first mastered the consumer applications of the technology.

Drucker[6] has emphasised the importance of the process which the Japanese call *kaizen*, which is aimed to improve a product or service so that, in two or three years, it becomes distinctly different and greatly improved. Every single step is important in leading towards the estimable goal of perfection, as inspired by the Zen tradition. Peters claims that this deeply ingrained habit is the essence of Japan's economic success; the cumulative effect of minor and continuous improvements – which may take many forms, such as miniaturization and product performance – is reflected in products and services which win acceptability in world markets. In Chapter 7, incremental improvement was seen to be a salient factor in product innovation).

In China, Japan's 'sparkling success', Peters maintains, rests on: (1) its commitment to the market (300 Japanese firms are compared with 170 US firms); (2) long-term investment in offices and service facilities in many cities; (3) the willingness of staff to learn the Chinese language, to tolerate 3–5-year assignments compared with the usual 2–4 years for Americans, and to accept less lavish accommodation – 'closer to the people' living; (4) the willingness to forgo the prospects of early profits in order to gain market share; and (5) the fact that, unlike American business operations, which are bureaucratic and legalistic, the Japanese, like the Chinese, cultivate more informal, personal bonds.

Drucker has speculated whether there will be more than one economic region in East Asia; there might be, he thinks, a region 'in which coastal China and the countries of south-east Asia coalesce around Japan'. It is feasible that the rapidly growing area of coastal China, from Tsientin in the north to Canton in the south, which accounts for about two-thirds of China's GNP, 'will establish itself as one region, with a Japanese-oriented south-east Asia as a second region. Drucker concludes that 'which way Asia will go will be among the key questions in the 1990s and in the early years of the 21st century'.[6]

NORTH AMERICAN FREE TRADE AGREEMENT (NAFTA)

In October 1992, the leaders of the USA, Canada and Mexico signed an agreement which provided for the gradual ending of tariffs and most other barriers to trade between them. Tariffs on some goods, such as agricultural products, were to be phased out over 15 years. This historic agreement, says Drucker, was triggered by the foundation of the EC and so far is purely economic in its intent, but 'it can hardly remain so in the long run'.[6]

After many months of tough political negotiations, President Clinton secured, in November 1993, the US Congress's approval of NAFTA. This agreement, effective from, 1 January 1994, will lead, over five years, to the elimination of customs duties on more than half of the 9,000 goods traded between the USA and Mexico.

In turn, Mexico will open up its highly protected financial sector and motor industry to US and Canadian companies. Mexico also hopes to attract increased inward investment through giving US and Canadian firms freedom to take profits out of the country. The implementation of NAFTA will test the political goodwill and trading flexibility of the three countries concerned. In particular, its success will be significantly affected by the stability of the Mexican economy, which does nearly 75 per cent of its trade with the USA; at the same time, Mexico accounts for around 10 per cent of the USA's total exports.

The new free-trade zone spanned by NAFTA covers a population of 370 million with a combined GDP/GNP of $6,854 bn, and directly challenges the EC's global significance based on a total population of about 340 million and GDP of £4,600m.

'OTHER' COMMON MARKETS

The EEC has been the model for common markets in other parts of the world as well as those specifically discussed: for example, the Latin American Integration Association (ALADI), the Grupo Andino (Economic Union of Andean Countries), the central American Common Market (MCCA), the Caribbean (CARICOM), and West Africa (ECOWAS). Drucker's pronouncements on the strong trend towards regionalism were quoted in the introduction to this section; from the review made of salient groupings of economies, this trend is certainly clear and appears to be irreversible.

FOUNDATIONS OF MODERN GLOBAL TRADING

The aftermath of the Second World War demanded radical restructuring of the ways in which countries carried out their economic activities. There was strong support for the view that the restrictive trading practices of the inter-war years should be abandoned, and that every effort should be made to liberalise world trade.

Three economic institutions were developed within the United Nations:

1. The *International Monetary Fund (IMF)* was established under the Bretton Woods Agreement of 1944 to promote exchange stability and to stimulate world trade by assisting countries which experienced temporary difficulties with their balances of payments.
2. *The International Bank for Reconstruction and Development (the World Bank)*, also established at Bretton Woods, was to provide capital forreconstruction following the ravages of war, to direct capital investment from the developed to the developing world and to promote expansion in world trading.
3. A projected body, the International Trade Organisation (ITO), failed to develop, and the *General Agreement on Tariffs and Trade (GATT)* was devised, in 1947, as a temporary measure, until such time as the ITO agreement could be ratified. As seems to happen from time to time, the temporary arrangement became permanent and GATT survived with these main objectives: (a) reduction in the number of tariffs and tariff rates; (b) elimination of non-tariff barriers (NTBs) and quantitative restrictions; (c) elimination of trade discrimination, as typified by the UK–Commonwealth preference arrangements; (d) easier access by developing countries to the markets of the developed countries; and (e) establishing rules of procedure governing international trade, and offering opportunities for discussion, negotiation and conciliation between member countries.

Bartlett and Ghosal[19] have stated that the protectionist trend of earlier decades was reversed as successive negotiations and agreements under GATT created an environment with fewer tariff and non-tariff barriers than had been seen since the early 1900s.

GATT, with about 110 member countries and associates accounting for over 80 per cent of total world trade, is now a well-established and influential organisation concerned with the encouragement of free-trading across the world. It is expected that, under the single market arrangements of the EC, the GATT multilateral system will be strengthened in accordance with the general concept of mutual benefits and reciprocity. Non-tariff barriers, in particular, are likely to be given special scrutiny.

GATT's second review of EC trade policies, which was issued in May 1993, was cautiously favourable; it was felt that the single market had enhanced market flexibility and improved business opportunities for both internal and external suppliers. In general, the EC was considered to have made its markets more open; fears of a 'fortress Europe' appear, so far, to be unfounded. However, some concern was expressed about the extension of preferential trading agreements, which might apply to 75 per cent of EC external trade. GATT also observed that EC agriculture generally continues to be highly protected, about 50 per cent of farm incomes being derived from price and other supports. However, the EC's commitment not to take unilateral action in pursuit of trade grievances where multilateral remedies are feasible attracted GATT's commendation. In general, GATT's second report confers a cautious and qualified approval to EC trade developments.

ORGANISATION FOR ECONOMIC CO-OPERATION AND DEVELOPMENT (OECD)

This Paris-based, intergovernmental organisation was set up in 1961 with a membership of 20 countries, including the UK, the USA and Canada, to increase the national incomes of members by 50 per cent over the period 1960–70. Today, the OECD, with around 24 members, including Japan (1963) and Finland (1968), and with special-status membership for Australia, New Zealand and the former Yugoslavia, provides data on multinationals' economic performance and publishes economic reports which are considered to be generally reliable, although some problems have been encountered in the past stemming from product/market definitions and comparable research methodologies. The OECD also publishes guidelines for multinational enterprises covering, for example, general policies, disclosure of information, competition, financing, taxation and employment policies.

The OECD's interests include long-term economic development, including science and education, and the environment.

BUSINESS AND SOCIETY

The concept and practice of business have been under searching scrutiny for some years; the activities of large corporations in particular have been ruthlessly examined by 'activist' groups which, for various motives, have energetically attacked some of the practices of industries and even individual firms.

Priorities and values are endlessly debated in the mass media as well as in private discussions. Information is no longer the prerogative of the rich, leisured or educated classes. The spontaneous optimism generated by what appeared to be the unlimited growth of industry and technological innovation over most of the western world has been shattered by the growing realisation of the problems which rapid expansion has inevitably brought with it. Threats as well as enticing prospects seem much more immediate. Some people feel that the whole system of modern technology, for instance, 'is like an uncontrollable and unpredictable juggernaut which is sweeping society along in its wake. Instead of technology serving human beings it sometimes seems to be the other way about.'[20]

Paradoxically, in some ways living is safer, but in other directions it is more precarious. Medical science has helped to prolong life and has overcome many of its illnesses; but psychological disorders have proliferated. Modern systems of transport have made the world a much smaller place, yet at the same time have brought once distant threats alarmingly near.

> It is only comparatively recently that most of us have been made aware of the fact that we live in a world of finite size and limited resources. Hitherto we have expected this finite world to provide an increasing population with an adequate

> supply of food and to satisfy its insatiable material wants in a never-ending spiral of growth.[20]

Dissident voices were few some twenty years ago; there was no 'market' for views about the disamenities of modern industrial society. Economic growth was widely believed to contain the solutions to mankind's problems: material prosperity would lead to 'the greatest happiness of the greatest number'.[21] This myth has been dismissed by many who are now beginning to count the costs of attaining some of the dubious benefits of economic progress. Mishan has acidly commented that men are unable to enjoy the present because they are restlessly pursuing 'with greed the rewards of the future'.[22] He thought that men could not escape feeling that they were but units of exploitation geared to the economic machine which grinds relentlessly on, devoid of conscience or human feeling. They are caught up in the 'whirling-dervish economy' characterised by Dennis Gabor as largely dependent upon 'the continual consumption of rapidly wearing articles'. Technology has brought to mass markets many material necessities and luxuries of life, but has also produced widespread waste and pollution.[23]

People in general live in a more sophisticated style than even a generation ago, let alone a hundred years. Many seem willing to exchange personal freedom and initiative for state-run systems of health and social welfare, which are now proving to be incapable of satisfying the heavy demands placed upon them. Large, impersonal organisations have replaced the intimate family firms which had strong ties with their customers and workpeople. Industry has become concentrated into a small number of gigantic corporations whose policies often appear to be misunderstood or mismanaged. Powerful élites in government, the trade unions and the public administration are increasingly influencing, and limiting, the personal lives of millions. Intervention in practically every aspect of industrial and personal activity by 'interested' authorities has become the norm in the mixed, controlled economy. From government ministries and town halls flows an incessant stream of exhortations, guides and threats aimed at directing and controlling the diverse activities of modern life.

Society itself is far from stable; old standards of behaviour have largely been declared outmoded. The relative roles of men and women are endlessly debated; campaigns for equality of opportunity have met with measurable success. Equal pay, which has existed in the professions for some years, has now rapidly extended to commerce and industry. Discrimination against the employment of women is now a statutory offence in the United Kingdom. In addition to personal emancipation, women have largely gained economic independence. Improved educational opportunities, the wide acceptance of birth control practices, smaller families and better health care have all helped to give women a new role in society where, as equals, they can compete with men in professional and business careers.

Life styles have been revolutionised by the advent of electronic entertainment and communication. Cultural values are disseminated widely and swiftly; consumption of many goods and services is no longer dictated by social class membership.

Rigid social stratification is not so apparent, although clearly inequalities of income, power and prestige still exist. Differences tend to rely less on money than a generation ago; better educational opportunities have given birth to the 'meritocracy' who occupy positions of influence in both the private and public sectors of the economy.

Within the short span of two generations, a new industrial state has evolved in many western countries. In the UK, socialisation of the economy was extended on a wide scale, but this creaking mechanism is now being disbanded as privatisation programmes take effect. The 'technological revolution' of the post-war era has had significant social and political impacts as well as economic consequences. Industry and commerce now operate in an environment which is overtly critical and even hostile. The parameters of management are vastly different from those which have been traditionally accepted by business and society for many years.

The concept of countervailing power in society has been noted in the United States, where the interplay of various value sources in farm life, small towns, churches, business, education and so on have shaped individual values and, in sum, the values of society. If business organisations have now reached a stage where they have unacceptable dominance in society, 'then society must restore its *countervailing* influence and business leadership must increase its ability to discern the social consequences of decisions and develop the ability to set social goals'.[24]

Participation in management decision making and in public affairs is increasingly demanded by those who live in democratic societies. As a society becomes more affluent and better educated, its members grow more sensitive to official and business policies.

Some large corporations are leading the way in accepting their responsibilities to society. Xerox has declared that its basic philosophy as a corporation is involvement in the problems of society. Employees are granted social and service leave up to 12 months, during which they may, without personal loss, 'make their contribution to a better society'.[24]

If three words could be said to mirror the mood of modern society, they might well be agitation, representation and participation. People at virtually all levels of society have quickly learned how to make their voices heard in the market-place; and the mass media have frequently encouraged the trend towards organised and articulate criticism of trading practices. Company directors should accept that their responsibilities do not stop at the balance sheet; greater skill and sensitivity in communications should be developed (see Chapter 10).

Caveat emptor, the traditional 'buyer beware' philosophy is seen as fast eroding. The most constructive consumer-orientated programme that a company could undertake would be to improve the quality of its products and its commercial behaviour.

BUSINESS ETHICS

More than 200 years ago, Adam Smith perceived that the interests of society followed naturally from the entrepreneur's concern with business success:

> Generally, indeed [the entrepreneur] neither intends to promote the public interest, nor knows how much he is promoting it, . . . by directing that industry in such a manner as its product may be of the greatest value, he intends only his own gain and he is in this, as in so many other cases, led by an invisible hand to promote an end which was not part of his intention.[25]

This is an elegantly phrased case for approving the preoccupation of business managers with running efficient organisations, from which, unintentionally, their success is shared by many members of society. Adam Smith's views reflected a mature and realistic understanding of business motivation and, at the same time, recognised that while self-interest acts as a spur to business development, the successes which may result will affect the lives of many and, indeed, may be projected as in the 'public interest'.

The chairman of Ciba-Geigy believes that, since industry is a part of society, it is affected by changing values which 'alter the framework within which enterprises exist'. Entrepreneurs should, therefore, take note of changing values and be prepared to face up to issues that are now being ventilated in, for instance, the media, about business behaviour, the use of scarce resources, the social acceptability of economic growth, etc.

> Where earlier, belief in progress and trust in the inherent meaning of the drive onward and upward imparted strength, today, questions are posed more urgently about meaningful progress . . . If short-term success were the only measure for social legitimisation of an enterprise, then I would be worried about the future of our free-market system.[26]

Sceptics take a distinctly reserved view of industry's concern with wider issues; the concept of business ethics tends to be dismissed as a contradiction in terms: an incongruous mismatch of entrepreneurial motivations and moral inhibitions. Business is about making money, which is difficult enough in today's highly competitive markets. But, says the Institute of Business Ethics, founded in October 1986 from an initiative by the Christian Association of Business Executives, and also supported by leaders of the Jewish and Islamic communities in the UK, 'Good ethics are good business, you don't have to choose between the two. You can get away with most behaviour in the short run, but you can't stay in business in the long term without an ethical approach to your product, your market and your employees.'[27]

The pragmatic approach can be contrasted with that of the 'moralists', who take the view that 'business ethics are an integral part of the individual's humanity',[27] and that no real difference exists between business ethics and personal ethics, i.e. they are inseparable and universally applicable. Professor Jack Mahoney SJ, first director of the Business Ethics Centre at King's College, London, has declared that business cannot be quarantined from ethical principles – it depends on them for its existence because it 'takes a certain level of honesty, of loyalty and respect for property granted within and without its walls. It cannot, in short, be played in a social vacuum.' Furthermore, just as business behaviour cannot be isolated from ethics, ethics cannot be quarantined from business. There must be a 'dialogue between the business community and the rest of society'.[28]

The Co-operative Bank launched an ambitious advertising campaign in 1992, which was deliberately designed to communicate the bank's ethical stance on a number of key issues, such as arms exports, environmental damage, cosmetics testing on animals, and human rights; these were found to be salient issues, from a survey of 30,000 of the Bank's 1.5 million customers. The managing director 'makes no secret that the ethical stance is designed to win new business'.[29]

KPMG International surveyed about 50 leading international financial institutions, and concluded that:

> Ethics and morality have emerged in 1989 as posing a real challenge to the chief executive officers of banks, and, in a different way, to those of security houses ... Insider dealings, problems with Chinese walls, drug money, commission payments to intermediaries and politicians, and lending to the 'wrong' regimes, are all causes of criticism in the industry.[30]

It is, perhaps, easier to be ethical when the temptations of high rewards seldom, if ever, arise; scruples may be suppressed when lucrative opportunities occur readily, as the notorious City scandals of recent years have sadly shown.

In 1992, Digital published a survey[31] of 429 UK managers across a broad spectrum of industry and commerce, which revealed that 82 per cent understood the importance of corporate values to the success of their organisations, including overall profitability. The report stressed that corporate values 'literally permeate and influence continuously every stage of the business process. Values in this context mean those shared beliefs and convictions which really do govern people's behaviour.' (See also the discussion in Chapter 5 on basic corporate values and mission statements). The linkages between corporate values and ethical issues are apparent. Values, explicit or otherwise, come from top management, which have the responsibility of 'clarifying and sharpening' them, and ensuring that they are well understood throughout their organisations, and that they are reflected in the behaviour of staff at all levels.

All members of an organisation should know the difference between acceptable and unacceptable behaviour – which is more than 'just knowing the law'.[32] Leadership in these matters should come from top management; otherwise, misconceptions and even malpractice may arise.

Nynex, the 'Baby Bell' company serving the north-eastern USA, received extremely unfavourable publicity as the result of 'wild, lewd parties thrown in Florida in the 1980s' by employees; this crisis led to a fundamental review of its business ethics. Nynex's chairman stated that the company was interested in ethics not because it was trying to create an 'ethics society or subculture' at the company, but because it was 'trying to make ethical behaviour an everyday norm ... basically, we believe ethics makes good busines sense'.[33]

The company implemented a five-part programme of recovery: (1) outside experts were appointed to see where corporate behaviour needed to be improved; (2) an office of ethics was set up at headquarters, run by a senior executive with direct access to the chairman and responsible to the board's audit committee; (3) similar offices were established in each of Nynex's business units – these had 'hot lines' to report misconduct; (4) a single code of business conduct was devised to replace differing codes in separate business units; and (5) company-wide training in business ethics was organised. Despite early sceptical responses and as the training programme progressed, 'participants began to discover that there were many grey areas in their work that needed clarification'.[33]

A survey[34] by the Institute of Business Ethics in 1992 indicated that 29 per cent of 164 leading British companies had a written ethical code in 1991 compared with 18 per cent in 1987. Of these, only about two-thirds had codes which adequately detailed policies, examples and actions to be taken, and only a very small number showed that they applied any method of evaluating the effectiveness of their policies in practice.

In 1988 Edinburgh University published a survey[35] which indicated that 42 per cent of 74 respondents from the top 200 companies which were sampled stated that they had 'a written code of ethics of some sort, setting down the company's approach towards employees, shareholders, consumers, the environment or society at large'. Only four companies, however, referred to the document as a 'code of ethics'; various other titles were used. Guidelines were used, some quite detailed, covering a range of issues, such as share dealing, hospitality and attitudes towards the environment.

The Institute of Business Ethics gives the following reasons why ethical codes are becoming more widely adopted in Britain: (1) recognition by companies of the need to be seen by shareholders as ethical; (2) response to pressure from graduate recruits; and (3) response to peer pressure from competitors, as a growing number embrace ethical policies. It seems, says the IBE, that good practice always advances by a mixture of altruism and self-interest.[34]

The British subsidiaries of North American companies are reported to take the subject of business ethics most seriously. For instance, Unisys has a full-time corporate ethics officer who, with a small staff, is responsible for monitoring and enforcing standards and organising an extensive training programme.[35]

At the instigation of the accountancy bodies and the London Stock Exchange, the Committee on the Financial Aspects of Corporate Governance was officially formed in 1991, and a year later published its report, which was 'presented as a draft for public comment'. This included a 19-point code of practice covering the following main areas: responsibilities of boards of directors; the role of executive directors; the role of non-executive directors; and accounting controls and reporting mechanisms. The code is voluntary and the spirit is essentially one of self-governance – no new company legislation is envisaged. The report attracted some sharp criticisms for its alleged lack of teeth, dependence on a voluntary code, and tendency to vagueness in some of its views.[36]

Business ethics, it has been said,[37] have become a growth industry since Robert Maxwell and others decided that the difference between their money and that in their businesses belonging to others was too trivial to bother them. Voluntary codes, which have sprouted like mushrooms, are clearly limited in their power; no code of business ethics is likely to inhibit those who subscribe to a 'greed is good' morality.

But apart from financial skulduggery, there are other aspects of business ethics which deserve consideration. A particularly sensitive ethical problem arose, for instance, when the chief executive of the US conglomerate Tenneco learned that he had a brain tumour. Michael Walsh decided to make a complete and immediate disclosure to securities analysts and the press. His action gained the strong approval of many US lawyers and management consultants. It should be added that, under US securities law, publicly quoted companies are obliged to disclose facts 'material' to their businesses. In making his dramatic statement, Mr Walsh observed: 'Little deceptions become big deceptions. Pretty soon all your energies are going into managing the problem, not the business.'[38]

Ethical behaviour also extends to relationships with suppliers, e.g. paying bills within a reasonable time period; to standards of negotiation with customers, particularly in certain overseas countries where bribery and corruption are virtually everyday practice; to staff relationships, including health and safety provisions; to customers who buy products in the expectation of good value for money, safety in use, etc.; and to communities, both adjacent to factories and more distant, who may be affected, for example, by industrial pollution. A further area of ethical responsibility concerns relationships with competitors, which was highlighted by the alleged 'dirty-tricks' campaign waged by British Airways against its rival, Virgin Atlantic.

Ethical behaviour in business expands the responsibilities of management; decisions involving ethics permeate an organisation. Most businesses do not face major ethical dilemmas, and conduct their day-to-day transactions without dramatic problems of this kind arising. But this does not mean that ethical issues do not exist – they may not be perceived or recognised. Examples are the ways in which health and safety regulations are observed in small workshops, where employees may not be in a position to bargain for improved working conditions; deliberately failing to keep vehicles properly maintained so that they become potential hazards to drivers and the public; and tolerating slackness in industrial processing, which may lead to the escape of noxious fumes or other pollutants – this particular aspect will be discussed more fully in the next section.

In the USA, courses on business ethics have been run for some years at, for example, the Harvard Business School and New York's Columbia University Business School. The former offers a nine-session non-graded module: Decision-making and Ethical Values; ethical aspects of corporate behaviour are also included in accounting, marketing and other business programmes through case studies. Inputs on business ethics are made by leading UK business schools, such as London, Manchester and Warwick. *Business Ethics: A European review* is published by

Blackwell, and in the USA, the *Journal of Business Ethics* (Kluwer) is now in its twelfth volume. In 1991 the Co-operative Bank endowed a chair in corporate responsibility at Manchester Business School, and in 1993 Mr Stanley Kalms, chairman of the Dixon's group of electrical goods retailers, donated £1m to the London Business School for a chair in business ethics and social responsibility. This chair will be held by Professor Jack Mahoney SJ, former principal of Heythrop College, University of London and, as noted earlier, founder director of the King's College Business Ethics Research Centre. In addition to the chair, Dixon's bequest will enable a research and teaching programme in ethics and responsibility to be organised.

ENVIRONMENTAL ISSUES

ECONOMIC USE OF SCARCE RESOURCES

The extraction and use of scarce natural resources by modern industries has alarmed many who have studied trends over the past decades. The dire prospect that at present rates of consumption the world's supply of several vital natural resources, such as minerals and oil, will soon be exhausted has become the focus of attention of scientists, technologists and diverse range of professional experts, apart from catching the headlines of the mass media.

Various estimates have been published of the likely life of available resources; the period of time during which basic metals like copper, lead and zinc will be available has been projected as less than 50 years. Controversy exists about the methods by which some of these statistics have been computed, but there is general alarm about the contemporary rates of extraction and the reserves which are known to exist at the present time.

Even if mining exploration and extraction techniques can add substantially to the world's supply of strategic raw materials, political and economic factors have intervened dramatically and prices have soared.

The concept of *sustainable development* has been promoted zealously by many organisations and individuals for some years. One of the problems, however, is general agreement on what constitutes sustainable develoment and how this creed can be put into practice.

The World Bank's report on development and the environment defined sustainable development as 'development that lasts', and stated that the key to growing sustainably is not 'to produce less but to produce differently'. It asserted that the link between economic growth and the environment depends on four factors: (1) *structure*: the goods and services produced; (2) *efficiency*: the quantity of inputs per unit of output; (3) *substitution*: the ability to substitute for scarce resources; and (4) *technology and management*: the environmental damage per unit of input or output.[39]

A sustainable development strategy is projected as having three elements: (1) *build on positive links*: appropriate energy prices, for example, will also improve the environment; (2) *break the negative links*: introduce appropriate incentives and discentives; and (3) *clarify and manage uncertain links*: where the consequences of human activity are unknown, the response should be the search for information, combined with precautionary measures.[39]

However, these rather neatly stated approaches have to be put into practice in real and imperfect market conditions where, for instance, entrenched vested interests are active; there is also the likelihood of value judgements being used to assess the welfare of future generations against economic advantages for those living today.

RECYCLING OF MATERIALS

Reclamation and recycling of many materials have developed to a level hitherto unknown. Ferrous metals have consistently relied on reclamation, with recycled material representing about 50 per cent of new production. Also, almost half of the non-ferrous metals used in the UK are now derived from recycled scrap. In the paper industry, recycling is now an important activity which is expected to develop still further as woodpulp prices continue to spiral. Lubricating oils are now being reprocessed after use, and although so far representing a minuscule proportion of total oil sales, there are indications that this commercial activity will extend significantly. Because the raw materials in glass represent only about 13 per cent of the finished product, there is no great economic incentive for the manufacturers to reclaim glass containers, etc. However, recycled glass accounts for about 22 per cent of new production of glass containers. 'Bottle banks' are evident in some towns and, presumably, apart from their economic purpose, also fulfil a valuable public relations role for the glass industry.

Recycling saves a large proportion of the energy needed to manufacture a product from original raw materials: there is, for example, a 62 per cent energy saving in the case of recycled scrap ferrous metal, a 96 per cent saving in the use of recycled aluminium, and a 63 per cent saving in the use of scrap zinc.[40]

In addition to significant savings in energy consumption, recycled materials have other important advantages: they are cheaper than new materials; they avoid the dumping of large quantities of used materials in land-fill sites; and, most of all, they reduce dependence on finite natural resources.[39]

Over recent years, several industries have realised that they must accept responsibilty not only for the manufacture and marketing of their products, but also for arrangements to recycle these in due course. In 1989 the Aluminium Can Recycling Association was set up by five leading manufacturers (three in the USA, one in France, and one in Germany) to promote the recycling of aluminium beverage cans across Europe and North America. British Alcan also announced in 1989 that it was building Europe's first can-recycling plant near Warrington, Cheshire.[41]

The Industry Council for Electronics and Electrical Equipment Recycling was formed in the early 1990s by electronics companies such as Hewlett-Packard, IBM,

ICL and BT, retailers like Thorn–EMI Rehtals and Boots, and waste disposal experts such as Mayer Cohen, Mann and the Bird Group (representing the recycling industry). The association developed as result of a report by the Centre for Exploitation of Science and Technology (CEST) about end-of-life electronics. It was predicted that six million items of electronic equipment (old televisions, photocopiers, personal computers, radios, toasters, etc.) would be dumped into British land-fill sites by 1995. It is hoped to make electronics recycling a commercial proposition.[42]

At Venray in Holland, where Rank Xerox has its European distribution base, old photocopiers which have been collected from its customers are stripped down and thoroughly cleaned, and the components processed for re-use. 'Remanufactured' machines are offered at 80 per cent of the cost of a new machine to those customers who are content not to have the latest technology. This pioneering strategy anticipates new European environmental legislation which may require all electronics manufacturers to re-use old components. Other companies are planning to tackle the problems associated with redundant products: Canon, for instance, intends to establish a remanufacturing plant in Scotland.

It was reported[43] in 1992 that BMW had teamed with a vehicle salvage company specialising in German executive cars in the UK's first dedicated car dismantling and recycling plant. Eventually, this operation should handle 2,500 cars per annum, and a network of 15 is planned for the UK.

The Rover Group has announced a full recycling programme in co-operation with the Bird Group, one of Europe's largest materials reclamation and recycling concerns. VW, Mercedes, Fiat and other leading car manufacturers have also set up or are planning recycling operations in expectation of EC-wide legislation governing car scrapping and recycling.

The packaging industry, with its extremely wide range of products, has a particularly noticeable impact on the environment. Glass-bottle banks, as already noted, are now fairly well-established features of urban areas; used plastics packaging and aluminium cans are now likewise collected. Biodegradable containers may eventually almost replace traditional materials, but meanwhile members of the packaging industry have a daunting task as they seek technical solutions which will also be acceptable to the many organisations – environmental groups, health and safety officials, etc. – interested in specific aspects of their products.

The disposal of waste materials is becoming increasingly complex. In Germany, for instance, if the packaging has a green dot, it is placed in a special yellow bin and not the usual black container. However, this sophisticated arrangement has suffered a setback, because the Duales System Deutschland (DSD), the nation-wide rubbish collection enterprise which operates the green dot system, is under investigation by the Federal Cartel Office.[44]

France has set up an 'ecoemballage' scheme – still in its infancy – which 'requires municipalities to collect packaging products already marked out for sorting'; so far, however, the French do not appear to have acquired the habit of sorting their own rubbish. Arthur D. Little, the US management consultancy group, is reported to be devising DSD-type organisations for the 'more orderly Austrians'.[44]

Some concern has been expressed about the threatened large-scale export of waste products from some European countries for processing in, for example, the UK, and the impact that large shipments would have on the stability of the market for home-based salvage schemes is being evaluated.

SUBSTITUTION OF SCARCE SUPPLIES

High prices and the difficulty of obtaining regular supplies of basic natural materials have encouraged many manufacturers to use substitute materials that are cheaper and readily available. Plastic mouldings, for example, have replaced brass fittings; chipboard is widely used in place of wood. In some cases it is not technically feasible to replace natural materials, e.g. silver for photographic emulsions. With some kinds of substitution, problems tend to be compounded because a new level of demand is created for materials such as plastics, products of the petrochemicals industry, which derive from limited world reserves of oil or natural gas.

Some of these problems may be solved by a more intelligent and integrated approach to product design, including the application of value analysis (see the discussion later in chapter).

ENVIRONMENTALISM

A generation ago, Levitt observed: 'When Pittsburgh's steel mills shut out the sun at high noon 30 years ago, the need for pollution control was obvious. But there was no market then; nobody thought of doing anything about the smog, even though techniques for controlling it were available.'[45]

Eventually, however, public interest in 'the environment' began to arise; this emerging preoccupation was spotted by the mass media, which, ever keen to espouse popular causes, soon discovered that atmospheric pollution, oil and chemical spillages, industrial effluents, ozone depletion and the destruction of marshlands and rain forests – to name but a few of the many issues involved – had become newsworthy. Journalists assiduously unearthed information, for example, about sulphur dioxide and nitrous oxide emissions from coal-burning and oil-burning power stations, which result in acid rain not only in the UK but further afield, as in Norway.

Today, virtually everyone in developed countries is aware of the impact of the twin philosophies of 'consumerism' and 'environmentalism' on the decisions taken by politicians, industries, public authorities, etc. Lobbying has become the norm in contemporary society: legislation and public opinion have developed a symbiotic relationship which has resulted in dramatic changes in attitudes and behaviour towards, for instance, the use of fossil fuels and water pollution. The European Commission has actively pursued policies aimed at achieving common standards of environmental protection, and further measures affecting, for example, vehicle exhaust systems are planned.

The decline of the smoke-stack industries in developed countries has, of course, contributed to the generally improved quality of air. On the other hand, the rapid growth in road traffic has now become a major source of urban pollution, aggravated by traffic congestion in city and town centres across the UK and elsewhere. Vehicle exhausts spew out carbon monoxide, oxides of nitrogen and hydrocarbons; and in sunshine, the latter two are involved in photochemical reactions which form secondary pollutants.[46] The car industry, stimulated by rising public expectations as well as legislation, has introduced catalytic converters which help to reduce environmental pollution. Millions have been spent on developing feasible versions of an electric car; GM, Ford and Chrysler are co-operating closely in such a venture, watched with great interest by metal producers who foresee prospective new markets for lead and nickel.[47]

The chemical industry has also attracted considerable and largely unfavourable attention over recent years; the phenomenon of 'chemophobia' has been used to describe the almost spontaneous negative response that occurs when the industry and its products are mentioned.[48]

Following a disastrous fire, in November 1986, at a chemicals warehouse operated by Sandoz, 30 tonnes of toxic waste were discharged into the Rhine. The effects of this calamity were widespread, reaching France, Germany and the Netherlands, and pressure was put on the Swiss chemicals and pharmaceuticals industry to improve its pollution control procedures. Ciba-Geigy, Sandoz and Roche, the major firms whose factories lie on both sides of the Rhine at Basle, have had to incur massive expenditure on improving their production facilties. Ciba-Geigy, which because of its size is responsible for larger volumes of chemical waste than either Sandoz or Roche, spent over £100m on environmental protection in the Basle area in the decade up to 1989, and a similar cost will be incurred over the next 10-year period.[49]

Ciba-Geigy's chairman has stated that 'It will no longer be sufficient to have good products, and efficient organisation, and a strong balance sheet . . . you have to win the acceptance of the people who live near your plants. People will have to believe in your professional competence and your ability to handle technology.'[50] Instead of focusing on 'end-of-pipe' solutions, i.e. removing and destroying harmful chemicals in effluents, Ciba-Geigy has declared that it is increasingly aiming for process improvements, so that toxic waste is minimised. Where this has not been possible, the company has withdrawn, for environmental reasons, certain products from the market.[49]

In Germany, the giant chemical companies – Bayer, BASF and Hoechst – have also faced strong adverse criticism and, like the Swiss and others, have had to take radical steps to improve their production processes, which for generations have heavily polluted the environment.

In the USA, the Superfund Amendments and Reauthorization Act (SARA), passed in 1986, required companies to report their emission levels of 300 chemicals. Until 1984, Dow had never actually tallied up its pollutants, and when, under duress, it along with 85 other chemical companies did so, it 'discovered that the company was releasing 10m pounds of dangerous chemicals into the environment'.[51] As the result of substantial investment and concerted efforts, Dow cut emissions and pollutants by more than 50 per cent.

It has been said[51] that, like zero defects, zero discharge is not a task that can be completed quickly – it is an objective, perhaps never entirely achieved, which indicates, however, the need for continuous improvement.

In November 1990, ICI announced[52] plans to double environmental expenditure to £1bn world-wide over the next five years, with the intention of cutting output of all wastes, particularly those of a hazardous nature, by at least 50 per cent by 1995. All new ICI plants will be built to standards likely to be encountered in the most environmentally demanding country in which they operate the processes in question. Like Ciba-Geigy, ICI will gradually switch its environmental control efforts from end-of-pipe measures to changes in manufacturing processes.

CFCs (chlorofluorocarbons), used in the production of plastics, pesticides, refrigerants, packaging and pharmaceuticals, have caused great concern to environmentalist groups, such as Friends of the Earth, and Greenpeace, which have campaigned consistently for the phasing-out of this environmentally harmful chemical compound. Scientific evidence has shown that CFCs damage the ozone layer, exposing the earth to cancer-inducing radiation.

ICI, once one of the world's major producers of CFCs, has invested heavily to develop alternatives to CFCs, such as HFC134a, which does not harm the world's ozone layer because it contains no chlorine, being a hydrofluorocarbon. But HFC134a is opposed by environmentalists on the grounds that it may exacerbate the greenhouse effect.

Du Pont, which has also been actively engaged in developing alternatives to CFCs, including HFC134a, has accelerated the phasing-out of CFC production in developed countries.[53]

Another large corporation, AT&T, the US telecommunications and electronics group, took an important step in 1988 in phasing out CFCs. It started to use an alternative and biodegradable solvent called Bioact EC-7 in its electronic circuit board factories and offered the technical know-how to other electronics companies. AT&T's pioneering action was warmly praised by environmentalist groups and by the US Environmental Protection Agency.[54]

In 1988, eight large manufacturers of toiletries operating in the United Kingdom – Beecham, Carter Wallace, Colgate–Palmolive, Cussons, Elida Gibbs, Gillette, L'Oréal, and Reckitt and Colman, accounting for 65 per cent of British sales of toiletry aerosols, agreed to phase out by the end of 1989 all aerosols containing chemicals which damage the ozone layer.

In February 1993, Candy, the Italian group making white goods, announced the introduction of what it claims to be the world's first mass-produced refrigerators which use HFC134a – two years ahead of the EC's requirement to phase out CFCs.

One of the problems about CFC usage is that existing systems, designed to use this compound, cannot use any known alternative as a direct, drop-in replacement without modification or redesign.[53]

The Swedish-based group Electrolux invested the equivalent of £4.6m in 1989, and was able to remove half of the CFC content from the insulation used in its ranges of freezers and refrigerators. This significant step was regarded as the first on the way to total elimination of CFCs from its products. Volvo also plans to abandon the use of CFCs in the plastics and cooling systems used in its cars. The Swedish Pulp and Paper Association admitted that its industry has been forced to develop environmentally friendly products, like bleach-free coffee filters, nappies, food packaging and handkerchiefs, because of pressure from customers who have been influenced by the activities of environmental pressure groups.

In 1992, ICI opened up a plant at Billingham in north-east England to produce Biopol, the first fully biodegradable commercial plastic, which is made in an industrial fermenter by bacteria that convert sugar (refined from corn or beet) into a polymer. A cheaper source of basic ingredients could be genetically engineered potatoes. Initial production is 300 tons per annum: this necessarily affects costs, which are higher than its petrochemicals equivalent. However, it is claimed that bioplastics will become more economic through scientific and technological developments. 'Farming for plastics could then grow into a large agri-business.'[55]

Large industrial groups have clearly made significant contributions to solving some of the problems of pollution which, for long, have been regarded as inevitable for economic progress. While their activities have not been entirely altruistic and seem at times to bear the imprint of late converts, they are now generally alert to the need to do more than legislation demands in the fields of environmental protection, health and safety procedures, etc.

This change of heart is reflected in comments by the head of the international division of Du Pont: 'For much of our reputation we have to blame ourselves as an industry. We haven't done enough to say how well we are doing economically and to talk about some of the good things we do . . . Public concern about chemicals is often based on ignorance.'[56] Perhaps the public's earlier attitudes are understandable, particularly when, in 1983, the chairman of the Dow Chemical Company stated: 'We play our cards close, maybe because we have a high regard for the value of technical information. We don't back down easily or compromise. We are perceived as prickly, difficult and arrogant.'[57] He admitted, however, that there was need to improve their public image, which had suffered from their traditional entrenched attitudes.

The Chemical Industries' Association in the UK conducts regular surveys of public perceptions of the chemical industry. In 1987, it found that less than one-third of people held favourable views of the industry, and nearly half thought it did not care about the environment. Over 90 per cent were concerned or very concerned about chemical pollution, while over three-quarters felt that the industry seriously damaged the environment, and more than eight out of ten respondents worried about plant safety.[58]

Tom Burke, director of the Green Alliance, has declared that three social forces interact to sharpen the difficulties facing industry as a whole: 'the growing strength of the pressure groups, the emergence of the green consumer, and the political maturing of the environment as an "issue".'[58]

A survey of the British public's interest in 'green issues', made in 1989, found that 42 per cent claimed to have consciously chosen one product over another for environmental reasons – specifically because of environmentally friendly packaging, formulation or advertising.[59] The range of products investigated related to personal care, household duties and food.

In 1990 the Cranfield School of Management[60] surveyed the 'green' policies of 200 small companies in the UK, of which 34 per cent were in the manufacturing sector, just over two-thirds were more than five years old, and 39 per cent had annual turnovers above £2m. From the findings it is apparent that green issues have not yet made much impact on small businesses in general. For example, 81 per cent of all firms stated that they produced no pollution of any kind, hazardous or otherwise; 49 per cent said that they took almost no measure to protect the environment, but 16 per cent reported that they took 'a lot of energy conservation measures'; 75 per cent of manufacturing firms and 60 per cent of non-manufacturing firms supported no environmental projects or organisation, although 43 per cent of manufacturing and 54 per cent of non-manufacturing firms rated green issues as very important for the world at large. Only 13 per cent of manufacturing and 10 per cent of non-manufacturing companies considered environmental issues when selecting suppliers. However, the findings may not be entirely factual because only 14 per cent of manufacturers and 8 per cent of non-manufacturers had actually conducted environmental audits to establish levels of pollution and energy wastage.

ENVIRONMENTAL AUDITS

These involve systematic examinations of companies' activities, such as measures to control or eliminate pollution or recycling of waste products, and are becoming standard practice in many large companies in the USA, where stringent regulations on environmetal safeguards are being enforced by authorities like the Environmental Protection Agency. As noted earlier, the Superfund Amendments and Reauthorization Act (SARA) requires companies to report emission levels of 300 chemicals. Further, the widespread recourse to litigious remedies has caused American companies to be wary about environmental issues in general, so as to avoid costly law suits. Environmental law in the USA is now big business; law firms have grasped this new opportunity to add to their very profitable activities. Insurance companies are reported[61] to have either refused to write policies or greatly increased premiums on pollution-sensitive plants which do not operate an audit.

In 1991, Dow Chemical founded a Corporate Environmental Advisory Council, with up to 14 members from around the world who will meet periodically. Dow's president has stated that 'the public has a right to know what we are doing and a right to contribute to our decision-making process'.[62]

Many large European companies have adopted environmental auditing. Like their American counterparts, Pilkingtons is facing up to the effects of more rigorous environmental legislation and the huge liabilities that might be incurred as the result of serious environmental disasters. Such firms are also more sensitive, as we have seen, to unfavourable media comment and public opinion on their pollution record.

Shell instigated, in 1990, an environmental audit of its various business activities so that specific action could be taken. National Westminster Bank, with Coopers Lybrand Deloittes, also undertook, in the same year, an environmental audit of its entire domestic operations; this thorough investigation covered property management, information technology, vehicles, supplies, waste management, etc. Apart from the useful economies which resulted, NatWest felt that the exercise gave it a valuable insight into the practical problems associated with environmental pollution. It has adopted a policy of examining its business customers' environmental record when considering their applications.[63]

In April 1992, the British Standards Institution (BSI) launched a new environmental management standard, BS7750, which indicates the systems and procedures necessary for a sound environmental performance. BS7750, like the quality standard BS5750, can be verified by external assessors.

Business in the Environment (BIE), founded in 1992 by Business in the Community (BIC) and the accountants KPMG Peat Marwick, produced a set of case histories to illustrate particular aspects of environmental problems and policies. The EC is also active in this area of environmental auditing and has drafted 'Eco-Audits'.

The UK Association of Environmental Consultancies approved, in 1993, a code of practice to regulate the activities of its members in the rapidly growing consultancies offering advice. As in the USA, there has also been a dramatic increase in the number of lawyers engaged in environmental issues.

Effective environmental management must now be regarded as one of the burgeoning responsibilities which organisations of many kinds have to accept. Business directors and managers cannot just keep their heads down and hope it will all blow over and soon be forgotten. New standards of corporate responsibility are now demanded on all sides. 'The environmental movement is not at odds with corporate interests; it is at odds with the slow pace of inevitable corporate change. The challenge for environmentalists is to make their case in a language managers can understand. The challenge for managers is to listen.'[51]

Environmental concern has also given attractive opportunities for companies specialising in pollution-control products and services, e.g. catalytic converters, electronic monitoring equipment, and filtration systems. The Centre for Exploitation of Science and Technology estimated, in 1991, that the UK would spend £140bn, the EC £860bn, and the USA £1,060bn in pollution-control technology. Extensive markets also exist in the newly industrialising economies; these will require professional expertise in addition to technical equipment. A few British water companies are already active in these areas, and as these developing countries tackle their environmental problems, further help will be needed.

STRATEGIC IMPORTANCE OF QUALITY AND DESIGN

TOTAL QUALITY MANAGEMENT (TQM)

Of the many management theories which have been introduced and zealously promoted over the post-war years, total quality management (TQM) has been one of the most enduring. Despite its critics, it has stood the test of time, largely, perhaps, because of the essential simplicity and relevance of its philosophy: that quality could be measured and therefore improved.

The pursuit of quality in manufacturing has been followed with messianic fervour over many years by W. Edwards Deming, Joseph Juran and Armand Feigenbaum, who laid the foundations of TQM theory. Deming and Juran were statisticians at Western Electric's Hawthorne plant who had developed statistical control techniques; Feigenbaum was head of quality at General Electric Company in the USA, and responsible for the term 'total quality control'. Deming argued that all processes 'are subject to some level of variation that is likely to diminish quality. Therefore, every process, whether it involves people or machines, is only as good as mangement's ability to control the levels of variation.'[64] Later, he was to extend his professional interests to the wider fields of management development, which he crystallised in 14 guiding precepts; among these was the need to break down barriers between departments so that people in different functions of a business work together to tackle common problems.

These American pioneers introduced, in the early 1950s, the theme of quality and the principles of quality control to the Japanese, who were faced with the problems of fundamental restructuring and redirection of their production efforts after the Second World War. Much of Japan's impressive economic regeneration and industrial growth has been attributed to the powerful influence of TQM theory. In 1951 the Japanese Union of Scientists established the Deming Prize, which has stimulated many major Japanese companies to focus on improving standards of quality, training and statistical systems of control. Through the next three decades, Deming, Juran and Feigenbaum continued to guide Japanese industrialists as they aimed to revolutionise their standards of production. Juran, for example, produced in 1951 a notable innovatory text, the *Quality Control Handbook*, as a result of which he was invited to give a series of lectures in Tokyo on this vital topic. Following this significant event, he developed long-lasting links among Japanese industrialists who, he said, were fully prepared, at top management level, to commit themselves and their companies to acquiring expertise in the management of quality.[65]

Meanwhile, the radical improvements in Japanese products aroused little interest among western companies, who seemed to suffer from widespread complacency. Deming was virtually unknown in the USA, until in 1980 he featured in a television documentary, 'If Japan, why can't we?' which described the competitive challenges now offered by Japan. Startled by his hard-hitting observations, some major US corporations, including Ford, contacted Deming and engaged his consultancy services. Ford's corporate objectives, relationships with suppliers, training programmes, and new compensation and bonus plans were influenced by Deming's 14-point scheme.[64]

In 1983, Xerox in the USA and Rank Xerox in Europe were also been stirred by the growing threat to their copier market from Japanese products. After carefully analysing the nature and extent of the competitive challenge, the two companies launched a comprehensive quality programme, which has enabled them to counter the decline in their market shares. Other leading companies, such as IBM, AT&T and GE have also espoused TQM.

In 1987 the Malcolm Baldrige National Quality Award was set up; two awards a year are made in each of the three categories: manufacturing, service and small business. Companies which nominate themselves for a Baldrige Prize – named after a US Commerce Secretary who died in a rodeo accident – submit applications detailing their quality practices and performances; those selected are scrutinised by a visiting team of examiners. Points are awarded under seven categories as follows: customer satisfaction, quality results, human resource development and management, management of process quality, leadership, information and analysis, and strategic quality planning. Particular emphasis is placed on acknowledging that the customer is the most important judge of a company's quality.

Critics have argued that the Baldrige scheme, unlike the Deming award which inspired it, lacks a coherent philosophy, the criteria being merely broadly descriptive rather than prescriptive. However, the US award is defended because it has succeeded in alerting management to the need for TQM. Motorola, a Baldrige award-winning company, has definite views about the advantages to be derived from commitment to quality management throughout a business: 'The difference between the alert business leader's attention to quality today versus 10 years ago is like night and day.'[66] Motorola claims that TQM has saved it millions in its manufacturing operations.

Not everyone, of course, is convinced about the virtues of TQM; to some degree it may be suffering from a backlash from the early heady days of its introduction, when over-enthusiastic claims were made by zealous converts to the theme of quality management. A survey of 500 US manufacturing and service companies by Arthur D. Little revealed that only a third felt that the TQM programmes significantly influenced their competitiveness.

In the UK, A.T. Kearney conducted a similar study of over 100 British firms. While 80 per cent of quality programmes were reported to have no tangible benefits, it was also suggested that most of these programmes failed because of the lack of realistic goals which were capable of being measured against well-defined criteria. It was recommended that, to be successful, TQM programmes should have a greater focus on customers and that employees should be given more authority to make decisions. Kearney's study also commented that companies which 'have successfully introduced TQM are twice as likely to have made an objective study of their competitors through "benchmarking" '.[67] Further, in cases where TQM had not produced tangible results, the responsibility often lay with the quality manager rather than a director.

Four characteristics are said[67] to feature in companies which practise TQM successfully: (1) emphasis on tangible results; (2) insistence on performance measurement; (3) an integrated programme: and (4) a clear commitment from top management. Also, it is important that the ownership of TQM programmes remains with a company instead of being passed to outside consultants. Another vital factor for success is to ensure that the means do not obscure the ends: to keep firmly in mind that the principal purpose of TQM programmes is to give customers better service – it is not about designing bureaucratic systems which impede decision making by those who have to deal directly with customers.

Teamwork, shared responsibilities, creative problem solving and speedy action are some of the qualities needed by those who contribute to TQM programmes. Customers' expectations should be monitored and evaluated against specific criteria, such as product quality and availability. The theme of TQM is *total* dedication to all aspects of satisfying customers' needs; it is a demanding task and one which, in dynamic market conditions, is never actually completed. Competitors – at home and abroad – will soon find a way to improve further the latest product introduced into a market.

A survey[68] of 224 large manufacturing companies in 14 European countries was conducted by INSEAD, the Fontainebleu-based business school, in 1990. It emphasised the need for quality in all aspects of manufacturing, which was perceived as *the* competitive issue of the 1990s. INSEAD was also involved in another research project[69] – with Waseda University in Tokyo, and the University of Boston – to find out what 500 of the world's top manufacturing companies saw as the most important competitive priorities facing them in the next five years. As with the earlier research survey, the findings reflected the salience of quality throughout a firm's operations, including the spin-off disciplines of just-in-time (JIT) manufacturing, etc.

Of particular interest, though, were the subtle but distinct differences in manufacturing priorities throughout the industrialised world. US manufacturers placed greater importance on competitive pricing than Europeans, who focused on quality and delivery. While the Japanese also emphasise quality and quality-related issues, they particularly stressed their ability to make rapid design changes in highly customized products: they were extremely flexible in their production facilities and strategies.

Throughout the world – but particularly in the USA – companies also attached growing importance to staff training and management development as vital to their successful operations.

Dr W. Edwards Deming, who died in December 1993 at the venerable age of 93, was arguably one of the most influential figures in modern industrial management theory and practice. The messianic fervour with which he pursued the theme of quality through every aspect of an organisation's activities undoubtedly laid the foundations for the vast improvements which have characterised many industrial and consumer products and services over recent years. With Juran, whose work on quality production techniques closely paralleled his own, Deming started a revolution in management philosophies and practices which is still active today.

In Chapter 2 it was noted that Toyota and other Japanese car-makers had set up assembly plants in the UK, and operated JIT delivery systems. As part of its quality programme, Toyota whittled down would-be suppliers of components from 2,000 to 150. This rigorous process of selection was undertaken by a number of multidisciplinary teams which evaluated 400 prospective suppliers against the following criteria: (1) management capability and attitudes; (2) production and manufacturing facilities, and level of investment in technology; (3) quality control systems and philosophy; and (4) research and development capability. The remaining successful 250 companies were asked to submit firm estimates. Prototype contracts were placed with approved firms, which were then invited to attend a series of meetings at which Toyota's business philosophy was fully explained, and detailed instructions were given about expected standards of performance from suppliers. Suppliers meeting Toyota's exacting demands receive production parts contracts, and are regarded by Toyota as partners in the business of making quality cars. Technology 'help' teams have been organised by Toyota to advise and support its component suppliers.[70]

Velcro, the patent fastener-makers, faced in 1985 an ultimatum from General Motors: meet GM's standards or it would find another supplier. Velcro was given 90 days to start a total quality control programme at its US plant in Manchester, New Hampshire. GM quality control specialists told Velcro that they were *inspecting* quality into the product, not *manufacturing* quality into the product, and demanded that quality should be maintained throughout production to avoid existing wastage of between 6 and 8 per cent.

Although Theodor Krantz, president of Velcro, confesses to a prejudice against using quality consultants, the urgency of the problem forced him to engage their services. An education programme for employees was started and a statistical process control system was instituted. In addition, a steering committee on quality was formed from heads of sales, finance, personnel, marketing, manufacturing, R&D, quality and MIS, and also the president.

At the end of 90 days, GM expressed its satisfaction with Velcro's progress in improving quality standards, and gave it six months to prepare for thorough inspection. As the president observes:

> Naturally, we were pleased at this reprieve, but we really had only scratched the quality surface. It takes a lot more than 90 days for, say, the loom operator on the third shift really to believe in quality and act on that belief. It was a long time

> before we got quality instilled throughout the organisation, before people were making changes for Velcro instead of for GM.[71]

Nevertheless, significant changes did occur: wastage, for example, was cut by 50 per cent over 1986–7, and by 45 per cent in 1987–8.

Velcro regained GM's confidence, but then the car manufacturer set new standards of quality. Krantz remarks: 'Even as our quality improved, the standard against which we are measured was moving as well . . . What was acceptable three years ago is no longer good enough.' He reflected that the well-thought-out logic of Deming, Juran and other proponents of TQM was irrefutable: (1) do it right first time; (2) employees are happier and more satisfied making good parts than bad ones; (3) quality should be an important purchasing criterion; (4) people must be trained properly; and (5) teamwork is vital to success.

Krantz recognised the necessity of committing everyone in the business to the achievement and maintenance of quality throughout manufacture. It was important, therefore, to encourage people on the factory floor, 'who know the process better than their boss or anybody up the line', to take an active part by submitting ideas on how manufacturing processes could be changed and lead to improved quality of products. 'Continuous improvement' teams were organised; these were originally headed by supervisors, but hourly paid employees are sometimes now in charge. Also, a material review board, consisting of a rotating group of salaried and hourly paid workers, meets daily to examine closely substandard material from each unit's production, discuss causes of the defects, and encourage corrective action in order to avoid similar problems.

Krantz stresses that, in a manufacturing company, the word 'quality' tends to be almost automatically related to manufacturing, whereas other functions, such as marketing and sales, should be involved in ensuring that the concept of quality permeates the entire business. With this firmly in mind, about half of Velcro's quality improvement teams are in departments other than manufacturing. 'A tenet of quality', states Krantz, 'is that you have inside customers as well as outside customers, and you have to satisfy both. When the paychecks are not correct, your inside customers get very upset.' Sales operations are also checked for the quality of service to customers, including effective handling of complaints.

Velcro declares that it is a customer-driven business 'where quality is in the eye of the customer'; this means that customers' *perceptions* should be studied carefully. Their needs will vary according to the purposes for which Velcro fasteners are used: in some cases, such as the car market, durability, reliability and capability are critical performance factors, but the weave on the tapes' backing need not necessarily be entirely uniform. But for a textile company appearances are important, as well as efficient technical features.

Krantz comments that quality is relative to customers' expectations and needs, and Velcro products involve a varying mix of technical, chemical and aesthetic attributes. Experience over the years since GM's shattering ultimatum has been fully used by Velcro to ensure that it retains its strong competitive position. This is particularly critical since Velcro's patents expired in 1978, and it has had to face competition from the Far East. Velcro Industries NV, the American company's parent, also operates plants in Europe, Asia and the Pacific Rim.

The British Standards Institution (BSI) (see Chapters 4 and 9) introduced in 1979 a quality management system of business procedure, BS5750, which has been adopted by many thousands of companies. BSI has stressed that quality management is quite different from quality control: the former is a documented procedure of quality management designed to eliminate, or at least trace and rectify, faults; the latter is concerned with screening products or services to weed out any that are faulty, and it is not a comprehensive product quality management system.

BS5750 is now International Standard ISO 9000 and European Standard EN 29000. The International Organisation for Standardisation (ISO) was founded in 1947 and is a federation of 96 countries which appoint committees to establish international standards. These take precedence over national or European standards. The ISO is not active in the electrical industry, which is the responsibility of the International Electrotechnical Commission (IEC). The European Committee for Standardisation (CEN) was founded in 1961, but until 1985 had little to do because standards were established either by national bodies or by ISO/IEC. Since that time, it has been given the responsibility of producing standards to back up EC directives; wherever possible, these are based on national or international standards.

However, responsibility for the electrical industry is handled by another organisation: the European Committee for Electrotechnical Standardisation (CENELEC). Telecommunication standards are covered by the European Telecommunications Standards Institute (ETSI).[72]

The European Organisation for Testing and Certification (EOTOC) was formed in January 1992 to establish the mutual recognition by certification and testing of the various European organisations involved in the setting of standards. This should assist companies by eliminating the need for separate certification in each country with which they trade.

The *CE Mark* indicates that a product meets the minimum specification required by the relevant EC directive. The *BSI Kitemark* is awarded, or licensed, by the BSI to firms producing goods to accepted national or international standards; it is not applicable to services or procedures.[72]

As can readily be seen from this necessarily short account of standards systems, professional guidance would be advisable in specific cases. As already stated in Chapter 9, the BSI and the DTI offer consultancy advice.

PRODUCT DESIGN: CREATIVE CONTRIBUTION TO MARKETING SUCCESS

Costs of labour, raw materials and overheads are rising inexorably; competition is keener than ever and is truly global in its effects; buyers are more demanding and knowledgeable; and supplies of essential materials and components are often in peril. Every weapon in the management armoury should be mobilised in the counter-attack; among the most valuable of these is product design.

No firm can ignore the function of design and expect to survive and prosper, especially when competitors from distant parts of the world are prepared to make design appeal a significant marketing attraction. Design is an integral part of a product; it is the fusion of utility and beauty so that maximum motivation to buy is created. But even an ideal design is not likely to be successful without the support of the other factors in the marketing mix, e.g. sensitive pricing, effective distribution and expert promotion.

A carefully planned marketing strategy integrates design policy with the other factors which contribute to profitable business. There is a reciprocal relationship between design and price, methods of distribution, etc. Only if these various factors are closely co-ordinated and organised can marketing strategies really achieve corporate objectives. Design policies must be drawn up within the overall marketing plan, to which they should make a distinctive and carefully integrated contributions. (See Chapters 5 and 6 on product policy.)

AESTHETIC APPEALS ARE *RELEVANT TO INDUSTRIAL PRODUCTS*

The aesthetics of design are not restricted to consumer products, as Theodore Levitt[73] has indicated. A panel of highly experienced technical directors was shown a testing machine, one version of which had a front panel designed by the engineers who had developed the equipment; the alternative machine, intrinsically identical, was fitted with a control panel designed by professional industrial designers. This latter version attracted twice the purchase intention compared with the engineers' design.

Another insight into the influence of design in technical products concerns a Canadian pump manufacturer who was asked why he thought it necessary to have his range of machines redesigned because, after all, they were only used underground. His reply reflected commercial acumen: 'Maybe, but they are not bought underground.'[74]

The added values of good styling have been shown to influence buying decisions, even though the effects may not be at a conscious level or openly admitted.

DESIGN CONTRIBUTES TO PROFITABILITY

A striking example[75] of the contribution to profitability made by effective design relates to the driver's cab of an excavator, which was redesigned to give all-round vision. This not only made the driver's job easier and safer, but also resulted in a significant reduction in the time taken to train drivers. In another case, a spectrometer proved difficult to demonstrate because it could not be carried easily in a representative's car and was too bulky to take inside a laboratory. Professional designers were able to reduce the size by half through rearranging the components, thus directly helping the sales campaign.

Simon Engineering of Dudley, West Midlands, designed what it claims to be the world's highest firefighting platform, which, mounted on a load vehicle, can rise up to 62 metres to reach 20 storeys – twice the height of a fire brigade's longest escape ladder. Utilising a boom, the Simon Super Snorkel is extremely flexible, being able 'to reach up, over and around obstructions so that firemen can direct large jets of water on to blazing buildings from a safe distance.'[76] In addition, the entire structure had to be capable of retracting to a size that would enable it to negotiate congested city streets, and of complying with international commercial vehicle regulations. In developing this complex product, Simon Engineering had help from the Design Council design consultancy scheme.

Product design, according to Juran,[77] is an essential part of product development: 'it is the activity of defining the product features required to meet customer needs'. These should: (1) meet customers' needs and also the needs of suppliers; (2) meet competitive challenges; and (3) minimise costs incurred by both customers and suppliers. It will be seen, therefore, that Juran takes a comprehensive view of the role of design, which should result in benefits for both buyers and sellers.

Experienced marketers plan their products so that they offer a 'package of benefits' to their customers. This creative approach acknowledges that people, whether they are buying for their individual needs or for organisations, are influenced by many motivations: economic, social, cultural and psychological. To assume that price is always the dominant buying influence reflects too narrow a conception of buying behaviour. Products may be acquired because of the desire to own something of unusual beauty or exclusivity; too low a price may, in fact, be a deterrent.

> Rarely does one motive alone influence human behaviour; motivations interact and modify the effects of single motives; for example, consumers may be motivated by economy to choose the lowest-priced brand of a product but, at the same time, they will also be motivated by safety, security or risk factors. So they tend to select well-known brands, even though lower-priced alternatives may be available.[78]

Product design is playing an increasingly important part in buying decisions; better educated, more widely travelled and experienced buyers are assessing products far more critically than a few years ago. Some domestic products, e.g. vacuum cleaners, floor polishers and spin dryers, are fundamentally the same mechanically as their predecessors of over a generation ago. But in many cases, by clever restyling, designers have been able to extend the life cycle of these products.

Innovation – one of the prime responsibilities of marketing management (see Chapter 7) – is closely linked to design; indeed, the two are working partners in the task of attracting a flow of new business to a firm. Although it is widely recognised that successful innovation is one of the most difficult areas of business, the role of the designer is frequently limited to his or her professional specialism. But market-orientated design is unlikely unless designers and marketing executives work in partnership, sharing their respective individual expertise. Industrial design has a purpose: to attract and keep customers in competitive markets.

The crucial role of innovation in the design process is well illustrated by two companies in the health-care products market. Keeler, based in Windsor, developed an instrument called a tonometer for diagnostic tests for glaucoma. This non-contact, quick and painless test measures the pressure inside the eye by directing a puff of air at it and then measuring the strength of the puff needed to flatten the cornea. Varian-TEM in Sussex developed the innovatory product Ximatron-C, which locates malignant tumours to within 0.5 mm, enables radiographers to give lower radiation doses and so reduces the risk of damaging healthy cells.[79]

Industrial design should take account of the many scientific and technical factors which influence the development of products, such as thermodynamics, engineering and other specialisms; the needs of customers must, of course, always be borne in mind, as well as the nature and extent of competition, environmental conditions, innovation policies, etc.

DESIGN IS NOT JUST A PRETTY FACE

Product design should not be merely cosmetic or some kind of face-lift; apart from aesthetic appeal, products should function well: they should provide the fundamental satisfactions which buyers expect. In designing furniture, for example, problems of ergonomics arise. Chairs should be shaped so that they are comfortable to sit in and support vital areas of the body such as the spine. With tools, it is essential that they work efficiently and are safe to use; integrated design ensures that components, such as handles, are styled for ease in holding, reducing muscular fatigue and improving safety in use.

Some years ago a notable NEDO report on manufacturing industry defined product design as both engineering design and aesthetic design, 'both of which are important and should be used in tandem. Too often industrial design considerations predominate in consumer goods, to the detriment of engineering design, and the reverse is true of engineering capital goods.' Good design is perceived to increase the value added to the resources of a business; it is not just a peripheral activity, but plays a core role in the development of markets. Unfortunately, however, as the NEDO report observes, products tend to be designed 'in isolation from all the other key functions'.[80]

At a relatively late stage of development, product designs are often modified to meet market needs which were inadequately identified earlier. In other cases, designs are changed at a late stage because of production problems or cost constraints that are suddenly brought into discussions. Such wasteful behaviour could be avoided if the design function were integrated into the early planning stages and adequate market information were available and shared among designers, marketers and production and finance specialists.

The NEDO report recommends that companies 'should designate an appropriate member of their boards to take on the design function as a prime responsibility'. Design should be regarded as part of the investment decisions made by companies. (This point should be considered in relation to innovation strategies: see Chapter 7.)

Design can make a direct contribution to the development of high-added-value products, which are essential for the development of UK industrial output, especially in overseas markets. But the design function must accept the disciplines of commercial management and accept that design specifications should be drawn up only after market enquiries have been made.

In September 1983 a report[81] was commissioned by the Department of Education and Science in association with the Design Council to identify what skills, knowledge and attitudes industry requires from industrial designers and how far these requirements are being fulfilled.

A survey covered about 300 individuals in 130 manufacturing and other companies in the United Kingdom, France, Germany, Italy, Scandinavia and the Netherlands. Eighty-five UK manufacturing companies were interviewed, of which 78 gave information about their designers.

Among the principal findings of this systematic survey were the following: 23 UK companies had a separate design budget; 20 UK companies had a designer at board or equivalent level (these companies generally made products heavily dependent on design); it was felt that designers were not sufficiently willing to offer alternative solutions to a design problem, and did not adequately appreciate the value of seeing the product in its market context; there was general agreement that basic design skills were the most important, followed by those needed to adapt to a corporate environment – about 20 per cent of respondents regarded the latter as a particular cause of dissatisfaction, and cited designers' inability to work to deadlines and also to communicate effectively with other management; there was an above-average shortfall in industrial designers' awareness of commercial realities; and designers were perceived to be insufficiently aware of market needs, and seemed to want to educate public taste rather than respond to it.

In continental Europe, the percentage of companies with separate design budgets was about twice that of the United Kingdom. In general, European companies rated highly the contribution of design to commercial success, and it was judged likely to become even more important: Italian, Scandinavian and West German companies were far more aware of the importance of industrial design to market sucess than French or UK companies; 'adapting to the corporate environment' was rated rather lower by European companies than by UK companies; but foreign language proficiency and the ability to assess customer feedback were rated more important in Europe than in the United Kingdom.

There was overall agreement in the United Kingdom and abroad that more emphasis on corporate skills in design education would improve company competitiveness. It was interesting to note that design education abroad is no better in this respect than in the United Kingdom; moreover, European firms regard British design education as superior in general.

Successful companies appeared to combine an *excellent* performance in one of the following five perceived criteria – identification of market opportunity, competitive pricing, quality and performance, delivery and aesthetic appeal – with *adequate* performance in all the others.

It is essential to plan and control the development and design of products. The techniques of marketing research should be applied to testing new product designs and monitoring the market performance of existing products. The investment costs of new products are heavy, and it is vital for marketing management to have objective information about their product ranges; this includes an assessment of design trends (see Chapters 4 and 5).

The findings of the DES report should be contrasted with the ways in which the design function is handled by Japanese industrialists, such as Sharp, Sony, Canon and Ricoh, where it is regarded as a strategic weapon and has the same status as other functions of the business. As discussed earlier in this chapter, the Japanese *kaizen* process reflects their dedication to continuous product/service improvement:

> Whereas western companies allow successful products to roll on indefinitely, their Japanese competitors innovate continually. This not only keeps their product lines fresher and broader, it also enables them to sustain constantly active design and development departments. This, in turn, helps them accelerate the product development process – a common target of most companies these days, but one which many western companies are finding elusive.[82]

PROFITABLE DESIGN IS A TEAM EFFORT

Product design depends on effective teamwork; the complexity of modern equipment increasingly demands a synthesis of skills. If the design function is to be effective, it should be integrated into virtually every aspect of a company's organisation and at all levels.[83] Close integration of marketing efforts, including design, has already been advocated in Chapter 1.

About 20 years ago, McKinsey made a study of the manufacturing operations of UK firms and their foreign competitors; the findings, which were disturbing, are still instructive today. The study found, for instance, that overseas companies tend to spend a 'much greater proportion of overheads on engineering and marketing but considerably less on functions related to production'. In other words, they 'spend more on getting the design right and much less subsequently on getting the product made'. What the UK lacks is competence in manufacturing engineering; there are not enough manufacturing engineers and they are not given sufficient status in their firms.

Product design largely dictates the processes of manufacture and the costs involved; it is central to the whole concept of profitability. Yet the same principle of integrated design is

> missed by many British industries ... Too often British product design progresses from concept to finished product with little or none of this essential feedback. The gleam in the researcher's eye is converted into a prototype by a development engineer whose primary objective is to produce something that works as well as possible. Then, the manufacturing engineer creates the facilities and processes to make the prototype in quantity. Finally, others try to sell it and maintain it.[84]

This uncoordinated approach to product design can result in severe diseconomies in production; costs of processing cheaper materials may outweigh the initial savings.

McKinsey emphasised that manufacturing engineers in overseas companies have considerable authority in the development of products. Instead of the widespread British practice of a *linear* approach to design, a *cyclical* one is adopted. Development prototypes are subject to critical commercial and technical evaluation. There is constant feedback from the various departments of a business – production, purchasing, marketing and costing – to eliminate snags: several redesigns may be necessary before a product is finally approved for production. (See Chapter 1 on corporate performance inputs.)

A major UK firm employs only six graduate engineers in product design, exclusively in development engineering. Its US competitors, whose output was only 50 per cent greater, had nearly 400 graduates employed, mostly in manufacturing engineering. 'The American company's production overhead staff, however (schedulers, chasers, storemen, quality inspectors, and so on) are fewer by a factor of 30. And, not surprisingly, the US product is cheaper, more reliable, and can be delivered faster.'[84]

Ideally, designers should work, as McKinsey has recommended, in partnership with other functional managers in companies. These cover all the diverse activities to be found in industrial organisations: costing, financial control, purchasing, production, marketing research and marketing, including promotional activities. These functions should be viewed as complementary rather than competitive. (See Chapter 1 for detailed discussion of the interfaces of marketing.)

It was proposed some time ago that designers should be included in corporate long-range planning teams: 'A new type of engineer has begun to emerge who may eventually provide the element in the forward planning team which is still normally lacking. This engineering specialisation is sometimes called "industrial design", sometimes "design engineering".' Engineering, and technological and social sciences, may be fused 'to produce a multi-discipline man, part scientist, part technologist, part artist'.[85] This type of industrial designer has an enormously important part to play in the profitable marketing of products, and also in the provision of amenities in the public sector.

The research unit of the School of Industrial Design (Engineering) at the Royal College of Art has contributed most valuably to the public health services by designing many appliances for handicapped people. Also, in a project concerned with improving the design of a range of dental equipment, it was found that the policy of bringing the designer into the heart of business discussions resulted in more effective solutions. 'Time and again, the presence of the designer at the market researcher's elbow led to the formulation of vital secondary questions, and of the market researcher at the designer's elbow led to more valid interpretation of the answers.'[86]

Marketing executives and designers should exchange ideas about ways in which the design of existing products could be improved, as well as being closely involved in the design development stages of new products. James Pilditch, writing of consultant design services, referred to the misguided kindness which inhibits some clients from briefing designers thoroughly because 'we don't want to impose our ideas on you'. Designers, says Pilditch, need good briefing: 'Describe the problem and your objectives. Describe the market, customer, competition, cost targets and your production capability . . . The more the designer knows of your problem and situation, the better.'[75]

Designers might be encouraged to attend sales conferences; they would be able to learn about reactions of customers, and of the sales force, to product improvements and also new models. Designers might occasionally accompany selected members of the sales force and meet customers at first hand. If a company is active in exporting, designers should visit these territories and see for themselves the conditions under which their products have to operate or be consumed. From these personal visits, designers' creative talents will be stimulated, and they will gain insight into the needs of those who actually use the products they design.

Designers should also be prepared to learn about the business techniques of costing, production planning, marketing and the related activities that are necessary for the profitable exploitation of their designs. Professional designers accept that their skills have to be exercised within the resources of the companies for which they are working. Designers may, perhaps, profitably extend their knowledge to modern techniques such as those used in operational research management.

Computer-aided design and manufacture (CAD/CAM) has enabled designers and production engineers to work even more closely together. From the early days of development in the aerospace and motor industries, these advanced techniques have spread to other industries and to comparatively small-scale businesses. As the prices of computer hardware and software have been significantly reduced, new applications have opened up, which have helped small firms as well as large companies to keep their competitive edge.

OBTAINING DESIGN SKILLS

The services of a skilled designer are not limited to large companies which are able to absorb the costs of relatively sophisticated management structures. Some consumer product companies, e.g. the larger firms in the textiles and pottery tableware industries, have traditionally had a staff of resident designers. Many companies, however, use the services of consultant designers; these may also contribute to, and complement, the work being undertaken by staff designers. The old commercial criterion of 'make or buy' may be applied. In complex areas of business activity such as law or taxation, many companies, although having members of staff qualified as general practitioners, call in the services of specialists when expert knowledge in depth is required in connection with particular problems. Specialised design skills may likewise be acquired.

The Design Council (28 Haymarket, London SW1), whose interests include industrial products, can assist firms in the difficult task of finding the right designer for their particular range of products. The Design Selection Service maintains a detailed record of designers which enables them to match a firm's needs and an individual designer's skills and experience. For a nominal fee, the Design Council will discuss the design problems facing a firm and present it with a short list of suitable designers.

The professional association for industrial designers is the Chartered Society of Designers (CSD), formerly the Society of Industrial Artists and Designers (12 Carlton House Terrace, London SW1). It offers manufacturers a Design Advisory Service, and will provide enquirers with full details of designers who are considered to have knowledge and experience relevant to specific design projects. The CSD also maintains a central library of photoprints, proofs, specimens of design work, etc., which may be inspected by prospective clients. In addition, the CSD keeps a register of qualified designers who are seeking staff appointments; these are matched against vacancies notified by client companies, and arrangements can be made to circulate specific vacancies to all members of the CSD.

Design fees are normally based on the time involved in fulfilling a commission; in addition, business expenses attributable to the work undertaken are charged. Occasionally, designers prefer to accept minimum fees and recoup themselves largely on a royalty basis. One well-known hardware manufacturer obtained by licensing arrangements access to a fundamental new design for its range of products. It proved to be a highly profitable negotiation.

Firms of *all* sizes, and over a wide spectrum of industry, can have access to the skills of professional designers; there is no valid argument for ignoring the design content of products of all kinds. An effective design policy should be developed as part of the overall marketing strategy of progressive companies. The UK once led the world in the excellence of its products; British manufacturers should regain their prestige by ensuring that the services of professional designers are used fully in the development and improvement of their products.

VALUE ANALYSIS AND VALUE ENGINEERING

Value analysis is defined by British Standards as 'a systematic interdisciplinary examination of design and other factors affecting the cost of a product or service in order to define means of achieving the specified purpose most economically at the required standards of quality and reliability'. It involves an analytical approach to the design and manufacture of products so that costs of production are rigidly controlled or reduced while efficient functioning is not impaired in any way. 'In an engineering sense VA is a technique used to examine ways of redesigning a product so that it costs less to build or functions more effectively, or both. Quality must not be sacrificed to cut costs.'[87]

Value engineering refers to the analytical approach, outlined above, applied to *new* products at the design stage, while value analysis is the term used to describe systematic investigation of *existing* products.

As with several other management techniques, value analysis originated during the Second World War when there were considerable problems in the availability and costs of manufacturing supplies. In the United States, pioneering work in this area was undertaken by the General Electric Company, where value analysis was developed into a systematic and disciplined technique. Interest in this approach continued after the war, and in 1959, the Society of American Value Engineers was founded in Washington, DC. In the 1950s, the US Department of Defense adopted value analysis as a formal requirement for all government contracts. Value analysis has now spread widely, although it has been adopted less enthusiastically in the United Kingdom than in the United States.[88]

The British Productivity Council published 16 case studies in value analysis; in seven of the cases it was advantageous for firms that were buying equipment to encourage suppliers to contribute their technical expertise in solving production problems. Again, the importance of the industrial salesperson in these negotiations is clear. Effective industrial selling entails considerable analytical and creative ability backed up by adequate technical knowledge, as well as the skill to communicate ideas persuasively (see Chapters 4 and 5).

A US capital goods company's policy was to sell the largest, highest-powered, most maintenance-free units possible. Customers, however, began to request smaller, less costly units 'without the rugged engineering characteristics required for maintenance-free operation'. Marketing management recommended that the product line should be radically redesigned, but the manufacturing and technical experts strongly opposed this, arguing that the current design and cost structure were superior to those of any competitors. What was needed, in their opinion, was more selling effort: their views were backed by top management. The company lost a substantial share of its market before the president ordered the whole range to be redesigned. 'Now that he has, things are looking up . . . it is unrealistic, of course, to expect a dramatic turnaround'.[89]

Products should be designed for ease of manufacturing as well as for their aesthetic appeals. A manufacturer of compressors redesigned one of its product ranges and eliminated 56 per cent of its production costs; likewise, a manufacturer of paper shredders cut production costs by a quarter, following a redesign exercise. Infrared Engineering, an Essex-based small manufacturer of industrial measuring instruments and control systems, decided to revamp equipment used to measure the moisture content of paper and board. Existing equipment had remained unchanged for over 15 years and was difficult to make and service, and some of the original components were difficult to obtain. Under the Enterprise Initiative Scheme, the company rather hestitantly called in a professional design consultancy, which 'challenged every assumption we had made about the product'.[90] After radical redesign, which included incorporating microprocessor technology and a bar code reader, the equipment was easier to assemble and more reliable in use; moreover, manufacturing costs fell by up to 25 per cent, the weight was reduced from 8 to 5½ kg and the engineering director said that these design changes contributed to a 50 per cent increase in sales in what had been a static market.[91]

DESIGNING SAFER PRODUCTS

A particularly pressing demand on designers is to ensure that products should be safe to use. Safety factors are now increasingly important buying motivations, and safety lobbying – which has developed strongly in the USA the 1960s, when Ralph Nader campaigned vigorously against the manufacturers of a car that was declared to be unsafe at any speed – has led to legal acceptance of the principle of strict product liability. Manufacturers and distributors are held accountable for product-related injuries, where 'a court or jury determines that a product's design, its construction, or its operating instructions and safety warnings make it unreasonably dangerous or hazardous to use'.[92]

Liability suits grew at an intimidating rate in the USA between 1974 and 1990, over half of them concerning asbestos-related cases. The damages awarded have also grown spectacularly, inflated to some extent by the contingency fee basis on which most plaintiffs' lawyers operate in these cases. American product liability legislation is also complicated in practice because of varying interpretations of strict liability in different states.

In Britain as long ago as 1893, the Sale of Goods Act conferred extensive rights on buyers who were, in general terms, entitled to goods of merchantable quality fit for the purpose for which they were sold. But this protection was reduced in two ways: by privity of contract (by which contracts in English law are normally only binding on the parties who made them) and by exclusion clauses. The latter were rendered illegal by legislation passed in the 1970s; the former disappeared under strict product liability legislation.

New product liability legislation in Europe has followed from the EEC Directive on Liability for Defective Products of 25 July 1985, which required each member state to introduce legislation to comply with the directive by July 1988. The UK was the first country to implement the European directive by the introduction of the Consumer Protection Act 1987, which came into force on 1 March 1988. Product liability forms part 1 of the Act. The other members of the European Community have various methods of protecting consumers from the results of product failure.

Under the Consumer Protection Act, product liability means that people injured by defective products may have the right to sue for damages, and any person who supplies a defective product will be liable for any damage it causes. Product liability relates to manufacturers, processors, suppliers of raw materials and components, importers, and own-label branded goods. Liability under the Act is not restricted to consumer goods; apart from unprocessed agricultural products, all other goods are included. The General Safety Requirement (GSR) applies a standard of 'reasonable safety' to most consumer goods supplied in the UK. Contraventions may lead to criminal proceedings. The GSR is closely linked to recognised product standards. As with safety regulations, an offence may be committed although no one may have been injured.

Formerly, those injured had to prove a manufacturer negligent before being compensated; this proof of negligence is no longer necessary in order to sue for damages. However, a producer may be able to reduce the impact of defective goods by pleading contributory negligence in the use of a certain product. Among several other defences which a producer could offer is that the state of scientific and technical knowledge at the time the products were under its control was such that any defects would not have been discovered. The degree of safety of a product is that which a person may generally be entitled to expect, after taking into account all circumstances.

While the product liability legislation brings Europe closer to the US practice which has existed for over 20 years, it has been drafted to avoid the draconian penalties which have imposed insufferable burdens on American companies. The product liability and safety provisions of the Consumer Protection Act 1987 provide for compensation for: (1) death; (2) personal injury; and (3) private property valued above £275. The plaintiff must be able to show that, on the balance of probabilities, the defect in the product caused the alleged damage. Claims can be made up to 10 years after the product was supplied, but legal proceedings must start within three years of the alleged injury from a defective product.

Businesses need to take out adequate insurance cover related to their responsibilities under the Act, install efficient product recall systems, check design and manufacturing standards in both their own factories and those of their suppliers, and ensure that records are maintained in view of their potential liability over the years.

Of course, risk can never be entirely eliminated – no product can be absolutely safe under all conditions of usage. This move towards higher safety standards and the improved legal protection of consumers follows the general trends in business and society.

Howard Abbott[93] advocates devising a *product design specification*, from inputs by various functional areas of management. This analysis details, for example, the likely users of a product, foreseeable types of misuse, the kinds of environment (temperature, humidity, vibration, noise, etc.) in which a product might be used, the proximity of children or animals, and other factors likely to affect product performance. The outcome of this systematic evaluation is a brief to which the designer can work. A formal design review system is also recommended as an important factor in risk reduction.

Designers and product development managers need to work closely to ensure that products reach the market only after rigorous evaluation of their safety features. This responsibility includes checking advertising copy so that it does not contain exaggerated claims about product features and applications. The requirements of liability legislation are rigorous, so a company should seek professional advice on its particular situation.

CUSTOMER SERVICE

THE CREATIVE ROLE OF SERVICING

In Chapter 2 the growth of the modern service economy was traced, and the dependence of the national economy on non-tangibles was seen to be of major importance. The concept of the augmented product was also discussed: that a business deal may often mean far more than a tangible product. Surrounding the core product may be 'added values' created by skilful marketing that provides customers with many benefits, such as technical training, after-sales service and comprehensive warranties. At the same time, these technical and other forms of service back-up can significantly increase the sales value of orders in both home and export markets.

The tendency to integrate the servicing function, and to improve its status within the firm, is a step towards greater efficiency. For too long, the service side of many organisations has been regarded rather as a nuisance than as offering management unique opportunities to back up their products and secure further profitable business. Today, efficient marketing should include first-class servicing arrangements. Before VW developed its British marketing operations, several regional warehouses, strategically based, were organised to ensure that spare parts could be obtained with minimum delay. A similar strategy was followed, some years later, by Renault, which built a huge new parts distribution centre at Reading to feed component supplies to regional stores throughout the United Kingdom.

One of the most irritating feelings which people tend to have from time to time is that what they are or what they think is of little concern to the faceless organisations – public or private – with which they are 'forced' to transact business. No *person* seems to be interested in them and their problems; they are about as significant as a flea on an elephant. Even if they manage to secure a listener, their complaints seem to be little heeded, or they are met with stunning indifference or crass rudeness. Eventually even the 'silent majority' grow tired of such malpractice and seek, wherever possible, alternative sources of supply. In many markets, these replacement products will attract others to change their buying preferences.

Marketers should, therefore, improve their communications with distributors and with end-users. Some companies have set up 'hot-lines' (toll-free direct telephone calling), which are growing in popularity. Callers can receive accurate information about, for example, parts and equipment from specially trained service consultants who have access to microfilmed data. This creative approach to servicing customers illustrates how astute firms can add to the satisfactions offered to their customers, especially if they are experiencing difficulties in obtaining supplies for vital equipment. Customer loyalty is worth a great deal of thought and effort.

Complaints often arise from bad communication or the entire absence of it. For instance, customers should be advised in good time of possible delays in the shipment of certain products or in the execution of some services. Goodwill can be fostered by keeping customers informed about likely shortages of raw materials or components, often outside the control of individual firms.

By improving servicing arrangements for complaints, a whole new era of marketing prospects can be opened up. Customers will respond to genuine efforts to provide them with greater benefits. New products are more likely to be adopted if those at present used have been backed up by satisfactory service. With some products, especially where intrinsic differences among competitive lines are small, the quality of service back-up may be the deciding factor in placing business. (See also Chapter 3: Post-decisional dissonance.)

PLANNING CUSTOMER SERVICE

Maintaining a high level of customer service clearly entails costs; these have to be justified. In profit-orientated organisations, success will, in the final issue, be measured by the higher level of profitability achieved by adopting more comprehensive sales-servicing policies. Sometimes immediate results may not be spectacular, it may take time to win back lost customers and to reassure those who were on the brink of departure.

Some years ago, the *Harvard Business Review*[94] gave three examples of where customer service had proved really effective: a supplier to the oil industry attributed a 5 per cent increase in sales directly to the improved delivery service and reduced number of stock shortages which it had achieved several months before; a tool manufacturer's use of air freight had enabled it to enter a new market; and a food manufacturer evaluated its customers' real service needs, redesigned its entire distribution system, and thereby saved $2 million annually.

Although the companies cited had applied different solutions to their problems, each had evaluated the contribution of the service element to marketing success, and had followed a six-step programme for customer service management. This phased plan is as follows:

1. Define the elements of service.
2. Determine the customer's viewpoint.
3. Design a competitive service 'package'.
4. Develop a programme to sell service.
5. Market-test the programme.
6. Establish performance controls.

The first stage requires marketers to identify the precise nature of the service to be supplied to their customers. In the case of industrial products, aspects of service could range from order-processsing time through to efficient maintenance calls. Other elements could be delivery time for spares, consistent quality, etc. This preparatory analysis should be undertaken thoroughly and as objectively as possible, perhaps by an independent consultant.

The next stage should take note of three important aspects of the customer's view of service: (1) additional elements of service perceived to be important by customers (more information about products, more convenient invoicing, etc.); (2) the economic significance of each element of service to the customer (these require careful checking); and (3) the rating of competitors' service levels by the customer (clues may be given to help in designing more attractive services).

Designing a competitive service 'package' follows the same principles as in the development of tangible products (see earlier chapters on marketing research principles). Customers' service needs should be analysed and the effects, for example, of certain delivery periods should be assessed:

> If failure to deliver the product within ten days after receipt of a customer's order will shut down his plant, the minimum service level required is obvious. Similarly, if all competitors are meeting a seven-day delivery schedule, there is a strong indication that the company should do at least as well.[94]

If additional levels of service are planned, the likely impact on customers' businesses should be carefully assessed. 'Sometimes better service can even be provided at lower cost – for example, by shipping parts of a product line by air freight rather than use field warehouses.' Operational research techniques may usefully be employed in assessing the most effective methods of providing specific types of service.

The fourth phase – selling the service – is critical. An ingenious service is of no real value until it is used by those for whom it was planned. Like new products, novel services require expert marketing. This includes planned selling, good publicity and all the other elements of an effective marketing mix.

The fifth phase – market-testing – applies to services some of the valuable techniques used for several years with products. Pilot marketing schemes, suitably controlled and researched, may be extremely useful in assessing total market demand and in amending certain elements of a service before it is launched nationally.

The final phase relates to the establishment of quantitative standards of performance for each service element. Causes of variance should be analysed and corrective action taken. Often, of course, services present special problems because some elements, e.g. delivery, are outside the direct control of the marketer. But alternative methods may be devised to overcome some of these handicaps to good service.

There is little logic in developing an extensive network of regional warehouses capable of giving virtually instant deliveries if orders received at head office take up

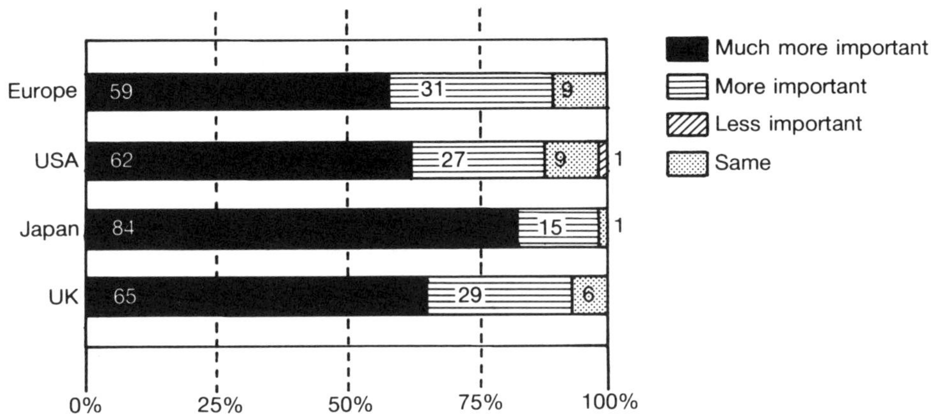

FIGURE 11.1 Importance of customer service compared with five years ago (Source: Digital[96])

to a week to process. It is likely to be more effective to ensure that orders are processed within 48 hours, while the speed of delivery may be less critical than its reliability. Customers will have many motivations for buying, e.g., product quality or technical advice, and as discussed in Chapters 2 and 3, suppliers should establish the relative strengths of these interrelated factors when developing comprehensive customer-service arrangements. Hakansson's research, it will be recalled from Chapter 3, lays particular emphasis on building effective buyer–seller relationships in industrial markets.

In Chapter 2 it was noted that the distinction between 'hard'manufacturing skills and 'soft' service skills is increasingly artificial and arbitary. 'A successful company will need to be able to blend both skills. A successful economy will need both a healthy manufacturing sector and a thriving service sector.'[95] Both are vital for the development of modern economies, and so that industry and commerce can build strong comparative advantages across world markets.

Digital published, in 1991, the findings of a very wide-spanning survey[96] (three continents, 19 countries and almost 4,000 executives) of how managers view service as part of their everyday jobs, and their perceptions of its importance in the future. While this world-wide survey showed that many similarities existed, it also revealed the influence of cultural attitudes. Courtesy, for instance, featured very highly in Japanese service priorities; in addition, the Japanese achieved higher levels of commitment to service than US or European companies.

Although there is general agreement that companies' attitudes to providing service have changed markedly over recent years, the Japanese lead the field, as indicated in Figure 11.1.

Companies' views of the future importance of customer service are shown in Figure 11.2, and it will be seen that, while the UK leads both Europe and the USA it falls far behind Japan.

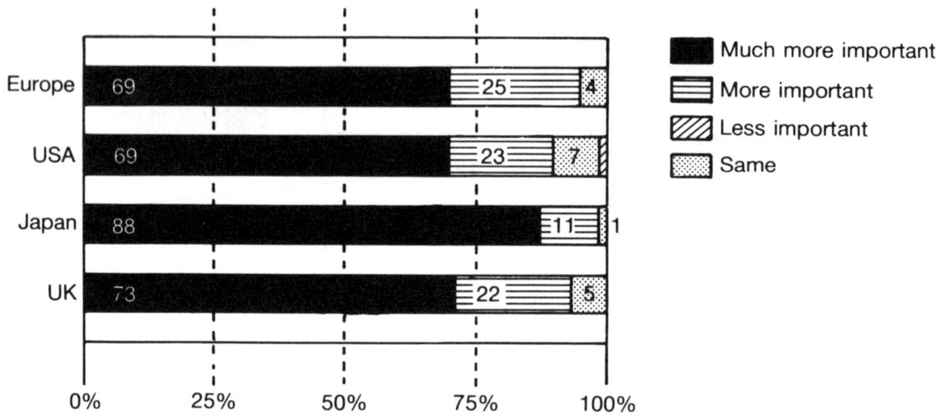

FIGURE 11.2 Expected significance of customer service in next five years (Source: Digital[96])

TABLE 11.1 External reasons for improving customer service

	Europe	*USA*	*Japan*	*UK*
Service is more important as a differentiator	4.3	4.4	4.6	4.4
Competition is fiercer	4.1	4.3	4.6	4.2
Customers are more demanding	3.9	4.0	4.5	4.1
Development of advanced information technology	3.2	3.3	4.2	3.2
Shortening life cycle of products and services	2.7	2.7	3.7	2.7

Note: Responses are based on a 5 to 0 scale (5 = very important, 0 = least important) and are given as average mean scores.
Source: Digital.[96]

The three 'western' groups' reasons for improving customer service are broadly similar, with emphasis on service as a differentiator between products with virtually the same physical characteristics. But there are striking differences in Japanese responses related to information technology and shortened life cycles compared with those of the USA and Europe, as Table 11.1 shows.

The survey states that these distinct variations confirm that Japanese companies use IT for such crucial areas as flexible, lean manufacturing, which enables them to offer rapid delivery of customised products; and the emphasis on shorter life cycles provides customers with the stimulus of new products. (Refer to earlier discussions on Japanese innovation strategies.)

As indicated in Table 11.2, 'western' groups of companies tended to use the same methods to discover and anticipate customer's needs, whereas the Japanese appear to have tried everything with great vigour. In response to questioning, however, 80 per cent of all groups said that they had concentrated more on specific

TABLE 11.2 Methods used to discover and anticipate customers' needs

	Europe (%)	*USA (%)*	*Japan (%)*	*UK (%)*
Regular discussion sessions with the salesforce	88	88	99	88
Regular meetings between customers and senior management	85	82	98	88
Market research of potential customers	85	74	98	84
Customer questionnaires	73	73	99	74
Customer 'clinics' on products/services	65	64	99	65
Comment cards attached to products	54	56	99	47

Source: Digital.[96]

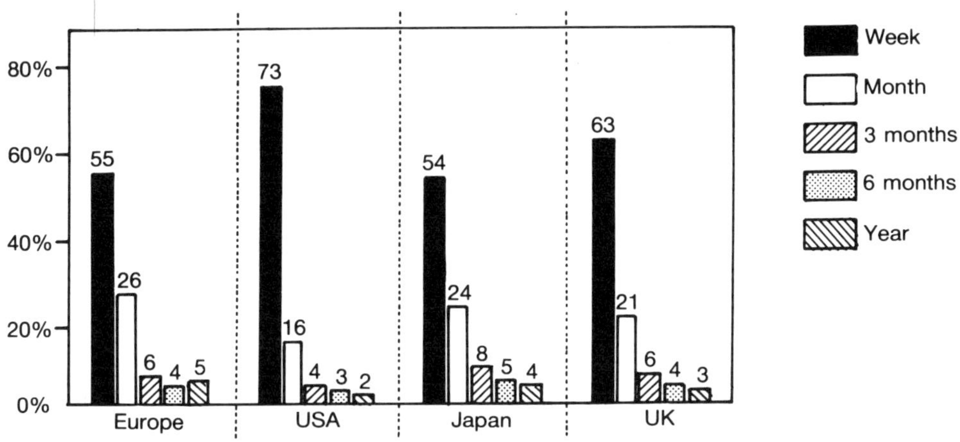

FIGURE 11.3 Frequency of personal contacts with customers (Source: Digital[96])

types of customer over the last two years, indicating that there is a general trend towards focusing on identified market segments.

Answers to a follow-up question revealed that 20 per cent of managers paying regular visits to customers did not regard such visits as effective for measuring levels of customers' satisfaction.

The degree to which companies keep closely in touch with their customers is reflected in Figure 11.3, which shows that, while nearly two-thirds of UK firms reported that they had talked to a customer in the last week, the Americans scored even higher at 73 per cent.

The various findings quoted so far suggest that, while UK companies tend to lag behind their Japanese counterparts, they are fairly committed to providing customers with service. But in common with the other groups, UK companies are sadly lacking in practical action programmes. Figure 11.4 shows that regular

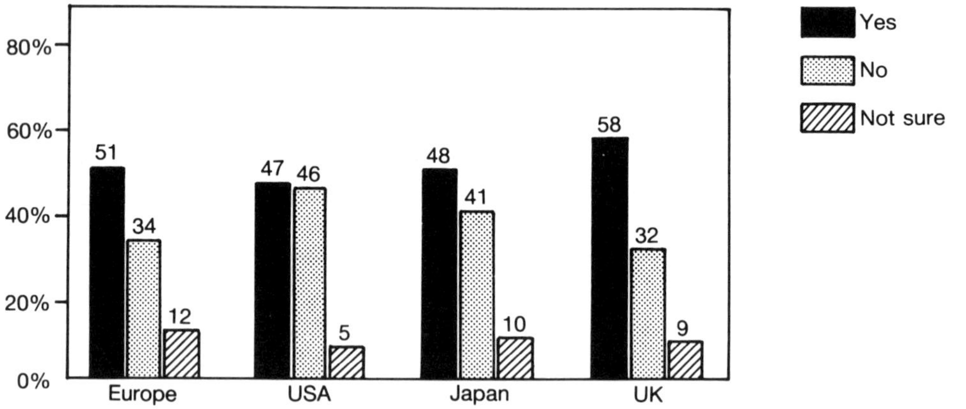

FIGURE 11.4 Use of regular reports and analyses on customer satisfaction (Source: Digital[96])

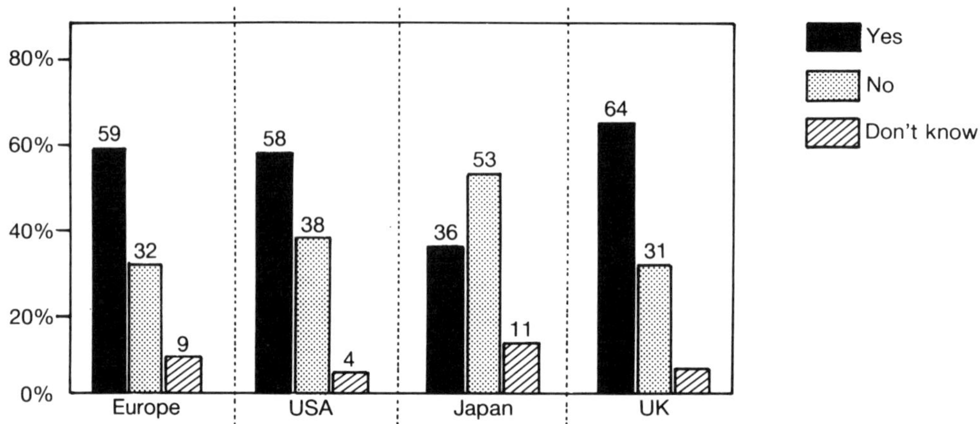

FIGURE 11.5 Incidence of quantified performance standards on key service issues (Source: Digital[96])

reports and analyses related to customers' levels of satisfaction are far from standard practice. This generally inadequate attention is also evident when respondents were asked whether their companies have quantified performance standards on most of the key issues (see Figure 11.5).

Systematically studying competitors' goods and services seems to be almost totally neglected; 'total commitment', as shown in Figure 11.6, is disturbingly low at less than a quarter of all firms surveyed. This suggests that the majority are content with relatively superficial knowledge of their competitors' products and services, and, presumably, are content to develop their marketing strategies, including product development, without rigorously evaluating competition.

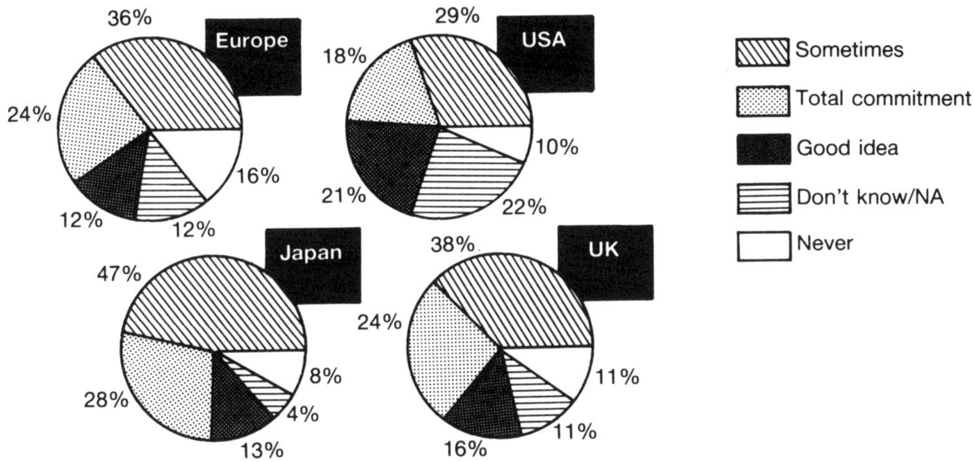

FIGURE 11.6 Systematic evaluation of competitors' products and services (Source: Digital[96])

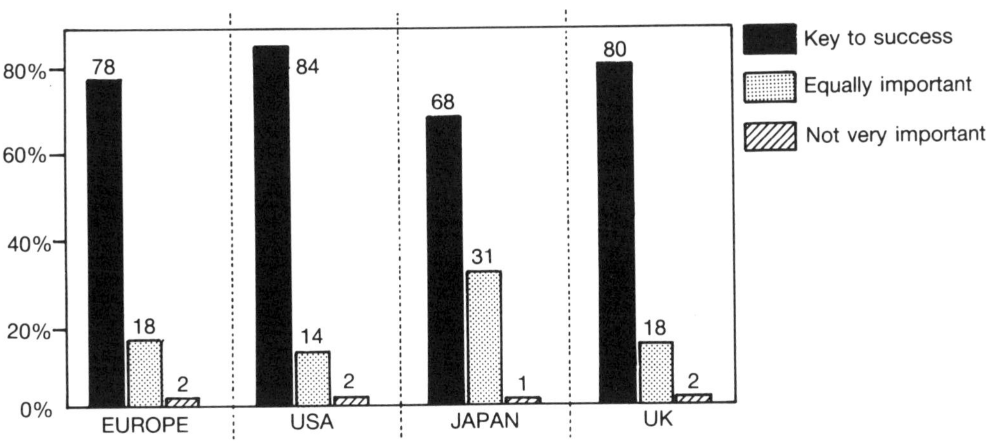

FIGURE 11.7 Importance of improving quality and service to customers (Source: Digital[96])

Yet, UK managers firmly believe that improving quality and service to customers is one of the keys to competitive success, as shown in Figure 11.7.

Consumer goods companies are highly regarded over the world for their general level of service to customers; in the UK, retailers and industrial goods firms take second and third places respectively. Government departments are generally rated very low, although the Japanese seem to take a slightly more favourable view of their civil servants, as shown in Table 11.3.

TABLE 11.3 Organisations/institutions rated for offering best service to customers/clients

Business sector	*Europe*	*USA*	*Japan*	*UK*
Consumer goods companies	3.2	3.2	3.5	3.2
Retailers	3.1	2.9	3.3	3.1
Industrial goods companies	3.1	3.0	3.0	2.9
Financial institutions	3.1	2.8	3.1	2.8
Transport companies	2.8	2.7	3.1	2.5
Government departments	1.2	1.3	1.9	1.4

Note: Responses are based on a 5 to 0 scale (5 = high, 0 = low) and are given as average mean scores.
Source: Digital.[96]

This extensive survey revealed the following major issues:

1. There are no quick and easy solutions – painstaking and integrated efforts have to be made if a company wants to build up a reputation for quality and service.
2. Fundamental changes in the attitudes and behaviour of staff are of paramount importance, hence the need for effective training in providing customer service. (In the UK, only 38 per cent of managers and 34 per cent of non-managers received training in customer service.)
3. Systematic ways of measuring customer satisfaction should be devised and implemented. (Some 90 per cent of respondents thought that service was the most important way a company could differentiate its products competitively, but only half received regular reports on customer satisfaction.)
4. Be alert and fully aware of what competitors are doing; institute regular comparative evaluations of performance, in general and also specific terms.
5. Bridge the gap between awareness that service is the competitive edge, as 95 per cent of respondents said, and actual implementation, which 50 per cent of respondents carried out.
6. Japanese companies are giving the provision of customer services the same intensive attention and detailed implementation that they applied to product quality.

GENERATING SUCCESSFUL ENTERPRISES

The generation of successful enterprises is clearly vital for economic and social prosperity. Various initiatives have been tried over the years; the small firms sector of the economy, in particular, has attracted special interest because policy-makers in both Europe and North America have pinned their hopes on the propensity of small firms to generate new employment. Such job creation depends, of course, on small companies being able to develop, produce and market successfully goods and services which are likely to satisfy the identified needs of specific kinds of customer.

Further, these innovative enterprises have to survive in the highly competitive conditions which prevail in virtually all markets today. Unfortunately, small firms have high mortality rates which are closely associated with size; even those with turnovers in the £50,000–90,000 range suffer a failure rate twice that of big businesses.

Small enterprises originate in many ways; successful entrepreneurs match their technical strengths with sound financial and marketing skills. Viable businesses have a sound core concept and a distinctive set of competences which gives them unique market appeal.

VARIOUS STRATEGIES FOR GENERATING NEW ENTERPRISES

'Spin-off' approach

Many large companies originate products and product concepts which, although potentially attractive, lie outside their main fields of activity – or perhaps are judged not to be likely to generate demand on a scale commensurate with corporate policies. Such potential products may well grow significantly in time, but the short- and medium-term prospects are deemed to be restricted. However, these kinds of product, frequently of high-added-value content, may well be the backbone of sucessful small businesses.

Large companies may also have talented technical and commercial executives who are bursting to start their own business – they may in fact have been responsible for originating specific product ideas and been involved in developing these over some years. In some cases, companies may be willing to give members of their staff opportunities of taking over such product; these could be the core of new businesses set up by them with the approval and, perhaps, 'life-line support' of their companies.

'Foster'companies may take an active role in releasing business concepts which have been initiated in-house and encouraging their staff to take these ideas and turn into real enterprises. The executives would need special help in setting up these businesses.

Comparatively limited information is readily available about the concept of the spin-off and its applications. In the United Kingdom, Rank Xerox pioneered two approaches in order to encourage its staff to consider setting up viable businesses (these are not mutually exclusive and some degree of overlap is inevitable):

1. *Xanadu* (Xerox association of networks and distributed utilities) was set up about 10 years ago with a membership of 200-plus small firms and an aggregate turnover of £20 million. These companies have been set up by staff who left Rank and who were offered, on a short-term basis, the use of space; no capital funding was involved. These entrepreneurs meet about once a month and exchange ideas, etc.
2. *Networking* covers Rank staff who have left to start up their own business and who contract to provide part of their output to Xerox; these firms must set up as limited companies.

The spin-off approach appears to have attractive potential for generating new businesses within parameters of risk significant below those characterising new small ventures.

Management buy-out (MBO)

This entrepreneurial activity has had remarkable growth in the United Kingdom: in 1977 there were 13 deals involving a few millions pounds; in 1986 there were 261 deals worth £1.2bn; and by 1989 MBOs achieved a record £6.38bn, with an average deal size of £14.3m. Then, however, rising interest rates and economic stringencies severely affected MBO activities, many of which had been in the retail sector. In 1992, 520 deals worth £3bn were completed, and in the first quarter of 1993, only seven deals with a total value of £390m were made. This downward trend has also been affected by the lack of investor confidence following some well-publicised MBO failures.

The 'shake-out' of industrial conglomerates over the past decade or so has activated alert management to seek financial support from the City institutions to buy out specific parts of the businesses which employ them. The venture capital industry has developed particular expertise in helping these entrepreneurs. In addition, receiverships have offered opportunities to enterprising executives to bid for viable parts of businesses. In the past, the joint-stock banks, leading firms of accountants and equity investors like 3i, Prudential Venture Managers and Kleinwort Benson, have offered money and expertise in MBO transactions. However, the high-leveraged deals of the 1980s are unlikely to return to prominence in the foreseeable future.

Some MBOs have sold out to large groups within a fairly short time, making millionaires of several of their founders. Premier Brands, for example, was a £300m venture by the senior management of Cadbury Typhoo, the former beverages and food group of Cadbury Schweppes plc, which within three years was sold out to Hillsdown Holdings in May 1989. The buildings products company Caradon was sold by its MBO team to the then MB Group, after only four years. Istel, a computer services company bought from the Rover Car Company by a group of employees for £35m in 1987, was sold by them to AT&T for £180m in September 1989.

A leveraged buy-out is similar to an MBO and has been popular in the USA. Transactions are usually initiated by financial groups rather than by management of the companies concerned. The term 'leveraged buy-out' refers to the inherent nature of the deals, which involve high levels of borrowing or leverage against the security offered by firms' assets.

MBOs in the USA

For several years, very large leveraged deals featured strongly in the USA, such as the Beatrice Companies (food and consumer products group) $6.2bn deal in April 1986. The leveraged buy-out is usually transacted by an investment bank which breaks up a group for maximum resale value of its constituent companies or divisions. Management itself does not have a significant role in these US deals. In March 1988, Colt Industries, the large US conglomerate making automative and aerospace components as well as the famous Colt revolvers, announced a $600m leveraged buy-out. The new company, Colt Holdings, was formed by Morgan Stanley Leveraged Equity Fund and includes senior managers of Colt.

In 1992, however, an air of dreary inactivity was reported to hang over MBO activities because of the crisis in the US commercial banking sector, ailing property assets and the recession, which has rendered it difficult to project future trends, including vital cash-flow estimates. This pronounced down-turn seems unlikely to experience any dramatic improvement in the near future. As and when the economic cycle reaches an optimistic phase, buy-out activities may well return to popularity. Meanwhile, firms which were involved earlier in MBOs are actively engaged in reducing high levels of borrowing with either equity or less expensive debt securities.[97]

Management buy-in

This is another phenomenon of the enterprise culture which developed around 1987, and involved the purchase of a business by a hand-picked team of outside managers plus financial backers. Buy-ins are now generally regarded as considerably more risky than buy-outs, because the incoming management team is likely to lack intimate knowledge of the company in question.

Hybrid deals

Some deals, involving both existing and incoming managers, have been awarded the arguable title of *bimbos*. These hybrid deals appear to have attracted favourable opinions from external investors because they strengthen existing management teams through the infusion of new expertise, as happened with Whitworths Produce Group, a vegetable pre-packing and processing business, which was bought from Booker plc for £11m in the early 1990s.

Intrapreneurship

Harnessing entrepreneurial activities *inside* a business and organising project teams have already been discussed in Chapter 7 on innovation strategy. Intrapreneurship, however, involves setting up a small company with the objective of exploiting commercially certain technologies and skills which may have significant market potential.

Pilkingtons has combined four separate energy-related centres of expertise in a small company – Pilkington Energy Advisers Ltd (PEAL) – to offer a comprehensive energy consultancy service. PEAL was founded in April 1987 with an initial capitalisation of £2 million; nine of the ten staff were transferred from within the Pilkington Group, with plans to increase to a total of 22 within two years.

Earlier attempts to organise and develop energy-related skills in the Pilkington group had not been successful because of the absence of a 'champion'. PEAL, however, was the answer to this problem, operating with complete professional independence although remaining within the group. Whether this policy will be relaxed and PEAL made completely self-standing remains to be seen. So far it has all the signs of developing into a healthy new business activity, exploiting skills which had previously been restricted.

Other entrepreneurial activities

These include licensing, leasing, franchising and joint ventures (see Chapters 2, 7 and 9), and various other forms of management buy-out, e.g. employee buy-out. Opportunities clearly still exist for those with business acumen and entrepreneurial, technological, financial and marketing skills.

New approaches can release and channel energies which might otherwise lie untapped or become dissipated in frustrating experiences in mammoth organisations. New small businesses have a particular characteristic that gives them a competitive edge: they are owner-managed, and decisions can be taken quickly. This rapid reaction to changing circumstances and close attention to the needs of customers are qualities which, unfortunately, are often not evident in large firms. Flexibility, adaptation and the development of high-added-value products and services are the greatest strengths of small and developing businesses.

PROCESS RE-ENGINEERING

Rather like total quality management, process re-engineering has thrust itself on management, promising dramatic improvements in productivity, specifically through the redesign of white-collar business processes. As Drucker points out, a great deal of service work does not differ significantly from the work of making and doing things, and can realistically be described as 'production work'. However, in order for service functions such as dealing with customers' enquiries, handling delivery problems and the many other types of routine activity with which most organisations are involved to be truly productive, some 're-engineering' is necessary. This entails the adoption of new approaches to the tasks of both knowledge workers and service workers.

Unlike manufacturing production processes, where workers are typically involved with serving the needs of machines, in 'knowledge work and in practically all service work the machine serves the worker';[6] tasks are not imposed – they need to be determined. This is a dramatic departure from the traditional work-study approach and the so-called scientific management principles enunciated by Frederick Taylor and others, which for many years had such a powerful influence on the design of production tasks.

Rank Xerox, the Marlow-based organisation, has undertaken a fundamental restructuring of its extensive business activities, including a reorganisation of its European marketing operations. As a result, seven 'uniform basic processes' will replace the freedom of operations traditionally enjoyed by each of its European offshoots. These standard processes will cover virtually every aspect of the company's activities, including product development, order handling and servicing functions.

This radical programme of process re-engineering will be firmly controlled by top management and senior executives directly responsible for the effective implementation of each process. Bernard Fournier, the French-born managing director of Rank Xerox, and his top colleagues will monitor the new re-engineering programmes.

Rank Xerox's dedicated commitment to process re-engineering followed the findings of a quality improvement team, which reported in 1992 that the company's current return on assets was far below that necessary if Rank Xerox was to be able to call itself 'the most productive company' in its industry. Concurrently, the organisation is implementing a variety of behavioural and cultural initiatives at all levels of staff.[98]

SUMMARY

The modern marketing environment is characterised by dynamic changes and challenges. Some of these are technical and economic, while others are political, social and behavioural.

Sensational political upheavals in eastern Europe and the disintegration of the Soviet Empire, the extension of the EC and the foundation of the single European market, and the rising significance of Japan and the Pacific Rim countries in world trading have all added to the competitiveness and turbulence of markets for goods and services of many kinds. Regionalism is a predominant characteristic of world trading.

The social responsibilities of business are increasingly debated, and 'action groups' encourage critical, and often hostile, attitudes to specific industries and firms. Agitation, representation and participation seem to mirror the mood of modern society. Organisations of all kinds cannot ignore their newly perceived roles in society. To keep strictly within legal limits is a lamentably inadequate corporate policy. Business ethics are being discussed widely, and environmental issues are increasingly influencing corporate policies.

The strategic importance of quality in design and throughout all the functions of a business is attracting increasing interest from all sectors of industry. Profitable design is a team effort which demands a synthesis of skills, including value analysis and value engineering. Safety in use is a serious aspect of product design which is growing in importance with the requirements of product liability legislation.

Giving customers adequate levels of service is vital in competitive markets; servicing of customers adds to the 'augmented product' value, which helps companies to differentiate their products.

The generation of successful enterprises is vital for economic and social prosperity. Various initiatives have been tried: spin-off, networking, management buy-out, intrapreneurship, etc. Small and medium-sized enterprises (SMEs) now feature prominently in the United Kingdom and in other economies, and have contributed significantly to employment in virtually all sectors.

REFERENCES

1. de Jonquières, Guy, 'Clearing up after communism', *Financial Times*, 3 July 1992.
2. Wiesner, Jerome B., 'Technological innovation and social change', *Economic Impact*, vol. 16, no. 4, 1976.
3. Schön, Donald A., *Beyond the Stable State*, Maurice Temple Smith, London, 1971.
4. Porter, Michael E., *Competitive Strategy*, Macmillan, New York, 1980.
5. Ansoff, H. Igor, *Business Strategy*, Penguin, Harmondsworth, 1969.
6. Drucker, Peter F., *Post-Capitalist Society*, Butterworth-Heinemann, Oxford, 1993.
7. 'The Single Market: not yet', *The Economist*, 10 April 1993.
8. Sutherland, Peter, 'Stronger than nations', *Daily Telegaph*, 28 May 1992.
9. Davidson, Ian, 'It started with coal, iron and steel', *Financial Times*, 19 January 1993.
10. Marsh, David, 'Wider still and wider', *Financial Times*, 19 January 1993.
11. Done, Kevin, 'Hard slog to make the marriage work', *Financial Times*, 7 September 1993.
12. Lorenz, Christopher, 'Here, there and everywhere', *Financial Times*, 10 November 1993.
13. Rodger, Ian, 'Japanese strive to become good Europeans', *Financial Times*, 20 January 1988.
14. Prowse, Michael, 'Report of its death an exaggeration', *Financial Times*, 8 January 1993.
15. 'Survey of eastern Europe', *The Economist*, 13 March 1993.
16. Hague, Paul, *The Industrial Market Research Handbook*, Kogan Page, London, 1992.
17. Keegan, Warren J., *Global Marketing Management*, Prentice-Hall, Englewood Cliffs, NJ, 1989.
18. Peters, Tom, *Thriving on Chaos*, Macmillan, London, 1987.
19. Bartlett, Christopher A., and Ghosal, Sumantra, *Managing Across Borders: The transnational solution*, Century Hutchison, London, 1989.
20. Freeman, Christopher, *The Economics of Industrial Innovation*, Penguin, Harmondsworth, 1974.
21. Kempner, Thomas, Macmillan, Keith and Hawkins, Kevin, *Business and Society: Tradition and Change*, Allen Lane, London, 1974.
22. Mishan, E.J., *The Costs of Economic Growth*, Penguin, Harmondsworth, 1972.
23. Gabor, Dennis, *The Mature Society*, Secker and Warburg, London, 1972.
24. Whitaker, John H., 'The supremacy of the business ethic', *Business and Society Review*, no. 10, summer 1974.
25. Smith, Adam, *An Inquiry into the Causes of the Wealth of Nations*, Methuen, London, 1961.
26. Krauer, Alex, 'Changing values in the changing responsibilities of industry', *Ciba-Geigy Journal*, no. 3, 1989.
27. Benady, Alex, 'Ethics man is good for business', *Sunday Telegraph*, 20 October 1991.
28. Lloyd, John, 'Ethics and business at loggerheads?', *Financial Times*, 10 June 1988.

29. Jack, Andrew, 'Banking on an ethical approach', *Financial Times*, 30 April 1992.
30. Fidler, Stephen, 'Financial sector worried over question of principle', *Financial Times*, 31 October 1989.
31. *Corporate Values: The bottom line contribution*, Digital Equipment Co., Reading, 1992.
32. Lorenz, Christopher, 'Flying in the face of corporate ethics', *Financial Times*, 22 January 1993.
33. Dickson, Martin, 'Baby Bell's bad behaviour', *Financial Times*, 14 May 1993.
34. Jack, Andrew, 'Time comes to mind corporate Ps and Qs', *Financial Times*, 8 May 1992.
35. *Corporate Codes of Ethics in Large UK Companies*, Department of Business Studies, University of Edinburgh, 1988.
36. Cohen, Norma, 'Code of Practice relies on threat of public censure', *Financial Times*, 28 May 1992.
37. 'Ethics men speak in many codes', *Daily Telegraph*, 6 May 1992.
38. Dickson, Martin, 'When fatal illness is a public affair', *Financial Times*, 25 January 1993.
39. Wolf, Martin, 'Key is not to produce less – but differently', *Financial Times*, 2 June 1992.
40. Hunt, John, 'Recycling: new interest worldwide', *Financial Times*, 31 October 1989.
41. Gooding, Kenneth, 'Aluminium producers woo the green vote', *Financial Times*, 16 June 1989.
42. Vail, Simon, 'Recycling group for electronics', *Financial Times*, 15 July 1992.
43. Griffiths, John, 'Scrapyard no longer the end of the road for cars', *Financial Times*, 2 December 1992.
44. Genillard, Ariane, 'Falling victim to its own success', *Financial Times*, 27 January 1993.
45. Levitt, Theodore, 'Think before you leap', *Harvard Business Review*, vol. 47, no. 3, 1969.
46. Cookson, Clive, 'Blots on the city scape', *Financial Times*, 19 February 1992.
47. Gooding, Kenneth, 'Emission-free car shows its mettle', *Financial Times*, 27 February 1993.
48. Mackinnon, A. M., 'The chemical industry under attack', *Ciba-Geigy Journal*, no. 3, 1981.
49. Cookson, Clive, 'The way to make a clean break', *Financial Times*, 10 April 1991.
50. Marsh, Peter, 'Ciba-Geigy cleans up its public image', *Financial Times*, 4 November 1987.
51. Klevier, Art, 'What does it mean to be green?', *Harvard Business Review*, vol. 69, no. 4, 1991.
52. Cookson, Clive, 'Big increases in spending', *Financial Times*, 13 March 1991.
53. 'Du Pont speeds up phase-out', *Financial Times*, 10 March 1993.
54. Kehoe, Louise, 'AT&T finds solution that dissolves ozone problems', *Financial Times*, 3 February 1988.
55. Cookson, Clive, 'It grows on trees', *Financial Times*, 12 August 1992.
56. Marsh, Peter, 'Marketing higher value niches', *Financial Times*, 22 January 1990.
57. Anderson, Jack, 'Dow vs the dioxin monster', *Fortune*, 30 May 1983.
58. Burke, Tom, 'Is there a common agenda?' in 'Environment and industry – towards a common agenda', *Royal Society of Arts Journal*, vol. 137, no. 5394, 1989.
59. McIntosh, Andrew, 'The impact of environmental issues on marketing and politics in the 1990s', *Journal of the Market Research Society*, vol. 33, no. 3, 1991.

60. *How green are small companies?*, Cranfield School of Management, 1990.
61. Thomas, David, 'An upsurge of interest', *Financial Times*, 13 March 1991.
62. Knight, Peter, 'Advice to a director to turn green', *Financial Times*, 22 January 1992.
63. Lascelles, David, 'Paper chase', *Financial Times*, 26 February 1992.
64. Gabor, Andrea, 'The man who changed the world of quality', *International Management*, vol. 43, no. 3, 1988.
65. Holberton, Simon, 'Prophets with converts in a far-off land', *Financial Times*, 3 October 1990.
66. Dickson, Martin, 'Bouquets and barbed ire', *Financial Times*, 3 February 1992.
67. Taylor, Paul, 'Faith in the religion of quality is starting to waver', *Financial Times*, 21 October 1992.
68. De Meyer, Arnoud, and Ferdows, Kasra, *Removing the Barriers to Manufacturing*, INSEAD, Fontainebleau, 1990.
69. De Meyer, Arnoud, *Factories of the Future*, INSEAD, Fontainebleau, 1991.
70. Griffiths, John, 'How Toyota filters its component suppliers', *Financial Times*, 10 April 1991.
71. Krantz, K. Theodor, 'How Velcro got hooked on quality', *Harvard Business Review*, vol. 67, no. 5, 1989.
72. Batchelor, Charles, 'Standard bearers', *Financial Times*, 25 May 1993.
73. Levitt, Theodore, 'The morality of advertising', *Harvard Business Review*, vol. 48, no. 4, 1970.
74. Pilditch, James, *Marketing*, November 1971.
75. Pilditch, James, 'Five questions about design', *The Director*, October 1974.
76. Strutt, Mike, 'Tall order for rescue work', *Financial Times*, 21 July 1987.
77. Juran, J. M., *Juran on Leadership for Quality: An executive handbook*, Free Press, New York, 1989.
78. Chisnall, Peter M., *Marketing: A behavioural analysis*, McGraw-Hill, Maidenhead, 1985.
79. Abrahams, Paul, 'A competitive line to British inventiveness', *Financial Times*, 28 January 1988.
80. Corfield, K. G., *Product Design*, NEDO, London, 1979.
81. *The Industrial Design Requirements of Industry*, Design Council, London, 1983.
82. Lorenz, Christopher, 'Unleashing the potential of design', *Financial Times*, 27 October 1989.
83. Lorenz, Christopher, 'Plugging design right into the organisation', *Financial Times*, 11 September 1989.
84. Holland, Roger, 'Industrial Britain's Achilles' heel', *The Director*, May 1974.
85. Black, Misha, 'The function of design in long range planning', *Long Range Planning*, June 1972.
86. Archer, Bruce, 'Design and management for the 70s', *Design*, June 1969.
87. Tavernier, Gerard, 'Where value analysis is a way of life', *International Management*, February 1975.
88. British Productivity Council, *Sixteen Case Studies in Value Analysis*, BPC, London, 1964.
89. Ames, Charles B., 'Trappings vs substance in industrial marketing', *Harvard Business Review*, vol. 48, no. 4, 1970.
90. Batchelor, Charles, 'A valuable competitive tool', *Financial Times*, 27 June 1989.
91. Batchelor, Charles, 'The product's face is the company's fortune', *Financial Times*, 12 November 1991.

92. Malott, Robert H., 'Let's restore balance to product liability law', *Harvard Business Review*, vol. 61, no. 3, 1983.
93. Abbott, Howard, *Safer by Design: The management of product design risks under strict liability*, Design Council, London, 1987.
94. Hutchinson, William M., and Stolle, John F., 'How to manage customer service', *Harvard Business Review*, vol. 46, no. 6, 1968.
95. Leadbetter, Charles, 'Taking a hard look at developing soft skills', *Financial Times*, 14 January 1991.
96. *Service: The new competitive edge – a survey of executive opinion in the UK*, Digital Equipment Co., Reading, 1991.
97. Tait, Nikki, 'Activity still sluggish', *Financial Times*, 3 December 1992.
98. Lorenz, Christopher, 'Time to get serious', *Financial Times*, 25 June 1993.

REVIEW AND DISCUSSION QUESTIONS

Q1 From your reading of this chapter, what would you say are the typical responses of (a) European companies and (b) non-European companies to the introduction of the single European market?

Q2 Discuss critically the opinion sometimes expressed that business ethics are really of little concern to most managers, particularly in today's highly competitive markets.

Q3 A British manufacturer of machine components wishes to export to an attractive but relatively undeveloped market, where it is known that all foreign suppliers incorporate a 5 per cent 'dash' allowance in their market development costs. In your role as export marketing manager, present an appraisal of the situation facing the company if it seeks to exploit this market. Include recommendations for action, together with supporting arguments.

Q4 What is the nature and scope of TQM (total quality management), and how is this management philosophy put into practice? Select an industry known to you and assess the impact of TQM on competitive activity.

Q5 Environmental lobbying and legislation have had far-reaching effects on industrial policies and practices over recent years. Select any industrial product/process with which you are familiar and describe in some detail the effects which 'environmentalism' has had on its operations.

Q6 Customer service programmes are being given more attention by industrial as well as consumer goods manufacturers, and have become important elements of their competitive marketing strategies. Outline the parameters of a customer service programme for a firm marketing heavy-duty tyres for equipment used in the construction and agricultural sectors.

Index